Crucial Readings in Special Education

Scot Danforth
University of Missouri, St. Louis

Steven D. Taff
University of Missouri, St. Louis

PEARSON

Merrill
Prentice Hall

Upper Saddle River, New Jersey
Columbus, Ohio

Library of Congress Cataloging-in-Publication Data

Crucial readings in special education / [edited by] Scot Danforth and Steven D. Taff.
    p. cm.
    Includes bibliographical references.
    ISBN 0-13-089929-1 (pbk.)
    1. Special education--United States. 2. Children with disabilities--Education--United
States. I. Danforth, Scot. II. Taff, Steven D.

LC3981.C77 2004
371.9--dc21   2003044497

Vice President and Executive Publisher: Jeffery W. Johnston
Acquisitions Editor: Allyson P. Sharp
Editorial Assistant: Kathleen Burk
Production Editor: Linda Hillis Bayma
Production Coordination: Emily Hatteberg, Carlisle Publishers Services
Design Coordinator: Diane C. Lorenzo
Cover Designer: Jason Moore
Production Manager: Laura Messerly
Director of Marketing: Ann Castel Davis
Marketing Manager: Amy June
Marketing Coordinator: Tyra Poole

This book was set in Life Roman by Carlisle Communications, Ltd. It was printed and bound by
R.R. Donnelley & Sons Company. The cover was printed by Phoenix Color Corp.

Pearson Prentice Hall™ is a trademark of Pearson Education, Inc.
Pearson® is a registered trademark of Pearson plc
Prentice Hall® is a registered trademark of Pearson Education, Inc.
Merrill® is a registered trademark of Pearson Education, Inc.

Pearson Education Ltd.   Pearson Education Australia Pty. Limited
Pearson Education Singapore Ptd. Ltd.   Pearson Education North Asia Ltd.
Pearson Education Canada, Ltd.   Pearson Educación de Mexico, S.A. de C.V.
Pearson Education—Japan   Pearson Education Malaysia Pte. Ltd.

10 9 8 7 6 5 4 3 2 1
ISBN: 0-13-089929-1

Preface

The days of confident clarity of purpose and action in the field of special education in the United States are behind us. In the 1970s and 1980s, a relatively young profession bolstered by new federal legislation and astronomical growth in the numbers of professionals burst forward with tremendous optimism. The reasons for this wide-eyed optimism were many. Legal battles over the rights of students with disabilities had resulted in not only court victories breaking down walls of segregation but also a federal law mandating the education of all children regardless of disability. Funding for research, training, and program development initiatives flowed freely. And a new science called "behavior modification" was coupled with an old science of psychological measurement to form what appeared to be a promising knowledge foundation for the expanding and hopeful field.

But the optimism of a youthful profession soon transformed into the complexity and conflict of adolescence. In the 1980s and 1990s, special educators realized that the victory of a guaranteed education for all students had been only a defeat of segregation. Public education was very willing to segregate within the boundaries of public schools by excluding students with disabilities from general buildings and classrooms. The attention of many special educators turned to the new antisegregation movement—inclusive education. Yet even this goal divided special educators into two groups: those who sought the radical reform of public schools and communities and those who sought politically milder objectives concerning student performance and skills.

Simultaneous to the inclusion debate was the serious questioning of the optimistic sciences of psychological measurement and behavioral technology and the practical value, political leanings, and theoretical meaning of these knowledge bases. Issues concerning quantitative and qualitative research methodologies were just the "tip of the iceberg" as the field ruminated over deep philosophical questions about science and belief.

By the turn of the century, one could look back to view the simple clarity of purpose and professional practice that marked the field of special education during the 1970s and most of the 1980s as a brief stage of innocence in the historical development of this field. *What to do* and *why to do it* were questions that seemed neatly settled to the young profession. From that ostensible consensus, it seemed that this profession could move forward toward lofty goals for students and families. By the beginning of the twenty-first century, these very questions—ethical, practical, and political—are open to examination, critique, and discussion across the profession.

The most recent development in this brief history of modern special education is what we call *the challenge of disability studies*. Quite simply, people with disabilities have united in many quarters to question the ways that they are understood and treated by the nondisabled majority, including the nondisabled professionals who make up special education, rehabilitation, and the other disability service fields. While the young field of special education put much emphasis on viewing human activity and identities from the standpoint of an objective science touted as unbiased and accurate, disabled scholars, writers, and activists have questioned the inherent ableism and overwhelming power of the perspective of the nondisabled professional fields. Who gets to define the meaning of disability? Can one truly understand disability if one does not have a disability? Can a nondisabled person claim to hold an objective, unbiased perspective on a way of living that is foreign to his experience? What kinds of ableism hide behind the social sciences and professions that claim to have the best knowledge of disability? These questions and others are now at center stage as special education and the disability service fields contend with a new level of complexity and challenge.

The naïve optimism of special education in 1975 has aged and changed. It is currently weathering into what we hope will be a different brand of optimism, what we would describe as a more mature hopefulness. The field is becoming humbler, more hesitant, more critical about what we think we know. Frequently, special educators are acknowledging that the perspectives on any issue or topic are multiple, and disagreement across the perspectives is a sign of a healthy democracy. In many circles, top-down monologue is giving way to egalitarian dialogue as persons who are disabled and their families increasingly take valuable seats at decision-making tables.

Our goal when putting together this group of readings is to support this move toward a new, more mature form of optimism and hope in the field of special education. We want to do justice to the complex and ultimately uncertain nature of the profession of special education in this current era of challenges and questions. Rather than long nostalgically for a simpler time when optimism came more easily, our goal is to honor the maturation of this field into debate and complication by attending to the widest range of concepts and professional practices possible. Our reason for doing so arises out of our deep conviction that the daily work of special educators and other disability service personnel is incredibly multifaceted and contingent.

In this text, we have gathered together readings that we believe are crucial to the intellectual and practical development of advanced educators working with students who have disabilities. We neither endorse nor reject any of the ideas put forth in these pages. We fully support the necessity of hearing, digesting, and discussing these readings. These are words and ideas that deserve to be honored with serious thought, that deserve to be traded and tested in active dialogue, and that deserve to be pulled apart and unpacked in vigorous criticism. A teacher who takes the time and makes the effort to seriously consider the ideas within these readings opens many doors of personal and professional growth, allowing an opportunity for a deepening and broadening of both theory and practice.

TEXT CONTENT

One logical way of organizing this text would have been to gather readings under common disability headings: a few on "learning disabilities," a few on "emotional/behavioral disorders," and so forth. We have avoided this tactic out of our conviction that a number of serious topics and concerns cut across these categorical subfields. While there are undoubtedly issues specific to certain subfields that deserve our attention, we would do better to wander purposefully across the various categorical boundaries, appreciating the problems and possibilities that exist across the social grain rather than within the standard categorical nooks.

We have gathered readings that address what we consider to be vital topics of concern, areas to which our eyes and minds and hearts should focus, questions that our dialogues should raise and flesh out. Some of these topics are fairly obvious. Almost any special educator would speak to the importance of these. Others are more obscure, bringing forward oft-neglected but highly valuable kinds of research and theory.

The chapters are as follows:

- **Chapter One**—Historical and Sociological Analyses of Disabilities Issues
    Often, we have little notion where the current ideas and practices shared by special educators originally developed or how they came to be prominent. Historical, sociological, and philosophical scholarship has often been overlooked by the field as we have

prided ourselves on practicality. Yet, as these readings demonstrate, an understanding of the cultural, conceptual, and political developments that surround and inform our work is indispensable to any educator hoping to make a meaningful and ethically defensible impact.

- **Chapter Two**—Special Education Research and Thought

  As noted earlier, the "science" of disability, first constructed and touted by the field of special education, has been critically questioned and reformulated in the past two decades. These readings provide a quick introduction to the central issues that have energized special educators of many ideological stripes.

- **Chapter Three**—The Challenge of Disability Studies

  The new interdisciplinary field of "disability studies" is growing quickly in North America, the United Kingdom, and elsewhere (see www.uic.edu/orgs/sds/ for the Society for Disability Studies or www.aera.net for the Disability Studies in Education Special Interest Group of the American Educational Research Association). These readings provide a healthy glimpse of the central themes of this work and the ways that it seriously challenges special educators to think and act in new ways.

- **Chapter Four**—Public Policy Issues

  From the start, special education in the United States has been supported by legal leverage and filled with policy questions. How should a democratic society best educate those individuals commonly understood to differ in significant and marked ways? These readings introduce a series of yet unresolved issues that are pertinent to special and general educators alike.

- **Chapter Five**—Transition Issues and Practices

  Too often, the field of special education has framed disability concerns as childhood issues with insufficient attention to the lifespan of persons who are disabled. The subfield of "transitions" addresses the practicalities of planning and programming for adult life, while also raising many important issues about the lives of persons with disabilities after they leave public education.

- **Chapter Six**—Relationships Between Schools and Parents, Families, and Communities

  While Individual Education Plans (IEPs) seemingly assure the parents of students with disabilities of a pivotal role in the planning processes, all special educators know tales of too common, antagonistic relationships between parents/families and public schools. The divisions and conflicts often loom large, and the challenges of creating better working relationships continue to confront this profession. These readings call upon educators to question both belief and practice in order to create more healthy and productive working relationships between schools and parents/families.

- **Chapter Seven**—Instructional Practices

  Both the location and the method of instructing students with disabilities have been hot topics for research and debate in many circles. At times, it seems as if special educators are searching for the magic feather, the silver bullet, the cure, the one best way. At other times, the profession is attempting to adapt the most current practices of general educators to a diverse group of students. At all times, how to best teach the difficult to teach is a crucial concern. Given the incredible amount of research on instructional practices, these readings provide a quick but informative introduction to this large area of research and development.

- **Chapter Eight**—Social, Emotional, and Behavioral Issues in the Classroom

  In practice-oriented texts, this section might be called "behavior management" or "classroom management." We are construing the issues a bit more broadly by including a variety of writings, not only about how to lead a safe and productive classroom, but also about social conflict, deviant behavior, and mental health issues. These readings help us explore our understandings of human behavior and the roles of professionals in relation to working with students who behave in odd, deviant, or disruptive ways.

ACKNOWLEDGMENTS

We express our gratitude to the following reviewers for their helpful suggestions: Linda Backus, University of Vermont; Greg Conderman, St. Ambrose University; Kathryn Haring, University of Oklahoma; Michael Kallam, Fort Hays State University; Sheldon Maron, Portland State University; and Marshall Zumborg, Wayne State University.

Discover the Companion Website Accompanying This Book

The Prentice Hall Companion Website: A Virtual Learning Environment

Technology is a constantly growing and changing aspect of our field that is creating a need for content and resources. To address this emerging need, Prentice Hall has developed an online learning environment for students and professors alike—Companion Websites—to support our textbooks.

In creating a Companion Website, our goal is to build on and enhance what the textbook already offers. For this reason, the content for each user-friendly website is organized by topic and provides the professor and student with a variety of meaningful resources. Common features of a Companion Website include:

For the Professor—

Every Companion Website integrates **Syllabus Manager**™, an online syllabus creation and management utility.

- **Syllabus Manager**™ provides you, the instructor, with an easy, step-by-step process to create and revise syllabi, with direct links into Companion Website and other online content without having to learn HTML.
- Students may log on to your syllabus during any study session. All they need to know is the web address for the Companion Website and the password you've assigned to your syllabus.
- After you have created a syllabus using **Syllabus Manager**™, students may enter the syllabus for their course section from any point in the Companion Website.
- Clicking on a date, the student is shown the list of activities for the assignment. The activities for each assignment are linked directly to actual content, saving time for students.
- Adding assignments consists of clicking on the desired due date, then filling in the details of the assignment—name of the assignment, instructions, and whether it is a one-time or repeating assignment.
- In addition, links to other activities can be created easily. If the activity is online, a URL can be entered in the space provided, and it will be linked automatically in the final syllabus.
- Your completed syllabus is hosted on our servers, allowing convenient updates from any computer on the Internet. Changes you make to your syllabus are immediately available to your students at their next logon.

For the Student—

- **Overview and General Information**—General information about the topic and how it will be covered in the website.
- **Web Links**—A variety of websites related to topic areas.
- **Content Methods and Strategies**—Resources that help to put theories into practice in the special education classroom.
- **Reflective Questions and Case-Based Activities**—Put concepts into action, participate in activities, examine strategies, and more.
- **National and State Laws**—An online guide to how federal and state laws affect your special education classroom.
- **Behavior Management**—An online guide to help you manage behaviors in the special education classroom.
- **Message Board**—Virtual bulletin board to post and respond to questions and comments from a national audience.

To take advantage of these and other resources, please visit the *Crucial Readings in Special Education* Companion Website at

www.prenhall.com/danforth

Contents

Chapter Seven

Instructional Practices

Chapter Eight

Social, Emotional, and Behavioral Issues in the Classroom

NOTE: Every effort has been made to provide accurate and current Internet information in this book. However, the Internet and information posted on it are constantly changing, and it is inevitable that some of the Internet addresses listed in this textbook will change.

THE EASIEST WAY TO ENHANCE YOUR COURSE
Proven Journals • Proven Strategies • Proven Media

www.EducatorLearningCenter.com

Merrill Education is pleased to announce a new partnership with ASCD. The result of this partnership is a joint website, www.EducatorLearningCenter.com, with recent articles and cutting-edge teaching strategies. The Educator Learning Center combines the resources of the Association for Supervision and Curriculum Development (ASCD) and Merrill Education. At www.EducatorLearningCenter.com you will find resources that will enhance your students' understanding of course topics and of current educational issues, in addition to being invaluable for further research.

How will Educator Learning Center help your students become better teachers?

- 600+ articles from the ASCD journal *Educational Leadership* discuss everyday issues faced by practicing teachers.
- Hundreds of lesson plans and teaching strategies are categorized by content area and age range.
- Excerpts from Merrill Education texts give your students insight on important topics of instructional methods, diverse populations, assessment, classroom management, technology, and refining practice.
- Case studies, classroom video, electronic tools, and computer simulations keep your students abreast of today's classrooms and current technologies.
- A direct link on the site to Research Navigator™, where your students will have access to many of the leading education journals as well as extensive content detailing the research process.

What's the cost?

A four-month subscription to Educator Learning Center is $25 but is **FREE** when used in conjunction with this text. To obtain free passcodes for your students, simply contact your local Merrill/Prentice Hall sales representative, and your representative will give you a special ISBN to give your bookstore when ordering your textbooks. To preview the value of this website to you and your students, please go to www.EducatorLearningCenter.com and click on "Demo."

Introduction

Examining the Practical Implications of Special Education Paradigms of Social Thought

In 1986, Tom Skrtic challenged special education professionals to open their minds to ideas and possibilities previously untapped and undeveloped by disability researchers and practitioners. He criticized the field of special education for remaining stalled in a limited vision that consisted of a single paradigm of social thought and a small handful of psychological theories. His critique claimed that the profession constricted its own ability to bring about meaningful changes in the lives of people who have disabilities, in their families, in public schools, and in society, by remaining chained to a very limited set of traditional ideas. The field of special education has largely ignored Skrtic's critique, for the most part allowing the field to languish in the limitations of old concepts and approaches.

The purpose of this book is to accept Skrtic's challenge by presenting a wide array of ideas about disability, education, and society that intentionally expand and deepen the terrain of special education thought. Our goal is to challenge special educators to think in new ways and to modify what we assume to be true about disability, education, and our profession. Our purpose is not to neatly present new answers, but to engage our colleagues in what are likely to be new questions. Hopefully, this book will open opportunities for thoughtful dialogues about important and complex matters of imminent social and ethical concern.

In this introduction, we present our translation of the four paradigms of social thought that Skrtic (1991, 1999; see also Burrell & Morgan, 1979) offered as a way of framing current disability research and scholarship. Skrtic encouraged special educators to expand from a tradition embracing one strand—positivism—to the intentional cultivation of all four strands: positivism, interpretivism, radical humanism, and radical structuralism. We accept Skrtic's challenge while adding a fifth position, a postparadigmatic or postmodern stance that critiques the other four. Although this discussion will (necessarily) be philosophical, our ultimate purpose is to examine the practical implications of the various ways of thinking within special education practice. We will look closely at what each of the five philosophical positions means in the professional practice of special educators who hold to those systems of belief. Our assumption is that what educators believe matters deeply and is closely connected to what they do. The bottom line on belief is action, the ways that people use ideas to guide their activities. We will examine the different varieties of belief about disability, education, and society in order to understand more about what special educators do or might do in the future.

Figure 1 represents four paradigms of modern social thought—radical structuralism, radical humanism, interpretivism, and positivism—as well as the postparadigmatic or postmodern position (see Burrell & Morgan, 1979; Skrtic, 1991, 1996). The four paradigms are deep, underlying systems of belief about the social world and how we know it. These are complex philosophical systems that teachers and researchers often hold as assumed truths. Some educators are highly aware of what they and others believe. Others are very unaware, and proceed as if their beliefs are as self-evident as the noses on their faces. Our goal for this chapter is to

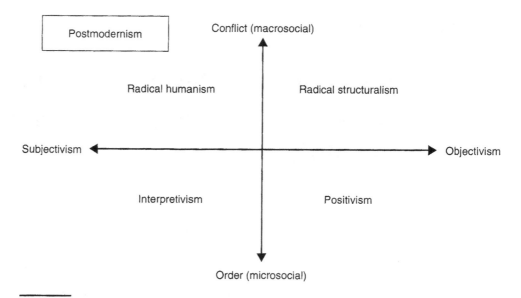

Postmodernism

Conflict (macrosocial)

Radical humanism   Radical structuralism

Subjectivism ←————————————————→ Objectivism

Interpretivism   Positivism

Order (microsocial)

Figure 1

Forms of social thought in special education.
Adapted from Burrell, G. & Morgan, G. (1979). *Sociological paradigms and organizational analysis.*
London: Heinemann.

bring these deep beliefs out into the open for discussion and scrutiny. *Our* belief is that such matters make a profound difference in the attitudes and actions of disability professionals.

In Figure 1, the vertical axis represents the ways that special educators think about society, the sociological theories that individuals hold and use. The axis creates a continuum from *Order* (bottom) to *Conflict* (top). On the *Order* end, the belief is that society is stable and consistent, and people basically agree on values and ways of life. The current arrangement of political power, wealth, and status is acceptable and should be maintained. Progress is created in a rational, incremental fashion, through research and planning by experts. Therefore, the primary goal of special education is to help nonconforming individuals fit into or cope with the social norms and requirements of the larger society.

On the *Conflict* end, the belief is that society consists of many social groups, such as social classes and races, that struggle with one another over crucial cultural issues such as the distribution of wealth, employment opportunities, social status, political power, and opportunities to create human dignity. The nature of society is problematic and in need of critique and reform in order to bring about a more just and fair way of life for all. The central themes of conflict theories focus on issues of social and political inequality—the ways in which the current social arrangement perpetuates and masks social injustices that bring about suffering in the lives of individuals, families, and communities. Progress occurs through intentional citizen action that creates government reforms, changes laws, alters economic structures, and enlightens social attitudes. Therefore, the primary goal of special education is to dramatically change the social norms and requirements of the schools and society in order to support greater equality, freedom, and dignity for persons with disabilities.

The horizontal axis represents the ways that special educators think about knowledge. Specifically, it represents the kinds of knowledge that individuals believe are the most trustworthy or the most useful. This axis runs a continuum from *Objectivism* to *Subjectivism. Objectivism* is typically the belief held by natural (or "hard") scientists. The best kind of human knowledge is created through the procedures and standards of modern science. A knower or researcher must be distant and detached from the object of study. He or she should be emotionless, objective, neutral, unbiased, and free of values. The usual claim in the field of special education is that these standards can be met through adherence to agreed-upon social science research procedures. Ideally, the procedures would involve the mathematical measurement of the object of study, because reliable and valid measurement is held as the pinnacle of objectivist research knowledge.

On the other end of the spectrum, *Subjectivism* is a belief that a person knows and understands best, not through detachment and distance, but through direct interaction that creates an intimate and personal understanding of the object of study. If you want to know about something, you have to be there to experience it yourself. Subjectivism values human experience as a process and form of knowledge. One can never be neutral or free of values. How can a person do anything without valuing something? Also, emotions are not viewed as negative, distorting aspects of consciousness that ruin perspective. All knowers are assumed to be biased, emotional, ideological, and idiosyncratic. Each person comes to know and understand in a way that directly reflects the object of study and the person who does the studying. Subjectivism holds that there is no single, authoritative truth about any issue. All we have are the variety of truths that individuals and groups arrive at through their own limited and value-laden perspectives.

The horizontal and vertical axes produce a neat illustration of the four paradigms of modern, social thought. We have added a fifth strand—postmodernism—that rests off the map (so to speak) in the direction of *Subjectivism* and *Conflict.* These five strands of social thought consist of a series of assumptions about the social world, how we know the social world, and the most promising forms of human action for special educators.

As Skrtic (1991, 1996) notes, the positivist paradigm has historically been the most dominant within special education research and practice. Most special educators have been thoroughly trained in the positivistic system of thought. To a great extent, this is common to all helping professions, including social work, psychology, and psychiatry. When these professions developed in the early 1900s, they sought political legitimacy and public acceptance by claiming to have scientific ways of understanding social problems (Brown, 1992; Jones, 1999; Kirschner, 1986). By the late twentieth century, special educators and other professions began to question the social utility of positivistic science in light of alternative ways of viewing the world. In the following sections, we will explore both traditional and nontraditional systems of belief by outlining these five strands of social thought and their historical and philosophical underpinnings. We will then examine what each specific strand means to special educators who embrace it, keeping one eye on the well-being of students, families, schools, and the American society we share. As we describe what each paradigm of social thought means to special education practice, we encourage readers to keep in mind that despite the domination of positivism in this profession, most teachers blend together beliefs from two or more of the paradigms in their daily work.

POSITIVISM: A BRIEF OVERVIEW

Positivism currently dominates special education research and practice. It is characterized by an emphasis on the microworld of individuals and deems social reality as objective, orderly, and rational (Skrtic, 1995). The positivist view, while historically influenced by a variety of disciplines, is perhaps most commensurate with the philosophical strand of realism. Positivist modes of thought are direct descendants of the means of inquiry utilized in the natural sciences. Realist and empiricist perspectives innate to the natural sciences hold that there are static laws of nature that are knowable, and that these laws exist independently, regardless of human perception, thought, or experience. According to the realist canon, the scientific laws that govern nature can only be discovered via select methodologies, most prominently reduction, objectivity, quantification, and verification. In the pursuit of absolute knowledge, these methodologies must be rigorously and universally applied.

In terms of special education, the adoption of positivism has led to the notion that scholars and researchers should delineate "what works" and what does not, thereby supplying practitioners with research-based prescriptions for effective instruction. Consequently, for the benefit of children with disabilities, only empirically verified instructional methods should be included in the special education knowledge base. Dudley-Marling (1996) critiques the positivist position in the modern world of special education accordingly:

> Herein lies the attraction of quantitative research, applied behavior analysis, and other reductive methods. Constructing the "perfect certainty . . . man wants" requires that the world be reduced to tiny bits . . . removed from the uncertain world of practical activity. This quest for certainty accounts for the privileging of knowing over doing (as if these are separable), which, in the world of education, relegates teachers as doers to the role of (mere) workers carrying out the designs of researchers who are the knowers (p. 110).

Teachers as Technicians: Positivism in Action

How does a positivist system of belief guide a special educator at work? What professional activities are supported through this way of thinking? While the history and philosophy of positivism may be foreign to many special educators, for we tend not to know where our central ideas come from, the actual practices emanating from this worldview are very familiar.

A positivistic special educator is a *technician* working within a vast project that is viewed as highly scientific, a project that borrows concepts of diagnosis and treatment from the field of medicine. The teacher is a technician who utilizes the systems of measurement, diagnosis, and treatment developed and validated by scientific researchers. This project values knowledge that carries the authority of quantitative social science. The purpose of that social science is to discover the truth about disability conditions and professional interventions. The technical task of the teacher is to properly apply that knowledge in daily action with children and families.

Central to this technical task is the positivistic concept of disability. From the positivist standpoint, a disability is an "individual condition of functional limitations" that can be objectively diagnosed by a professional who uses a combination of standardized measures and clinical judgement (Hahn, 1983, 1985). Frequently, special educators describe these conditions using lists of characteristics. Most introductory textbooks in the field are filled with these lists. The characteristics themselves are context free descriptions of bodily or psychological deficits, faults, or abnormalities that require correction. The characteristics are expressed in a framework of words and ideas borrowed from the most prominent, positivistic profession—medicine. The result is a standard grammar of disability through which disability is framed in a metaphor of disease (Blatt, 1999). Disability is a permanent condition of biophysical or psychological abnormality that one "has," and that inheres to the body and mind of the individual in the manner of illness or disease. This condition can be best understood (or "diagnosed," a term borrowed from medicine) by professionals who use standardized forms of measurement (such as intelligence testing) that compare specific forms of functioning to statistical norms, thereby verifying and locating the areas of deficit or abnormality. This framework is further augmented by the medical concepts of treatment and cure, brought about by professional intervention.

Professional actions are focused on increasing functioning in areas of measured deficit in order to bring about a higher degree of normalization of the individual. From the positivist perspective, a teacher's job is to precisely enact the specific programs and practices verified by positivistic social science to increase measurable functioning in areas of ability deficit. Teachers utilize some degree of clinical or professional judgement in the application of scientifically validated interventions to specific cases, but teachers generally do not wander into activities not supported by positivistic research.

INTERPRETIVISM: A BRIEF OVERVIEW

The interpretivist paradigm is characterized by order, subjectivity, and a "micro" focus (Burrell & Morgan, 1979). In common with positivism, interpretivisim shares a quest for order and an emphasis on the individual. However, in marked contrast, the interpretivist view concentrates on analysis of the subjective experience of individuals. Interpretivism, as it stands in special education research and practice today, is concerned with individual narratives—"letting people tell their stories" (Ferguson & Ferguson, 1995, p.105). An individual's telling of a story acts as an interpretation for others to understand that experience, the particulars and idiosyncrasies of that life, and that individual's perspective on the world.

Perhaps the most influential philosophical underpinning for the interpretivist framework comes from the phenomenological movement. Phenomenology is commonly defined as the study of individual human experience and the ways in which the world is understood through such experience. Therefore, the focus is on consciousness, perception, and the development of meaning for the individual—it is one's perceptions of the world and reflection upon those perceptions that establish meaning. A phenomenologist concentrates on the detailed description of action and experience in the world as it is lived—"the investigation of the immediate data prior to all scientific thematization" (Lyotard, 1991, p. 33). Thus, phenomenology rejects the notion of a presupposed objective reality.

As an approach to inquiry, interpretivism is very specific and subjective, therefore, not at all generalizable. The individual's story is the key—how people interpret and relay their experience and how listeners perform a second-order interpretation of one's original experience. For interpretivism, there are no pure "facts," because facts always come packaged in a contextual situation. Reality is not prepackaged, standardized, and identical for every person. The goal of interpretivism is not prediction, control, or obtaining immutable fact. Instead, the focus is on understanding.

Bruner (1996) considers narrative to be an essential element both in the formation of the individual self and in the creation of meaning in a transactional context. "What characterizes human selfhood is the construction of a conceptual system that organizes, as it were, a 'record' of agentive encounters with the world" (Bruner, 1996, p. 36). It is of this record of "agentive encounters"—experience in the world—that interpretivism seeks understanding. We are active residents in the world, not simply passive reactors to an unchanging landscape of facts and objects. The world is the context in which our experiences reside. "There is no inner man, man is in the world, and only in the world does he know himself" (Merleau-Ponty, 1962, p. xi). Primordial meanings derived from experience help to determine the form and function of our thoughts. The goal of interpretivism is to impart meaning via narrative interpretation of that experience.

Teachers as Relationship Artists: Interpretivism in Action

How does an interpretivist system of belief guide a special educator at work? What professional activities are supported through this way of thinking?

The interpretivist special educator is a *relationship artist* who views her personal connections with students and their families as the most promising way to understand them and assist them. Much of this work involves careful and devoted listening to the words of students and families. This teacher believes that the best source of useful knowledge comes directly from the individual who receives the services and that individual's loved ones. Interpersonal connection and emotional intimacy are held to be prime sources of wisdom and guidance along the way.

An interpretivist tends to hold a highly flexible model of disability, allowing him to adjust to the values and self-definitions of the many individuals he serves. He believes that disabilities are socially constructed. That is, they are culturally agreed-upon ways of describing and defining certain individuals who the culture, as a whole, views as falling outside the boundaries of dominant social norms. He finds the positivistic, functional limitations model of disability to be too rigid, too bureaucratic, and too deficit-focused to be helpful in understanding an individual. His approach is more holistic and personal, more akin to the way one would understand and appreciate a friend than the way that a meteorologist would study a tropical storm or the way an entomologist would study the life cycle of a dragonfly. He focuses closely on the ways that the student views herself and her own life. His task is to build a trusting connection with that individual so that he can, to the greatest extent possible, hear and understand the life story of the individual student. If he can understand the nuanced rhythms and idiosyncratic features of the student's autobiography, he can play a role in supporting the student's development toward the fulfillment of her dreams and desires. That role is developed and nurtured within the sphere of a caring interpersonal relationship (Noddings, 1984, 1992).

At best, the interpretivist special educator is also aware that she, too, brings a rich and deep life story into her interactions and relationships with students. Not only is the student impacted by the ongoing, interpersonal connection. So, too, is the teacher. This teacher views her classroom as a complex, dynamic, social space where living autobiographies mingle into one another's stories, changing all involved in ways seen and unseen, understood, and not understood. The goal within that space is twofold: to create opportunities for individuals to steer their own life stories in directions they view as positive and hopeful and to create opportunities for individuals to play positive and supportive roles in the development of the life stories of their classmates. The vehicle of all of this is the interpersonal relationship.

RADICAL HUMANISM: A BRIEF OVERVIEW

Radical humanism occupies a paradigmatic position characterized by conflict, subjectivity, and a "macro" focus (Burrell & Morgan, 1979). Radical humanists wish to replace tyranny and oppression in society with democratic social processes that seek equality and freedom. They view man as "a being of praxis, of practical activity which seeks to challenge, destroy, and transcend the limitations that everyday existence places upon his ability to develop as a free, creative being" (Sher, 1978, p. 2). To the radical humanist, social analyses cannot be objective in nature. Instead, radical humanists center their attention on ideological structures such as culture and values, and the effects of such structures on individual human interpretation and consciousness (Skrtic, 1991). Radical humanists strive to make the world more "transparent," therefore exposing hidden power relations and inequities on a societal scale (Kiel, 1995). A keystone of the radical humanist perspective lies in the challenge to increase human freedom and to offer choice without ideology. By exposing the inequities of ideologies, radical humanists hope to foster a more democratic society. From this standpoint, the freedom of the individual is seen as the condition for the freedom of society as a whole. *"The principle of human self-realization* presupposes social equality and social conditions . . . not only for *some* but for *all* members of society" (Golubovic, 1978, p. 176).

Marxist humanism, a fundamental springboard for the radical humanist paradigm, acknowledges the necessity of challenge and criticism in any examination of social issues. Here, the critique takes place within the context of social life, where "confirming evidence will be sought in practical experience, and supporting arguments will be derived from principles expressing basic human needs and rights" (Markovic, 1978, p. 27–28). One important variant of Marxist radical humanism is critical theory. Philosophers of the Frankfurt School, such as Adorno, Horkheimer, and Marcuse subscribed to this variant. Prevailing ideologies, and the power discrepancies born from them, were the chosen targets of their philosophical assault. For the critical theorists in particular, a chief concern was the reification of ideological norms by a "mass culture" and the consequential loss of individuality, subjectivity, and capability for critical thought. The critical theorists assailed what they saw as the theoretical neutrality of positivism, and argued for a different approach in which one "takes sides in the interest of struggling for a better world" (Giroux, 1983, p. 19).

Radical humanists are often described as reformers, not revolutionaries (Kiel, 1995). A useful way to examine this aspect of the radical humanist position is exemplified in Hacking's (1999) "grades of commitment," which he uses to classify social constructionists. According to Hacking's scheme, humanists would most likely fall into the category of "unmaskers." Unmaskers seek to undermine ideologies and cultural institutions. They wish to "strip it of false appeal or authority" (Hacking, 1999, p. 20). They prefer to point out discrepancies between what we believe and how the world actually is. The final goal of this activity is social action to bring about change toward greater freedom, equality, and human growth.

Teachers as Social Reformers: Radical Humanism in Action

How does a radical humanist system of belief guide a special educator at work? What professional activities are supported through this way of thinking?

The humanistic special educator is a *social reformer* who views her work as social action directed toward the construction of a more democratic and just society. In a style similar to the interpretivist, the humanistic special educator views interpersonal relationships as the primary modality of her work with students, families, and colleagues. Relationships and dialogue between people are where social action occurs.

Where the humanist diverges from the interpretivist is not so much in method as in final goals. While the interpretivist tends to maintain the small, local focus on nurturing the hearts and minds of his students, the humanist tends to also emphasize the macrosocial picture, the development of strong hearts and able minds for the purpose of building a more just and equal society. The humanist believes that the well-being of individuals, and the vitality of individual life stories, are inseparable from the welfare of the community, society, and the international community. In this sense, an individual's experience and perspective is valued by the humanist, but it is never divorced from a broader vision of the social whole to which that individual belongs.

Like the interpretivist, the humanist believes that disabilities are socially constructed identities that are placed on individuals who are judged to be deviant or problematic by social authorities such as schools and hospitals. Unlike the interpretivist, the humanist will not quietly accept any aspect of the dominant deficit-based, functional limitations model of disability. To the humanist, the standard procedures of measurement and diagnosis used within special education systems are a means of making an unjust and dehumanizing process appear to be scientific and professional. The humanist views this as a systematic way of demeaning and oppressing entire groups of people—a cruel way of convincing the labeled and the unlabeled that persons with disability labels are *failed normals* (Goffman, 1963), or lesser humans who need segregation and correction. Central to the work of the humanist is the active, vocal unmasking of this oppression in an attempt to change the minds of colleagues, therefore to change the systems that perpetuate the injustice.

The task of unmasking oppression occurs in two directions, in the teacher's work with students and in her activities throughout the school, community, profession, and society. The humanist takes seriously the democratic notion that all people are inherently equal. This is a fact, regardless of individual differences in body, mind, or ability. Her work is to bring to light the myth of individual defectiveness—individual lesser value—so that all people can discuss and evaluate it on ethical terms. This process seeks the development of more positive and hopeful social identities and roles for all oppressed people, especially those with disabilities or disability labels.

RADICAL STRUCTURALISM: A BRIEF OVERVIEW

As a paradigm of social thought, radical structuralism falls into the realm of objectivity and macroscopic focus (Burrell & Morgan, 1979). Radical structuralists seek to affect social change by demonstrating how oppression occurs within the essential structures of society. The radical structuralist views the world as a place of conflict, and sees the potential for domination and inequality, even in democratic societies (Tomlinson, 1995). The emphasis of radical structuralism is on large scale change in concrete categories such as race, gender, and socio-economic class (Skrtic, 1991). This approach differs from the radical humanist perspective, which sets its sights more on the subjective aspects of individual consciousness. Within this paradigm, radical action and change must take place at the center of societal conflict itself—laws, bureaucracies, economies, governments, and technologies. Radical structuralist perspectives, while sharing an objective focus with the positivists, purport to offer a more realistic portrayal of reality as a world, not of order and rationality, but one characterized by conflict and social upheaval. Unlike positivism, the radical structuralist paradigm does not approach conflict in terms of deviance from societal norms. Radical structuralism, rather, views conflict and change as a product of power struggle and coercion.

The radical structuralist paradigm is primarily (though not exclusively) influenced by two wellsprings of thought: materialist Marxism and structuralism, particularly the version forwarded in the anthropology by Lévi-Strauss. One Marxist notion representative of the radical structuralist position is that of social conflict, more specifically, a clash between those who have power and those who lack it. Marx argued that alienation results from the objectification of human labor, which leads to a social rift comprised of the "haves" and the "have-nots." Therefore, an imbalance in social power, which generates conditions ripe for oppression, is constructed. Radical structuralists wish to change these social power imbalances. For Marx, as well as the radical structuralist, the result of conflict and radical change is dissolution of oppression and emergence of a more egalitarian society.

Structuralism, broadly speaking, posited that the material and events of the world are composed of underlying structures that are universally linked. Lévi-Strauss's structuralist anthropology was an attempt to uncover deep universal mental structures as they manifest themselves in social transactions (Kurzweil, 1980). Specifically, Lévi-Strauss concentrated on the analysis of myth in order to bring out the universal structures of humanity. Myths—narratives constructed to illustrate a culture's origins—allowed for social discourse in the absence of individual voice (Champagne, 1990). Devoid of this voice, myth could be analyzed without concern for "the narrator, narratee, or the succession of events in which the story was told" (Champagne, 1990, p. 24). Therefore, the structures identified by Lévi-Strauss were decontextualized to the point where cultural history and subjectivity held no sway. Lévi-Strauss's analysis of myth supplied a foundation for the objective study of other institutional artifacts, namely, the province of the radical structuralist.

Teachers as Revolutionaries: Radical Structuralism in Action

A special educator who subscribes to theories of radical structuralism views himself as a social activist who seeks to strategically overturn or subvert the deeply ingrained political, economic, legal, and bureaucratic structures that oppress persons with disabilities. Like the humanist, his goal is to work closely with persons with disabilities (and others) in order to unmask the internal and external barriers to social equality. The structuralist agrees with the humanist that these barriers include the negative attitudes and stigmatizing beliefs many people have about disabilities and the disabled. He differs from the humanist in his belief that changing attitudes and habits of thinking is far less important than changing the deep economic and political structures that trap the disabled in poverty, unemployment, and institutional incarceration.

A handy example, which helps us understand the transgressive work of the revolutionary teacher within the many layers of the social environment, can be drawn from the physical environment. In many cities and towns, disability activists have worked for years to remove the many physical barriers that block wheelchairs from full access to buildings, parks, busses, stadiums, and movie theaters, as well as all other public places. One aspect of this ongoing work is lobbying legislatures and bus companies to guarantee that all busses are accessible to people who use wheelchairs. This purposeful activism has included the full range of political activity, from the gentle persuasion of legislative hearings and city council meetings to the civil disobedience of public protests.

The revolutionary teacher embodies this same spirit and intent, in regard not only to the physical environment of the school, but also in relation to the social environment. Radical structuralists tend to struggle fiercely for the inclusion, social participation, and competent education of students with disabilities in general classrooms. The organizational and bureaucratic division between "general" and "special" education is viewed as a barrier to respect, equality, relationship, and dignity for disabled students. Additionally, this barrier is seen as a way of systematically limiting the opportunities for nondisabled or nonlabeled students to interact with students with disabilities, thereby teaching nondisabled students that some humans are unacceptable and are worthy of segregation.

POSTMODERNISM

Briefly summarizing postmodernism can be as difficult and dangerous as trying to erase the spots from a leopard. It is safe to say that postmodernism arose in the late twentieth century as a number of intellectual movements critiquing the closed hegemony of modern thought. That critique has implicated all four of the paradigms of social thought examined here, although the greatest emphasis has been placed on overturning the objectivist end of the continuum—the traditions of structuralism and positivism. In that complex and wide ranging critique, the single most prominent idea put forward by postmodern philosophers has been the rejection of social science as a universal, generalizable way of accurately discovering and describing the truth about human social activity. To the postmodernists, the objectivists' claim to a method that "finds" the truth of the matter and a language to accurately represent the social world is a power move, an attempt to garner power to a small group of elite voices while suppressing and silencing nonscientific alternatives (Bernstein, 1992; Rosenau, 1992). Let us briefly look at two strands of postmodern thought, the French and the American, before examining the practical implications for special educators.

French Postmodern Thought

The French postmodern tradition includes work by Derrida (see Danforth & Rhodes, 1997), Lyotard (1984), and Foucault (1965, 1977, 1980). Much of the emphasis within the French tradition has focused on the politics of language—the ways in which specific kinds of linguistic discourse create and maintain social privilege and oppression. One aspect of this has been a thorough critique of the language of positivist science as a means of objectifying disenfranchised groups such as the poor and the disabled, thereby accruing authority to scientists and silencing the perspectives of the poor and disabled. Language use in both writing and speech is viewed by the French postmodernists as an "agonistic" (Lyotard, 1984) political terrain, a social realm of struggle where social identities and life possibilities and limitations are carved out between the tensions of opposing interests. What a person or group is called, how a person or group is described, and how individuals and groups are viewed matter deeply and have profound consequences. Life paths of wealth and power or subjugation and poverty rely on the cultural framing of identities and social relationships through language.

In Foucault's work (1965, 1977, 1980; see also Danforth, 2000), modern professions such as medicine, psychiatry, and teaching, as well as modern institutions such as prisons and schools, are cast not as the positive social forces one might assume them to be. Modern professions and institutions created to seemingly facilitate order and democracy, are tools of social control that discipline school students, psychiatric patients, and prisoners toward docility and conformity. Foucault rejects the scientific basis that these professions claim as their foundation. He exposes science as a political lever utilized to gain legitimacy and power in the field of social problems. His work provides a graphic reminder to special educators of the dark side of professions and institutions, the side that hides behind upbeat notions of scientific progress and public service.

American Postmodern Thought

The American tradition of postmodern thought is neopragmatism, a revised version of the pragmatism of William James (1907, 1909a, 1909b, 1912), John Dewey (1920, 1929, 1938), and Jane Addams (1902). In the early 1900s, these pragmatists initiated what West (1989) calls "the American evasion of philosophy." What these thinkers evaded was the basic epistemological question—"What is truth?"—because they viewed this question as a dead end that yielded little practical support to people attempting to live in intentional and ethical ways. They set aside the age-old mission of universal, certain truth for the specificity and uncertainty of human judgement within actual experiences. They attempted to foster both individuality and community within a liberal democracy by acknowledging the practicality of viewing truth as multiple and variable across situations. They demoted truth from statements that apply across time and place to ideas that work for real people in real situations, ideas that people can use to accomplish worthwhile goals.

Teacher as *Bricoleur:* Postmodernism in Action

A *bricoleur* is a versatile person who finds, creates, and modifies intellectual and practical tools to fit the specific situations she faces. The special educator who is informed by postmodern thought seeks the political and humanistic ends espoused by the humanist and the structuralist. As West (1993, p. 105) explains, "The moral aim and political goal of such intellectual activity are the creation of greater individual freedom in culture and broader democracy in the economy and society." This points toward a vision of public schools and communities that accept, respect, and support all people, regardless of ability or disability. Traditions of segregation and stigmatization are actively replaced with new social habits of inclusion and dignity. Yet these goals are not assumed to depend on the truthfulness of a certain knowledge base or research project. The *bricoleur* seeks these goals through her creative and insatiable habit of finding tools and making ways to take practical steps in democratic directions.

The common disability researcher's promise to progressively unlock the hidden truths of learning disabilities or mental retardation is a dull mantra to the postmodern special educator, a stale salesman's pitch about the timeless and universal brilliance of his tools. To this teacher, all ideas put forward—whether they are from colleagues, supervisors, researchers, students, parents, poets, or janitors—are tools that may be helpful or unhelpful in a given situation. The key is to critically and continuously sift through the many ideas offered—the many ways of thinking about disabilities, teaching, and humanity—in order to borrow, combine, and refashion them toward greater utility in specific circumstances.

The postmodern teacher does not believe that the researchers from any of the four strands of social thought are unlocking mysteries of disabilities or validating effective practices. This teacher reads research, or hears conference presentations, with an irreverent and democratic impulse, peeling away the authority of the researchers' language and universal intentions in order to seek useful tools for social change.

This teacher also borrows the tools of the humanist and the interpretivist who teaches that listening deeply to the words of disabled persons and their families is crucial. The voices of the disabled and labeled, as well as the perspectives of their families, must be included in the ongoing democratic conversation of issues and possibilities. The common professional tendency to hear these voices as biased and lesser than the scientific findings is rejected wholesale by the postmodern special educator. While the scientific traditions have often positioned persons as either the "able us" or the "disabled them," the postmodern *bricoleur* seeks concrete ways to create alliances with disabled individuals, with families, and with the disability community.

WHAT LIES AHEAD?

The pages of this book contain previously published articles and excerpts from books that include offerings from all five strands of social thought (see Figure 2). Many combine multiple strands in a single essay or research study. We have selected what we view as a broad array of challenging materials that present diverse views that refuse superficial consensus. In doing so, we assume that the complex social and ethical issues that face our profession require not a bland conformity to a single goal and common set of practices but a rich and thoughtful, democratic dialogue about both means and ends. Although intellectual conformity can be temporarily comforting, we believe that an open ear to the current critiques of special education coming both from within the field and from the disabled community requires our open minds and courageous hearts.

As a group, these readings display and challenge the narrowly positivistic tradition of the field of special education. They ask us to explore complex human issues with sensitivity and humility, to reconsider the value of our goals within the social world, and to critically examine our own beliefs and actions in light of these goals. They require us to learn new languages, hear previously unheard voices, try out new visions, and construe disability in seemingly strange ways. Perhaps most of all, they implore us to view our work through lenses both political and ethical, asking us to think deep and long about how our beliefs and actions matter.

We have structured this book into two sections, each of which contains four chapters. The chapters consist of a wide array of previously published works. We have attempted to include both well-known, classic articles in the field, as well as some little known, unique perspectives. At all times, our intention has been to draw from as many disciplines as possible and raise as many crucial issues as possible.

In Section One, *Social, Historical, Theoretical, and Philosophical Foundations of Special Education,* we have gathered articles that explore broad social and political issues that are vital to practitioners in the field. This section examines the structures and stories that lay deep behind the obvious practicalities of everyday teaching. The articles flesh out the dimensions of that background that give meaning to the everyday foreground, helping us understand how special education as a field and special education teaching have become what they are. Inherent in these chapters is the notion that the current state of affairs in the field might have turned out differently, and might still change direction, given the right constellation of social forces and human effort. The story (or stories) of special education is complex, and much about how we got here or what we are currently trying to do can be argued on many sides. Moreover, the story (or stories) is far from over. The plot continues to thicken with our work each day.

In Section Two, *Issues and Innovations in Special Education Practices,* we focus more explicitly on pedagogical practices, what professionals do or might do in their daily work.

Positivism

Horner, R. H. & Carr, E. G. (1997). Behavioral support for students with severe disabilities: Functional assessment and comprehensive intervention. *The Journal of Special Education, 31*(1), 84–104.

MacMillan, D., Gresham, F. M., & Forness, S. R. (1996). Full inclusion: An empirical perspective. *Behavioral Disorders, 21*(2), 145–159.

Interpretivism

Ferguson, P., Ferguson, D., & Jones, D. (1988). Generations of hope: Parental perspectives on the transitions of their children with severe retardation from school to adult life. *Journal of the Association for Persons with Severe Handicaps, 13*(3), 177–187.

Gallagher, D. (1998). The scientific knowledge base in special education: Do we know what we think we know? *Exceptional Children, 64*(4), 493–502.

Harry, B. (1992). Making sense of disability: Low-income, Puerto Rican parents' theories of the problem. *Exceptional Children, 59*(1), 27–40.

Radical humanism

Biklen, D. (1990). Communication unbound: Autism and praxis. *Harvard Educational Review, 60*(3), 291–314.

Brantlinger, E. (1997). Using ideology: cases of nonrecognition of the politics of research and practice in special education. *Review of Educational Research, 67*(4), 425–459.

Taylor, S. J. & Bogdan, R. (1989). On accepting relationships between people with mental retardation and non-disabled people: Towards an understanding of acceptance. *Disability, Handicap, & Society, 4*(1), 21–36.

Radical structuralism

Carrier, J. G. (1986). Sociology and special education: Differentiation and allocation in mass education. *American Journal of Education, 94*, 281–312.

Oliver, M. (1992). Changing the social relations of research production? *Disability, Handicap, and Society, 7*(2), 101–114.

Postmodernism

Danforth, S. (1997). On what basis hope? Modern progress and postmodern possibilities. *Mental Retardation, 35*(2), 93–106.

Smith, P. (1999). Drawing new maps: A radical cartography of developmental disabilities. *Review of Educational Research, 69*(2), 117–144.

Figure 2
Published examples of forms of social thought in special education.

Rather than break these practices down into sections by disability type or in terms of the severity of the disability, we have categorized these into general areas of professional activity.

Despite the size of this volume, we are very aware that we have ignored or given short treatment to many important issues and concerns. Educators who work with students considered to have "low incidence" disabilities are likely to find little that directly addresses problems and practices in their field. It is our hope that, by providing an expansive and thought provoking series of works, we have given even these professionals much to chew on and learn from.

In the end, the best we can do is open ourselves and our circles of professional and personal connection to dialogues that challenge us deeply and repeatedly, that ask us to question what we think we know and reimagine what we think we are doing. We aim this volume of readings toward the goal of a more creative, cooperative, and practical dialogue among professionals, families, and persons with disabilities.

References

Addams, J. (1902). *Democracy and social ethics.* New York: Macmillan.

Bernstein, R. J. (1992). *The new constellation: the ethical-political horizons of modernity/postmodernity.* Cambridge, MA: MIT Press.

Blatt, B. (1999). *In search of the promised land: The collected papers of Burton Blatt.* Washington, DC: American Association on Mental Retardation.

Bruner, J. (1996). *The culture of education.* Cambridge, MA: Harvard University Press.

Burrell, G., & Morgan, G. (1979). *Sociological paradigms and organizational analysis.* London: Heinemann.

Champagne, R. A. (1990). *French structuralism.* Boston, MA: Twayne Publishers.

Danforth, S., & Rhodes, W. C. (1997). Deconstructing disability: A philosophy for inclusion. *Remedial & Special Education, 18*(6), 57–66.

Danforth, S. (1999). Pragmatism and the scientific validation of professional practices in American special education. *Disability & Society, 14*(6), 733–751.

Danforth, S. (2000). What can the field of developmental disabilities learn from Michel Foucault? *Mental Retardation, 38*(4), 364–369.

Danforth, S. (2001). A pragmatic evaluation of three models of disability in special education. *Journal of Developmental & Physical Disabilities, 13*(4), 343–359.

Dewey, J. (1920). *Reconstruction in philosophy.* New York: H. Holt and Co.

Dewey, J. (1929). *The quest for certainty: A study of the relation of knowledge and action.* New York: Minton, Balch.

Dewey, J. (1938). *Logic: The theory of inquiry.* New York: H. Holt and Co.

Dudley-Marling, C. (1996). Acknowledging the why of method. In L. Heshusius & K. Ballard (Eds.), *From positivism to interpretivism and beyond: Tales of transformation in educational and social research* (pp. 108–114). New York: Teachers College Press.

Ferguson, P. M., & Ferguson, D. L. (1995). The interpretivist view of special education and disability: The value of telling stories. In T. M. Skrtic (Ed.), *Disability and democracy: Reconstructing special education for postmodernity* (pp. 104–121). New York: Teachers College Press.

Foucault, M. (1965). *Madness and civilization: A history of insanity in the age of reason.* New York: Pantheon Books.

Foucault, M. (1977). *Discipline and punish: The birth of the prison.* New York: Pantheon Books.

Foucault, M. (1980). *Power/knowledge: Selected interviews and other writings, 1972–1977.* New York: Pantheon Books.

Giroux, H. (1983). *Theory & resistance in education.* New York: Bergin & Garvey Publishers, Inc.

Goffman, E. (1963). *Stigma: Notes on the management of spoiled identity.* Upper Saddle River, NJ: Prentice Hall.

Golubovic, Z. (1978). Self-realization, equality, and freedom. In G. S. Sher (Ed.), *Marxist humanism and praxis* (pp. 175–182). Buffalo, NY: Prometheus Books.

Hacking, I. (1999). *The social construction of what?* Cambridge, MA: Harvard University Press.

Hahn, H. (1983). Paternalism and public policy. *Society, 20,* 36–46.

Hahn, H. (1985). Introduction: Disability policy and the problem of discrimination. *American Behavioral Scientist, 28*(3), 293–318.

James, W. (1909a). *The meaning of truth.* New York: Longmans, Green.

James, W. (1909b). *A pluralistic universe.* New York: Longmans, Green.

James, W. (1907). *Pragmatism, a new name for some old ways of thinking: Popular lectures on philosophy.* New York: Longmans, Green.

James, W. (1912). *Essays in radical empiricism.* New York: Longmans, Green.

Kiel, D. C. (1995). The radical humanist view of special education and disability: Consciousness, freedom, and ideology. In T. M. Skrtic (Ed.), *Disability and democracy: Reconstructing special education for postmodernity* (pp. 135–149). New York: Teachers College Press.

Kurzweil, E. (1980). *The age of structuralism: Levi-Strauss to Foucault.* New York: Columbia University Press.

Lyotard, J. F. (1984). *The postmodern condition: A report on knowledge.* Minneapolis: University of Minnesota Press.

Lyotard, J. F. (1991). *Phenomenology.* (B. Beakley, Trans.). Albany, NY: State University of New York Press.

Markovic, M. (1978). Reason and historical praxis. In G. S. Sher (Ed.), *Marxist humanism and praxis* (pp. 19–33). Buffalo, NY: Prometheus Books.

Merleau-Ponty, M. (1962). *Phenomenology of perception.* (C. Smith, Trans.). London: Routledge & Kegan Paul Ltd.

Noddings, N. (1984). *Caring, a feminine approach to ethics and moral education.* Berkeley, CA: University of California Press.

Noddings, N. (1992). *The challenge to care in schools: An alternative approach to education.* New York: Teachers College Press.

Rosenau, P. M. (1992). *Post-modernism and the social sciences: Insights, inroads, and intrusions.* Princeton, NJ: Princeton University Press.

Sher, G. S. (1978). *Marxist humanism and praxis.* Buffalo, NY: Prometheus Books.

Skrtic, T. M. (1991). *Behind special education: A critical analysis of professional culture and school organization.* Denver, CO: Love Publishing Company.

Skrtic, T. M. (1995). The functionalist view of special education and disability: Deconstructing the conventional knowledge tradition. In T. M. Skrtic (Ed.), *Disability and democracy: Reconstructing special education for postmodernity* (pp. 65–103). New York: Teachers College Press.

Tomlinson, S. (1995). The radical structuralist view of special education and disability: Unpopular perspectives on their origins and development. In T. M. Skrtic (Ed.), *Disability and democracy: Reconstructing special education for postmodernity* (pp. 122–134). New York: Teachers College Press.

West, C. (1989). *The American evasion of philosophy: A genealogy of pragmatism.* Madison, WI: University of Wisconsin Press.

West, C. (1993). *Keeping faith: Philosophy and race in America.* New York: Routledge.

Part One

Social, Historical, Theoretical, and Philosophical Foundations of Special Education

Chapter One

Historical and Sociological Analyses of Disabilities Issues

1.1   The Discovery of Hyperkinesis:

Notes on the Medicalization of Deviant Behavior

Peter Conrad

INTRODUCTION

The increasing medicalization of deviant behavior and the medical institution's role as an agent of social control has gained considerable notice (Freidson, 1970; Pitts, 1968; Kitterie, 1971; Zola, 1972). By *medicalization* we mean defining behavior as a medical problem or illness and mandating or licensing the medical profession to provide some type of treatment for it. Examples include alcoholism, drug addiction, and treating violence as a genetic or brain disorder. This redefinition is not a new function of the medical institution: psychiatry and public health have always been concerned with social behavior and have traditionally functioned as agents of social control (Foucault, 1965; Szasz, 1970; Rosen, 1972). Increasingly sophisticated medical technology has extended the potential of this type of social control, especially in terms of psychotechnology (Chorover, 1973). This approach includes a variety of medical and quasi-medical treatments or procedures: psychosurgery, psychotropic medications, genetic engineering, antibuse, and methadone.

This paper describes how certain forms of behavior in children have become defined as a medical problem and how medicine has become a major agent for their social control since the discovery of hyperkinesis. By discovery we mean both origin of the diagnosis and treatment for this disorder, and discovery of children who exhibit this behavior. The first section analyzes the discovery of hyperkinesis and why it suddenly became popular in the 1960's. The second section will discuss the medicalization of deviant behavior and its ramifications.

"The Discovery of Hyperkinesis: Notes on the Medicalization of Deviant Behavior" by P. Conrad, 1975. *Social Problems* 23(1), pp. 12–21. Copyright © 1975 by the Society for the Study of Social Problems. Reprinted by permission.

THE MEDICAL DIAGNOSIS OF HYPERKINESIS

Hyperkinesis is a relatively recent phenomenon as a medical diagnostic category. Only in the past two decades has it been available as a recognized diagnostic category and only in the last decade has it received widespread notice and medical popularity. However, the roots of the diagnosis and treatment of this clinical entity are found earlier.

Hyperkinesis is also known as Minimal Brain Dysfunction, Hyperactive Syndrome, Hyperkinetic Disorder of Childhood, and by several other diagnostic categories. Although the symptoms and the presumed etiology vary, in general the behaviors are quite similar and greatly overlap.[1] Typical symptom patterns for diagnosing the disorder include: extreme excess of motor activity (hyperactivity); very short attention span (the child flits from activity to activity); restlessness; fidgetiness; often wildly oscillating mood swings (he's fine one day, a terror the next); clumsiness; aggressive-like behavior; impulsivity; in school he cannot sit still, cannot comply with rules, has low frustration level; frequently there may be sleeping problems and acquisition of speech may be delayed (Stewart et al., 1966; Stewart, 1970; Wender, 1971). Most of the symptoms for the disorder are deviant behaviors.[2] It is six times as prevalent among boys as among girls. We use the term hyperkinesis to represent all the diagnostic categories of this disorder.

THE DISCOVERY OF HYPERKINESIS

It is useful to divide the analysis into what might be considered *clinical factors* directly related to the diagnosis and treatment of hyperkinesis and *social factors* that set the context for the emergence of the new diagnostic category.

Clinical Factors

Bradley (1937) observed that amphetamine drugs had a spectacular effect in altering the behavior of school children who exhibited behavior disorders or learning disabilities. Fifteen of the thirty children he treated actually became more subdued in their behavior. Bradley termed the effect of this medication paradoxical, since he expected that amphetamines would stimulate children as they stimulated adults. After the medication was discontinued the children's behavior returned to premedication level.

A scattering of reports in the medical literature on the utility of stimulant medications for "childhood behavior disorders" appeared in the next two decades. The next significant contribution was the work of Strauss and his associates (Strauss & Lehtinen, 1947) who found certain behavior (including hyperkinesis behaviors) in postencephaletic children suffering from what they called minimal brain injury (damage). This was the first time these behaviors were attributed to the new organic distinction of minimal brain damage.

This disorder still remained unnamed or else it was called a variety of names (usually just "childhood behavior disorder"). It did not appear as a specific diagnostic category until Laufer, Denhoff, and Solomons (1957) described it as the "hyperkinetic impulse disorder" in 1957. Upon finding "the salient characteristics of the behavior pattern . . . are strikingly similar to those with clear cut organic causation" these researchers described a disorder with no clear-cut history or evidence for organicity (Laufer et al., 1957).

In 1966 a task force sponsored by the U.S. Public Health Service and the National Association for Crippled Children and Adults attempted to clarify the ambiguity and confusion in terminology and symptomology in diagnosing children's behavior and learning disorders. From over three dozen diagnoses, they agreed on the term "minimal brain dysfunction" as an overriding diagnosis that would include hyperkinesis and other disorders (Clements, 1966). Since this time M.B.D. has been the primary formal diagnosis or label.

In the middle 1950's a new drug, Ritalin, was synthesized, that has many qualities of amphetamines without some of their more undesirable side effects. In 1961 this drug was approved by the FDA for use with children. Since this time there has been much research published on the use of Ritalin in the treatment of childhood behavior disorders. This medica-tion became the "treatment of choice" for treating children with hyperkinesis.

Since the early sixties, more research appeared on the etiology, diagnosis and treatment of hyperkinesis (cf. DeLong, 1972; Grinspoon & Singer, 1973; Cole, 1975)—as much as three-quarters concerned with drug treatment of the disorder. There had been increasing publicity of the disorder in the mass media as well. The *Reader's Guide to Periodical Literature* had no articles on hyperkinesis before 1967, one each in 1968 and 1969, and a total of forty for 1970 through 1974 (a mean of eight per year).

Now hyperkinesis has become the most common child psychiatric problem (Gross & Wilson, 1974, p. 142); special pediatric clinics have been established to treat hyperkinetic children, and substantial federal funds have been invested in etiological and treatment research. Outside the medical profession, teachers have developed a working clinical knowledge of hyperkinesis' symptoms and treatment (cf. Robin & Bosco, 1973); articles appear regularly in mass circulation magazines and newspapers so that parents often come to clinics with knowledge of this diagnosis. Hyperkinesis is no longer the relatively esoteric diagnostic category it may have been twenty years ago; it is now a well-known clinical disorder.

Social Factors

The social factors affecting the discovery of hyperkinesis can be divided into two areas: (1) The Pharmaceutical Revolution; (2) Government Action.

1. The Pharmaceutical Revolution. Since the 1930's the pharmaceutical industry has been synthesizing and manufacturing a large number of psychoactive drugs, contributing to a virtual revolution in drug making and drug taking in America (Silverman & Lee, 1974).

Psychoactive drugs are agents that effect the central nervous system. Benzedrine, Ritalin, and Dexedrine are all synthesized psychoactive stimulants which were indicated for narcolepsy, appetite control (as "diet pills"), mild depression, fatigue, and more recently hyperkinetic children.

Until the early sixties there was little or no promotion and advertisement of any of these medications for use with childhood disorders.[3] Then two major pharmaceutical firms (Smith, Kline and French, manufacturer of Dexedrine, and CIBA, manufacturer of Ritalin) began to advertise in medical journals and through direct mailing and efforts of the "detail men." Most of this advertising of the pharmaceutical treatment of hyperkinesis was directed to the medical sphere; but some of the promotion was targeted for the educational sector also (Hentoff, 1972). This promotion was probably significant in disseminating information concerning the diagnosis and treatment of this newly discovered disorder.[4] Since 1955 the use of psychoactive medications (especially phenothiazines) for the treatment of persons who are mentally ill, along with the concurrent dramatic decline in inpatient populations, has made psychopharmacology an integral part of treatment for mental disorders. It has also undoubtedly increased the confidence in the medical profession for the pharmaceutical approach to mental and behavioral problems.

2. Government Action. Since the publication of the USPHS report on MBD there have been at least two significant governmental reports on treating school children with stimulant medications for behavior disorders. Both of these came as a response to the national publicity created by the *Washington Post* report (1970) that five to ten percent of the 62,000 grammar school children in Omaha, Nebraska were being treated with "behavior modification drugs to improve deportment and increase learning potential" (quoted in Grinspoon & Singer, 1973). Although the figures were later found to be a little exaggerated, it nevertheless spurred a Congressional investigation (U.S. Government Printing Office, 1970) and a conference sponsored by the Office of Child Development (1971) on the use of stimulant drugs in the treatment of behaviorally disturbed school children.

The Congressional Subcommittee on Privacy chaired by Congressman Cornelius E. Gallagher held hearings on the issue of prescribing drugs for hyperactive school children. In general, the committee showed great concern over the facility in which the medication was prescribed; more specifically that some children at least were receiving drugs from general practitioners whose primary diagnosis was based on teachers' and parents' reports that the child was doing poorly in school. There was also a concern with the absence of follow-up studies on the long-term effects of treatment.

The HEW committee was a rather hastily convened group of professionals (a majority were M.D.'s) many of whom already had commitments to drug treatment for children's behavior problems. They recommended that only M.D.'s make the diagnosis and prescribe treatment, that the pharmaceutical companies promote the treatment of the disorder only through medical channels, that parents should not be coerced to accept any particular treatment,

and that long-term follow-up research should be done. This report served as blue ribbon approval for treating hyperkinesis with psychoactive medications.

DISCUSSION

We will focus discussion on three issues: How children's deviant behavior became conceptualized as a medical problem; why this occurred when it did; and what are some of the implications of the medicalization of deviant behavior.

How does deviant behavior become conceptualized as a medical problem? We assume that before the discovery of hyperkinesis this type of deviance was seen as disruptive, disobedient, rebellious, antisocial, or deviant behavior. Perhaps the label "emotionally disturbed" was sometimes used, when it was in vogue in the early sixties, and the child was usually managed in the context of the family or the school or in extreme cases, the child guidance clinic. How then did this constellation of deviant behaviors become a medical disorder?

The treatment was available long before the disorder treated was clearly conceptualized. It was twenty years after Bradley's discovery of the "paradoxical effect" of stimulants on certain deviant children that Laufer named the disorder and described its characteristic symptoms. Only in the late fifties were both the diagnostic label and the pharmaceutical treatment available. The pharmaceutical revolution in mental health and the increased interest in child psychiatry provided a favorable background for the dissemination of knowledge about this new disorder. The latter probably made the medical profession more likely to consider behavior problems in children as within their clinical jurisdiction.

There were agents outside the medical profession itself that were significant in "promoting" hyperkinesis as a disorder within the medical framework. These agents might be conceptualized in Becker's terms as *moral entrepreneurs*, those who crusade for creation and enforcement of the rules (Becker, 1963).[5] In this case the moral entrepreneurs were the pharmaceutical companies and the Association for Children with Learning Disabilities.

The pharmaceutical companies spent considerable time and money promoting stimulant medications for this new disorder. From the middle 1960's on, medical journals and the free "throwaway" magazines contained elaborate advertising for Ritalin and Dexedrine. These ads explained the utility of treating hyperkinesis and urged the physician to diagnose and treat hyperkinetic children. The ads run from one to six pages. For example, a two-page ad in 1971 stated:

MBD ... MEDICAL MYTH OR DIAGNOSABLE DISEASE ENTITY What medical practitioner has not, at one time or another, been called upon to examine an impulsive, excitable hyperkinetic child? A child with difficulty in concentrating. Easily frustrated. Unusually aggressive. A classroom rebel. In the absence of any organic pathology, the conduct of such children was, until a few short years ago, usually dismissed as ... spunkiness, or evidence of youthful vitality. But it is now evident that in many of these children the hyperkinetic syndrome exists as a distinct medical entity. This syndrome is readily diagnosed through patient histories, neurologic signs, and psychometric testing— has been classified by an expert panel convened by the United States Department of Health, Education and Welfare as Minimal Brain Dysfunction, MBD.

The pharmaceutical firms also supplied sophisticated packets of "diagnostic and treatment" information on hyperkinesis to physicians, paid for professional conferences on the subject, and supported research in the identification and treatment of the disorder. Clearly these corporations had a vested interest in the labeling and treatment of hyperkinesis; CIBA had $13 million profit from Ritalin alone in 1971, which was 15 percent of the total gross profits (Charles, 1971; Hentoff, 1972).

The other moral entrepreneur, less powerful than the pharmaceutical companies, but nevertheless influential, is the Association for Children with Learning Disabilities. Although its focus is not specifically on hyperkinetic children, it does include it in its conception of Learning Disabilities along with aphasia, reading problems like dyslexia, and perceptual motor problems. Founded in the early 1950's by parents and professionals, it has functioned much as the National Association for Mental Health does for mental illness: promoting conferences, sponsoring legislation, providing social support. One of the main functions has been to disseminate information concerning this relatively new area in education, Learning Disabilities. While the organization does have a more educational than medical perspective, most of the literature indicates that for hyperkinesis members have adopted the medical model and the medical approach to the problem. They have sensitized teachers and schools to the conception of hyperkinesis as a medical problem.

The medical model of hyperactive behavior has become very well accepted in our society. Physicians find treatment relatively simple and the results sometimes spectacular. Hyperkinesis minimizes parents'

guilt by emphasizing "It's not their fault, it's an organic problem" and allows for nonpunitive management or control of deviance. Medication often makes a child less disruptive in the classroom and sometimes aids a child in learning. Children often like their "magic pills" which make their behavior more socially acceptable and they probably benefit from a reduced stigma also. There are, however, some other, perhaps more subtle ramifications of the medicalization of deviant behavior.

THE MEDICALIZATION OF DEVIANT BEHAVIOR

Pitts has commented that "Medicalization is one of the most effective means of social control and that it is destined to become the main mode of *formal* social control" (1971, p. 391). Kitterie (1971) has termed it "the coming of the therapeutic state."

Medicalization of mental illness dates at least from the seventeenth century (Foucault, 1965; Szasz, 1970). Even slaves who ran away were once considered to be suffering from the disease *drapedomania* (Chorover, 1973). In recent years alcoholism, violence, and drug addiction as well as hyperactive behavior in children have all become defined as medical problems, both in etiology or explanation of the behavior and the means of social control or treatment.

There are many reasons why this medicalization has occurred. Much scientific research, especially in pharmacology and genetics, has become technologically more sophisticated, and found more subtle correlates with human behavior. Sometimes these findings (as in the case of XYY chromosomes and violence) become etiological explanations for deviance. Pharmacological technology that makes new discoveries affecting behavior (e.g., antibuse, methadone, and stimulants) are used as treatment for deviance. In part this application is encouraged by the prestige of the medical profession and its attachment to science. As Freidson notes, the medical profession has first claim to jurisdiction over anything that deals with the functioning of the body and especially anything that can be labeled illness (1970, p. 251). Advances in genetics, pharmacology, and "psychosurgery" also may advance medicine's jurisdiction over deviant behavior.

Second, the application of pharmacological technology is related to the humanitarian trend in the conception and control of deviant behavior. Alcoholism is no longer sin or even moral weakness, it is now a disease. Alcoholics are no longer arrested in many places for "public drunkenness," they are now somehow "treated," even if it is only to be dried out. Hyperactive children are now considered to have an illness rather than to be disruptive, disobedient, overactive problem children. They are not as likely to be the "bad boy" of the classroom; they are children with a medical disorder. Clearly there are some real humanitarian benefits to be gained by such a medical conceptualization of deviant behavior. There is less condemnation of the deviants (they have an illness, it is not their fault) and perhaps less social stigma. In some cases, even the medical treatment itself is more humanitarian social control than the criminal justice system.

There is, however, another side to the medicalization of deviant behavior. The four aspects of this side of the issue include (1) the problem of expert control; (2) medical social control; (3) the individualization of social problems; and (4) the "depoliticization" of deviant behavior.

1. The Problem of Expert Control. The medical profession is a profession of experts; they have a monopoly on anything that can be conceptualized as illness. Because of the way the medical profession is organized and the mandate it has from society, decisions related to medical diagnoses and treatment are virtually controlled by medical professionals.

Some conditions that enter the medical domain are not ipso facto medical problems, especially deviant behavior, whether alcoholism, hyperactivity, or drug addiction. By defining a problem as medical it is removed from the public realm where there can be discussion by ordinary people and put on a plane where only medical people can discuss it. As Reynolds states,

> The increasing acceptance, especially among the more educated segments of our populace, of technical solutions—solutions administered by disinterested politically and morally neutral experts—results in the withdrawal of more and more areas of human experience from the realm of public discussion. For when drunkenness, juvenile delinquency, sub par performance and extreme political beliefs are seen as symptoms of an underlying illness or biological defect the merits and drawbacks of such behavior or beliefs need not be evaluated. (1973, pp. 220–221)

The public may have their own conceptions of deviant behavior but that of the experts is usually dominant.

2. Medical Social Control. Defining deviant behavior as a medical problem allows certain things to be done that could not otherwise be considered; for example, the body may be cut open or psychoactive medica-

tions may be given. This treatment can be a form of social control.

In regard to drug treatment Lennard points out: "Psychoactive drugs, especially those legally prescribed, tend to restrain individuals from behavior and experience that are not complementary to the requirements of the dominant value system" (1971, p. 57). These forms of medical social control presume a prior definition of deviance as a medical problem. Psychosurgery on an individual prone to violent outbursts requires a diagnosis that there was something wrong with his brain or nervous system. Similarly, prescribing drugs to restless, overactive, and disruptive school children requires a diagnosis of hyperkinesis. These forms of social control, what Chorover (1973) has called "psychotechnology," are very powerful and often very efficient means of controlling deviance. These relatively new and increasingly popular forms of social control could not be utilized without the medicalization of deviant behavior. As is suggested from the discovery of hospice, if a mechanism of medical social control seems useful, then the deviant behavior it modifies will develop a medical label or diagnosis. No overt malevolence on the part of the medical profession is implied: rather it is part of a complex process, of which the medical profession is only a part. The larger process might be called the individualization of social problems.

3. The Individualization of Social Problems. The medicalization of deviant behavior is part of a larger phenomenon that is prevalent in our society, the individualization of social problems. We tend to look for causes and solutions to complex social problems in the individual rather than in the social system. The medical perspective of diagnosing an illness in an individual lends itself to the individualization of social problems. Rather than seeing certain deviant behaviors as symptomatic of problems in the social system, the medical perspective focuses on the individual diagnosing and treating the illness, generally ignoring the social situation.

Hyperkinesis serves as a good example. Both the school and the parents are concerned with the child's behavior; the child is very difficult at home and disruptive in school. No punishments or rewards seem consistently to work in modifying the behavior; and both parents and school are at their wit's end. A medical evaluation is suggested. The diagnoses of hyperkinetic behavior leads to prescribing stimulant medications. The child's behavior seems to become more socially acceptable, reducing problems in school and at home.

But there is an alternate perspective. By focusing on the symptoms and defining them as hyperkinesis we ignore the possibility that behavior is not an illness but an adaptation to a social situation. It diverts our attention from the family or school and from seriously entertaining the idea that *the "problem" could be in the structure of the social system.* And by giving medications we are essentially supporting the existing systems and do not allow this behavior to be a factor of change in the system.

4. The Depoliticization of Deviant Behavior. Depoliticization of deviant behavior is a result of both the process of medicalization and individualization of social problems. To our western world, probably one of the clearest examples of such a depoliticization of deviant behavior occurred when political dissenters in the Soviet Union were declared mentally ill and confined in mental hospitals (cf. Conrad, 1972). This strategy served to neutralize the meaning of political protest and dissent, rendering it the ravings of mad persons.

The medicalization of deviant behavior depoliticizes deviance in the same manner. By defining the overactive, restless and disruptive child as hyperki-netic we ignore the meaning of behavior in the context of the social system. If we focused our analysis on the school system we might see the child's behavior as symptomatic of some "disorder" in the school or classroom situation, rather than symptomatic of an individual neurological disorder.

CONCLUSION

I have discussed the social ramifications of the medicalization of deviant behavior, using hyperkinesis as the example. A number of consequences of this medicalization have been outlined, including the depoliticization of deviant behavior, decision-making power of experts, and the role of medicine as an agent of social control. In the last analysis medical social control may be the central issue, as in this role medicine becomes a de facto agent of the status quo. The medical profession may not have entirely sought this role, but its members have been, in general, disturbingly unconcerned and unquestioning in their acceptance of it. With the increasing medical knowledge and technology it is likely that more deviant behavior will be medicalized and medicine's social control function will expand.

Notes

1. The USPHS report (Clements, 1966) included 38 terms that were used to describe or distinguish the conditions that it labeled Minimal Brain Dysfunction. Although the literature attempts to differentiate MBD, hyperkinesis, hyperactive syndrome, and several other diagnostic labels, it is our belief that in practice they are almost interchangeable.

2. For a fuller discussion of the construction of the diagnosis of hyperkinesis, see Conrad (1976), especially Chapter 6.

3. The American Medical Association's change in policy in accepting more pharmaceutical advertising in the late fifties may have been important. Probably the FDA approval of the use of Ritalin for children in 1961 was more signifi-cant. Until 1970, Ritalin was advertised for treatment of "functional behavior problems in children." Since then, because of an FDA order, it has only been promoted for treatment of MBD.

4. The drug industry spends fully 25 percent of its budget on promotion and advertising. See Coleman, Katz, & Menzel (1966) for the role of the detail men and how physicians rely upon them for information.

5. Freidson also notes the medical professional role as moral entrepreneur in this process: "The profession does treat the illnesses laymen take to it, but it also seeks to discover illness of which the laymen may not even be aware. One of the greatest ambitions of the physician is to discover and describe a 'new' disease or syndrome . . . " (1970, p. 252).

References

Becker, H. S. (1963). *The outsiders.* New York: Free Press.

Bradley, C. (1937, March). The behavior of children receiving Benzedrine. *American Journal of Psychiatry, 94,* 577–585.

Charles, A. (1971, October). The case of Ritalin. *New Republic, 23,* 17–19.

Chorover, S. L. (1973, October). Big brother and psychotechnology. *Psychology Today,* pp. 43–54.

Clements, S. D. (1966). *Task force 1: Minimal brain dysfunction in children* (National Institute of Neurological Diseases and Blindness, Monograph no. 3). Washington, DC: U.S. Department of Health, Education, and Welfare.

Cole, S. (1975, January). Hyperactive children: The use of stimulant drugs evaluated. *American Journal of Orthopsychiatry, 45,* 28–37.

Coleman, J., Katz, E., & Menzel, H. (1966). *Medical innovation.* Indianapolis: Bobbs-Merrill.

Conrad, P. (1972). *Ideological deviance: An analysis of the Soviet use of mental hospitals for political dissenters.* Unpublished manuscript.

Conrad, P. (1976). *Identifying hyperactive children in the medicalization of deviant behavior.* Lexington, MA: D. C. Heath & Co.

DeLong, A. R. (1972, February). What have we learned from psychoactive drugs research with hyperactives? *American Journal of Diseases in Children, 123,* 177–180.

Foucault, M. (1965). *Madness and civilization.* New York: Pantheon.

Freidson, E. (1970). *Profession of medicine.* New York: Harper & Row.

Grinspoon, L., & Singer, S. (1973, November). Amphetamines in the treatment of hyperactive children. *Harvard Educational Review, 43,* 515–555.

Gross, M. B., & Wilson, W. E. (1974). *Minimal brain dysfunction.* New York: Brunner/Mazel.

Hentoff, N. (1972, May). Drug pushing in the schools: The professionals. *Village Voice, 22,* 21–23.

Kitterie, N. (1971). *The right to be different.* Baltimore, MD: Johns Hopkins University Press.

Laufer, M. W., Denhoff, E., & Solomons, G. (1957, January). Hyperkinetic impulse disorder in children's behavior problems. *Psychosomatic Medicine, 19,* 38–49.

Lennard, H. L., & Associates. (1971). *Mystification and drug misuse.* New York: Harper & Row.

Office of Child Development. (1971, January 11–12). *Report of the conference on the use of stimulant drugs in treatment of behaviorally disturbed children.* Washington, DC: Department of Health, Education, and Welfare, January 11–12.

Pitts, J. (1968). Social control: The concept. In D. Sills (Ed.), *International Encyclopedia of the Social Sciences* (Vol. 14). New York: Macmillan.

Reynolds, J. M. (1973). The medical institution. In L. T. Reynolds & J. M. Henslin (Eds.), *American society: A critical analysis* (pp. 198–324). New York: David McKay.

Robin, S. S., & Bosco, J. J. (1973, December). Ritalin for school children: The teachers' perspective. *Journal of School Health, 47,* 624–628.

Rosen, G. (1972). The evolution of social medicine. In H. E. Freeman, S. Levine, & L. Reeder (Eds.), *Handbook of medical sociology* (pp. 30–60). Englewood Cliffs, NJ: Prentice-Hall.

Ryan, W. (1971). *Blaming the victim.* New York: Vintage.

Silverman, M., & Lee, P. R. (1974). *Pills, profits and politics.* Berkeley: University of California Press.

Sroufe, L. A., & Stewart, M. (1973, August). Treating problem children with stimulant drugs. *New England Journal of Medicine, 289,* 407–421.

Stewart, M. A. (1970, April). Hyperactive children. *Scientific American, 222,* 794–798.

Stewart, M. A., Ferris, A., Pitts, N. P., & Craig, A. G. (1966, October). The hyperactive child syndrome. *American Journal of Orthopsychiatry, 36,* 861–867.

Strauss, A. A., & Lehtinen, L. E. (1947). *Psychopathology and education of the brain-injured child* (Vol. 1). New York: Grune & Stratton.

Szasz, T. (1970). *The manufacture of madness.* New York: Harper & Row.

U.S. Government Printing Office. (1970, September 29). *Federal involvement in the use of behavior modification drugs on grammar school children of the right to privacy inquiry: Hearing before a subcommittee of the committee on government operations.* Washington, DC, 91st Congress, 2nd session.

Wender, P. (1971). *Minimal brain dysfunction in children.* New York: John Wiley.

Zola, I. (1972, November). Medicine as an institution of social control. *Sociological Review, 20,* 487–504.

1.2   A Pupil and a Patient

Hospital-Schools in Progressive America

Brad Byrom

Around the turn of the twentieth century, a new definition of disability emerged in the United States. As Americans moved from a nineteenth-century system of beliefs rooted in Protestant ideology to a modern culture embedded in secular ideologies, a new understanding of disability evolved. Beginning around 1890, with the creation of the first institutions most aptly referred to as "hospital-schools" and the opening of the first programs for the vocational training of "cripples," an approach to the problem of disability emerged that became known as *rehabilitation*.[1]

In examining the words and deeds of those involved in the movement, it is apparent that the years between 1890 and 1920 constitute a distinctive period in disability history. The movement acted as a bridge spanning the gap between nineteenth-century supernatural and post-1920 medical explanations of disability. The reformers who led this movement identified what they called "crippledom" as a serious social and economic problem. The term *cripple* referred to individuals with mobility impairments, such as amputees and paraplegics. But more than a physical description, in common usage the term also indicated economic dependency. In relying on charity, reformers believed, cripples became immoral characters who siphoned off the lifeblood of the economy. The elimination of dependency among cripples became the focus of the rehabilitation movement.

In attempting to solve the riddle of dependency, reformers struck an uneasy balance between social approaches to disability that sought to reform cultural attitudes and individual or medical approaches intended to correct flaws in disabled people. This balance is evident not only in the discourse that sur-

rounded the rehabilitation movement but in the structure and purpose of the institutions created. Some reformers, whom I describe as "social rehabilitationists," emphasized the need for social and cultural change and saw little need to change the disabled person through surgery, physical therapy, or other such methods. "Medical rehabilitationists," by contrast, viewed the individual as the central problem of disability and focused their efforts on orthopedic surgery, moral education, and other solutions centering on repair of the individual.[2] Yet it is also important to realize that neither group outwardly rejected the tenets of the other. In fact, most rehabilitationists reflected a bit of each perspective in their writings. Thus, it is best to see the differences between the two groups as points along a continuum, separated by degrees of emphasis, rather than as diametrically opposed positions.

The approach taken by medical rehabilitationists forms the core of what is defined by scholars in the field of disability studies as the "medical model." Those who employ this model define disability in the language of medicine, which lends scientific credibility to the notion that physical and mental abnormalities are at the root of all problems encountered by disabled individuals. Medical rehabilitationists absolved society of any complicity in the exclusion of disabled people from such social functions as employment, marriage, and even access to public institutions such as schools or government buildings. On this point social rehabilitationists clearly differed. Yet, somewhat surprisingly, neither group rejected the ideas of the other or even seemed aware of the contradictions within the movement. Instead, many, if not most, blurred the lines between the social and medical perspectives in their own writings, expressing elements of both approaches in their calls for reform.

By settling on a middle ground between the two approaches, rehabilitationists inadvertently slowed,

Byrom, B. (2001). A pupil and a patient: Hospital-schools in progressive America. In P. K. Longmore & L. Umansky (Eds.), *The new disability history. American perspectives* (pp. 133–156). New York: New York University Press. Reprinted by permission.

but did not prevent, the full development of the medical model. In an age noted for its devotion to science and the expert, the slow growth of the medical paradigm demands an explanation. This explanation can be found by looking to the position of the "scientific experts" most directly connected to the rehabilitation movement—orthopedic surgeons.

In the first decades of the century, orthopedists lacked the credibility necessary to dominate the rehabilitation movement. Over the century or so prior to 1890, they gained recognition in the medical community as the specialists best suited to the care of cripples.[3] Despite their uncontested position in medical circles, they failed to gain preeminence in the rehabilitation movement until the conclusion of World War I. Known in the nineteenth century as "sawbones" or worse, early-twentieth-century orthopedic surgeons failed to earn unquestioned control of rehabilitation and were forced to share leadership with businessmen, social scientists, teachers, and other "progressive," reform-minded individuals. These individuals came together to answer the most fundamental questions concerning disability: Did older, nineteenth-century notions of divine causation still have validity in the twentieth century? Were cripples primarily a product of individual, physical impairment? Or rather, were they victims of stereotypes and social discrimination?

In cities such as Boston, New York, and Cleveland, reformers of the 1890s began to address these questions with unprecedented enthusiasm. The conclusions they reached rejected supernatural causes, explaining "disability" as a product of the interaction between physical impairment and social prejudice. The final explanation, while laced with contradictions, was a compromise between the opinions of social and medical rehabilitationists.

The nearly unanimous opinion among reformers that employment provided the best solution to the problem of disability also fit well with the development of a program planted on the middle ground. To rehabilitationists, the greatest problem facing the cripple was rejection from the workplace.[4] Enforced unemployment denied cripples access to something many considered the most fundamental right and responsibility of citizenship. To rehabilitationists and other Progressives, citizenship was a fairly uncomplicated matter, at least as it applied to males. It involved a give and take. The obligation of every male citizen was to work. Through work, men contributed to the economic well-being of the nation, set an example for younger generations, and symbolized the most prized aspect of the American character—independence. Without work, men became parasites feeding off the labors of others. Not only a duty, work also served as America's promise to its male citizens—a promise thought to benefit the individual in immeasurable ways.[5] In the words of one rehabilitationist, it provided "the only opportunity for real happiness." Only through employment could a man "look up at the sky every night and say 'I too, am doing my work in your world, O God!'"[6] To rehabilitationists, dependent cripples symbolized the antithesis of American citizenship, challenging America's identity as the land of opportunity. Such a situation necessitated reform.

The rehabilitationists' emphasis on employment led some to define "cure" as a physical improvement that increased an individual's chances of getting a job.[7] They even referred to certain aspects of rehabilitation itself as the "work cure."[8] The focus on work encouraged reformers to look beyond the disabled individual for an explanation of disability in society. This belief gained credence after a group of New York reformers canvassed local businesses and discovered that many employers assumed "that a cripple must be a beggar" and therefore denied job opportunities even to well-qualified, "reconstructed" cripples. The persistence of such beliefs convinced some advocates that rehabilitating the cripple required a change in cultural attitudes. "Until we can get public opinion more friendly towards the employment of cripples," wrote one rehabilitationist, "our placement cannot be extensive."[9] To achieve such a state of mind, social rehabilitationists made a top priority of convincing the public to hire cripples on equal terms with the nondisabled.

In the nineteenth century, Americans viewed cripples as members of the "afflicted" class—individuals suffering from divinely inspired physical conditions that left them dependent on the goodwill of more fortunate Americans.[10] Protestant religious doctrine reinforced the perception of the disabled person as dependent by teaching that a good Christian provided for "the lame, the halt and the blind," much as Jesus of Nazareth had done. The first institution created for crippled children in the United States fit well into this set of beliefs. During the Civil War, the New York Hospital for the Ruptured and Crippled became the first institution to address the problem of the crippled child. Construction of the hospital began after the dramatic appearance of disabled beggars on the streets of New York City in the early 1860s. The unique economic conditions produced by the war encouraged hundreds of disabled people—a startling number of whom were children—to beg for alms. Their presence so shocked and offended the sensibilities of some New Yorkers that an influential and well-to-do group united to create an institution designed to eliminate the problem.[11]

Dr. James Knight served as the first superintendent of the hospital. A model of medical conservatism during his twenty-four years as surgeon-in-chief,[12] Knight decried unproven or risky surgical procedures. He castigated those who practiced heroic surgery as "arrogant and mendacious exponent[s] of adventurous treatment"[13] and himself performed no more than seventy or eighty operations, mostly minor, on the approximately 180 children who entered the hospital during any given year. Yet he did treat his patients in other ways. He used orthotic devices to correct or brace disabled limbs, a dietary regime and physical exercise, as well as moral instruction, academic education, and vocational training to bring his pupil-patients into conformity with nondisabled norms.

Though considered something of a medical prude by more aggressive contemporaries and later rehabilitation-era orthopedists such as his successor Virgil Gibney, Knight constructed an institution that superficially resembled the Progressive Era hospital-school. His approach was not unlike that of the rehabilitationists in that he intended not only to provide crippled children with medical care but to prevent them from becoming mendicants by instilling in them the desire and skills to become moral citizens. But on closer examination, the comparison between Knight and the rehabilitationists breaks down. He set out less to "cure" children than, in a word frequently employed in his discharge reports, to "relieve" them. He attained relief through the use of minor medical procedures to ease painful or potentially dangerous conditions and through the use of educational, vocational, and moral training. If crippled children could be taught the immorality of begging while developing a small degree of earning capacity, he had fulfilled his mission and had relieved his charges.[14] Rarely did he achieve what rehabilitationists considered a cure—the conversion of the dependent cripple into "an earning, serving unit."[15] While rehabilitationists mirrored Knight's distaste for dependency, they carried this focus further, defining the problem of disability in terms of citizenship. In many ways, Knight's hospital foreshadowed the efforts of the rehabilitationists, but with less confidence, less public support, and a focus more narrowly trained on the individual. In this way, Knight contributed as much to the development of the medical model as he did to the rehabilitation movement. Though clearly an opponent of

aggressive medical practices, and in fact, a man dedicated as much to education as to surgery, he nonetheless believed that the crippled child rather than society was most in need of repair. He made no apparent effort to change public attitudes toward employment of the cripple, not did he agitate for any significant social change. In this sense, he differed from "adventurous" surgeons only in the means employed to correct the crippled child.

By the early twentieth century, the growing focus on correction of the individual exhibited by Knight and his more aggressive successors seemed to signal the coming of the medical model. Late-nineteenth-century changes in the medical profession supported this trend. Medical innovations from anesthesia to X rays provided surgeons with newfound respect. Meanwhile, the establishment of professional medical organizations, the creation and refinement of medical journals, the development of an increasingly specialized medical lexicon, and the reform of medical schools added great prestige to the medical profession. Such changes allowed physicians to gain unprecedented control over illness.[16] For their part, orthopedists established their own medical journals (including the *American Journal of Orthopedic Surgery*), surgical innovations, and institutions in which to perform their craft.

Beginning in the 1890s, individual philanthropists along with a number of organizations (most notably fraternal organizations such as the Rotarians and the Shriners) began working to create institutions that they believed would greatly improve the lives of crippled children; they then secured the help of orthopedists to achieve this goal.[17] The mostly nondisabled men and women who directed the rehabilitation movement not only worked with disabled children but also engaged in the accompanying effort to rehabilitate disabled military veterans injured in World War I and civilians injured in the "industrial army."[18] The institutions they created provided orthopedists with a base from which to develop their burgeoning specialty.

Of course, all this greatly benefited the orthopedists' reputation, a fact that would seem to suggest increased medical authority over physical disability, followed by the rapid emergence of a medical model to dominance in shaping societal understanding of disability. Yet certain events intervened that not only slowed the rise of the orthopedic profession and the development of the medical model but complicated both the rehabilitationists' agenda and public perceptions of disability. To begin with, doctors did not dominate rehabilitation. Many of the philanthropists and reformers who helped create the rehabilitation movement ended up sharing control with medical practitioners in each of its two main areas of work: hospital-schools and vocational rehabilitation. Leaders of the movement included businessmen, medical doctors, nurses, sociologists, bureaucrats, politicians, publicists, and even a few disabled adults.

Of those who came to the movement from outside the medical profession, Douglas C. McMurtrie and Joseph F. Sullivan were the most influential. The opinions of each, at least prior to 1920, reflect the social rehabilitationists' perspective. As a prosperous businessman in the craft of printing, McMurtrie's wealth and position allowed him to become a filter through which the vast bulk of information concerning the movement passed. His writings reflected the belief "that the greatest handicap is not a loss of limb or other disability but the weight of public opinion."[19] To him, the most important aspect of rehabilitation involved changing traditional attitudes toward disabled people. McMurtrie held the nondisabled primarily responsible for the dependency that characterized America's crippled population.

Sullivan expressed similar views, though he approached the subject from a vantage point that the nondisabled McMurtrie could not—as a self-proclaimed cripple. After contracting polio at an early age, Sullivan lost muscle function in both legs and one arm. Throughout his childhood, he met with great difficulty gaining physical access to school and social acceptance in the workplace. Perhaps this experience led him, unlike many of his contemporaries, to conclude that cripples comprised "a noble class of humanity" whose greatest need was opportunity.[20] Like McMurtrie, he entered the publishing profession. As an editor of small newspapers and magazines, and as author of numerous articles in larger publications, Sullivan served as an advocate for disabled children for over twenty years. During this time, he consistently argued that disability emanated from "a social arrangement that virtually condemns the cripple to mendicancy," rather than from the physical limitations of the individual.[21] To Sullivan and other, like-minded reformers, the problem of disability began in childhood—or, more precisely, in school.

Prior to 1920, Sullivan rarely wavered in his position that education and opportunity were the only tools needed for the success of the cripple. Nevertheless, he agreed with McMurtrie and other rehabilitationists that, in some ways, it was necessary to adapt the crippled child to an inaccessible world. The most significant way in which he voiced this belief was through his support of surgical intervention. In doing so, he failed to recognize that his support of orthopedic surgery not only aided the rise of that profession to greater status but unwittingly contradicted the social rehabilitationists' oft-repeated argument that "the great sufferings of crippledom" had little to do with one's "physical conditions."[22] Even an individual as self-consciously committed to social rehabilitation as Sullivan found his way to the middle ground between social and medical explanations of disability.

At the opposite end of the spectrum from Sullivan and McMurtrie, others in the rehabilitation movement placed little blame on society. Instead, they argued that the real source of disability lay in the physical and moral failings of the individual. Of those who expressed this opinion, many, if not most, came from a background in the medical sciences.[23] Medical rehabilitationists discovered a pathological process that explained the peculiar "mental kinks" they believed present in most individuals who lived with a disability for an extended period of time. Augustus Thorndike typified this outlook. As an orthopedic surgeon, he became familiar with the efforts around Boston (a leading city in the rehabilitation movement) to provide crippled children with industrial training. Within the industrial schools, he wrote, "all teachers realize the mental warp of the cripple, and struggle to overcome it."[24] To Thorndike and like-minded individuals, the cripple was a product of an ambiguous process of moral degeneration in which feelings of worthlessness, magnified by alcohol and reinforced by the pity of friends and families, produced a shiftless personality.

Charles H. Jaeger, a doctor who worked with both adult and child cripples, provides another example of the victim-blaming practiced by medical rehabilitationists. He explained the acquisition of a dependent spirit in a theory born of both the social and medical sciences:

Well-intentioned but ill-advised friends and relations coddle the patient. He is cared for and supported until he has lost his ambition to work. In his idle hours he seeks solace and companionship in the saloon. This environment still further aids in the moral decline [of the individual into dependency]. It is an easy step to beg for the money thus needed, and when he once finds out how profitable this is, he loses his desire to work.[25]

In the expression of their dependency theories, medical rehabilitationists conceived of dependency itself as something of a pathological process, through which the individual gradually became incapable of independence. Yet Thorndike's theory did not outwardly reject the assertions made by his counterparts, the social rehabilitationists. Though placing primary blame for the dependency that rehabilitationists equated with disability on the cripple, both Thorndike and Jaeger agreed that blame for the cripple's dependent status came "from both himself and the employer." Even to the staunchest of medical rehabilitationists, disability was understood as a product of individual failings coupled with a cultural understanding of disability that encouraged the dependency of the cripple.

Rehabilitationists of all stripes seem to have accepted that long-term disability created an entrenched and all-but-impossible sense of dependency in the individual. In turn, this belief led to the logical conclusion that, if long-term mendicant cripples made poor candidates for rehabilitation, then children made the best subjects. Further, the best subjects of all were those who lacked the dependency-generating comforts of the well-to-do. Thus, in the scheme of rehabilitation, poor children represented the best subjects, whereas affluent adults represented the worst. "These poor, neglected children," Jaeger concluded, "not spoiled by over-indulgence or schooled in depravity, have proven that, with a little care and effort expended along right lines, the problem of the cripple can be solved."[26]

Medical rehabilitationists had other reasons for the focus on indigent children. For one, children provided little resistance to medical authorities and therefore made ideal patients for a developing medical specialty that lacked the confidence of the American public. Their very dependency, their young ages, and the requirement of many hospital-schools that their parents give the institution temporary custody meant that orthopedists had broad control over the direction of their patients' medical regime. Thus, for orthopedists, indigent children made the ideal subjects for their developing medical specialty.

Rehabilitationists also focused on children because of the appeal children held for philanthropists. In their fund-raising campaigns, hospital-school administrators relied heavily on the sentimental appeal of their young charges, whether they were soliciting from wealthy philanthropists or state legislators. Thus, with the exception of the war years (1917–1919), when fears of an insufficient labor force encouraged Americans to rehabilitate adult males, children from working-class families provided the focus of rehabilitation efforts.

Rehabilitationists on both sides of the fence appeared oblivious to, or at least willing to overlook, the obvious contradictions that existed between the social and medical approaches to rehabilitation. In all their writings, Sullivan and McMurtrie never directly challenged the position of medical rehabilitationists.[27] For their part, Jaeger, Thorndike, and like-minded reformers never expressed opposition to the social rehabilitationists' position. Instead, all seem to have accepted without question the existence of a middle ground between the two perspectives in a move that, wittingly or not, kept the movement united. Apparently unrecognized by rehabilitationists on either side, however, was that in playing the role of the mugwump, each side effectively weakened its fundamental thesis. Calls for new medical facilities to treat crippled children weakened social arguments that claimed only society needed to change. Similarly, medical arguments blaming individual impairment for disability lost force in the face of assertions that social discrimination caused disability.

Further complicating matters, medical rehabilitationists typically presented one set of views in the popular media and another in trade and academic journals, where the only audience expected was other rehabilitationists. In the popular press, medical rehabilitationists exonerated the cripple of complicity in dependent status. A stream of articles featuring stories of successful cripples appeared in popular magazines such as *The Outlook, Ladies' Home Journal,* and *American Magazine.* Though not all such articles came from rehabilitationists, many did, and most such stories appeared between 1917 and 1921, at the peak of the rehabilitation movement.[28] These brief biographies detailed the great obstacles overcome by disabled individuals who had attained employment and generally supported the notion that society alone was responsible for the dependency of the disabled person. Given a chance, all cripples could succeed. Meanwhile, in journals intended primarily for other rehabilitationists, such as the *American Journal of Care for Cripples,* medical rehabilitationists contradicted such claims, placing blame for dependency and disability squarely on the individual. Indeed, the very efforts to reform cripples surgically and morally contradicted many of the claims made in popular magazines. The inconsistency of medical rehabilitationists served important functions. By presenting the cripple as a capable individual, rehabilitationists helped open up the job opportunities for cripples necessary for their vocational success; in locating fault in them, orthopedists justified their own work and the institutions they built.

Consensus as to the ultimate objective of rehabilitation—employment of the cripple—bound the two rehabilitation perspectives together. In fact, some went so far as to suggest that "productive workers . . . are no longer classified as cripples, and dare not be so regarded."[29] Virtually all rehabilitationists, no matter what type of institution they created, shared the common goal of employment for the cripple. Most agreed that to succeed required a combination of education and medical care.

Rehabilitationists initially placed primary emphasis on training the minds and bodies of young cripples through the hospital-school. Though boys were clearly the primary object of the rehabilitation movement, girls were included in numbers that in some institutions may even have exceeded those of their male counterparts. Given that the ultimate goal of the movement prior to 1920 was employment or preparation for employment, this is a somewhat surprising finding. Most Americans of the time still objected to the employment of large numbers of women. And, while girls were trained primarily for traditional women's jobs such as sewing and teaching, they were encouraged to continue through high school and even into college in a day in which the education of most girls from working-class families ended before high school.[30]

Why did rehabilitationists give such special consideration to crippled girls? The explanation lies in the very different conception of the roles of disabled and nondisabled women. It was widely believed that the crippled woman was unfit for marriage and thus would need to find some means of support. Writing in 1919 as a middle-aged woman, an anonymous cripple recalled the day some decades earlier on which she became engaged. The announcement "aroused a storm of disapproval and dismay; of pity for the man, pity for the woman and dire predictions for both." Relatives had long since explained to the would-be bride that "married life was too exacting" and that she was too "unattractive." Courageously, she rejected this advice and soon disproved the predictions of her relatives.[31] The story illustrates the difficulties faced by women who sought acceptance in the traditional role of housewife. It also helps explain the willingness of rehabilitationists to provide crippled girls with greater access to education.

For both boys and girls, then, rehabilitationists created the hospital-school. In all, U.S. rehabilitationists built some seventy institutions fitting the hospital-school mode over the thirty-four-year span between 1890 and 1924, and yet the history of these institutions has scarcely been touched upon.[32] Hospital-schools ranged in size from modest facilities of less than thirty "pupil-patients" to large institutions with hundreds of beds. Though diverse in their physical

structure and mission, they shared a commitment to providing the crippled child with varying levels of both medical treatment and education. In the early years of the hospital-school, between roughly 1890 and 1915, education held an equal, if not superior, position to medicine on the agendas of many such institutions. During this time, few were willing to trust the fate of the crippled child solely to orthopedists, even though orthopedists generally conducted only those operations that posed little or no threat to the patient's life.[33]

Reformers employed the term *rehabilitation* to refer not only to the surgical and therapeutic treatment of cripples but to the rehabilitation of public attitudes toward disabled people.[34] In this important way they differed from their predecessors and complicated America's move toward the medical model. Those who emphasized the reshaping of public attitudes pointed to flaws in American society to explain the problem of disability. In doing so, they evinced the influence on the rehabilitation movement of emerging social sciences such as sociology and psychology. By the 1890s, researchers in the social sciences had concluded that childhood was a formative period in which social values were instilled—values that could not be easily replaced in later life.[35] Thus rehabilitationists demonstrated a particular concern with addressing the problem of idleness before it took root in the child. In studying the lives of children in the poorest areas of both rural and urban America, researchers discovered a number of factors that inhibited the child's growth into moral citizenship. A poor diet, unhealthy air, cramped living conditions, and disability all conspired to hinder the development of critical values in the working-class child.[36] Reformers intended to overcome such obstacles through the unique combination of medicine and education offered in the hospital-school.

For adults, a different institution was deemed necessary—vocational rehabilitation. The most important example was the Red Cross Institute for Crippled and Disabled Men in New York City.[37] This institute, which worked closely with the Surgeon General's Office during World War I, was created in 1917 as an experiment in the rehabilitation of adult male cripples. The "greater work" of the agency, headed by Douglas McMurtrie, was "in the abstract field of research and public education." The institute began its work with "a general educational movement . . . to create an enlightened public opinion towards the physically handicapped, so that they will be regarded from the standpoint of their capabilities rather than their disabilities. This is undoubtedly the most important phase of the whole question."[38]

To accomplish this goal the institute created a publicity service that regularly issued press releases to over eleven hundred newspapers nationwide, encouraging "comment that might be helpful to the cause of the disabled." A speakers bureau equipped with slides and film reels organized vast meetings at Carnegie Hall and the Hippodrome, canvassed hundreds of New York-area businesses seeking commitments to hiring cripples, and sent out a circular along with AT&T bills to over 1 million New York residents.[39] Through these and other publicity devices, institute leaders hoped to convince the public to consider the cripple a competent and capable citizen.

Despite placing primary emphasis on changing public opinion, the institute nonetheless ended up on the middle ground between social and medical rehabilitation with regard to adaptation. Outwardly, U.S. rehabilitationists claimed to use something known as the "American method" in making workplace adaptations. In the American method, "the cripple is regarded as the fixt [sic] element, and the device or method is adapted to the individual who uses it." This method stood in contrast to the European method, in which individuals were adapted to particular jobs, sometimes even using prosthetic devices that created a literal connection between man and machine.[40] The American method would seem to represent a social approach to the problem, since it required adaptation of a social barrier, while the European method more closely approximated a medical approach. In reality, however, American rehabilitationists hedged on their policy of not adapting men to jobs. The Institute for the Crippled and Disabled, for instance, maintained a workshop for the construction of artificial limbs, braces, and appliances in an effort to make cripples more employable. As an institute publication explained, "A limp is less objectionable to an employer than crutches."[41]

After 1920, vocational rehabilitationists drifted toward the medical model. During the 1910s, the Institute for Crippled and Disabled Men had been used as a training ground for those who would soon enter the mainstream workforce. Eventually this policy changed in a way that, to insiders, must have seemed subtle. In retrospect, however, the establishment of a sheltered workshop in May 1927 signaled a major shift in the institute's approach to rehabilitation. The workshop was intended as a way station of sorts between "homebound" workers and "regular employ-

ment."[42] Yet the move had tremendous symbolic significance. The increasing number of sheltered workshops that emerged around the country beginning in the Progressive era served as a symbol of the cripple's inferior status in the job market. It was, in effect, an admission by institute leaders that not all cripples were fit for regular employment, at least not without specialized training.

Though superficially a very different facility, the rehabilitation movement's other major institutional contribution, the hospital-school, was also built on rehabilitation's middle ground during the 1910s, then slipped into full embrace of the medical model in the 1920s. Rehabilitationists used the term *hospital-school* to describe institutions that combined varying degrees of education (moral, vocational, and academic), socialization, and medical practice. They were not purely medical institutions. Even the staunchest proponent of orthopedic surgery could agree that "the medical and surgical treatment of the physical ills of the body should always be supplemented by a similar effort to educate the mind of the cripple."[43] This idea was the backbone of the hospital-school, an institution unique to the rehabilitation era with a name that clearly illustrates the competing interpretations of disability that comprised the middle ground.

Not unlike institutes of vocational rehabilitation, hospital-schools were created to act as a temporary haven for crippled children from an outside world seemingly hostile to their very existence. Many attempted to create a physical environment in which the child could be entirely independent. In her 1914 study of institutions for crippled children, Edith Reeves placed great importance on the presence of adaptive equipment in evaluating such schools, while providing the modern observer with a glimpse into the workings of the hospital-school. Though few could afford to make all the adaptations Reeves applauded, institutions unencumbered by funding restraints created a few models that are most suggestive of what rehabilitationists hoped to accomplish.

During the 1910s, the Widener Memorial School for Crippled Children in Philadelphia set the standard of care. Thanks to the philanthropy of P. A. B. Widener, who donated some $4 million to the institution, rehabilitationists were able to construct a prototype hospital-school that reflected the values of both social and medical rehabilitationists. Social rehabilitationists were no doubt pleased by the existence of a gymnasium equipped with the latest in adaptive equipment. Accessibility for mobility-impaired children was of prime concern. Elevators provided access to upper floors in the main buildings, and thresholds were eliminated from all doorways. Buildings were connected by glass-enclosed passageways that were heated in the winter. Adjustable desks and seats provided schoolchildren with accessible seating. Widener's medical facilities were also state of the art. Occasional use of the gymnasium for therapy rather than recreation, along with a surgical suite "comparable with those in the most completely modern general hospitals," reminded children that, despite the accessibility of their current accommodations, the burden of adaptation was ultimately theirs.[44]

Some institutions, such as the Van Leuven Browne Hospital School, the Minnesota State Hospital and School for Indigent Crippled and Deformed Children, and the Massachusetts Hospital School, maintained a strong, if not dominant, medical element. Of thirty-two institutions in a 1914 study of institutions for crippled children constructed during the rehabilitation era (1890–1914), all but one provided an orthopedic surgeon or other doctor with access to their pupil-patients. Some of these doctors were residents, though many others appear to have been visiting physicians.

In contrast to this medical presence, twenty-five of the institutions provided children with regular access to academic education, through resident teachers, visiting teachers, or nearby schools for crippled children. In addition, twenty-two of the institutions offered children some form of vocational training. These statistics suggest that the vast majority of the institutions created during the rehabilitation era supplied the basic ingredients of a hospital-school—institutions that included both education and medicine.

While physicians often became the most important individuals within such institutions, their authority did not go unchecked. To begin with, physicians ran relatively few hospital-schools. As of 1914, doctors held chief administrative positions at fewer than one-fourth of all such facilities. Statistics from that year reveal that doctors ran only seven of the thirty hospital-schools that provided the name of their superintendents. Of the twenty-three institutions with medical laypersons in charge, twenty-one superintendents were listed with the title Miss, Mrs., or Sister, while another two were listed as Mr. and Father.[45] The high number of women in charge of such institutions is probably explained by traditional gender roles. The assignment of women to the role of caregiver—whether as mother, educator, or nurse—

made them the logical choice for the care of crippled children. Most administrators left few, if any, written records of their own ideological position within the rehabilitation movement. Still, it is clear that the majority worked to develop institutions that paid more than passing consideration to both the education and the medical treatment of the crippled child. They, too, seem to have sought out the middle ground.

The authority of the orthopedists within the rehabilitation movement was further limited by the poor reputation of the orthopedic profession. At the turn of the century, many Americans, especially members of the working-class poor families for whom most hospital-schools were constructed, shunned orthopedists as charlatans bent on turning crippled children into subjects of experimentation. And in fact, at teaching hospitals, which mostly served indigent populations and where most children were admitted, doctors referred to their patients as "clinical material."[46] Doubts concerning the efficacy of orthopedic treatment extended to the middle and upper classes and even plagued orthopedists themselves. Despite their faith in science, prior to World War I few rehabilitationists believed orthopedics was capable of curing the crippled child, though they proved far more willing to try than working-class parents wanted.[47] Within the medical establishment, the responsibility for treating crippled children had long since been conferred on the orthopedic surgeon. Yet, from the time the first orthopedic hospital for crippled children opened its doors in the United States during the Civil War, only the boldest of orthopedists were willing to make the claim of being able to fully cure physical disability. Most clung to the cautious path of medical conservatism first tread by James Knight and other nineteenth-century orthopedists who made relieving rather than curing their goal.[48]

Most hospital administrators also shunned orthopedists, though for reasons related to economics more than reputation. The early twentieth-century practice of orthopedics involved a time-consuming combination of surgery followed by months of therapy. In many cases, this formula had to be repeated several times to attain physical changes that, with some imagination, might be labeled a "cure." From the perspective of hospital administrators, the lengthy therapies and questionable results produced by such practices conflicted with the bottom-line exigencies of the modern hospital. Whereas nineteenth-century hospitals acted primarily as convalescent homes, the modern, twentieth-century hospital emerged as something of a profit-making enterprise. Though most hospitals still relied heavily on philanthropy, the efficiency-minded Progressive Era hospital administrator, who emphasized the bottom line, demanded an institution that did more than nurse the sick. Besides, philanthropists generally gave their support to hospitals with the highest reputations, and reputations were based largely on the number of patients "cured" in a given hospital. The skepticism of the public and the priorities of hospital administrators kept orthopedics on the periphery of medical respectability.[49]

The conclusion that medical practice did not dominate the hospital-school is further supported by an analysis of discharge policies in 1914. The conditions under which children were discharged demonstrated a commitment not only to medical care but to education and vocational training. Hospital-schools discharged pupil-patients for a number of reasons, but only five institutions established policies based purely on medical considerations.[50] Two others released children only if educational opportunities could be found elsewhere, while thirteen did so only after the pupil-patients were able to secure a job and find another home.[51] Flexibility was the key to most discharge policies. At the Widener Memorial School, for instance, where the parents of admitted children "signed an indenture binding [the] child over to the trustees of the institution until he shall reach his majority (21 years of age)," pupil-patients might gain an early release "if ready to begin wage-earning."[52] Similarly, at the Massachusetts Hospital School, children might be permitted to stay for long periods of time, even after all medical avenues had been exhausted, if it was thought the child could benefit from further education.[53] At the Minnesota State Hospital and School, discharge policies allowed pupil-patients to remain until "benefited as much as possible."[54] In this way, children could receive something more than medical treatment—they could be provided with the educational and vocational tools necessary to assume the responsibilities of moral citizenship.

Thus, circumstances conspired to prevent orthopedists from dominating the rehabilitation movement and, in the process, provided an opening for social rehabilitationists.[55] In this context, Sullivan, McMurtrie, and other social rehabilitationists found room for the expression of a perspective that challenged, however unintentionally, the basic tenets of the medical model. Yet none of these men committed himself to a position that denied medicine a role in solving the problem of

disability. Even in the years prior to World War I, when orthopedic practice remained mired in doubts, the attitude expressed by social rehabilitationists toward medicine is best described as ambivalent. They neither promoted nor condemned surgical intervention.

By the mid-1910s, the middle ground began to shift toward the medical side of the rehabilitation movement. A growing number of reformers began emphasizing the importance of surgical and therapeutic intervention over education. The major reason for this change centered on the improved reputation of orthopedic practice. With its startling and unprecedented casualty rates, World War I produced a wealth of "clinical material" on which the orthopedist was able to develop his craft. Many of the casualties suffered impairment of one or more limbs—injuries that came to be referred to as "orthopedic handicaps." A number of American doctors, including such notable hospital-school orthopedists as H. Winnett Orr and Fred H. Albee, left for the battlefields of Europe even before the United States entered the war. The unusual circumstances surrounding battlefield surgery allowed orthopedists to develop innovative methods for repairing injured muscles, bones, and tendons. On returning to America, orthopedists brought with them greater knowledge, greater confidence, and, most important, greater respect in the eyes of their critics.[56] All that they lacked was clinical material. For many orthopedists, the hospitals that served America's disabled children would fill this need. The old strictures of conservatism that governed institutional practices in centers of orthopedics such as the Hospital for the Ruptured and Crippled loosened in the mayhem of total war.[57] From the outset of the rehabilitation era, orthopedic surgeons established their presence in hospital-schools, often without charge, thereby gaining a reputation as possibly the most philanthropic members of the medical profession.[58] This reputation combined with the new-found regard earned in World War I to help create a thriving medical specialty.[59]

Though it is difficult to gauge the exact level of involvement of orthopedists, the experiences of one asylum turned hospital-school and the pupil-patients there provide some indication of how changes in the orthopedic profession impacted on hospital-schools between 1900 and 1920. At the outset of its existence in 1907, the Van Leuven Browne Hospital School, much like other institutions for crippled children founded shortly after the turn of the century, was far less a hospital than a small asylum. Though doctors routinely visited and provided medical care, no surgeries were performed on the thirty or so pupil-patients living there until 1917.[60] This all began to change, however, with the conversion of Van Leuven Browne into the Michigan Hospital School. As the institution changed names, construction began on a new facility in the Michigan countryside that would increase capacity to two hundred pupil-patients. More important, a new administration allowed orthopedic surgeons, for the first time, to enter the lives of the children in the hospital-school.[61]

In 1919, a teenage girl wrote a note of thanks to her doctor and teacher at the Michigan Hospital School. The brief letter was relatively unremarkable, noting the educational and physical improvements she had made in her sixteen months at the institution. The letter appeared in the *Hospital School Journal* with a number of similar missives from other children who had been in the hospital-school. This teenage girl signed off with apparent affection: "I still remain a patient and a pupil,—Delphina."[62] Delphina entered the Michigan Hospital School at a time of transition. Neither completely a student nor exclusively a patient, her closing illustrates the tension within an institutional form that was neither fully hospital nor fully school, that accepted neither a social model of disability nor a medical model. By 1919, however, the experiences of pupil-patients like Delphina strongly suggested the direction in which hospital-schools, along with the American cultural definition of disability, was headed.

In 1913, another young pupil-patient named Edward Claypool had entered the same facility, then called Van Leuven Browne Hospital School. According to his own account, he had spent his first six years as a virtual prisoner in his home. Once at the institution, he reveled in the friendships and freedoms he discovered. Surrounded by other crippled children, living in a fairly accessible environment, and participating in both physical and intellectual activities designed for the physically disabled child, Edward gained access to a world from which he had previously been excluded. From the example of teachers and administrators at the small institution, two of whom were disabled themselves, he came to realize that a world of potential existed that he had never dared imagine. From the day he entered Van Leuven Browne in December 1913, he found that he "never again knew what it meant to be lonesome."[63]

But as Van Leuven Browne became a hospital-school, things began to change. The facility, which had once focused almost exclusively on educating

and socializing disabled children, increasingly turned to medicine as a solution to the problem of disability. An orthopedic surgeon, William E. Blodgett, was enlisted and began a regular round of student examinations. Fortified by the increasing respect given to his profession as a result of World War I, he made regular use of surgery as a tool of rehabilitation. By 1918, surgery had become a part of the routine of daily life in the institution, now referred to as the Michigan Hospital School. Over the course of the next five years, Claypool underwent six surgeries aimed at allowing him to discard his crutches and braces. Yet, despite Blodgett's surgical efforts, at the age of fourteen Edward still required braces and crutches in order to walk.[64]

Changes in admission policies soon followed the upswing in orthopedic activity. Prior to 1920, most hospital-schools accepted all children regardless of whether or not their "condition" was amenable to surgical intervention.[65] By the 1920s, hospital-schools increasingly restricted entrance to those who could be aided by orthopedic surgery. The Michigan Hospital School exemplified such changes, deciding sometime after 1917 to accept only crippled children whom surgery would benefit. By 1924, the one-time Van Leuven Browne Hospital School had become part of the larger Michigan Children's Hospital. This final transformation reflected a larger national trend in which relatively small institutions that featured a mixture of education and medical care were absorbed or replaced by far larger, more exclusively medical institutions. Reflecting the same trend, whereas the *American Journal of Care for Cripples* (published 1914–1919) had focused on crippled children and primarily on their education, by the 1920s, periodicals such as the *Hospital School Journal* and the *Crippled Child* increasingly concentrated on curing cripples. Meanwhile, in terms of the cultural understanding of disability, the transformation of Van Leuven Browne signified the full emergence of the medical model of disability. With the coming of the medical model, social explanations of disability such as those that prevailed in the rehabilitation era virtually disappeared for the next half century. The experiences of Edward Claypool and others make it clear that with the increasing prestige and power of the orthopedic profession, the hospital-school, and American thought in general, was being pulled from the middle ground of the rehabilitation period toward the soon-to-be dominant medical model of disability. Joseph F. Sullivan provides the clearest sign of the medical model's ascendancy. By 1919 he devoted as much attention to the promotion of surgery as to education in his *Hospital School Journal.* He even wrote in favor of legislation "making it compulsory for parents to surrender their children to the authorities of the [Michigan Hospital School] when deemed expedient that the children might be treated in due time."[66] As the reputation of orthopedists improved, Sullivan and other social rehabilitationists who had once expressed ambivalence toward surgical intervention fell in line with the medical model.

Notes

1. The first institution referred to as a "hospital-school" was not created until after 1900. The first institution created in the mold of the hospital-school, however, was the New York Hospital for the Ruptured and Crippled, opened in 1863. This institution was followed closely by the New York Orthopedic Hospital, which opened in 1866. After this, no other significant institutions of this type were created until the 1890s. During this decade, several hospital-schools were created, including the House of St. Giles the Cripple in New York City (1891), the James Kernan Hospital and Industrial School near Baltimore (1895), and the State Hospital for Indigent Crippled and Deformed Children in St. Paul, Minnesota (1897). See Edith Reeves, *Care and Education of Crippled Children in the United States* (New York: Russell Sage Foundation, 1914); 168–233.

2. Social rehabilitationists and their counterparts, medical rehabilitationists, were separated not only by their competing explanations of the problem of disability but also by their backgrounds. Most social rehabilitationists did not come from a medical background, whereas many (though certainly not all) medical rehabilitationists did. Most rehabilitationists should be classified as neither, as they blended elements of each in addressing the problem of disability.

3. Little motivation existed for anyone to challenge the orthopedists' medical dominion over crippledom. It was commonly believed that cripples came primarily from the ranks of the poorest Americans, and therefore there was little profit to be made in caring for them.

4. The negative economic impact of unemployed disabled people is the topic of Garrard Harris, *The Redemption of the Disabled* (New York: D. Appleton and Company, 1919). Alice Willard Solenberger discusses the "Parasitic Cripple" and other types of unemployed crippled in *One Thousand Homeless Men* (New York: Charities Publication Committee, 1911), chaps. 3–6.

5. Numerous studies stress the importance of the work ethic in Progressive America. Among the most important of these are Daniel Rodgers, *The Work Ethic in Industrial America, 1850–1920* (Chicago: University of Chicago Press, 1978); and Herbert Gutman, *Work, Culture, and Society in Industrializing America: Essays in American Working-Class and Social History* (New York: Random House, 1977).

6. Elias Parker Butler, "Exit Mr. Tumult and Miss Shouting," *Carry On* 1 (October–November 1918): 12.

7. See, for instance, Harry E. Mock, "Reclamation of the Disabled from the Industrial Army," *Annals of the American Academy of Political and Social Science* 80 (November 1918): 29–34. Mock writes that a man is "disabled" only while "the doctor is helping cure him." Afterward, even if impairments remain, a man is "no longer classed as a cripple" if he "trains himself for work and becomes a productive citizen."

8. "The 'Work-Cure' for Crippled Soldiers," *Literary Digest* 62 (July 19, 1919): 24.

9. Gertrude R. Stein, "Placement Technique in the Employment Work of the Red Cross Institute for Crippled and Disabled Men," in Douglas C. McMurtrie, ed., *Publications of the Red Cross Institute for Crippled and Disabled Men* 1 (May 6, 1918): 10.

10. For a discussion of nineteenth-century views of disability, see Douglas C. Baynton, *Forbidden Signs: American Culture and the Campaign against Sign Language* (Chicago: University of Chicago Press, 1996), 102. The twentieth-century medical model of disability is discussed in Michael Oliver, *The Politics of Disablement* (New York: St. Martin's Press, 1990) 1–4; and Robert Bogdan, *Freak Show: Presenting Human Oddities for Amusement and Profit* (Chicago: University of Chicago Press, 1988), 274–78.

11. The "ruptured" were children with hernias.

12. The vast majority of surgeons, even in the rehabilitation era, were conservatives. Even Knight's successor, Virgil Gibney, was said to approach surgical intervention "with fear and caution." See Fenwick Beekman, *Hospital for the Ruptured and Crippled: A Historical Sketch Written on the Occasion of the Seventy-fifth Anniversary of the Hospital* (New York: privately printed, 1939), 47.

13. Ibid., 13.

14. Ibid., 29–47; Charles E. Rosenberg, *The Care of Strangers: The Rise of America's Hospital System* (New York: Basic Books, 1987).

15. Mock, "Reclamation of the Disabled," 30.

16. The standard history of medical professionalization in the United States is Paul Starr's seminal book *The Social Transformation of American Medicine: The Rise of a Sovereign Profession and the Making of a Vast Industry* (New York: Basic Books, 1982).

17. It should be pointed out that, while medical laymen were behind the creation of many such institutions, a number were created by orthopedists as well. See Katherine W. Ambrose Shrady, "The History of the Federation of Associations for Cripples." *American Journal of Care for Cripples* 1 (1914): 21.

18. Many of the most prominent reformers in the movement to aid crippled children, including Douglas C. McMurtrie and Dr. Fred H. Albee, were also leaders in the movement to rehabilitate America's soldiers.

19. Douglas C. McMurtrie, *The Disabled Soldier* (New York: MacMillan Company, 1919), 26.

20. Joseph F. Sullivan, *The Unheard Cry* (Nashville: privately printed, 1914), 37.

21. Joseph F. Sullivan, "A Plea to the Legislators of Michigan," *Hospital School Journal* 7 (November–December 1918): 4.

22. Ibid.

23. It should be pointed out, however, that not all doctors fixed the blame for disability wholly on the individual.

24. Augustus Thorndike, "Industrial Training for Crippled Children About Boston," *American Journal of Care for Cripples* 1 (1914): 19.

25. Charles H. Jaeger, "Trade Training for Adult Cripples," *American Journal of Care for Cripples* 1, 2 (June 1915): 68.

26. Ibid., 69.

27. Sullivan did challenge the idea that some individuals were beyond help and should be rejected by society as a result of physical inadequacies. See Joseph F. Sullivan, "Who Are the Unfit? A Question and a Reply to a College Professor," *Hospital School Journal* 9 (May–June 1921): 11.

28. The Surgeon General's Office and the Red Cross Institute for Crippled and Disabled Men each maintained a large publicity department that worked to encourage publications to produce just such types of articles. Examples include B. C. Forbes, "A Genius Who Never Walked a Step," *American Magazine* 89 (April 1920): 9–11; Norman Blake, "How One Man Overcame," *Ladies' Home Journal* 34 (November 1917): 64; Lacy Simms, "Useful as Other Men Are," *The Outlook* 120 (September 11, 1918): 54–57.

29. Charles A. Lauffer, "The Injured in Industry," *Carry On* 1 (June 1919): 11.

30. They also received training in a few occupations, such as stenography and secretarial work, that were transitioning to the women's sphere in the early twentieth century.

31. "What I Faced in My Life," *Ladies' Home Journal* 30 (February 1919): 13.

32. Not all these institutions were called hospital-schools. See Henry Howard Abt, *The Care, Cure and Education of the Crippled Child* (Elyria, Ohio: International Society for Crippled Children, 1924), passim.

33. Frederick Fox Cartwright, *The Development of Modern Surgery* (New York: Thomas Y. Crowell Company, 1967), 146–57. Instead, orthopedists focused largely on therapeutic measures such as bracing, stretching, and dieting, while other, social rehabilitationists worked to educate cripples and to alter public opinion concerning the cripple.

34. The double meaning of *rehabilitation* is illustrative of what separates this period from the subsequent period. Rehabilitation featured (and continues to feature) a focus on correcting the individual, by providing him or her with medical services or employment services. But to social rehabilitationists, the term also signified a rehabilitation of society and, in particular, social norms relating to disability. Though prior to the 1910s reformers did not employ this or any other specific term to describe their work (they spoke only of the "care, cure, and education" of crippled children), during World War I, as the movement peaked, *rehabilitation* gained widespread use.

35. Michael B. Katz, *In the Shadow of the Poorhouse: A Social History of Welfare in America* (New York: Basic Books, 1986), 115.

36. A few examples of studies that emphasized the problems presented by disability include Willard's, *One Thousand Homeless Men*; Nels Andersen, *The Hobo: The Sociology of the Homeless Man* (Chicago: University of Chicago Press, 1923); and F. C. Laubach, "Why There Are Vagrants" (published privately by the Municipal Lodging House of New York City, 1910).

37. Later referred to as the New York Institute for the Crippled and Disabled and today known as the International Center for the Disabled (ICD).

38. Howard R. Heydon, "The Supremacy of the Spirit," *Annals of the American Academy of Political and Social Science* 80 (November 1918): 55.

39. John Culbert Faries, *Three Years of Work for Handicapped Men: A Report of the Activities of the Red Cross Institute for Crippled and Disabled Men* (New York: Institute Crippled and Disabled Men, 1919), 70–75.

40. "Putting the Crippled on the Pay-Roll," *Literary Digest* 54 (March 10, 1917): 617–18.

41. Institute for the Crippled and Disabled, *Some Things a Ten-Year-Old Knows about Cripples* (New York: privately printed, 1928), 7.

42. Ibid., 9.

43. Newton M. Shaffer, M.D., professor of Orthopaedic Surgery, Cornell University, "On the Care of Crippled and Deformed Children," *New York Medical Journal* 68 (July 9, 1898): 37–40. Reprinted in William R. F. Phillips and Janet Rosenberg, eds., *The Physically Handicapped in Society* (New York: Arno Press, 1980), 38.

44. Reeves, *Care and Education of Crippled Children*, 171–83.

45. These statistics were derived from ibid., 141–201.

46. For an appraisal of working-class attitudes toward orthopedic surgeons, see "The Medical Department," *Hospital School Journal* 11, 1 (March–April 1923): 5–6; and Joseph F. Sullivan, "The Social Service Work of the M.H.S.," *Hospital School Journal* 8, 4 (February–March 1920): 5.

47. Many rehabilitationists did believe, however, that disability could, by and large, be prevented.

48. John Duffy, *From Humors to Medical Science: A History of American Medicine* (Chicago: University of Illinois Press, 1993), 200.

49. See Arthur J. Gillette, "The Advantage of a State Hospital for Indigent Crippled and Deformed Children in the Advancement of Orthopedic Surgery in the State," *American Journal of Orthopedic Surgery* 14, 5 (May 1916): 259–64 (also printed and circulated in pamphlet form); and

Arthur J. Gillette, "Sixty Years of Surgery," *Hospital School Journal* 11, 1 (March–April 1923): 6.

50. These hospital-schools discharged pupil-patients after a cure was affected or after dispensary care could be substituted for institutional care.

51. Reeves, *Care and Education of Crippled Children,* 141–201. Seven institutions discharged children after they had been "benefited as much as possible," a policy description that is too vague to draw conclusions from.

52. Ibid., 175.

53. Ibid., 163.

54. Ibid., 166.

55. At least, this was the case until World War I, when the extensive experience gained by orthopedic surgeons in the war improved both the knowledge and reputation of orthopedic surgeons. See Cartwright, *Development of Modern Surgery,* 157.

56. In particular, Albee's bone-grafting procedure was perfected in Europe, providing the orthopedist with a variety of new surgical options. See Fred H. Albee, *A Surgeon's Fight to Rebuild Men* (New York: E. P. Dutton & Co., 1943), 17.

57. Cartwright, *Development of Modern Surgery,* 157.

58. Reeves, *Care and Education of Crippled Children,* 28.

59. For the connections between war, surgery, and the crippled child, see Roger Cooter, *Surgery and Society in Peace and War: Orthopaedics and the Organization of Modern Medicine, 1880–1948* (Hampshire, England: Macmillan Press, 1993).

60. Most asylums and hospital-schools associated with a surgeon by 1910. Van Leuven Browne delayed its association with orthopedists because of a longstanding commitment to osteopaths.

61. See "The Medical Department," *Hospital School Journal* 11, 1 (March–April, 1923): 5; and "An Epochal Day," *Hospital School Journal* 8, 4 (February–March 1920): 3.

62. "As They Were and As They Are Now," *Hospital School Journal* 7 (May–June 1919): 3.

63. Edward Claypool, "What the Michigan Hospital School Has Meant to Me," *Hospital School Journal* 9, 6 (May–June 1921): 3.

64. Ibid.

65. I have arrived at this conclusion by comparing evaluations of admissions procedures in Reeve's 1914 study *The Care and Education of Crippled Children* with Abt's 1924 study *The Care, Cure and Education of the Crippled Child.*

66. Joseph F. Sullivan, "An Important Clause," *Hospital School Journal* 8 (September–October 1919): 3.

1.3 Sociology and Special Education:

Differentiation and Allocation in Mass Education

James G. Carrier

Although special education provision has been expanding rapidly over the past 30 years, sociologists of education have shown little interest in the topic. This may be because the main themes in existing sociological studies that bear on special education, reviewed here, do not address the central structural concerns of the sociology of education. This paper presents a structural framework for the analysis of special education, seeing it as one of the ways in which schools perform their reproductive task by differentiating children and allocating them to different educational treatments. This framework is then used to analyze the different histories of special education in England and the United States.

The sociology of education has been a boom industry within academic sociology for the past few decades.

Carrier, J. G. (1986). Sociology and special education: Differentiation and allocation in mass education. *American Journal of Education, 94,* 281–312. Copyright © by the University of Chicago. All rights reserved.
0036 6773/86/9403-002501.00

New theoretical frameworks have been put forward and old frameworks have been refurbished and put to good use. New styles of empirical investigation have emerged and empirical studies have been done that really do deserve the overworked adjective "landmark." New specialist journals have appeared, new books have come out, and, one expects, an exciting time has been had by all.

Well away from all the noise and clatter of the sociology of education, an important change was taking place within education itself, one that almost all the noisemakers have ignored. This change was the explosion, another overworked word that really does apply, in special education—the provision of separate curricula or pedagogies for educationally anomalous children, usually outside of the normal classroom.

In 1948, just over 1.2 percent of American school-aged children were enrolled in special education programs in local public schools; hardly noticeable, much less worth worrying about. A decade later, however, in 1958, this had grown to 2.1 percent. In another decade, it was 4.4 percent, and in yet another decade, the 1978 figure was a respectable 8.2 percent. Not only was this percentage just about doubling every decade, noteworthy enough in itself, but also because of the growth in population after World War II, the base on which it was computed was rising smartly too. The rise in the absolute number of children in special education is, therefore, even more impressive. There were 357,000 children in these programs in 1948, 837,000 in 1958, 2,252,000 in 1968, and 3,410,000 in 1978, almost a tenfold increase to a group the size of the state of Connecticut, with a bit of Rhode Island thrown in to take up the surplus (see, generally, Chandler 1981, p. 102; Dunn 1973, pp. 18–19). Even more impressive, in 1974–75, the U.S. Office of Education estimated that 12.6 percent of the total child population was in need of special education (Anderson, Martinez, and Rich 1980, p. 7). In other words, we are talking about one child in eight on the government's own estimate. Some unofficial estimates were higher.

A similar state of affairs existed in England, though there the boom began rather later. In 1960, the number of full-time pupils in special classes was 61,099. By 1970, this rose by more than one-third, to 83,342. And by 1978, there were 122,484 such pupils, though 22,653 of these were severely retarded children not included in the 1970 figures (Ford, Mongon, and Whelan 1982, p. 24). Additionally, the late 1960s and 1970s saw sharp expansion in informal provision outside of special schools. In all, the Warnock Committee estimated (1978, pp. 37–38) that in 1976–77 about 6.5 percent of schoolchildren in England and Wales were receiving special education of some sort, though the committee asserted that one child in six was in need of special education.

Clearly, important things have been happening in special education. The purpose of this paper is to relate these things to the sociology of education, in the belief that sociologists, educators, and special educators will benefit. If this paper is successful, sociologists will gain by seeing the ways in which sociological models have been used to describe and explain different aspects of special education and the ways in which special education relates to central questions within the sociology of education. Educators and special educators will gain because these sociological models inevitably cast special education institutions, policies, and practices in terms of more general issues and processes in society. This puts special education in a broader context and so helps show the broader implications of what special educators do as well as the broader forces that both shape and limit the opportunities for change.

One reason to relate sociology and special education is that even though so much has been happening in special education, sociologists generally have failed to sit up and take notice. This may reflect the belief that educational handicaps are like physical handicaps, as educational psychologists and special educators have argued—objective physiological conditions objectively defined, the very objectivity of which robs them of any broader significance—or it may reflect the belief that the growth of special education is simply the consequence of the growing theoretical and empirical sophistication of the field. Such beliefs will not do. Scientific research plays a role in educational psychology and many educational handicaps do have physiological correlates, but educational handicaps are not simply an objective reality that has only recently been discovered.

It might be felt that special education is sociologically uninteresting for another reason; it is just one more manifestation of a growing general humanitarian concern for the unfortunate. Worthy, perhaps, but sociologically rather dull. Many people in special education do see the identification and treatment of handicapped children as a moral imperative for a society with pretensions to civilization, but it is difficult to see how anyone could take such an unproblematically rosy view of humanitarian motives after the publication of such books as Michel Foucault's *Madness and Civilization* (1965) or Anthony Platt's *The Child-Savers: The Invention of Delinquency* (1969).

Instead, educational handicaps and the fields of educational psychology, which studies them, and special education, which treats them, are social products that are affected by social forces, reflecting social interests, and amenable to sociological analysis. I need to stress this point. It is not enough to say that there are such things as educational handicaps and that certain children have them. Such a view is questionable even for so self-evident a condition as blindness, which, as Robert Scott (1969) has shown, is not fixed and absolute but profoundly social. And if this is so for an apparently objective condition like blindness, it will be much more so for the sorts of mild disabilities that Sally Tomlinson (1982, pp. 65–67) has called the nonnormative conditions, those for which there is little normative agreement about signs, symptoms, and diagnosis, conditions that characterize the bulk of children in special education: learning disability, mild retardation, and emotional disturbance.

For example, there may be a normative consensus that there are people who are completely mute and that this is a disabling condition. But when we move to milder forms of speech abnormality, agreement becomes more tenuous because the criteria for judgment become harder and harder to define and defend. When does a slight lisp become impaired speech? When does speech variation become speech pathology? If a boy pronounces "something" as "sumfingk," is this variation from the standard to be explained sociologically as characteristic of a certain region and class—which suggests that we should accept it as valid—or is this to be explained in terms of the physiology of the mouth and throat—which means in effect that we treat it as an aberration to be corrected?[1] Similarly, when we move from profound to mild retardation, neuropathology, or psychological disorder, we leave the realm of normative consensus and relative certainty and encounter debate and interpretation; we leave those cases in which a medically based, clinical orientation is a roughly adequate way of approaching and understanding the condition and the people who have it; and we encounter cases in which a clinical outlook needs to be supplemented by sociology.

In the balance of this paper, I will show how sociology can be used and has been used to supplement, to challenge, and even to supplant a clinical view. I do this first by summarizing and systematizing a number of the ways in which sociologists have dealt with aspects of special education or with areas that parallel those aspects closely. This task inevitably involves criticism of the work summarized. This criticism is based partly on what strikes me as difficulties in some of the studies involved. The more basic ground of this criticism is, however, much less subjective; the failure of sociologists of special education to attract the interest of the sociology of education more broadly.

This failure, I argue, comes from the failure to relate special education to the central concern of much of the work done in the sociology of education, and indeed the history of education, over the past 15 years— the way in which education reflects the class structure of Western societies. This relationship exists, and the bulk of this paper is intended to make it explicit. I do so first by laying out a theoretical model of education, special education, and social structure and then by presenting a brief, illustrative application of the model to American and English educational history over the past century.

SOCIOLOGY AND SPECIAL EDUCATION

Pupils identified as mildly handicapped have real difficulties in school. The question is, however, What contribution can sociology make to understanding the forms the conditions and difficulties take, the ways in which they are understood, the establishment of programs to deal with them, the sorts of children identified as being educationally handicapped, and the ways in which they are identified?

One of the earliest researchers in this area was Lewis Dexter, who argued that in American society the stupid are discriminated against because of their stupidity per se "and not because the stupidity is relevant to the task, claim or situation" in which the discrimination occurs (Dexter 1964, p. 40). Dexter is thus pointing out that the meaning of "stupidity," and mental ability in general, is a cultural construct, not explicable solely in terms of the facts that are supposed to support it. The corollary is that these meanings and the sorts of people to whom they are attached as identities are shaped by a range of social influences, from the minutiae of social interaction to long-term changes in the fundamental orientation of society.

Many of those who have followed Dexter have consciously sought to undercut existing cultural constructions of handicap, especially retardation, by showing that handicapped people are not as disabled as they are commonly thought to be (see Pougiales 1983). One such researcher is David Goode (e.g., 1980, 1984), who has demonstrated that severely handicapped children are more competent with those people with whom they have a long-term, intimate relationship (such as parents and custodial nurses) than they are with those whose interactions with them are more sporadic and clinical (such as physicians, child psychologists, and speech therapists). His point takes on urgency when he notes (1984, p. 232) that often short-term interactions are the basis of decisions about "how and where a client will live, what training or education he will receive, the kinds of interpersonal relationships he will experience and even, on occasion, whether he will live or die." Another such researcher is Robert Bogdan, one of whose main concerns is to challenge the stereotyping he calls "handicapism" (Bogdan and Biklen 1977). Thus, he has criticized the negative stereotype of the handicapped in films (Bogdan, Biklen, Shapiro, and Spelkoman 1982) and demonstrated their inaccuracy by collecting life histories of people labeled mentally retarded that show that in many, and perhaps most, ways they are indistinguishable from the rest of the population (Bogdan and Taylor 1976, 1982).

In addition to raising questions about the validity of the cultural construction of handicaps and other identities related to education, sociologists have investigated the ways in which these identities are attached to individual children and along the way have raised doubts about the accuracy and objectivity with which they are applied. One of the earliest studies concerned with this question is *The Educational Decision-Makers* (1963), Aaron Cicourel and John Kitsuse's study of guidance counseling in an American secondary school. They found that being "college material" or an "underachiever" was more than just a matter of scholastic record or a given discrepancy between aptitude and achievement that was objectively and causally related to a pupil's academic prospects. Rather, counselors made informal personal judgments about a pupil's attitudes, tastes, and demeanor and advised that pupil in such a way that their informal judgments became self-fulfilling. For instance, the pupil who wanted to go to college but who was not "college material" was not advised that certain courses were necessary for college admission and was even advised not to take them.

Other researchers also have sought to identify the ways in which identities are applied by social actors and institutions and the consequences thereof. Jane Mercer (1968, 1973) studied the mentally retarded, noting that retardation was not an objective attribute but a status earned by certain sorts of social performance that are specific to certain social institutions and relations.[2] Likewise, David Hargreaves studied labeling in English secondary schools (esp. Hargreaves, Hester, and Mellor 1975), and he shows that teachers used the labels that they attached to pupils to justify their educational achievement; that pupils very often responded to being labeled deviant by further deviance, which solidified the label; and

that the application of labels affected the curriculum and pedagogy that pupils were offered and thus their educational achievement, which echoes a number of points Cicourel and Kitsuse made. Since Hargreaves's studies there has been a rapid expansion in special units for disruptive pupils in English schools, and Delwyn Tattum (1982) has shown that many people are assigned to the units because of the sort of interaction and labeling Hargreaves describes. Ford, Mongon, and Whelan (1982) use the same approach in their analysis of maladjusted children in English schools.

These studies share an orientation that is radically sociological, arguing that being college material (Cicourel and Kitsuse 1963), mentally retarded (Mercer 1968, 1973), a high- or low-stream pupil (Hargreaves 1982), a disruptive pupil (Tattum 1982), or a maladjusted child (Ford, Mongon, and Whelan 1982) is not to be explained in terms of whether or not the child's individual attributes match some objective set of criteria but in terms of how the application of the identity or label is shaped by the child's situation and interactions in which he is involved and of how that application affects the way in which the child is treated and thus his educational career. In general, these studies have focused on the labeling process itself, ignoring the broader factors within the labeling institution that affect the labeling process, though this question has attracted sociological interest. In *Special Education*, Carl Milofsky (1976) shows how the identification of children as educationally handicapped and their placement in special programs were affected significantly by the institutional and professional relationships that existed between the personnel involved: classroom teachers, special educators, educational psychologists, and school administrators. Moreover, he shows how political and budgetary constraints shaped the institutional setting in which these relationships occurred and thus indirectly influenced the relationships themselves and through them the sorts of children who were labeled.[3] Sally Tomlinson pursues this tack in *Educational Subnormality* (1981), a study of the administrative practices entailed in the identification of children as mildly retarded and their placement in special programs in Birmingham, England. She shows that assessment and placement decisions were affected strongly by their institutional framework and by the different occupational and professional interests, resources, and prerogatives of those involved. In short, Milofsky and Tomlinson show that the identification of children as handicapped is more explicable in terms of social and institutional processes than in terms of medical or psychological knowledge.

The institutional framework within which labeling occurs is, of course, not isolated and self-contained. Rather, it is affected by events taking place within the larger society. The event that has attracted the greatest attention from those concerned with the handicapped (e.g., Conrad and Schneider 1980) has been what they see as the increasing dominance of the medical profession (see Fox 1977) and the increasing dominance of a medical construction of deviance. Thus, the increasing authority of the medical profession in society is reflected by the growing influence of a medical-therapeutic orientation in both special education and the government agencies concerned with education. Deborah Bart in particular has argued that special education has adopted this orientation in part in an attempt to gain respectability by cloaking itself in a medical aura. This results in a growing acceptance of a therapeutic model by those who are involved with children and a growing institutional importance for those most closely associated with that model—physicians. She notes, for instance, "the presence of medical practitioners within the field, especially pediatricians, neurologists and psychologists, as well as in the field's curricular and professional practices" (1984, p. 109). This results in a growing tendency to identify educationally anomalous children as sick, as having some clinical shortcoming that calls for therapeutic intervention. This has the sociologically important consequence of directing "attention away from the social and structural [influences on children's school performance], since it takes the individual as its unit of concern" (Bart 1984, p. 111; see also Carrier 1983).

The studies that I have described by no means exhaust the topic, but they do illustrate what appear to be the main threads in the budding sociology of special education in England and the United States: the study of the cultural understanding of handicaps, the meaning of handicap identities, the social interactions in which identities are applied to children, the institutional settings of those interactions and the ways in which they affect labeling, and broader social changes that affect both the institutions that apply the labels and the sorts of labels that are applied and thus how children are labeled and what they are labeled with.

In spite of work that shows that special education has a clear social dimension, interest in the topic has not really penetrated the sociology of education in either Britain or America. I want to suggest two

reasons that may account for this. One is that many of the labeling and deviance studies that I have referred to sit uneasily together and may not form a whole persuasive enough to make the sociology of special education appear coherent and attractive to other sociologists interested in education. After all, these studies involve very different sorts of identities: the mentally retarded are not, really, that similar to underachievers, delinquents, or even disruptive pupils. Moreover, some of the work is not, at face value, immediately applicable to special education: studies of how children are labeled underachievers or of how the nature of interaction affects judgments about the abilities of the severely retarded are not the same as studies of special education. Handicapped children are not the same as children in special education—an important distinction to make because the bulk of children in special education would not be considered handicapped outside of school. Interactionists have established this point but often fail to see its implications for the sociology of special education. Children who are in special education are not just, or perhaps even, handicapped. Rather, agents of a particular social institution have identified them as having particular attributes that warrant teaching them in a particular way.

This leads me to the second reason why these sorts of studies of educational handicaps have not attracted a wider audience: generally they have not related the processes that they study to the special role that education plays in industrial society, though obviously this is more the case for the more interactionist studies and less for the more institutional ones (but even these accept, e.g., medicalization as a broader social force without really attempting to relate it to social structure or change [e.g., Bart 1984; Conrad 1976]). Moreover, the relatively smooth linkages that I have traced in the preceding pages, between individual labels and labeling on the one extreme and the broad, society-wide influence of medical models on the other, exist so far as I know only in this paper. Certainly it is not a concern discussed commonly in the sociology of special education literature. It seems quite likely that this inattention to social-structural issues reflects the influence of deviance theories on the sociology of special education, especially Talcott Parsons's model of the sick role as a form of deviance (1951, pp. 428–79) and Hargreaves's work on deviance in secondary schools.

My purposes in the balance of this paper are, first, to lay out a model that relates special education explicitly to central concerns within the sociology of education, particularly to the relationship between education and the social structure. The model that I will present also relates special education to other practices within education that serve similar purposes, thereby emphasizing the ways in which special education is linked to mainstream education. Second, I will try to account for the growth in special education by linking it to shifts in broader social processes and orientations. I will illustrate this linkage by comparing English and American educational systems over the past century, using the differences between them to try to account for the fact that special education was established and flourished later in England than it did in the United States. These histories will of necessity be extremely brief and must ignore factors that a more leisurely pursuit would allow. I include both histories in the hope that my presentation will have some attraction to those unfamiliar with America's education history as well as those unfamiliar with England's. The models, arguments, and histories that I present here are, of course, tentative. I have neither the space nor the knowledge to do more than present a sketch that may help to show how special education relates to education more generally and why it should be of greater interest to sociologists of education.

SPECIAL EDUCATION AND SOCIAL STRUCTURE

Although it has been the subject of substantial criticism in the past few years (e.g., Arnot and Whitty 1982; but see Hargreaves 1982), I think it reasonable to begin with basic reproduction theory (e.g., Althusser 1971; Bourdieu and Passeron 1977; Bowles and Gintis 1976; see generally Giroux 1983), the idea that the operation of education reflects, justifies, and reproduces the social order. This theory is attractive because it explicitly and inextricably links education to the society in which it exists. It identifies a process that appears to be common to a large number of societies—the reproduction of social inequality—and it says that in certain sorts of society, education is a prime agent of this process, thereby providing a parsimonious sociological explanation of the fact that education systems in advanced societies function to sort children, to differentiate them, and to allocate them to different educational treatments.

In societies without mass schooling, children are sorted prior to entering school by a number of institutions and broader social processes so that those who,

because of class, geographical location, sex, language, race, religion, or anything else, are judged unsuited to education do not enter school in the first place. In societies with mass schooling, it is usually pupils rather than children who are sorted: those already enrolled in school are differentiated by the school itself and allocated to different sorts of education.

Although differentiation and allocation are related as part of an overall sorting process, they are distinct analytically. Allocation consists of educating children in different curricula and using different pedagogies or, in extreme cases, excluding them from school. On the other hand, differentiation occurs when children are judged to be more or less suited to that combination of pedagogy and curriculum that offers the best chance of finishing the educational career that leads to material and social success in adult life. Although my main concern here is differentiation based on attributes of the child, many different criteria can be the basis of differentiation, some of them recognized by the society as being totally unrelated to a pupil's merit. For example, American children who attend public school are differentiated geographically and allocated the educational treatment the state offers. And to the degree that states differ in the quality of education that they (or, until recently, the different school districts) offer, this can have substantial consequences.

Differentiation and allocation vary in different ways. Differentiation can be anything from an official act of the school, a formal labeling of the child as genius, female, or black where these are significant categories, to the personal, unofficial, and at times probably even unconscious judgment by a teacher that a child is troublesome, bright, or the like. As this suggests, differentiation can range from the most objective assessment of the pupil to the most subjective reaction; from the most formal and explicit to the inarticulate and subconscious; from a decision based on the most objective and substantial attributes to one based on the most ephemeral. Similarly, allocation can range from the major, formal placement of the child in a separate educational program to the minor, subtle, and informal ways in which teachers teach some of their children differently from others (see Keddie [1971] and Rist [1970] for case studies and Reid, Clunies-Ross, Goacher, and Vile [1981] for a more systematic study).

This focus on differentiation and allocation situates special education in a broader framework of educational practices and relates it systematically to the focus of interactionist concerns: classroom life, pupil careers, deviance, and handicap. And it does so without losing sight of the institutional nature of special education and the role it and other forms of sorting play in the school and the society at large, for it links sorting directly to reproduction. Just as reproduction can take place without the conscious intent of educators, so special education solidifies and perpetuates poor educational performance in spite of the desire of special educators to help the child. As studies of special education have shown (e.g., Milofsky 1974; Weatherly and Lipsky 1977), the meliorative desires of special educators often count for little in the face of opposing educational forces.

I said that prior to mass schooling, sorting routinely took place largely by nonenrollment—those unsuited to school simply did not go—implying that only with mass schooling did the schools need to develop internal sorting mechanisms and thus that mass schooling is a necessary condition for the development of special education. However, it is not a sufficient condition for the simple reason that sorting can operate and be made legitimate in terms of a variety of ideologies. In a previous attempt to deal with these legitimating ideologies (Carrier 1984), I drew a distinction between egalitarian and inegalitarian beliefs, those that reject the idea that there are fundamental social class or ascriptive differences between children and those that assert that there are such differences.

Rethinking the material and some of the unresolved difficulties this distinction presented has led me to adopt a distinction put forward by Steve Barnett and Martin Silverman (1979, p. 56): the distinction between a symbolism of substance, based on "ideas such as natural substance . . . which people believe to be real [and] internal to the individual" and under which different sorts of people are fundamentally different, and a symbolism of contract, reflecting "notions about individuals (more or less) freely entering into agreements to do certain things in accordance with certain standards or rules" and under which there are no "different sorts" of people, because all are formally equal and unique individuals. Returning to my earlier egalitarian-inegalitarian distinction, to a degree substantialist ideologies are inegalitarian and contractualist ideologies are egalitarian, but the relationship between these two dimensions turns out, on closer inspection, to be more complex.

A contractualist ideology is egalitarian, in the sense that it sees children as unique individuals—with individual differences no doubt, but not classifiable as different types or sorts.[4] This ideology can appear radical at times, for it identifies any social class differences between pupils that may appear as superficial and artifactual, generated by unjust, inegalitarian social forces that educators ought to counter and correct. Particularly pertinent for my concerns in this paper, the focus of contractualism on individual attributes provides a justification both for meliorative intervention to correct individual shortcomings and for the proliferation of optional courses and different curricula to cater to individual tastes and aptitudes. It is in this area that the contradiction between contractualism and capitalism, with which this ideology is particularly associated (see below), is contained. This ideology exerts an equalizing influence, pulling all people onto the same general level. At the same time it exists within a capitalist, which is to say unequal, system, one that entails both social inequality and an ideology that justifies that inequality. In education this tension is both contained in and contained by the idea of individual differences, itself an ambiguous notion that can refer to differences between pupils in terms of their educational interests, which does not necessarily imply inequality, or to differences in ability, which necessarily does.

The question of a substantialist ideology is not so simple. In principle, this is inegalitarian, for it sees children as naturally falling into qualitatively different sorts. However, anticipating some of what I have to say later in this paper, substantialism can appear egalitarian if there is one type or sort that is culturally defined as overwhelming all the others. In this case, the practical effect is an egalitarian educational system: pupils should all get the same education but only because all pupils are expected to be of the same type, whereas children of other types are thought to be so unlikely to become pupils that they can be ignored. Of course, should these other sorts of children become more visible, the fundamentally inegalitarian nature of this substantialist ideology would become more apparent. Whether it appears as egalitarian or not, substantialism, by its focus on immutable types, provides no justification for large-scale meliorative programs. Because the types are different, they are expected to do different things and are judged on different standards. Likewise, because individual differences are not at issue, education tends to be uniform within types.

Barnett and Silverman's (1979) distinction is particularly pertinent because they see contractual symbolism "as an historical development of the capitalist mode of production" (p. 56). It is especially suited to capitalism because it focuses on performance—"the basis of a wage which allows the extraction of surplus value" (p. 51)—and because it reflects and allows the sort of abstract and depersonalized domination by mystified entities such as "the marketplace" and "supply and demand" that capitalism entails (pp. 54, 56). The link between contractualism and capitalism helps provide a theoretically more adequate explanation of the development of special education. It becomes possible to go beyond intermediate factors and get at more fundamental ones. Increasing institutional support for therapeutic models, growing willingness on the part of governments to spend money on clinically defined forms of educational abnormality, and increasing parental pressure for special education, all of which have been instrumental in making special education and educational psychology grow, themselves become not poorly explained independent causes but different manifestations of the same growing contractualism, itself a product of the increasing penetration of capitalist practices and values in society and culture.

In the rest of this paper, I will present brief sketches of education in England and Wales and in the United States. My purpose is to present a broad outline of changes in educational ideology and practice in these two places and to relate these changes to the development of special education as a sorting device. In other words, I will provide illustrative material for the abstract theoretical notions of the last few paragraphs. Because of this limited purpose and because of limitations of space and my own knowledge, I will not be able to deal with a number of topics that would have to be considered in a more thorough presentation.

First, I restrict myself to formal varieties of sorting. This is in spite of the fact that the arguments that I have made suggest that one should also look at all the forms of sorting that may have helped the schools fulfill their reproductive task. These would include the range of semiformal and informal varieties that, until quite recently, have been the ephemeralities of education: undocumented, unstudied, and largely lost beyond recall.

Second, I restrict myself to the past and avoid any serious attempt to deal with present issues or practices. I make, for example, only minor reference to the Education for All Handicapped Children Act of the United States, the Education Act of 1981 of England and Wales, and related issues. These events are still so recent and education in each country is undergoing so much fiscal and ideological flux that it is not possible to make the sort of summary judgment that one can with, for example, *Brown* v. *Board of Education* in the United States or even Circular 10/65 in England and Wales. Although I do make

some comments on recent events in both countries, my intentions are to be suggestive and to indicate how present issues and practices can be seen as the working out of broader social and historical processes.

Third, these histories are too brief to allow much attention to the more immediate, local causes of changes in practice and thought that both embody the forces that I have sketched out and necessarily modify and qualify the sort of simple, tentative model that I have presented. However, where more detailed research has been done that addresses the issues of concern in this paper, it tends to support my general interpretation. For instance, Gillian Sutherland's (1984) exhaustive and detailed analysis of changes in the use of educational psychology in England and Wales from 1880 to World War II ends up explaining differences in practices in terms of differences between the lingering strength of substantialist ideology, espoused by the landed elite in many localities, and the growing central government ideology of contractualism. As brief as these sketches are and as brief as they must be in a paper of this sort, they will also show that the spread of contractualism was by no means a uniform movement throughout all branches of education and all educators.

EDUCATION IN ENGLAND AND WALES

In nineteenth-century England, significant education legislation was linked with the Reform Acts, a linkage that is not fortuitous. The first important state involvement in education began one year after the Reform Act of 1832, when Parliament granted £20,000 to charity organizations to assist with school construction costs, an annual grant that rose to £800,000 by 1861 (Evans 1975, pp. 19–21). This link was more striking with the Reform Act of 1867 and the momentous Forster's Education Act of 1870. The 1867 Act gave workers numerical dominance in certain electorates, increasing the likelihood of eventual working-class control of Parliament. Agitation for education reform, which was intended to tame and instruct the newly enfranchised classes, followed. This intention is illustrated by the views of Robert Lowe, Chancellor of the Exchequer in the Gladstone government formed in late 1868. Lowe (quoted in Simon 1974c, p. 356) said that the eventual inheritors of Parliament had to "be educated that they may appreciate and defer to a higher cultivation when they meet it; and the higher classes ought to be educated in a very different manner, in order that they may exhibit to the lower classes that higher education to which, if it were shown to them, they would bow down and defer."

This substantialist belief that the children of the different social classes were qualitatively different types that required different sorts of schooling characterizes early English mass education and is nicely illustrated by the contrast between the 1870 Act and the Endowed Schools Act of 1869. The 1870 Act laid the basis for free state schooling for the working classes, which became compulsory over the next decade. It established locally elected school boards and empowered them to levy taxes to run local schools, commonly called "board schools." On the other hand, the 1869 Act allowed the reorganization of "grammar schools," with the result that many were able to exclude the poor local scholars whom they were often originally endowed to teach (Simon 1974a, pp. 97–112), and some were thereby able to become the great "public schools."

By 1870, then, the foundations of inegalitarian mass schooling had been laid, "consciously designed to establish different types of schools for different social classes" (Simon 1974a, p. 97) and underpinned by a substantialist view of social class. There were board schools for the poor and public schools for the elite. In the middle were the grammar schools, which the Taunton Report divided into three grades in 1868: the top for the children of top professionals and the leisured class; the bottom for the children of farmers, traders, and superior artisans; and the middle for the children of other professionals, established merchants, and the military. The first half of the twentieth century saw the extension of this structure to secondary education as demand for more education grew. A series of government reports—Hadow in 1926, Spens in 1938, and Norwood in 1943—urged the expansion and ramification of state secondary schooling, regularized in the Education Act of 1944. By World War II, England had a tripartite system of state secondary schooling: grammar schools on the top, "secondary modern schools" on the bottom, and the relatively rare "technical schools" in the middle.

While this system remained stratified, the ideology and practices underlying it were not static. Although the change was erratic and spotty (Sutherland 1984), the basis of differentiation gradually evolved away from a substantialist view of social classes as types to the more contractualist view of individual merit as embodied in the 11 + examination, a measure of general intelligence developed largely under the influence of Cyril Burt (Quicke 1982, chap. 1). In many respects the 11 + exam was inegalitarian because gen-

eral intelligence is a social construct, because assessed intelligence appears to be a function of social class and education, and because the supposed objective neutrality of the examination was vitiated by the extensive streaming of English primary schools. In spite of these qualifications, the shift to the 11 + examination marked a fundamental, if glacial, liberalization of English education, for it replaced the Taunton Report's idea that children should be grouped into qualitatively different sorts with the idea that children differed only quantitatively, with the consequence that the child of no class was barred simply because of class membership from access to any stream of state schooling.[5]

One aspect of this shift was the idea that since pupils differed in degree rather than kind, a tripartite structure makes little sense: pupils should be getting more or less of essentially the same education rather than fundamentally different educations. The lurching development of comprehensive education since World War II marked just this restructuring. A brief flurry of support for comprehensives just after the war faded with the defeat of Labour in 1951, and it was not until the return of Labour in 1964 and the Ministry of Education's Circular 10/65 of 1965 that comprehensive education really took hold. Thus, in 1960, 4.7 percent of children in maintained (i.e., state) secondary schools in England and Wales were in comprehensive schools. By 1965, the figure was only 8.6 percent, but then it took off: 1968—20.9 percent; 1973—50 percent; 1979—85.9 percent (Bellaby 1977, pp. 11–12; Rogers 1980, pp. 13–14).

The spread of comprehensives coincided with another change in English educational ideology. The Spens Report in 1938 marked official support for the use of intelligence as the basis of differentiation, as assessed by the 11 + examination. This was, as I said, a token of a move away from substantialist ideology, but only a partial move because general intelligence was taken to be innate and hence in some way substantial. This move was extended in the 1960s, when the Newsom Report in 1963 and the Plowden Report in 1967 focused on the role of relative social advantage and disadvantage in shaping performance. Although this change was not as profound as the earlier adoption of intelligence as a device for differentiation, it had the important implication that many of the differences between children of different classes are contingent on social processes and hence are devoid of implications for the child's fundamental worth or ability (e.g., Bernstein 1971). Children each have an individual identity, and the task of the schools is to compensate for the illegitimate and somewhat artificial social forces that produce apparent class differences and so bring this individual identity to the surface.

Special education followed the development of mass education and the gradual emergence of contractual ideology. The first government commission that investigated educational provision for the handicapped was established at about the time of the onset of mass education: the Royal Commission on the Blind, the Deaf, the Dumb and Others of the United Kingdom reported in 1889—after having its brief expanded to include the retarded—and the first local authority programs for the education of the handicapped were established in the 1890s. However, because the dominant ideology was substantialist with sorting by social type in a multi-track system, only gradually evolving into innate ability, the milieu was not conducive to the growth of special education. This is illustrated by the response to reforms proposed by the Hadow Report in 1926. According to John Quicke (1982, p. 7), a number of important people on the Board of Education "were quite open about their elitism and would have agreed . . . that the majority of children should be educated according to the class to which they belonged," and they were successful in resisting reform. It may have been true, as Quicke (p. 11) argues, that early expansion of special education was disrupted by the financial difficulties brought on by World War I and the depression that followed, but it seems likely that the money would have appeared had there been the political will.

In any event, by the outbreak of World War II there was little special education, and educational psychology generally was undeveloped, in part because these fields did not have the necessary base of a contractualist ideology to legitimate them. What there was consisted of psychometriec on the one hand and the child guidance movement for the disturbed and delinquent on the other, itself established through American influence and support. Both educational psychology and its parent discipline were poorly established in universities: by 1939 there were only six chairs. Furthermore, though the London County Council, the largest and most progressive education authority, had an official psychologist as early as 1913, the post was so marginal that it remained vacant for 17 years following Cyril Burt's resignation in 1932 (see, generally, Quicke 1982, chap. 1).

World War II marked a change. The Education Act of 1944, although regularizing and maintaining a hierarchical structure, was floated on a tide of "education for all," and, significantly, it was the first act

that obliged local education authorities to provide special education. Even so, between the war and the contractualist swing under Labour in the 1960s, special education grew slowly: between 1950 and 1960 the proportion of pupils in special schools rose only from 7.5 per thousand to 8.6 per thousand. On the other hand, as I noted in the beginning of this paper, by 1970 it was 10.1 per thousand, and in 1977 it was 13.9 per thousand (Booth 1981, pp. 293–94), though part of this increase resulted from the inclusion of the severely educationally subnormal (severely retarded) in the local education authorities' area of responsibility in 1971. Including provision for pupils outside special schools, the Warnock Committee reported that (1978, pp. 37–38) about 6.5 percent of school children in England and Wales were receiving special education in 1976–77.

This growth in special education enrollment in the 1960s and 1970s was matched not only by a marked expansion of educational psychology but also by a marked reorientation, one that was in line with the developing contractualist concern with pupils' individual attributes. Practitioners began to abandon the routine application of brute measures of mental ability and to adopt instead what they saw as more subtle techniques of assessment. This change was reflected in the development of more sensitive tests, most notably the British Ability Scales (see Quicke 1982, pp. 43–44), intended to allow a much more detailed assessment of pupils' mental attributes and performance and thus much more detailed differentiation and allocation. This was also a time of increased official concern for special education, with a host of government commissions, reports, and the like that considered special educational needs and provisions, capped by the Warnock Committee itself, the only government committee in this century established to investigate all forms of educational handicaps and special education.

The Warnock Report exemplifies the link between egalitarian, contractualist ideology and special education in a system of mass schooling. One reason for the report was the feeling that the criteria and framework of special education were illegitimate, reflecting not substantial differences between different types of children but illegitimate differences brought about by social inequality or even educational and bureaucratic convenience—a point reflected in many studies of the sort discussed in the beginning of this paper. Critics (e.g., Galloway and Goodwin 1979; Hegarty and Pocklington with Lucas 1981) were arguing that classroom practice should be liberalized to accommodate a broader range of pupils, while special education categories should be de-reified, partly to eliminate labels that stigmatize pupils. The Warnock Committee embraced the latter idea but then proceeded to estimate that at any one time one pupil in six needed special educational provision and that one pupil in five would need such provision at some point in his school career. So, in fact, increased egalitarian contractualism and the desire to expand special education came together in the report. Furthermore, given the existing distribution of performance and measured ability among English children, expansion would increase the number of poor and immigrant children in special education, so strengthening the reproductive mechanism that had been weakened by the move to comprehensives and resolving the contradiction between the individualist egalitarianism of contractualism and the class-based inegalitarianism of capitalism.[6]

In sum, in the past 120 years, English education has moved from an inegalitarian substantialism to an egalitarian contractualism, though this did not become pronounced until after World War II, and especially after about 1960. This reflected, perhaps, the relative autonomy of educational systems, in this case the ability of the noncapitalist elements of the English elite to influence education policy and practice (see Sutherland 1984, chaps. 9 and 10). This is in line with Turner's (1960) description of English education as part of a system of sponsored mobility: more open than the strict inegalitarianism of the late nineteenth and early twentieth centuries but not the egalitarian system that emerged with Labour ascendency in the late 1960s and 1970s. Furthermore, as the conception of differences between pupils changed from a substantialist to a contractualist form, so allocation moved from forced streaming into qualitatively different curricula and pedagogies to comprehensive education, buttressed by a mushrooming special education establishment.

EDUCATION IN THE UNITED STATES

American educational history, even the small number of general aspects that bear on my argument, is much more difficult to summarize than English. Whereas English education can be presented in terms of government commissions, reports, and policies, always bearing in mind the point that there have been "wide variations in terms of deference to or defiance of central directives" (Simon 1974b, p. 11), no such central structure existed for most of American educational history. Even so, it is possible to pick out major trends, so this section will be more than just a catalog of particularities.

Whereas England maintained a weakening but still markedly inegalitarian ideology until the 1964 Labour victory, America had an egalitarian view of education as early as the late eighteenth century. This was strongest in Puritan New England, and especially in Massachusetts, which, by 1789, required all towns with 50 families or more to provide six months of education annually for all children. In 1827, the state compelled school districts to levy taxes to support schools and, in 1834, subsidized school districts. The Mid-Atlantic states moved slower. New York did not require school taxes until 1849, and it abolished all fees in 1867. Pennsylvania, on the other hand, was supporting schools in 1834, and by 1837 there were tax-supported common schools in over three-quarters of the state's school districts. Slowest of all was the South, where there was no public schooling of importance until Reconstruction. For instance, the only pre–Civil War legislation in Virginia was a law in 1846 permitting free schooling. In the frontier states of the Upper Midwest, free common schooling came quickly after statehood, encouraged by the Land Ordinance of 1785, which established the framework of government for the region prior to statehood and which set aside land for public schools. With the exception of the South, then, tax-supported common public elementary schooling was in place by mid-century, well ahead of the English Education Act of 1870.

However, I think one can tentatively identify this as egalitarianism within the main type in a substantialist system. James Coleman's description of the four key elements of this ideology shows that it lacks the concern with individual attributes that is a part of contractualist egalitarianism: "(1) Providing a *free* education up to a given level which constituted the principal entry point to the labor force. (2) Providing a *common curriculum* for all children, regardless of background ['a common curriculum that would not exclude (them) from higher education' (p. 12)]. (3) Partly by design and partly because of low population density, providing that children from diverse backgrounds attend the *same school*. (4) Providing equality within a given *locality*, since local taxes provided the source of support for schools" (1968, p. 11). The most striking evidence that this egalitarianism applied only to the dominant social sort, which probably was conceived of as independent petty agriculturalists, merchants, and craftsmen, was the almost complete absence of education for blacks, as well as the emergence of a more overt inegalitarian substantialism in the face of growing immigration and the development of significant concentrations of proletarians in urban areas, especially in New England, as the nineteenth century wore on.

At around the turn of the century, however, American egalitarian ideology underwent a significant change. As my discussion earlier in this paper suggested, the sort of common-curriculum ideology that Coleman describes was not compatible with mass schooling, for it did not provide legitimate ways of sorting pupils. At about the time of mass compulsory schooling, roughly in the 1890s, however, this older ideology was replaced by a new one. The school superintendent of Boston put the change this way in 1908: "Until very recently [the schools] have offered equal opportunity for all to receive *one kind* of education, but what will make them democratic is to provide opportunity for all to receive such education as will fit them *equally well* for their particular life work" (quoted in Kirp 1974, p. 11).

This new egalitarian ideology was linked to the rise of Progressivism in the early twentieth century. It argued for a contractualist, child-centered approach, a recognition that because children are different, they should set their own pace and learn on their own so that their education reflects their unique constellation of personal attributes. This encouraged the development of educational psychology to help determine just what those individual attributes were, the proliferation of curricula to cater to them, and the development of pupil guidance and counseling to help assure that pupils took proper advantage of the choices available to them.

The machinery of sorting began to spread, particularly at the secondary level, which was expanding rapidly: enrollments doubled every decade from 1880 to 1930, when 4.5 million children were in school, more than half of those aged 14–17. Of course there had been some sorting going on for several decades. By the Civil War, high schools in a number of urban areas were offering three curricula: classics as a preparation for college; a teacher-training course; and English, the most popular, for those not involved in the other two. However, curricula proliferated around the turn of the century, permitting greater sorting, as business and commercial courses, science, home economics, industrial arts, and many others were established. Although this was, perhaps, just as reproductive as the more inegalitarian English system (Karier, Violas, and Spring 1973), the ideology was distinctly American: not the class distinctions of the Taunton Report and Robert Lowe or even the somewhat more egalitarian 11 + examination but the attributes and aptitudes of individuals, "the diverse needs and proclivities of the expanding high school population" (Oakes 1983, p. 330), leading ultimately to the idea of self-sorting, with pupils choosing the curriculum best suited to their needs and abilities.

Thus, by the early years of this century, American education had mass schooling and a developing contractualist ideology that was transforming the old substantialist ideal of common schooling into one of schooling appropriate to the individual child (see, generally, Bowles and Gintis 1976, chaps. 6, 7; Cohen and Lazerson 1977; Nasaw 1979, part 1; Tyack 1977). This early conjunction of contractualism and mass schooling helps explain some of the differences between England and the United States in educational psychology, special education, and pupil guidance and counseling. These fields developed earlier in the United States: Dewey, the founder of progressive education, was, after all, American; mass intelligence testing began in the United States in the army in World War I; and the Child Guidance Movement was spread to England from the United States.

A striking sign of these differences is the fact that America put a much higher proportion of pupils into special education years earlier than did England. Demonstrating this is complicated by the fact that special education in the two countries is construed and administered somewhat differently, so American enrollment figures include those in special schools and in classes attached to regular schools, whereas English figures include only the former. However, special classes in regular schools are relatively recent in England, though their rapid growth in the 1970s does cause real problems of interpretation. Even bearing these caveats in mind, the difference is clear. To begin with, special education in Britain was of so little moment that the government did not start to collect systematic figures for England and Wales until 1950, whereas the American government thought it was worth gathering systematic data much earlier, in 1922, and complete data in 1932. As early as 1940, 1.1 percent of the school-age population from kindergarten to grade 12 in the United States was enrolled in special education, a figure that England did not achieve until 1970. In 1950, .75 percent of English schoolchildren were in special education, compared with 1.2 percent for the United States (Booth 1981, p. 293; Dunn 1973, pp. 18–19). As the postwar English shift to a more contractualist and egalitarian ideology would lead one to expect, however, the difference between the two countries has decreased. In the United States in 1978, 8.2 percent were in special education, while, as I said, the Warnock Committee's estimate for England and Wales for 1976–77 was 6.5 percent.

I have argued that the early expansion of special education, educational psychology, and other forms of sorting based on the individual pupil's constellation of attributes was a consequence of the conjunction of mass schooling and a contractualist ideology. My discussion thus far has left out two important issues: the place of blacks in American education and the fact, with which I began this paper, that the great boom in American special education occurred after World War II, especially during the 1960s and 1970s. These are related, and I want to deal with them now.

In one sense egalitarianism permeated even the castelike position of American blacks, at least at the ideological level, for their position was subsumed under the slogan of "separate but equal." This egalitarianism began to take on a more contractualist form, particularly after World War II and especially after *Brown* v. *Board of Education* in 1954, which declared that separate never could be equal. This was followed by decisions that attacked discrimination in all areas of education (see Kirp 1968). The assault on racial segregation marks an important extension of contractualism, occurring about the same time as the shift to egalitarianism in English educational ideology.

As a result of the *Brown* ruling, a number of school systems were forced to find other ways of sorting pupils, and many introduced or expanded ability grouping and increased provision for the mildly retarded and to a lesser extent the emotionally disturbed. Particularly with respect to blacks, this resembles the introduction of the 11 + examination in English education. The most famous instance of this was the Washington, D.C., school system, which began tracking based on IQ test results "shortly after it was ordered to dismantle its dual school system" (Kirp 1974, p. 38), a policy that was attacked successfully in the landmark case of *Hobson* v. *Hansen*.[7] Similarly, the denial of legitimacy to inegalitarian substantialist bases of sorting led to the search for devices that could both explain the poor performance of blacks in contractualist terms and be used to sort pupils. The prime example of this sort of model is cultural deprivation theory, which salvaged the substantial ability of poor blacks while savaging their performance and prospects. Thus, the relationship between mass education, contractualist ideology, and

special education is repeated in miniature in the ending of racial segregation in the schools.

A contractualist egalitarian wave swept through American special education just as in England, with the same perverse results. A series of court cases and political movements in the late 1960s and 1970s, coupled with growing rejection of the segregation of the educationally handicapped and of the traditional categories of exceptionality (described in Kirp 1974, 1977), culminated in the Education for All Handicapped Children Act of 1975, intended to end the exclusion of any child from school because of handicaps, guarantee special education to all pupils in need of it, provide procedural safeguards to prevent the dumping of pupils in special education, and reduce the segregation of handicapped children in the schools to a minimum (Reid and Hresko 1981, pp. 178–96). Although, like the English reforms of about the same time, this was enacted against a background of growing distrust of special education, the law aimed as much at expanding special education as regulating it. This is because one of its main purposes was to assure that all those entitled to special education received it. Although we are still too close to the act to see it in historical perspective and to be able to see the consequences of its implementation and practical operation, there is evidence to suggest that it is serving to strengthen special education (Weatherley and Lipsky 1977) and that the "assumption that parents want a mainstream educational setting for their children is false" (Kirst and Bertken 1983, p. 162).

CONCLUSIONS

In this paper I have laid out a sociological model that links special education to the core structural concerns of the sociology of education, and I have used this model to discuss the differences in special education in England and the United States. The model begins with the assertion that schools, in order to carry out their reproductive task, have to differentiate children and allocate them to different curricula and pedagogies. This sorting can take many forms, and I suggested some of the ways in which differentiation and allocation can be expected to vary.

Seeing special education in terms of variations in differentiation and allocation emphasizes the ways in which it is an extension of regular education practices in a contractualist system. Furthermore, this in turn points out one danger in the institutional approaches to the sociology of special education that I discussed earlier in this paper. Although these are a corrective to the more purely interactionist studies, their institutional focus may end up making special education, which has a distinct institutional structure and place within the educational system, appear too distinct, too qualitatively different from mainstream education. Certainly there are differences between special and general education, and it will not do to conflate the two, for indeed it may be just these institutional aspects that define special education. But equally there are elements and purposes that underlie and unite the two, and it would be misleading to ignore them.

Identifying special education as one form of sorting is only part of an adequate sociological analysis, for the question remains. Under what conditions does it arise and become significant? The historical sketches suggest that the conjunction of two broad social factors is important. The first is a system of mass education, which requires that sorting occur within the school rather than in the society, influencing who goes to school and who does not. The second is a contractualist ideology, which focuses attention on the attributes of individual children and justifies meliorative programs.

In any event, with the conjunction of contractualism and mass education, children cease to be a stratified and clearly differentiated collection of social sorts that can be graded as finely as is done in the Launton Report and allocated to clearly distinct educations or to no education at all. Instead, they are seen as a mass of individuals, each with an individual constellation of tastes, abilities, and aptitudes. In this situation, schools are obliged to differentiate children who differ only quantitatively and to allocate them to educations that differ only quantitatively and to do so in terms of theories and techniques of assessment that deal with that individual constellation.

The schools, then, are caught in a bind. Under the reproductive model with which I started this discussion, they are required to be sensitive to the class origins and attributes of children. At the same time the contractualist ideology requires that sorting, if it is to be legitimate, needs to be explained in terms of individual attributes. In fact, this ideology denies legitimacy to sorting that is overtly based on class membership or attributes.

To digress for a moment, this suggests that special education is likely to be more egalitarian than general education in contractualist systems. When classroom teachers make assessments of their pupils, they are under much less public scrutiny than are special educators and educational psychologists, especially when these latter are deciding whether a child should be placed in special education. This, after all, was one of the main points of the Education for All Handicapped Children Act. Thus, general educators are free to use substantialist criteria, being told (as one teacher I know reported) that "Barbara certainly is not a B pupil, because her mother was a whore and her father was of no account." In both England and the United States, special education decisions are regulated by legislation that, reflecting the strength of contractualist ideology, imposes an individualistic orientation, requiring that decisions be justified, at least, in terms of the child's individual attributes.

To resume, schools and the agencies and actors that have been able to influence them cope with this tension between the social orientation of reproduction and the individual orientation of contractualism by basing formal sorting, the sorting for which schools are publicly accountable, on models that treat class-cultural attributes in terms of individual abilities and aptitudes, abnormalities and shortcomings. Tomlinson's nonnormative handicaps, described earlier, can do the job nicely. Furthermore, it is no accident that these are the largest categories by far in special education: about 55 percent of English children in special education in 1977 and about 58 percent of American children in special education in 1978, rising to 85 percent if the speech impaired are excluded from the total figure. It is no accident that these categories have increased much more than special education generally over the last quarter-century in both countries, and it is no accident that, with the possible exception of learning disabilities, these categories predominate among the lower classes of society, the subordinate position of which, reproduction theory indicates, the schools endeavor to reproduce by relegating the lower classes to less desirable streams (Booth 1981, p. 294; Chandler 1980, p. 20; Dunn 1973, pp. 19–20).

In this paper I have tried to locate special education directly in the center of the main issue within the sociology of education—the way in which education is related to social class, to the structure of society. In doing so my purpose has not only been to suggest ways in which the sociology of education might broaden its scope. Rather, it has also been to suggest that those who are interested in or part of special education need to see the enterprise in terms of its social backdrop. Such a broadened perspective will not provide instant answers to why special educators are doing what they do or to what special educators ought to do. It will, however, make apparent the fact that special education is part of a much larger social process. As such, special education and special educators are constrained by forces beyond their control, for instance, the forces emanating from the organization of labor and the nature of employment in capitalist society. These forces affect fundamental ways that human identity and merit are defined and so limit the socially acceptable ways in which schools can classify, educate, and certify children. Within these limits, schools and special educators have a certain degree of freedom to maneuver, to alter practices and policies, and within these limits, narrower explanatory frameworks may be quite useful in providing detailed accounts of why educators and special educators do what they do. Even though they may be difficult to identify at a distance, the limits imposed by these broader social forces are real. They and the social and historical framework that identifies them must be kept in mind by those who want to answer fundamental questions of why special education exists and how it can be changed and expected to change. In presenting this broadened perspective. I have been obliged to simplify some complex material and to leave some potentially fruitful lines of argument undeveloped. I want to conclude with some speculations that involve recomplicating some of my simplifications and developing some of the abandoned arguments.

Although I have treated educational ideologies as either substantialist or contractualist, it should be obvious that real ideologies are not purely one or the other. Instead, the move to contractualism is gradual and uneven, and I have no reason to assume it is complete. If this movement continues, it will put increasing pressure on special educators in particular but also on educators more generally to change the ways in which they do things.

Even though special education is much more egalitarian than the old English ideology or American ideology in the era of racial segregation, it still has a marked substantial aspect, for it asserts a qualitative difference between normal and handicapped children and between different sorts of handicapped children. Furthermore, it is this substantialism that gives a sharp edge to those interactionist and labeling studies that argue that substantialism is a mirage, that in many cases children are stigmatized as handicapped as a result of the merest social contingencies or the vagaries of administrative convenience. Consequently, those identified as handicapped are not uniformly and qualitatively different from normal

people, a point that is complemented by attacks on the lay and professional stereotypes of the handicapped. Following Barnett and Silverman, it is worth noting that these interactionist criticisms are part of the extension of capitalist ideology and social relations in education.

These attacks and the changing ideological climate of which they are a part put pressure on special education to abandon its substantialism and to adopt instead a contractualist concern with performance. This observation helps make sense of a change in special education that I have not been able to discuss in this paper—the growth of behaviorist approaches— which possess an ideology that is avowedly nonsubstantial and concerned exclusively with performance. Not only has behaviorism become increasingly popular in special education over the past 20 years but it has also been granted official legitimacy in the United States in the Education for All Handicapped Children Act of 1975, which has a clear behaviorist orientation (Odle and Galtelli 1980; Reid and Hresko 1981, p. 185).[8]

This suggests that special education as it has existed for the last century—the discovery of substantial pathologies or abnormalities that affect educational performance, the identification and treatment of these in handicapped children, and the development of curricula and pedagogies specially suited to them—may very well be an artifact of the gradual and uneven move to contractualism. As this move continues, concern should focus more on performance, as the growth of behaviorist special education indicates. This would break down even further the barriers between normal and handicapped children, and in extreme form it would do away with the latter category altogether and so would strengthen mainstreaming still more. This, coupled with the individualism of contractualist educational ideology, would lead to education becoming unitary in form, with all pupils in a single classroom. However, curriculum and pedagogy would be individually oriented, geared to the performance of each child separately, so that sorting would occur openly in the main classroom as part of official ideology and practice, with each child's performance monitored and his or her education adjusted accordingly. This, of course, is the technique of individually guided instruction, recently gaining ground in both American and English education (for the United States, see Popkewitz, Tabachnick, and Wehlage [1982]; for England, see Reid et al. [1981] and Wallace and Tickle [1983, p. 234]).

Notes

I gratefully acknowledge the encouragement and assistance of Len Barton, now of Bristol Polytechnic, and Achsah Carrier and Peter Smith of the University of Papua New Guinea. As will become clear, portions of this paper are substantially revised versions of Carrier (1984).

1. Males predominate in all categories of educational exceptionality (Gillespie and Fink 1974). The significance of gender in special education has not been studied extensively, which makes it impossible to produce a thorough sociological model of special education.

2. Many people took this conclusion to undercut the idea that mental retardation is a clinically identifiable condition that children have or do not have. As the studies contained in Carol Whalen and Barbara Henker (1980) illustrate, however, Mercer's findings can be taken to show only that mental defect or abnormality is complex and that its manifestations vary with the child's setting.

3. Milofsky thinks that the educational handicap that he studies is real. His objection is not that pupils get labeled but that they get labeled improperly, and especially that those who really are handicapped are likely to lose out to disruptive nonhandicapped pupils.

4. This contractualist egalitarian view has been noted by other commentators, albeit under other names. Arthur Jensen refers to it as the "average children" concept. He says, "The average children concept is essentially the belief that all children, except for a rare few born with severe neurological defects, are basically very much alike in their mental development and capabilities, and that their apparent differences in these characteristics as manifested in schools are due to rather superficial differences in children's upbringing at home, their preschool and out-of-school experiences, motivations and interests, and the educational influences of their family background" (1969, p. 4). My thanks to one of this journal's anonymous referees for bringing this to my attention.

5. This illustrates the inadequacy of the sort of ahistorical arguments put forward by Stephen Gould (1981), e.g., who criticizes IQ and the 11 + exam as repressive and stultifying. His lack of historical sensitivity makes him unable to see the liberalizing effect that they had on English educational thought and practice.

6. Even those who urged that classrooms should accommodate a broader range of pupils were urging changes that would increase sorting. Although such a change might decrease sorting by special education, it would increase it in regular education because reformers were urging that "education offered by ordinary schools becomes more differentiated" (Hegarty et al. 1981, p. 1).

7. A similar situation occurred in California in 1947. Under threat from civil suits, the state legislature eliminated the requirement that Mexican-Americans be taught in segregated schools. "That same year, the legislature created programs for educable retarded children" (Lazerson 1983, p. 40).

8. My argument here would seem to be contradicted by the increasing unedicalization of special education, discussed earlier in this paper. However, the contradiction is more apparent than real, for many medicalized forms of deviance are defined and identified behaviorally and treated symptomatically. Although an underlying substantial pathology may figure in these forms of abnormality, it does so decreasingly, and for many practitioners it is of little or no relevance. The clearest examples of thus are hyperkinesis (e.g., Whalen and Henker 1980) and learning disability (e.g., Carrier 1977).

References

Althusser, Louis. "Ideology and Ideological State Apparatuses." In *Education: Structure and Society*, edited by B. Cosin. Harmondsworth, England: Penguin Books, 1971.

Anderson, Robert, David Martinez, and Lydall Rich. "Perspectives for Change." In *Implementing Learning in the Least Restrictive Environment*, edited by J. Schifani, R. Anderson, and S. Odle. Baltimore: University Park Press, 1980.

Arnot, Madeleine, and Geoff Whitty. "From Reproduction to Transformation: Recent Radical Perspectives on the Curriculum from the USA." *British Journal of Sociology of Education* 3 (1982): 93–103.

Barnett, Steve, and Martin Silverman. *Ideology and Everyday Life.* Ann Arbor: University of Michigan Press, 1979.

Bart, Deborah. "The Differential Diagnosis of Special Education: Managing Social Pathology as Individual Disability." In *Special Education and Social Interests*, edited by L. Barton and S. Tomlinson. London: Croom Helm, 1984.

Bellaby, Paul. *The Sociology of Comprehensive Schooling.* London: Methuen, 1977.

Bernstein, Basil. "Education Cannot Compensate for Society." In *School and Society: A Sociological Reader*, edited by B. R. Cosin, R. Dale, G. Esland, and D. Swift. London: Routledge & Kegan Paul, 1971.

Bogdan, Robert, and Douglas Biklen. "Handicapism." *Social Policy* (March/April 1977), pp. 14–19.

Bogdan, Robert, Douglas Biklen, Arthur Shapiro, and David Spelkoman. "The Disabled: Media's Monster." *Social Policy* (Fall 1982), pp. 32–35.

Bogdan, Robert, and Steven Taylor. "The Judged, Not the Judges: An Insider's View of Mental Retardation." *American Psychologist* 35 (1976): 47–52.

Bogdan, Robert, and Steven Taylor. *Inside Out: The Social Meaning of Mental Retardation.* Toronto: University of Toronto Press, 1982.

Booth, Tony. "Demystifying Integration." In *The Practice of Special Education*, edited by Will Swann. Oxford, England: Basil Blackwell, 1981.

Bourdieu, Pierre, and Jean-Claude Passeron. *Reproduction in Education, Society and Culture.* London: Sage, 1977.

Bowles, Samuel, and Herbert Gintis. *Schooling in Capitalist America.* London: Routledge & Kegan Paul, 1976.

Carrier, James. "Social Influences on the Development of Scientific Knowledge: The Case of Learning Disability." Ph.D. dissertation, University of London, 1977.

Carrier, James. "Masking the Social in Educational Knowledge: The Case of Learning Disability Theory." *American Journal of Sociology* 88 (1983): 948–74.

Carrier, James. "Comparative Special Education: Ideology, Differentiation and Allocation in England and the United States." In *Special Education and Social Interests*, edited by L. Barton and S. Tomlinson. London: Croom Helm, 1984.

Chandler, B., ed. *Standard Education Almanac 1980–1981.* Chicago: Marquis Who's Who Books, 1980.

Chandler, B., ed. *Standard Education Almanac 1981–1982.* Chicago: Marquis Who's Who Books, 1981.

Cicourel, Aaron, and John Kitsuse. *The Educational Decision-Makers.* Indianapolis: Bobbs-Merrill Co., 1963.

Cohen, D., and M. Lazerson. "Education and the Corporate Order." In *Power and Ideology in Education*, edited by Jerome Karabel and A. H. Halsey. New York: Oxford University Press, 1977.

Coleman, James. "The Concept of Equality of Educational Opportunity." *Harvard Educational Review* 38 (1968): 7–22.

Conrad, Peter. *Identifying Hyperactive Children: The Medicalization of Deviant Behavior.* New York: D. C. Heath & Co., 1976.

Conrad, Peter, and Joseph Schneider. *Deviance and Medicalization: From Badness to Sickness.* St. Louis: C. V. Mosby Co., 1980.

Dexter, Lewis. "On the Sociology and Politics of Stupidity in Our Society." In *The Other Side: Perspectives on Deviance*, edited by H. Becker. New York: Free Press, 1964.

Dunn, Lloyd. "An Overview." In *Exceptional Children in the Schools*, edited by L. Dunn. New York: Holt, Rinehart & Winston, 1973.

Evans, K. *The Development and Structure of the English Educational System.* London: University of London Press, 1975.

Ford, Julienne, Denis Mongon, and Maurice Whelan. *Special Education and Social Control.* London: Routledge & Kegan Paul, 1982.

Foucault, Michel. *Madness and Civilisation.* New York: Random House, 1965.

Fox, Renee. "The Medicalization and Demedicalization of American Society." In *Doing Better and Feeling Worse: Health Care in the United States*, edited by John Knowles. New York: W. W. Norton & Co., 1977.

Galloway, D., and C. Goodwin. *Educating Slow-Learning and Maladjusted Children: Integration or Segregation?* London: Longman, 1979.

Gillespie, Patricia, and Albert Fink. "The Influence of Sexism on the Education of Handicapped Children." *Exceptional Children* 41 (1974): 155–62.

Giroux, Henry. "Theories of Reproduction and Resistance in the New Sociology of Education: A Critical Analysis." *Harvard Educational Review* 53 (1983): 257–93.

Goode, David. "The World of the Congenitally Deaf-Blind: Toward the Grounds for Achieving Human Understanding." In *Mental Retardation: A Phenomenological Approach*, edited by J. Jacobs. Springfield, Ill.: Charles C. Thomas, Publishers, 1980.

Goode, David. "Socially Produced Identities, Intimacy and the Problem of Competence among the Retarded: A Synthesis from Three Observational Studies." In *Special Education and Social Interests*, edited by L. Barton and S. Tomlinson, London: Croom Helm, 1984.

Gould, Stephen. *The Mismeasure of Man*, New York: W. W. Norton, 1981.

Hargreaves, Andy. "Resistance and Relative Autonomy Theories: Problems of Distortion and Incoherence in Recent Marxist Analyses of Education." *British Journal of Sociology of Education* 3 (1982): 107–26.

Hargreaves, David, Stephen Hester, and Frank Mellor. *Deviance in Classrooms.* London: Routledge & Kegan Paul, 1975.

Hegarty, S., and K. Pocklington, with Dorothy Lucas. *Educating Pupils with Special Needs in the Ordinary School.* Windsor, England: NFER-Nelson, 1981.

Jensen, Arthur. "How Much Can We Boost IQ and Scholastic Achievement?" *Harvard Educational Review* 39 (1969): 1–123.

Karier, Clarence, Paul Violas, and Joel Spring. *Roots of Crisis.* Chicago: Rand-McNally & Co., 1973.

Keddie, Nell. "Classroom Knowledge." In *Knowledge and Control*, edited by M. Young. London: Collier-Macmillan, 1971.

Kirp, David. "The Poor, the Schools, and Equal Protection." *Harvard Educational Review* 38 (1968): 635–68.

Kirp, David. "Student Classification, Public Policy, and the Courts." *Harvard Educational Review* 14 (1974): 7–52.

Kirp, David. "Law, Politics, and Equal Educational Opportunity: The Limits of Judicial Involvement." *Harvard Educational Review* 47 (1977): 117–37.

Kirst, Michael, and Kay Bertken. "Due Process Hearings in Special Education: Some Early Findings from California." In *Special Education Policies*, edited by J. Chambers and W. Hartman. Philadelphia: Temple University Press, 1983.

Lazerson, Marvin. "The Origins of Special Education." In *Special Education Policies*, edited by J. Chambers and W. Hartman. Philadelphia: Temple University Press, 1983.

Mercer, Jane. "Labelling the Mentally Retarded." In *Deviance: The Interactionist Perspective*, edited by E. Rubington and M. S. Weinberg. London: Collier-Macmillan, 1968.

Mercer, Jane. *Labelling the Mentally Retarded.* Berkeley: University of California Press, 1973.

Milofsky, Carl. "Why Special Education Isn't Special." *Harvard Educational Review* 44 (1974): 437–58.

Milofsky, Carl. *Special Education: A Sociological Study of California Programs.* New York: Praeger Publishers, 1976.

Nasaw, David. *Schooled to Order: A Social History of Public Schooling in the United States.* New York: Oxford University Press, 1979.

Oakes, Jeannie. "Limiting Opportunity: Student Race and Curricular Differences in Secondary Vocational Education." *American Journal of Education* 91 (1983): 328–55.

Odle, Sara, and Barbara Galtelli. "The Individualized Education Program." In *Implementing Learning in the Least Restrictive Environment*, edited by J. Schifani, R. Anderson, and S. Odle. Baltimore: University Park Press, 1980.

Parsons, Talcott. *The Social System.* Glencoe, Ill.: Free Press, 1951.

Platt, Anthony. *The Child-Savers: The Invention of Delinquency.* Chicago: University of Chicago Press, 1969.

Popkewitz, Thomas, Robert Tabachnick, and Gary Wehlage. *The Myth of Educational Reform.* Madison: University of Wisconsin Press, 1982.

Pougiales, Rita. "Review Essay: The Working Papers of the Socio-behavioral Group, Mental Retardation Research Center, UCLA. *Anthropology and Education Quarterly* 14 (1983): 131–39.

Quicke, John. *The Cautious Expert.* Milton Keynes, England: Open University Press, 1982.

Reid, D. Kim, and Wayne Hresko. *A Cognitive Approach to Learning Disabilities.* New York: McGraw-Hill Book Co., 1981.

Reid, Margaret, Louise Clunies-Ross, Brian Goacher, and Carol Vile. *Mixed Ability Teaching: Problems and Possibilities.* Windsor, England: NFER-Nelson, 1981.

Rist, Ray. "Student Social Class and Teacher Expectations: The Self-fulfilling Prophecy in Ghetto Education." *Harvard Educational Review* 40 (1970): 411–51.

Rogers, Richard. *Crowther to Warnock.* London: Heinemann, 1980.

Scott, Robert. *The Making of Blind Men.* New York: Russell Sage Foundation, 1969.

Simon, Brian. *Education and the Labour Movement 1870–1920.* London: Lawrence and Wishart, 1974. (*a*)

Simon, Brian. *The Politics of Educational Reform 1920–1940.* London: Lawrence and Wishart, 1974. (*b*)

Simon, Brian. *The Two Nations and the Educational Structure 1780–1870.* London: Lawrence and Wishart, 1974. (*c*)

Sutherland, Gillian. *Ability, Merit and Measurement: Mental Testing and English Education 1880–1940.* Oxford, England: Clarendon, 1984.

Tattum, Delwyn. *Disruptive Pupils in Schools and Units.* Chichester, England: John Wiley & Sons, 1982.

Tomlinson, Sally. *Educational Subnormality: A Study in Decision-Making.* London: Routledge & Kegan Paul, 1981.

Tomlinson, Sally. *A Sociology of Special Education.* London: Routledge & Kegan Paul, 1982.

Turner, Ralph. "Sponsored and Contest Mobility." *American Sociological Review* 25 (1960): 855–67.

Tyack, David. "City Schools: Centralization of Control at the Turn of the Century." In *Power and Ideology in Education*, edited by Jerome Karabel and A. H. Halsey. New York: Oxford University Press, 1977.

Wallace, Gwen, and Les Tickle. "Middle Schools: The Heart of Schools in Crisis." *British Journal of Sociology of Education* 4 (1983): 223–40.

Warnock Report. *Special Educational Needs: Report of the Committee of Enquiry into the Education of Handicapped Children and Young People.* Cmnd 7212. London: HMSO, 1978.

Weatherley, Richard, and Michael Lipsky. "Street-Level Bureaucrats and Institutional Innovation: Implementing Special Education Reform." *Harvard Educational Review* 47 (1977): 171–97.

Whalen, Carol, and Barbara Henker, eds. *Hyperactive Children: The Social Ecology of Identification and Treatment.* New York: Academic Press, 1980.

Chapter Two

Special Education Research and Thought

2.1   Using Ideology:

Cases of Nonrecognition of the Politics of Research and Practice in Special Education

Ellen Brantlinger

This critical review focuses on 13 articles and 5 book chapters by prominent special education scholars. These authors write in support of a continuum of special education services and recommend that only the results of empirical research should inform special education practice. They also express wariness about the concept of inclusion and the direction of the inclusion movement. In touting the superiority of their own scholarship, they accuse inclusion supporters of being political, subjective, and ideological. This article challenges the supposed neutrality of the special education status quo and the moral grounding of the reviewed authors' position. Drawing from the insights of theorists who study ideology, the analysis sheds light on the ideological nature of the reviewed authors' own writing. The major recommendation put forth in this article is that scholars and other professionals need to think seriously about the impact of their educational preferences on the least powerful members of society if equity in schooling is to be realized.

When "Inclusive Schools Movement and the Radicalization of Special Education Reform" by Fuchs and Fuchs (1994) appeared in *Exceptional Children*, I was puzzled: Why would a respected journal publish an attack on the leaders of the inclusion movement when the authors offered no coherent alternate vision for the education of students identified as having disabilities? My initial response—and apparently that of others—was to ignore this piece, or at least not descend to its level and engage in a shouting match. That article, however, appeared to set a standard. Subsequent papers of a similar tone and/or perspective by other eminent special education scholars followed in the major special education journals (see entries marked with asterisks in the reference list). Though these pieces were ostensibly written to rally support for traditional special education services, the authors took the opportunity to criticize inclusion advocates for their lack of empiricism and their "rhetoric." While noting ideology on the other side, they implied that they write from a privileged, nonideological position. Collectively, these papers have stimulated an abundance of behind-the-scenes conversations, but to my knowledge a

thorough analysis of their arguments, their style, their "science," and their visions has not appeared in print.

Although I urge *Review of Educational Research* readers to think about how arguments put forth this article have implications beyond special education. I write as a supporter of inclusion, and my review is aimed at a specific set of articles and chapters all recently written by well-known special education scholars. The authors are influential because of their multitude of publications, frequent citations in special education literature, positions on editorial boards of journals, and active involvement in and leadership of organizations for special education professionals. They have also received substantial federal funding; their articles and chapters often end with notes acknowledging grants from the U.S. Department of Education.

It will be apparent to some readers that my views align with a critical model of social science (Anderson & Irvine, 1993; Fay, 1987) and that the forms of schooling I advocate are consistent with Dewey's progressive ideas about democratic education (see E. Robertson, 1992). Although situated in these perspectives, my critique is multifaceted, in that it covers a number of complex issues related to educational scholarship and practice. It draws from various theories and scholarly disciplines. Finding fault on many sides and at many levels may seem to be a shotgun approach, yet the various facets are so intermeshed and entangled that focusing on all of them seems necessary for a substantive review.

Brantlinger, E. (1997). Using ideology: Cases of nonrecognition of the politics of research and practice in special education. *Review of Educational Research, 67*(4), (425–459). Reprinted by permission of the publisher.

Specifically, in this critical review I will (a) provide an overview of the trends and issues in special education for those who are unfamiliar with the field, (b) point out common themes in the reviewed papers, (c) summarize how the reviewed authors make their case against inclusion, (d) hypothesize about the motives that provoked the papers, (e) show how special education—not inclusion—is the real bandwagon, (f) make explicit the beliefs that underlie their version of best (special) education practice, (g) delineate the beliefs that undergird support for inclusion, (h) demonstrate that their use of ideology to denigrate the case made by inclusion leaders is a naive misuse, (i) outline informed theories about ideology, and (j) illustrate the ways in which ideology permeates their position and their papers. More generally. I make the case that an endorsement of pre-inclusion, business-as-usual special education is unfounded and unwise, in that it will not further the aims of democratic education.

Before I begin my analysis, it is essential to stress three caveats. First, my critique is aimed only at the papers marked with asterisks in the reference list and is not meant to be generalized to other work by the same authors. I acknowledge their contributions to my field. Second, my focus on these special education scholars is not intended to convey that they are the only ones who believe their own work is apolitical and nonideological. Just because I pinpoint the ideology of the reviewed authors does not mean that I deny its existence in inclusion philosophy or in my thinking and writing. Ideology is "at work in everything we experience as reality" (Zizek, 1994, p. 17). Third, I would like to emphasize that the incentive for my attack on the attackers does not arise from their having criticized my work. They have not. Nor have I any ties to people they attack. If these papers had been written by unknown figures or published in less prominent journals, I would have ignored them. It is precisely because all of the authors are influential people in my field that I feel it is necessary to speak up and talk back to power. In documenting their abuse of scholarly standards and their ways of undermining best educational practices, I risk seeming unscholarly and vindictive myself. That is a risk I take, albeit with trepidation.

AN OVERVIEW OF DEVELOPMENTS IN SPECIAL EDUCATION

Because not all *RER* readers may be familiar with the field, I provide a brief background of the trends and issues in special education, in order to place the debate about inclusion in context.

The field of special education has burgeoned, a trend that began with an upsurge in the 1950s and has continued into the 1990s. New types of disability have sprung into existence.[1] The proportion of students categorized as disabled and the number of professionals designated to serve their needs has grown exponentially. Professional organizations and journals have proliferated at a corresponding rate. Those within the field were and are occupied with tightening definitions of disability: determining eligibility for services; establishing "due process" testing, classifying, and service provision routines; developing distinct special education pedagogy and curriculum; and designing a cascade of service delivery arrangements from special schools to self-contained classes to resource rooms to inclusion classes (see Deno, 1970). Rights of people with disabilities as well as special practices were codified through federal and state laws.

Originally, special education was synonymous with separate schools and self-contained classrooms. Guided by the concept of *least restrictive environment* (LRE), mainstreaming figured prominently in the special education discourse of the 1970s and 1980s.[2] Yet mainstreaming was typically done on a voluntary basis; special education teachers got permission from general education colleagues for their students to spend time in the others' classes. As might be expected in such circumstances, implementation happened according to the idiosyncratic styles of teachers and schools. It was not widespread. Furthermore, in spite of LRE mandates in successive laws, specialized head count funding provided the stimulus to classify more and more students as disabled. Another impetus for high rates of identification was the pressure felt by administrators who are held accountable for students' performance on high-stakes, standardized tests (McGill-Franzen & Allington, 1993). Because students identified as having disabilities are not always required to take group tests, if low-achievers are classified as handicapped, their scores are eliminated and their district will appear to be more successful.

Approval for the expansion of special education has come from those who believe it benefits students who receive services. However, its growth has not gone uncontested. As the field and its proponents grew, so did opposition. Much of the challenge to the concept and practice of special education came from within. In 1968, Lloyd Dunn wrote a provocative and often cited article in which he suggested that special education might fundamentally be doing more harm than good. Dunn and Jane Mercer (1973) were especially concerned about the possibility that bias might underlie the schools' labeling and segregating disproportionate numbers of minority pupils. In posthumously published letters, Blatt (1979) expressed doubt about the category labeled *learning disability*, as well as the motives behind its inception. Grant and Sleeter (1986) grouped handicap status with class, race, and gender in a critical analysis of ways in which social stratification occurs in schools. Others (e.g., Algozzine & Ysseldyke, 1983; Hahn, 1989; Skrtic, 1991) criticized disability labeling. Sleeter (1986) saw disability as a social construct that resulted from institutions' inability to accommodate diversity. Gartner and Lipsky (1987) questioned the validity of the "medical model," which defines disability as a disease or essential trait of certain people. These insiders recommended rethinking pull-out programs; some felt that special education should be discontinued as a separate system.

Many who oppose pull-out classes are particularly troubled by the persistence of disproportionate numbers of students of color and students from low-income families who are classified as disabled and removed from general education for special services (see Artiles & Trent, 1994; E. Brantlinger, 1993, 1994; Harry, 1992, 1994; Mercer, 1973; P. Robertson, Kushner, Starks, & Drescher, 1994; Utley, Haywood, & Masters, 1991). This apparent overrepresentation can be interpreted two ways: Either schools are neutral and kids are flawed, or something is amiss with schools. Those who support the status quo in (special) education buy into the first interpretation. Advocates of inclusion see the disproportionate labeling of minorities as a powerful indicator that something is wrong. A second bothersome tradition is that although teachers refer students for special services—and although psychometricians inevitably find many of these students eligible for services—efficacy studies fail to show positive results from pull-out services. Evidence reveals that integrated classes spur social and achievement gains (Oakes & Guiton, 1995). A third concern is that students are not consulted about their feelings and preferences. When asked, most state a desire to be in heterogeneous groups (Elbaum, Schumm, & Vaughn, 1997) and general education classrooms (E. Brantlinger, 1994).

Those opposed to hierarchically stratified systems do not single out special education. Tracking and remedial programs are faulted on similar grounds. Examining the actual proponents of separate educational programs, Kantor and Lowe (1995) found that "no black constituency demanded compensatory education; nor did any organized black group participate in the formulation of federal legislation that endorsed compensatory practices" (p. 9). Wrigley (1982) provides similar historical evidence that Chicago working classes fought vocational programs through labor unions. Because they felt a separate system was inherently unequal, they wanted their children to be part of a comprehensive curriculum. After analyzing the widespread adoption of compensatory education in the sixties and seventies, Watt (1994) concluded, "Americans are dominated by the egoistic conception of equality as equality of opportunity to compete for society's prizes," rather than an "alternate, noncompetitive conviction that all people are equally and uniquely valuable, and have the same claim on the respect of their fellows and the benefits of the society" (p. 227). The latter view supports the distribution of resources endorsed by Rawls (1972) in *A Theory of Justice* (see also Christensen & Rizvi, 1996; Howe, 1996).

The rationale for integrating students with disabilities with a range of peers in general education classrooms came from many, including Dunn (1968). The first broad-based movement to advocate the full-time education of students with disabilities in general classrooms, the Regular Education Initiative (REI), was articulated by Margaret Wang and her colleagues (Reynolds, Wang, & Walberg, 1986; Wang & Walberg, 1988). Its popularity was fueled by a speech by United States Office of Education Assistant Secretary Madeline Will (1986). Backed by Lilly (1986), Pugach (1988), and others, *inclusion* grew out (or is a renaming) of REI. Although definitions vary, inclusion is associated with students who fall in the range of mild disabilities and have some academic proficiency. The rationale for *full inclusion,* or the integration of students with moderate and severe disabilities into general education, was enunciated by Stainback and Stainback (1988, 1992, 1996) and Lipsky and Gartner (1987, 1996) and endorsed by the Association for Persons with Severe Handicaps (TASH). The field has since become replete with a multitude of books and articles that detail how collaboration and coteaching might occur, how curriculum and pedagogy can meet the needs of a range of students in integrated classes, and how schoolwork can be adapted to support individuals' learning. In addition to suggestions from the special education professional community, the literatures on cooperative grouping, detracking, and constructivism recommend ways to make student integration and inclusion successful. For most supporters, inclusion does not mean a cessation of special school funding, nor does it mean simply dumping children into the mainstream without support. A poignant account by Bullough and Baughman (1995) illustrates the disasters that can result from that. Most advocate meeting the diverse needs of students and teachers by coteaching among teachers who have supportive and complementary proficiencies.

In the past decade, the impact of the idea of inclusion on policies and practices of special and general education has been profound. Although some straddle a middle ground as they attempt to understand what inclusion means for them, many have come out as strong, unbending proponents or opponents. Using the language of civil rights, advocates of inclusion describe pull-out programs as segregated and discriminatory. Those on the other side feel that inclusion does not meet the special needs of all students with disabilities. Internal conflict is not unique to special education; parallel divisiveness is evident within language arts (see Smith, 1997) and other subject areas. For instance, there is little consensus among educators and the lay public about voucher systems, school choice, integrated classes for students of mixed achievement levels, and bilingual and multicultural education (see review by Sleeter, 1995). Opposing ideas about schooling are often embedded in polarized views on broader political and social issues. These disputed domains engender conflicted perspectives and the articulation of strong stands, as spokespersons attempt to persuade others of the worthiness of their positions.

UNITING THEMES IN THE REVIEWED AUTHORS' SCHOLARLY WORK

My review includes articles and chapters by scholars who have a range of interests and use different research methods. Yet five themes run through their work. One is a deep suspicion about inclusion's aims and outcomes. A second is the desire to retain traditional placements. Fuchs and Fuchs (1994) write in "support of a strong, independent special education" (p. 295) and allege that Kauffman, Hallahan, Gerber, Semmel, and others have the same purpose. Third, by endorsing special education traditions, they convey the idea that broader school structures are fair and not in need of restructuring. A fourth uniting theme is a technical orientation which boasts the superiority of incremental reform based on the findings of empirical studies. Kauffman (1996) worries about the "haphazard or inverse relationship between popular intervention procedures and reliable research data" and recommends that "future research . . . be directed

toward finding ways to suppress the tendency to accept unsubstantiated claims for methods and materials and to construct a culture of support for research-based practices" (p. 55). A fifth commonality is the authors' rejection of any need for moral grounding of professional practices. As Schumm and Vaughn (1995) write, "Politicians, parents, and professional educators are reacting to the inclusion movement based on emotions, personal beliefs, moral and civic responsibilities, and perceptions of justice and equality" (p. 169). Although these orientations are not entirely unique to special education, Malouf and Schiller (1995) do identify field-linked conceptions of the reasons for and place of research:

> The perspective reflected in much of the general education literature emphasizes the potential of research as a source of new educational approaches and understandings—a "wellspring" for educational innovations. A contrasting perspective [that of special education] places greater emphasis on the role of research as a "proving ground" to test the effectiveness of educational approaches (much as medical research tests treatments) before they are used in practice. (p. 422)

Rizvi and Lingard (1996) write, "Special education thus developed as a technical field, located within a positivist framework, concerned with issues of diagnosis, assessment and causes of disability and appropriate forms of treatment" (p. 10). In contrast to the deep analysis, theory building, and varied research epistemologies and designs included in many education journals and conferences, most special education publications and organizations seem philosophically and methodologically conservative and monolithic.

Having identified themes shared by these various authors—and because it is cumbersome to repeatedly refer to them as the "reviewed authors"—it seems appropriate to give them a title. I was tempted to dub them *anti-inclusionists,* but most claim that inclusion should be part of the continuum of special education services. Their wish to preserve a pre-inclusion status quo might establish them as *conservatives.* However, in accusing the supporters of inclusion of fitting into the right-wing agenda of reducing government spending, some (e.g., Fuchs & Fuchs, 1997; Kauffman, 1995a) appear to reject a conservative label for themselves. They do call inclusionists "radical." Because of their support for traditional educational structures and research methods, the designation *traditionalist* seemed appropriate.

THE LACK OF EMPIRICISM IN THE CASE AGAINST INCLUSION

A perusal of other publications by traditionalists leaves little doubt that they can do empirical work; however, few of the reviewed papers could be judged to fall into that class. Like the Dunn (1968) article they so disparagingly cite, most are position papers: The authors try to convince readers of the soundness of their views while delegitimatizing the arguments of inclusionists. This behavior is not unusual. Indeed, selective reviews are endemic to scholarly work. Yet some of these authors go beyond typical position-paper practice and provide prime examples of the flaws delineated in Dunkin's (1996) article "Types of Errors in Synthesizing Research in Education." These include the exclusion of relevant literature, unexplained selectivity of sources, lack of discrimination between sources, wrongly reporting details,[3] erroneously summarizing positions and suppressing contrary findings,[4] and stating unwarranted conclusions and generalizations.[5] Dunkin warns that because readers cannot be expected to check the validity of claims by going to original sources, the trustworthiness of a synthesis becomes suspect when errors are discovered in it. The potential impact of fallacious renderings seems especially harmful when they are done by authors so prominent in the field.

The most blatant scholarly offense occurs in *The Illusion of Full Inclusion: A Comprehensive Critique of a Current Special Education Bandwagon* (Kauffman & Hallahan, 1995). The editors' preface begins,

> In one of his most memorable essays, "Bandwagons Also Go to Funerals," the late Burton Blatt (1979) cautioned special educators about advocacy unrestrained by careful analysis and reliable data. A decade and a half later, Blatt's cautions need forceful reiteration, for in 1994 special education is in danger of riding the bandwagon called full inclusion to its own funeral. (p. ix)

The trouble with quoting someone who can no longer speak for himself and appropriating part of a title from someone who cannot give his permission is that readers who do not have access to Blatt's publications are led to believe that Blatt would agree with the editors' and contributors' disapproval of inclusion. A pretense of speaking for Blatt and having Blatt on their side is created. The most egregious act is not doing him the justice of printing his rather brief letters in their entirety. One must conclude that

this omission is intentional. Why? Because his arguments are similar to those made by Lipsky and Gartner (1987) and disputed by traditionalists: Disability is a social construct that can be illogical, damaging, and imbued with others' vested interests. Kauffman and Hallahan's biased selectivity in publishing only part of the letters is a prime example of the type of distortion of citations that Dunkin (1996) warns against.

Blatt and Kaplan's (1974) book *Christmas in Purgatory*, which graphically and disturbingly illustrated institutional life, persuaded many to support deinstitutionalization. Yet some traditionalists use that movement as a negative example, to warn against endorsing inclusion. One wonders how Blatt would have reacted to its wholesale panning, as when Fuchs and Fuchs (1994) write of "deinstitution's failure" (p. 302) and their view is seconded by MacMillan, Gresham, and Forness (1996, p. 146). Blatt wrote that "if our early heroes had devoted themselves to cultivating beneficial social conditions for people with special needs rather than becoming obsessed with the pathology of difference, a whole other story of human service might have developed," and this leads one to suspect that Blatt would have been pleased to see group homes and people who would have been institutionalized prior to the 1970s in productive jobs and enjoying events in the community.

Another oddity about Kauffman and Hallahan's (1995) commemoration of Blatt is that his letters contain the "errors" that traditionalists censured in Dunn and REI and inclusion spokespersons: "lack of scholarly rigor," "failing to review evidence in a scholarly manner," "advocacy papers" that "advanced a point of view" (MacMillan, Semmel, & Gerber, 1994, pp. 30, 32, 34); "moral and polemical rather than empirical" (Semmel, Gerber, & MacMillan, 1995, p. 48). Semmel et al. reject comparisons of racial and special education segregation: "Dunn's legacy has been a tendency to hold special education unfairly accountable for many of the structural and ideological limitations of the larger public schooling system that produces and defines it" (p. 55). Yet they chose to be included in a volume with a title derived from someone who argues that the learning disability category is a hobbyhorse of the drug companies and a "powerful variant of the industrial-medical-educational monolith" (Blatt, 1979, p. 19). Blatt's position is "left-wing." Moreover, his letters contradict claims that early practices were validated by research prior to implementation: "In my own field, the histories of the almost infinite methodologies and uncountable attempts to prevent disabilities or ameliorate their devastating effects also inadvertently recount the many wrong paths we have taken" (p. 17). Presumably, these "wrong paths" were not always "empirically substantiated" before they were tried.

The Motives Behind the Attack on Inclusion

Traditionalists constitute a discourse community, that is, one that produces knowledge (Bensimon, 1995) and establishes conditions for who speaks and what gets heard (Bakhtin, 1981). Because it is institutionally sanctioned, their discourse is powerful (Britzman, 1991); its "regime" or "politics of truth" (Foucault, 1980) sets standards for the field. Special education is engulfed in bureaucratic rationality with an ideology of "professionalism" or "expertism" instantiating power relations (Tomlinson, 1996; Troyna & Vincent, 1996). In general, professionals are the chief beneficiaries of (scientific) knowledge; by controlling its circulation, they create an indoctrination that solidifies and privileges their own status (Wrong, 1979).

While validating empiricism and sanctioning the educational status quo, traditionalists discredit inclusion supporters and, with emotional intensity, offer reasons why their ideas should be dismissed. Much of the criticism is aimed at Dunn, Gartner, Lipsky, the Stainbacks, and Wang, but others surface as worthy of blame. When inclusion supporters came up with a paradigm for schooling that coincided with broader reform initiatives and had widespread appeal—that is, when an alternate discourse and discourse community began to have power—they constituted a threat to those who had fared well in prior special education scholarly and professional circles. This hypothesis is consistent with Taylor's (1995) rejoinder to the Fuchses, who "present themselves as 'pragmatists' and the voice of moderation," yet "if the extremist nature of inclusive education movement were self-evident and its positions were so flawed, this kind of language [i.e., strident attacks] would be unnecessary" (p. 305). No doubt traditionalists would dispute my claims. Not always conscious of their power, agents are genuinely mystified by anyone calling attention it (Cicourel, 1993). Yet, whose security is threatened and which interest groups will protect their turf must be understood by reformers (Mirel, 1994). The "interest of bureaucrats is the survival and expansion of their bureaus, the size of their budgets, and their own careers" (Weiss, 1995, p. 574).

Understanding Context: Bandwagons Within Bandwagons[6]

Traditionalists repeatedly use the bandwagon metaphor in reference to inclusion. They do not see special education as a bandwagon, but do acknowledge that "as a field we have a history of embracing untried treatments" (MacMillan, Gresham, & Forness, 1996, p. 145); "increasing numbers of students, inconsistent and diverse identification practices, and inconclusive data about program efficacy" (Kavale, Fuchs, & Scruggs, 1994, p. 70); "unparalleled and unprecedented growth experienced since the formal recognition of learning disabilities" (Kavale, 1995, p. 150); "efficacy studies of special versus regular classes provided ambiguous and contradictory evidence, at best" (Semmel et al., 1995, p. 46); "extremely low rates of return of students from special classes to general education" (Fuchs, Roberts, Fuchs, & Bowers, 1996, p. 214); the "misidentification" of ethnically and culturally diverse children with serious emotional disturbance who are "overreferred to the juvenile justice system" (Forness, 1988, p. 130). Traditionalists' own statements provide evidence that the inclusion movement is contained within, and is a reaction to, the encompassing bandwagon of special education.

What Is Their Drumbeat? Where Is Their Parade Going?

Fuchs and Fuchs (1994) worry that inclusion leaders are "out of step with general education's steady drumbeat" and "march to a beat of their own" (p. 303), yet rarely do they make their own rhythms audible, nor do they connect the beats to a whole song. They see inclusionists' discourse as "rhetoric," but there is a scarcity of detail in their papers about practices they actually endorse. The lack of a coherent breakdown of the beliefs and values that undergird their educational preferences leaves others with the task of deciphering messages embedded in their papers to deduce where they stand. The beliefs (see Table 1) explain variations in student achievement, provide rationale to justify special classes and other stratifying arrangements, and undergird the anti-inclusion position. Such beliefs surely obstruct or diminish the success of inclusive school practices.[7]

The Values Which Undergird Inclusive Schooling

After that explicit rendering of the beliefs and values that are implicit in traditionalists' support for

Table 1

Beliefs that undergird traditional special education structures.

(1) Disabilities are innate conditions of certain human beings; those "with disabilities" are essentially different.*

(2) Pupils who achieve above or below the norm are appropriately referred to as gifted and talented, learning disabled, or mentally handicapped. Pupils with problematic attitudes or behaviors are emotionally handicapped, conduct disordered, socially maladjusted, or ADHD/ADD.**

(3) Diversity is problematic in both school and society.

(4) The grade level statistical norm is the proper achievement level for all pupils of a certain chronological age.***

(5) Pupils who achieve below the norm or act uniquely will improve significantly (i.e., "catch up to" their peers or "straighten up") if they receive specialized, intensive, individualized instruction.****

(6) Academic support or behavioral interventions for students "with disabilities" are most effectively provided in separated settings.*****

(7) Competitive school structures are natural, fair, and expected; therefore, stratified ranking and homogeneous grouping of students are inevitable.

(8) Learning is developmentally linear—it follows a narrow path that mirrors or matches the incremental levels of academic subject matter and literacy skills—and takes place one sequential step at a time.***

(9) Traditional subject-matter-centered and academically oriented content comprises the best curriculum for most students.

(10) Special education teachers are more successful than general education teachers in instructing students identified as disabled.******

(11) The practices and structures of the institution of school are neutral and therefore have little or no deleterious effect on pupils.

---

*"Physicians, psychologists, and social workers do not seriously entertain the idea that sickness, mental illness, and social deprivation will be totally eliminated any time soon" (Hallahan & Kauffman, 1995b, p. 61).
**See the debate about learning disabilities between Kavale, Fuchs, and Scruggs (1994) and Algozzine, Ysseldyke, and McGue (1995).
***In reintegrating children, Fuchs, Roberts, Fuchs, and Bowers (1996) suggest "doing it case by case so that they have the academic skills and school behaviors required by the mainstream setting prior to entry" (p. 216).
****"Moving children successfully 'up' the cascade presupposes that special educators are willing and able to provide individualized intensive instruction that prepares students for the academic, behavioral, and social requirements of the next LRE" (Fuchs, Roberts, Fuchs, & Bowers, 1996, p. 215).
*****Schumm and Vaughn (1995) claim, "The evidence that does exist concerning students with learning disabilities suggests that they do not fare well in the general education classroom" (p. 169).
******"There is little evidence that educators know how to deliver such instruction to all students with high- or low-incidence disabilities in full inclusion schools" (Fuchs & Fuchs, 1997, p. 231).

the continuation of the cascade of special education services, my next step is to show that inclusive schooling is also based on a clarifiable belief system (Table 2). Although these 11 beliefs ground my own support for inclusion, they reflect ideas generated by inclusion spokespersons.[8] General education scholars (e.g., Mason & Good, 1994; Oakes & Guiton, 1995) offer persuasive evidence that mixed classes benefit pupils and that degrading labels are damaging (Franklin, 1994; LeCompte & Dworkin, 1991). "Inclusive beliefs" also coincide with progressive philo-sophies.[9] Readers should contrast the beliefs in Table 1 with those in Table 2.

A Correction in Locating Where the Onus Lies

It is important to counter traditionalists' denunciation of inclusionists for wanting "dramatic change without a carefully conceptualized blueprint" (Fuchs & Fuchs, 1994, p. 298), and their charge "from an empirical perspective" that "there be clear specification of what constitutes full inclusion" before it is implemented (MacMillan, Gresham, & Forness, 1996, p. 145).

Table 2
Beliefs that undergird inclusive schooling.

(1) Human commonalities cut across the socially constructed categories of race, class, disability, gender, sexual orientation, and achievement level.

(2) Human diversity is natural and expected. It is unnecessary and damaging to label people according to how they vary from a norm.

(3) Individual and group diversity contributes positively to classroom climate, learning outcomes, and community quality.

(4) It is natural and normal for any chronological or cross-age grouping arrangement to include students with a broad range of behaviors, academic achievement levels, learning styles, and other competencies.

(5) Individuals of varying achievement levels and competency and behavioral patterns can learn together. Although they may learn different things at different rates, their learning is enhanced by contact and interaction.

(6) It is best for all children to be in socially inclusive learning environments. An important mode of both academic and social learning is imitation of admired peers and adults. The classroom should be a place where all children are active and valued and where families feel welcome.

(7) Competitive activities encourage an individualistic and egocentric ethos in students. Because it is best for students to learn that the welfare and success of all people is of equal importance, collaboration, cooperation, and mutual support are preferred forms of interpersonal interaction.

(8) Knowledge and competence are purposefully constructed in a variety of ways from a range of meaningful phenomena in enriched and stimulating contexts.

(9) Classrooms should be places where challenging, practical, and relevant experiences take place and where authentic, important questions are asked. Education should encourage the formation and expression of informed views, lifelong learning, an active search for solutions to serious societal problems, caring for others, and constructive community participation.

(10) A basic requirement of any teacher education program should be to prepare preservice and inservice teachers to successfully include and engage diverse learners in inclusive classrooms. Teachers with different expertise can co-teach for optimal social and academic results for pupils.

(11) There is a strong tendency for schools to be structured so that powerful members of society are advantaged and those with little power are oppressed by being given stigmatizing labels and being placed in limiting environments. School funding formulas result in vast differentials of spending such that rich students have more and better human and material resources than poor students. For a society to become and remain democratic, it is essential that these tendencies be controlled.

These demands are based on two faulty assumptions: (a) that disability is an agreed upon, innate "condition" which necessarily requires unique treatment, and (b) that the natural place for students with disabilities is some form of separated setting or treatment. In contrast, inclusionists believe that all students belong in socially comprehensive classrooms and that the onus is on those who would alter that status to show that students, as individuals or groups, benefit from other (pull-out) settings. Most inclusion advocates agree that there are compelling and unavoidable reasons for students to sometimes be in restricted settings, such as when they are severely depressed, suicidal, or violent

toward others. Unfortunately, as Goffman (1961) theorized in *Asylums,* when institutions exist they tend to be used. Therefore, a substantial dismantling of separated educational structures is recommended.

AN IDEOLOGICAL CRITIQUE OF TRADITIONALISTS' WORK

This review so far has provided an overview of debates within special education, identified flaws in traditionalists' scholarship, and delineated the premises that underlie inclusive and separated educational structures and practices. Yet, as the title promises, its primary purpose is to document how the reviewed authors (mis)use ideology and how ideology saturates their work. To this end, I provide a conceptual framework by summarizing theories about ideology, which I then apply to traditionalists' work. But first, some examples of how traditionalists locate ideology in the writing and position of inclusionists.

Multiple Sightings/Citings of Inclusionists' Ideology

Traditionalists denounce inclusionists and dismiss ideas for transformative school reform on the grounds that they are derived from ideology. As MacMillan, Gresham, and Forness (1996) write,

> Fuchs and Fuchs (1994) clearly chronicle how The Association for Persons with Severe Handicaps (TASH) emerged as the ideological leader in the inclusive schools movement and how the rhetoric of its leading spokespersons . . . became increasingly radical. Clearly, the impetus for advocates of full inclusion was never empirically driven, but rather ideologically driven, and spokespersons frequently employed offensive statements, misrepresentations of extant evidence, and tortured logic to attract followers. (p. 147)

Accusing others of "improper rendering of empirical data," Kavale, Fuchs, and Scruggs (1994) note,

> Complicating the process is a tendency to misinterpret research findings for ideological reasons. The Ysseldyke et al. (1982) study serves as a prime example; it often has been used as the basis for suggesting that [learning disabled] and [low-achieving] groups cannot be distinguished unequivocally. In the present case, it is absolutely necessary that the conventional interpretation be revisited since the political implications are enormous: Special education as we know it may be transformed radically if some have their way. (p. 77)

They claim this "explanation related to values" has resulted in "a distortion of the entire process of policy development," and "even the application of sound reason cannot overcome the adverse effects of data misinterpretation" because "the zeitgeist in special education over the past several years has been embodied in ideas about unified systems and inclusive schools" (p. 70).

While marking inclusionists as ideological, traditionalists assume—or attempt to create the impression—that their own work is nonideological. Kavale and Forness (in press) distinguish "scientific" advocacy from "political" advocacy, where the latter "takes on the nature of the dominant political philosophy of the time" (p. 8). However, according to Zizek (1994), "When some procedure is denounced as 'ideological par excellence' one can be sure that its inversion is no less ideological" (p. 4). Their readiness to recognize ideology in others and their failure to see that it permeates their own work indicates that they are naive, perhaps because they have "not read widely cross-nationally or cross-disciplines" (Delamont & Atkinson, 1995, p. 3) and hence remain uninformed by important, relevant work in other fields. Because they refer to others' ideology so pejoratively, their ignorance cannot be excused as benign.

Traditionalists misuse the concept of ideology by equating "being idealistic" with "being ideological" and confusing "having ideology" with "being ideologues" (see Table 3). They might have been advised by Bourdieu (in Bourdieu & Eagleton, 1994):

> I tend to avoid the word 'ideology' because it has very often been misused, or used in a very vague manner. It seems to convey a sort of discredit. To describe a statement as ideological is very often an insult, so that this ascription itself becomes an instrument of symbolic domination. (p. 266)

If traditionalists stuck to panning inclusionists for idealism or demagoguery, however, they would be on safer theoretical grounds. Because they support status quo practices, they locate ideology in inclusionists' hope for radical school change. Yet, informed theorists note that ideology's real strength is in preserving existing social structures and power relations (Martin, 1994). Claiming that "both occupy the same terrain," Britzman (1991) distinguishes "authoritative discourse with unitary [dominant] meanings" from "internally persuasive discourse with renegade knowledge" which "pulls one away from norms and admits a variety of contradictory social discourses" but is "denied all privilege" (p. 21).

The Nature and Role of Ideologies

Ideologies are systems of representations (images, myths, ideas) which, in profoundly unconscious ways,[10] mediate one's understanding of the world (Althusser, 1976). As "anonymous discourse on the social" (Thompson, 1984, p. 27), ideologies are discursively constructed of a complex of narratives that are intertextually composed of other (religious, scientific) texts, so that they seem familiar and are respected (Althusser, 1971; Bakhtin, 1981). One function of ideology is to insulate beliefs and believers from criticism (Burbules, 1992). For example,

Table 3
Traditionalists' depictions of supporters of inclusion.

The enemy in battle

"no holds barred critique of special education" (Fuchs & Fuchs, 1994, p. 96)

"rallying cry today is 'inclusive schools'" (Fuchs & Fuchs, 1994, p. 295)

"even met, on occasion, to coordinate tactics" (Fuchs & Fuchs, 1994, p. 297)

"instigating more aggressive forms of mainstreaming" (Fuchs & Fuchs, 1994, p. 297)

"TASH took the field by storm" (Fuchs & Fuchs, 1994, p. 299)

"TASH leadership seized control of the reform movement" (Fuchs & Fuchs, 1994, p. 300)

"marshal it in support" (Semmel, Gerber, & MacMillan, 1995, p. 45)

The dreamer out of touch with reality

"embracing illusory rhetoric" (Kauffman & Hallahan, 1995, p. ix)

"attractive platform," "appealing sheen" (Kauffman & Hallahan, 1995, p. ix)

"popular but misguided rhetoric," "illusion of support" (Kauffman & Hallahan, 1995, p. x)

"lofty, idealized goals" (Hallahan & Kauffman, 1995b, p. 61)

"feel good approach" (Fuchs & Fuchs, 1992, p. 93)

"clinging to a vision, romantic, insular" (Fuchs & Fuchs, 1994, p. 304)

"out of step," "march to their own beat" (Fuchs & Fuchs, 1994, p. 303)

"zealous reformers" (Semmel, Gerber, & MacMillan, 1995, p. 39)

"naive environmentalism" (MacMillan, Semmel, & Gerber, 1994, p. 468)

The demagogue

"broad, sweeping generalizations" (MacMillan, Semmel, & Gerber, 1994, p. 476)

"much-publicized position" (Fuchs & Fuchs, 1994, p. 295)

"using tactics cleverly aimed to curry favor" (Fuchs & Fuchs, 1994, p. 297)

"TASH spokespersons appear disciplined, well organized, articulate, and politically connected" (Fuchs & Fuchs, 1994, p. 297)

"focus on a single issue, identify with a precisely defined constituency, and use rhetoric effectively" (Fuchs & Fuchs, 1994, p. 299)

"enjoying success in shaping state and national policy, is a relatively small and insular group" (Fuchs & Fuchs, 1994, p. 301)

"zealous advocates," "march to their own beat" (Fuchs & Fuchs, 1994, p. 303)

Boudon (1994) cites the strength of the egalitarian myth in the United States, which is in reality a stratified society, to show how ideology validates and protects the status of the middle class (p. 180).

Rationality's place in ideology is debated (see Larrain, 1992). Boudon (1989) maintains that although the irrational has a residual place in the creation and diffusion of ideologies, they occur "not in spite of but because of human rationality" (p. 24). As "common sense beliefs about political and social matters," they are based "directly or indirectly on scientific authority" (p. 73). Validated by the rational, ideologies still "resonate with individuals' needs, anxieties, passions, and fantasies" (Cookson, 1992, p. 95). Ideology connects to the psyche through "master signifiers" (Lacan, 1982), or such identity-bearing words as *masculine, White, smart, conservative, pragmatist,* and *scholar.*

Ideologies present plausible explanations of social life that establish the basis for solidarity (Burbules, 1992). They are recognizable in texts by the ways in which authors set themselves apart from Others.[11] Identity and in-group unity are ideologically constructed through dichotomous, binary categories which create borders between insiders and outsiders (Bakhtin, 1984). Distinction depends on exclusion; individuals and groups define and redefine themselves through marking out what is pure and normal, and by projecting despised attributes onto Others and pointing them out as inappropriate and contaminating (Morrison, 1993; Stallybrass & White, 1986). Thus, outsiders reciprocally affect power holders.

Power in modern societies is located in the middle class (Gouldner, 1979), a class composed of highly skilled wage earners; managers and such professionals as social workers, teachers, psychiatrists, and researchers (see Lamont, 1992). Gaining from the existence of subordinate classes,[12] the middle class puts forth its knowledge as *the* legitimate knowledge and circulates ideas that reinforce its advantaged position—a phenomenon referred to by Gramsci (1971) as "hegemony of the ruling class." The middle class controls cultural capital through institutions which generate class distinctions and contain the struggles of subjugated classes (E. O. Wright, 1989). Ideology conceals power relations by "allowing the dominant class to appear not as a class but as representative of the whole society" (Larrain, 1992, p. 52). Power embedded in institutions allows practices to redound to interests of the powerful (professionals, high-income groups) without the conscious knowledge of whose interests are being served (Lukes, 1974). Credentialed experts retain a sense of their validity by relying on tradition, deference to authority, and inherited privilege (Gouldner, 1979). By creating class distinctions and positional epistemologies, the intelligentsia contribute to the reproduction of the symbolic and material interests of dominant classes; because knowledge and interests are fused, entitlements associated with social location endow individuals with varying degrees of power to make decisions, pursue ends, and realize interests (Bourdieu, 1984).

Ideologies and institutions are coterminous; they take form and are articulated through networks of templates or blueprints for practice (Geertz, 1973). Ideology saturates architecture and such school routines and rituals as pupil grading and grouping (Stanley, 1992). Embodied in social life, institutions produce orientations which then reconstitute ideology. The circular, reciprocal interaction between ideology and institutions explains why schools remain stable over time: Cultural constructions of "real school" are so powerful that reforms are inevitably altered (Tyack & Tobin, 1994). Habermas (1978) sees institutions as collective manifestations of a repetitive compulsion that defend rigidly uniform behaviors and function to regulate oppression. As with individual neuroses, institutional pathologies have damaging consequences that cause suffering. Although created to address social tensions, institutions evolve into hierarchical bureaucracies that resist change and generate ideologies that naturalize their existence (Popkewitz, 1991). Recognizing that reform efforts fail to have much impact on school structures and practices, many (e.g., Cuban, 1988; Fullan & Hargreaves, 1992; Sarason, 1990; Smylie, 1994) note that [traditional] beliefs of students, parents, and school personnel impede and obstruct change. Various stratifying systems that sort and rank students arise in spite of reform efforts to suppress them (Hargreaves, 1996; Wells & Serna, 1996).

British sociologist John B. Thompson (1990) formulates a critical conception of ideology to show how "symbolic forms intersect with relations of power" and "meaning is mobilized to establish and sustain relations of domination" (p. 56). His definition of ideology as "meaning in the service of power" (Thompson, 1984, p. 7) is fitting for this review. Thompson (1990) claims that domination occurs when "established power relations are systematically asymmetrical" and "particular agents have durable power that is inaccessible to other agents" (p. 59). His modes of ideological operations and symbolic strategies include a range of actions, utterances, images, and texts which are produced and recognized by people as meaningful constructs (see Table 4). Cautioning that the modes overlap, are mutually reinforcing, and are not the only way ideology operates, Thompson sees symbolic construction as ideological only if it intersects with relations of domination. Thompson's breakdown provides a means for identifying the ways ideology is manifested in the reviewed papers.

Ideology in Traditionalists' Scholarly Writing

The overview of theories about ideology was necessarily cursory, but should prepare readers to follow my examples of how ideology pervades the traditional special education scholars' discourses. I urge readers to refer to Table 4 as I locate the modes and strategies in representative quotations from the authors' papers. In addition, relevant ideological modes

Table 4

Thompson's (1990) modes of ideological operations and strategies of symbolic construction.

Legitimation: Relations of domination are represented as just and worthy of support.

  Rationalization: A chain of reasoning defends a set of social relations or institutions and seeks to persuade an audience of their worthiness of support.

  Universalization: Institutional arrangements which serve the interests of some are represented as serving the interests of all.

  Narrativization: Justifying actions are embedded in stories.

Dissimulation: Relations of domination are concealed, denied, obscured, or represented in ways that deflect attention.

  Displacement: Positive or negative connotations are transfered to other objects or individuals.

  Euphemization: Institutions, actions, or social relations are (re)described in terms that elicit a positive evaluation.

Unification: Individuals are embraced in a collective identity, irrespective of any differences and divisions.

  Standardization: A certain framework is promoted as the shared and acceptable basis of symbolic exchange.

  Symbolization of unity: A collective identity is diffused through a plurality of groups.

Fragmentation: Individuals and groups capable of mounting a challenge to a dominant group are dispersed.

  Differentiation: There is a focus on divisions, distinctions, and characteristics that disunite individuals and groups.

  Expurgation of the other: An enemy, either within or without, is constructed and portrayed as evil, harmful, or threatening and requiring resistance.

Reification: A transitory, historical state of affairs is represented as if it were natural, permanent, and outside of time.

  Naturalization or essentialization: A social creation is portrayed as the inevitable outcome of innate characteristics.

  Eternalization: Phenomena are deprived of social-historical character by emphasizing their permanent, unchanging nature.

  Nominalization: Attention is focused on certain central and salient themes at the expense of other marginal or decentered ones.

  Passivization: Certain actors and agencies are ignored and deleted.

---

will be cross-referenced (in brackets) to quotations and descriptions of actions.

This ideological critique is organized around how ideology is infused in traditionalists' (a) reifying disability categories and naturalizing services, (b) believing the meritocratic creed, (c) allowing bias to remain invisible, (d) creating a shared identity, (e) constructing standard-bearer status, (f) touting a neutral science, (g) recalling an ideal past, (h) recognizing contaminating opponents, (i) foretelling an endangered field, (j) portraying personal victimization, and (k) undermining inclusion with cynicism. I reemphasize that my critique is not meant to locate ideology solely in traditionalists' writing. Ideology permeates all thought and practice. Although it is beyond the purview of this paper to apply Thompson's typology to the work of inclusion supporters, I invite others to do so.

Reifying disability and naturalizing special services. Traditionalists write as if disability were innate rather than socially constructed and as if special education were an inherent part of schooling rather than an evolved practice [reification, naturalization, eternalization]. Their "rhetoric of substantial difference and unique needs" (Sapon-Shevin, 1993, p. 27) provides the grounding for separated treatment. "Cultural deprivation," "remediation makes normal," and "need for individualized instruction" are stories that legitimate pull-out services [narrativization, differentiation, rationalization, expurgation of the other].

Disability categories and discourse about educability came about with the advent of mental testing and the concepts of norm and normal (Richardson, 1994). Normality, intelligence, and competence are heavily infused with scientific, medical, legal, academic, and discipline-based discourses. The technical nature of language promotes labels' image as scientifically correct and thus impervious to criticism [universalization, eternalization, standarization]. Yet, technical academic discourses (naming, ordering, classifying) are "practices of power that produce effects which are deeply inscribed on the oppressed" (Ladwig & Gore, 1994, p. 234). The labeled tend to be relatively powerless and hence vulnerable to such epithets as "at risk," "culturally deprived," and "mentally handicapped." These "conditions" provide the incentive for middle-class professionals to study, intervene, and gain employment. Traditionalists imply that progress results from experiments with new remedial approaches. Zizek (1994) concludes, "The purely formal operation of looking for newer technological solutions to everyday problems which bring about the effect of scholarly depth, while ignoring crises such as homelessness and ecological disaster, is perhaps ideology at its purest" (p. 16).

A dissimulation strategy, euphemization, is apparent in how difference is (re)described so as to elicit positive evaluation. Special educators have been obsessive in their endless defining, refining, redefining, renaming, and disputing of disability categories (see Forness, Kavale, & Denti, 1995; Kavale, 1995; Kavale et al., 1994; MacMillan, Siperstein, & Gresham, 1996; McIntyre & Forness, 1997). As successive official labels take on negative connotations they are replaced with temporarily neutral ones. The "feeble minded" and "imbeciles" are transformed to "mental deficients," then to "mentally retarded," and then to "students with special needs" and "those in need of substantial support." Education that results from failure is "special." Placements are "opportunity rooms" or "learning centers." With a charitable, *we*-are-doing-good-for-*them* image, special education blesses "patient" and "dedicated" professionals and disguises insidious effects on powerless students by euphemisms and silences. Yet, it has a heightened responsibility for being accountable because it serves students and families who are especially vulnerable to fraudulent treatment claims (Malouf & Schiller, 1995).

Believing the meritocratic creed. The extent and seriousness of race and class bias in schools is well documented,[13] but a subliminal message of the traditionalist position is that school is neutral. These scholars voice concern about disruptive students but fail to ask how school influences behavior (see E. Brantlinger, 1991; Zane, 1994) [nominalization, passivization]. Disputing the idea of meritocracy—that schools provide equal opportunity and reward competence and diligence evenhandedly—Connell (1993) sees modern education as central to legitimating inequality. It is symbolically violent, because it is in schools that people are taught societal ranking systems as if they are scientific and neutral (Delamont, 1989). Schools accomplish exclusion through such routine practices as special education. Thus education contributes to social hierarchies, advantage and poverty, and the negative or positive identities of groups and individuals. Schools not only produce unequal distributions of personal capital but the ideologies that legitimate inequality (Bourdieu & Eagleton, 1994). Location in the social structure frames what is seen and what is felt to be significant (Banks, 1995); academics are well served by education, but "should never forget there are many others who have been much worse served" (Connell, 1993, p. iii).

Allowing bias to remain invisible and unaddressed. For Fuchs and Fuchs (1994), the "Dunnian view" (that special education is biased and ineffective) is "recrudescent" (p. 295). MacMillan, Semmel, and Gerber (1994) downplay the significance of the phenomenon of overrepresentation of African American children in special education (pp. 21–22), but empathize: "When Jensen (1969) commented on black-white differences in IQ, he was vilified" (p. 20). They conjecture, "Stigmatization is a social process related to rejection. It stems from people's attitudes and behavior, not from terminology" (p. 43) [rationalization]. Nevertheless, claims about the links between labels, stigma, and self-esteem are well substantiated (Christensen, 1996; Edgerton, 1967; Goffman, 1963; Meekosha & Jakubowicz, 1996). Schumm and Vaughn (1995) find fault with teachers' claims that including students with disabilities makes their work too hard or is detrimental to other students. They recognize that these attitudes may be a "real" reason for many special education referrals. Nevertheless, traditionalists persistently maintain that the reason for special placement is that it benefits classified children—that inclusion is for their sake rather than for the convenience of others [nominalization, passivization]. This lack of recognition of the painful aspects of labeling indicate an inability to identify with those who are labeled and separated [differentiation, dissimulation].

It is important to examine texts for points pushed to margins or left out of discourse (Gottdiener, 1993). Padeliadu and Zigmond (1996) use what might appear to be an impeccable research design, yet its validity is seriously compromised by their failure to address the social class status of their subjects—a variable shown to be of importance in students' perceptions of special education (E. Brantlinger, 1994). In positional alignment with other traditionalists, they preface their report with a note that "arguments for mainstreaming are often based on ambiguous empirical data," "philosophical approaches," and "attitudinal barriers erected by various interest groups" rather than "empirical data that supports a particular model of service delivery" (p. 15). They ask, "Is there anything special that you don't like about this class?" but do not report responses to the question. It is no surprise that they find that students "like special education" and conclude by warning against eliminating pull-out options.

Based on studies of the attitudes of special and general education teachers, Vaughn, Schumm, Jallad, Slusher, and Saumell (1996) state, "The majority of teachers had strong, negative feelings about inclusion and felt the decision makers were out of touch with classroom realities" (p. 96). Submerged in the report, however, is a quote from a teacher: "I have too many . . . that want to look alike, think alike, dress alike, etcetera. I mean the kids beg me, for example, if we have an assembly not to walk in the same door they did because I was strictly identified as an LD teacher" (p. 104). In any gathering of special education teachers, remarks regarding students' embarrassment about special education are prevalent. It is imperative for these researchers to ask, Why, if students are so enthusiastic, do they care so much about disguising their special education status? Again, a sign of psychological insularity and lack of identification with or empathy for labeled students is non-recognition of their feelings.

Creating a shared identity. Traditionalists quote one another and praise those who share their sentiments for their astuteness, scholarly methods, and true accounts. Fuchs and Fuchs (1994) say, "By focusing on the REI and inclusive schools movement, we give short shrift to those who view some reformers' characterizations of special education as distorted and unfair" (p. 295), and then go on to list others in their own camp [symbolization of unity]. Collective identity is also apparent in "gratuitous advice" given to leaders of inclusion, a "message which we suspect is on the tip of many tongues" (Fuchs & Fuchs, 1994, p. 304). They claim to speak for many,

but denounce TASH leaders' "willingness to speak for all" (p. 304) [displacement, fragmentation].

Constructing standard-bearer status. Traditionalists, who have had the power to set the rules for scholarly discourse in special education, promote empiricism as the acceptable basis of symbolic exchange [universalization, naturalization, standardization, eternalization]. They herald their own work as disinterested, objective, logical, neutral, and pragmatic—a quality of work that supposedly sets them apart from inclusion scholars' rhetoric, subjectivity, advocacy, and ideology. Recall that ideology is recognizable in authors' creation of binaries. Semmel et al. (1995) state, "The subsequent quarter century has been marked by much confusion between advocacy on one hand and scholarship on the other" (p. 40). "The more negative result of Dunn's assault on pre-EHA special education, however, has been to reawaken tension between visionaries and pragmatists, a tension that historically fills the air with more rhetoric than scholarship" (p. 55) [expurgation of other, differentiation]. This self presentation indicates that *empiricist* is an identity-bearing word or a "master signifier" (see Lacan, 1982) that lends an "honorable and dignified complexion to social conduct" (Apter, 1964, p. 16). Ideology is situated even in claims to empiricism.

Fuchs and Fuchs (1994) distinguish their facts from Others' beliefs, although they do waver:

If harboring a biased view on inclusion is a sin, then we admit our guilt. However, we have little interest in browbeating or proselytizing. Our primary aim is to explain how the field's reformist impulse has been radicalized and why we believe this is undesirable. In the interest of fairness and scholarship, we try to distinguish between facts and beliefs. (p. 296)

Bensimon (1995) claims that "facts" are not so different from beliefs—they, too, reflect shared values, normative controls, and consensus among members of certain groups [standardization, reification]. Moreover, bestowing the status of fact on concepts renders the special interests, privileges, and power relations of the community that produced them invisible [dissimulation].

Touting a neutral science. Promoting the superiority of positivist social science, traditionalists narrate:

Another lesson to be learned from our history is that approaches designed to meet the needs of children with disabilities should be adopted on the basis of empirical validation, and not based on ideology, persuasive slogans, or the volume and stridency of voices advocating a particular treatment or position. It has been noted elsewhere (MacMillan, Semmel, & Gerber, 1994) that one of the unfortunate legacies of Lloyd Dunn's 1968 influential article has been the tendency for policy in special education to be influenced more by ideology than by research. (MacMillan, Gresham, & Forness, 1996, p. 146)

Kavale and Forness (in press) declare, "When politics is dominant, decision-making dynamics change, advocacy, ideology, and philosophy come to the fore at the expense of the analytical, logical, and rational" (p. 96) [narrativization, legitimation, expurgation of other, symbolization of unity, standarization].

Traditionalists are not alone in assuming that technical research is apolitical and nonideological (see Goodman, 1995). Yet, the idea of "objectivity"—of having no interests—is a "pseudo-scientific maneuver that imputes a spurious air of rationality" (Wrong, 1979, p. 196). Although national agendas (e.g., Nation at Risk, Goals 2000) are spurred and reinforced by positivist social science and technocratic solutions to political problems (Howe, 1994), there is a need to "scrutinize claims to knowledge that are validated through the exercise of reason on behalf of western rationalism" (Roth, 1992, p. 693). Rational thought, liberal political theory, empiricist epistemology, and capitalist economics were from the beginning interfused in deeply conflicting ways (P. M. Brantlinger, 1996).

Recalling an ideal past. Nostalgia for the past, tacit support for the status quo, and wariness about change riddle the traditionalists' work. In spite of their insistence that new practices be "proven" before being tried and their sense of an ideal time when implementing only proven practices was in vogue, a more realistic account reveals that "the disabled"—and professionals recruited to serve them—expanded in spite of disputed definitions (see Algozzine & Ysseldyke, 1983; Algozzine, Ysseldyke, & McGue, 1995; Kavale, Fuchs, & Scruggs, 1994; MacMillan, Siperstein, & Gresham, 1996; McIntyre & Forness, 1997) and vacillating visions of appropriate treatment or schooling. Labels and services always evolve according to the values, preferences, imaginings, and logics of a myriad of professionals—a pattern that did not start with those who opposed a separated special education. Evidence for this claim comes from the eugenics movement, in which people with disabilities were institutionalized and involuntarily sterilized to prevent disabilities in future generations and to diminish the strain on or threat to society of *their* being in

our midst. Dugdale (1877), Goddard (1914), and others who supported such transgressions on human rights saw themselves as scientists and were perceived as such by people of their time. In retrospect, most of us would challenge their science.

Recognizing and defining a contaminating opponent. Military metaphors and analogies cast inclusion supporters as evil, threatening enemies with sinister motives (again, see Table 3). Other construed faces are the ignorant person innocently bumbling into dangerous territory and the "radical," "presumptive," and "misleading" "extremist" (Fuchs & Fuchs, 1994, p. 299). Goldfarb (1991) notes, "When one thinks and acts ideologically, opponents become enemies to be vanquished" (p. 9) [expurgation of the other, fragmentation, narrativization, rationalization].

In regulating their own behaviors, traditionalists ignore the rigid standards imposed to judge leaders of inclusion. Traditionalists repeatedly use the driving-a-wedge metaphor as they accuse inclusionists of polarizing the field [displacement]. Semmel et al. (1995) refer to those who compare special education to racial segregation as "helping to drive a powerful ideological wedge between advocates for special education and advocates for ethnic and racial minorities" (pp. 39–40). They attribute this "wedge" to "the 'tragedy' of Dunn's 1968 article" (p. 40), rather than to the strain that results when a separate system is created in which poor children and children of color are vastly overrepresented [nominalization, passivization].

Fuchs and Fuchs (1994) claim that inclusionists' perspective is "increasingly insular and disassociated from general education's concerns" (p. 294). They situate support for inclusion almost exclusively in TASH leadership—a "relatively small and insular group" of "zealous advocates" (p. 301)—and identify those opponents' motives by saying that "the power to influence must be heady stuff for the leaders of full inclusion." Yet they turn around and admit inclusionists' popularity and impact: "There can be no doubt about TASH's profound impact on the policy environment" (p. 300); "the sun surely is shining on the current movers and shakers of special education reform" (p. 305). After representing TASH as "enjoying success in shaping state and national policy," Fuchs and Fuchs warn, "If clear skies are overhead, black clouds may be crowding for room on the horizon" (p. 304). "Recognize, too, that you're probably at the apex of your power" (p. 305).

Hedging about whether inclusion supporters can be lumped with the political right, Kauffman (1995a) still projects its purposes onto them: "REI bears all the markings of the Reagan-Bush agenda for education aimed at decreasing federal support for education, including the education of vulnerable children and youth" (p. 130). Similarly, Fuchs and Fuchs (1997) warn,

> Viewed through a conservative prism of supply-side economics and reduced government spending, calls for full inclusion—eliminating special education placements and redeploying resources into mainstream settings—will be understood to mean that all children can survive on a regular education diet; that monies saved by downsizing special education can be returned to taxpayers. (p. 229)

While some traditionalists report that inclusion advocates have right-wing leanings, Kavale and Forness (in press) assert, "The unremittingly racist, exclusivist, and undemocratic trends assumed in these basic class conflict perspectives about LD are red herrings that cloud rational argument" (p. 46). "The Marxist analysis also fails to recognize . . . [that mental retardation, behavior disorder, and learning disability] represent authentic realities and not simply policy conveniences" (p. 48). "With all programs aimed at enhancing school success, the only reasons for the Marxists' distress must reside in the politics of envy" (p. 50). By condemning reform efforts as "extremist" or "radical," conservatives attempt to silence reformers and dissenters. Yet it is unlikely that many Marxists line the ranks of inclusion spokespersons. Poplin and Heshusius, whom Kavale and Forness dismiss as Marxist, write about phenomenology, holism, and constructivism. I read their work as postmodern; postmodernists typically see such "grand or meta-narratives" as Marxism as reductive. In contrast, I might legitimately be spotted as left-wing and Marxist because I stress the importance of the economic base on social relations and status rankings in institutions in this society. Thus, I believe that economic disparities should be addressed as well as school inequities. I believe that my position is rare among inclusion advocates.

Foretelling an endangered field. In a two-page preface of premonitions and prophecies,[14] Kauffman and Hallahan (1995) introduce their book as "a tool to warn of the dangers of embracing the illusory rhetoric of full inclusion" and "for informing educators, advocates for students with disabilities, and policymakers of the disaster that we can still avoid—if we quickly, forcefully, and effectively unite to steer the full inclusion bandwagon away from its collision" (p. x). Semmel et al. (1995) write

Looking simultaneously at the past and at the future, we fear that contemporary reform rhetoric about "full inclusion," as well as about consultative and collaborative models of service delivery, will not only fail to benefit from the tragic past experience, but also will command such little real commitment of resources as to be a farce. (p. 43)

Kauffman (1995b) claims, "Many of us are dispirited by what we perceive to be a very serious, immediate, and nearly insurmountable threat to the welfare of the children we are concerned about, especially their educational welfare. The threat we see is the rapid erosion of placement options for students with learning disabilities, emotional and behavioral disorders, and mild mental retardation" (p. 225). He continues, "Full inclusion ideology seems to imply that the congregation of students in neighborhood schools for general education purposes is sacrosanct" (p. 229) [narrativization, expurgation of other].

In spite of a lack of proof that pull-out classes improve school achievement and social adjustment—indeed, in spite of evidence that such classes are detrimental—traditionalists blame inclusionists for "program advocacy . . . that gives the distinct impression to legislators and others concerned with special education that we know what works and how to best serve children with disabilities" (MacMillan, Semmel, & Gerber, 1994, p. 476). Again, I must emphasize that the onus is on those who would take students out of general education classrooms to prove that the alternatives are effective.

Portraying personal victimization. Traditionalists feel persecuted. Kavale (1995) writes, "Fuchs, Scruggs, and I were maligned as 'big-footed' men with a 'serious cross to bear.' Once the relationship of Algozzine et al. to REI is demonstrated, we possess the whole story of their misinterpretation" (p. 145). Hallahan and Kauffman (1995b) project their feelings onto teachers, simultaneously becoming the "defenders of teachers":

> Today's special educators are made to feel like pariahs when critics describe the profession as segregationist . . . and suggest that good teaching would obviate the need for special education. . . . If we were to believe its most vitriolic critics, special education teachers are responsible for harming children irreparably by labeling them and segregating them from their friends, all in order to provide them with instruction that is less adequate than what they would receive in general education. (p. 61) [unification, displacement, rationalization, narrativization, fragmentation]

The academic freedom enjoyed by pillars in a field does not include the right to be free from criticism. Yet, when they are requested to be sensitive to the damaging impact of educational practices, they belittle this concern by countering that they are being asked only to be politically correct. As Kavale, Fuchs, and Scruggs (1994) complain,

Although the political bandwagon marches forward, it would behoove special education . . . to [use] research evidence . . . only when there is a scientifically, not politically correct interpretation of research data so that policy analysis can incorporate reason and achieve rational solutions beyond the advocates' impassioned plea. (p. 77)

Their use of the politically correct put-down, as well as their sense of being victims, resembles conservatives' claims that they are oppressed by prevailing leftist ideologies or radicals determined to brainwash them or force their views on them. Despite conservatives' complaints, radical students and faculty face more oppression on campus; conservative correctness remains the greatest threat to freedom of expression (Wilson, 1995).

Undermining inclusion with cynicism. Cynicism about inclusion prevails in the reviewed papers. Cynicism is a problematic form of ideology (Goldfarb, 1991; Zizek, 1994) that is destructive because it results in the bypassing of sustained constructive, informed dialogue about serious issues. Cynics dismiss others' ideas without having to put their own alternative plans on the table for scrutiny [fragmentation, displacement].

When writers are sarcastic, it is assumed that they disagree with what they mock. After claiming that Dunn "rhetorically mused" (p. 39) about whether separate classes were justifiable, Semmel et al. (1995) themselves muse, "Another quarter century passes, and in 1993 we now find zealous reformers wondering aloud if much of special education is justified. Echoing some of the same arguments made by Dunn (unproved efficacy, possible harm), contemporary reformers . . ." (p. 39).
They continue,

With Dunn's unwitting assistance, special education in the late 1960s and early 1970s was successfully cast as one of the villains in the civil rights melodrama. The "smoking gun" was "overrepresentation" of minority students in classes for students with mental retardation. . . . (p. 41)

They apparently refute the merit and validity of these concerns.

One use of sarcasm is to ridicule others' accomplishments. All reviewed authors are prolific in publishing and professional networking; similar acts by inclusionists are viewed with contempt [differentiation, expurgation of the other]. Referring to those who "set the tone of the debate," Fuchs and Fuchs (1994) write,

Reynolds and Wang assumed high-profile roles by writing frequently in visible journals and organizing prestigious conferences. REI supporters generated a handful of tactics to restructure the special education-general education relationship and to move greater numbers of students with disabilities into mainstream classrooms. Some strategies were downright ingenious, others irritatingly vague or inconsistent. Several were cleverly aimed to curry favor with special and general education communities. (p. 297)

Under the heading "Reformist Rhetoric Hardens," they express strong, disparaging sentiments about TASH spokespeople:

In our view, [TASH] took the field by storm; they rushed into a vacuum created by others' inaction, no doubt intimidating by their vigor alone many who disagreed with their radical message. TASH spokespersons . . . appear disciplined, well organized, articulate, and politically connected. They tend to focus on a single issue, identify with a precisely defined constituency, and use rhetoric effectively. (pp. 299–300)

After damning networking by inclusion leaders, Fuchs and Fuchs do an about-face and advise them to "choose compromise over principles" and "transform adversaries into allies" (p. 305). They blame inclusionists for views that are "increasingly insular and dissociated from general education concerns" (p. 295), yet offer a "pessimistic prediction about the current movement's success in forging a productive alliance with general education" (p. 294); "many researchers and advocates (e.g., Kauffman, Hallahan, Gerber, Semmel) have claimed that general education cannot be trusted to always respect the needs of special needs children" (p. 295). These authors rarely say that inclusion, in principle, is a bad idea. Indeed, the case against inclusion is mainly made on grounds that because of contemporary attitudes and conditions, students with disabilities will not fare well in inclusive classrooms. Cicourel (1993) argues that agents seek to rationalize power imbalances they benefit from by claiming their temporary or necessary status.

RHETORIC AND REASON: RESTATING THE VALUE OF INCLUSION

Special education classification and pull-out arrangements have continued since, and in spite of, the sage warnings of such paragons of my field as Burton Blatt and Lloyd Dunn, as well as the REI and inclusion movements. From the perspective of one who supports reform that integrates and includes diverse students, the sad and discouraging part of the actual legacies of Dunn, Blatt, and others is that they have had too little rather than too great an impact. Traditionalists must be held accountable for some hindering of inclusive school reform. MacMillan, Gresham, Semmel, and Gerber call position papers empirical work. Schumm, Vaughn, and Zigmond silence social class and race in studies of students' attitudes about special education. Kavale and Forness ferret out Marxism in Others' writing—and dismiss arguments on those grounds. Kauffman and Hallahan see doomsday looming. And the Fuchses denounce "the other side" for polarizing the field.

In spite of the very political nature of these publications, the problematic themes of "neutrality of special education" and "objectivity of research" surface repeatedly. Traditionalists are quick to see ideology in others, but do not turn the gaze inward and recognize it in their own practice. In shedding light on how ideology infuses special education traditionalists work, I do not deny its presence in inclusionists' stand. There are, however, important differences. Inclusionists' ideology can be considered organic, in that it dwells on emancipatory or transformative ideas for eliminating oppression from social structures (Gramsci, 1971). Arriving at organic ideologies means struggling to intervene in the terrain of common sense by taking steps to counteract familiar, taken-for-granted practices (Hall, 1988) and treating the regularities of everyday life as problematic (Delamont & Atkinson, 1995). Barrett (1994) distinguishes organic ideologies from "the polemics of ideologues who use rhetoric to retain their personal interests in certain social structures" (p. 236). Second, a perusal of inclusion spokespersons' work reveals that they are explicit about values, educational philosophies, theories of learning, and goals for society (i.e., their ideologies). Perhaps openness, simplicity, and logical coherence in expressions of ideology are deficiencies rather than virtues. Watt (1994) notes the tendency for dominant ideology, or the accepted orthodoxy of a society, to take on corrupted

forms rather than being the best theoretical expressions of ideals. Third, inclusionists accept nontraditional learning theories, instructional practices, and research methods. Finally, and perhaps most importantly, they are optimistic about school reform and individual transmutability. In contrast, traditionalists privilege empirical knowledge but do not tie it to any explicit value base or theory of society. Atheoretical studies that are devoid of serious engagement with the concept of society are "a stunning example of social amnesia" (Shapiro, 1993, p. xvi). Although theories are not inherently beneficial, socially useful theories result from dialogue between people's everyday activities and their visions of an equitable, humane society. If scholars fail to address deep cultural and structural causes of inequality, they are unlikely to have a constructive impact on the democratic ends that could be achieved through schooling (Banks, 1995; Howe, 1996; McCarthy, 1993; Meier, 1993). Fair educational decisions will never be made if they are based on knowledge that maintains the status quo by not forcing recognition of unequal power relations (Anderson & Irvine, 1993). Endorsing technical research as progress can be tenable and laudable only when the basic structures of schools as well as other parts of the societal infrastructure are fair and enhancing to the full range of United States citizens.

I have openly situated my perspective in critical social science and progressive education philosophy, and I have detailed the beliefs and ideals that underpin my preferences for certain types of schooling (see Table 2). In holding what I believe are inclusive, progressive, and democratic beliefs, I admit to an orientation toward utopian visions of school and society. Watt (1994) claims that mainstream theorists see utopian thinking or "the effort to plan an ideal society founded on a simple, coherent, rationally planned set of ideals" as "a fine thing provided that it does not enjoy much success in practice" (p. 246). Although idealistic, I am realistic in knowing that utopia is a vision, perhaps remote, but one that inspires, provides direction for action, and suggests forms for mundane practice. Utopia is not easily or ever attainable, but it is important to optimistically keep an eye on the prize in everyday actions. I also believe that it is essential that all educators and the general public identify the values and societal implications of the school practices they endorse. As Rizvi and Christensen (1996) state, "While it is impossible to explicate a definitive definition of social justice, it is nonetheless important to look at the various ways in which considerations of justice relate to the practice of education" (p. 2).

Notes

1. Forness, Kavale, and Denti (1995) write, "There have traditionally been seven special education categories, i.e., physical handicaps, visual impairments, hearing impairments, mental retardation, speech or language disorders, learning disabilities, and serious emotional disturbance. The current annual report to Congress on IDEA now lists 10 categories. Multiple handicaps, other health impairments, and deaf-blindness were added over the years to the original seven; autism and traumatic brain injury have been added in the past year. This brings the total to 12 categories" (p. 226).

2. Least restrictive environment (LRE) was integral to the 1975 Education of All Handicapped Children Act (P.L. 94-142) and its 1990 update, the Individuals with Disabilities Education Act (IDEA, P.L. 101-476). The LRE clause mandates that classified students spend the maximum "appropriate" amount of time with typical peers in mainstream general education settings.

3. In a response to Fuchs and Fuchs (1994), Taylor (1995) wrote, "Parenthetically, Fuchs and Fuchs misrepresented my own published work; my 1988 article (Taylor, 1988) provided a philosophical, conceptual, and empirical critique of the related concepts of 'least restrictive environment' and the 'continuum' ('cascade of services model'), but it said nothing about the elimination of special education or 'ridding the educational landscape of professionals called "special educators" ' (p. 301). Having said that, I suppose that I should be thankful to Fuchs and Fuchs for elevating the influence and importance of my ideas in our field and bestowing on me the leadership of TASH. In actuality, I am merely a TASH member and the Editor of *Mental Retardation*, a journal published by the American Association on Mental Retardation" (p. 302).

4. Claiming "ample evidence suggesting the need to be cautious about inclusion of children with serious emotional or behavior disorders in regular classrooms," MacMillan, Gresham, and Forness (1996, p. 153) proceed to cite position papers written by themselves and colleagues.

5. For example, Fuchs, Roberts, Fuchs, and Bowers (1996) state that "a majority of the disability community in the United States supports separate special education placements" (p. 214) and cite Kauffman and Hallahan (1995) as providing evidence to back this statement. None exists in that source.

6. MacMillan, Semmel, and Gerber's (1994) "The Social Context of Dunn: Then and Now" contextualizes Dunn's 1968 article in the history of the times.

7. Studies designed to examine educational beliefs and tacit knowledge (concepts that resemble and share characteristics with ideology) have been directed mainly at practicing and preservice teachers (see McDiarmid, 1990)—an action that I, too, am guilty of (see E. Brantlinger, 1996). Teachers are scrutinized rather than preeminent scholars, who might be assumed to have more power to influence school policies. The practice of directing the gaze down-ward and outward and not upward or inward parallels the behaviors of sociologists (and other scholars) who, even though they claim to be looking for solutions to social ills, inevitably focus on the least powerful (i.e., poor rather than middle class, Black rather than White, and children and families rather than industrialists and politicians) in searching for reasons for disparities in social outcomes (S. E. Wright, 1993). Researchers assemble data about attitudes and behaviors of "disadvantaged" children and families, yet pervasive belief patterns can and should be discerned at home, in ourselves and other researchers, where we are likely to find the causes of racism, sexism, and classism. I might also point out that studies of thinking rarely focus on the misconceptions about people and education which interfere with best practices (Brookhart & Freeman, 1992).

8. The Stainbacks' tenets of inclusion are that all children attend neighborhood schools with a "natural proportion" of students with disabilities, services are based on needs rather than labels, support takes place in general education classrooms, curriculum is adapted when necessary, resources are shared by all students, a sense of community is intentionally fostered, diversity is valued, and interdependence, collaboration, and natural support networks are encouraged for both students and school personnel (Stainback & Stainback, 1992, pp. 34–39).

9. Dewey held that democratic communities require socially generous attitudes, units small enough for face-to-face communication, and awareness of interdependence (E. Robertson, 1992). Giddens (1994) envisions a "dialogic democracy" in which social solidarity is constructed through "active trust, reciprocity, mutuality, and shared authority" (p. 127). For Opotow (1990), a "moral community" has collective considerations of fairness, personal sacrifices for others, and reallocations of community resources. "Discourse and action concerning public schools provide an opportunity for citizens to become concerned not only about what is good for themselves and their own children but what is necessary to bring about a more just and effective society" (Tyack & Hansot, 1982, p. 296).

10. "Consciousness" is the elements of mental life which are discursively accessible to the individual's own awareness (E. O. Wright, 1985, p. 245).

11. When *Other* is spelled with an uppercase *O*, it denotes that a process of othering or constructing someone as essentially different from self is occurring.

12. Advantaged position depends on others' inferior status. Middle-class students benefit from having low-income students serve as negative referents with whom to compare their own achievements (E. Brantlinger, 1993). Middle-class helping professionals have jobs because Others are designated as "in need of services." Being employed, they continue to be middle class. The working classes and poor do not gain employment through the expansion of social services; they remain unemployed or marginally employed.

13. There is an abundance of evidence about social class and racial impact on the nature and quality of students' schooling (E. Brantlinger, 1993, 1994; Coleman, 1969; Grant & Sleeter, 1986; Kozol, 1991; Sizer, 1984; Wells & Serna, 1996). Middle-class, college-educated parents have a propensity to be integrated into school affairs and information networks, to be knowledgeable about school placements, and to exert an influence over their children's education by intervening in educational decisions made by school personnel (E. Brantlinger, 1987; E. Brantlinger, Majd-Jabbari, & Guskin, 1996; David, 1980, 1993; Gewirtz, Ball, & Bowe, 1995; Lareau, 1989; Useem, 1992). Observing a double standard among middle-class professionals, Bingham, Haubrich, White, and Zipp (1990) found that teachers who rated the inner-city schools where they taught as "good schools" would not send their own children to them. The inversion of middle-class power is the dearth of power of subordinate groups. Fine (1992) notes that by virtue of social class, ethnicity, race, gender, or disability, people with low ascribed status cannot control the forces that limit opportunities. Because economic inequality has increased, the stratification of society and schools has in-tensified (Nelson, 1995). Meier (1994) recommends that the purpose and nature of schools be examined so that their means and ends align better, and that "schools must be places where important questions are asked and important answers are heard" (p. 85). Similarly, noting that consequences like pollution mainly affect the poor, while decision makers can live in healthier, better protected areas, Mlicki (1996, p. 86) advocates the studying of real problems in school.

14. They foretell: "Special education is in danger of riding the bandwagon called 'full inclusion' to its own funeral"; "largest bandwagon ever, one having gathered such great mass and momentum that it seems to many unstoppable"; "astute observers immediately warned that this bandwagon, although just forming, had all the potential for mischief of a loose cannon"; "within 10 years, its size, velocity, and direction have become potentially fatal not only to those on board but to the entire special education community through which it is traveling"; "an illusion that may trick many into jumping on the bandwagon but is sure to produce disappointment, if not outrage, in its riders when the juggernaut crushes the students it was to defend" (pp. x–xi).

References

Asterisks indicate articles and chapters included in the critical review.

Algozzine, B., & Ysseldyke, J. E. (1983). Learning disabilities as a subset of school failure: The oversophistication of a concept. *Exceptional Children, 50,* 242–246.

Algozzine, B., Ysseldyke, J. E., & McGue, M. (1995). Differentiating low-achieving students: Thoughts on setting the record straight. *Learning Disabilities Research and Practice, 10*(3), 140–144.

Althusser, L. (1971). Ideology and the ideological state apparatus. In B. Brewster (Trans.), *Lenin and philosophy, and other essays* (pp. 229–236). New York: Monthly Review Press.

Althusser, L. (1976). *Essays in self-criticism* (G. Lock, Trans.). London: New Left Books. (Original work published 1974)

Anderson, G. L., & Irvine, P. (1993). Informing critical literacy with ethnography. In C. Lankshear & P. L. McLaren (Eds.), *Critical literacy: Politics, praxis, and the postmodern* (pp. 81–104). Albany: State University of New York Press.

Apter, D. E. (1964). Introduction. In D. E. Apter (Ed.), *Ideology and discontent* (pp. 15–46). New York: Free Press of Glencoe.

Artiles, A. J., & Trent, S. (1994). Overrepresentation of minority students in special education: A continuing debate. *Journal of Special Education, 27,* 410–437.

Bakhtin, M. (1981). *The dialogic imagination* (C. Emerson & M. Holquist, Trans.). Austin: University of Texas Press. (Original work published 1975)

Bakhtin, M. (1984). *Rabelais and his world* (H. Iswolsky, Trans.). Bloomington: Indiana University Press.

Banks, J. A. (1995). The historical reconstruction of knowledge about race: Implications for transformative teaching. *Educational Researcher, 24*(2), 15–25.

Barrett, M. (1994). Ideology, politics, hegemony: From Gramsci to Laclau and Mouffe. In S. Zizek (Ed.), *Mapping ideology* (pp. 235–264). New York: Verso.

Bensimon, E. M. (1995). Total quality management in the academy: A rebellious reading. *Harvard Educational Review, 65,* 593–611.

Bingham, R. D., Haubrich, P. A., White, S. B., & Zipp, J. F. (1990). Dual standards among teachers: This school is good enough for other kids but not my child. *Urban Education, 25,* 274–288.

Blatt, B. (1979). Bandwagons also go to funerals. *Journal of Learning Disabilities, 12*(4), 17–19.

Blatt, B., & Kaplan, F. (1974). *Chrismas in purgatory: A photographic essay on mental retardation.* Syracuse, NY: Human Policy Press.

Boudon, R. (1989). *The analysis of ideology* (M. Slater, Trans.). Chicago: University of Chicago Press, (Original work published 1986)

Boudon, R. (1994). *The art of self-persuasion: The social explanation of false beliefs* (M. Slater, Trans.), Cambridge, England: Polity Press. (Original work published in 1990)

Bourdieu, P. (1984). *Distinction: A social critique of the judgment of taste.* Cambridge, MA: Harvard University Press.

Bourdieu, P., & Eagleton, T. (1994). Doxa and common life: An interview. In S. Zizek (Ed.), *Mapping ideology* (pp. 265–277). New York: Verso.

Brantlinger, E. (1987). Making decisions about special education placement: Do low-income parents have the information they need? *Journal of Learning Disabilities, 20*, 95–101.

Brantlinger, E. (1991). Social class distinctions in adolescents' reports of problems and punishment in school. *Journal of Behavioral Disorders, 17*, 36–46.

Brantlinger, E. (1993). *The politics of social class in secondary school: Views of affluent and impoverished youth.* New York: Teachers College Press.

Brantlinger, E. (1994). High-income and low-income adolescents' views of special education. *Journal of Adolescent Research, 9*(3), 384–407.

Brantlinger, E. (1996). The influence of preservice teachers' beliefs about pupil achievement on attitudes toward inclusion. *Teacher Education and Special Education, 19*(1), 17–33.

Brantlinger, E., Majd-Jabbari, M., & Guskin, S. L. (1996). Self-interest and liberal educational discourse: How ideology works for middle-class mothers. *American Educational Research Journal, 33*(3), 571–598.

Brantlinger, P. M. (1996). *Fictions of state: Culture and credit in Britain, 1694–1994.* Ithaca, NY: Cornell University Press.

Britzman, D. P. (1991). *Practice makes practice: A critical study of learning to teach.* New York: State University of New York Press.

Brookhart, S. M., & Freeman, D. J. (1992). Characteristics of entering teacher candidates. *Review of Educational Research, 62*, 37–60.

Bullough, R. V., Jr., & Baughman, K. (1995). Inclusion: A view from inside the classroom. *Journal of Teacher Education, 46*(2), 85–92.

Burbules, N. C. (1992). Forms of ideology-critique: A pedagogical perspective. *International Journal of Qualitative Studies, 5*, 7–17.

Christensen, C. (1996). Disabled, handicapped or disordered: 'What's in a name?' In C. Christensen & F. Rizvi (Eds.), *Disability and the dilemmas of education and justice* (pp. 63–78). Philadelphia: Open University Press.

Christensen, C., & Rizvi, F. (Eds.). (1996). *Disability and the dilemmas of education and justice.* Philadelphia: Open University Press.

Cicourel, A. V. (1993). Aspects of structural and processual theories of knowledge. In C. Calhoun, E. LiPuma, & M. Postone (Eds.), *Bourdieu: Critical perspectives* (pp. 89–115). Cambridge, England: Polity Press.

Coleman, J. S. (1969). *Equal educational opportunity.* Cambridge, MA: Harvard University Press.

Connell, R. W. (1993). *Schools and social justice.* Philadelphia: Temple University Press.

Cookson, P. W., Jr. (1992). The ideology of consumership and the coming deregulation of the public school system. In P. W. Cookson, Jr. (Ed.), *The choice controversy* (pp. 83–102). Newbury Park, CA: Corwin Press.

Cuban, L. (1988). Constancy and change in schools (1880s to the present). In P. W. Jackson (Ed.), *Contributing to educational change: Perspectives on research and practice* (pp. 85–105). Berkeley, CA: McCutchan.

David, M. E. (1980). *The state, the family and education.* London: Routledge & Kegan Paul.

David, M. E. (1993). Parents, gender, and education. *Educational Policy, 7*(2), 184–205.

Delamont, S. (1989). *Knowledgeable women: Structuralism and the reproduction of elites.* London: Routledge.

Delamont, S., & Atkinson, P. (1995). *Fighting familiarity: Essays on education and ethnography.* Cresskill, NJ: Hampton.

Deno, E. (1970). Cascade system of social education services. *Exceptional Children, 37*, 229–237.

Dugdale, R. (1877). *The Jukes: A study of crime, pauperism, disease, and heredity.* New York: Putnam.

Dunkin, M. J. (1996). Types of errors in synthesizing research in education. *Review of Educational Research, 66*, 87–97.

Dunn, L. M. (1968). Special education for the mildly retarded: Is much of it justifiable? *Exceptional Children, 35*, 5–22.

Edgerton, R. B. (1967). *The cloak of competence: Stigma in the lives of the mentally retarded.* Berkeley: University of California Press.

Elbaum, B. E., Schumm, J. S., & Vaughn, S. (1997). Urban middle-elementary students' perceptions of grouping formats for reading instruction. *The Elementary School Journal, 97*(5), 475–500.

Fay, B. (1987). *Critical social science.* Ithaca, NY: Cornell University Press.

Fine, M. (1992). *Disruptive voices: The possibilities of feminist research.* Ann Arbor: University of Michigan Press.

Forness, S. R. (1988). Planning for the needs of children with serious emotional disturbance: The National Special Education and Mental Health Coalition. *Behavioral Disorders, 13*(2), 127–139.

Forness, S. R., Kavale, K. A., & Denti, L. G. (1995). The struggle to include the handicapped. *Contemporary Education, 66*(4), 226–232.

Foucault, M. (1980). Truth and power. In C. Gordon (Ed.), *Power/knowledge: Selected interviews and other writings, 1972–1977* (pp. 109–133). New York: Pantheon.

Franklin, B. M. (1994). *From "backwardness" to "at-risk": Childhood learning difficulties and the contradictions of school reform.* Albany: State University of New York Press.

Fuchs, D., & Fuchs, L. S. (1992). Limitations of a feel-good approach to consultation. *Journal of Educational and Psychological Consultation, 3*(2), 93–97.

Fuchs, D., & Fuchs, L. S. (1994). Inclusive schools movement and the radicalization of special education reform. *Exceptional Children, 60*(4), 294–309.

Fuchs, D., & Fuchs, L. S. (1997). Editorial: Lessons from welfare "reform." *Journal of Special Education, 30*(3), 229–231.

Fuchs, D., Roberts, P. H., Fuchs, L. S., & Bowers, J. (1996). Reintegrating students with learning disabilities into the mainstream: A two-year study. *Learning Disabilities Research and Practice, 11*(4), 214–229.

Fullan, M., & Hargreaves, A. (Eds.). (1992). *Teacher development and educational change.* Washington, DC: Falmer.

Gartner, A., & Lipsky, D. K. (1987). Beyond special education: Toward a quality system for all students. *Harvard Educational Review, 57*, 367–395.

Geertz, C. (1973). Ideology as a cultural system. In C. Geertz (Ed.), *The interpretation of cultures* (pp. 197–207). New York: Basic Books.

Gewirtz, S., Ball, S. J., & Bowe, R. (1995). *Markets, choice and equity in education.* Buckingham, England: Open University Press.

Giddens, A. (1994). *Beyond left and right: The future of radical politics.* Stanford, CA: Stanford University Press.

Goddard, H. H. (1914). *Feeblemindedness, its causes and consequences.* New York: Macmillan.

Goffman, E. (1961). *Asylums: Essays on the social situation of mental patients and other inmates.* Garden City, NY: Doubleday.

Goffman, E. (1963). *Stigma.* Englewood Cliffs, NJ: Prentice-Hall.

Goldfarb, J. C. (1991). *The cynical society: The culture of politics and the politics of culture in American life.* Chicago: University of Chicago Press.

Goodman, J. (1995). Change without difference: School restructuring in historical perspective. *Harvard Educational Review, 65*(1), 1–29.

Gottdiener, M. (1993). Ideology, foundationalism, and sociological theory. *The Sociological Quarterly, 34*(4), 653–671.

Gouldner, A. (1979). *The future of intellectuals and the rise of the new class.* New York: Oxford University Press.

Gramsci, A. (1971). *Selections from the prison notebooks* (Q. Hoare & G. N. Smith, Trans.). New York: International Publishers. (Original work published 1929–1935)

Grant, C. A., & Sleeter, C. E. (1986). *After the school bell rings.* Philadelphia: Falmer.

*Gresham, F. M., & Forness, S. R. (1996). Full inclusion: An empirical perspective. *Behavioral Disorders, 21*(2), 145–159.

Habermas, J. (1978). *Knowledge and human interests* (2nd ed., J. Shapiro, Trans.). London: Heinemann. (Original work published 1971)

Hahn, H. (1989). The politics of special education. In D. Lipsky & A. Gartner (Eds.), *Beyond special education* (pp. 225–242). Baltimore: Paul H. Brooks.

Hall, S. (1988). The toad in the garden: Thatcherism among the theorists. In C. Nelson & L. Grossberg (Eds.), *Marxism and the interpretation of culture* (pp. 35–73). Urbana: University of Illinois Press.

*Hallahan, D. P., & Kauffman, J. M. (1995a). From mainstreaming to collaborative consultation. In J. M. Kauffman & D. P. Hallahan (Eds.), *The illusion of full inclusion: A comprehensive critique of a current special education bandwagon* (pp. 5–17). Austin, TX: Pro-Ed.

*Hallahan, D. P., & Kauffman, J. M. (1995b). Toward a culture of disability. In J. M. Kauffman & D. P. Hallahan (Eds.), *The illusion of full inclusion: A comprehensive critique of a current special education bandwagon* (pp. 59–74). Austin, TX: Pro-Ed.

Hargreaves, A. (1996). Revisiting voice. *Educational Researcher, 25*(1), 12–19.

Harry, B. (1992). *Cultural diversity, families, and the special education system.* New York: Teachers College Press.

Harry, B. (1994). *The disproportionate representation of minority students in special education: Theories and recommendations.* Alexandria, VA: National Association of State Directors of Special Education.

Howe, K. R. (1994). Standards, assessment, and equality of educational opportunity. *Educational Researcher, 23*(8), 27–33.

Howe, K. R. (1996). Educational ethics, social justice and children with disabilities. In C. Christensen & F. Rizvi (Eds.), *Disability and the dilemmas of education and justice* (pp. 46–63). Philadelphia: Open University Press.

Jensen, A. R. (1969). How much can we boost IQ and scholastic achievement? *Harvard Educational Review, 39*, 1–123.

Kantor, H., & Lowe, R. (1995). Class, race, and the emergence of federal education policy: From the New Deal to the Great Society. *Educational Researcher, 24*(3), 4–11, 21.

*Kauffman, J. M. (1995a). The regular education initiative as a Reagan-Bush education policy: A trickle-down theory of education of the hard-to-teach. In J. M. Kauffman & D. P. Hallahan (Eds.), *The illusion of full inclusion: A comprehensive critique of a current special education bandwagon* (pp. 125–155). Austin, TX: Pro-Ed.

*Kauffman, J. M. (1995b). Why we must celebrate a diversity of restrictive environments. *Learning Disabilities Research and Practice, 10*(4), 225–232.

*Kauffman, J. M. (1996). Research to practice issues. *Behavioral Disorders, 22*(1), 55–60.

*Kauffman, J. M., & Hallahan, D. P. (Eds.). (1995). *The illusion of full inclusion: A comprehensive critique of a current special education bandwagon.* Austin, TX: Pro-Ed.

*Kavale, K. A. (1995). Setting the record straight on learning disability and low achievement: The tortuous path of ideology. *Learning Disabilities Research and Practice, 11*(3), 145–152.

*Kavale, K. A., & Forness, S. R. (in press). The politics of learning disabilities. *Learning Disabilities Quarterly.*

*Kavale, K. A., Fuchs, D., & Scruggs, T. E. (1994). Setting the record straight on learning disability and low achievement: Implications for policy making. *Learning Disabilities Research and Practice, 9*(2), 70–77.

Kozol, J. (1991). *Savage inequalities: Children in America's schools.* New York: HarperPerennial.

Lacan, J. (1982). Desire and the interpretation of desire in Hamlet. In S. Felman (Ed.), *Literature and psychoanalysis* (pp. 11–52). Baltimore: Johns Hopkins University Press.

Ladwig, J. G., & Gore, J. M. (1994). Extending power and specifying method within the discourse of activist research. In S. Gitlin (Ed.), *Power and method: Political activism and educational research* (pp. 227–238). New York: Routledge.

Lamont, M. (1992). *Money, morals, and manners: The culture of the French and American upper-middle class.* Chicago: University of Chicago Press.

Lareau, A. (1989). *Home advantage: Social class and parental intervention in elementary education.* London: Falmer.

Larrain, J. A. (1992). *The concept of ideology.* Hampshire, England: Gregg Revivals (Routledge).

LeCompte, M. D., & Dworkin, A. G. (1991). *Giving up on school: Student dropouts and teacher burnouts.* Newbury Park, CA: Corwin Press.

Lilly, M. S. (1986, March). The relationship between general and special education: A new face on an old issue. *Counterpoint,* p. 10.

Lipsky, D. K., & Gartner, A. (1987). Capable of achievement and worthy of respect: Education for handicapped students as if they were full-fledged human beings. *Exceptional Children, 54,* 69–74.

Lipsky, D. K., & Gartner, A. (1996). Equity requires inclusion: The future for all students with disabilities. In C. Christensen & F. Rizvi (Eds.), *Disability and the dilemmas of education and justice* (pp. 145–155). Philadelphia: Open University Press.

Lukes, S. (1974). *Power: A radical view.* London: Macmillan.

*MacMillan, D. L., Gresham, F. M., & Forness, S. R. (1996). Full inclusion: An empirical perspective. *Behavior Disorders, 21*(2), 145–159.

*MacMillan, D. L., Semmel, M. I., & Gerber, M. M. (1994). The social context of Dunn: Then and now. *The Journal of Special Education, 27,* 466–480. (Reprinted in *The illusion of full inclusion: A comprehensive critique of a current special education bandwagon,* pp. 19–38, by J. M. Kauffman & D. P. Hallahan, Eds., 1995, Austin, TX: Pro-Ed)

MacMillan, D. L., Siperstein, G. N., & Gresham, F. M. (1996). A challenge to the viability of mild mental retardation as a diagnostic category. *Exceptional Children, 62*(4), 356–371.

Malouf, D. B., & Schiller, E. P. (1995). Practice and research in special education. *Exceptional Children, 61*(5), 414–424.

Martin, J. R. (Ed.). (1994). *Changing the educational landscape: Philosophy, women, and curriculum.* New York: Routledge.

Mason, D. A., & Good, T. L. (1994). Effects of two-group and whole-class teaching on regrouped elementary students' mathematics achievement. *American Educational Research Journal, 30,* 328–360.

McCarthy, C. (1993). Beyond the poverty of theory in race relations: Nonsynchrony and social difference in education. In L. Weis & M. Fine (Eds.), *Beyond silenced voices: Class, race and gender in United States schools* (pp. 325–346). Albany: State University of New York Press.

McDiarmid, G. W. (1990). Challenging prospective teachers beliefs during early field experience: A quixotic undertaking? *Journal of Teacher Education, 41*(3), 12–20.

McGill-Franzen, S., & Allington, R. L. (1993). Flunk 'em or get them classified: The contamination of primary grade accountability data. *Educational Researcher, 22*(1), 19–22.

McIntyre, T., & Forness, S. R. (1997). Is there a new definition yet or are our kids still seriously emotionally disturbed? *Beyond Behavior, 7*(3), 4–9.

Meekosha, H., & Jakubowicz, A. (1996). Disability, participation, representation and social justice. In C. Christensen & F. Rizvi (Eds.), *Disability and the dilemmas of education and justice* (pp. 79–95). Philadelphia: Open University Press.

Meier, D. (1993). Transforming schools into powerful communities. In R. Takanishi (Ed.), *Adolescence in the 1990s: Risk and opportunity* (pp. 199–202). New York: Teachers College Press.

Meier, D. (1994, Winter). A talk to teachers, *Dissent,* pp. 80–87.

Mercer, J. R. (1973). *Labeling the mentally retarded.* Berkeley: University of California Press.

Mirel, J. (1994). School reform unplugged: The Bensenville New American School Project, 1991–1993. *American Educational Research Journal, 31,* 481–518.

Mlicki, M. K. (1996). Five questions to the research on social dilemmas. In W. W. Gasparski, M. K. Mlicki, & B. H. Banathy (Eds.), *Social agency: Dilemmas and education praxiology: The international annual of practical philosophy and methodology, Vol. 4* (pp. 79–91). New Brunswick, NJ: Transaction.

Morrison, T. (1993). *Playing in the dark: Whiteness and the literary imagination.* New York: Vintage.

Nelson, J. I. (1995). *Post-industrial capitalism: Exploring economic inequality in America.* Thousand Oaks, CA: Sage.

Oakes, J., & Guiton, G. (1995). Matchmaking: The dynamics of high school tracking decisions. *American Educational Research Journal, 32*(1), 3–33.

Opotow, S. (1990). Moral exclusion and injustice: An introduction. *Journal of Education, 165,* 75–98.

*Padeliadu, S., & Zigmond, N. (1996). Perspectives of students with learning disabilities about special education placement. *Learning Disabilities Research and Practice, 11*(1), 15–23.

Popkewitz, T. S. (1991). *A political sociology of educational reform: Power/knowledge in teaching, teacher education and research.* New York: Teachers College Press.

Pugach, M. (1988). Special education categories as constraints on the reform of teacher education. *Journal of Teacher Education, 39*(3), 52–59.

Rawls, J. (1972). *A theory of justice.* Cambridge, MA: Harvard University Press.

Reynolds, M. C., Wang, M. C., & Walberg, H. J. (1986). The necessary restructuring of special and regular education. *Exceptional Children, 53,* 391–398.

Richardson, J. G. (1994). Common, delinquent, and special: On the formalization of common schooling in the American states. *American Educational Research Journal, 31,* 695–723.

Rizvi, F., & Christensen, C. (1996). Introduction. In C. Christensen & F. Rizvi (Eds.), *Disability and the dilemmas of education and justice* (pp. 1–8). Philadelphia: Open University Press.

Rizvi, F., & Lingard, B. (1996). Disability, education, and the discourses of justice. In C. Christensen & F. Rizvi (Eds.), *Disability and the dilemmas of education and justice* (pp. 9–26). Philadelphia: Open University Press.

Robertson, E. (1992). Is Dewey's educational vision still viable? *Review of Research in Education, 18,* 335–381.

Robertson, P., Kushner, M. L., Starks, J., & Drescher, C. (1994). An update of participation rates of culturally and linguistically diverse students in special education: The need for a research and policy agenda. *The Bilingual Special Education Perspective, 14*(1), 1–9.

Roth, J. (1992). Of what help is he? A review of Foucault and education. *American Educational Research Journal, 29,* 683–694.

Sapon-Shevin, M. (1993). Gifted education and the protection of privilege: Breaking the silence, opening the discourse. In L. Weis & M. Fine (Eds.), *Beyond silenced voices: Class, race and gender in United States schools* (pp. 25–44). Albany: State University of New York Press.

Sarason, S. B. (1990). *The predictable failure of school reform.* San Francisco: Jossey-Bass.

*Schumm, J. S., & Vaughn, S. (1995). Getting ready for inclusion: Is the stage set? *Learning Disabilities Research and Practice, 10*(3), 169–179.

*Semmel, M. I., Gerber, M. M., & MacMillan, D. L. (1995). A legacy of policy analysis research in special education. In J. M. Kauffman & D. P. Hallahan (Eds.), *The illusion of full inclusion: A comprehensive critique of a current special education bandwagon* (pp. 39–57). Austin, TX: Pro-Ed.

Shapiro, H. S. (1993). Introduction. In H. S. Shapiro & D. E. Purpel (Eds.), *Critical social issues in American education* (pp. xiii–xxi). New York: Longman.

Sizer, T. (1984). *Horace's compromise: The dilemmas of the American high school,* Boston: Houghton-Mifflin.

Skrtic, T. M. (1991). *Behind special education: A critical analysis of professional culture and school organization,* Denver: Love.

Sleeter, C. E. (1986). Learning disabilities: The social construction of a special education category. *Exceptional Children, 53,* 46–54.

Sleeter, C. E. (1995). An analysis of the critiques of multicultural education. In J. A. Banks & C. A. McGee Banks (Eds.), *Handbook of research on multicultural education* (pp. 81–94). New York: Macmillan.

Smith, J. K. (1997). The stories educational researchers tell about themselves. *Educational Researcher, 26*(5), 4–11.

Smylie, M. A. (1994). Redesigning teachers' work: Connections to the classroom. *Review of Research in Education, 20,* 129–177.

Stainback, S., & Stainback, W. (1988). Educating students with severe disabilities in regular classes. *Teaching Exceptional Children, 21,* 16–19.

Stainback, S., & Stainback, W. (1992). Schools as inclusive communities. In W. Stainback & S. Stainback (Eds.), *Controversial issues confronting special education: Divergent perspectives* (pp. 29–44). Boston: Allyn & Bacon.

Stainback, S., & Stainback, W. (Eds.). (1996). *Inclusion: A guide for educators.* Baltimore: Paul H. Brookes.

Stallybrass, P., & White, A. (1986). *The politics and poetics of transgression.* Ithaca, NY: Cornell University Press.

Stanley, W. (1992). *Curriculum for utopia: Social reconstructionism and critical pedagogy in the postmodern era.* Albany: State University at New York Press.

Taylor, S. J. (1988). Caught in the continuum: A critical analysis of the principle of the least restrictive environment. *Journal of the Association for Persons With Severe Handicaps, 13*(1), 41–53.

Taylor, S. J. (1995). On rhetoric: A response to Fuchs and Fuchs (1995). *Exceptional Children, 61*(3), 301–302.

Thompson, J. B. (1984). *Studies in the theory of ideology.* Berkeley: University of California Press.

Thompson, J. B. (1990). *Ideology and modern culture: Critical social theory in the era of mass communication.* Stanford, CA: Stanford University Press.

Tomlinson, S. (1996). Conflicts and dilemmas for professionals in special education. In C. Christensen & F. Rizvi (Eds.), *Disability and the dilemmas of education and justice* (pp. 175–186). Philadelphia: Open University Press.

Troyna, B., & Vincent, C. (1996). 'The ideology of expertism': The framing of special education and racial equality policies in the local state. In C. Christensen & F. Rizvi (Eds.), *Disability and the dilemmas of education and justice* (pp. 131–144). Philadelphia: Open University Press.

Tyack, D., & Hansot, E. (1982). *Managers of virtue: Public school leadership in America, 1820–1980.* New York: Basic Books.

Tyack, D., & Tobin, W. (1994). The "grammar" of schooling: Why has it been so hard to change? *American Educational Research Journal, 31,* 453–479.

Useem, E. L. (1992). Middle schools and math groups: Parents' involvement in children's placement. *Sociology of Education, 65,* 263–279.

Utley, C. A., Haywood, H. C., & Masters, J. C. (1991). Policy implications of psychological assessment. In H. C. Haywood & D. Tzuriel (Eds.), *Interactive assessment* (pp. 445–469). New York: Springer-Verlag.

*Vaughn, S., Schumm, J. S., Jallad, B., Slusher, J., & Saumell, L. (1996). Teachers' views of inclusion. *Learning Disabilities Research and Practice, 11*(2), 96–106.

Wang, M. C., & Walberg, H. J. (1988). Four fallacies of segregationism. *Exceptional Children, 55,* 128–137.

Watt, J. (1994). *Ideology, objectivity, and education.* New York: Teachers College Press.

Weiss, C. H. (1995). The four "I's" of school reform: How interests, ideology, information, and institution affect teachers and principals. *Harvard Educational Review, 65*(4), 571–592.

Wells, A. S., & Serna, I. (1996). The politics of culture: Understanding local political resistance to detracking in racially mixed schools. *Harvard Educational Review*, 66(1), 93–118.

Will, M. C. (1986). Educating children with learning problems: A shared responsibility. *Exceptional Children, 52*, 411–415.

Wilson, J. K. (1995). *The myth of political correctness: The conservative attack on higher education.* Durham, NC: Duke University Press.

Wright, E. O. (Ed.). (1985). *Classes.* New York: Verso.

Wright, E. O. (1989). A general framework for the analysis of class structure. In E. O. Wright (Ed.), *The debate on classes* (pp. 3–48). New York: Verso.

Wright, S. E. (1993). Blaming the victim, blaming society or blaming the discipline: Fixing responsibility for poverty and homelessness. *The Sociological Quarterly, 34*(1), 1–16.

Wrigley, J. (1982). *Class politics and public schools: Chicago 1900–1950.* New Brunswick, NJ: Rutgers University Press.

Wrong, E. H. (1979). *Power: Its forms, bases and uses.* New York: Harper and Row.

Ysseldyke, J. E., Algozzine, B., Shinn, M. R., & McGue, M. (1982). Similarities and differences between low achievers and students classified learning disabled. *The Journal of Special Education, 16*, 73–85.

Zane, N. (1994). When "discipline problems" recede: Democracy and intimacy in urban charters. In M. Fine (Ed.), *Chartering urban school reform: Reflections on public high schools in the midst of change* (pp. 122–135). New York: Teachers College Press.

Zizek, S. (1994). Introduction: The spectre of ideology. In S. Zizek (Ed.), *Mapping ideology* (pp. 1–33). New York: Verso.

2.2　The Crisis in Special Education Knowledge:

A Perspective on Perspective

Thomas M. Skrtic

Special education is a conglomeration of a number of sub-fields. Historically, the sub-fields have been organized around so-called categories of "exceptionality" or "disability." As such, each sub-specialty within special education has its own professional knowledge, which reflects the presumed differences among the categories of exceptionality. Nevertheless, behind the surface differences each of the sub-fields subscribes to a basic foundation of general special education knowledge. What is of interest here is this tradition of general special education knowledge, which, for convenience sake, we will refer to simply as *special education knowledge.*

Another challenge in discussing special education knowledge is deciding on whose version to accept as the genuine article. To draw a crude analogy,

asking the special education community about the nature of its professional knowledge is like asking a school of fish about the nature of water. Neither group can be depended upon for an adequate answer because these matters are so basic to them that they are largely taken for granted. Thus, bringing a number of perspectives to bear upon the subject will be helpful. The best way to do this is to consider some of the criticisms of traditional special education knowledge. There is no shortage of such criticism.

Special education knowledge follows a threefold model of professional knowledge (Schein, 1972, p. 43):

1. An *underlying discipline* or *basic science* component upon which the practice rests or from which it is developed.

2. An *applied science* or "engineering" component from which many of the day-to-day diagnostic procedures and problem solutions are derived.

Skrtic, T. M. (1986). The crisis in special education knowledge: A perspective on perspective. *Focus on Exceptional Children, 18*(7), 1–16. Reprinted by permission.

3. A *skills and attitudinal* component that concerns the actual performance of services to the client, using the underlying basic and applied knowledge.

According to the model, special education knowledge is grounded in the *theoretical knowledge* of an underlying discipline or basic science. At the applied science level of the model, theoretical knowledge is translated into *applied knowledge*, or models, techniques, and procedures for application to the day-to-day problems of practice. Finally, special education's theoretically grounded applied knowledge yields *practical knowledge*, which is transmitted to the special education practitioner—in the form of knowledge, skills, attitudes, and norms—through an extended program of training and indoctrination that constitutes professional education in special education. The performance of special education professional services to clients—by the special education teacher, clinician, or therapist—is based on practical knowledge, which is conceptualized as the result of applying theoretical knowledge to solving problems of special education practice.

Historically, two general types of criticism of special education knowledge are found: practical and theoretical. These can be understood in terms of the above model of special education professional knowledge. *Practical criticism* refers to criticism of special education practical knowledge—the knowledge and skills that underwrite the actual performance of services to the client by the professional special education practitioner. As we will use the term, *theoretical criticism* refers to criticism of both special education theoretical and applied knowledge—both the theoretical knowledge of the underlying discipline or basic science and the applied knowledge engineered from theoretical knowledge by special education applied researchers.

PRACTICAL CRITICISM OF SPECIAL EDUCATION KNOWLEDGE

Of the two general types of criticism, practical criticism has been the most visible and has had the greatest impact on the way special education services are delivered to students. Practical criticism, centered on the actual practice of special education, has been mounted by parents, consumers and advocates, and, to some extent, special educators themselves (e.g., Dunn, 1968; Blatt & Kaplan, 1966). Historically, critical debate has revolved around the relationship between regular and special education in terms of the identification, placement, and education of students with disabilities. In fact, much of today's special education practice has evolved as a response to yesterday's practical criticism. Although this mutually-shaping relationship between practical criticism and changes in practice can be traced over the entire history of special education, in the modern era its most intense and fruitful phase was the 10-year period from 1965 to 1975.

At the height of the social-political ferment of the 1960s, parents and consumers and advocates used the period's increased sensitivity to human and civil rights to mount a case against special education as it was practiced at that time. This particular round of practical criticism led to victories in courtrooms and statehouses across the country and eventually in the U.S. Congress, which ultimately redefined special education practice under the rubric of the statutory mandate of Public Law 94-142, The Education for All Handicapped Children Act of 1975.

PL 94-142 essentially mandates a free, appropriate public education for all students with disabilities in the least restrictive—most integrated—environment possible. It changed special education practice by changing its structural relationship to regular education and by extending to students and their parents certain constitutional rights and procedural safeguards, including due process of law. Of course, PL 94-142 did not end critical commentary on special education practice. Public debate and legal action over the precise meaning of "appropriate education" and "least restrictive environment," among other concepts, have continued over the 10 years of the law's implementation (Turnbull, 1986).

But the point to be made here is that practical criticism led to changes in special education practice. An important point to grasp is that the changes brought about by PL 94-142 did not result from theoretical criticism. The law itself (and the changes in practice that have resulted from it) was the product of moral, ethical, legal, and political arguments against special education practice at that time (Ballard-Campbell & Semmel, 1981; Biklen, 1985).

THEORETICAL CRITICISM OF SPECIAL EDUCATION KNOWLEDGE

Ultimately, theoretical criticism of special education knowledge is also criticism of special education practice. But, as it is used here, it is essentially criticism of the manner in which basic science theory is applied at the applied science level of special education knowledge. Thus, the targets of theoretical criticism are special education applied researchers, developers, and policy analysts within universities and at all levels of government. Whereas practical criticism of special education has been mounted primarily by consumers and advocates, theoretical criticism tends to come from the academic disciplines—primarily from the social sciences—and is based on three claims: *atheoretical, confounded theory*, and *wrong theory*.

The Atheoretical Claim

The first type of theoretical criticism is based on the claim that special education applied research and practice operate in the absence of any guiding theory (e.g., Bogdan & Kugelmass, 1984; Rist & Harrell, 1982; Tomlinson, 1982). It is argued that, instead of being grounded in the theories of an underlying discipline or basic science, special education applied research and practice are guided by a narrow set of unconscious assumptions. Bogdan and Kugelmass (1984) summarized special education's unconscious assumptions as follows:

(1) Disability is a condition that individuals have; (2) disabled typical is a useful and objective distinction; (3) special education is a rationally conceived and coordinated system of services that help children labelled disabled; (4) progress in the field is made by improving diagnosis, intervention and technology. (p. 173)

While not denying the accuracy of the Bogdan and Kugelmass analysis of special education's assumptions—indeed, I believe that these are precisely the basic beliefs that implicitly serve as guides for research and practice in special education—when examined more closely, they reveal that the "atheoretical" part of their claim cannot be justified. The first two assumptions—that disability is a condition that people have, and that disabled/typical is a useful and objective distinction—derive directly from theories of deviance in the basic sciences of psychology and biology. The third assumption—that special education is a rationally conceived and coordinated system of services—actually has two theoretical sources. The first source is the positivist theory of knowledge, which serves as the foundation for the dominant model of professional knowledge (Schon, 1984; Schein, 1972; Glazer, 1974). Special education, like all professional fields, implicitly believes that its knowledge is the end product of a rational system of

knowledge production. The second source of this assumption is a general theory of organizational rationality, which until recently has dominated thinking and writing about all organizations, including schools (see Clark, 1985; Weick, 1985). It has been so central to the organization of industrialized societies that it permeates the consciousness of all industrialized people, even if they don't realize it.

The fourth assumption—about the nature of progress—derives from the notion of cumulative knowledge that underwrites the positivist theory of knowledge, as well as the dominant conceptualization of scientific progress (discussed later). The point is that, although special education research and practice are guided by unconscious beliefs, one can hardly claim that these beliefs have no theoretical basis at all. The real problem for special education is the unconscious—and thus noncritical—nature of these basic beliefs, and not whether they are grounded in theory.

The "Confounded Theory" Claim

The second type of theoretical criticism is based on the claim that special education applied research and practice confound theories. The best example of this type of criticism is Jane Mercer's (1973) explanation of the way biological and psychological theories of deviance are confounded within the clinical perspective of mental retardation. Derived from medicine and psychology, the clinical perspective is the familiar frame of reference that guides research and practice in the helping professions, including special education. This perspective contains two contrasting theories of "normal/abnormal": the pathological model from medicine (biology), and the statistical model from psychology.

The *pathological model* defines impairments according to the presence or absence of observable biological symptoms. Biological processes that interfere with system preservation are "bad," or pathological; those that enhance the life of the organism are "good," or healthy. Thus, the pathological model is bipolar: At one pole is normal (i.e., the absence of pathological symptoms and health), at the other pole is abnormal (i.e., the presence of pathological symptoms and illness or "unhealth"). The pathological model is essentially evaluative: To be abnormal is to be unhealthy; this is "bad" and should be prevented or alleviated.

The *statistical model* is based on the concept of the normal (or bell-shaped) curve: In essence, an individual's attributes can be described by his or her relative position in a frequency distribution of other persons measured on those attributes. Whereas the pathological model defines abnormality as the presence of observable pathological symptoms, the statistical model defines abnormality according to the extent to which an individual varies from the average of a population on a particular attribute. Unlike the bipolar pathological model, which defines only one type of abnormality, the statistical model defines two types of abnormality: abnormally large and abnormally small amounts of the measured characteristic. Whereas the pathological model is evaluative (pathological signs are always "bad"), the statistical model is evaluatively neutral; whether high is "good" and low is "bad" or high is "bad" and low is "good" depends on the attribute being measured. And whether it is "good" or "bad" to be high or low on any particular attribute is defined by society. As far as the attribute of intelligence, in our society abnormally high is "good," and abnormally low is "bad."

Both models are used to define mental retardation—the pathological model for assessing *biological* manifestations and the statistical model for assessing *behavorial* manifestations, which are not comprehensible within the pathological model. Although instances of moderate to severe/profound mental retardation are associated with observable patterns of biological symptoms, and are thus comprehensible under the pathological model, most individuals labeled "mildly mentally retarded" do not show any biological signs. In these instances the statistical model is used and a low score on an intelligence (IQ) test is accepted as a symptom of pathology. The problem is that when the models are used in conjunction with one another, the tendency is to transpose them, turning behavioral patterns into pathological signs. Mercer (1973) explained the confusion by saying that:

> The implicit logic that underlies this transformation is as follows: Low IQ = "bad" in American society: a social evaluation. "Bad" = pathology in the pathological model. Therefore, low IQ = pathology. Thus, IQ, which is not a biological manifestation but is a behavioral score based on responses to a series of questions, becomes conceptually transposed into a pathological sign carrying all of the implications of the pathological model. (pp. 5–6)

Although Mercer identified a number of negative implications of the conceptual transposition, the primary implication—and the point of interest here—is the fact that mental retardation ends up being regarded as an *attribute* of the individual. The clinical perspective regards mental retardation as a pathological condition, and the pathology is considered to be an objective condition that individuals have. Although Mercer limits her criticism to the area of mental retardation, the same type of criticism has been made for special education research and practice in the area of learning disabilities (Rist & Harrell, 1982; Schrag & Divorky, 1975), and particularly in the area of emotional disturbance (Algozzine, 1976, 1977; Apter, 1982; Hobbs, 1975; Rhodes, 1970; Ross, 1980; Swap, 1978). Together with mild mental retardation, these areas make up the majority of all students identified as disabled.

The "Wrong Theory" Claim

The third type of theoretical criticism rests on the claim that special education applied/practical knowledge is based on the wrong theory, or that it relies too narrowly on one or more theories to the exclusion of others. Most instances of this type of criticism have been mounted by sociologists and political scientists who argue that special education depends too heavily or exclusively on theory derived from the discipline of psychology and the associated disciplines behind the field of medicine—ultimately, biology. The argument is that, by their very nature, these disciplines place the root cause of all disability and deviance within the person, and exclude from consideration causal factors that lie in the larger social and political processes external to the individual. In addition, social scientists see diagnosis, intervention, and technology based in the behavioral and biological sciences as superficial because these do nothing to assess, alter, or circumvent the social-political-cultural context of "disability."

Whereas the behavioral and biological sciences study organisms and consider disability to be an objective condition that people have, the social sciences study social and political systems and processes and consider deviance to be a subjective condition that is societally created and maintained (see Gould, 1982; Szasz, 1961; Goffman, 1961, 1963; Scheff, 1966; Scott, 1969; Braginsky & Braginsky, 1971; Lemert, 1967; Davis, 1963; Wiseman, 1970; Bogdan, 1974; Gubrium, 1975; Biklen, 1977; Taylor & Bogdan, 1977). And this is more than an academic argument. Many of the social scientists who raise the issue are ultimately concerned with the impact of social and political processes on people and society. From their perspective, in the extreme, special education in industrialized societies is an arm of education that creates and works against the social-political interests of powerless groups (Sarason & Doris, 1979; Smith, 1985; Barton & Tomlinson, 1984; Tomlinson, 1982; Farber, 1968).

THE IMPACT OF CRITICISM OF SPECIAL EDUCATION KNOWLEDGE

Practical criticism—mounted by parents, consumers and advocates, and, in a more limited way, special educators themselves—was successful in bringing about changes in the way special education is practiced in public education, as those changes have been embodied in PL 94-142. But, as noted, criticism of special education's practical knowledge does not resort to a critique of special education's theoretical or applied knowledge. Thus, it has had no effect on special education's unconscious assumptions. That is, although PL 94-142 brought about substantial changes in the organization and practice of special education, it rests on the same set of basic beliefs about the nature of disability, special education as a helping profession, and progress in the field. The first three assumptions—that disabilities are conditions people have, that disabled/typical is a useful and objective distinction, that special education is a rationally conceived and coordinated system that helps students who are labeled disabled—stand unaltered. Moreover, according to the fourth assumption, PL 94-142 is perceived as improved diagnosis, intervention, and technology—an example of progress.

Unlike practical criticism, which at least has resulted in visible changes in the organization and practice of special education within public education, theoretical criticism has had few, if any, meaningful consequences for research or practice in special education. People from a number of disciplines and fields, including special education, have criticized special education's unconscious assumptions, or have attempted to convince the professional community of special education to expand its disciplinary base to include social and political theories of deviance. But no general movement has been launched to alter special education policy and practice or to reorient its research based on these insights.

Discussing the impact of theoretical criticism of special education applied research on the effectiveness of special education practice, Bogdan and Kugelmass (1984, p. 173) summarized the state of affairs succinctly by saying that, "In short, most research has been *for* special education (serving the field as it conceived of itself), not *of* special education, that is looking at the field from an alternative vantage-point."

Special education applied research leaves unanswered, and treats as unproblematic, fundamental questions about its unconscious assumptions.

Thus, on one hand is practical criticism, which has resulted in visible changes in the way special education is practiced but has had no effect on theory or the taken-for-granted assumptions that derive from it. On the other hand is theoretical criticism, which has had virtually no impact on theory, research, or practice in special education. Special education practice has been altered by PL 94-142, but only within the frame of reference of special education's traditional assumptions about the nature of disability, special education as a helping profession, and progress in the field. Does PL 94-142 represent progress? Undoubtedly it does. But progress in this sense is only a limited sort of progress; it is progress *within* a particular frame of reference or set of basic assumptions.

I am arguing that real progress in special education will require a different frame of reference. At a minimum, it will require that special education take seriously the critics of its theoretical and applied knowledge, and thus of its taken-for-granted assumptions. It will require criticism in the classical sense—self-reflective examination of the limits and validity of special education knowledge. But the problem is that the professional community of special education will not readily accept theoretical criticism, precisely because it contradicts its basic assumptions about the nature of disability, special education as a helping profession, and progress in the field.

Of course, one could argue that, as a professional community, special education demonstrated its ability to accept criticism—and even to engage in self-criticism—during the period leading to passage of PL 94-142. But most of that was practical criticism or criticism that could be deflected onto the regular education system. Special education could accept it because at bottom it did not contradict or conflict in any way with its basic assumptions. Theoretical criticism, however, is more difficult to accept precisely because it contradicts those assumptions. Moreover, the problem is more than an inability to accept theoretical criticism. It is largely an inability to understand it.

Professionals in all fields are prepared for practice—whether practice is service delivery or applied research—through a process that shapes their thought and behavior to conform to the established knowledge of the profession. The process requires total submission to the authority of the profession, an acceptance on faith of the profession's knowledge. Professional induction *is* the efficient inculcation of the inductee with a commitment to a particular way of seeing the world and operating in it.

Special education professionals—teachers, administrators, teacher trainers, applied researchers—ordinarily have difficulty understanding theoretical criticism because it is based on a view of the world and special education that falls outside of special education's established knowledge. Persons inside the professional community and their theoretical critics on the outside literally are inhabitants of different conceptual worlds. They slice up the social world differently; they speak different languages and employ different concepts. Moreover, professional autonomy means that nothing has compelled the special education professional community to listen to its critics. All judgments as to the adequacy of special education knowledge are left to the profession itself. And, of course, special education's inability to see itself as others do is not particularly unusual. This is an inherent characteristic of all professional communities. They all create and maintain their own conventionally-based reality. Each is an insulated sub-culture of conventional knowledge. Each is a way of seeing.

THE CASE FOR MULTIDISCIPLINARY SPECIAL EDUCATION KNOWLEDGE

The fact that special education *can* view itself from alternative vantage-points can be demonstrated through two approaches: longitudinal and cross-sectional. The *longitudinal* approach—looking at the same entity over time—is simple. To understand that special education can be viewed in different ways, one need only compare special education today with what it was at any given point in its past history. In this sense, the history of special education is the history of the redefinition of special education practice. We can see, for example, that special education practice in the 1940s was substantially different than it was in the 1960s, or than it is today. Here again, however, we must not lose sight of the fact that these changes have been largely changes in *practice*. Theoretical and applied knowledge—and thus the unconscious assumptions of the profession—have not changed.

In contrast, the *cross-sectional* approach looks at one entity from different perspectives. Conventional special education knowledge about the nature of disability is the result of the particular disciplinary base of theoretical knowledge that has been used and the manner in which it has been applied. Given the dominant model of professional knowledge and the nature of

professional education, the special education professional community not surprisingly is deeply committed to a biological-psychological explanation of disability. Nevertheless, we know that alternative theoretical conceptualizations of deviance, and thus alternative forms of potential special education knowledge, exist. A substantial body of literature, deriving primarily from sociological, political, and cultural theories of deviance, and which provides many different perspectives on virtually every aspect of the notions of special education and "disability," is available.

Once one accepts the position that special education and "disability" can be viewed in alternative ways and, more important, that each perspective has different implications for children labeled disabled and their parents and families, the argument that special education *should* consider itself and its professional knowledge from alternative vantage-points is self-evident on ethical and moral grounds. For special education to continue to rely on an exclusively biological/psychological explanation of "disability" has no defensible argument.

Today's special education knowledge is not inherently "correct." It is a matter of history—a history that could have taken a different course. If special education knowledge were to have had a broad base in, say, sociology, political science, anthropology, psychology, and biology, instead of a narrow base in psychology and biology, members of the professional community would think and act in very different ways. They would inhabit a different conceptual world, speak a different language, and employ different concepts. If this were so, the very notion of "disability" and the approach taken would be substantially different. Diagnosis, intervention, and technology would not be directed exclusively at the individual but would just as likely be directed at the conceptual and material structures, systems, and processes external to the individual. Things such as organizations, institutions, and belief systems—not just children and youth—would be targets.

Special education should expand its disciplinary base beyond psychology and biology to include the various social, political, and cultural sciences. Like most of the theoretical critics cited above, I believe that special education knowledge should be multidisciplinary. "Multidisciplinary" is not the same as "interdisciplinary." Interdisciplinary refers to collaboration among professionals in the performance of services to clients. The case for interdisciplinary professional practice is a familiar argument by now (see Schein, 1972) and is based on the fact that many of the challenges society faces today are so complex that no single profession can deal with them effectively. This is not to miminize the need for interdisciplinary professional *practice*. Given the complexity of problems in special education practice, interdisciplinary collaboration—among regular and special education practitioners, among various types of special educators, and among special education and related services professionals—is a necessity. The point to make is that special education *knowledge* should be multidisciplinary, as well. Special education requires a substantial reorientation of theoretical, applied, and practical knowledge, and a concomitant revision in the professional education curriculum of special education.

This reorientation would begin with a multidisciplinary theoretical critique of special education knowledge—a self-reflective examination of the limits and validity of special education knowledge from the alternative perspectives of the various social sciences. And, of course, the multidisciplinary theoretical analysis would be facilitated greatly by the fact that a number of alternative disciplinary analyses currently exist. Moreover, to be adequate, this substantially top-down analysis must incorporate the essentially bottom-up practical criticism of current special education practice, opening up the possibility of uniting in one democratized discourse the interests of theorists, applied scientists, practitioners, and consumers and advocates.

Even if the professional community of special education could be persuaded to carry out a multidisciplinary theoretical critique and to adopt a multidisciplinary orientation, however, these measures would not be sufficient to reorient special education knowledge. Today, theoretical criticism and a multidisciplinary orientation are simply not enough.

METATHEORETICAL CRITICISM OF SPECIAL EDUCATION KNOWLEDGE

A multidisciplinary theoretical criticism and a multidisciplinary reorientation of special education knowledge are not sufficient because the very notions of "theory" and "discipline" themselves are under attack today. The basis of the reorientation of special education knowledge must go beyond theoretical criticism: The professional community of special education must attempt a metatheoretical critique of its professional knowledge. To understand the meaning of metatheoretical criticism, several additional concepts are introduced here.

Central among these are the concepts of paradigm and paradigm shift.

Paradigms and Paradigm Shifts

For the past two decades the terms *paradigm* and *paradigm shift* have been associated most often with the influential work of Thomas Kuhn (1962, 1970a). Kuhn used these concepts in an analysis of scientific development in the physical or "hard" sciences, such as physics and chemistry. Kuhn reserved his analysis exclusively for the physical sciences, making no claim for its application to the social sciences. Nevertheless, Kuhn's work has had a profound effect on the social sciences, despite his reluctance to apply it there.

Although the concept of a paradigm was the central element in Kuhn's analysis of scientific progress, he was neither clear nor consistent about what he meant by it. Masterman (1970) counted 21 different uses of the term in Kuhn's original work, which she reduced to three broad types of paradigms. Of the three types of paradigms—metaphysical, sociological, and construct—the metaphysical paradigm represents the broadest use of the term and subsumes the other two. A *metaphysical paradigm is a total world view or gestalt within a given scientific community or sub-community.*

> The metaphysical paradigm is the broadest unit of consensus within a given science. It serves to define the broad parameters of the field, or subareas within a field, giving the scientist a broad orientation from which to operate. (Ritzer, 1980, p. 5)

In this sense, Kuhn used paradigm to mean a way of "seeing," a general organizing principle governing perception, a "map" that describes for scientists which entities exist (and which do not) and how they behave.

Broadly construed, then, a paradigm is a set of explicit or implicit presuppositions or basic beliefs that scientists use to provide coherence to their picture of the world and how it works. These presuppositions or basic assumptions are metatheoretical assumptions. They are *meta*theoretical assumptions because they are *beyond*, or are more fundamental than, theories themselves. Metatheoretical assumptions are more fundamental than theories because observation—which, according to the conventional view of theory, is the rock bottom upon which theory is founded (see Feigl, 1970)—is itself strongly influenced by a prior conceptual system of metatheoretical assumptions (see Mulkay, 1979; Shimony, 1977).

A metaphysical or metatheoretical paradigm (hereafter simply paradigm) can be thought of as a special lens through which the world can be viewed. This lens has the peculiar property that, while it may enhance the clarity with which some things can be viewed, it does not allow one to view other things. A paradigm is a particular lens, a particular way of seeing. A paradigm shift occurs when we abandon one lens (or way of seeing) for a different one. The new lens or paradigm provides a different way of seeing the world and making sense of it.

Kuhn revolutionized our understanding of scientific knowledge by using the concepts of paradigm and paradigm shift to distinguish between continuous and discontinuous scientific progress. Continuous scientific progress—what Kuhn called "normal science"—progresses by gradual additions to a knowledge base. Normal science is a highly cumulative enterprise that refines, extends, and articulates a paradigm that already exists. An accepted paradigm is essential for scientific work because it unrandomizes nature and thus permits scientists to know what data are, what methods and instruments are necessary to retrieve them, and what concepts are relevant to their interpretation (Kuhn, 1970a).

Although normal science or continuous scientific progress is the typical image of scientific work, Kuhn's thesis is that it is only a necessary prelude to discontinuous scientific progress—real scientific discovery that uncovers new and unsuspected phenomena and invents radical new theories. Discontinuous scientific progress—what Kuhn called "revolutionary science"—is characterized by discontinuous breakthroughs that demand an entirely new set of metatheoretical assumptions—or, a new paradigm—for understanding data. Discoveries of this sort begin with the recognition and extended exploration of an anomaly, which is a violation of the paradigm-induced expectations of normal science. When the anomaly comes to be seen as more than just another normal science problem, the transition to paradigm crisis has begun. As the anomaly continues to resist, many of the field's most eminent scientists come to view its resolution as *the* subject matter of their field, which intensifies the crisis to the point where the rules of normal science are blurred. The paradigm exists, but few practitioners now can agree entirely about what it is.

Loosening of the paradigm's rules gives rise to extraordinary research and philosophical analysis. Extraordinary research includes attempts to isolate and magnify the anomaly, random experimentation, and generation of speculative theories. Philosophical analysis is directed toward exposing—often for the

first time—the metatheoretical assumptions that underwrite the current paradigm and the contemporary research tradition. Together, extraordinary research and philosophical analysis loosen the paradigm's stereotypes and begin to provide the incremental data necessary for a fundamental paradigm shift. Sometimes the structure these procedures give the anomaly foreshadows the shape of the new paradigm. More often, however, the new paradigm emerges all at once—"sometimes in the middle of the night, in the mind of a man deeply immersed in crisis" (Kuhn, 1970a, p. 90). In any event, the shift to a new paradigm is revolutionary science. Normal science rests on the mutual acceptance of a given paradigm among a community of scientists; revolutionary science requires a paradigm shift. After the shift, the stage is set for the process to repeat itself.

Kuhn's view of scientific development as discontinuous progress placed him at odds with the prevailing view of scientific progress and the growth of knowledge. In effect, it introduced a major anomaly into the dominant paradigm of positivist knowledge. In place of the conventional assumption of cumulative, convergent, and objective knowledge, Kuhn substituted the idea that science and knowledge are discontinuous, divergent, and subjective.

The Subjectivity of Science and Knowledge

A key element in Kuhn's original work was that the process by which one paradigm replaces another paradigm is essentially a political phenomenon, a process of persuasion and conversion, with the victorious paradigm being the one that wins the most converts (Ritzer, 1980). Thus, irrational and subjective factors may affect and even determine the emergence of a new paradigm. In the face of criticisms that he overemphasized irrationality in scientific work (see Lakatos & Musgrave, 1970), Kuhn subsequently retreated from this position (Kuhn, 1970b). Nevertheless, it was this aspect of his analysis that was most attractive to those who have extended his work.

Using Kuhn's thesis to frame their work, proponents have argued that indeed paradigms in the physical sciences rise and fall as a result of subjective, not objective, factors (e.g., Bloor, 1976; Law, 1975; Phillips, 1973; Knorr, Krohn, & Whitley, 1981). Krohn (1981, p. xi) summarized the first body of empirical work on scientific practice—the ethnographic and detailed historical study of actual scientific activity—by saying that "[physical] scientists are literally constructing their world rather than merely describing it." Kuhn's work was important for what it had to say about the role of culture and tradition in the production of knowledge. His analysis of the conventional nature of knowledge and the nature of convention itself contradicted the common perception that science and knowledge are objective, and advanced the idea that both depend on their cultural context for meaning and interpretation.

Barry Barnes (1982, p. 10) noted the significance of the subculture in science, and the communal activity of the organized practitioners who sustain it, when he said that "the culture is far more than the setting for scientific research; it is the research itself." The image of the scientist as an objective and impersonal observer in the process of knowledge discovery is being replaced by the image of the scientist as craftsperson who, bound by the culture of a particular place and time, creates knowledge that is assumed to be of temporary utility and validity (Ravetz, 1971). This revised image of science and scientific work has necessarily caused a revision in the very legacy of knowledge. Once conceived as "a separate verbal and symbolic high culture [with] the power to reveal, order and enlighten . . . [it] is being brought down to earth, demystified as a human construction, in the natural as well as the social [sciences]" (Krohn, 1981, p. xii).

At this point we can begin to see the parallels between the work of the basic scientists and the work of the applied scientists and professional practitioners. The latter groups operate on the basis of received knowledge—that is, knowledge that each accepts on faith from higher levels in the hierarchy of professional knowledge. Although this is the case for applied researchers and professional practitioners, the assumption had been that the theoretical knowledge of the basic sciences was itself objective knowledge about reality. The key point to grasp is that, like the applied scientist and professional practitioner, basic scientists operate on the basis of received knowledge. Theirs is not objective knowledge but, rather, knowledge received by looking at the world through the lens of a particular paradigm or set of metatheoretical assumptions.

From Kuhn's description of the induction of physical scientists into scientific communities, we can see now that all three groups—basic scientists, applied researchers, and professional practitioners— are inducted into subcultures of conventional knowledge, which they "receive" on faith as the only way of unrandomizing the complexity of their particular worlds of practice. Like the craftsperson, each is bound by the culture of a particular place and time. Like the image of science and the legacy of knowledge, the role of basic scientist has been demystified and brought down to earth.

Social Scientific Thought

Although Kuhn reserved his conception of paradigms and paradigm shifts exclusively for the physical sciences, further extensions of his work have allowed an understanding of the paradigmatic status of the social sciences. Masterman (1970) made an important contribution in this regard in using the concept of a paradigm to distinguish four types of sciences: paradigmatic, nonparadigmatic, dual paradigmatic, and multiple paradigmatic. For Masterman, a *paradigmatic science* is one having broad consensus within the scientific community on a particular paradigm. Examples of a science achieving the paradigmatic state are relatively few, but some do exist. Physics is the primary example. Until the birth of the Einsteinian paradigm in this century, physics was dominated by the Newtonian paradigm. Although some scientists doubted the Newtonian paradigm, physics during the period between Newton and Einstein is perhaps as close as a science can come to the paradigmatic state.

Nonparadigmatic science is the situation in which no consensus exists on a paradigm. Before Newton, physics presumably lacked consensus and therefore was, at that point in its development, a nonparadigmatic science. The *dual paradigmatic* state exists immediately before a Kuhnian scientific revolution, when two paradigms—the older, crisis-ridden paradigm and the new, emerging paradigm—are vying for the dominance that only one of them ultimately will achieve. The Newtonian paradigm dominated physics until increasing anomalies set it up for defeat by the Einsteinian paradigm (see Clark, 1971), but at the point when both paradigms were competing for dominance, physics was a dual paradigm science.

The final type of science discussed by Masterman is the *multiple paradigmatic* science, in which several viable paradigms compete unsuccessfully for dominance within the scientific community. The multiple paradigm state is particularly important for our purposes because it permits differentiation between the physical and social sciences on the basis of their paradigmatic status. The various physical sciences (more or less) are paradigmatic sciences. The birth of a particular physical science can be thought of as the point at which it emerged from a nonparadigmatic state and achieved its paradigmatic status. From there, its history is a series of discontinuous progressions in which normal science—now possible because of paradigmatic consensus—produces the anomalies necessary to create a crisis big enough to yield a scientific revolution, and thus a new paradigm.

On the other hand, the social sciences are multiple paradigm sciences. Unlike the physical sciences, in which one paradigm dominates until crisis and revolution replace it in toto with another paradigm, multiple paradigms co-exist in the social sciences. This means that scientific revolutions in the Kuhnian sense are virtually impossible in the social sciences because there is no dominant paradigm to be overthrown. Although the social sciences always have had revolutionary ways to think, all of the paradigms for thinking about the social world emerged—relative to the way physical science paradigms emerge—more or less together. Each one is a viable way to understand the social world, and each has had its own followers.

Allegiances have shifted throughout history, and one or another paradigm has dominated particular regions of the globe. But no general consensus—and thus no single dominant paradigm of social scientific thought—has been reached. Not only has this precluded revolutionary science, but it also has made normal science more difficult because, as Ritzer (1980) noted, social scientists are forced to spend an inordinate amount of energy engaging in the politics of winning converts and defending their flanks against attack from rival paradigms.

Burrell and Morgan (1979) conceptualized the multiple paradigms in the social sciences by considering the relationship between two dimensions of intellectual tradition: philosophy of science, and theories of society. Philosophy of science is a branch of philosophy that studies the reasoning processes behind the concepts, presuppositions, and methodology of science. Among other things, philosophers of science are concerned with the consequences of scientific knowledge for matters such as our perception of reality and the validity and limits of our sources of knowledge (Angeles, 1981). Burrell and Morgan used four traditional strands of debate within philosophy of science to formulate the philosophy of science or "objective-subjective" dimension of their analysis: ontology (the nature of reality), epistemology (the nature of knowledge), human nature (the nature of human action), and methodology (the nature of inquiry).

According to Burrell and Morgan (also see Morgan & Smircich, 1980), the *realist* assumes that the social world exists "out there," independent of an individual's appreciation of it, and that it is virtually as hard and concrete as the physical world. The *nominalist*, in contrast, assumes that the social world external to individual cognition is made up of names, concepts, and labels that serve as tools for describing, making sense of, and negotiating the external world. The *positivist* seeks to explain and predict social events by searching for regularities and determinate causal relationships. Growth of knowledge is seen as essentially a cumulative process in which new information is added to the existing stock of knowledge and false hypotheses are eliminated. The *anti-positivist*, conversely, assumes the social world to be essentially relativistic—understandable, but only from the point of view of the individuals directly involved in the activities to be investigated. Anti-positivists reject the notion of "observer" as a valid vantage point for understanding human activities.

Determinists assume that humans respond mechanistically or even deterministically to the situations encountered in their external world. *Voluntarists* ascribe a much more creative human role. Free will and autonomy are assumed and humans are seen as creating their environments, controlling them rather than being controlled by them. *Nomothetic* methodologies are adopted by social scientists who treat the social world as if it were a hard, objective, external reality. The search is for universal laws that explain and govern the one, concrete, objective social reality that is presumed to exist. *Idiographic* methodologies are adopted by those who assume the importance of the subjective experience of individuals in creating their social world. The principal concern for social scientists using idiographic methodologies is to understand the ways individuals create, modify, and interpret the social world in which they find themselves.

The extreme positions of the objective-subjective dimension are reflected in two major intellectual traditions that have dominated social science for 200 years. Objectivist social science is logical positivism, the dominant position in the West, which:

> . . . reflects the attempt to apply the models and methods of the natural sciences to the study of human affairs. It treats the social world as if it were the natural world, adopting a "realist" approach to ontology . . . backed up by a "positivist" epistemology, relatively "deterministic" views of human nature and the use of "nomothetic" methodologies. (Burrell & Morgan, 1979, p. 7)

The subjectivist position, German idealism, stands in complete opposition to positivism in that:

> ... it is based upon the premise that the ultimate reality of the universe lies in "spirit" or "idea" rather than in the data of sense perception. It is essentially "nominalist" in its approach to social reality ... "antipositivist" in epistemology, "voluntarist" with regard to human nature and it favours idiographic methods as a foundation for social analysis. (Burrell & Morgan, 1979, p. 7)

Burrell and Morgan used the terms "sociology of regulation" and "sociology of radical change" to describe the extreme positions on their "nature of society," or "order-conflict," dimension. Sociology of regulation—the dominant position in the West—reflects the value position of theorists who are concerned about explaining society's underlying unity and cohesion. Conversely, theorists of the sociology of radical change view modern society as being characterized by conflict, modes of domination, and contradiction. They are concerned with people's emancipation from existing social structures.

Ritzer (1980) proposed another way to think about the same intellectual territory covered in the Burrell and Morgan analysis. He used the same objective-subjective dimension but substituted a "levels of social reality" dimension in place of Burrell and Morgan's order-conflict dimension. Ritzer used a "macroscopic-microscopic" dimension in which the magnitude of social phenomena—that is, social reality ranging from whole societies to social acts—differentiates among theoretical positions. Ritzer's "microscopic" level corresponds to the "order" end of Burrell and Morgan's order-conflict dimension, and his "macroscopic" level corresponds to the "conflict" position. In either case, when the two dimensions are counterposed orthogonally, they produce four paradigms of social scientific thought based on mutually exclusive views of the social world and how it might be investigated. Each of the four paradigms—what we will refer to, following Burrell and Morgan, as the functionalist, interpretive, humanist, and structuralist paradigms—rests on a fundamentally different set of metatheoretical assumptions about the nature of science and of society (i.e., the nature of social science).

The *functionalist paradigm* is the dominant framework for social science in the Western world. It is firmly grounded in the sociology of regulation, takes a more or less microscopic view of social reality, and studies its subject matter from an objectivist point of view. It seeks to provide rational explanations of social affairs using an approach to science premised in the tradition of logical positivism. As such, it:

> ... reflects the attempt, *par excellence,* to apply the models and methods of the natural sciences to the study of human affairs ... The functionalist approach to social science tends to assume that the social world is composed of relatively concrete empirical artifacts and relationships which can be identified, studied and measured through approaches derived from the natural sciences. (Burrell & Morgan, 1979, p. 26)

The functionalist paradigm is equivalent to what Ritzer referred to as the "micro-objective" approach to social science. Theorists operating from this vantage-point are concerned with explaining social life by concentrating on microscopic social phenomena such as patterns of behavior, action, and interaction.

Interpretive theorists are only implicitly committed to regulation and order. They assume that the social world is cohesive, ordered, and integrated, but (unlike the functionalists) they are oriented toward understanding the ongoing processes through which humans subjectively create their social world. The *interpretive paradigm* addresses the same social issues as the functionalist paradigm, but it is concerned with understanding the essence of the everyday world as an emergent social process. When a social world outside the consciousness of the individual is recognized, it is regarded as a network of assumptions and intersubjectively shared meanings. The interpretive paradigm corresponds to Ritzer's micro-subjective level of social reality. Theorists of this persuasion are concerned with understanding the various facets of the social construction of reality—the way people create and share meaning (see Berger & Luckmann, 1967).

Although humanists share a view of social science with the interpretive paradigm, their frame of reference is the sociology of radical change. The *humanist paradigm* views society with a prime concern toward the importance of transcending the limitations of existing social structures. Humanism views the ideological superstructures with which people interact as a screen between them and their true consciousness. Thus, society is viewed as being antihuman—as inhibiting human development and fulfillment. Humanist theorizing centers on a critique of the status quo, from what Ritzer called the "macro-subjective" level of social reality. As such, humanists concentrate on the influence of ideological structures—culture, norms, and values—on human action.

Like humanism, the *structuralist paradigm* mounts a critique of the status quo and advocates change. But it takes this stance from the perspective of the objectivist, thus sharing an approach to social science with the functionalist paradigm. Structuralists view contemporary society as being characterized by fundamental conflicts that generate change through political and economic crisis. Whereas humanists are concerned with ideological structures and individual consciousness, structuralists focus their critique upon material structures—including social arrangements—and are concerned with the consciousness of entire classes of individuals. Structuralist theorists occupy Ritzer's macro-objective level and approach social science with a concern to explain social entities such as society, law, bureaucracy, architecture, technology, and language.

The basic point is that the approach social scientists take depends on their metatheoretical assumptions with respect to the nature of the social world and how it may be investigated. The particular combination of metatheoretical assumptions explicitly or, as is most often the case, implicitly defines the paradigm and provides the frame of reference of social scientists who work within it. Each paradigm produces knowledge that is based on a unique brand of insight. Each paradigm is a way of seeing.

The Paradigm Shift in Science and Civilization

From Kuhn, and the extensions of his original work, we can see that the very notions of paradigm and paradigm shift support a subjectivist philosophy of science. Whether we think of the process of total paradigm replacement in the physical sciences, or the process of competitive co-existence among multiple paradigms in the social sciences, the idea that paradigms exist in the minds of humans, who then operate under their received meaning, is the type of thinking about knowing that is possible only from a subjectivist view of science and knowledge. The concepts of paradigm and paradigm shift can exist only in the interpretive and humanist paradigms. They are conceptually impossible in the two objectivist paradigms, which assume a single objective reality as one of their metatheoretical assumptions.

Further evidence for a paradigm shift in the physical and social sciences was provided by Schwartz and Ogilvy (1979) in their analysis of the 20th century Kuhnian paradigm shifts in physics,

chemistry, brain theory, ecology, evolution, mathematics, philosophy, politics, psychology, linguistics, religion, consciousness, and the arts. They argued that, taken together, the manifestations of these disciplinary shifts characterize an emergent world view in the formal disciplines that is moving away from objectivism and positivism and toward a subjectivist view of science and knowledge.

At yet a broader level of human consciousness, Schwartz and Ogilvy argued that the values inherent in the disciplinary paradigm shift foreshadow an emergent shift in the entire consciousness of Western civilization. Evidence supporting this assertion, of course, is all around us. Our current world view itself is the result of the 17th century scientific revolutions that collectively became the Enlightenment. The Newtonian world view emanating from that paradigm shift is reflected today in every aspect of our social order. Its models and metaphors are embedded in our language, our history, our science. These mental maps of the world are the foundations of Western values and beliefs—the very values and beliefs that made the functionalist paradigm the dominant social science paradigm in the West. In the future, according to Schwartz and Ogilvy, Western values and beliefs will conform to the subjectivist metatheoretical assumptions.

The Meta-Leap to Antifoundational Knowledge

According to Schwartz and Ogilvy, even though science and civilization have shifted paradigms before, the current paradigm shift is even more revolutionary because this time the patterns of change have themselves changed. Not only do we appear to be at the threshold of a new paradigm or world view, but we know that there *are* paradigms. This awareness itself is part of the new paradigm because it took a shift to the subjectivist paradigms before we could comprehend a paradigm or a paradigm shift. Our current paradigm amounts to the view that there are no such things as paradigms; only the "facts" are important—seeing is believing.

But now Western science has begun to take seriously the proposition that what we believe determines much of what we see, and that the notion of an objective science is illusionary. Until this century, the assumption was that we could study the social world objectively by using the methods and models of the physical sciences. Now we have discovered that even in the physical world inquiry affects results. Our disciplines themselves are not neutral to the world. Believing is seeing.

The common view that social science is a neutral, technical process that reveals or discovers knowledge is being replaced by an appreciation of social sciences as a distinctively human process through which knowledge is created. Each paradigm produces a unique brand of insight. Historically, debate in the social sciences has been premised on a foundational view of knowledge, which has led to arguments over the "best" way of doing research or the "best" theory to explain social phenomena. But today, debate is moving beyond considerations of a single research method, theory, or paradigm, and social scientists are beginning to call for an antifoundational, reflective discourse about and appreciation of the variety of available research logics, theoretical positions, and paradigmatic perspectives (see Morgan, 1983; Soltis, 1984). Moreover, recognition of the selection of a particular research strategy, theory, or paradigm as problematic and value-laden is forcing us to recognize social science as a political, moral, and ethical undertaking as much as a technical one.

The Paradigmatic Status of Special Education Knowledge

Special education's disciplinary base in biology (medicine) and psychology yields an approach to diagnosis, intervention, and technology grounded in diagnostic-prescriptive teaching and behavioristic theory. Diagnostic-prescriptive teaching is the attempt to design instructional programs on the basis of test performances. Of the two theoretical models within the diagnostic-prescriptive approach—ability-training and task-analysis—Salvia and Ysseldyke (1981) noted the preference in special education for the latter because of the lack of reliable and valid norm-referenced assessment devices necessary to actualize the ability training model.

The task-analysis model is based on the application of behavioristic theory to instruction in specific skills. Complex instructional goals are task-analyzed into subskills and taught using a hierarchy of behavioral procedures for skill acquisition (see White & Haring, 1976). The teacher is conceptualized as a technician applying a technology of teaching commonly referred to as "systematic instruction," which:

. . . has grown out of the experimental analysis of behavior, which, as a scientific discipline, sought to find a systematic interpretation of human behavior based on generalized principles, or laws, of behavior. The goal of this search for laws of behavior was much the same as in any other branch of science—to make reliable predictions (Skinner, 1953). The development of behavior analysis has been rigorously scientific, beginning with basic laboratory research and slowly generalizing the results to social situation. (Haring, 1978, p. 21)

Burrell and Morgan (1979) locate behaviorism in the extreme objectivist region of the functionalist paradigm.

Skinner's perspective is a highly coherent and consistent one in terms of the four strands of the subjective-objective dimension of our analytical scheme. Ontologically, his view is firmly realist; epistemologically, his work is the archetype of positivism; his view of human nature reflects a determinism of an extreme form; the highly nomothetic methodology reflected in his experimental approach is congruent with these other assumptions. (Burrell & Morgan, 1979, p. 103)

This places special education knowledge in the most extreme objectivist region of the functionalist paradigm (see Heshusius, 1982).

THE CASE FOR MULTIPARADIGMATIC, MULTIDISCIPLINARY SPECIAL EDUCATION KNOWLEDGE

Special education can and should view itself from alternative vantage-points. You will recall that the fact that special education can view itself from alternative vantage-points was demonstrated using both a longitudinal and a cross-sectional explanation. The basic concept to grasp about the cross-sectional explanation at this point is that, in addition to the possibility of considering special education knowledge from a number of alternative disciplines, the very nature of those disciplines necessitates consideration of special education knowledge from the multiple paradigms of social scientific thought. As we have seen, to consider any of the social science disciplines as a unitary body of thought is simply inadequate.

Once one accepts the position that special education can be viewed in alternative disciplinary ways, and that each perspective has different implications for the lives of children labeled disabled and their parents and families, there is no morally or ethically defensible argument for special education to continue to rely on an exclusively biological/psychological interpretation of "disability." At this point we can extend the moral and ethical argument by referring to the multiple paradigmatic status of the social sciences and the notion of antifoundational knowledge. That is, given that we know that multiple paradigms exist in the social sciences, and that no particular paradigm is inherently correct, and that each paradigm has different implications for children labeled disabled and their parents and families, there is no morally defensible argument for the special education community to rely exclusively on a functionalist conceptualization of the social sciences.

Special education should expand its disciplinary base beyond psychology and biology to include the various social, political, and cultural sciences. At a minimum, special education knowledge should be multidisciplinary. But given the multiparadigmatic status of the social sciences and the antifoundational implications of the paradigm shift, an adequate response would require that special education adopt a multiparadigmatic, multidisciplinary stance. This stance would begin with a multiparadigmatic, metatheoretical critique of special education knowledge—an antifoundational, self-reflective examination of the limits and validity of special education knowledge from the alternative perspectives of the multiple paradigms of social scientific thought. And it would end with a democratized, multiparadigmatic, multidisciplinary reorientation of all levels of special education knowledge and concomitant modifications in the curriculum of special education professional education. This reorientation of special education professional knowledge would produce a community of special education professionals who think and act in ways that are substantially different from their contemporary counterparts.

But, of course, a number of factors are working against the possibility of a reorientation of special education knowledge. Paradigm shifts take time and are bitterly resisted. Moreover, the meta-leap to antifoundational knowledge itself requires a prior paradigm shift. Nevertheless, as we have seen, there are some encouraging developments on all of these fronts. In fact, there even has been some movement in the field of special education, both at the level of practice (Heshusius, 1982) and at the level of applied research (Stainback & Stainback, 1984). In both cases, the argument has been for a shift from the functionalist to the interpretive paradigm, which of course reflects the broader paradigm shift in science and civilization.

As might be expected from the foregoing discussion, the (published) reactions of the special education community to these proposals has been decidedly negative (see Ulman & Rosenberg, 1986;

Simpson & Eaves, 1985). In both cases, the defenders of the prevailing functionalist paradigm evaluate and dismiss the proposals of the advocates for the interpretive paradigm exclusively on the basis of functionalist criteria, which they implicitly assume to be foundational—and thus the only criteria that exist. They demonstrate no recognition of the possibility of alternative frames of reference, to say nothing of the possibility of antifoundational knowledge. Although the original proposals and the advocates' responses to the defenders' reactions to them (Heshusius, 1986; Stainback & Stainback, 1985) were informative and thought provoking, the exchange could hardly be called a discourse. Exchanges like this serve the purpose of educating the field and introducing anomalies, but what is needed is a sustained discourse in which all participants recognize the existence—and the moral and political implications—of multiple paradigms and antifoundational knowledge.

If an informed discourse of this nature could be initiated and sustained in a manner that would enhance special education's capacity for reflective self-criticism, two additional problems potentially would arise. First, there is the danger of the discourse becoming a substitute for action. Given the moral and political implications of the nature of special education knowledge, we do not have the luxury of time; every day counts. Second, there is the danger that the discourse will remain at the level of paradigms. As Morgan and Smircich (1980) noted, such a debate might lead to merely replacing one dominant paradigm with another dominant paradigm. We must not lose sight of the implications of antifoundational knowledge. The discourse must be raised to the meta-level of the multiple paradigms of social scientific thought and not be permitted to degenerate into a narrow debate over "the best paradigm."

Finally, even if such a discourse could be mounted and sustained to the point at which it would produce a fundamental and ongoing reorientation of special education knowledge and professional education, it would not be sufficient to substantially alter the actual practice of special education. Special education is not an island. It is merely a subsystem within the larger system of public education. Criticism of special education knowledge and practice necessarily will spill over into criticism of the knowledge base and practice of general education. In a sense, this article is a start in that direction, for virtually everything that has been said in it applies equally well to general education knowledge.

In summary, I believe that special education knowledge should be paradigmatic and multidisciplinary. Arriving at this point will require the initiation of a multiparadigmatic, metatheoretical critique of special education knowledge in the context of a democratized, informed, sustained discourse on the moral, ethical, and political implications of the choice of a frame of reference on the lives of children and youth and their parents and families. And it will be essential to expand the critique and the discourse to the entire system of public education in this country.

References

Algozzine, B. (1976). The disturbing child: What you see is what you get? *Alberta Journal of Education Research, 22,* 330-333.

Algozzine, B. (1977). The emotionally disturbed child: Disturbed or disturbing? *Journal of Abnormal Child Psychology, 5* (2), 205-211.

Apter, S. J. (1982). *Troubled children, troubled systems.* New York: Pergamon Press.

Ballard-Campbell, M., & Semmel, M. (1981, August). Policy research and special education: Research issues affecting policy formation and implementation. *Exceptional Education Quarterly,* pp. 59-68.

Barnes, B. (1982). *T. S. Kuhn and social science.* New York: Columbia University Press.

Barton, L., & Tomlinson, S. (Eds.). (1984). *Special education and social interests.* London: Croom-Helm.

Berger, P. L., & Luckmann, L. (1967). *The social construction of reality.* New York: Doubleday.

Biklen, D. (1977). Exclusion. In B. Blatt, D. Biklen, & R. Bogdan (Eds.), *An alternative textbook in special education.* Denver: Love Publishing.

Biklen, D. (Ed.). (1985). *Achieving the complete school: Strategies for effective mainstreaming.* New York: Columbia University.

Blatt, B., & Kaplan, F. (1966). *Christmas in purgatory.* Boston: Allyn & Bacon.

Bloor, D. C. (1976). *Knowledge and social imagery.* London: Routledge & Kegan Paul.

Bogdan, R. (1974). *Being different: The autobiography of Jane Fry.* New York: John Wiley.

Bogdan, R., & Kugelmass, J. (1984). Case studies of mainstreaming: A symbolic interactionist approach to special schooling. In L. Barton & S. Tomlinson (Eds.), *Special education and social interests* (pp. 173-191). London: Croom-Helm.

Braginsky, D., & Braginsky, B. (1971). *Hansels and Gretels.* New York: Holt, Rinehart & Winston.

Burrell, G., & Morgan, G. (1979). *Sociological paradigms and organizational analysis.* London: Heinemann Educational Books Ltd.

Clark, D. L. (1985). Emerging paradigms in organizational theory and research. In Y. S. Lincoln (Ed.), *Organizational theory and inquiry: The paradigm revolution* (pp. 43-78). Beverly Hills, CA: Sage Publications.

Clark, R. (1971). *Einstein: The life and times.* New York: Avon Books.

Davis, F. (1963). *Passage through crisis.* Indianapolis: Bobbs-Merrill.

Dunn, L. M. (1968). Special education for the mildly retarded: Is much of it justifiable? *Exceptional Children, 35,* 5-22.

Farber, B. (1968). *Mental retardation: Its social context and social consequences.* Boston: Houghton Mifflin.

Feigl, H. (1970). The "orthodox" view of theories: Remarks in defense as well as critique. In Radnew & Winokur (Eds.), *Minnesota studies in the philosophy of science* (Vol. 4). Minneapolis: University of Minnesota Press.

Glazer, N. (1974). The schools of the minor professions. *Minerva, 12*(3), 346-364.

Goffman, E. (1961). *Asylums: Essays on the social situation of mental patients and other inmates.* Garden City, New York: Doubleday/Anchor Books.

Goffman, E. (1963). *Stigma.* Englewood Cliffs, NJ: Prentice-Hall.

Gould, S. J. (1982). The mismeasure of man. New York: W. W. Norton.

Gubrium, J. (1975). *Living and dying at Murray Manor.* New York: St. Martin's Press.

Haring, N. G. (1978). *Behavior of exceptional children: An introduction to special education.* Columbus, OH: Charles E. Merrill.

Heshusius, L. (1982). At the heart of the advocacy dilemma: A mechanistic world view. In *Exceptional Children, 49*(1), 6-13.

Heshusius, L. (1986). Paradigm shifts and special education: A response to Ulman and Rosenberg. *Exceptional Children, 52*(5), 461-465.

Hobbs, N. (1975). *The futures of children: Categories, labels, and their consequences.* San Francisco: Jossey-Bass.

Knorr, K. D., Krohn, R., & Whitley, R. (Eds.). (1981). *The social process of scientific investigation.* Boston: D. Reidel Publishing Co.

Krohn, R. (1981). Introduction: Toward the empirical study of scientific practice. In K. D. Knorr, R. Krohn, & R. Whitley (Eds.), *The social process of scientific investigation* (pp. vii-xxv). Boston: D. Reidel Publishing.

Kuhn, T. S. (Ed.). (1962). *The structure of scientific revolutions* (1st ed.). Chicago: University of Chicago Press.

Kuhn, T. S. (Ed.). (1970a). *The structure of scientific revolutions* (2nd ed.), Chicago: University of Chicago Press.

Kuhn, T. S. (1970b). Reflections on my critics. In I. Lakatos & A. Musgrave (Eds.), *Criticism and the growth of knowledge.* Cambridge: Cambridge University Press.

Lakatos, I., & Musgrave, A. (Eds.). (1970). *Criticism and the growth of knowledge.* Cambridge: Cambridge University Press.

Law, J. (1975). Is epistemology redundant? *Philosophy of the Social Sciences, 5,* 317–337.

Lemert, E. (1967). *Human deviance, social problems, and social control.* Englewood Cliffs, NJ: Prentice-Hall.

Masterman, M. (1970). The nature of a paradigm. In I. Lakotos & A. Musgrave (eds.), *Criticism and the growth of knowledge.* Cambridge: Cambridge University Press.

Mercer, J. R. (1973). *Labeling the mentally retarded.* Berkeley: University of California Press.

Morgan, G. (Ed.). (1983). *Beyond method: Strategies for social research.* Beverly Hills, CA: Sage Publications.

Morgan, G., & Smircich, L. (1980). The case for qualitative research. *Academy of Management Review, 5,* 491–500.

Mulkay, M. J. (1979). *Science and the sociology of knowledge.* London: Allen & Unwin.

Phillips, D. (1973). Paradigms, falsifications and sociology. *Acta Sociologica, 16,* 13–31.

Ravetz, J. R. (1971). *Scientific knowledge and its social problems.* Oxford: Clarendon Press.

Rhodes, W. C. (1970). A community participation analysis of emotional disturbance. *Exceptional Children, 36,* 306–314.

Rist, R., & Harrell, J. (1982). Labeling and the learning disabled child: The social ecology of educational practice. *American Journal of Orthopsychiatry, 52*(1), 146–160.

Ritzer, G. (1980). *Sociology: A multiple paradigm science* (rev. ed.). Boston: Allyn & Bacon.

Ross, A. O. (1980). *Psychological disorders of children* (2nd ed.). New York: McGraw-Hill.

Salvia, J., & Ysseldyke, J. E. (1981). *Assessment in special and remedial education.* Boston: Houghton Mifflin.

Sarason, S. B., & Doris, J. (1979). *Educational handicap, public policy, and social history.* New York: Free Press.

Scheff, T. J. (1966). *Being mentally ill: A sociological theory.* Chicago: Aldine Publishing.

Schein, E. H. (1972). *Professional education.* New York: McGraw-Hill.

Schon, D. A. (1984). *The crisis of professional knowledge and the pursuit of an epistemology of practice* (Report for the Harvard Business School). Cambridge: Harvard.

Schrag, P., & Divorky, D. (1975). *The myth of the hyperactive child.* New York: Pantheon.

Schwartz, P., & Ogilvy, J. (1979). *The emergent paradigm: Changing patterns of thought and belief* (Analytic Report 7. Values and Lifestyle Program). Menlo Park, CA: SRI International.

Scott, R. (1969). *The making of blind men.* New York: Russell Sage Foundation.

Shimony, A. (1977). Is observation theory-laden? A problem in naturalistic epistemology. In R. G. Colodny (Ed.), *Logic, laws and life.* Pittsburgh: University of Pittsburgh Press.

Simpson, R. G., & Eaves, R. C. (1985). Do we need more qualitative research or more good research? A reaction to Stainback and Stainback, *Exceptional Children, 51* (4), 324–329.

Skinner, B. F. (1953). *Science and human behavior.* New York: Free Press.

Smith, J. K. (1984). The problem of criteria for judging interpretive inquiry. *Educational Evaluation & Policy Analysis, 6* (4), 379–391.

Soltis, J. F. (1984, December). On the nature of educational research. *Educational Researcher,* pp. 5–10.

Stainback, S., & Stainback, W. (1984). Broadening the research perspective in special education. *Exceptional Children, 50,* 400–408.

Stainback, S., & Stainback, W. (1985). Quantitative and qualitative methodologies: Competitive or complementary? A response to Simpson and Eaves. *Exceptional Children, 51* (4), 330–334.

Swap, S. (1978). The ecological model of emotional disturbance in children: A status report and proposed synthesis. *Behavioral Disorders, 3* (3), 156–186.

Szasz, T. S. (1961). *The myth of mental illness.* New York: Hoeber-Harper.

Taylor, S., & Bogdan, R. (1977). A phenomenological approach to "mental retardation." In B. Blatt, D. Biklen, & R. Bogdan (Eds.), *An alternative textbook in special education.* Denver: Love Publishing.

Tomlinson, S. (1982). *A sociology of special education.* Boston: Routledge & Kegan Paul.

Turnbull, H. R. (1986). *Free appropriate education: The law and children with disabilities.* Denver: Love Publishing.

Ulman, J. D., & Rosenberg, M. S. (1986). Science and superstition in special education. *Exceptional Children, 52* (5), 459–460.

Weick, K. L. (1985). Sources of order in underorganized systems. In Y. S. Lincoln (Ed.), *Organizational theory and inquiry: The paradigm revolution* (pp. 106–136). Beverly Hill, CA: Sage Publications.

White, O. R., & Haring, N. G. (1976). *Exceptional teaching: A multimedia training package.* Columbus, OH: Charles E. Merrill.

Wiseman, J. (1970). *Stations of the lost.* Englewood Cliffs, NJ: Prentice-Hall.

2.3 The Newtonian Mechanistic Paradigm, Special Education, and Contours of Alternatives:

An Overview

Lous Heshusius

The concept of paradigm as a set of ontological and epistemological benchmarks is the basis for a discussion of the influence the Newtonian mechanistic paradigm has exerted over special education theory, research, and practice. Discussions of "malcontents" with the mechanistic paradigm across the social sciences and within special education are noted. Recent literature in the field of special education is critiqued for renaming theories as paradigms, thereby leaving mechanistic assumptions in place. The contours are then drawn of theoretical reorientations and of the emerging alternative holistic paradigm and its importance for special education. It is concluded that we do not have paradigms or paradigm shifts within the field, but that the field is part of a paradigm that is undergoing change across the sciences and social sciences.

Increasingly, the concepts of paradigm and paradigm shifts are becoming major foci of discussion across the sciences and social sciences. As guest editors Adelman and Taylor note in their introduction to an article by Torgesen (1986), within special education far too few broad overviews of paradigms and theories have been provided. It is important to note, however, that there are different meanings attached to the term "paradigm" by different authors and within different disciplines. Kuhn (1970), in his major treatise on scientific revolutions, brought the term "paradigm" into fashionable use. He employed the term, though, in at least 21 different ways to include metaphysical, sociological, and more directly concrete meanings (see Masterman, 1970; Note 1).

For the purpose of the present paper I use the term paradigm in a focused metaphorical sense, rather than equating it, as is perhaps more typical within the social sciences, with model of inquiry (see, e.g., Popkewitz, 1984) or with theory (as is the case in some fields of study, including in the field of learning disabilities—an observation I will return to later). In doing so I draw largely from contemporary philosophy of science and from the literature on new paradigm thinking.

From "The Newtonian mechanistic paradigm, special education, and contours of alternatives: An overview" by L. Heshusius, 1989, *Journal of Learning Disabilities*, *22*(7), pp. 403–415. Copyright ©1989 by PRO-ED, Inc. Reprinted with permission.

The concept of paradigm-as-metaphor points to a distinctly more fundamental level at which questions can be asked than is the case at the level of theory, or of model of inquiry. Paradigm-as-metaphor directs attention to the most fundamental ways in which we think about the concept of reality in the first place and how it is allowed to be known, not just within scientific inquiry, but in all of life. Paradigm-as-metaphor refers to the values, beliefs, perceptions, and practices that collectively constitute the decisions we make about what counts as real, and how we allow each other to know about it.

Within scientific inquiry, paradigm-as-metaphor gives rise not only to theory and research methodology but also to criteria for problem selection and for evaluation (Capra, 1986; Lakoff & Johnson, 1980; LeShan & Margenau, 1982; Lincoln & Guba, 1985; Ogilvy, 1986; Prigogine & Stengers, 1984; Sadawa & Caley, 1985).

Paradigm-as-metaphor represents what Lincoln and Guba (1985, p. 15) call "the ultimate benchmarks against which *everything else* is tested" (emphasis theirs). It does not directly delineate the phenomena of interest as does theory, but rather presents a "way of seeing" that is also a way of not seeing. (Indirectly, of course, the paradigmatic assumptions manifest themselves also in how theory conceives of its phenomena in the first place.) Paradigm-as-metaphor represents the beliefs by which we ultimately think and act. "Paradigms represent a distillation of what we *think* about the world (but cannot prove)" (Lincoln & Guba, 1985, p. 15). Paradigms, when made self-conscious and articulated, make explicit how we think about how we think about the phenomena of interest in any area of our lives. Paradigms describe who *we* are in our epistemological makeup. Understanding paradigms is "a knowing that we know how we know" (Ogilvy, 1986, p. 14). It demands a self-consciousness of ourselves as knowers, an understanding that we, as knowers, are *part of* the paradigm we function within. The process of becoming self-conscious about our ultimate benchmarks is bound to happen when the paradigm we un-self-consciously live by reaches its limitations. Then the full extent of its characteristics emerges (Capra, 1982, 1986; Kuhn, 1970; Lincoln & Guba, 1985; Prigogine & Stengers, 1984).

Many substantial accounts now exist that trace the dominant paradigm of the last three centuries to the rise of the natural sciences in the seventeenth century: It has been Newtonian, mechanistic assumptions that have guided intellectual and practical life since that time. A dawning self-consciousness about the paradigmatic boundaries we have lived within can be found in publications by increasing numbers of scientists, and philosophers and historians of science (e.g., Berman, 1984; Bernstein, 1983; Capra, 1982; Hesse, 1980; Jantsch, 1980; LeShan & Margenau, 1982; Prigogine & Stengers, 1984; Wolf, 1981).

Mechanistic assumptions are captured by the metaphor of the machine, initially set forth by Descartes in his *De Homine*, a theory of man and animals as machines. The subsequent enormous influence of the machine metaphor upon the study of human behavior has been explicitly described by many (e.g., Capra, 1982; Koestler, 1967; LeShan & Margenau, 1982; Von Bertalanffy, 1967, 1968).

While discussions of the Newtonian mechanistic paradigm-as-metaphor typically relate to scientific inquiry, many sources are also available describing its influence on other areas in life (e.g., Capra, 1982 [economy, ecology]; Dodson-Gray, 1982, and French, 1985 [patriarchy]; Fox, 1983 [religion]; LeShan & Margenau, 1982 [art, ethics]; Lewis, 1983 [politics & economics]).

In the social sciences, similar discussions are appearing in areas of study directly related to special education, such as psychology, research methodology, and curriculum inquiry (e.g., Doll, 1986a, 1986b; Gergen, 1985; Lincoln & Guba, 1985; Polkinghorne, 1983; Sadawa & Caley, 1985; Smith & Heshusius, 1986; Valle, 1981).

In the remainder of this paper I will (a) address the assumptions about the nature of reality and the nature of knowledge claims that underlie Newtonian mechanistic thought, particularly in relation to special education theory and practice; (b) discuss the discontent with mechanistic thought and the calls for a paradigm change across the social sciences; (c) note conceptual misunderstandings within the field of special education that stand in the way of paradigmatic change, notably the recent tendency to rename theories as paradigms and the accusation of "fuzziness" against those who advocate new paradigmatic thought; (d) address the importance for special education of what I have called theoretical "reorientations"; and (e) outline the assumptions about what counts as real, how we can know about it within the emerging nonmechanistic, holistic paradigm, and its importance for special education theory, practice, and research.

THE NEWTONIAN MECHANISTIC PARADIGM AND SPECIAL EDUCATION

References in Figure 1 explicitly trace how the tenets of the Newtonian mechanistic paradigm have directly dictated our conceptions of the learner and the teacher, instructional and assessment practices, research methods, theory building, and the criteria we choose for problem selection and evaluation. Without exception, the authors take a very critical perspective, engaging in creative discontent, or in what Gould (1981, p. 32) refers to as "positive debunking." Debunking is not a negative exercise (as it would be within the mechanistic paradigm where science moves toward truth in an additive fashion, by gathering more and more data) but a positive and necessary act, since science advances not by addition, but by replacement through a process in which the old is transformed by new understandings (Gould, 1981; Kuhn, 1970; LeShan & Margenau, 1982; Prigogine & Stengers, 1984).

Accounts of the Newtonian mechanistic paradigm point to the belief in *simplicity* as the foundation of the paradigm. All complexity is to be broken down into components; translated into practice, this leads to, for instance, task analysis and isolated skill training. The whole is understood by understanding the components as logically and sequentially arranged—assumptions that lead to mastery learning, programmed materials, and behavioral objectives. Thus, causality, prediction, certainty, and control become inherently possible, leading to predictive instruments,

KEY ASSUMPTIONS OF THE MECHANISTIC PARADIGM	TRANSLATIONS INTO SPECIAL EDUCATION THEORY AND PRACTICE
The Nature of Reality: • is objective. Fact can be separated from value, the observer from the observed, the knower from the known • is understood through a mathematical symbol system • is reductionistic. The dynamics of the whole can be understood from the properties of the parts • consists of components. Knowledge of pieces adds up to knowledge of the whole • can be known with certainty with the gathering of sufficient data **The Nature of Progress:** • is deterministic. All events have direct causes and consequences • is additive, incremental, sequential, and continuous, which leads to prediction and control • is the same regardless of personal meaning and context **The Nature of the Organism:** • is reactive	• attempts to objectify knowledge and knowing; only that which can be reliably measured gains the status of formal knowledge; categorization of exceptionalities by objective diagnosis; right-wrong answers, errorless learning • quantification and ranking (statistically significant findings, frequency counts, test scores) as indices of children's recall abilities; diagnostic testing • learning equates lengthy sequences of processes, behaviors, and learning strategies; focus on deficits within the student • isolated skill training, worksheets, bottom up approaches to literacy; task analysis; learning equates mastery of predetermined, known curriculum outcomes • predictive instruments, search for causality in diagnosis; answers to problems lie in "more research" and "more data" • casual linkages between diagnosis and instruction; task analysis, mastery learning; precision teaching; programmed and sequentialized materials; controlled vocabulary; daily charting; curriculum-based assessment; "individualized" education (meaning the same for all the students but at their own pace) • behaviorism, stimulus control, reinforcement, input-output models; unidirectional control of curriculum by teacher

(Synchronized)

Figure 1

Key assumptions of the mechanistic paradigm and special education. Sources: Doll, 1986a, 1986b; Fisher & Rizzo, 1974; Heshusius, 1982, 1984b, 1986a, 1986b; Iano 1986, 1987; Mitchell, 1980; Poplin, 1984a, 1984b, 1984c, 1985.

diagnostic testing, and diagnostic/prescriptive teaching. In Newton's universe, time and space flowed uniformly and continuously (reflected in measured curriculum and curriculum-based assessment), and all movement was controlled by outside forces (assumptions that are reflected in stimulus control and systematic reinforcement practices). Fact was separated from value, the observer from the observed, the knower from the known.

Quantification, with the rise of mechanistic thought, became *the* epistemologically privileged way by which to make valid knowledge claims. The hu-

manities, the arts, intuitive knowing, personal knowing, inner knowing, were no longer considered valid ways to know. Measuring and ranking (that is, assigning numbers to things and to relations between things) *became* knowing. One doesn't even have to reflect about how the obsession with quantification and ranking is translated into special education practice: It permeates all we do. During the seventeenth-century rise of the natural sciences, God was seen by Galileo, Descartes, and Newton as a "chief mathematician of the Universe"; "Geometry existed before the creation, is coeternal with the mind of God, is

God himself," wrote Kepler (cited in LeShan & Margenau, 1982, p. 246). Paraphrasing Bohm (1980, pp. 21–22), before the rise of science, to "measure" something meant to understand the totality of inner proportions, to understand its "innermost being." A measure was a form of insight, and a person's actions following on ways indicated by such insight would bring about orderly action and harmonious living, in terms of physical health, social order, and mental harmony. Such insight was gained, not by conforming to external standards, but by creative insight and understanding of the deeper meaning of the structures and proportions of that which one wished to understand. It has only been since the rise of seventeenth-century science that to measure something has come to mean comparison to an external standard only, and has become routinized, habitual, and relatively gross and mechanical.

The failure of the Newtonian mechanistic paradigm to understand human behavior is reflected in a disarray in the social sciences. Sarason (1981, p. 14) describes this "disarray" as follows:

[Social scientists] will admit that something is (and went) wrong, that the promise of social science has not paid off; that the world of affairs does not conform to social science models and paradigms; ... that perhaps the natural science conception of solutions is not applicable to social problems.

The failure of the Newtonian mechanistic paradigm is also reflected in the strong contemporary calls for personal, intuitive, and inner knowing and in the call for the humanities and the arts to take their place alongside science in the formal study of human behavior (see, among many others, Frye, 1981; LeShan & Margenau, 1982; Prigogine & Stengers, 1984; Randall, 1984; Scully, 1980; Winkler, 1985; and within special education, Blatt, 1984; Heshusius, 1988). None of this is to say that there is no place for quantification at all, but that quantification can no longer be equated with formal, epistemologically privileged knowing. It is to say that a judgment of significance, which within mechanistic thought is a quantitative/statistical one, must become a human judgment.

Reflection on the assumptions of mechanistic thought will demonstrate their synchronizing nature. Together they display internal coherence and interdependence. Each assumption, as Lincoln and Guba (1985, p. 85) also point out, is a raison d'être for the others. One can't exist without instantly drawing on all others.

It may be helpful to note that different names are used at different times to refer to the mechanistic paradigm. Besides the term *mechanistic* or *Newtonian* (used by Berman, 1984; Capra, 1982; Doll, 1986a, 1986b; Heshusius, 1982; LeShan & Margenau, 1982), the term *component* or *atomistic* is also used (Capra, 1982), as well as the terms *reductionistic* (Poplin, 1985), *natural science* (Fisher & Rizzo, 1974), and *rational/technical paradigm* (Iano, 1986). A close look at Figure 1 will show that these different labels stress individual assumptions. Given the synchronizing nature of all assumptions, the different labels merely reflect the particular dimension the author is emphasizing. All other assumptions, however, are instantly implied. Similarly, whichever practice results as a manifestation of a particular mechanistic assumption, others are implied. One cannot, for instance, plan instruction by stipulating quantitatively measurable behavioral objectives without engaging in other manifestations of the mechanistic paradigm such as objectification and fragmentation of knowledge, right and wrong answers, task analysis, and reduced complexity of learning to predetermined sequences of behaviors.

Within the field of special education, Mann and Phillips (1967) must have been among the first to point to the danger of fragmentation resulting from our imitation of the natural sciences' emphasis on manipulation of precisely delineated variables. Fisher and Rizzo (1974), Heshusius (1982), and Poplin (1984b, 1985) explicitly analyze the mechanistic Newtonian paradigm as paradigm-as-metaphor and relate its general characteristics to special education practices. With regard to assessment, Iano (1987) and Doll (1986b) specifically address the influence of the mechanistic paradigm. Doll analyzes the measured curriculum in terms of Newtonian assumptions: The atomistic units of instruction and the linear sequencing and behavioral language in which the curriculum is described constitute a "modern day reincarnation of the seventeenth century's view of stability and order" (Doll, 1986a, p. 21). Curriculum-based assessment (CBA), as practiced and advocated in special education, constitutes such Newtonian reincarnation. According to Tucker (1985, p. 200), gauging the degree of achievement according to CBA "can only happen when the expected curricular outcomes are known and measurable and where there is a method for the ongoing measurement of student progress." Objectification of knowing and of knowledge, additive and linear progress, quantification, right and wrong answers, mastery learning, and lack of consideration for context, meaning, and personal purposes are reflected in Tucker's statement. CBA is no more than a "course to be run," to use Doll's (1986b, p. 11) expression (see also Iano, 1987). In a profound sense, CBA, like all manifestations of mechanistic/reductionistic thought, has the answer before asking the question. Rather than a process of inquiry that leads to insights about children's learning, measured curriculum approaches such as CBA are processes of justification that are both dictated by and justify mechanistic assumptions about teaching and learning.

Mechanistic thought as translated into the never-ending search for objectivity, causality, and certainty in diagnoses and categorization of exceptionalities is specifically discussed by Iano (1986), Heshusius (1982), and Poplin (1985). The mechanistic need to fragment in order to know, as expressed in task analysis, isolated skill training, endless worksheets, behavioral objectives, and so forth, is in one way or another addressed by all the above-noted references. The deficit-driven nature of our field resulting from reductionist conceptions of learning problems is frequently critiqued as well. The boredom that flows from mechanistically informed instruction and from the characterization of the human organism as reactive is specifically addressed by Heshusius (1982, 1984b), Mitchell (1980), Poplin (1984b, 1985), and Smith (1983, 1986).

The machine-like quality of the human being is at times blatantly acknowledged. For instance, Johnson (1977) devotes only 1 out of 12 chapters to "research directed at the individual," and here we read: "[In a case study] information is not limited to test scores and observations. Talking to the student may be necessary. The researcher *may* need to see the student as a human being in order to better understand certain problems" (p. 320; emphasis added). Clearly, in none of the other chapters does Johnson deem it necessary to consider the human being. The following excerpt from a special education early childhood text is an example of the machine metaphor taking the form of behavioral objectivism: "Given Susie with her coat on and the verbal command 'take off your coat,' Susie will grab one edge of the coat at the chest within 10 seconds 5 out of 5 times for 3 consecutive days" (Thurman & Widerstrom, 1985, p. 179).

Specific to the field of learning disabilities, Poplin (1985) provides perhaps the most systematic analysis of the translations of mechanistic thought into our dominant theoretical approaches. Comparing the medical model, the psychological process model, the behavioristic model, and the cognitive learning strategies model, Poplin concludes that their differences are at a surface level and are not nearly as important as their commonalities, which have rarely been reflected upon. Each model shares a mechanistic/reductionistic heritage in which the child has to be reduced in order to be understood. Each model (a) assumes that the problem of not learning is within the student; (b) segments learning into pieces (be it pieces of auditory/visual processes, pieces of behavior, or pieces of cognition); (c) is deficit driven, linking directly to instruction the perceived problems in the pieces of processes, behaviors, or cognition; (d) conceives of teaching as unidirectional; that is, the teacher gives to the student the preset tasks in a preordained sequence; (e) assumes that there are correct and incorrect strategies, facts, behaviors, and processes, that is, strategies, behaviors, and so forth, that directly, linearly, and indisputably flow from the theoretical assumptions of the particular theory; and (f) reduces life goals almost exclusively to school goals. There is insufficient evidence of generalization and maintenance for each model, which Poplin sees as a result of their common mechanistic/reductionistic heritage.

A powerful solidification of mechanistic thought is seen in the mandates of Public Law 94-142. As Reid and Hresko (1981) observed, behaviorism (which is the quintessential expression of Newtonian mechanistic thought) was legalized in Public Law 94-142 through the stipulation that goals need to be stated in the language of quantitatively measurable behavioral objectives (see also Poplin, 1985, and Heshusius, 1986a).

THE "FAMILY OF MALCONTENTS"

Special educators who critique mechanistic assumptions have clearly joined what Gergen and Gergen (1982, p. 128) call "the family of malcontents." Increasing numbers of scholars across the social sciences have outlined this discontent with mechanistic, natural science assumptions. Lather (1986, p. 261), for instance, speaks of the "rich ferment" in the field of social science research methodology and of the "dramatic shift" in our understanding of scientific inquiry away from mechanistic assumptions. Bernstein (1983) compares the Cartesian "Age of Reason" with the contemporary "Rage Against Reason" (that is, reason as narrowly defined by Cartesian/Newtonian assumptions). Gould (1981, p. 24) refers to our obsession with quantifying and ranking human behavior as the "ranking fallacy," by which he means, "our propensity for ordering complex variation as a gradual ascending scale." Gergen (1985) speaks of the profound threat that contemporary thought poses to the traditional Western conception of objective, individualistic, ahistoric knowledge. Iano (1986) notes the mushrooming of a literature of discontent.

These references represent only a very small number of members within this "family of malcontents." Without doubt, the social sciences are in turmoil and the discontent is centrally focused on the inadequacies of the ultimate, paradigmatic benchmarks of mechanistic thought.

CONCEPTUAL MISUNDERSTANDINGS WITHIN SPECIAL EDUCATION

As a result of this discontent, some major theoretical reorientations are occurring in an attempt to correct for some of the inadequacies of existing approaches. At a still more fundamental level, the formulation of an alternative, holistic paradigm is emerging. Within the field of special education, however, at least two conceptual misunderstandings inhibit exploration of substantial theoretical and paradigmatic alternatives. These are the renaming of theories as paradigms, and the accusation of "fuzziness" associated with those who stray from the mechanistic path. Without doubt, additional issues encumber the formulation of new knowledge, such as the difficulties of established legal mandates, policies, and practices; one's own, often unconscious, investment in established ways of thinking; the mere courage it requires to go against established practices, and so forth. I will deal only with the two conceptual misunderstandings, since they seem at this point to be most prevalent in the literature.

RENAMING THEORIES AS PARADIGMS: CREATING AN ILLUSION OF FUNDAMENTAL CHANGE

Within the field of learning disabilities, several authors have been renaming existing theories as paradigms. I believe this is unfortunate, in that the impression is created that something essential has changed or that a new level of inquiry has been reached, when in fact only variations in theory (however important they may be) are discussed while leaving the fundamental mechanistic paradigmatic assumptions firmly in place. Ritzer (1975) has expressed similar concerns within the field of sociology.

To clarify the distinction between theory and paradigm-as-metaphor, it is important, I believe, to be aware of both the different levels of inquiry possible and the different focus of these levels: the level of theory, directly delineating specific phenomena, and the level of paradigm-as-metaphor, delineating the assumptions we hold of reality and of knowing itself (regardless of the phenomena of interest). Even Kuhn (1962, 1970), whose many meanings of the word *paradigm* included theory as one definition, never equates the two. As Masterman (1970) notes with reference to Kuhn's work, a paradigm already exists and functions when the theory is not there. Within a paradigm one can change, modify, or expand a "part" (e.g., a theory, a model, a research method, or a criterion for evaluation) without ever changing the paradigmatic benchmarks as such; that is, *how* we think about how we think about the phenomena of interest.

Torgesen (1986) provides an example of the confusion over paradigms and theories. He discusses three major theories within the field of learning disabilities (neuropsychological, information processing, and applied behavioral analysis theory), but renames them as paradigms. In a brief attempt to distinguish paradigm from theories, Torgesen (1986, p. 400) states that theory is "more narrowly focused" than paradigms, that theories are "systems of propositions and hypothetical constructs that are developed to explain specific phenomena." Indeed, and that is precisely what neuropsychological, information processing, and applied behavioral analysis theories do, and always have done. In the remainder of Torgesen's article, the paradigm/theory confusion appears in his use of the terms "paradigms," "paradigmatic pluralism," "theoretical confusion," and "theoretical coherence" to refer to these same three theories or the relations between them. His recommendations for the future do not go beyond extending the existing theories. Torgesen leads the reader to believe that we have as many paradigms in the field as we once had theories, which must mean that there is no difference between these two concepts that makes a difference.

Radencich (1984) provides a particularly strong illustration of the confusion the concept of paradigm has wrought in the field. After stating that the learning disabilities (LD) field needs to be grounded in a "paradigm or a theoretical framework" (p. 79), Radencich moves from equating "paradigm" with "a field of study" (p. 80) to asserting that we had "a process of modality paradigm" (p. 82), while on the same page contending that we are "finding ourselves in a preparadigm stage." Radencich then moves on to the assertion that "the modality model did constitute a paradigm of sorts" (p. 82), followed by the statement that the LD field is "undergoing a scientific revolution" (p. 86) (which means that one paradigm is being replaced by a new one). Radencich concludes that we are "still searching for a common paradigm" (p. 87). Such confusion may be a natural part of the processes that occur when established knowledge and its foundations are questioned, and as such it may be helpful in upsetting the established order, which is necessary before fundamental change can occur. It is not helpful, however, to clarify the concept and functions of paradigms and of levels of inquiry.

Kavale and Forness (1985, p. 13) also use the concept of paradigm in analyzing the field of learning disabilities, but unlike Torgesen, who proposes three paradigms, Kavale and Forness propose only one: They change the Strauss and Werner theory into a "paradigm" (quotation marks are theirs) on the basis of the fact that theories in the LD field have not substantially deviated from it. The Strauss and Werner "paradigm" is later referred to as a "fundamental theoretical orientation." The latter, of course, is true: The Strauss and Werner theory was a prototype for all theories in learning disabilities, that is to say, theories in the LD field have been a variation on the same set of theoretical propositions. This, Kavale and Forness show in detail. Serving as a prototype does not, however, change a theory into a paradigm. It still is what it is: a set of propositions about a specific set of phenomena, not a set of beliefs, values, and assumptions about what counts as real and how we are allowed to claim knowledge. Kavale and Forness conclude that, although we do have a Strauss and Werner "paradigm," the LD field is (somehow, nevertheless) "really in a preparadigmatic period" because we don't have a firm foundation yet (p. 19).

What is necessary next, Kavale and Forness (1985, p. 19) state, in order to move from a preparadigmatic to a paradigmatic period, is to question whether the natural sciences model provides the most appropriate model for understanding LD phenomena: As is argued in the present paper, the natural science, mechanistic paradigm *has been* the paradigm under which we have functioned. It has provided us, not with a set of propositions about specific phenomena such as learning disabilities, as do theories, but with a metaphor to live by. Clearly, the Strauss and Werner theory is not at the same level of explanatory power as is the mechanistic, natural science paradigm. One does not speak of "the natural science theory" as one

speaks of, for instance, a psychoneurological theory, because the former provides a metaphor, not a set of specific propositions to directly denote phenomena of interest. From this perspective, Strauss and Werner did not initiate a paradigmatic framework, as Kavale and Forness (1985) state; rather, they initiated a theoretical framework against the backdrop of the Newtonian paradigm. Thus, it is argued here that the field of special education/learning disabilities does not contain paradigms within itself, nor does it constitute a preparadigm stage; rather, it *is part of* a paradigm that has dominated the sciences and social sciences for several centuries.

"FUZZINESS": A CASE OF MISTAKEN IDENTITY

Under Newtonian mechanistic assumptions of objectivity, predictability, certainty, control, and so forth, accusations of fuzziness, mere intuition, and being anti-science are quickly leveled against those who are engaged in the formulation of nonmechanistic thought. Lloyd's (1987) response to Iano's (1986) paper (in which Iano argues for an alternative paradigm conceptualization for the study of teaching) and the response by Ulman and Rosenberg (1986) to my earlier work (Heshusius, 1982) reflect such reactions. There is a fear in these reactions that, if we let go of fundamental mechanistic assumptions, we will collapse into either chaos or nothingness (see particularly Ulman & Rosenberg, 1986). Or the formulation of alternative thought is seen as constituting art rather than science (see particularly Lloyd, 1987). Others misinterpret or minimize the extent and seriousness of the paradigmatic differences, as does Carnine (1987, pp. 42–43) in his response to Iano (1986), by declaring that we should drop the "unnecessary battle" and go on with our work because there are really "no substantial differences." A different reaction still is that engaging in a nonmechanistic paradigm means engaging in a sort of watered-down science. According to Forness and Kavale (1987, p. 47), we can do it, and even should do it, but then "our level of aspirations for scientific inquiry must be lowered in order to be realistic." Lowering scientific aspirations, however, is a compromise of expectations, not a transformation of assumptions. If is saying, too bad we can't get there completely, but we may get there halfway. The belief in the possibility of certainty, objectivity, prediction and control, separation of fact and value, of observer and observed, and so forth, is steadily left in place. It is clear that Forness and Kavale, too, continue to think that the methods we borrowed from the natural sciences are not only capable of explaining human behavior, but are ultimately the most privileged ones and continue to constitute real science. Likewise, their support of the curriculum as "a course to be run" in the form of curriculum-based assessment, firmly leaves in place the mechanistic assumptions about learning as outlined earlier.

At the heart of these reactions, then, lies the continuous belief in mechanistic assumptions. The accusations of "fuzziness" and being "anti-science" are mirror images of these assumptions, which is to say, they give rise to each other and are parasitic upon each other. As Lakoff and Johnson (1980, p. 189) note, each defines itself in opposition to the other, therefore each *is* the other, but sees the other as enemy. Any disturbance of mechanistic beliefs will automatically trigger the fuzziness accusation. Iano (1986, p. 59) states similarly, with regard to the charge that "anything goes" in an alternative paradigm (a charge closely related to that of fuzziness) that such a charge is but a mirror image of mechanistic dogma and implies that no "real" truth or knowledge is to be had at all if not through the established methods of traditional science: If you cannot know mechanistically, you cannot know. The point is that *once* the mechanistic assumptions are seen to hold up no longer, the accusation of fuzziness (or engaging in anti-science, or in a kind of watered-down science) when not adhering to them is instantly rendered irrelevant: Such an accusation cannot hold up when that which gave rise to it in the first place is seen to be no longer adequate (see also Bernstein, 1983, and Rorty, 1982).

In a holistic paradigm, mechanistic assumptions are replaced by assumptions that directly emerge from human knowing. As will be noted in the section on the emergent holistic paradigm, the paradigm shift constitutes a profound shift from the machine metaphor to a human metaphor. We do not collapse into nothingness or fuzziness, but transform our understanding into something qualitatively, and therefore fundamentally, different. We rid our thinking of *both* "objectivity" and "fuzziness," as both are a measure of exactly the same: One portrays the presence of the possibility of certainty and of control, the other its absence, but both are centrally preoccupied with the Cartesian/Newtonian belief in the possibility of certainty and control and its related set of paradigmatic assumptions. The contemporary paradigm shift is transforming the very concept of science itself and along with it the concepts of "Objectivity," "Method," and "Research."

The contemporary turbulence and ferment that within the constraints of a mechanistic paradigm are seen as fuzziness, chaos, and anti-science, from the vantage point of a conscious and close examination of the paradigmatic boundaries themselves contain the roots and the information needed to move into the articulation of alternative paradigm thinking. To do so, much of what is sacred needs to be relinquished. The difficulties experienced in doing so both individually and as a community are indeed enormous, as many have elaborated upon (e.g., Bernstein, 1983; Gergen, 1985; Kuhn, 1970; LeShan & Margenau, 1982).

THEORETICAL REORIENTATIONS

Processes of Social Interchange

Out of the malcontent with mechanistic assumptions, theories are emerging that address the specific phenomena of learning (and of not learning) in ways that attempt to transform certain assumptions of mechanistic thought. Alternative sociological theories of exceptionalities have of course been with us for some time, for example, viewing exceptionalities as social constructions rather than as deficits within the person (see, e.g., Blatt, Biklen, & Bogdan, 1977; Bogdan & Taylor, 1982; Tomlinson, 1982, with regard to mental retardation, and Carrier, 1983, and Sleeter, 1986, with regard to learning disabilities). Here it is the more recent theoretical trends that define *knowledge and knowing as a result of processes of social interchanges* we want to briefly refer to for their importance for the field of special education. Knowledge and knowing are seen no longer as a matter of mental representation, as mapping the "truth-out-there" onto one's own mind, as mechanistic thought would have it, but are seen as direct outcomes of processes of social interactions. As Gergen (1985, p. 270) states, "knowledge is not something people possess somewhere in their heads, but rather something people do together." While one may argue, correctly I believe, that yet another too simplistic monism is created by lodging everything within social interchange and nothing in a person's head, there is nevertheless much of importance in conceptualizations that focus on social interchanges as a medium through which knowledge and knowing come about. These conceptualizations pose a fundamental problem for the presumably objective, acontextual, individually acquired, and ahistoric knowledge base that mechanistic thought presents. Within these developments, cognitive anthropology and anthropological psychology have been particularly informative. Erickson's (1984) overview of research shows, for example, that mental abilities (including linguistic and mathematical) once thought relatively, or even absolutely, context independent (as presumed by classical learning theory and Piagetian developmental theory), are much more labile. Human reasoning, in fact, seems to consist of understandings that are constituted in the context of personal use and purpose. In education, by changing settings, tools, meanings, and symbols, and by changing the social forms of relations among people, one has profoundly changed the nature of the situation, the learning task, and the demands on the ability of the child. This view would explain, for instance, Sarason's (cited in McKean, 1985, p. 25) surprise when he arrived one morning at the institution for individuals with mental retardation to hear that several of the residents he had tested and found wanting in intelligence had escaped from the institution. Residents who had not been able to successfully trace their way out of a simple maze had plotted their way out of a 24-hour supervised institution. From this point of view, as Erickson (1984) states:

> . . . it is not surprising that a child can display arithmetic competence while dealing with change at the grocery store and yet seem to lack that performance when doing what seems to be the "same" arithmetic problem on a worksheet or at the blackboard . . . [Even] the picture of a coin is not a coin, and relations with the teacher and fellow students are not the same as relations with a store clerk. . . . The nature of the task in the store and in the classroom is very different and so is the nature of the abilities required to accomplish it. (p. 529)

Differences in performance, states Erickson (1984), such as the arithmetic problem referred to above (and Sarason's subjects' differential performance on maze tests versus in a real life, purposeful situation) do not merely lie on the dimension of abstract-concrete, as we have mostly assumed, but on the dimension of problem definition by self or other. When the person has ownership in the very formation of the problem, he or she goes through a series of decision-making points, each one involving abilities as well as processes of social interchange that do not come into play when, for instance, doing problems on worksheets or tracing mazes. It is not just that learning tasks are "out of context," as Erickson (1984, p. 533) notes, but that they are *in a context* in which the

power relations and processes of social interchanges are such that the child has no influence on problem formulation, and the tasks offer no context of personal use and purpose.

Resistance Theory

Resistance theory is also grounded in the web of social interchanges and processes and particularly challenges the passive-reactive nature of the human being as characterized by mechanistic thought. Resistance theory was articulated to account for active noncooperation and resistance by both students of less privileged classes who are defined by schools as having less worth than others, and high school students who see schools as alienating and boring institutions. The students' defiance provides a more acceptable self-image to themselves than does agreement with the school's definition of them (Erickson, 1984; Giroux, 1983; Willis, 1977). Resistance theory may well serve to explain some of the behaviors of special education students, who are also being defined by schools as less worthy, or at least, as less "normal" or not "regular," and who are often bored under mechanistically conceived instruction. McDermott (1974, 1977), for instance, shows in a detailed microanalysis of videotapes how students in a lowest reading group worked actively at not reading. The students constructed a situation in which the teacher cooperated, apparently without being aware of it, and in which they received far less reading instruction than did the better readers. Similarly, Miller (1985), in an ethnographic study involving 175 hours of observation, described how children with learning problems integrated into regular classrooms worked hard at not working. They were overwhelmed by the amount of work that needed to be done and actively found many ways of otherwise occupying themselves that largely went unnoticed by the teachers, who nevertheless complained that these children were never ready with their work. While conventional LD theories would likely assess these students as inattentive, having a short attention span, being hyperactive, or the like, resistance theory provides a framework for understanding these children's behavior as active resistance to a situation they find threatening, boring, or otherwise intolerable.

Another example of resistance theory can be seen in an interview with an adult with LD (Heshusius, 1984a) reflecting on his school years. He not only actively but also very consciously had resisted anything that could have put him on the spot as a poor reader. Such active and conscious resistance shaped his behavior in school in dramatic ways as he was determined not to "lose face." The system, however, reinterpreted his resistance behavior as further evidence of his deficits and labeled him emotionally disturbed in addition to learning disabled. Meek, Armstrong, Austerfield, Graham, and Plackett (1983), in their 3-year participant observation study, provide a sensitive account of how a group of poor readers at the secondary level used resistance as a personal/political act. Resistance theory shows special education students as active, purposeful beings who have reasons for behaving as they do within their specific context and within specific processes of social interchanges. It raises questions such as: To what extent, and for what reasons and under what conditions do special education students engage in active resistance and work, as Erickson (1984) phrases it, on further "achieving" their own failure? And to what extent do we reinterpret active resistance behavior as further evidence of their deficits and low ability?

Toward a Theory of Empowerment

A third and related theoretical orientation that places behavior and knowing within processes of social interchanges, and views the student as an active, self-organizing being, could be referred to as an empowering orientation. This orientation sees as the main purpose of teaching the empowerment of the student. Education is viewed as an agent of change in the service of those who have been judged inadequate. It represents a struggle for personal meaning and for possibilities, but always within the framework of the histories and experiences of those who have been judged inadequate by the system.

Within special education, an empowering approach moves away from remediation (which is adjustment to the system), directing teaching toward activities that allow students the fullest expression of who they are and where they are going. Holzman and LaCerva (1986) describe how they use the empowering approach with high school students with LD. Initially, their work was informed by, among others, Paulo Freire, who developed literacy programs for illiterate peasants in the third world, based upon an empowering theory of learning. Increasingly their work has become more explicitly influenced by Vygotsky's theories. Vygotsky postulates development of higher psychological processes as a series of qualitative transformations that arise through dialectical processes that are sociocultural and historical in nature. Such grounding defies any approach emerging from simple stimulus-response models or medical models that pos-

tulate innate ability or deficiencies as a point of departure. Vygotsky views learning as a dialectical social-historical activity, not a private, mentalistic, or inside-the-head activity. He stresses the need to create an environment of social interchanges in which educational methods are used that are adapted to who the students are in their historical/social setting:

> What do we need to build learning? We usually think of learning materials in a very limited way—as books, pens, paper, minds, intelligence, the teacher, etc., but that only scratches the surface of what is available. What about the histories of the students— their individual as well as collective histories, and of you, the teacher; their emotions, their wants, needs, desires, skills, hobbies, joys, loves, pain, their conflicts—and yours? In the building of the social environment for learning and development to take place, we must use what we have. This means that nothing is off limits; everything should be considered potentially useful in the process. (Holzman & LaCerva, 1986, p. 5)

These may indeed be "unorthodox building materials" (Holzman & LaCerva, 1986, p. 5), but they are the most serious set of building blocks for learning one can think of, and they take utterly seriously the commonplace saying that we need to motivate students. Motivating here does not mean designing nice activities for students to do. It means understanding students in *who they are* and letting instruction emerge in a dialectical manner in the process of coming to understand them and in assisting them to become empowered as persons. This means, as Freirian theory also holds, that educators have to work with the personal, historical, and political experiences students bring to school and make these experiences the object of debate and confirmation. It means legitimizing such experiences in order to give those who live and move within them a sense of affirmation and to provide the conditions for students to fully be who they are through learning.

Holzman and LaCerva (1986) describe, among other examples, how they taught social studies to a class for students with LD in an inner city multiracial high school in New York. These were students who could not and would not write or read and who wanted to "burn all textbooks." The teachers reorganized the students' understanding of what learning could be from an empowering perspective. They involved the students directly in generating discussions of major issues in their personal lives by starting a unit on poverty and racism in America. Exchanges about painful events were engaged in, and these issues were then related to how three different social studies texts presented "history" to them. One text was a college text of the 1960s, a period of great social movements, one was a new, very conservative college text, and the third was a text chosen for them as learning disabled students with simple vocabulary and few concepts, centering only around the history of great (white) men. Students came to see how accounts of history are constructed under constraints of the time period and external purposes and interests. They then decided they needed a text that came out of their own experience and started to rewrite the text collectively from a more personal/political perspective:

> They caught on quite quickly. In fact, they began to question *me* about how I knew what I was talking about. They began to work actively, giving expression to their life histories, including their anger, but not as victims. They were now engaging in the cooperative, socially meaningful activity of producing a useful history book. (Holzman & LaCerva, 1986, p. 13)

As Erickson (1984, p. 84) stresses, a full appreciation of the role of context, personal purpose and use, and of processes of social interchanges would fundamentally reshape our conceptualizations of and approaches to both assessment and instruction. I believe it would particularly affect special education as our dominant theories and models for assessment and instruction have been, more than in any other field within education, explicitly based on the assumption that learning problems are lodged within the individual (problems, variously assessed as deficits, defects, delayed development, disabilities, disorders, deficiencies, auditory or visual memory deficits, faulty learning, deficits in cognitive strategies, and so forth).

THE EMERGENT ALTERNATIVE HOLISTIC PARADIGM

Elsewhere (Heshusius, 1982) when discussing the mechanistic paradigm in relation to special education, I noted that special education has not been wrong so much as it has attempted to do what we now know is impossible: to force the innately unpredictable into the predictable, the unmeasurable into the measurable, and wholeness into fragmentation. It has attempted to transform teachers and students into reactive individuals.

Paradigms do not offer "right" and "wrong" answers, nor perfect solutions. Rather, they provide sets of fundamental assumptions that are adequate (or no longer adequate) to generate the pertinent questions of the time and possibilities for their answers.

We have been told that now that legal mandates are in place and we have recorded progress in terms of numbers served and test scores obtained, we need to start asking questions of quality. The difficulty is that mechanistic thought can only conceive of first translating qualitative questions back into quantitative formulations so they are measurable and otherwise adhere to mechanistic assumptions. While the latter have been adequate in terms of the assessment and instruction of academic skills in restricted settings and with regard to controlled tasks and in terms of quantitatively measuring the outcomes of such learning, they have not been adequate in understanding the *nature* of the processes and the nature of social interchanges through which learning does or does not occur. They have not resulted in significantly increasing students' meaningful functioning in their day-to-day interactions (see Iano, 1986; Poplin, 1984c; Reid & Hresko, 1981). They have nothing to say about the place and importance of dialectics, nor about novelty. They do not address the question of how students actually construct the meaning of their school situation, and therefore they can't tell us anything about what really motivates students. They do not inform us about the impact the relationship between teacher and student *as persons* has on the student's learning. They have nothing to say about the ethical and moral dimensions of all we do.

It is generally acknowledged that the emergence of a holistic paradigm started with the revolutionary discoveries in quantum physics that signaled the demise of Newtonian mechanistic assumptions. Fundamental changes in the understanding of the very structure of reality and of knowing at the subatomic level show that the observer and the observed are *not* separate, as mechanistic assumptions would have it. The observer shapes, and in a profound way, creates the observed. In addition, particles, the ultimate pieces of the Newtonian mechanistic universe, turn out to be not particles, but relations in the form of ever-changing electromagnetic field interactions. Systems, from molecules to complex human organizations, are now understood not through stimulus-response and deterministic frameworks but through active self-organizing, self-regulating principles that form unexpected properties that cannot be predicted from their antecedents.

Recently, Rhodes (1987) directly and explicitly relates the empowerment view of the child as a generator of her or his own reality (rather than as a receptor) to the discoveries of quantum physics by acknowledging that the separation between knower and known, between self and world, is erroneous (see Valle, 1981, for a similar discussion within psychology).

The contemporary paradigm shift, then, is centrally concerned with the shift from a machine metaphor to a human metaphor. Prigogine and Stengers (1984, p. 23) speak of art forms as the new metaphor to characterize the pivotal importance of the inner and intuitive ways of knowing in today's science (Prigogine is a Nobel laureate chemist). Lincoln and Guba (1985, pp. 61–62) refer to the shift in metaphor from "machine to human being," or from "reality as a machine toward reality as a conscious organism." Philosopher of science Bernstein (1983) speaks about the shift from a "Rationality of Method" to a "Human Rationality." Valle (1981) speaks of a "person-world view." And within the field of special education, Iano (1986) speaks of the shift from a "Natural Science Model" to a "Human Science Model." This fundamental shift characterizes emergent thinking in virtually every major discipline. The axioms of the emergent paradigm represent "the analytic residue remaining after the particulars of physics, chemistry, brain theory, mathematics and so on have been 'boiled off' " (Lincoln & Guba, 1985, p. 65).

THE EMERGENT PARADIGM AND SPECIAL EDUCATION

Relative to human behavior, the holistic paradigm holds the human being (in our case, the student, the teacher, and the researcher) as both active and reflexive. "Active," *not* as defined by traditional science (that is, actively displayed in reaction to a task, question, or stimulus provided by someone else), but "immanently active," to use Von Bertalanffy's (1968) terminology: active as existing within, as self-generated, meaning giving, as actively constructing and transforming reality. Behavior is seen to occur because active choices are constantly made based upon perceptions of purpose and meaning rather than because of the explanatory power gained from external, "objective" knowledge and the collection of more data. As LeShan and Margenau (1982, p. 147) state: "The assumption—which has now collapsed—that if you have enough data you can know what is going to happen, was a comfortable one." Central to contemporary understanding is that *purpose* is the driving force, and replaces conventional cause-and-effect relations. Openness of systems, self-organizing and self-regulating principles, progress through transformation guided by what we experience as the purpose of our actions (or the purpose of systems), are now seen as the keystones of our understanding of the nature of reality, including human behavior. Science is now understood to be epistemic (as the observer and the observed are not separate) rather than objective and independent of the human observer or measurer. That is, our own consciousness about the way we know needs to be explicitly included in the description of the phenomena. (For elaborations on the above, see, among others, Battista, 1982; Berman, 1984; Bohm, 1980; Capra, 1982, 1986; Cousins, 1985; LeShan & Margenau, 1982; Prigogine & Stengers, 1984; Wolf, 1981.)

Holistic assumptions reverse the reductionistic/mechanistic position: It is not the case that the dynamics of the whole can be understood from the properties of the parts, but rather, that the properties of the parts can only be understood from the dynamics of the whole. The whole is both different from and more than the sum of its parts. Knowledge of "parts" does not lead to knowledge of the whole. There are no fixed and reliable linkages among the "parts." For our purposes, it means that learners are always learning and that the learner not only is actively involved but actively initiates this process, by constantly judging the personal relevance of what is to be learned relative to what she or he already knows. And when we think that the learner is not learning, the learner is learning nevertheless, although not necessarily of course what we would like her or him to be learning.

Our theories of learning disabilities will depend on our constructs of learning abilities. Just as we do not have one theory of how the blood circulates or how the heart works for those persons who are healthy, and suddenly a different theory of how the blood circulates or how the heart works for those who are not, we should not have one theory of learning that is holistic for those who learn normally and quite another theory that proposes mechanistic assumptions of learning for those who do not manage to learn well in our schools. Yet, that is what seems to be happening at present, when whole language theories, for instance, are increasingly seen as more adequate explanatory systems by which to understand how a human being learns to talk, read, and write and then turn to programmed materials, worksheets, mastery learning, direct instruction, errorless learning, measured curriculum, and so forth, for students who do not learn as well as we want them to.

Holistic education is not a matter of a new set of prescriptive strategies and techniques. Since holism understands human behavior and growth as immanently active, meaning constructive, self-organizing, and self-regulating, there cannot be a sequentially organized, prescriptive approach to "how to be holistic": Once it is understood how holistic assumptions are fundamentally different from mechanistic ones, one starts *thinking* differently about the nature of learning, teaching, assessing, and about curriculum. Authors collectively point to the following translations of the holistic paradigm into educational principles.

Learning is understanding *relations* rather than pieces of knowledge. It is the personal/social/cultural construction of meaning by the child, based on who the child is and on what she or he knows (not based on how *we* understand what needs to be learned). Learners always bring their own personal, social, cultural, and political histories, purposes, and interpretations to the situation, whether we are aware of it or acknowledge it or not. Learning occurs at various but equally valid levels, including kinesthetic, intuitive, and nondiscursive.

Progress is transformative, rather than additive and incremental. Progress occurs when concepts are seen in new ways. As the human organism is self-regulating and immanently active, what is learned is not necessarily directly and solely "caused" by how or what we teach. What is learned and how it is learned cannot be controlled by superimposing measurement theory, and cannot be captured by simple input-output or closed feedback loop models. New knowledge is not added on to previous knowledge, but transforms the old, just as past knowledge influences and shapes the nature of new knowledge.

There is no one best way to teach or to assess. Attentiveness to how *the child* thinks and reasons in a nonpunitive environment is essential. Teaching is a fundamental pedagogical engagement before it is an instructional one, containing immediate social, cultural, moral, and political dimensions. Teachers capitalize on children's natural curiosity and natural interests. The teacher becomes a "reflective practitioner" (see Schon, 1983) instead of an "executor of prescription" (Heshusius, 1982).

Assessment focuses on what students do over time in purposeful (to the student) engagements, in natural, interactive settings. We can no longer separate the question of what this learner needs to learn from the question of how this learner constructs meaning in this situation. "Errors" are not wrong pieces of knowledge but ways of making sense that provide insights into how the child thinks and reasons. Assessment also includes assessing the actual teacher/student match (see also Messick, 1984, p. 5), the actual teacher/student instructional interactions, the value of the curriculum in the first place, and the motivational readiness of the child (see also Adelman & Taylor, 1986). Clearly, then, the very criteria by which we evaluate learners change: from testing, and from counting and ranking correct responses to controlled tasks, to documenting and assessing real life processes and accomplishments.

Possibilities and choices are essential in a curriculum for human learning. A holistic curriculum, for all learners, stresses the interdependencies among concepts and areas of study (reading–writing–oral language; language–math; history-geography-social movements–the arts, etc.). It stresses the interdependencies among individuals and the larger world around them, leading not just to getting to know the community, but also to attending to crucial real life issues of our times, for example, global awareness and ecology.

More specifically, well-known scholars in literacy acquisition who base their research and theory building on holistic principles have started to bring their work to the field of special education (see Church & Newman, 1986, and Smith, 1983, in reading, and Graves, 1985, in writing). Further, holistic language activities for children labeled learning disabled are offered by Rhodes and Dudley-Marling (1988), Leigh (1980), McNutt (1984), and Weaver (1988), and for hearing impaired children by Ewoldt (1982). Holistic criteria for planning and evaluation are discussed by Dudley-Marling (1986) and by Hasselbrüs (1982).

Once holistic educational principles are grasped, one cannot go back to worksheets, isolated skill training, stipulating short-term quantitatively measurable behavioral objectives, IQ testing, CBA, and so forth (see Note 2).

RESEARCH WITHIN AN ALTERNATIVE PARADIGMATIC FRAMEWORK

Within alternative paradigmatic thought, the concepts of "research" and "method" naturally undergo a transformation according to the different assumptions about what counts as real and how we can know.

Various forms of inquiry that have emerged within alternative paradigmatic thought include phenomenological research, qualitative/interpretive research, ethnography, naturalistic research, human science research, open ideological research, research as praxis, and research for empowerment. Their commonality lies in the rejection of mechanistic assumptions, and they overlap to a considerable degree in their specific inquiry strategies and assumptions. Their differences are of emphasis and purpose (for overviews of issues and approaches see, e.g., Jacob, 1987; Lather, 1986; Morgan, 1983; Polkinghorne, 1983). These forms of inquiry collectively hold to the view of the person as an immanently active, meaning-constructing being, to the importance of context, and to the pivotal role of the "lived experience." This fundamentally changes the role of the subject in traditional inquiry to that of research-participant. Understanding of the natural, real life context is seen as crucial to gain insights, and inquiry occurs in real life settings and in relation to real life events. The role of the researcher in these forms of inquiry changes from a measurer, controller of variables, and executor of research design to that of a careful and aware listener, observer, absorber, participator, organizer of data, and able narrator. The privileged symbol system for data gathering, data organization, reporting of findings, and a judgment of significance shifts from a mathematical symbol system to the language of our everyday discourse. "Method" is no longer an unambiguous set of fixed rules but is defined as organized inquiry and careful accounting of data gathering and analysis strategies, which are always in the service of, rather than in control of, the research question, the context, and the flow of events. Quantification through application of conventional method is no longer seen to be epistemologically privileged to render knowledge claims. To quote Lincoln and Guba (1985, p. 156): "The necessity for human judgment is not only *not* an embarrassment, but is elevated to the level of precondition" (emphasis theirs). In the present post-positivistic era, we are moving "Beyond Method" (Morgan, 1983). We are moving from a "rationality of method" to a "human rationality" (Bernstein, 1983).

Needless to say, such dramatic reconstruction of key dimensions of the processes of inquiry has brought about many debates between proponents of the different paradigms, a discussion of which, however, does not lie within the scope of this paper.

The impact of new paradigm inquiry on the field of special education research is not yet great, but it does exist. Some examples include the work by Bogdan and Taylor (1982), Edgerton (1967), and Heshusius (1981) in the area of mental retardation, Ewoldt (1985) in the area of hearing impairment, Miller (1985) and Sanders (1986) in the area of learning disabilities, Biklen (1985) in his inquiry into successful mainstreaming programs, and Mehan, Hertweck, and Meihls (1986) and Smith (1982) in the study of assessment decisions in school.

CONCLUSION

The purpose of this paper has been to show the emergence of a nonmechanistic paradigm. It is a paradigm that is emerging from our increased consciousness of having painted a now several centuries old picture of reality and of knowing, and finding it wanting. While holism is certainly not "just around the corner," not in our practice and not in mainstream academia, its influence is slowly but steadily becoming visible, not only in North America but internationally (e.g., Prigogine & Stengers, 1984; Van Steenbergen, 1986). As LeShan and Margenau (1982) and Polkinghorne (1983) note, it is the first time in 400 years that we are asking fundamental questions again. Much still needs to be further explored and articulated. However, it took the mechanistic paradigm over three centuries to work out its assumptions and implications in order to fulfill and then outlive its promises. It may well take longer for a holistic paradigm to do so, because it acknowledges understanding complexity, rather than reduction to simplicity, as its major task. Grasping complexity, guided by human rationality, will be far more difficult than inquiry informed by a machine metaphor of reality. But the effort will be more worthy of human beings, will result in more relevance, and is bound to be further-reaching.

AUTHOR'S NOTE

It is time to express my gratitude to Mary Poplin, Claremont Graduate School, John Smith and Loree Rackstraw, University of Northern Iowa, and Michael Wheeler, Dufferin-Peel School Board, Toronto, whose knowledge and sustained discussions have for many years fostered the development of my own understandings. I would also like to thank Carolyn Ewoldt, of York University, for her insightful comments on an earlier draft of this paper.

Notes

1. The metaphysical notion included paradigm as myth, a general epistemological viewpoint, something that defines a broad sweep or reality, or an organizing principle governing perception itself. The sociological notion included paradigm as a recognized scientific achievement, or a set of political institutions. The more direct concrete notion included paradigm as an actual classic work, an exemplar, or a grammatical paradigm (see Masterman, 1970). In the second edition of his work, Kuhn (1970, see postscript) acknowledges the confusion in his discussion of paradigms, and in his attempts to clarify the concept, emphasizes the notion of paradigm as a concrete examplar, which would come closest to the concept of theory and may have encouraged various scholars to misinterpret theories as paradigms, as Ritzer (1975) also has observed. Kuhn, however, does not equate paradigms with theories. He stresses, in fact, that his viewpoints on fundamentals stayed nearly unchanged. The postscript of his 1970 discussion does not exclude the metaphysical and sociological notions. A paradigm, also in the Kuhnian sense, as Masterman (1970) notes, already exists (and functions) when the theory is not there.

2. During my several years of teaching students in classes for students labeled learning disabled and in my present work with graduate students at York University (all practicing teachers and school administrators), the "way to holistic practice" is facilitated by keeping this set of educational principles literally pinned over our desks. They guide decision making and action in any concrete situation. Given the always present and immense pressures to function mechanistically that are built into the system, I have found (as have our students) that one needs a visible, immediately available clear reference to guide one's conceptualizations and actions throughout the day if one wishes to seriously engage in a paradigm shift. Of course, in the present climate, compromise will be almost always necessary as the system largely demands mechanistic procedures. However, and without losing one's job, *much can be done within one's own classroom, within one's own school, and much can be changed, however slowly, through networking and raising consciousness with colleagues, parents, and administrators. From our experience, one thing can be stated with certainty: There is no problem convincing children that holistic principles are more adequate.

References

Adelman, H.S., & Taylor, L. (1986). *An introduction to learning disabilities.* Glenview, IL: Scott, Foresman.

Battista, J.R. (1982). The holistic paradigm and general systems theory. In W. Gray, J. Fidler, & J. Battista (Eds.), *General systems theory and the psychological sciences (Vol. I)* (pp. 209–210). Seaside, CA: Intersystems Publications.

Berman, M. (1984). *The reenchantment of the world.* New York: Bantam Books.

Bernstein, R.J. (1983). *Beyond objectivity and relativity: Science, hermeneutics, and praxis.* Philadelphia: University of Pennsylvania Press.

Biklen, D. (1985). *Achieving the complete school, strategies for effective mainstreaming.* New York: Teachers College, Columbia University.

Blatt, B. (1984). On distorting reality to comprehend distortion. *Journal of Learning Disabilities, 17,* 627–628.

Blatt, B., Biklen, D., & Bogdan, R.B. (Eds.). (1977). *An alternative textbook in special education.* Denver: Love.

Bogdan, R.B., & Taylor, S.A. (1982). *Inside out. The social meaning of mental retardation.* Toronto: University of Toronto Press.

Bohm, D. (1980). *Wholeness and the implicate order.* Boston: Routledge & Kegan Paul.

Capra, F. (1982). *The turning point: Science, society and the rising culture.* New York: Simon & Schuster.

Capra, F. (1986). The concept of paradigm and paradigm shift. *Revision, Journal of Consciousness and Change, 9*(1), 11–17.

Carnine, D. (1987). A response to "False standards, a distorting and disintegrating effect on education, turning away from useful purposes, being inevitably unfulfilled, and remaining unrealistic and irrelevant." *Remedial and Special Education, 8*(1), 42–43.

Carrier, J.G. (1983). Explaining educability: An investigation of political support for the Children with Learning Disabilities Act of 1969. *British Journal of Sociology of Education, 4*(2), 125–140.

Church, S., & Newman, J.M. (1986). Danny. A case history of an instructionally induced reading problem. In J.M. Newman (Ed.), *Whole language, theory and practice* (pp. 169–179). Portsmouth, NH: Heinemann.

Cousins, N. (1985). *Nobel Prize conversations by Sir John Eccles, Roger Sperry, Ilya Prigogine, Brian Josephson.* Dallas: Saybrook Publishing.

Dodson-Gray, E. (1982). *Patriarchy as a conceptual trap.* Wellesley, MA: Roundtable Press.

Doll, W.E. (1986a). *Curriculum beyond stability, Schon, Prigogine, Piaget.* Paper presented at Bergamo Curriculum Conference, Bergamo, OH.

Doll, W.E. (1986b). Prigogine: A new sense of order, a new curriculum. *Theory Into Practice, 25*(1), 10–16.

Dudley-Marling, C. (1986). Assessing the written language development of learning disabled children: An holistic perspective. *Canadian Journal of Special Education, 2*(1), 33–43.

Edgerton, R. (1967). *The cloak of competence. Stigma in the lives of the mentally retarded.* Berkeley: University of California Press.

Erickson, F. (1984). School literacy, reasoning, and civility: An anthropologist's perspective. *Review of Educational Research, 54*(4), 525–546.

Ewoldt, C. (1982). *The Kendall demonstration elementary school language arts curriculum guide.* Washington, DC: Gallaudet University, KDES Outreach.

Ewoldt, C. (1985). A descriptive study of the developing literacy of young hearing-impaired children. *Volta Review, 87*(5), 109–126.

Fisher, C.T., & Rizzo, A.A. (1974). A paradigm for humanizing special education. *The Journal of Special Education, 8,* 321–329.

Forness, S.R., & Kavale, K.A. (1987). Holistic inquiry and the scientific challenge in special education: A reply to Iano. *Remedial and Special Education, 8*(1), 47–51.

Fox, H. (1983). *Original blessing. A primer in creation spirituality.* Santa Fe, NM: Bear & Co.

French, M. (1985). *Beyond power. On woman, men, and morals.* New York: Ballantine.

Frye, N. (1981). Where metaphors and equations meet: A convergence of the arts and sciences. *The Chronicle of Higher Education, 21*(7), 64.

Gergen, K. (1985). The social constructionist movement in modern psychology. *American Psychologist, 40*(3), 266–275.

Gergen, K., & Gergen, M. (1982). Explaining human conduct: Form and function. In P. Secord (Ed.), *Explaining human behavior: Consciousness, human action, and social structure* (pp. 127–154). Beverly Hills, CA: Sage.

Giroux, H.A. (1983). Theories of reproduction and resistance in the new sociology of education: A critical analysis. *Harvard Educational Review, 53*(3), 257–293.

Gould, S.J. (1981). *The mismeasure of man.* New York: Norton.

Graves, D.H. (1985). All children can write. *Learning Disabilities Focus, 1*(1), 36–43.

Hasselbrüs, P. (1982). I.E.P.s and a whole language model of language arts. *Topics in Learning & Learning Disabilities, 1*(4), 17–21.

Heshusius, L. (1981). *Meaning in life as experienced by persons labeled retarded in a group home: A participant observation study.* Springfield, IL: Thomas.

Heshusius, L. (1982). At the heart of the advocacy dilemma: A mechanistic world view. *Exceptional Children, 49,* 6–13.

Heshusius, L. (1984a). The survival story of a non-reader: An interview. *Journal of Learning Disabilities, 7,* 472–476.

Heshusius, L. (1984b). Why would they and I want to do it? A phenomenological-theoretical view of special education. *Learning Disability Quarterly, 7,* 363–368.

Heshusius, L. (1986a). Paradigm shifts and special education: A response to Ulman and Rosenberg. *Exceptional Children, 52,* 461–465.

Heshusius, L. (1986b). Pedagogy, special education, and the lives of young children: A critical and futuristic perspective. *Journal of Education, 168*(3), 25–38.

Heshusius, L. (1988). The arts, science, and the study of exceptionality. *Exceptional Children, 55*(1), 60–66.

Hesse, M. (1980). *Revolutions and reconstructions in the philosophy of science.* Bloomington: Indiana University Press.

Holzman, L., & LaCerva, C. (1986). *Development, learning and learning disabilities.* Paper presented at the Eighth International Conference on Learning Disabilities, Kansas City, MO.

Iano, R.P. (1986). The study and development of teaching: With implications for the advancement of special education. *Remedial and Special Education, 7*(5), 50–61.

Iano, R.P. (1987). Rebuttal: Neither the absolute certainty of prescriptive law nor a surrender to mysticism. *Remedial and Special Education, 8*(1), 52–61.

Jacob, E. (1987). Qualitative research traditions: A review. *Review of Educational Research, 57*(1), 1–50.

Jantsch, E. (1980). *The self-organizing universe: Scientific and human implications of the emerging paradigm of education.* Oxford, England: Pergamon Press.

Johnson, M.C. (1977). *A review of research methods in education.* Chicago: Rand McNally.

Kavale, K.A., & Forness, S.R. (1985). Learning disability and the history of science: Paradigm or paradox? *Remedial and Special Education, 6*(4), 12–23.

Koestler, A. (1967). *The ghost in the machine.* London: Hutchinson.

Kuhn, T.S. (1962). *The structure of scientific revolutions.* Chicago: University of Chicago Press.

Kuhn, T.S. (1970). *The structure of scientific revolutions.* Chicago: University of Chicago Press.

Lakoff, G., & Johnson, M. (1980). *Metaphors we live by.* Chicago: University of Chicago Press.

Lather, P. (1986). Research as praxis. *Harvard Educational Review, 56*(3), 257–277.

Leigh, J.E. (1980). Whole language approaches: Premises and possibilities. *Learning Disability Quarterly, 3,* 62–69.

LeShan, L., & Margenau, H. (1982). *Einstein's space and van Gogh's sky. Physical reality and beyond.* New York: Macmillan.

Lewis, F. (1983, November 13). Quantum mechanics of politics and life. *Des Moines Sunday Register,* pp. 1, 3.

Lincoln, Y.S., & Guba, E.G. (1985). *Naturalistic inquiry.* Beverly Hills, CA: Sage.

Lloyd, J.W. (1987). The art and science of research on teaching. *Remedial and Special Education, 8*(1), 44–46.

Mann, L., & Phillips, W.A. (1967). Fractional practices in special education: A critique. *Exceptional Children, 33,* 311–317.

Masterman, M. (1970). The nature of a paradigm. In I. Lakatos & A. Mosgrave (Eds.), *Criticism and the growth of knowledge* (pp. 59–89). Cambridge, England: Cambridge University Press.

McDermott, R.P. (1974). Achieving school failure: An anthropological approach to illiteracy and social stratification. In G.D. Spindler (Ed.), *Education and cultural process: Toward an anthropology of education* (pp. 82–118). New York: Holt, Rinehart & Winston.

McDermott, R.P. (1977). The ethnography of speaking and reading. In R. Shuy (Ed.), *Linguistics* (pp. 153–185). Newark, DE: International Reading Association.

McKean, K. (1985). Intelligence: New ways to measure the wisdom of man. *Discover, 6*(10). 25–41.

McNutt, G. (1984). A holistic approach to language arts instruction in the resource room. *Learning Disability Quarterly, 7*, 315–320.

Meek, M., Armstrong, S., Austerfield, V., Graham, J., & Plackett, E. (1983). *Achieving literacy. Longitudinal studies of adolescents learning to read.* Boston: Routledge & Kegan Paul.

Mehan, H., Hertweck, A., & Meihls, L. (1986). *Handicapping the handicapped. Decision making in students' educational careers.* Stanford, CA: Stanford University Press.

Messick, S. (1984). Assessment in context: Appraising student performance in relation to instructional quality. *Educational Researcher, 13*(1), 3–8.

Miller, C.M.M. (1985). *The viability of students with special learning needs remaining in regular classrooms: Perceptions of students, teachers, parents and administrators, and observations of teachers' responses to student diversity.* Unpublished thesis, York University, Toronto.

Mitchell, R.M. (1980). Is professionalism succumbing to a push-button mentality? *Counterpoint, 1*(2), 14.

Morgan, G.M. (1983). *Beyond method. Strategies for social research.* Beverly Hills, CA: Sage.

Ogilvy, J. (1986). The current shift of paradigms. Revision, *A Journal of Consciousness and Change, 9*(1), 11–17.

Popkewitz, T.S. (1984). *Paradigm and ideology in educational research. The social functions of the intellectual.* New York: Falmer Press.

Polkinghorne, D. (1983). *Methodology for the human sciences.* Albany: State University of New York Press.

Poplin, M. (1984a). Research practices in learning disabilities. *Learning Disability Quarterly, 7*, 2–5.

Poplin, M. (1984b). Summary rationalizations, apologies and farewell: What we don't know about the learning disabled. *Learning Disability Quarterly, 7*, 130–135.

Poplin, M. (1984c). Toward an holistic view of persons with learning disabilities. *Learning Disability Quarterly, 7*, 290–294.

Poplin, M. (1985). Reductionism from the medical model to the classroom: The past, present and future of learning disabilities. *Research Communications in Psychology, Psychiatry and Behavior, 10*(1&2), 37–70.

Prigogine, I., & Stengers, I. (1984). *Order out of chaos. Man's new dialogue with nature.* New York: Bantam Books.

Radencich, M.C. (1984). The status of learning disabilities: The emergence of a paradigm or a paradigm shift? *Learning Disabilities, 3*(7), 79–89.

Randall, F. (1984). Why scholars become storytellers. *The New York Times Book Review*, pp. 1, 31.

Reid, D.K., & Hresko, W.P. (1981). *A cognitive approach to learning disabilities.* Toronto: McGraw-Hill.

Rhodes, L.K., & Dudley-Marling, C.C. (1988). *Teaching reading and writing to learning disabled and remedial learners: A holistic perspective.* Portsmouth, NH: Heinemann.

Rhodes, W.C. (1987). Ecology and the new physics. *Behavior Disorders, 13*(1), 58–61.

Ritzer, G. (1975). Sociology: A multiparadigm science. *The American Sociologist, 10*, 156–167.

Rorty, R. (1982). Method, social science and social hope. In R. Rorty (Ed.), *Consequences of pragmatism* (pp. 191–229). Minneapolis: University of Minnesota Press.

Sadawa, D., & Caley, M.T. (1985). Dissipative structures: New metaphors for becoming in education. *Educational Researcher, 14*(3), 13–25.

Sanders, N. (1986). *Friendship perceptions of learning disabled students. A participant observation study.* Unpublished thesis, York University, Toronto.

Sarason, S.B. (1981). *Psychology misdirected.* New York: Macmillan-The Free Press.

Schon, D. (1983). *The reflective practitioner.* New York: Basic Books.

Scully, M.G. (1980). Social scientists, unable to explain some issues, turning to humanists. *The Chronicle of Higher Education, 20*(5), 1, 4.

Sleeter, C.E. (1986). Learning disabilities: The social construction of a special education category. *Exceptional Children, 53*, 46–54.

Smith, F. (1983). How children learn. In D. Carnine, D. Elkind, A.D. Henrickson, D. Meichenbaum, R.L. Sieben, & F. Smith (Eds.), *Interdisciplinary voices in learning disabilities* (pp. 187–214). Austin, TX: PRO-ED.

Smith, F. (1986). *Insult to intelligence.* New York: Arbor House.

Smith, J., & Heshusius, L. (1986). Closing down the conversation: The end of the quantitative-qualitative debate among educational inquirers. *Educational Researcher, 15*(1), 4–12.

Smith, M.L. (1982). *How educators decide who is learning disabled. Challenge to psychology and public policy in the schools.* Springfield, IL: Thomas.

Thurman, S.K., & Widerstrom, A.H. (1985). *Young children with special needs. A developmental and ecological approach.* Newton, MA: Allyn & Bacon.

Tomlinson, S. (1982). *A sociology of special education.* London: Routledge & Kegan Paul.

Torgesen, J.K. (1986). Learning disabilities theory: Its current state and future prospects. *Journal of Learning Disabilities, 19*, 399–407.

Tucker, J.A. (1985). Curriculum-based assessment: An introduction. *Exceptional Children, 52*, 199–204.

Ulman, J.D., & Rosenberg, M.S. (1986). Science and superstition in special education. *Exceptional Children, 52*, 459–460.

Valle, R.S. (1981). Relativistic quantum psychology. In R.S. Valle & R. von Eckarteberg (Eds.), *The metaphors of consciousness* (pp. 417–434). New York: Plenum.

Van Steenbergen, B. (1986, October). Holisme schreeuwt om kritische sympathie. *Elseviers Magazine*, pp. 81–92.

Von Bertalanffy, L. (1967). *Robots, men and minds.* New York: George Braziller.

Von Bertalanffy, L. (1968). *General system theory.* New York: George Braziller.

Weaver, C. (1988). *Reading process and practice.* From socio-psycholinguistics to whole language. Portsmouth, NH: Heinemann.

Willis, P.E. (1977). *Learning to labour.* Westmead, England: Saxon House.

Winkler, K.J. (1985). Questioning the science in social science. Scholars signal a 'Turn to Interpretation.' *Chronicle of Higher Education, 30*(17), 1–3.

Wolf, F.A. (1981). *Taking the quantum leap.* New York: Harper & Row.

2.4   On What Basis Hope?

Modern Progress and Postmodern Possibilities

Scot Danforth

Abstract: Modern and postmodern versions of hope as they apply to services for persons labeled as having mental retardation were examined. Proponents of modernism construct hope as relying on an ever-improving science to accurately comprehend mental retardation and other disabilities and the effectiveness of professional interventions. This myth of scientific progress is traced in various forms through American intellectual history to the development of special education as interventionist social science. Advocates of postmodernism cast doubt upon the grand narrative of modernism and critique modern social science as perpetuating stigmatized "mentally retarded" identities through the exercise of power. A rhetorical analysis of the current controversy over facilitated communication demonstrates the utilization of the language of modern science for its power effects in special education discourse.

Special education and hope seem to go hand in hand. Common sense tells us that individuals could not work to improve the lives of students with mental retardation without carrying and embodying hope in their professional practice. Despite the powerful and assumed role of hope in special education, it is an unexamined aspect of work in this professional field. My purpose in this paper is to provide a deep analysis of the philosophical and historical bases of hope in special education. I describe two separate and conflicting modes of hope: the modern version of hope as

Danforth, S. (1997). On what basis hope? Modern and postmodern possibilities. *Mental Retardation, 35*(2), 93–106. Reprinted by permission.

a project of progressive social science devoted to the comprehension and correction of mental retardation and other disability conditions, and a postmodern (Note 1) version of hope as an ongoing critique of the scientific ground and language by which individuals are habitually and casually devalued with disabling terms and identities such as "mental retardation." Although the modern version of hope promises a steady climb toward more enlightened findings and facts about mental retardation and services, for the postmodern mode claims that a critical dialogue is necessary, wherein professionals, parents, and, of course, labeled persons may confront, contest, and perhaps overturn the standard mental retardation construct.

Modern discourse in special education emerges from an American historical myth of scientific progress, what Gergen (1991) called "the grand narrative of modernism" (p. 30). This explanatory story extends from the Enlightenment rationalism of this nation's founding fathers to present day mainstream social science research to some faith-held, extrapolated future date when scientific knowledge and technological practice peak at a mastery of all necessary variables. This totalizing narrative links the revolutionary birth and subsequent political, economic, and moral rise of this democratic civilization with the deliberate advancement of science, industry, and technology. In the 20th century, this grand narrative of progress may be seen in the growth of interventionist social sciences (e.g., sociology, psychology, education, social work) and the many allied human service professions that ground their practices in these empirical research knowledges.

What does modernism mean for special education philosophy in the field of mental retardation? Modernist special educators hold that the profession should follow the lead of empirical social science to describe accurately the reality of mental retardation and identify the modes of intervention best suited to those conditions. From this perspective, hope lies in the gradual, scientific production of improved approximations of "truth" and the development of intervention technologies, practices, programs, and instruments "that work" according to the truth-clarifying research. Progress, the scientific development of increasingly accurate representations of human living and more powerful interventions to positively adjust that living, and the hope of helping special education students are taken to be conceptually and morally conjoined.

In stark and critical contrast, the post-modern professional concepts and practices (Note 2) of hope break from the modern tradition of progressive empiricism. Postmodern practices found hope not on the production of generalized, context-free facts about mental retardation and interventions but on the creation of human relationships and conversations in which "mental retardation" as a standard and overriding definition of self can be contested and more positive personal identities, roles, and activities constructed.

Proponents of postmodern positions critique modern empiricism and propose alternative possibilities for action. Postmodernists find the historical myth of scientific progress to be a socially constructed story of uncertain truth value, a narrative that relies on the naive assumption that human knowledge and ability are flowing in continuous motion through time toward perfection or eternal betterment. Lacking a transhistorical perspective from which to evaluate the truth value of modernism, postmodern scholars critique the sociopolitical effects of that narrative, finding it to be a dominating story with profound moral and political implications in the lives of the children served by special education programs. To postmodern special educators, the most notable result of modernism is not scientific progress but the reification of mental retardation as a "real" or "objective" phenomenon of human limitation and stigma in specific lives. Mental retardation, as fashioned in scientific discourse and daily practice, is perpetuated as a natural and unreproachable state, a ready and waiting deficient identity. From this critical analysis, new directions of hope allow us to ask: If the activities of modernist social scientists are not moving professional knowledge, practice, and hope for the improvement of children's lives forward, then how shall professionals, students, and families forge new forms of hope in special education?

In order to more fully compare modern and postmodern perspectives on hope, I must first explicate the philosophical concepts and historical roots of modern special educators' faith in the revelations of social science. This task requires tracing the development of the modernist grand narrative in its varied shapes through over 200 years of American history.

Following my exploration of the history of modern progress and the alternative concepts put forth by postmodern philosophy, I conclude this paper with an analysis of the current professional debate concerning the effectiveness of utilizing facilitated communication with students considered to have mental retardation and severe disabilities. My focus is on the way special education writers on both sides of the facilitated communication debate appropriate the words and phrases of modern science as a power language that excludes and silences the participation of the many nonscientific voices.

MODERNISM: HOPE AS SCIENTIFIC PROGRESS

Gergen (1991) noted that the:

grand narrative of modernism . . . is a story told by Western culture to itself about its journey through time, a story that makes this journey both intelligible and gratifying. The grand narrative is one of continuous upward movement—improvement, conquest, achievement—toward some goal. Science furnishes the guiding metaphor. Had science not demonstrated the capacity to defy gravity, extend the lifespan, harness human energies, and carry voice and image through the stratosphere?' Because of individual's capacities for reason and observation, as expressed in our scientific attitude, utopias were now within our grasp. (p. 30–31)

The dominant discourse among special educators in the field of mental retardation claims the value of modernist research to discover the pieces to the mental retardation puzzle and to find "what works" in practice with children and parents. The ultimate goal is to objectively unveil the approaches and tactics that can be confirmed to produce positive effects in the education and treatment of children with mental retardation. These "best practice" approaches, it is commonly stated, should then be generalized, encapsulated in standard form, and dispensed for use by professionals throughout the nation.

Professionals, family members, and students who pioneer pathways that are not supported by scientific knowledge, including those involved in inclusion programs and facilitated communication, are criticized by modernist special educators as promulgating "long-odds approaches . . . [that]) foster unrealistic hopes against formidable odds" (Kauffman, 1993, p. 12). From this vantage point, professional and nonprofessional activities that are supported by social science research are valued as contributions to a reality-based hope for concrete improvements in the education of "exceptional" students. Such hope is viewed as "realistic" or "truthful," unswayed by the power of overhyped fads and irrational emotional currents. In contrast, those innovations and developments not sanctioned by modernist social science are viewed as lacking a basis in reality. They are spirited "fanaticism," the long-short pipedreams and tomfoolery of persons lacking the reason of empirical science (in a later discussion I explore this notion in relation to the current debate over the use of facilitated communication).

For now, I ask: How have modernist special educators arrived at such a faith in the progress of social science? How has hope for the improvement of the lives of persons called "disabled" come to be viewed as inherently dependent on the progress of social science knowledge? In response to these questions, a brief historical analysis of the myth of scientific progress in America will be presented based on the works of Gergen (1991, 1994b), Randall (1940), and Marcell (1974).

AMERICAN MYTH OF SCIENTIFIC PROGRESS

Perhaps in America, as in no other Western country, the idea of progress has played the most powerful role in guiding and unifying a national sense of identity, history, and purpose. A New World burst forth from the political fervor of the Enlightenment to launch a uniquely American brand of progressive mentality. This American idea of progress, as it has developed through a wide range of intellectual ideas and popular movements over the past 2 centuries, has enabled citizens to create great unity in common interpretations of a victorious civilization rising up an ever-improving road. Stretching from the rationalism of the founding fathers to the current incarnation of progress in the professional application of modernist social science knowledge as redemption for a variety of social ills, this road brings us notably to our special education profession as intervention for the "social problem" of students with mental retardation. Although the central cultural meaning of progress was recast in varying forms and lights over those many decades, it remained ever closely tied to both modern science and a nationalistic, optimistic American identity.

Drawing from Marcell (1974) and Gergen (1991), I posit progress as a national phenomenon passing through four historical eras: rationalist (1750–1815), romantic (1815–1860), evolutionary (1860–1900), and modernist (1900–present). These eras should be viewed not so much as precise periods in American history than as provisional historical categories that allow me to trace the changing nature of the concept of progress over vast spans of time. Borrowing from Foucault's (1980) understanding of historical research, I view these categories as "fictions" of a sort, as late 20th century scholars' limited depictions of the past. My purpose in organizing and describing American history in this way is to examine the theme of progress through time.

Be aware that this history emphasizes progress as championed primarily by those privileged American populations that viewed themselves as benefiting from the growth and development of industry, technology, and public institutions of social control. Concepts and practices of progress typically were not directed by women, the poor, African Americans, children, persons considered to have disabilities, and new immigrants. These politically marginalized groups were often included in movements of progress insomuch as they served as persons to be sacrificed and controlled to the progressive benefit of the privileged class of men. Also, keep in mind that each of the three premodern historical distillations persist in various aspects of present America, social science, and special education. For example, much of the spirit (if not the practical orientation) of special education might easily be described as modern day romanticism, efforts growing from the heart and relying on love.

Rationalism

Many leading 18th century thinkers, including Thomas Jefferson, Benjamin Franklin, George Washington, and Thomas Paine, propounded a general philosophical position called *rationalism*. The common assumptions of rationalists centered around the orderly, mechanized structure of Nature and the ability of human reason to understand and thereby adjust Nature for man's own purposes and fulfillment. The rationalists often admixed their early rational science with theology, placing God at the helm of Nature. Essentially, God had constructed Nature as a sort of cosmic watchworks full of spinning reels, lifting levers, and tumbling cogs. He likewise endowed people with the rationality to decipher the static laws of Nature's machinery and utilize that knowledge to manipulate Nature for the greater benefit of humankind.

Progress, from this perspective, was viewed to be the gradual fruition of God's plan, the movement of humanity toward a fulfillment of Nature's laws in the context of society, a reflection of the natural in the social. The ways of humans, most specifically the form and operations of government in achieving a democratic social order, should be in accord with the divine laws of Nature. In the case of American rationalism, this meant that the institutions and principles of government must protect the rights of individuals to live free from unnecessary encroachment. Marcell (1974) stated:

Progress, it was assumed, would follow naturally from the establishment of political and social institutions whose form and function gave individuals the greatest freedom to exercise their foreordained rights. Seen in this light, history was the story of man's slow, progressive recognition of his own humanity, and progress became the special intention of the author of nature. (p. 57)

Certain individual rights—"life, liberty, and the pursuit of happiness"—were conceived of as "natural"

aspects of God's constant and unfailing design, to be reflected and supported in human social design.

Romanticism

Although the rationalism of early America involved humanity bowing down before God and the divine structure of things, it also carried a subtext that ironically promoted individualism. After all, it was humans who had the rational power to interpret the principles of the divine mechanism, humans both prostrate before God and oddly rising up as quasi-divine knowing subjects.

From the rationalist emphasis on the reasoning individual as transcendent knower came romanticism, the celebration of the internal subjectivities of the individual. Beneath the surface veneer of reason lay, as Gergen (1991) noted, "the world of the deep interior" (p. 20), a mysterious place populated by powerful essences: heart, soul, passion, imagination, and love. The acts of knowing truth, beauty, or goodness were no longer taken to be completely rational undertakings. The epistemological power of rationality was augmented or even supplanted by subjective sensibility, self-knowledge, and personal reflection. Look within to find one's truth and hold that truth dearly.

And what of progress? Although some aspects of romanticism (such as the skepticism of Thoreau about the benefits of technology) questioned the grand narrative of America progressing to a brighter tomorrow, romanticists primarily adopted the myth of progress and reerected it upon subjective foundations. Progress was not merely "out there" in the improving movement of a distant natural design, but one could sense and feel it internally through interior reflection. For example, Marcell (1974) quoted William Ellery Channing's romanticist advice:

Be true to our own convictions. Intimations from your own souls of something more perfect than others teach, if faithfully followed, give us a consciousness of spiritual force and progress. (p. 87)

Looking within, plumbing one's interior depths, would bring knowledge of what is true and natural, of the great potential for personal and social development. Such interior searching would demonstrate the inevitability of the upward slant of American history.

This faith in the progress of America produced a conservative, self-satisfied America. Most Americans of the early 19th century believed that imperfections or problems existing in American society should be left to run their natural course. The institutions of public life, developed and maintained in agreement with the grand natural design, would gradually solve any difficulties without intentional intervention by citizens. American optimism and confidence in the advancing motion of history precipitated a general laissez-faire attitude about social ills. Individuals should draw from within to improve themselves, but the broader social world would take care of itself.

Evolution

Charles Darwin's theory of evolution, appearing first in *Origin of the Species* in 1859, fueled the fires of argument on the issue of progress. Darwin provided opportunities for both the empiricist critique and the popular reinvention of the myth of progressive.

On the one hand, Darwin had delivered a meticulous empirical account, a work of precise observation outlining the minute operations of natural change. In doing so, he explained species transition not in reference to God and the grand mechanism of Nature but through an almost haphazard scheme of mere probability. Developments in nature, Darwin claimed, were greatly due to chance, a hypothesis running in direct confrontation with previous formalistic assumptions about the constant and reliable order of Nature.

From this line of reasoning arose the radical empiricists' stance of historical and secular neutrality, a denial of any knowledge of grand designs and an affirmation of the need to scientifically observe specific, distinct phenomena. This strict form of Baconian science attempted to ignore assumptions of social and historical progression in order to observe only the object of study in and of itself. Science, however, was already entangled in an historical, cultural tale of America perfecting civilization, and the self-proclaimed "neutral" empiricist could not help but go along for the nationalistic ride.

In fact, American scientists and citizens typically melded Darwin's challenging work with earlier concepts of historical progress to create a revived brand of progress. Popular author Herbert Spencer led a movement that subsumed the particular workings of natural and sexual selection under the larger story of the march toward natural and human perfection (Marcell, 1974). Spencer explained the theory of evolution as biological advance toward species perfection. He then extended this concept to the human social organism, claiming that society itself is evolving constantly toward higher, more efficient forms. Through Spencer's widely read books, writings far more popular than Darwin's own works, a recast evolutionary theory was enlisted to the support of the century-old story of the continuous improvement of scientific knowledge wedded to the betterment of American life. Progress, in post-Darwinian garb, moved ever forward as the bearer of hope. Political leaders, academics, and informed citizens typically comprehended the present in terms of the trusted, rising road ahead.

Modernism and Interventionist Social Science

As the 20th century dawned, it became clear to many that the practical application of natural science knowledge had brought a particular kind of progress, a proliferation of an urbanized, industrial, and technological culture. America had its factories, bridges, tall buildings, and enormous cities. Yet, the apparent fall-out of this capitalistic/technological expansion was a variety of social ills, including school failure, delinquency, crime, and poverty. The cure for these social ills and the hope for social progress became entrusted to the imitator of natural science: the new, developing social sciences and the social science professions. An experimental science of humanity and society would be unleashed to intervene in spaces of imperfection and weakness, suffering and disorder.

No depiction of the development of modern social science would prove adequate to the task of explaining the common philosophical ground behind the geometric growth of the fields of psychology, social work, education, and special education in this century. My analysis, therefore, is limited to the career of one of the early creators of interventionist social science, Lester Frank Ward, a man who may rightfully be called the father of American sociology. Although it would be a foolish stretch to claim that special education science was born of sociology, a brief analysis of Ward's philosophy of an interventionist social science provides great insight into modernist special education assumptions about the necessary and powerful role of empirical knowledge in relation to hopeful professional practice. Ward's extension of natural science principles into the nascent field of sociology demonstrates both the attempt of social science to imitate the obvious successes of the natural sciences and the continuing narrative of progress newly imbedded in the hope to heal American society.

Lester Frank Ward developed a science of human, social living based within the principles and evident success of natural science, growing from a specific interpretation of the work of Darwin (Marcell, 1974; Randall, 1940). Although many claimed that society evolved in a manner analogous to biological evolution, relying on haphazard advancement via probability, Ward disagreed. He theorized two distinct forms of evolution: (a) the Darwinian mode of genetic or natural evolution that described the random and slow progression of nature to more perfect forms and (b) a conscious, intentional mode of social evolution in which people applied his scientific knowledge to push social improvement along at an increased pace. Because humans may understand the operations of evolutionary development in the social sphere, they should then intervene to artificially boost the natural process, making social progress more efficient and less time-consuming.

The power to know the truths of Nature as articulated by the revolutionary era rationalists and as demonstrated by Darwin had gradually become the power to know the truths of Society. A rational social science would accurately describe human, social activity just as an earlier natural science had unlocked the laws of physical motion. Notably, as manifested in Ward's interventionist sociology, the modern social sciences combined the task of knowing truths with the related mission of affecting social change. A constantly improving comprehension of individual activity and social problems—a gradual but steady piecing together the pieces of the puzzle—would place the new social science in the most hopeful position of all: the cultural and historical place of redemptive power. Human problems could be solved through the faithful application of an interventionist brand of modern social science.

BIRTH OF SPECIAL EDUCATION AS INTERVENTIONIST SOCIAL SCIENCE

Where does the early development of special education fit in with this development of an interventionist, modern social science? More specifically, what was the connection between this social science and the work of early professionals and the development of early institutions in the field of mental retardation?

Space limitations in this paper demand that I address this issue in direct and brief fashion. The work of Henry Goddard in the first 2 decades of the 20th century provides us with a useful glimpse at the role of modern social science (namely, measurement psychology) in the growth of mental retardation as a construct and a legitimate professional field (Smith, 1985; Trent, 1994).

Conducting research at the Training School at Vineland with institutionalized, "mentally deficient"

persons, Goddard was one of the first American psychologists to import and apply the intelligence testing instruments of Binet and Simon. The intelligence test allowed specialists to "objectively" classify persons along a graded scale, to separate the "normal" from the mentally deficient, and to classify the mentally deficient within ranges of intellectual deficit.

Goddard's application of intelligence testing to the identification and categorization of mentally deficient persons was important for two reasons. First, the importation of the mathematical schemes of measurement from natural sciences provided a dramatic boost of legitimacy to the fields of psychology and early special education. These disciplines and professions accessed a source of tremendous power and credibility within Western society through alliance with the assumed accuracy, progressive motion, and morality of modern science. It is not surprising that Goddard's utilization of intelligence testing at Vineland quickly led to his rise as a leading psychologist in the field of mental deficiency and Vineland as the preeminent research and early special education teacher training site.

The second reason that Goddard's use of cognitive measurement was important involves the theorized relation between mental deficiency, immorality, and a range of early 20th century social problems. Trent (1994) described Goddard, his professional colleagues at institutions for the "feebleminded," and the public at-large as subscribing to a general fear of "the menace of feebleminded" (p. 131). In both popular and the scientific publications, social vices such as criminality, alcohol abuse, unemployment, and sexual promiscuity were linked to mental deficiency.

Goddard claimed that the relation between immoral behavor and mental deficiency was causal. Trent (1994) explained that

> Goddard was . . . convinced . . . about the causal relationship between social vice and mental deficiency. The linkage, he came to see, was simple. At least two-thirds of all feeblemindedness was the result of hereditary factors. . . . Added to this was the fact that a high proportion of social vices was linked to feeblemindedness. His preliminary studies suggested that crime did not cause the feebleminded to inherit feeblemindedness: logic would indicate, therefore, that feeblemindness affects rates of crime. (pp. 162–163)

The variety of social ills that concerned Americans could be explained primarily in terms of mental deficiency. Specifically, mentally deficient persons, due to their pathology, were the purveyors of social vices. In accordance with prominent scientific thought at the time, feeblemindedness was assumed to be genetically inherited. As Goddard fully explained in his famous study of the Kallikak family, immorality was being passed on from one feebleminded generation to the next.

Perhaps the greatest insight into the early development of special education as a scientific practice based in intelligence testing can be gleaned from an analysis of the connection between modern social science and the hope to cure America of social vices in Goddard's work. Through the use of intelligence testing, Goddard claimed to have discovered a new class of feebleminded persons whom he called "morons." This group was undoubtedly the most dangerous of the feebleminded menace. Morons, according to Goddard, had the physical characteristics of "normal" persons and the intelligence of high-range mental deficients. In essence, Goddard claimed that there was an entire group of feebleminded persons who remained undetected, who had intermixed with the normal population, and passed by appearance for normal. Given the propensity of the feebleminded to commit acts of social misconduct, the existence of this class of morons in the general population was a frightening prospect. Evil was hidden among the population, but who could say where? (Or, more accurately, who?)

Goddard and his colleagues at Vineland proposed that intelligence tests be used to identify the "immoral element" for purposes of exclusion and population control. He and many professional leaders at that time advocated that the feebleminded be completely isolated from the mainstream in residential institutions. In addition, he joined the then-popular eugenics movement, supporting the surgical termination of the reproductive capacities of mentally deficient persons. Through exclusion and eugenics, Goddard believed that feeblemindedness could be wiped out through scientific intervention, thus solving the vast array of American social problems and ensuring the continued progress of this society (Smith, 1985; Trent, 1994).

At the recent crest of this wave of modern progress rises present-day special education, a field devoted to the practical improvement of the lives of a specific group of children commonly viewed as social or educational failures. Proponents of the centrality of modern social science to special education continue the story of a progressing science in relation to the hopeful mission of helping students with men-

tal retardation and their families. From this modernist perspective, professional hope must rest on a faith in the grand narrative of scientific progress led by special education researchers.

But what if one, in agreement with philosophers Nietzsche and Foucault, holds no faith in the modernist story of progress? What if one does not believe that social science provides gradually improving pictures of social reality? What if the certain and upward motion of modern progress is viewed as neither certain nor upward-moving? Postmodern philosophers in many academic fields, including education and special education, are posing these and other critical questions about the truthfulness of the modernist account.

POSTMODERNISM AND HOPE IN SPECIAL EDUCATION

> What binds societies together are common vocabularies and common hopes. The vocabularies are, typically, parasitic on the hopes—in the sense that the principal function of the vocabularies is to tell stories about the future outcomes which compensate for present sacrifices.... To retain social hope, members of such a society need to be able to tell themselves a story about how things get better, and see no insuperable obstacles to this story's coming true. (Rorty, 1989, p. 86)

A postmodern philosophy of special education asserts that the current governing story, the guiding scheme of modern social science, no longer provides a valuable basis for hope and unity in the struggle to educate children described as "mentally retarded." Postmodernists typically eschew any universal guiding story as deceptive and totalizing, providing not generalizable or useful facts but a harmful privileging of some knowledges and vocabularies over others of lesser sociocultural power. In brief, the modernist grand narrative cannot be determined to be objectively true. Its maintenance and re-creation in daily practice relies on the faith and actions of persons who believe in the American myth of historical progress. Postmodernists claim that adherence to this historical tale by professionals, students, and families perpetuates the belief that certain persons in society have a deficit condition called "mental retardation" that requires professional intervention and institutional control. As a result, postmodern educators encourage a professional shift from the primary explanatory story of modern social science to a pluralistic, conversational arena in which a multitude of smaller, nongeneralizable stories may be told by the diversity of participants in special education (Gergen, 1991, 1994a, 1994b; Rosenau, 1992).

In the place of the dominating grand narrative, postmodernism supports a patchwork quilt of many stories, a provisional and ever-changing fabric honoring diverse cultural traditions and multiple versions of "the way it is." A place of many legitimate stories is an arena of dialogue and possibility, allowing individuals and groups to claim their voices, call out their own identities, and forge paths of action that need not comply with the scientific dictates of truth. The scientific goal of progressively finding and describing truth is thus replaced by the moral and political goals of supporting human freedom and community.

Postmodern special educators (Danforth, Rhodes, & Smith, 1995; Duplass & Smith, 1995; Sailor & Skrtic, 1995; Skrtic, 1991) contend that the hope of educating and supporting children considered to have disabilities can no longer be fueled and conceptualized through the modern social science story, that "insuperable obstacles to this story's coming true" (Rorty, 1989, p. 86) have indeed arisen. Scientific truth is in trouble.

Modern Truth in Crisis

A conceptual shift, "tectonic" in its implications has taken place. We ground things, now, on a moving earth. There is no longer a place of overview (mountaintop) from which to map human ways of life, no Archimidean point from which to represent the world. (Clifford, 1986, p. 22)

If university special educators wander dangerously across the positivistic doorstep to sample life at the academy, they may find philosophical crisis far beyond squabblings over the technical acceptability of new research methods, extending to powerful doubts concerning the project of finding and explaining truth itself. A number of movements described as postmodern or poststructural have struck at the very core of modern academic disciplines, contesting and undermining the underlying assumption that an objective world is knowable and may be established through the workings of a neutral, rational science. Gergen (1991), in his analysis of the academic upheaval, stated:

Most of the cherished beliefs that undergird the traditional goals of research and teaching are in eclipse. Some consider the demise of traditional assumptions to be an event little short of catastrophe, to part with the longstanding ideals of truth and understanding is to invite chaos, first in the academic world and then

in society generally. Others feel an innervating sense that history is at a turning point, that a new and exciting era is in the making. (p. 82)

This "catastrophe" or "turning point," depending on one's perspective, is evident through much of academia as postmodern concepts have swept into writings in numerous disciplines, including anthropology (Wolf, 1992), history (Featherstone, 1991; Hassan & Hassan, 1983), psychology (Gergen, 1991, 1994a, 1994b; Kvale, 1992), sociology (Denzin, 1991; Dickens & Fontana, 1994), philosophy (Poster, 1990; Rorty, 1979, 1989), and education (Giroux, 1991; Usher, 1994). The intellectual stir in opposition to the domination of the modernist scientific project is rising in many bubbling caldrons.

Not surprisingly, the knowledge base of special education is the subject of similar doubt and critique from postmodern perspectives (Danforth et al., 1995; Sailor & Skrtic, 1995). Skrtic (1991) described special education as one of a group of professions based in modern social science that has suffered a crisis of legitimacy since the 1960s. This crisis gained initial impetus from Kuhn's (1962) analysis of the social and paradigmatic nature of science.

Kuhn's (1962) analysis removed scientific activity from the realm of cold rationality and redefined it in terms of social negotiations among perspective-bearing human actors. The truth-producing capabilities of science, according to Kuhn, do not depend on the strict performance of dry and neutral procedures but flex and change within the social and political interactions of scientists. What is held to produce the theoretical ground of authorized research in a given scientific field is a matter of social agreement among those scientists who have the status and reputation that allow them to declare certain theories and hypotheses to be better than alternatives.

In the modernist vocabulary, we would say that scientists negotiate and agree upon the "biases" that will create the conceptual foreground to their discoveries. A mutually supported set of "biases" is often called a "paradigm," a world view, an assumed way of seeing, perceiving, and describing that allows persons to order experience into rational and livable explanations. Often, modernist researchers have no or little awareness of how their paradigmatic assumptions form a field of assumed truths that greatly determines what aspects of living will be called "data," what data will be collected, how that data will be symbolized and manipulated, and what hypotheses will ultimately be supported by the inquiry. Parallel to Freud's assertion that the hidden weavings of unconscious mental activity influence and determine behavior for reasons beyond conscious awareness, modernist researchers' unacknowledged paradigmatic framework surreptitiously provides the structural limitations, linguistic make-up, and conceptual substance of the knowledge they claim to "find" in the external world (Best, 1994).

The alternative postmodernism should not be viewed as laying claim to a "better" paradigm; a new process holier than the modern, mechanistic way of constructing meaning; a more "truthful" outline for delineating "what is the case." Instead, we should understand postmodernism as a mode of critical vigilance maintaining that no means of describing reality holds universal privilege over alternatives. All descriptions are viewed as limited and partial, confined and influenced by the linguistic and sociohistorical contexts from which persons speak and write. They are understood to be contingent on the sociocultural context, the language community of the speaker, the knower's paradigmatic predisposition, and the historical situation in which the representation occurs.

TRUTH, POWER, AND SPECIAL EDUCATION

The greatest danger of modern social science, from a postmodern position, concerns the overwhelming authority generally accorded to both the modernist account and the bearers of that account. Knowledge and power are interrelated, integrated socially and institutionally. Each depends on and is supported by the other. The danger of modernism is tyranny in mundane forms, proceeding from what Foucault (1980) described as the "general politics of truth" (p. 131), the regime of power running through the social procedures and mechanisms creating truth and manifested within the applications of truth in social practice. What is made true applies power in the lives of those who are the objects of the truth.

For example, in special education, a series of "objective" and psychometric descriptions of a student can justify a mental retardation diagnosis and extrusion to a special education classroom. A child's social identity is quickly refashioned from "normal" status to debilitated learner through procedures of truth and power, processes whose credibility relies on modernist claims of "value-free," rational operation in depicting an "objective truth." The diagnosis makes up merely one moment of the powerful drama by which a person's social identity is constructed in stigmatized form. The on-going services provided by professionals and institutions continue this devalua-

tion project by further reifying the mental retardation status in the life of the diagnosed and treated individual.

If, as the postmodernists contend, adherence to modernist grand narrative cannot be supported by claims to truthfulness or factuality, and if this history produces not so much hope as the social control of persons considered "abnormal," then special educators may choose to view special education science and disability as historical and bureaucratic artifacts of an international special education that may be questioned and contested on local levels. This practical contestation may bring about opportunities for the making of new stories, nongeneralizable tales of local identity generating valuable meaning for individuals and small educational communities. Students "disabled" by modernism may be re-defined or re-interpreted in terms and priorities that do not include disability concepts and descriptions.

As the hope generated by the myth of social science progress has faltered, space for the making of new versions of hope may arise in special education work with students considered to have mental retardation. Professionals may join with "persons who have disabilities" in their struggle to overturn disability constructs and roles in their own lives. Professionals can ally themselves with labeled persons, their families, and loved ones in efforts to transform social constructions of deficiency and incompetence into relationship-based and self-based understandings of personal power and efficacy.

Issues of power obviously highlight the chasm between modernism and postmodernism in special education. The current controversy surrounding the questioned effectiveness of facilitated communication as a method for some persons considered to have mental retardation and severe disabilities to communicate is a ripe opportunity for examining the implications of a postmodern philosophy in special education. I conclude this paper with an analysis of the rhetoric utilized in the facilitated communication debate, emphasizing the exercise of power in words. I encourage readers to view this as merely one application of postmodern philosophy to a prominent issue.

FACILITATED COMMUNICATION, LANGUAGE, AND POWER

The central issue among both proponents and critics of facilitated communication concerns the question of whether the typed words of facilitated communicators, persons bearing labels of autism, mental retardation, and severe disability, are truly the words authored by those persons. Instead of offering yet another opinion about what I believe to be the truth of the matter, I instead have analyzed the use of power within the various forms of discourse appropriated by prominent commentators, investigating the published words of both the proponents and the critics of facilitated communication. My interest in doing so lies in the way the proponents and critics utilize power in their arguments, the forms of language they gather to their task of constructing a "truthful" argument.

Given the expansive array of writings on both sides of the issue, I have focused my analysis on two specific texts: one in which the authors are proponents of facilitated communication (Biklen & Duchan, 1994) and one in which the authors criticize this approach (Green & Shane, 1994), published simultaneously in a recent special issue of the *Journal of the Association for Persons with Severe Handicaps.*

In an argument later echoed by Simpson and Myles (1995) and Jacobson, Mulick, and Schwartz (1995), Green and Shane (1994) offered an ardent critique of facilitated communication from the perspective of positivistic modern science. They explained that both the authors who support facilitated communication and those who oppose it have conducted observations of persons doing facilitated communication and have described those observations in the professional literature. Throughout their paper, Green and Shane discussed and portrayed the numerous written texts produced as a result of these many observations. How they portrayed these texts is the point of interest.

The language Green and Shane (1994) utilized in describing the many articles on facilitated communication, the many observation-based texts, effectively accomplished two tasks. First, they distinguished the set of critics' texts and the set of proponents' texts to be of two distinct types. Each type consists of a different substance and character than does the other. Second, they presented these types as contrasting in value. Green and Shane asserted that the facilitated communication critics' texts are greatly superior in value to the facilitated communication proponents' texts. One should, therefore, believe the critics and not the proponents. How did Green and Shane's text rhetorically accomplish these tasks? What language did they appropriate and utilize to render the two sets of texts as distinct and unequal?

The rhetorical accomplishment of this inequality of value relies on a contrast of terms I have arranged under the categorical headings of Science and Non-Science. Green and Shane (1994) appropriated the familiar language of Science as descriptors of the set of critical accounts of facilitated communication. In sharp contrast, they appropriated the language of Non-Science as descriptors of the set of accounts that support facilitated communication. Basically, they described the critical texts they support as representing "objective" accounts of the failure of facilitated communication. In fact, they summoned the term *objective* not less than 56 times over the course of their paper, hammering home the point repeatedly. In contrast, they weighed down the observational texts of the facilitated communication proponents with terms ranging from *subjective* to *inaccurate* to comparisons to such superstitious practices as Ouija boards and demon possession.

Table 1 lists a series of words and phrases that Shane and Green (1994) utilized to describe each of the two accounts of facilitated communication. Notice the final phrase in each column evidencing the myth of scientific progress as the narrative scheme guiding the authors' work. As modern knowledge marches forward, the facilitated communication critics are described as contributing to that moral, truthful advance while the facilitated communication proponents' work hinders that progress toward truth.

Shane and Green (1994) are not the first to present these two sets of terms, these two contrasting vocabularies that differentiate truth value according to the priorities of modernism. The average American adult has a fair understanding of the high cultural value commonly accorded to a rhetoric of objectivity and low cultural value often granted to a language of subjectivity. The special education leaders and researchers who make up the readership of the professional journals have been formally schooled in modernism, in the value of the Scientific and the questionable nature of the Non-Scientific. The Shane and Green text exercises power by drawing from the discourse of modernism, rhetorically propelling the facilitated communication critics' accounts to heights of truthfulness while trampling under the pro-facilitated communication accounts in the muck of superstition.

Turning to the Biklen and Duchan (1994) text in support of facilitated communication, I found an ironic attempt to do much the same, to link facilitated communication to the modernist project of science and power. The irony lies in the fact that both Crossley (1994) and Biklen (1990, 1993), the two leading figures in the development of facilitated communication, have apparently opposed the assessment of facilitated communication by means of experimental science. Not surprisingly, Jacobson et al. (1995) described these proponents of facilitated communica-

Table 1
Rhetorical analysis of Shane and Green (1994).

Language describing texts criticizing FC[a]	Language describing texts supporting FC
Objective (used 56 times)	Subjective
Controlled	Uncontrolled
Scientific research	Anecdotes
Rigorous	No empirical evidence from sound scientific research
Basic logic	
Fundamental facts	An ideology that engenders fanaticism
Unambiguous	Testimonials
Empirical	Incidental evidence
Well-controlled experimental analyses	Unreliable
Sound research	Unproven assertions
Extensive empirical evidence	Descriptive studies
Established facts	Nonexperimental observational methods
Scientific evidence	Misleading
Controlled, objective examinations	No objective information
The advancement of knowledge	Implausible arguments
	Inaccurate
	Indirect, naturalistic, incidental evidence
	No objective verification
	No empirical evidence
	Danger to scientific progress

[a]Facilitated communication.

tion as "anti-science." This seems confusing. Have the "anti-science" facilitated communication supporters appropriated the rhetoric of science in their text.

Biklen and Duchan (1994), much like Shane and Green (1994), created a dichotomy of terms in which the writings of the critics' and proponents of facilitated communication are outlined, differentiated, and compared. They drew a clear distinction between the substance and character of the critics, and proponents', written accounts of facilitated communication. This distinction relies on differences of philosophical orientation concerning the construct "mental retardation" and, more importantly, regarding approaches to special education research.

Biklen and Duchan (1994) readily and without substantial critique granted that the critics of facilitated communication are positivist researchers who produce acceptable research knowledge. The facilitated communication critics are undoubtedly scientific in their observations and writings concerning

facilitated communication. In appropriating the power of modern science to their opponents without a critique of positivism on philosophical, ethical, or political grounds, Biklen and Duchan left themselves little room to argue the case in favor of facilitated communication. If the facilitated communication critics are Scientific, and therefore truthful in calling facilitated communication ineffective at best, what convincing argument can be made on facilitated communication's behalf?

Backed into the rhetorical corner, Biklen and Duchan (1994) argued that they, too, are Scientific. They just do a different brand of social science. Instead of working within the tradition of positivism, the supporters of facilitated communication do research within the tradition of phenomenology, what Biklen and Duchan termed *experiential research*. They described this approach as a qualitative, ethnographic form of inquiry in which researchers maintain some of the usual standards of scientific work, for instance, avoiding bias. The argument is made that the two research approaches, positivism and the experiential approach, vary in terms of goals and methods but are each legitimate sciences in their own right.

The issue of whether phenomenology is scientific is not crucial to my purpose. What is of particular interest here in this analysis of the use of language by both sides of the facilitated communication issue is that *each side draws from the rhetoric of modern science for power and legitimacy in making their argument.* The power and apparent necessity of the scientific terminology as a component of a convincing argument concerning facilitated communication is evident. Even the so-called "anti-science" writers did not argue their case without appealing to the vocabulary of modern science for support.

This raises the question of whether any convincing argument or account of a given practice in the field of mental retardation and special education in general may be made without drawing from the powerful discourse of modern science. Is the field of special education so narrowly based that all writers and speakers who seek to be heard and valued must conform to the language and philosophy of modern science? Is the grand narrative of modernism the only story that will be heard?

Postmodern philosophers propose that the sources of hope in the field of mental retardation services erupt from precisely those mouths and writing (or typing) hands that do not speak the language of science. Beyond, under, and beside the booming voice of science, that discourse attempting to conform the activities of many to the truth declarations of few, are voices of hope. These are the contributions of parents, students, family members, front-line practitioners, and program directors. Where the modern quest of a uniform knowledge that informs and limits practice has failed; where the science-prescribed methods to be used with students of a certain label or diagnosis are set aside as irrelevant intrusions on the local task of figuring out what to do and how to do it; where the many partners in the Individual Educational Plan (IEP) and educational planning process no longer depend on the promised progress of research to find a better way; in all these and other spaces where a more equal and open dialogue may be developed between practitioners, parents, and students, the hope of postscientific forms of knowledge abounds. The small stories and the soft voices so often devalued and silenced as subjective and biased, unscientific and unknowing, may become genuine and full participants in conversations about pressing matters in the day-to-day education of students labeled as having mental retardation.

HOPE IN DISCOURSE BEYOND SCIENCE

A rather insistent interviewer once pressed the French philosopher Michel Foucault to agree that Marxism and psychoanalysis were really scientific (Foucault, 1980). Foucault declined to answer the question, commenting instead on the more crucial assumption behind the question. Obviously, the supporters of Marxism and psychoanalysis want their beliefs and ideas to be called "scientific." In doing so, they aspire to the power accorded to modern science as the dominant discourse of the 20th century.

At this point, Foucault (1980) posed a set of questions that, given my previous analysis of the attempts of both sides of the facilitated communication controversy to garner the power of modern science language to their arguments, is strikingly suitable to the postmodern goal of fashioning new forms of hope. In response to the interviewer's question, Foucault said:

> What types of knowledge do you want to disqualify in the very instant of your demand: 'Is it a science'? Which speaking, discoursing subjects—which subjects of experience and knowledge—do you then want to 'diminish' when you say: 'I who conduct this discourse am conducting a scientific discourse, and I am a scientist'? (p. 85)

Essentially, what Foucault said is that whenever a speaker or writer claims that his or her knowledge is scientific, that speaker or writer is making a claim to power. That individual is pushing his or her own words upward by accessing the stream of power ensconced in modern science rhetoric. In doing so, that speaker or writer is thereby diminishing the knowledges of other speakers and writers, of other "discoursing subjects" whose ideas and beliefs are not cast in the rhetoric of science.

Likewise, one might ask, when special educators utilize the discourse of modern science to discuss national issues such as facilitated communication or individual student practicalities in an IEP meeting, what knowledges and persons are being "diminished"? My assertion is that these knowledges, these voices, that are typically stifled, muffled, and devalued by science, are the voices of hope for the field of mental retardation.

Examples of such Non-Science voices within the professional literature are few for reasons made plain in my analysis of the facilitated communication commentaries. To be critical of modern science or to write in words beyond the language of science is to risk illegitimacy in professional circles. One who fails to tap into the language of modern science may be unconvincing to a readership greatly faithful to the progressive myth. It is my personal hope that the professional literature may be opened up to a postscientific dialogue involving a greater diversity and equality of contributors: parents, students (typed contributions from facilitated communicators!), teachers, and so on. Such a dialogue would seek democracy over science, community over "objective truth."

The most important conversations occur in schools and homes, where labeled students, family members, friends, and professionals create practices and relationships far from the gaze of researchers and professional authors. These spaces offer the greatest opportunities for the cultivation of hope beyond modern science, for the arrangement of services in which the individuals involved can place their faith and trust. Small groups of 3, 5, 10, or 12 persons devoted to the well-being of an individual labeled as having mental retardation have the opportunity to set aside scientific talk and disability constructs in favor of language and relationships that value the labeled individual. Within such local circles, the stigmatizing identity of mental retardation may be tossed out and replaced with understandings that seek to protect labeled persons from stigma and devaluation. This reconstructive and relational task disavows universal concepts of progress for the sake of hope.

Notes

1. A brief note concerning my use of the terms *postmodern* and *modern* throughout this paper is in order. To facilitate the introduction of philosophical concepts to special educators typically not schooled in these compelling languages and ideas, I have overstated the internal unity within the various philosophies currently called "postmodern" and those called "modern." Also, I have intentionally rendered the two modes of discourse as completely distinct from the other. The danger of these simplifications lies in the ignoring of the many debates among scholars concerning what postmodernism is or might be and how it is different or not so different from its modern philosophical predecessors. Readers should be informed that many postmodernisms have been and will continue to be put forth as scholars continue to write and talk. The brand of postmodernism I describe here is the result of my own combination of interpretations of the works of Foucault, Rorty, Gergen, and others. With my special educator's eye toward the well-being of persons described as having mental retardation, my reading of these authors emphasizes the link between modern science knowledge and power in professional research, organization, and practice.

2. In this paper I have focused on concepts without investigating teaching practices that are based on postmodern philosophy. For practitioners who want to know how postmodern ideas can be translated into practice, see writings by Duplass and Smith (1995) and Coelho de Amorim and Cavalcante (1992). These teachers present political forms of instruction in which teachers and students critique standardized disability labels and constructs. Also note that postmodern educators do not seek to replace the menu of scientifically authorized "best practices" with a new list of postmodern "best practices." Instead, the idea is one of supporting a development of specific practices by teachers, students, and families that meet the unique needs and goals of individuals students.

References

Best, S. (1994). Foucault, postmodernism, and social theory. In D. R. Dickens & A. Fontana (Eds.), *Postmodernism and social inquiry* (pp. 25–52). New York: Guilford Press.

Biklen, D. (1990). Communication unbound: Autism and praxis. *Harvard Educational Review, 60,* 291–314.

Biklen, D. (1993). *Communication unbound.* New York: Teachers College Press.

Biklen, D., & Duchan, J. F. (1994). "I am intelligent": The social construction of mental retardation. *Journal of the Association for Persons with Severe Handicaps, 19,* 173–184.

Clifford, J. (1986). Introduction: Partial truths. In J. Clifford & G. E. Marcus (Eds.), *Writing culture: The poetics and politics of ethnography* (pp. 1–26). Berkeley: University of California Press.

Coelho de Amorim, A., & Cavalcante, F. G. (1992). Narrations of the self: Video production in a marginalized subculture. In S. McNamee & K. Gergen (Eds.), *Therapy as social construction*. London: Sage.

Crossley, R. (1994). *Facilitated communication training*. New York: Teachers College Press.

Danforth, S., Rhodes, W. C., & Smith, T. (1995). Inventing the future: Postmodern challenges in educational reform. In J. L. Paul, D. Evans, & H. Rosselli (Eds.), *Integrating school restructuring and special education reform* (pp. 214–236). Orlando, FL: Harcourt Brace College Publishers.

Denzin, N. K. (1991). *Images of postmodern society: Social theory and contemporary cinema*. Newbury Park, CA: Sage.

Dickens, D. R., & Fontana, A. (1994). *Postmodernism and social inquiry*. New York: Guilford Press.

Duplass, D., & Smith, T. (1995). Hearing Dennis through his own voice. *Behavioral Disorders, 20*(2), 144–148.

Featherstone, M. (1991). *Consumer culture and postmodernism*. Newbury Park, CA: Sage.

Foucault, M. (1980). *Power/knowledge*. New York: Pantheon.

Gergen, K. J. (1991). *The saturated self*. New York: Basic Books.

Gergen, K. J. (1994a). Exploring the postmodern: Perils or potentials? *American Psychologist, 49*, 412–416.

Gergen, K. J. (1994b). *Realities and relationships*. Cambridge, MA: Harvard University Press.

Giroux, H. (1991). *Postmodernism, feminism, and cultural politics: Redrawing educational boundaries*. Albany: State University of New York Press.

Green, G., & Shane, H. C. (1994). Science, reason, and facilitated communication. *Journal of the Association for Persons with Severe Handicaps, 19*, 151–172.

Hassan, I., & Hassan, S. (1983). *Innovation/renovation: New perspectives on the humanities*. Madison: University of Wisconsin Press.

Jacobson, J. W., Mulick, J. A., & Schwartz, A. A. (1995). A history of facilitated communication: Science, pseudo-

science, and anti-science. *American Psychologist, 50*, 750–765.

Kauffman, J. (1993). How to achieve radical reform in special education. *Exceptional Children, 60*, 6–16.

Kuhn, T. S. (1962). *The structure of scientific revolutions*. Chicago: University of Chicago Press.

Kvale, S. (1992). *Psychology and postmodernism*. Newbury Park, CA: Sage.

Marcell, D. W. (1974). *Progress and pragmatism*. Westport, CT: Greenwood Press.

Poster, M. (1990). *The mode of information*. Chicago: University of Chicago Press.

Randall, J. H., Jr. (1940). *The making of the modern mind*. Cambridge, MA: Riverside Press.

Rorty, R. (1979). *Philosophy and the mirror of nature*. Princeton, NJ: Princeton University Press.

Rorty, R. (1989). *Contingency, irony, and solidarity*. New York: Cambridge University Press.

Rosenau, P. M. (1992). *Postmodernism and the social sciences: Insights, inroads, and intrusions*. Princeton: Princeton University Press.

Sailor, W., & Skrtic, T. (1995). American education in the postmodern era. In J. L. Paul, H. Rosselli, & D. Evans (Eds.), *Integrating school restructuring and special education reform* (pp. 418–432). Orlando, FL: Harcourt Brace College Publishers.

Skrtic, T. (1991). *Behind special education: A critical analysis of professional culture and school organization*. Denver: Love.

Simpson, R. L., & Myles, B. S. (1995). Facilitated communication and children with disabilities: An enigma in search of a perspective. *Focus on Exceptional Children. 27*(9), 1–16.

Usher, R. (1994). *Postmodernism and education*. New York: Routledge.

Wolf, M. (1992). *A thrice-told tale: Feminism, postmodernism, and ethnographic responsibility*. Stanford: Stanford University Press.

2.5

Macro-Social Validation:

Referencing Outcomes in Behavioral Disorders to Societal Issues and Problems

Hill M. Walker
Steven R. Forness
James M. Kauffman
Michael H. Epstein
Frank M. Gresham
C. Michael Nelson
Phillip S. Strain

Abstract: During the past two decades, the field of special education has become politicized and fragmented as a result of internal strife and turf battles among professionals. Special education often is perceived by professionals in other fields as strife ridden, expensive, litigious, consumed with legislative mandates and court orders, and ineffective. These perceptions have damaged special education's status and hindered its ability to pursue its agenda. By association, the field of behavioral disorders also has suffered from these perceptions. We need to rededicate ourselves to empirical inquiry and use our collective expertise to find solutions to problems that are of great concern to children and families as well as the larger society. In so doing, we may achieve a degree of macrosocial validation for our efforts. The term *macrosocial validation,* as used herein, refers to recognition, approval, and valuing of a field's professional activities by the larger constituencies affected by them, such as the general public, the U.S. Congress, and policymakers.

The field of behavioral disorders needs to broaden its agenda to address larger issues and problems of great concern to our society. These needed efforts include ensuring school safety; identifying children vulnerable to gang membership; intervening proactively to prevent school dropout; participating in delinquency prevention efforts; proactively addressing youth violence issues in collaboration with other disciplines and agencies; controlling the transport of dangerous weapons across school boundaries; and reducing bullying, sexual harassment, and mean-spirited teasing within the context of schooling. Professionals in the field of behavioral disorders have the skills, knowledge, and expertise to play a significant leadership role in targeting and positively impacting these social problems. However, we rarely assume such a leadership role in addressing them directly, nor do we

consistently promote our collective capabilities in this regard. We should consider the example of other professions, such as medicine and psychology, that make powerful public health contributions to solving problems of great concern to the larger society (e.g., drug and alcohol use among youth). In so doing, we may achieve a level of macrosocial validation for some of our contributions that does not currently exist. The absence of this validation does not serve us well in the continuing public debates about the value of general education, special education, and the allied subspecialties (Gresham & Lopez, 1996).

Perhaps in no field is there a more glaring disconnect between the availability of proven research-based methods and their effective application by consumers than in education. Commentaries by Carnine (1993, 1995) and Kauffman (1996) have done much to highlight the gaps that persist in the field of education in this regard. Educators often seem to resist empirically supported innovations that represent more effective practices. The specific reasons for such resistance are not always clear; however, their unfortunate effects are often palpable. For example, Kauffman (1981, 1993, 1996) has noted that the education profession is characterized by continuous change but little sustained improvement because the relationship between reliable, effective practices and their widespread adoption remains weak.

Many consumers and practitioners of education continue to embrace facilitated communication, the concept of multiple intelligences, and whole-language approaches to teaching beginning reading to children who are at risk for school failure in the face of mounting evidence of (a) the invalidity of the assumptions underlying these methods and (b) their demonstrated lack of effectiveness for the purposes for which they are used. Such ignorance or rejection of scientific evidence provides grim testimony to the validity of the assertions by Carnine and Kauffman (cf. American Speech-Language-Hearing Association, 1994; Green & Shane, 1994; Jacobson, Mulick, & Schwartz, 1995; Lieberman & Lieberman, 1990; Lyon & Moats, 1997). Substantial numbers of educators seem to ignore the concept of best practices and rely upon a hodgepodge of activities, unplanned curricula, and conceptually incompatible interventions to accomplish teaching, learning, and management goals.

THE MATURITY OF EDUCATION AS A PROFESSION

Carnine (1997) has made the case that, compared to medicine, psychology, and engineering, education is an immature profession. One of the hallmarks of such professional immaturity is the failure to develop and use cohesive knowledge bases in those contexts where it is possible. In education, there appears to be ample opportunity to achieve this goal—for example, in the domains of phonics-based approaches to teaching beginning reading and the use of behavior management procedures that produce reliable, socially valid outcomes. However, the first question that educators seem to pose regarding a potentially effective innovation is "Is it ideologically acceptable or politically correct?" rather than "How effectively does it work and what are its limitations of use?" (see Malysiak, 1997). As a result, many highly beneficial innovations enjoy only limited accessibility, and their potential impact on the lives of thousands of students and their families is diminished. Other professions tend to ask questions about the outcomes and conditions of use first rather than last.

A number of professions implement formal procedures on a regular basis to update, synthesize, and consensually validate their scientific knowledge bases in relation to topics of societal importance (e.g., effects of tobacco use on cancer rates). In many instances, medicine and psychology, through the national organizations and agencies that support their respective research and development efforts, have (a) designed consensual knowledge verification conferences to identify empirically derived principles and practices on which there is scientific agreement and (b) initiated multisite scientific studies in which key questions are investigated systematically and replicated across sites and by different groups of investigators. These scientific efforts lay the foundation for the development of solid knowledge bases that can advance understanding of a critical topic or problem. As such, they can be of enormous benefit to the fields involved and to the larger society.

In 1987, for example, the National Institutes of Health held a knowledge/best practices conference on what was currently known about learning disabilities from a variety of disciplinary perspectives (e.g., medicine, psychology, education). The results of this conference were highly influential and greatly increased congressional support of research on topics suggested by the conference. The conference led practitioners to focus more directly on phonemic awareness and early, systematic intervention efforts (Lyon & Moats, 1997): The National Institute of Mental Health funded a consensus project resulting in a structured diagnostic interview that has become the "gold standard" for determining the presence of a psychiatric diagnosis in children. It is used extensively in both research studies and clinical training situations (Shaffer et al., 1996).

Similarly, the U.S. Centers for Disease Control is in the process of implementing a consensus task force project on violence prevention that involves study groups of 40 experts in this area. This initiative is referred to as the *Violence Prevention Communication Plan for Preventing Youth Violence: The Best Practices Project* (Hammond, 1998). Its goals are to (a) systematically review the evaluation research in the field of youth violence prevention and (b) build upon existing research to develop background papers that could be used as planning guides at the appropriate community level.

Currently, the National Institute of Mental Health is funding a multisite study of attention-deficit hyperactivity disorder in which different promising approaches to treating this disorder (i.e., pharmacological, psychosocial, and combinations thereof) are being investigated systematically (Richters et al., 1995). When the results of this study are announced, there likely will be extensive exposure for it in the literature and the media, and the public will perceive that the professions of medicine and psychology jointly have made another substantive contribution to our collective quality of life. More important, the children and families affected by these social problems will benefit greatly from the improved quality of professional practice.

The resulting benefits to the professions that are perceived to account for these achievements, in terms of public image, status, and financial support for research, are enormous. A timely case in point involves the budget surplus funds that are becoming available to Congress for reinvestment. It is currently estimated, for example, that the budget of the National Institutes of Health will double in the next 5 years. While our field is unlikely ever to approach this standard of public valuing, we have the ability and the opportunity to demonstrate our societal value to a far greater extent than we currently do.

DEVELOPING AND PROMOTING SOLUTIONS TO PROBLEMS OF CONCERN TO THE LARGER SOCIETY

On a smaller scale, the field of behavioral disorders has the capacity to make substantive contributions to solving the numerous social problems that plague our society (e.g., truancy, drug and alcohol use, youth violence, lack of school safety and discipline, gang membership, school dropout). We have a well-developed knowledge base, much of which is empirically verifiable and reasonably well integrated, on the adjustment problems that at-risk, vulnerable children and youth manifest in the context of schooling. We also have a cadre of professionals committed to the use of applied research procedures in developing and verifying, through systematic replication, effective procedures and practices the professionals who serve these students can use to enhance the quality of their lives.

Our field can, and occasionally does, make highly valued contributions to issues that concern society, but we generally do not take advantage of our opportunities for demonstrating them to all of the audiences that count. Other than ourselves, the audiences that count are the children and families with whom we work, the general public, state and local policymakers, and the U.S. Congress. We need to promote our field's achievements and contributions aggressively and broadly among these constituencies.

IDEOLOGY VERSUS SCIENCE AS A VEHICLE FOR ADVANCING OUR PROFESSION

Unfortunately, the value of our contributions as a field has been masked and attenuated in some cases by internal conflicts of our own making. Although there are philosophical conflicts within all disciplines, the high visibility, costs, and litigious nature of special education seem to have highlighted our field's contentious debates regarding such issues as inclusion, consumer empowerment, and deconstruction. The public perception of what we do too often has been obscured by the vitriolic debates occurring over the past two decades. They have led to negative public appraisals of our field, and these appraisals, in turn, have received widespread exposure in the general education literature (e.g., Brantlinger, 1997) and national media (e.g., *U.S. News and World Report* and *60 Minutes*) and have damaged the reputation of special education. By association, the field of behavioral disorders also has been denigrated.

To the extent that we allow the subspecialty of behavioral disorders to be dominated by political or ideological issues, in the tradition of special education, we make ourselves vulnerable to the same outcomes that have so severely plagued it in recent times, the protestations of Brantlinger (1997) notwithstanding that every position is saturated with ideology. A highly politicized field is much more vulnerable to scientific bias, limited influence, and ineffective practice than one that guides itself primarily through empirical evidence (Kavale & Forness, in press). These outcomes have caused other professions to view us as incapable of managing our affairs and unable to resolve our differences. Probably as a natural consequence, some professionals and policymakers, perhaps for reasons of self-interest, have asserted that the field of special education should be dismantled (Gartner & Lipsky, 1987; Stainback & Stainback, 1991). Moreover, the unrelenting, attacking styles of many professionals involved in special education debates may have caused some sectors of the public to conclude that no expertise really exists in our discipline.

The merging and in some cases submerging of special education programs within curriculum and instruction departments in schools and colleges of education has been costly to special education. It has meant the loss of autonomy, status, influence, and resources (cf. Kauffman & Hallahan, 1993). It is likely that this development has been made possible, at least in part, by special education's persistent and contentious airing of its differences in public arenas. In many cases, these mergers have had the earmarks of a hostile corporate takeover.

The recent reauthorization of the Individuals with Disabilities Education Act (IDEA), for which the field of special education endured self-indulgent paroxysms of infighting and virulent turf battles among professionals and advocates over a 3-year period, illustrates just how fragmented and ineffective our field has become. Much like a disgusted parent who tires of endless squabbling among siblings, Congress finally called an end to it and mandated a settlement that perhaps did not satisfy any particular constituency. No one gains under such conditions of settlement, and our reputation with Congress suffers as a result.

Special education certainly is not well served by this public display of its fragmentation and its inability to agree on critical national legislation that benefits individuals with disabilities and their families. The notion of professional maturity in this context is indeed an oxymoron. To the extent that we continue to insist on using the club of often unpopular legislative mandates to achieve our goals, rather than making a persuasive case to the public regarding what we do, we also will continue to see erosion of support for our field, even among our friends and supporters within the education profession. We should be seeking allies and forming true working partnerships, particularly with professionals in general education; instead, we seem to insist on narrow ideological victories rather than suffer the quid pro quo of political compromise that other professions embrace as a necessary means to professional progress. If we continue on our contentious, single-minded, and often self-righteous path in this regard, we may ultimately suffer the refrain of the movie classic *They Shoot Horses, Don't They?*—being put out of our misery.

The development of a national agenda in our field for emotional or behavioral disturbance, depending on how it plays out, holds the potential to replicate the role of The Association for Persons with Severe Handicaps (TASH) in terms of its impact on the field of mental retardation (MR) and developmental disabilities (DD) (U.S. Office of Special Education Programs, 1994). TASH has advocated forcefully and aggressively for the hegemony of values in driving the MR/DD field. An unfortunate consequence of this advocacy has been relegation of scientific processes and outcomes to far less important status. In our view, the field of behavioral disorders is vulnerable to this same set of outcomes. For example, at the national conference of the American Institute for Research held in the spring of 1996 to showcase the national agenda, a number of advocates were publicly critical of professionals in our field and the value of the research activities in which we engage. Such rhetoric demonizes empirical inquiry and those who do it and legitimizes discrediting and devaluing of the scientific knowledge base in the field of behavioral disorders. Kauffman's (1997) appraisal of

the national agenda analyzes its implications, points out its limitations, and cautions us against uncritical acceptance of its premises—especially its implied pressures for the dominant role of values in driving policy and practices.

The national agenda should serve to stimulate dialogue among consumers, professionals, policymakers, and researchers about best practices and strategies for (a) securing additional federal and state support for addressing this increasing social need and (b) using the tools of empirical inquiry, scholarship, and proactive advocacy to enhance the lives of those most affected by it (i.e., children and youth, families, schools, community agencies). These important goals will not be realized if the national agenda serves instead as a vehicle for attacking empirical inquiry and those who conduct it by consumers, advocates, and others.

THE CHALLENGE OF POSTMODERNIST AND DECONSTRUCTIVIST PHILOSOPHIES

Within the past decade, postmodernism and deconstructionism, philosophies that reject the scientific method and deny the possibility of common or universal knowledge, have gained momentum in many fields, especially the social sciences and humanities. We refer to radical postmodern and deconstructivist philosophy together as *PD* because the two are often linked conceptually in the literature. These linkages include joint presentations of postmodern and deconstructivist ideas about special education (e.g., Brantlinger, 1997; Danforth, 1997; Danforth & Rhodes, 1997) and critiques of PD by scholars (e.g., Wilson, 1998).

The proponents of PD often criticize scientific understanding by claiming that it is decontextualized and does not acknowledge the construction of meanings. As incoherent as their critiques of science may be, advocates of PD have achieved substantial currency in the academic departments of many institutions of higher education today and pose a significant challenge to our field.

We understand that inquiry and learning always occur in, are affected by, and help to shape their social contexts. Sometimes the interactions of individuals and their social contexts are fortuitous, and sometimes they are deliberate. People construct meaning from their interactions with the social and material worlds they experience. These principles of social learning theory have been recognized and applied in the scientific analysis of human behavior for decades (cf. Bandura, 1977, 1978, 1986). They are not, as some may suggest, inventions of postmodern or deconstructivist philosophy. Indeed, the ways in which social contexts and the construction of meanings operate to influence behavior are seen by social learning theorists as legitimate and necessary topics of scientific study.

PD rejects the possibility of a science of human behavior and denies the superiority of social learning theory over more idiosyncratic ways of knowing and of finding order in the seeming disorder of human conduct. Indeed, PD suggests that we can know nothing but our own experience ("text" or "narrative" in PD lingo). The assertions of PD could be ignored were they mere philosophical amusement, but PD has become more than that. "One is tempted to place postmodernism in history's curiosity cabinet, alongside theosophy and transcendental idealism, but it has seeped by now into the mainstream of the social sciences and the humanities" (Wilson, 1998, p. 58). It is now being released into mainstream education and special education (cf. Brantlinger, 1997; Danforth, 1997; Danforth & Rhodes, 1977; Elkind, 1998; Sailor & Skrtic, 1996; Skrtic, Sailor, & Gee, 1996).

As Wilson (1998) and Gross (1998) have noted, scientists do not see PD as useful precisely because scientists seek meaning outside their own idiosyncratic experience and because they are held responsible for what they say. Not only are behavioral scientists held responsible for what they say, but they also must seek better solutions to important social problems, including many of the seemingly intractable problems involved in teaching difficult students more effectively. Better solutions to special education problems have not been put forward by PD proponents, who typically and perhaps mistakenly label their assumptions "paradigm shifts" (cf. Kauffman, in press). A paradigm shift occurs when an established theory can no longer explain the observations and results of experiments and a new paradigm emerges to replace the old theory or paradigm. In fact, PD suggestions that science is a misleading, if not an inferior, route to understanding tend to forestall further scientific inquiry. Where Kuhn (1996) saw structure in the revolutions of science, PD proponents tend to see chaos and a crisis of knowledge precipitated by crumbling structures. "Consider this rule of thumb: to the extent that philosophical positions both confuse us and close doors to further inquiry, they are likely to be wrong" (Wilson, 1998, p. 59).

Perhaps, as Wilson (1998) suggested, we need challenges such as PD to keep us vigilant and ready to reject erroneous ideas. Notwithstanding the value of PD as a foil, however, it is important for us not to let PD proponents capture the public imagination about special education. Most important, they must be held accountable for their assertions. It is also important that we prevent them from determining special education policy by our own default (i.e., by our failure to call attention to the reliability and value of the empirical evidence supporting our practices).

ADVOCATING AND PROMOTING THE ACHIEVEMENTS OF SPECIAL EDUCATION

Special education, through its federally funded programs of research and development, is responsible for numerous innovations that have led directly not only to an enhanced quality of life for individuals with disabilities but also to improved capacities in learning, adaptive behavior, and social development for individuals generally. These innovations include curriculum-based measurement procedures, positive behavioral support technology, transition models, supported employment, and procedures to study and influence aberrant as well as prosocial forms of behavior (e.g., functional behavioral assessment and analysis). All are examples of innovations originated in whole or in part by special education that have advanced the field of education profoundly and positively impacted related disciplines such as school psychology and counseling. Special education also has contributed to the areas of policy and advocacy in ways that have resulted in key benefits to the lives of individuals with disabilities. These include the training of general education teachers in early detection and classroom accommodations for children with learning or behavioral problems, strategies for individualizing their curriculum, and meaningful involvement of parents or guardians in educational decisions. These achievements need to be catalogued, synthesized, and promoted within educational and public arenas so our field receives proper credit for them.

The recognition and perceived value of our work should be so clear that there is no excuse for articles such as those of Detterman and Thompson (1997) in *American Psychologist*, which concluded that there is nothing special about special education, or Brantlinger (1997) in *Review of Educational Research*, who bemoaned the existence of special education as a distinguishable entity and concluded that it is designed to coerce the least powerful members of society. But there is no clear recognition of the value of our work. Just as Detterman and Thompson

(1997) provided much misinformation (see Forness, Keogh, MacMillan, Kavale, & Gresham, 1998) and Brantlinger (1997) lofted antiscientific and indefensible statements about special education research, we can expect more of the same from other professions and influential policymakers in the future. It is important to note in this regard that careful scholarship and informational accuracy are too often lost in the heat of such debates and in the eagerness to make a particular case. For example, Doug Fuchs (personal communication, May 1998) reported that there are myriad misstatements of fact and quotation errors from his articles alone as cited in Brantlinger (1997).

As a field, we should recommit to and reinvest in the research-based, empirically oriented strategies that have created such reliable and powerful innovations for serving the needs of individuals who have disabilities and other conditions of risk. Equally important, we must describe, promote, and advocate these innovations in ways that demonstrate their value and connect them to their research and funding streams and to the public concerns that give greater value to special education.

A CALL FOR ACTION

What is needed in the field of behavioral disorders is a rededication to a profession that (a) is research driven; (b) focuses upon what works rather than what feels, sounds, or looks good; (c) has the potential to enhance the lives of children and youth with emotional and behavioral disorders and their families; and (d) contributes to the larger public good. Aside from rededicating ourselves to this commitment, we should consider a strategy of macrosocial validation in which we publicly demonstrate, whenever possible, our ability to positively impact the issues and problems that drive public concern and fall within our realm of expertise. Just as the fields of speech-language pathology and school psychology, through their respective professional organizations, the American Speech-Language-Hearing Association and the National Association of School Psychologists, have been particularly effective in promoting the value of what they do with Congress and the general public, we are also capable of influencing a diverse group of stakeholders. As a profession, we are no less able in addressing larger societal concerns (Webber & Scheuermann, 1997).

Professionals in the field of behavioral disorders conduct research and produce knowledge that bears directly upon some of the most pressing social issues affecting our society; yet we are far down the list of professions perceived by Congress and the general public as having such solutions. It is unlikely that we will be invited to share our knowledge on these issues in key public forums if we continue as we have in the past. Most of the responsibility for this lack of awareness rests collectively with us. We have tended to pursue a relatively narrow, insular agenda of topics and outcome measures in our research activities. We select goals, intervention procedures, and outcome measures that make sense to us, that show some sensitivity or responsiveness to our intervention attempts, and that are acceptable to the targets of those efforts (Lloyd & Heubusch, 1996). As part of this process, we impress ourselves and our immediate constituencies with the changes we produce on such measures as the rate of out-of-seat behavior and talk-outs, academic engagement levels, number of words read correctly and math problems solved per minute, or our ability to reduce the number of times aggressive students hit each other at recess. These are useful achievements in the contexts of teaching and managing students and are not to be denigrated; however, they do *not* serve to capture public attention, nor do they effectively address major issues confronting society.

The public is far more concerned with critical policy issues and larger questions such as the following:

- How do I know my child is safe in school and on the way to and from school each day?
- My child reports being bullied or sexually harassed to the point of humiliation in school. What are you doing to solve this problem?
- How are you going about creating a sense of discipline in schools that are chaotic and are ruled by disruptive youth and in which teachers are afraid of students?
- How are you accommodating students who are clearly a danger to others?
- How do you stop your students from using anger and violence as a means of solving social problems and conflicts?
- How are you dealing with chronic truants and reducing dropouts, many of whom then live on the streets and adopt a criminal lifestyle?
- Why can't you prevent students from bringing weapons that cause injury and sometimes death to school?
- Why can't you detect childhood depression before it leads to suicide attempts?

- How are you helping children deal with the tragic consequences of abuse and neglect?

These are the pressing social validity questions that Congress, parents, and the public want answered. These constituencies are interested in such details as positive gains on a social skills rating measure or improvements in student self-reports or other reports of self-esteem only to the extent that they represent part of an *effective* solution to one of the questions just listed or questions like them.

It appears that neither the general public nor Congress becomes aware of or values many of the behavioral changes we celebrate in our professional forums. When federal bureaucrats representing educational research agendas go before Congress and attempt to make a case on behalf of what we do, they are invariably asked, "What difference does this make in a person's life?" or "How is society better off as a result of this work?" Usually the answers are not satisfactory because we are not able either to address these larger macrovalidity questions or to demonstrate our effects on them through research and development efforts. Until we do, our value in solving such larger societal problems will be viewed with ambiguity and skepticism by legislators, policymakers, parents, and the general public.

Strain and his associates (Strain, Steel, Ellis, & Timm, 1982) recently were funded to conduct a long-term follow-up assessment of adults and their offspring who received early intervention services from the Regional Intervention Program (RIP) 20 to 25 years ago. This investigation will assess the status of follow-up sample members on such important outcome variables as school history, performance and adjustment, criminality, drug and alcohol usage patterns, employment, contact with community social service agencies, and other variables that measure adjustment and quality of life. This investigation is an exemplar of the kinds of long-term strategies we need to consider adopting to determine the life impact of our interventions and treatments.

ELEMENTS OF A COMPREHENSIVE STRATEGY

We suggest four generic strategies for addressing the larger questions noted earlier. First, we need to reference, whenever possible, the measures and outcomes we record to these questions of public concern. In some instances, this will require longitudinal follow-up designs in which important relationships are demonstrated over time. For example, what impact does improving reading achievement for low-achieving readers in the primary grades have upon discipline problems, delinquent acts, and truancy in middle school? Does systematically teaching conflict resolution and anger management strategies in the primary and intermediate grades reduce violent and aggressive episodes among at-risk youth in middle and high school? What do documented gains on social skills measures have to do with preventing delinquency years later? These and related questions are difficult, time-consuming, and costly to answer. But unless we pose and pursue them, we will remain mired in short-term solution strategies that will never be sufficient either to develop good answers or to convince the larger society of the value of what we do. In other instances, the relationships we are seeking have been demonstrated, at least partially, through prior research. In such cases, we need to acknowledge and document those relationships whenever possible in the presentation of our research findings and to show how our outcomes advance or affect such relationships.

Second, we must show a greater willingness to collaborate with other professionals in the larger school or societal arena, rather than just in our own settings or programs. Educators have been viewed by families, courts, social agencies, and other professions as detached players who respond primarily to problems that lie within our own domains of responsibility and expertise. We should, for example, be developing the means to identify early those students who are vulnerable to violence or gang membership and then intervene proactively to deter them from doing so. This requires that the field of behavioral disorders become partners with general education, other disciplines, parent organizations, and social service agencies in addressing these problems comprehensively. Even though general educators often are not motivated to "own" such problems and address them proactively, we should continue to influence them to do so.

Third, we should be advocating strenuously for policies that support best practices in prevention. Identifying children just prior to or at the point of school entry who are at risk for emotional or behavioral disorders and intervening proactively with teachers, parents, peers, and other professionals to divert them from this path ought to be a standard practice in all school systems (Hoagwood & Erwin, 1997; Kavale, Forness, & Walker, in press; Walker et al., 1996). Proactive prevention of this type is an atypical practice at present in most school districts.

Frequently cited barriers to such practice are pejorative labeling and stigmatization resulting from early identification (i.e., political correctness inserted into a professional context), costs, attitudinal barriers, and logistical problems. In addition, a common reaction is that we should not screen and identify children for the possibility of emotional or behavioral problems because services do not currently exist to accommodate them. Are we saying the well is dry and will remain so? This is like saying we should not screen for early detection of cancer because we do not have enough resources at present to treat those who already are diagnosed with cancer. Unfortunately, these obstacles frequently have suffocated proactive efforts to mount effective prevention programs in schools. We suggest getting beyond such barriers and dealing constructively, on a firm reality base, with the urgent issues that demand our attention.

Within this context, we need to consider integrated prevention approaches involving true multidisciplinary collaborations that can result in cross-environment intervention planning and execution. It is essential that interventions designed to achieve primary, secondary, and tertiary prevention outcomes, respectively, be implemented and coordinated effectively within school and community contexts. We need to address the complex issues and tasks attendant upon increasing known effective practices for school-wide, district-wide, and even state-wide applications. This empirical and helping agenda also would facilitate addressing the critical issues of sustainability, fidelity, and range of effectiveness of these practices.

Fourth, as the major professional organization for our field, the Council for Children with Behavioral Disorders (CCBD) should be serving as a valuable resource to the larger educational community and society in terms of synthesizing and integrating the knowledge base on such key topics as reducing bullying and mean-spirited teasing, preventing youth violence in schools, enhancing school safety, and preventing school failure and dropout. These syntheses, with accompanying policy and practice recommendations, have been developed to great effect by other disciplines. For example, the two-volume document *Violence and Youth: Psychology's Response* (American Psychological Association, 1993) has been cited widely and is perceived as a useful contribution by the field of psychology to solving a serious societal problem. The National Association of School Psychologists has developed and published three valuable syntheses of the professional knowledge base: a compendium of techniques for dealing with learning and behavior problems in the regular classroom (Stoner, Shinn, & Walker, 1991), an analysis of the knowledge base on school violence and safety (Furlong & Morrison, 1994), and the book *Best Practices in School Psychology-III* (Thomas & Grimes, 1995).

CCBD and individual professionals need to work with the Office of Special Education Programs, other federal agencies, foundations, and additional funding sources (e.g., corporations) to develop support for multisite, longitudinal special education research efforts to test preferred practices in addressing the challenging behaviors of children and youth. CCBD should consider developing a consensus strategy, involving standing panels of experts, to determine recommended best practices. This strategy also could be used to certify programs and professionals who implement such practices.

Given that we have solutions to offer and something of value to say about these pressing issues, we should organize ourselves to say them articulately within the forums and contexts that matter. We have much to learn from professional organizations such as the American Psychological Association, the American Medical Association, the National Association of School Psychologists, and the American Speech and Hearing Association, all of which advocate effectively for themselves in the context of issues and problems that society desperately wants solved. To this end, researcers and scholars in our field need to translate their research findings into broad, meaningful strategies and practices so that professional organizations can disseminate them effectively to the relevant audiences. In addition, our findings and knowledge syntheses need to be carefully contextualized, using differing formats and presentation styles, so that divergent audiences (e.g., parents, policymakers, professionals, legilators) can act upon them effectively.

CONCLUSION

There is a pressing need for effective, practical solutions as our society shows persisting signs of social deterioration and incivility (Kauffman & Burbach, 1997). However, we will not accomplish these solutions through further politicization and fragmentation of the field of special education. The need for empirical research has never been greater in our field. We should rededicate ourselves to producing replicable and powerful outcomes that are socially valid (cf. Kauffman, in press). Empirical research provides us with a compass and sense of direction to find our way through the thickets of bias, assumption, and intuition. Rigorous research also allows us to pursue innovations, correct our course, and clarify the paths we choose to follow. Special education research, and most especially research in behavioral disorders, has revolutionized practices and dramatically improved the quality of life of thousands of individuals and their families. We can ill afford to abandon these impressive traditions in favor of ideology, turf battles, or political correctness infused into professional contexts (Walker, 1993).

Federal agencies across the board are being strongly encouraged by Congress to translate research into effective practices that can make a difference. Congress is keenly interested in seeing tangible results and applied forms of accountability from the research

it has funded previously. This creates a positive climate for pursuing the strategies described in this article.

We hope constructive debate will occur on the general issues raised herein and our field can come together in forming strategies that will enhance our perceived value and afford opportunities to share our collective expertise. We are aware that persuasive counterarguments can be made in relation to each of the key arguments presented in this article, but we are hopeful that a debate will ensue on the advisability of pursuing more vigorously the path described here, or one like it, and that counterarguments can be tested on their merits within the forums of professional and public debate. The results of these efforts may result in a level of macrosocial validation and recognition that will position our field well for the future (Gresham & Lopez, 1996).

References

American Psychological Association. (1993). *Violence and youth: Psychology's response.* Washington, DC: Author.

American Speech-Language-Hearing Association. (1994). *Technical report on facilitated communication.* Rockville, MD: Author.

Bandura, A. (1977). *Social learning theory.* Englewood Cliffs, NJ: Prentice-Hall.

Bandura, A. (1978). The self-system in reciprocal determinism. *American Psychologist, 33,* 344–358.

Bandura, A. (1986). *Social foundations of thought and action: A social cognitive theory.* Englewood Cliffs, NJ: Prentice-Hall.

Brantlinger, E. (1997). Using ideology: Cases of non-recognition of the politics of research and practice in special education. *Review of Educational Research, 67,* 425–459.

Carnine, D. (1993, December 8). Facts, not fads. *Education Week,* 40.

Carnine, D. (1995). *Enhancing the education profession: Increasing the perceived and actual value of research.* Eugene, OR: National Center to Improve the Tools of Educators (NCITE).

Carnine, D. (1997). Bridging the research to practice gap. *Exceptional Children, 63,* 513–522.

Danforth, S. (1997). On what basis hope? Modern progress and postmodern possibilities. *Mental Retardation, 35,* 93–106.

Danforth, S., & Rhodes, W. C. (1997). Deconstructing disability: A philosophy for inclusion. *Remedial and Special Education, 18,* 357–366.

Detterman, D. K., & Thompson, L. A. (1997). What is so special about special education? *The American Psychologist, 52,* 1082–1090.

Elkind, D. (1998). Behavioral disorders: A postmodern perspective. *Behavioral Disorders, 23,* 153–159.

Forness, S. R., Keogh, B. K., MacMillan, D. L., Kavale, K. A., & Gresham, F. M. (in press). What's so special about IQ: The limited explanatory power of cognitive abilities in the real world of special education. *Remedial and Special Education.*

Furlong, M. J., & Morrison, G. M. (Eds.). (1994). School violence and safety in perspective (9-article miniseries). *School Psychology Review, 23,* 139–261.

Gartner, A., & Lipsky, K. (1987). Beyond special education: Toward a quality system for all students. *Harvard Education Review, 57,* 367–395.

Green, G., & Shane, H. C. (1994). Science, reason, and facilitated communication. *Journal of the Association for Persons with Severe Handicaps, 19,* 151–172.

Gresham, F. M., & Lopez, M. (1996). Social validation: A unifying concept for school-based consultation research and practice. *School Psychology Quarterly, 11,* 204–227.

Gross, P. R. (1998). The Icarian impulse. *The Wilson Quarterly, 22,* 39–49.

Hammond, W. R. (1998). *Violence prevention communication plan for preventing youth violence: The Best Practices Project.* Atlanta, GA: Centers for Disease Control.

Hoagwood, K., & Erwin, H. (1997). Effectiveness of school-based mental health services for children: A 10-year research review. *Journal of Child and Family Studies, 6,* 435–451.

Jacobson, J. W., Mulick, J. A., & Schwartz, A. A. (1995). A history of facilitated communication. Science, Pseudoscience, and Antiscience Working Group on Facilitated Communication. *American Psychologist, 50,* 750–765.

Kauffman, J. M. (1981). Introduction: Historical trends and contemporary issues in special education in the United States. In J. M. Kauffman & D. P. Hallahan (Eds.), *Handbook of special education* (pp. 3–23). Englewood Cliffs, NJ: Prentice-Hall.

Kauffman, J. M. (1993). How we might achieve the radical reform of special education. *Exceptional Children, 60,* 6–16.

Kauffman, J. M. (1996). Research to practice issues. *Behavioral Disorders, 22,* 55–60.

Kauffman, J. M. (1997). Conclusion: A little of everything, a lot of nothing is an agenda for failure. *Journal of Emotional and Behavioral Disorders, 5,* 76–81.

Kauffman, J. M. (in press). Today's special education and its messages for tomorrow. *Journal of Special Education.*

Kauffman, J. M., & Burbach, H. J. (1997). On creating a climate of classroom civility. *Phi Delta Kappan, 79,* 320–325.

Kauffman, J. M., & Hallahan, D. P. (1993). Toward a comprehensive delivery system for special education. In J. I. Goodlad & T. C. Lovitt (Eds.), *Integrated general and special education* (pp. 72–102). Columbus, OH: Merrill/Macmillan.

Kavale, K. A., & Forness, S. R. (in press). The politics of learning disabilities. *Learning Disability Quarterly.*

Kavale, K. A., Forness, S. R., & Walker, H. M. (in press). Interventions for ODD and CD in the schools. In H. Quay & A. Hogan (Eds.), *Handbook of disruptive behavior disorders.* New York: Plenum.

Kuhn, T. S. (1996). *The structure of scientific revolutions* (3rd ed.). Chicago: University of Chicago Press.

Lieberman, I. Y., & Lieberman, A. M. (1990). Whole language versus code emphasis: Underlying assumptions and their implications for reading instruction. *Annals of Dyslexia, 40,* 51–76.

Lloyd, J. W., & Heubusch, J. D. (1996). Issues of social validation in research on serving individuals with emotional or behavioral disorders. *Behavioral Disorders, 22,* 8–14.

Lyon, G. R., & Moats, L. C. (1997). Critical conceptual and methodological considerations in reading intervention research. *Journal of Learning Disabilities, 30,* 578–588.

Malysiak, R. (1997). Exploring the theory and paradigm base for wraparound. *Journal of Child and Family Studies, 6,* 399–408.

Richters, J. E., Arnold, L. E., Jensen, P. S., Abikoff, H., Connors, C. K., Greenhill, L. L., Hechtman, L., Hinshaw, S. P., Pelham, W. E., & Swanson, J. M. (1995). NIMH collaborative multisite multimodal treatment study of children with ADHD: I. Background and rationale. *Journal of the American Academy of Child and Adolescent Psychiatry, 34,* 987–1000.

Sailor, W., & Skrtic, T. M. (1996). School-linked services integration: Crisis and opportunity in the transition to a postmodern society. *Remedial and Special Education, 17,* 271–283.

Shaffer, D., Fisher, P., Dulcan, M. K., Davies, M., Placentini, J., Schwab-Stone, M. E., Lahey, B. B., Bourdon, K., Jensen, P. S., Bird, H. R., Canino, G., & Regier, D. A. (1996). The NIMH Diagnostic Interview Schedule for Children version 2.3 (DISC-2.3): Description, acceptability, prevalence rates, and performance in the MECA study. *Journal of the American Academy of Child and Adolescent Psychiatry, 35,* 865–877.

Skrtic, T. M., Sailor, W., & Gee, K. (1996). Voice, collaboration, and inclusion: Democratic themes in educational and social reform initiatives. *Remedial and Special Education, 17,* 142–157.

Stainback, W., & Stainback, S. (1991). A rationale for integration and restructuring: A synopsis. In J. W. Lloyd, N. N. Singh, & A. C. Repp (Eds.), *The Regular Education Initiative: Alternative perspectives on concepts, issues, and models* (pp. 226–239). Sycamore, IL: Sycamore Press.

Stoner, G., Shinn, M. R., & Walker, H. M. (Eds.). (1991). *Interventions for achievement and behavioral problems.* Silver Spring, MD: National Association of School Psychologists.

Strain, P. S., Steel, P., Ellis, T., & Timm, M. A. (1982). Long term effects of oppositional child treatment with mothers as therapists and therapist trainers. *Journal of Applied Behavior Analysis, 15,* 163–169.

Thomas, A., & Grimes, J. (1995). *Best practices in school psychology-III.* Bethesda, MD: National Association of School Psychologists.

U.S. Office of Special Education Programs. (1994). *Development of a national agenda for emotional disturbance.* Washington, DC: Author.

Walker, H. M. (1993, April). *Acceptance remarks for the 1993 Council for Exceptional Children's Research Award.* San Antonio, TX.

Walker, H. M., Horner, R. H., Sugai, G., Bullis, M., Sprague, J. R., Bricker, D., & Kaufman, M. J. (1996). Integrated approaches to preventing antisocial behavior patterns among school-age children and youth. *Journal of Emotional and Behavioral Disorders, 4,* 193–256.

Webber, J., & Scheuermann, B. (1997). A challenging future: Current barriers and recommended action for our field. *Behavioral Disorders, 22,* 167–178.

Wilson, E. O. (1998, March). Back from chaos. *The Atlantic Monthly,* 41–62.

Chapter Three

The Challenge of Disability Studies

3.1   Changing the Social Relations of Research Production?

Mike Oliver

Abstract: This paper will argue that research on disability has had little influence on policy and made no contribution to improving the lives of disabled people. In fact, up to now the process of research production has been alienating both for disabled people and for researchers themselves. Neither positivist nor interpretive paradigms are immune from the characterisation of research as alienation, and hence it is suggested that the only way to produce unalienated research is to change the social relations of research production. This change will require the development of an emancipatory research paradigm and both the development of and agenda for such a paradigm are briefly considered.

INTRODUCTION

Disability cannot be abstracted from the social world which produces it; it does not exist outside the social structures in which it is located and independent of the meanings given to it. In other words, disability is socially produced. In the past 100 years or so, industrial societies have produced disability first as a medical problem requiring medical intervention and second as a social problem requiring social provision. Research, on the whole, has operated within these frameworks and sought to classify, clarify, map and measure their dimensions.

The late twentieth century has seen a crisis develop in these productions of disability because disabled people have recognised the medical and individual ideologies underpinning them. What is more, having done so, they are now engaged in a struggle to produce disability as social oppression. As this struggle continues and disabled people grow in strength, the crisis in disability production will deepen and researchers will be forced to answer the question Howard Becker posed 30 years ago: whose side are you on? Such are the fundamentals with which we are now dealing.

Returning to the question Becker posed all those years ago is apt, for the book in which he posed it was called *Outsiders*. More recently and in another context Chambers (1983) talks about researchers as out-

siders. He talks about the way academic researchers of all methodological persuasions have consistently misunderstood and distorted both the phenomenon of rural poverty and the experiences of the rural poor in the third world. His critique of what he calls 'rural development tourism' in many respects mirrors the critique of disability research provided by disabled people.

If research in two such disparate areas as rural poverty in the third world and disability in late capitalist society can be attacked on the same grounds, then the problems inherent in such research cannot be reduced to narrow methodological or technical issues. What is more, black people (Bourne, 1981) and women (Maguire, 1987) have provided similar critiques of race and gender research indicating that the problems inherent in such research are widespread.

It is to what can only be called the social relations of research production that the failures of such research can be attributed, and indeed, it is to these very social relations that attention must be focused if research, in whatever area, is to become more useful and relevant in the future than it has been in the past.

The social relations of research production provides the structure within which research is undertaken. These social relations are built upon a firm distinction between the researcher and the researched; upon the belief that it is the researchers who have specialist knowledge and skills; and that it is they who should decide what topics should be researched and be in control of the whole process of research production.

To leave these social relations of research production unchallenged is to leave the task of setting a research agenda for the 1990s in the hands of these

Oliver, M. (1992). Changing the social relations of research production? *Disability, Handicap, and Society*, 7(2), 101–114. Taylor & Francis Ltd.
http://www.tandF.co.uk/journals

experts. The very idea that small groups of 'experts' can get together and set a research agenda for disability is, again, fundamentally flawed. Such an idea is the product of a society which has a positivistic consciousness and a hierarchical social structure which accords experts an elite role. Agenda setting, whether it be in politics, policy-making or service provision, is part of a process of struggle and this is equally true of agenda setting in disability research.

Disability research should not be seen as a set of technical, objective procedures carried out by experts but part of the struggle by disabled people to challenge the oppression they currently experience in their daily lives. Hence the major issue on the research agenda for the 1990s should be; do researchers wish to join with disabled people and use their expertise and skills in their struggles against oppression or do they wish to continue to use these skills and expertise in ways in which disabled people find oppressive?

This leads to the final fundamental issue which will be addressed in this paper—the potential and significance of disability research under a different set of social relations of research production. In order to fully grasp this potential significance, my paper will locate the discussion historically, considering both the history of research generally and how disability research relates to this history, for any understanding that is not historically grounded can only be partial. The history of research will be discussed utilising a three stage historical schema as follows: the positivist stage, the interpretive stage and the emancipatory stage. This schema will then be used to discuss the history, development and future of disability research specifically.

Before discussing the history of research in any detail, however, it is necessary to provide some commentary on the contemporary 'state' of research in general and disability research in particular. There have been numerous attempts in recent years to consider the value and importance of social research (Bulmer, 1981; Kallen, 1982; Shotland & Mark, 1985; Finch, 1986; Heller, 1986; Wenger, 1987) with almost as many differing conclusions. For present purposes, in the following section, one such conclusion will be discussed; that of research as alienation.

At this point however, it is important emphasise that while much of the paper will be critical of research, it is nonetheless based upon the belief that social research has much to contribute to improving the quality of life for everyone in late capitalist society. That it has not done so, so far, is not because social

research has little to offer, but because the social relations of research production have resulted in the production of distorted findings which have been irrelevant to the policy process. Changing the social relations of research production will, at least, offer the possibility of developing a social research enterprise which is relevant to, and significant in, the lives of those people who are the subjects of this enterprise.

RESEARCH AS ALIENATION

The term alienation in its original Marxist sense referred to the process of labour whereby workers became estranged from the products they produced. In a powerful critique of most of what passes for social research, Rowan (1981) argues that alienation is the outcome of the process of this research. By this he meant

> . . . treating people as fragments. This is usually done by putting a person into the role of 'research subject' and only then permitting a very restricted range of behaviour to be counted. This is alienating because it is using the person for someone else's ends—the person's actions do not belong to that individual, but to the researcher and the research plan. (Rowan, 1981, p. 93)

For him, almost all social research has been alienating and alienation in all the four forms suggested by Marx are usually present; from the product of research, from the process itself, from other research subjects and, finally, from self.

The recent history of disability research, in Great Britain at least, can certainly be seen in the terms that Rowan (1981) describes above. The national disability survey undertaken by the Office of Population Censuses and Surveys (OPCS) on behalf of the British Government is a good example of such alienation. Since the publication of the findings of this research (Martin et al., 1988; Martin & White, 1988), despite promises to the contrary, the Government has failed to take any coherent policy initiatives based upon it. OPCS has not taken it further, considering that they have done what they were contracted to do. Disabled people and their organisations have either ignored it or disputed both its reliability and validity (DIG, 1988; Disability Alliance, 1988; Abberley, 1991).

Much of this was predictable in advance because of the alienation of disabled people from the process of research. They were not consulted about the research in advance; what issues should be investigated, how the research should be carried out and so

Table 1
Survey of disabled adults—OPCS, 1986.

Can you tell me what is wrong with you?

What complaint causes your difficulty in holding, gripping or turning things?

Are your difficulties in understanding people mainly due to a hearing problem?

Do you have a scar, blemish or deformity which limits your daily activities?

Have you attended a special school because of a long-term health problem or disability?

Does your health problem/disability mean that you need to live with relatives or someone else who can help look after you?

Did you move here because of your health problem/disability?

How difficult is it for you to get about your immediate neighbourhood on your own?

Does your health problem/disability prevent you from going out as often or as far as you would like?

Does your health problem/disability make it difficult for you to travel by bus?

Does your health problem/disability affect your work in any way at present?

on. Because of this the questions asked in the survey clearly locate the 'problems' of disability within the individual. (See Table 1 for a sample of these questions.) It would have been equally possible to have asked questions which located the problems of disability elsewhere. (See Table 2 for a sample of alternative questions.)

Further, in Rowan's terms, the researchers and the researched were alienated from each other in the way the research was carried out. Disabled people either filled in a postal questionnaire or were interviewed, not by the principal OPCS workers but by part-time interviewers. Further, as I have pointed out elsewhere,

> It is in the nature of the interview process that the interviewer presents as expert and the disabled person as an isolated individual inexperienced in research, and thus unable to reformulate the questions in a more appropriate way. It is hardly surprising that, by the end of the interview, the disabled person has come to believe that his or her problems are caused by their own health/disability problems rather than by the organisation of society. It is in this sense that the process of the interview is oppressive, reinforcing onto isolated, individual disabled people the idea that the problems they experience in everyday living are a direct result of their own personal inadequacies or functional limitations. (Oliver, 1990, p. 8)

Hence the research experience for all concerned was an isolating, individual one reinforcing the dominant idea of disability as an individual problem. Finally, according to Abberley (1991) it attempted to "de-

politicise the unavoidably political, to examine the complex and subtle through crude and simplistic measures."

This alienation from the most extensive and most expensive disability research ever carried out in Britain is not simply an isolated example but symptomatic of a wider crisis that exists between disabled people and the research community. As disabled people have increasingly analysed their segregation, inequality and poverty in terms of discrimination and oppression, research has been seen as part of the problem rather than as part of the solution (Oliver, 1987). Disabled people have come to see research as a violation of their experience, as irrelevant to their needs and as failing to improve their material circumstances and quality of life.

This wider crisis is not something which just affects disabled people for as Chambers (1983, p. 53) reflects in relation to research on rural poverty.

> Much of the material remains unprocessed, or if processed, unanalyzed, or if analyzed, not written up, or if written up, not read, or if read, not remembered, or if remembered, not used or acted upon. Only a minuscule proportion, if any, of the findings affect policy and they are usually a few simple totals. The totals have often been identified early on through physical counting of questionnaires or coding sheets and communicated verbally, independently of the main processing.

Other (oppressed) groups feel exactly the same (Bourne, 1981; Roberts, 1981). Women, for exam-

Table 2
Alternative questions.

Can you tell me what is wrong with society?

What defects in the design of everyday equipment like jars, bottles and tins cause you difficulty in holding, gripping or turning them?

Are your difficulties in understanding people mainly due to their inabilities to communicate with you?

Do other people's reactions to any scar, blemish or deformity you may have, limit your daily activities?

Have you attended a special school because of your education authority's policy of sending people with your health problem or disability to such places?

Are community services so poor that you need to rely on relatives or someone else to provide you with the right level of personal assistance?

What inadequacies in your housing caused you to move here?

What are the environmental constraints which make it difficult for you to get about in your immediate neighbourhood?

Are there any transport or financial problems which prevent you from going out as often or as far as you would like?

Do poorly-designed buses make it difficult for someone with your health problem/disability to use them?

Do you have problems at work because of the physical environment or the attitudes of others?

---

ple, have been advised by Finch (1986) to protect themselves from people like her and black people have been advised to tell researchers to 'fuck off' (Jenkins, 1971). Similarly, disabled people have been advised not to partake in research that does not fully involve them from the outset on the grounds of 'no participation without representation' (Finkelstein, 1985). Hence, in order to understand the crisis in disability research, it is necessary to understand the wider research crisis and how this has developed historically. This will be the subject of the next section.

HISTORY OF RESEARCH

Up until now, there is no doubt that social research has been dominated by positivism. This positivist paradigm has built into a number of assumptions about the nature of the social world and appropriate methods for investigating it. These assumptions consist of the following; a belief that the social world can be studied in the same way as the natural world—that there is a unity of method between the natural and social sciences; that the study of the social world can be value-free; that, ultimately explanations of a causal nature can be provided; and that the knowledge obtained from such research is independent of the assumptions underpinning it and the methods used to obtain it.

Each and all of these assumptions have been questioned over the years, not just in the social sciences (Cicourel, 1964; Giddens, 1979; Hindness, 1980) but in the natural sciences as well (Kuhn, 1961; Popper, 1972). This has given rise to what is almost a new orthodoxy, within the social sciences at least, which suggests that all knowledge is socially constructed and a product of the particular historical context within which it is located. This view of knowledge has spawned a new social research paradigm often referred to as the interpretive or qualitative paradigm.

The assumptions underpinning this are very different from those of the positivist paradigm; that there can be no unity of method for the social world is a meaningful place, a world full of active subjects not passive objects; that research should attempt to understand the meaning of events, not their causes; and that research is a product of the values of researchers and cannot be independent of them.

This new paradigm, itself been subject to much criticism, naturally from positivist researchers but also from others; critical theorists, Marxists, methodological anarchists and most importantly, the active subjects of this research. There is not the space to reproduce the debates with positivists nor to repeat the snipings of a ragbag of remote theorists. However, when one of the classic works in interpretive research, Robert Edgerton's *The Cloak of Competence*, which influenced a whole generation, is accused of serving "to deny members of his sample a voice with which to speak authoritatively about their own situation" (Gerber, 1990, p. 3), clearly all is not well within the paradigm.

Far more important than academic disputes, however, is the critique which has emerged from active research subjects who have argued that while the interpretive paradigm has changed the rules, in reality it has not changed the game. Interpretive research still has a relatively small group of powerful experts doing work on a larger number of relatively powerless research subjects. To put the matter succinctly, interpretive research is just as alienating as positivist research because what might be called 'the social relations of research production' have not changed one iota.

Not only that but the defects of both positivist and interpretive approaches merely reinforce one another.

> The positivist approach, by ignoring how . . . problems are always preinterpreted, effectively eliminates their . . . character; the interpretive approach, by insulating the self-understanding of practitioners from direct, concrete and practical criticism, effectively eliminates their problematic character. (Carr & Kemmis, 1986, p. 215)

As a consequence of this situation, there have been calls to develop another paradigm for social research—what has variously been called critical enquiry, praxis or emancipatory research.

This, even newer paradigm has a very different view of knowledge (theory) which must

> . . . illuminate the lived experiences of progressive social groups; it must also be illuminated by their struggles. Theory adequate to the task of changing the world must be open-ended, nondogmatic, informing, and grounded in the circumstances of everyday life. (Lather, 1987, p. 262)

Not only that but the social relations of research production also must fundamentally change so that both researcher and researched become changers and changed (Lather, 1987). Finally, of course, the methodology of research must also change building upon trust and respect and building in participation and reciprocity.

It is possible to see the development of positivist, interpretive and emancipatory research paradigms as

a historically located sequence and the next section will discuss disability research in precisely this way. It is also possible to provide models which link these paradigms to the policy making process; engineering, enlightenment and struggle approaches. Finally each of these paradigms and their linked policy models are underpinned by particular views of the nature of disability; as an individual, a social and a political problem (see Fig. 1).

However, it should be pointed out that this historically located sequence is not a fixed and absolute series of developmental stages but rather a set of trends. All three paradigms, their related policy models and their views of disability may exist at any one time and currently do; the dominance of the positivist paradigm has been challenged by the interpretive one in the last twenty years with emancipatory research currently emerging if not to challenge, then at least to question some of the assumptions of the other two.

DISABILITY RESEARCH

The history of research on disability is undoubtedly one that has been dominated by the positivist research paradigm both in terms of the research undertaken (Harris, 1971; Martin et al., 1988), and the assumptions underpinning it (Wood, 1980). There are two major problems with this domination; first that the experience of disability has been profoundly distorted; and secondly, the links between research and social change have been seen as relatively simplistic and rational, adopting a social engineering approach to the policy making process. These have caused major problems which need further discussion.

Unfortunately disability research has been unable to shake off the methodological individualism inherent in positivist social research of all kinds, which has been defined as follows:

> Methodological individualism is a doctrine about explanation which asserts that all attempts to explain social (or individual) phenomena are to be rejected (or, according to a current, more sophisticated version, rejected as 'rock-bottom' explanations) unless they are couched wholly in terms of facts about individuals. (Lukes, 1972, p. 110)

Disability research, therefore, has reinforced the individual model of disability (Oliver, 1983) seeing the

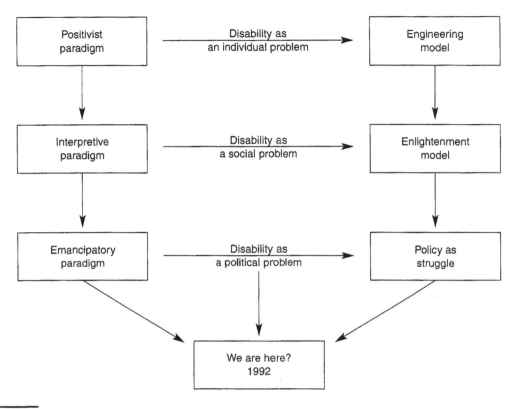

Figure 3.1
Social research and social policy.

problems that disabled people face as being caused by their individual impairments.

These rock-bottom explanations not only see disability as an individual problem but in so doing they reject other possible explanations.

> Methodological individualism is thus an exclusivist, prescriptive doctrine about what explanations are to look like. . . it excludes explanations which appeal to social forces, structural features of society, institutional factors and so on. (Lukes, 1972, p. 122)

Hence they fail to accord with disabled people's own explanations of the problems of disability which argue that these are caused by society; by the social restrictions it imposes and by its failure to acknowledge, let alone attempt to meet, the self-defined needs of disabled people (UPIAS, 1975).

The second problem that positivist research poses is that it assumes that the relationship between research findings and policy change is non-problematic. Given the facts, government will act and changes will occur for the better. This has been called 'the social engineering approach' and has been widely criticised both for its epistemological assumptions and for its failure to produce social change in the manner prescribed (Bulmer, 1981; Finch, 1986). Again this is certainly true of the lack of effect that this approach has had in the area of disability policy (Borsay, 1986a; Oliver, 1986).

For example, a sustained and extensive campaign for a national disability income over the last twenty years (DIG, 1989; Disability Alliance, 1989) has been based precisely on this approach;—countless studies have demonstrated the numbers and extent of poverty amongst disabled people to the point where everyone, including the Government, agrees with the evidence. Yet a national disability income is no nearer than it was when the campaign began over 20 years ago. This failure then, can only be explained in terms of the inappropriateness of the social engineering model as an explanation of policy change in general and disability policy in particular (Oliver & Zarb, 1989).

There have been some attempts in recent years to undertake disability research within the interpretive paradigm (Blaxter, 1980; Borsay, 1986b; Oliver et al., 1988) and while this has attempted to take the meaning of disability for disabled people themselves seriously, it has still been subject to criticisms. These criticisms centre, in the main, around the failure of this kind of work also to have any serious effect on services for disabled people and their quality of life.

Again it is possible to identify two main reasons for this; firstly, such research does not fundamentally alter the social relations of research production and not for nothing has this kind of research been called in another context "the rape model of research" (Reinharz, 1985) in that researchers have benefitted by taking the experience of disability, rendering a faithful account of it and then moving on to better things while the disabled subjects remain in exactly the same social situation they did before the research began.

A second criticism stems from the model of the policy making process that the interpretive paradigm presupposes; what is usually called the enlightenment model. This argues that there is no direct and explicit link between research and policy making but what research does instead is that it informs the policy making process; it provides a backdrop against which policy makers make decisions; it helps them to decide what questions to ask rather than to provide specific answers; and so on. This is all very well but it offers little in the way of immediate improvements in the material conditions of life for the disabled research subjects and again raises the issue of whether or not to participate in such research.

This disillusion with both the positivist and interpretive research paradigms has raised the issue of developing an emancipatory paradigm in order to make disability research more relevant to the lives of disabled people. The next section will consider what such a paradigm might look like in general before discussing its potential for disabled people.

EMANCIPATORY RESEARCH—ANOTHER NEW PARADIGM?

The development of such a paradigm stems from the gradual rejection of the positivist view of social research as the pursuit of absolute knowledge through the scientific method and the gradual disillusionment with the interpretive view of such research as the generation of socially useful knowledge within particular historical and social contexts. The emancipatory paradigm, as the name implies, is about the facilitating of a politics of the possible by confronting social oppression at whatever levels it occurs.

Central to the project is a recognition of and confrontation with power which structures the social relations of research production. To put it bluntly, research has been and essentially still is, an activity carried out by those who have power upon those who do not. Some 30 years ago much sociological research was criticised for its underdog mentality (Gouldner, 1975) and caricatured as being the "sociology of nuts, sluts and perverts" (Liazos, 1972).

Such criticisms apply with equal force today; people who are poor, unemployed, mentally ill, women, black people, disabled people and children are all frequently studied. In comparison research has uncovered little about the lives and activities of psychiatrists, bank managers, policemen, politicians, policy makers, political terrorists, captains of industry or even researchers themselves. As one policy researcher has put it

... the powerful are so rarely studied because they have the resources to protect themselves from scrutiny. (Taylor, 1985, p. 152)

However the importance of the emancipatory research paradigm is not attempts it might make to study the other end of existing power relations but to attempts it might make to challenge them. Such challenges are unlikely to be funded by institutions located within existing power structures and one suggested solution is to take money for studying one thing but then to shift the focus once the research has begun "from victim to victimiser, from the powerless to the powerful" (Jenkins, quoted in Wenger, 1987, p. 157).

Not all researchers, even those committed to developing an emancipatory paradigm, would find such an approach acceptable arguing that taking money for one thing and then doing something else is not only unethical but dangerous in the consequences it may have for the researcher, the discipline, the institution and the research community. For example, it is debateable whether the benefits and practical implications of the research by Cohen & Taylor (1972) on long-term imprisonment outweighed the damage done to relations between the Home Office and the research community because of the deceitful basis on which they gathered their data.

However, the development of an emancipatory paradigm is not simply about confrontation with or accommodation to the power structures which fund and resource research production; it is also about the demystification of the ideological structures within which these power relations are located. According to Giroux, researchers, along with other transformative intellectuals,

> . . . need to understand how subjectivities are produced and regulated through historically produced social forms and how these forms carry and embody particular interests. At the core of this position is the need to develop modes of enquiry that not only investigate how experience is shaped, lived and endured within particular social forms. . . but also how certain apparatuses of power produced forms of knowledge that legitimate a particular kind of truth and way of life. (Quoted in Sherman & Webb, 1988, p. 196)

Feminist research has probably made most progress in the demystification of existing ideological structures in that

> When feminist epistomologies are proposed, they not only set out to legitimise a new field of inquiry; often they also question the entire nature of the 'scientific project' and its underlying metaphysics. (Halberg, 1989, p. 3)

These epistemologies (and according to Harding [1987], there are at least two, feminist empiricism and feminist standpoint research) have also made progress in developing methodological strategies commensurate with the emancipatory paradigm.

The three key fundamentals on which such a paradigm must be based are reciprocity, gain and empowerment (Gollop, 1989). These fundamentals can be built in by encouraging self-reflection and a deeper understanding of the research situation by the research subjects (Lather, 1987). Unfortunately such a view can be criticised on precisely the same grounds as the previous two paradigms; the social relations of research production may not necessarily be changed

at all. Instead of research achieving social change (transformation) through engineering or enlightenment approaches to policy, it will achieve it through the empowerment of research subjects and the main technique for empowerment will be the encouragement of reciprocity.

While reciprocity is a worthwhile aim, claims to have achieved it (Oakley, 1981) have recently been called into question and it has been argued that within existing social relations of research production, researchers never reveal as much about themselves as they expect to be revealed (Ribbens, 1990). Further empowerment does not exist as the gift of few who have it to be delivered to those who do not; people can only empower themselves (Freire, 1972).

The issue then for the emancipatory research paradigm is not how to empower people but, once people have decided to empower themselves, precisely what research can then do to facilitate this process. This does then mean that the social relations of research production do have to be fundamentally changed; researchers have to learn how to put their knowledge and skills at the disposal of their research subjects, for them to use in whatever ways they choose. The task for emancipatory research is not, as is sometimes implied, to help the researched to understand themselves better, but to develop its own understanding of the lived experiences of these very subjects. This is, of course, a dialectical process in which research can play a significant part.

The importance of emancipatory research, therefore,

> . . . is in establishing a dialogue between research workers and the grass-roots people with whom they work, in order to discover and realise the practical and cultural needs of those people. Research here becomes one part of a developmental process including also education and political action. (Reason, 1988, p. 2)

Hence such research can challenge the social relations of research production, it can be about the self-understanding of researchers as well as researched and it need not be separated from wider processes of education and politics.

Empowerment through self-understanding is a process through which many oppressed groups are beginning to pass and emancipatory research can have a role to play in this. Such self-understanding is an essential pre-requisite to providing a redefinition of 'the real nature of the problem'. This process has been succinctly captured in a commentary on research on black issues.

> It was not black people who should be examined, but white society; it was not a case of educating blacks and whites for integration, but of fighting institutional racism; it was not race relations that was the field for study, but racism. (Bourne, 1981, p. 339)

This quote, 10 years later applies exactly to the 'state' of disability research; it is not disabled people who need to be examined but able-bodied society; it is not a case of educating disabled and able-bodied people for integration, but of fighting institutional disablism (Oliver, 1990); it is not disability relations which should be the field for study but disablism.

So, at last we can begin to identify a research agenda for emancipatory disability research; not the disabled people of the positivist and interpretive research paradigms but the disablism ingrained in the individualistic consciousness and institutionalised practices of what is, ultimately, a disablist society. These are the issues that disabled people have placed on the research agenda: the key issue for the research community is whether or not they can respond.

Bourne (1981) suggests three ways in which this new research paradigm can make a contribution to the combating of racism: (i) a description of experience in the face of "academics who abstract and distort black experience (however, unwittingly)"; (ii) a re-definition of the problem; and (iii) a challenge to the ideology and methodology of dominant research paradigms. To that list written more than 10 years ago, disabled people would want to add the following: (iv) the development of a methodology and set of techniques commensurate with the emancipatory research paradigm; (v) a description of collective experience in the face of academics who are unaware or ignore the existence of the disability movement; and (vi) a monitoring and evaluation of services that are established, controlled and operated by disabled people themselves.

CONCLUSIONS—THE WAY AHEAD

The argument presented here has suggested that existing research paradigms have proved inadequate and hence, will not be useful in trying to construct a disability research agenda for the future. Issues highlighted by disabled people have been identified and it has been suggested that they can only be tackled by building a new research paradigm which fundamentally changes the existing social relations of research production.

Finally, this new paradigm must throw off the shackles of methodological individualism with its inadequate and abstracted view of the individual for emancipatory research can only be really accomplished

> . . . on the basis of a view of unabstracted individuals in their concrete social specificity, who in virtue of being persons, all require to be treated and to live in a social order which treats them as possessing dignity, as capable of exercising and increasing their autonomy, of engaging in valued activities within a private space, and of developing their several potentialities. (Lukes, 1973, pp. 152–153)

Thus the transcending of methodological individualism produces a vision of society exactly the same as the one for which disabled people are currently struggling. The struggle to produce just such a social order is not one for disabled people alone and Howard Becker's question is revealed as false; we are all on each other's side.

REFERENCES

Abberley, P. (1991) The significance of the OPCS disability surveys, in: M. Oliver (Ed.) *Social Work: disabled people and disabling environments* (London, Kingsley).

Blaxter, M. (1980) *The Meaning of Disability* (London, Heinemann).

Borsay, A. (1986a) Personal trouble or public issue? Towards a model of policy for people with physical and mental disabilities, *Disability, Handicap & Society*, 1, pp. 179–196.

Borsay, A. (1986b) *Disabled People in the Community* (London, Bedford Square Press).

Bourne, J. (1981) Cheerleaders and ombudsmen: a sociology of race relations in Britain, *Race and Class*, 21, pp. 331–352.

Bulmer, M. (1981) *The Uses of Social Research: social investigations in public policy making* (London, Allen & Unwin).

Carr, W. & Kemmis, S. (1986) *Becoming Critical: education, knowledge and action research* (Lewes, Falmer Press).

Chambers, R. (1983) *Rural Development: putting the last first* (Harlow, Longman).

Cicourel, A. (1964) *Method and Measurement in Sociology* (New York, Free Press).

Disability Alliance (1988) *Briefing on the First Report from the OPCS Surveys of Disability* (London, Disability Alliance).

Disability Alliance (1989) *Poverty and Disability: breaking the link* (London, Disability Alliance).

Disablement Income Group (1988) *Not the OPCS Survey: being disabled costs more than they said* (London, Disablement Income Group).

Disablement Income Group (1989) *DIG's National Disability Income* (London, Disablement Income Group).

Edgerton, R. (1967) *The Cloak of Competence* (Berkeley, CA, University of California Press).

Finch, J. (1986) *Research and Policy: the uses of qualitative methods in social and educational research* (Lewes, Falmer Press).

Finkelstein, V. (1985) Paper given at *World Health Organisation Meeting*, 24–28 June, Netherlands.

Freire, P. (1972) *Pedagogy of the Oppressed* (Harmondsworth, Penguin).

Gerber, D. (1990) Listening to disabled people, *Disability, Handicap & Society*, 5, pp. 3–24.

Giddens, A. (1979) *New Rules of the Sociological Method* (London, Hutchinson).

Giroux, A. (1988) 'Critical theory and the politics of culture and voice.' Rethinking the discourse of educational research, in: R. Shearman & R. Webb (Eds), *Qualitative Research in Education: focus and methods*.

Gouldner, A. (1975) *For Sociology: renewal and critique in sociology today* (London, Pelican).

Harris, A. (1971) *Handicapped and Impaired in Great Britain* (London, HMSO).

Heller, F. (Ed.) (1986) *The Use and Abuse of Social Science* (London, Sage).

Hindness, B. (1980) *Philosophy and Methodology in the Social Sciences* (New York, Harvester).

Jenkins, R. (1971) *The Production of Knowledge in the IRR* (London, Institute for Race Relations).

Kallen, D., Kosse, G., Wagenaar, H., Kloprogge, J. & Vorbeck, M. (1982) *Social Science Research and Public Policy Making: a reappraisal* (Windsor, NFER-Nelson).

Kuhn, T. (1961) *The Structure of Scientific Revolutions* (Chicago, IL, Chicago University Press).

Lather, P. (1987) Research as praxis, *Harvard Educational Review*, 56, pp. 257–273.

Liazos, A. (1972) The poverty of the sociology of deviance: nuts, sluts and perverts, *Social Problems*, 20, pp. 102–120.

Lukes, S. (1972) *Individualism* (Oxford, Basil Blackwell).

Maguire, P. (1987) *Doing Participatory Research: a feminist approach* (Amherst, MA, University of Massachusetts).

Martin, J., Meltzer, H. & Elliott D. (1988) *The Prevalence of Disability among Adults* (London, HMSO).

Martin, J. & White, A. (1988) *The Financial Circumstances of Disabled Adults in Private Households* (London, HMSO).

Oliver, M. (1983) *Social Work with Disabled People* (Basingstoke, Macmillan).

Oliver, M. (1986) Social policy and disability: some theoretical issues, *Disability, Handicap & Society*, 1, pp. 5–18.

Oliver, M. (1987) Re-defining disability: some issues for research, *Research, Policy and Planning*, 5, pp. 9–13.

Oliver, M. (1990) *The Politics of Disablement* (Basingstoke, Macmillan).

Oliver, M. & Zarb, G. (1989) The politics of disability: a new approach, *Disability, Handicap & Society*, 4, pp. 221–239.

Popper, K. (1972) *Conjectures and Refutations* (London, Routledge).

Reason, P. (Ed.) (1988) *Human Inquiry in Action: developments in new paradigm research* (London, Sage).

Reinharz, S. (1979) *On Becoming a Social Scientist* (San Francisco, CA, Jossey-Bass).

Ribbens, J. (1990) Interviewing—an unnatural situation?, *Women's Studies International Forum*, 12, pp. 579–592.

Roberts, H. (Ed.) (1981) *Doing Feminist Research* (London, Routledge & Kegan Paul).

Rowan, J. (1981) A dialectical paradigm for research, in: P. Reason & J. Rowan (Eds) *Human Inquiry: a sourcebook of new paradigm research* (Chichester, John Wiley).

Sherman, R. & Webb, R. (Eds) (1988) *Qualitative Research in Education: focus and methods* (London, Falmer Press).

Shotland, R. & Mark, M. (Eds) (1985) *Social Science and Social Policy* (London, Sage).

UPIAS (1975) *Fundamental Principles of Disability* (London, Union of the Physically Impaired Against Segregation).

Wenger, C. (Ed.) (1987) *The Research Relationship: practice and politics in social policy research* (London, Allen & Unwin).

Wood, P. (1980) *International Classification of Impairments, Disabilities and Handicaps* (Geneva, World Health Organisation).

3.2   Divided Society

Simi Linton

I have the right when I go out and pay good money for a meal to enjoy it. The sight of a woman in a wheelchair with food running down her chin would make me throw up. I believe my rights should be respected as much as the rights of the person in the wheelchair . . . maybe even more so, because I am normal and she is not.

In my opinion, restaurants should have a special section for handicapped people—partially hidden by palms or other greenery so they are not seen by other guests.

—excerpts from two letters printed in an Ann Landers column, spring 1987

No person who is diseased, maimed, mutilated or in any way deformed so as to be an unsightly or disgusting object or improper person to be allowed in or on the public ways or other public places in this city, shall therein or thereon expose himself to public view, under penalty of nor less than one dollar nor more than fifty dollars for each offense.

—from the Municipal Code of the City of Chicago

It is in the formal and informal, the explicit and the tacit, the overt and the covert that society works to divide up the human community and oppress some of its members. The above example of public rules and private thoughts (revealed in the safety of anonymity) may not seem to have much force. Federal law prohibits such discrimination, and public expression of these sentiments would be scorned in many circles and the speakers branded as unsympathetic or uncharitable, not to mention unsophisticated. But the underlying ethos has not dissolved with shifting practices; it remains a virulent force with new manifestations.

As Young (1990) notes:

The objectification and overt domination of despised bodies that obtained in the nineteenth century, however, has receded in our time, and a discursive commitment to equality for all has emerged. Racism, sexism, homophobia, ageism, and ableism, I argue, have not disappeared with that commitment, but have gone underground, dwelling in everyday habits and cultural meanings of which people are for the most part unaware. (124)

To Young's comments I would add that in addition to the everyday habits and cultural meanings, there remain policies and practices that serve to control and marginalize disabled people. Unfortunately, these barriers to the integration of disabled people are often not fully visible, at least not to the untrained observer. They function like the "glass ceiling" that women come up against when attempting to advance in business. But it would be a mistake to say that the barriers that women or disabled people encounter are truly invisible. For instance, the policy to exclude women from private clubs where business deals are clinched might be made visible by looking at the by-laws of such clubs, or by testing the admissions practices. The practices within the clubs can be revealed by conducting research on the behaviors and habits of their members to find out how they transact business while seeming to talk about golf. Of course it would take extraordinary methods to expose all the structural inequities that exist in the business world and other significant arenas that privilege some groups' participation and success. Moreover, as Marx and others have instructed us, these local events are often controlled by forces beyond the purview of those acting at that site, making it even more difficult to gain access to the information (Gorelick 1996). Nevertheless, it is important to recognize that by call-

Linton, S. (1998). Divided society. In *Claiming Disability: Knowledge and Identity,* (pp. 34–70). New York: NYU Press. Reprinted by permission.

ing the barriers invisible we run the risk of implying that they are so amorphous and intangible that we can't document them and can't change them.

A watchful outsider might recognize some of the more obvious barriers that exclude disabled people from participation in society but may have the false impression that there are few hidden barriers. It may seem that if ramps are built to get into all the polling places, sign language interpreters are provided at public functions, and the Constitution is transcribed into Braille, we will have done away with the inequities. But redressing second-class citizenship, 66 percent unemployment, incarceration in institutions, and separate and unequal education will take more than these mechanical changes (Shapiro 1993).

Although an enormous amount of research is yet to be done to document the complex history of these practices and to catalogue their current manifestations, we can review what is already known about humans' response to disability to see that disability has been conceptualized and responded to in a variety of ways throughout history and across human cultures. It is not a singular history. There isn't, as some might imagine, a clear stream of progress from prehistory to the present moment. Nor is it accurate to valorize the United States and other Westernized countries for exemplary practices and an enlightened vision.

This chapter examines the variations in social arrangements that have existed throughout history and currently exist around the world. Of course, it is not possible to provide a complete history of humans' response to disability. Some significant examples have been chosen in order to demonstrate the variation and to expose some of the problems that have occurred in the documentation and interpretation of that history. Disabled people have existed predominantly as marginal figures, their contributions and perspectives are not generally noted. Researchers outside disability studies have not been actively interested in this history nor in examining the meaning and function of disability in the lives of the few well-known people with disabilities.

The disability history that does exist is heavily dominated by the perspectives of scholars from the United States and Western Europe, whether they are looking at their own country's practices or others', leaving even more obscure the perspectives from the remainder of the world. Further, these reports usually do not make differentiations along gender, class, or race lines; therefore, many of the statements made about "treatment of disabled people" are not truly for the whole population. The most fundamental prob-

lem, though, is that disabled people's voices are almost completely absent from this picture, and so the understanding of disabled people's place in these situations is filtered through the experience of people who have never been in that place.

VARIATIONS

Although there are variations across time and cultures in response to disability, there are patterns that can be traced. An article by Hanks and Hanks written in 1948 provides a useful starting point for organizing the available evidence into a typology or classification system. While their study, *The Physically Handicapped in Certain Non-Occidental Societies,* predates the formal presentation of social models of disability by some thirty years, it is focused on the social variables that structure participation of disabled people in selected societies. It is a strength of the report that they looked primarily *at* social participation rather than at treatment or care provided to disabled people, and that they looked *to* the social structure for the explanation of the degree of integration or participation of disabled people in each society rather than to the nature of the disability itself or the psychological makeup of disabled individuals. Astonishingly, they also in some instances point out class and gender differences in disability experience in instructive ways. There are also some limitations to their schema, to their interpretations, and to the data they looked to for evidence.

Hanks and Hanks analyzed practices in a number of cultures, with a particular interest in response to physical disability in "non-Occidental" societies. A limitation of their material, therefore, for the present analysis is that practices related to people with other disabilities are not included; relatively few countries were actually studied; and Westernized and/or industrialized countries are not included. The few gender and class differences they did note are inadequate to the complexity that exists, and, further, their descriptions fall short of the meaning that these differences have for the people they describe. Another limitation is that their conceptualization of response to disability into the five domains they chose limits the range of practices that can be studied. Therefore, I have added a sixth category and reworked some of the descriptive material to include an even broader range of data and more contemporary examples. In a number of places, I have indicated ways that a more explicit and differentiated scheme could be fashioned from the data and theoretical formulations that have emerged since their study. These caveats aside, the

Hankses' original categories, Pariah, Economic Liability, Tolerant Utilization, Limited Participation, and Laissez-faire, as amended, are described below, along with the sixth category, Active Participation and Accommodation that I have added.

1. Pariah. The first category, Pariah, is described by Hanks and Hanks (1948) as cultures in which disabled people are "denied all claims to succor by the protective group and [are] deemed a threat to the group itself" (13). I have amended this to read that disabled people are denied most if not all claims to succor and to rights by the dominant nondisabled majority and are deemed a threat to the group itself. This revision alters the category in three significant ways. The addition of "rights" and "dominant group" makes explicit the power differentials in these situations in which nondisabled people determine what resources, if any, will be made available to disabled people. I have eliminated the Hankses' term "protective group" because it assumes that protection is the desired behavior. Although the definition of *pariah* in many dictionaries is solely "social outcast," typical usage and other dictionaries also incorporate more active and virulent meanings, such as Merriam Webster's "despised by society." Throughout history there have been groups whose religious beliefs or social customs sanctioned practices that were harmful, and often lethal, for disabled people. Therefore, the practices discussed in this category reflect more than the passive meaning, that the individual is an outcast; rather, the examples support the stance of "casting out" or harming these despised members of society.

Denying or withholding resources or protection is one set of responses to disabled people deemed pariahs. Hanks and Hanks (1948) state that the practice of denying all protection and care is "most frequent in India" (13), where the family is put at risk by having a disabled member because its social position is thereby threatened. The family may deny the individual protection. However, a woman is told to care for, indeed worship, her disabled husband even if his family abandons him. Women with disabilities, it seems, would not expect the reciprocal response from their husbands.

Directly harming or killing disabled people is an even more aggressive means of managing the perceived threat. It is ironic that the Hankses, writing in the late 1940s, pointed toward India, when evidence of what was probably the most comprehensive example of systematic violence toward disabled

people was known. Granted their focus was on "non-Occidental" societies, but they wrote "most frequent in India" and other phrases in an absolute manner, implying its unequivocal status. Nazi Germany took specific actions to eliminate disabled people and succeeded in annihilating 200,000 "disabled men, women and children . . . 'Lebensunwertes Leben'— life unworthy of life—was the concept Nazi doctors used to justify their practice of direct medical euthanasia" (Shapiro 1993, 271). Disabled people threatened the idea of Aryan perfection, constructed around a very narrow band of acceptable behavior, appearance, and genetic makeup. (The contributions of the United States to the early eugenics movement on which Nazi practices were built is discussed in the next chapter.)

A most profound example of withholding care and "succor" can be seen in the United States, in the history of many of our institutions and asylums. In the early 1970s Geraldo Rivera described the conditions at the Willowbrook State School that were "not unlike Nazi deathcamps. At Willowbrook, Rivera told his viewers, one hundred percent of all residents contracted hepatitis within six months of entering the institution. . . . Many lay on dayroom floors (naked) in their own feces" (Trent 1994, 258). A more recent example, affecting people with a broader range of disabilities, is reported by Asch and Fine (1988, 23) from a *New York Times* article from 1984. "An inquiry into California's community care facilities for the mentally and physically disabled and for the elderly found that 'daily, throughout the state, residents of community care facilities are being sexually abused, beaten, fed spoiled food, forced to live with toilets that don't work.' "

There are varying reports on the degree to which infanticide has occurred in the past or still does. Scheer and Groce (1988) note that infanticide of disabled newborns is not commonly practiced in developing countries, despite popular beliefs to the contrary. However, a number of examples of disabled children being killed at birth or shortly thereafter have been documented. These practices, though, also target children not considered disabled by Western definitions, such as babies with extra fingers or twins. For instance, Nichols (1993) reports that among the Ashantis of central Ghana infants with six fingers are killed at birth and with "the Igbo and some other groups infanticide sometimes occurred following the birth of twins" (32).

Mallory (1993) describes how the Songye tribe of Zaire divides all children with physical anomalies into three categories: ceremonial, miserable, or faulty.

"Miserable children are those born with albinism, dwarfism, or hydrocephaly." They are not seen as human beings; rather, they are thought to be supernatural beings and are accorded "an inferior status in the tribe, and little is done to make their lives comfortable or meaningful" (18). The Igide of Nigeria are reported to "tolerate" certain "minor birth defects" but other "abnormal babies are usually killed and thrown away by the Ebih priest" (Nichols 1993, 32). The practice of "throwing away," or abandoning babies on river banks or in the bush, is practiced by the Igbo with twins and by the Ashantis with "severely" retarded infants because both groups of infants are thought to be animal-like. Whyte (1995) reports that these practices have tapered off in recent times and that there is increased conflict between the parents, who often wish to have the infant live, and the will of the elders of the tribe, who may wish to conform to ritual practices. Ross (1983) reports that "infanticide in hunting and gathering societies was probably universally practiced in instances of congenital birth defects" and also notes that there are "ethnographic references to the ritual disposal of adolescents and adults when they had become physically disabled and were unable to be ambulatory or fulfill certain tasks." Ross later says that these actions are taken "only when selective pressures were beyond the control of the particular group in question" (137).

A recent report in the *Atlantic Monthly* on orphanages in China demonstrates how vulnerable babies born with disabilities are there. It should be noted that other infants are also vulnerable in those institutions, particularly girls. Anne Thurston (1996) reported that for years friends had been telling her "that severely handicapped infants—those with incapacitating infirmities requiring full-time care—are routinely allowed to die" (40). Other infants are placed in "dying rooms" as well, although it appears that the practice is more systematic and probably more generally accepted when the infants are disabled. A doctor with whom Thurston spoke, "a man of great compassion," pointed out that the "best of his people have suffered the most egregious persecution . . . [therefore] does it not follow that those of so little official worth—the handicapped and abandoned—should be allowed to die" (40). This statement is Thurston's paraphrase, and hence it is not possible to tell whether the word "official" as a modifier of "worth" is the doctor's view, Thurston's, or the government's. However, "the best of his people" is said straightforwardly and implies its opposite, the worst. Comments such as these come out in public unchecked when the speaker assumes that there is consensus on the official worth of disabled people.

In the reports of Chinese and African practices, a number of explanations are provided for these practices that emanate from commonly held belief systems. For instance, the *Buddhist*, belief that "a severe handicap [is] . . . evidence of a heinous crime in a previous life" and the Confucian belief that "a severely handicapped child would be incapable of fulfilling the immutable demands of filial piety and thus unable to behave as a proper human being" (Thurston 1996, 40) are mentioned. Nichols, in discussing the derivations of African practices, makes an important distinction between beliefs that emerge from what he calls "*pragmatic spirituality*" and those attributable to "*blind superstition*" (1993, 29). His objective is to take a more serious look at belief systems that have often been dismissed as "primitive" or "barbaric" and to demonstrate the humanitarian and practical responses evidenced in African cultures. It is ironic, and unfortunate, that a metaphoric use of *blind* is employed in this context, particularly because, in contrast to pragmatic spirituality, which is thought to reflect knowledge and utility, blind superstition is in "bondage to ignorance" (29). All these pragmatic and metaphysical explanations provide useful material for analysis, but a rigorous examination of the practices themselves needs to be made. Ritual "disposal" of disabled people and infanticide are murder and therefore individual acts, no matter what function they are serving and no matter what complex long standing imperatives they fulfill.

The recent debates about euthanasia, currently being called "physician-assisted suicide," and about prenatal screening and selective abortion in North America and in Europe have raised concerns about the "right to life" of disabled people. The Supreme Court in the United States is deliberating on the legality of physician-assisted suicide, and the issue is being debated throughout the press. Disabled people and allies, in demonstrations outside the Court in January 1996 and in other fora, have been pointing out that "suicide" implies a fully voluntary act, and for many disabled people and poor people there are coercive forces that act on their choices. Particularly in the climate of managed care, where the economic imperatives that guide a physician's choices are increasingly powerful, the supposed "expense" of disabled people's lives make us more vulnerable to coercion. Further, physicians are not reliable judges of the value and worth of disabled people's lives. Nat Hentoff (1997b) reports that Dr. Katherine Foley, cochief of the Pain and Palliative Care Service at the Memorial Sloan-Kettering Cancer Center, said in an interview that "physicians consistently underestimate the quality of living for those individuals who are disabled."

For a number of years disabled people have been watching the Netherlands, where "Dutch doctors have been empowered to help patients kill themselves, and, increasingly, physicians there have been directly killing patients without being asked to" (Hentoff 1997a). Hentoff asked a television interviewer how the "Dutch people can justify not only this 'quality of life' killing of adults, which brings back memories of Nazi occupiers—but also the liquidating of 'defective' children." It is particularly horrible that today the Dutch appear complicit in these actions when just over fifty years ago, Dutch physicians gave up their medical licenses rather then join the Nazi medical association. A study conducted in 1995 revealed that "23 percent of the doctors interviewed reported that they had euthanized a patient without his or her explicit request," and in some cases made the initial suggestion that "death should be embraced."

Less egregious than murder but socially and personally devastating is the practice of ostracizing and vilifying members of a society. Two recent reports from Japan provide examples of behaviors that have existed and continue in many places in the world. The headline of a *New York Times* article by N. D. Kristof (1996) declares, "Outcast Status Worsens Pain of Japan's Disabled." Osamu Takahashi, now age forty-nine and the director of a center for disabled people in Japan, told the reporter that

[he] never went to any school and was hidden in the house from birth until the age of 26. While the rest of his family are together, he was served meals alone in his room. His family allowed him out of the house only about once a year, and then mostly at night so the neighbors would not see . . . [and] that view still survives in some households. (3)

The term *outcast* seems to have particular saliency for disabled people in Japan. Other people interviewed for the article described discrimination in housing, education, and employment but emphasized the pain and frustration of being social outcasts. S. Sesser (1994) reported in the *New Yorker* on the particularly painful experience that people who are HIV positive have in Japan. "With the sick and the disabled ordinarily feeling like outcasts, it's not surprising that those Japanese infected with H.I.V. are the most reclusive of all" (64).

Disabled people around the world who are deemed pariahs by their own families and communities have lived through the terrible pain of being denied succor by the very persons to whom it would be most natural to turn. Practices ranging from withholding attention, food, love, and education to denying them life itself have been documented. For the most part the practices described here are not unique to that particular culture. Many disabled people around the globe have stories to tell of abuse and marginalization. As the rest of this chapter will demonstrate, casting out and vilifying disabled people is the extreme end of a long and complex continuum.

2. Economic and Social Liability. I've changed the Hanks and Hanks (1948) original category, Economic Liability, to Economic and Social Liability to permit inclusion of examples of disabled people's being seen as impairing the economic well-being, as well as the vitality and viability, of a society. Even if disabled people are not considered pariahs, those who are thought to bring harm directly to individuals or to the group, there are situations or cultures where disabled people are unwelcome because they are thought to drain resources or deflect attention from other needs. Included in this category are the more extreme examples, couched in survivalist rhetoric, that invoke a lifeboat image of a society abandoning the "weaker" members to aid the survival of the group. Responses to these imperatives range from containment and control to abandonment and annihilation, all enacted ostensibly to conserve resources and protect the interests of the majority. This section does not survey practices across different countries but, rather, traces liability themes by describing the emergence of modern approaches to disability from the seventeenth through twentieth centuries in the United States and Europe.

The modernist "solution" to disability was the institutionalization of disabled people and the medicalization of all responses to disability. These were understood to be benchmarks of progress in the modern era. There are at least two competing ideas at work here. One is the belief that in the modern, industrialized world scientific and technological competence, coupled with advanced humanitarian and moral development, would lead the way toward the highest level of care and of concern ever evidenced. However, those modernist ideals mean the society would not tolerate being bogged down by those who can't keep up, who are thought to drain resources, or who remind us in any way of the limitations of our scientific capabilities. In both ideas, the issues of efficiency prevail, leading to actions taken to contain the perceived negative social and economic impact of disability on society, even when glossed with an altruistic facade.

In the early years of the founding of the United States, and during a similar time frame in Europe, there were few facilities where disabled people were housed or cared for in systematic ways. Disabled people lived in their communities and occupied roles ranging from shoemaker to town fool to despised outcast. Their roles and degree of acceptance depended on a number of factors, including type of community, whether rural or urban; nature of the disability; status of the family; and gender, race, or personality of the individual. Paul Starr (1982) writes that "in the colonial period, the mentally ill, along with other classes of dependents, were treated as a local responsibility, primarily within their own or other families" (72). Early in the history of this country, individuals who would today be labeled mentally retarded were absorbed into communities with varying degrees of acceptance and support. Before the advent of large institutions, there were a few places, such as convents, where groups of disabled people were housed. What is apparent is that whatever ways disabled people were accommodated, the response was local and informal. For some disabled people, these situations were relatively comfortable. However, because of the idiosyncratic and arbitrary nature of these accommodations, disabled people were more likely to be ostracized than they were to be functioning members of the community. Further, even if work and participation in religious activities were possible, they may not have had opportunities for friendship, love, and intimacy. More systematic responses were to come, with varying outcomes for disabled people.

From the seventeenth through the twentieth centuries, a number of economic and philosophical factors affected community life for disabled people. Fraser and Gordon (1994) describe a transformation in policies for those in need and, moreover, in the whole idea of "dependency." America imported from England the model social legislation embodied in the Poor Relief Act of 1601 and it "did more than influence American laws—for the first 150 years of the colonies' existence, it was American law" (Groce 1992, 7). The

act acknowledged a responsibility to "disabled in need" but with a clear distinction made between those who were deemed worthy of such help and those who were not (7–8). The act may have given some disabled people more consistent financial support and relieved families of some financial responsibilities, but it also functioned to make more rigid the dividing lines between those for whom dependency was "deemed natural and proper" and those for whom receiving assistance was a source of shame.

During the seventeenth century, dependency on public assistance became more stigmatized. Whereas in the early days of the colonies "dependency" was considered a social relationship between one group and another, for instance, between workers and land-owners, increasingly *dependency could also designate an individual character trait* (Fraser and Gordon 1994, 315). A differentiated reading of dependency along gender and race lines emerged: women and the "dark races" were deemed acceptable as dependents, but it was considered shameful for white males to accept public assistance. Further, "dependency was deemed antithetical to citizenship" (315), which was also related to race and gender, and to disability. The condition of dependency was considered acceptable by the dominant majority for some groups, but it deprived recipients of the rights of citizenship and forced people to appear helpless in order to insure continued receipt of benefits.

America's glorification of independence has not served disabled people well. Individual worth came to be increasingly judged in terms of financial and social independence, a goal very, very few disabled people, nonwhites, and women could reach.

In the nineteenth century, there was a shift from the belief that disability was caused by supernatural agency[1] to a biological explanation that held that treatment, or some form of rehabilitation, was the logical response to disability (Longmore 1987). That shift marked the birth of an enormous "care" industry and along with it a variety of institutions, asylums, and state schools. Following the Civil War, a more comprehensive generalized approach to dealing with people in need of support developed that took the financial burden off families and communities. Trent (1994) reports, "[T]he shift from local to state responsibility for many groups of the disabled poor—the mad, the blind, the deaf, and the delinquent—[and] care for feeble-minded people became part of a response to rapid changes in the social and economic fabric of American life" (39). Contributing to medical and state intervention were the growth of cities and the mobility of families. The population density in cities resulted in "a higher concentration of the insane . . . and a greater demand for order and security" (Starr 1982, 72). Trent also traces the development of a medicalized response to people with mental retardation in the United States and the birth of orphanages, asylums, and state-operated schools. These appeared throughout the country in the early eighteenth century; however, most would not admit children with physical and mental disabilities (11).

Specialized institutions and residential schools emerged with varying ideas about the people who lived in them and their needs. In the United States, there came to be more and more institutions organized around a particular type of disability. Within institutions, a number of notions shaped goals and practices. The most significant for disabled people was the increasing influence of medical personnel and practices. Although medicine didn't overtly claim expertise in reducing the economic liability posed by disabled people, it did corner the market on attempts to contain the perceived negative social impact of disability. This is most clearly seen in the growing influence of medicine on the response to mental illness and the shift from the mid-nineteenth century to the early twentieth century from custodial care of people with mental illnesses to belief in the efficacy of prevention and cure. Although superintendents of custodial institutions often had medical training, their work came to be seen as policing and restraining people. The medical establishment launched attacks on asylums, asserting their practice was unscientific because they were offering custodial care with no proven ability to treat or cure.

Adolf Meyer led the "mental hygiene" movement, a program that elevated the role of psychiatrists in not only treatment but prevention. The institutions that emerged in the twentieth century became teaching hospitals and research centers. Along with this trend in institutional care, spurred by a new orientation to scientific progress, came a belief in aftercare, which "looked not to the chronic, but to the curable patient, not to custody but to *adjustment*, not to continued dependence but to *independence*" (Rothman 1980, 313). The practices were reminiscent of the way some communities had responded to mental illness before the growth of institutions.

Of course, had this push toward independence and productivity for people with mental illness and other disabilities been successful, and had the government assured the type of support and equality of opportunity that would have allowed disabled people to live in the community, the history of disabled people in the twentieth century would look much different than it does. Some of the innovative medical interventions and growing expertise might then have been coupled with a commitment to independent living, active participation in the community, and, possibly, with concern for rights and equality. Instead, institutionalization and medical control became the norm for many disabled people.

The idea that disabled people are, in an absolute sense, an economic and social liability is rarely challenged. The belief that disabled people impede progress or increase the vulnerability of a society, particularly when it is under siege, has never been tested, and certainly has never been tested in a society that works to maximize the productivity and participation of disabled people. The financial stability of society does not seem to be the factor that determines greater degrees of acceptance and participation. Indeed, Hanks and Hanks (1948) conclude their discussion of this category by commenting that economic considerations alone don't determine response to disability. They remind us that although some of the groups they discuss resort to infanticide or other means of eliminating disabled people when there are scant resources, "the Paiute of the Great Basin of North America, who had an almost equally precarious margin of existence, neither practiced infanticide nor abandoned their disabled . . . ." And the Australians, who "had a slim margin of surplus" did practice infanticide but "seem not to have disposed of the physically handicapped" (16).

In the current climate in the United States of managed health care, there is a deep fear among disabled people that our lives will be weighed on an economic scale. In Michael Bérubé's (1996) book about his family's experience of having a child born with Down syndrome, he speaks poignantly of that fear:

> Among the many things I fear coming to pass in my children's lifetime, I fear this above all: that children like James will eventually be seen as "luxuries" employers and insurance companies cannot afford, or as "luxuries" the nation or the planet cannot afford. I do not want to see a world in which human life is judged by the kind of cost-benefit analysis that weeds out those least likely to attain self-sufficiency and to provide adequate "returns" on social investments. (52)

3. Tolerant Utilization. One can infer from the examples provided under the Hankses' (1948) category

Tolerant Utilization that they recognized situations in which disabled people, although often marginal figures in the society, are allowed to participate to the extent that they have the ability to fulfill certain roles and duties designated by the nondisabled majority as necessary. Disabled people's actions therefore are at the will and bidding of the nondisabled majority. For instance, during World War II disabled people worked in record numbers because so many "able-bodied" people were at war. During this time women (both disabled and nondisabled) were also employed in positions never before open to them. At the close of the war, these groups returned to their previously low levels of employment and to the restricted range of positions they were allowed to occupy.

Another example of disabled people being utilized as needed by the society are situations in which they are considered more useful or practical in certain roles than nondisabled people. For instance, the utilization of hearing-impaired and deaf workers on assembly lines where noisy machinery is used or of people of short stature in tight spaces where larger workers cannot fit. Although gainful employment is always desirable in a drastically underemployed group and there is a certain peculiar logic to these solutions, given the economic vulnerability and low social status of men and women with disabilities, these situations are ripe for exploitation. Further, the particular health and safety issues for these workers and the lack of control or free will in such situations make them highly dubious opportunities.

Disabled people have also served at the dominant culture's pleasure as fools and jesters in a royal court, and in such social institutions and rituals as freak shows and carnivals. People have been put on public display in circuses and other more sedate institutions, such as museums and medical facilities. (Bogdan 1988, 1996; Thomson 1996). A man described as the "Elephant Man" and a woman called the "Hottentot Venus" were put on view in medical and scientific settings, as well as in commercial venues. People have worked in these areas out of economic necessity or because they were under the "care" of medical personnel and had little opportunity to pursue other goals. Either as scientific specimens or amusements displayed for profit, people with disabilities were denied basic rights and freedoms. Although the large buttocks and genitalia of the "Hottentot Venus" are not disabilities by most current legal and typical definitions, her body and that of the "Elephant Man" were considered pathological by social standards.

A final example boldly illuminates the utilitarian and exploitive nature of some people's ideas about disabled women and men, and about women in general:

> When geneticist Sharlene George was interviewed for admission into a graduate program at Stanford University in 1967, the department chair said: "Miss George, do you know why I'm interviewing you? It's because this year I'm reduced to the lame, the halt, the blind, and the women." (Todd 1984, 44)

The next three categories, Limited Participation, Laissez-Faire, and Participation and Accommodation, are presented together and then used to discuss the continuum in educational practice in the United States from the seventeenth century to the present.

4. Limited Participation. The category Limited Participation is the least specific in the Hankses' typology and the examples provided are the most ambiguous, yet I find the term useful to describe situations in which disabled people's roles and status are largely derived from their ability to be productive in terms of the standards set by the dominant majority. This idea is based on an individual model of disability, the idea that it is up to the individual to demonstrate worth and competence. It promotes a false sense of acceptance because the norms and standards of the able-bodied majority are imposed and held up as the ideal to which all should aspire. Whereas the previous category, Tolerant Utilization, speaks to the society's control not only of criteria for performance but of domains in which competence can be demonstrated, Limited Participation indicates the society's willingness to accept a disabled person among its ranks in any domain in which she or he can "keep up" with the nondisabled.

5. Laissez-Faire. In the Hankses' (1948) description of their last category, Laissez-Faire, "a steadfast relation to the protective group, despite handicap," is observed and "the obligation of the extended family to shelter and provide for its unfortunates continues, whether they are able to give their labor or not" (18–19). I've eliminated the terms "protective group" and "provide for its unfortunates," two ideas that do not capture the more complex relations that occur among disabled and nondisabled people, and propose instead that the category include situations in which relations between nondisabled and disabled people exist, and where the family and community provide varying degrees of support for disabled people, whether they are able to work or not. Although in such situations the society does not overtly exclude disabled people, it does not work toward accommodation, social justice, and equity with respect to them.

I am proposing that the idea of noninterference implied by the term *laissez-faire* applies to the social structures and not to specific responses to disabled people. Indeed, in such situations there may be various types of concern displayed for disabled people and interventions provided, yet if the norms of the able-bodied majority are centered and held up as the ultimate goal of all people, and the society makes no effort to reconstruct its goals or acceptable means of achieving them to reflect a broader range of citizens, the society has adopted a laissez-faire approach to disability. In such situations, the dominant group decides what disabled people need and attempts to meet those needs but does little to engage with disabled people as a constituency to work together to set the terms of accommodation. Disabled people then are left in the unenviable position of having to keep up with norms and standards but with no opportunity to shape them.

6. Participation and Accommodation. I've added the last category, Participation and Accommodation, to the Hankses' typology in order to report on the moments and places in which a proactive stance is evident toward the equitable participation of all members of the society. These are admittedly rare events, but there are some examples of concerted efforts to accommodate all members of the group and to adapt the procedures and standards typically imposed to reflect a range of abilities, interests, and needs. This does not mean lowering standards in an absolute sense; it means that greater flexibility is evident and a broader range of objectives are set. These actions are based on moral, practical, religious, and/or rights-based approaches to full participation of all members of society.

Throughout the history of the United States, education for disabled children has assumed many forms, from complete denial of formalized instruction to a few recent examples of exciting, well-informed, and inclusive classrooms where disabled and nondisabled children learn together in cooperative groups designed to maximize the participation of all children in the learning process. Between these extremes, disabled children have experienced a variety of learning environments.

There are segregated settings, including classrooms in institutions; specialized residential and day schools, designed either for children with specific disabilities or for mixed disability groupings; and separate special education classrooms within a general education school. A variety of other types of placements for disabled children have emerged since the 1975 passage of PL94-142, "which guaranteed an education for the nation's eight million children with disabilities . . . in the least restrictive environment, that is with nondisabled children whenever possible" (Shapiro 1993, 166). These options include the common practice of placing some children who are identified as "special education" students in a general education class for one or two periods a day, or, for a few children, in the those classrooms for whole day, if they can keep up with the academic curriculum. This practice of incorporating students in general education for part or all of the day is generally known as "mainstreaming," even though that is not a legal term. The total integration of all disabled children in general education is known as "inclusion" and exists currently in a number of isolated schools and in a few school districts around the country. In inclusive schools all children attend their neighborhood school, and are placed in classes based on age rather than on test results, evaluation, diagnosis, or past performance. Although inclusion is a very recent project of schools, there has not been a straightforward historical march from complete denial of education for those considered outcasts or pariahs through to totally inclusive and integrated classrooms.

The education system throughout the history of the United States exemplifies the range of responses demonstrated in the six categories presented in this chapter. The three categories just presented, Limited Participation, Laissez-Faire, and Participation and Accommodation, are particularly useful in distinguishing among the recent approaches to educating disabled children. Although the connections between the Hankses' typology and the educational practices described here are somewhat forced, I will describe how the ideology underlying each of their categories might lead to particular educational practices. When disabled people are considered pariahs, education, if provided at all, is aimed at containment and control. It might also have a taming function: to civilize creatures seen as not quite human. Any of the general goals of education—intellectual development, acculturation, employment, or preparation for participation in the democracy—would not be considered useful or worthwhile for people thought to be a threat to society, or incapable or unworthy of citizenship. However, to the extent that education is thought to decrease the dangerous, unwanted characteristics of disabled people, then it would be conducted in a situation isolated from others, with goals of social control and order imposed rather than individual enhancement. These agendas were more obvious in institutions and asylums of the past, but I am not convinced that the ideology has disappeared. At any given moment, whether in an institution of the eighteenth or twentieth century, or a general education school today, the idea that disabled people are to be controlled can influence a number of different types of educational initiatives.

When education is guided by the idea that disabled people are Economic and Social Liabilities, then instruction will be geared toward decreasing the drain. Indeed, any educational intervention, short of the most proactive, rights-based approach to the education of all children, can be seen as responding to a need to reduce the economic and social burden disabled people are thought to represent. Rather than see the mission of education of disabled children in terms of intellectual and social development, preparing them to partake in the rights and pleasures of citizenship, the orientation that guides this approach is more focused on vocational training and on the tools and skills needed to become productive and self-sufficient. Similar interpretations have been made along class and race lines of the imperatives that drive education.

These liability themes emerge in, debates over what is the most cost-efficient means of educating disabled students. When moral and pedagogically based arguments for inclusive education are presented, they are often countered by economic arguments presented at school board meetings or in legislative bodies about the drain that educating disabled children is on community resources. However, the concerns raised about allocating resources to disabled children's education are based on local and immediate economic analyses. Broader, long-term analyses are often not part of these discussions, thereby bypassing recognition of the long-term consequences of denying children equitable education and the long-term gains that could be realized from an educated and prepared cadre of disabled children. In addition to the economic liability themes, concerns are also raised about whether the presence of disabled children in a general education classroom deflects attention from the needs of the nondisabled children. Each of these is a practical problem but also an ethical problem. My purpose here is to uncover the ethos that drives the decisions.

The values that underlie the Tolerant Utilization approach may subtly influence a school toward preparing disabled people to fulfill the functions that the nondisabled majority are in need of. Recall that in this category are the situations in which disabled people, though treated as marginal figures in the society, are incorporated as needed if they have the ability to fulfill certain roles and duties designated by the nondisabled majority as useful. Therefore, pedagogy and curriculum are not guided by a concern for equality of opportunity but, rather, a utilitarian vision of educating disabled people. Special education classrooms, institutional settings, and sheltered workshops whose curriculum is influenced by this restricted and stereotyped vision of appropriate roles of disabled people qualify as examples in this category.

The categories Limited Participation and Laissez-Faire apply to situations in which standards for disabled people's performance are set by the dominant majority, and it is up to the individual to demonstrate worth and competence in terms of these criteria. This description could apply to schools that have mainstreaming programs for some disabled children and separate special education classes for others. Children with physical disabilities or sensory impairments may be mainstreamed for a few or all periods a day in general education classes if they can keep up with the academic level of the class. In settings such as these you often see students popped in and out of classrooms, put into a general education reading class if they show skill in this area but returned to the special education classroom or to a resource room if their skill is not considered equivalent to the general education students.

Some schools with mainstreaming programs have created wonderful, innovative programs to incorporate some of the disabled children into their general education classes. These programs provide more systematic interactions between nondisabled and disabled children, and the school provides support for some disabled children in more integrated classroom environments, even if the disabled children are not able to engage in or complete all the same tasks that nondisabled children can. Disabled children are eligible for such programs if they can keep up in most academic areas with the children identified as nondisabled. If they are not able to meet those requirements, segregated specialized education is provided, designed on a priori decisions made about their academic and social capabilities. Although the class or the school does not overtly exclude disabled people, it does not work toward full accommodation or equity with respect to disabled children.

In situations such as these, the basic structure of schools and classrooms remains unchanged, but some disabled children are shifted into general education as long as they can keep up and their presence results in minimal alteration of the prevailing structure. The children's welfare may be of great concern to the school and the community, yet the vision of what can or should be done to create a more equitable environment is limited.

My objective here is not to indict the much-maligned special education teachers or programs. There is probably as broad a range of quality of education in general as in special education. The point is that mainstreaming and other moderate solutions are token programs that cull from the special education rosters the children who are most like the "mainstream." The system places them in classrooms where their presence is contingent on their behaving as much like the nondisabled children as possible. If drooling or having spasms or a speech impairment is not within the school's or the district's criteria for acceptable behaviors for mainstreamed classrooms, the child will be locked out of general education. This places the mainstreamed children in the awkward position of having to look and act as nondisabled as possible to maintain their position in general education and, as a result, it marginalizes even more the disabled children who can never play those parts. Further, and rarely discussed, mainstreamed children lose the opportunity to be with other disabled children. Mainstreaming doesn't erase the line between disabled and nondisabled people; it just draws the line between acceptable and not acceptable a little to the left or, if you're sitting on the opposite side, to the right.

For the past ten years in particular, the practices in most school districts have hovered between those whose overt structure resembles the Limited Participation and Laissez-Faire models. The other ideas, that disabled people are pariahs, social and economic burdens, and people to be utilized in society if and when they are needed, filters through educational discourse in more covert and intangible ways.

Recall that the distinguishing features of the last category, Accommodation and Participation, are that a proactive stance is taken toward equitable participation, and where procedures and standards are adapted to include everyone. The newest model of education, full inclusion, is the closest to such an accommodating environment. It differs from all the categories above in that in its most thorough and successful forms, all children go to their neighborhood school and all are incorporated in general education classes with appropriate supports and accommodations. The pedagogical practices and curriculum are designed to reach a broad range of children, and in-

tegration and active participation are goals the school is committed to. Whereas the practice of mainstreaming has been restricted primarily to children with physical disabilities and sensory impairments, the inclusion model incorporates all children, whatever their disability, in a general education classroom. Therefore, children with mental retardation, autism, or mental illnesses, those who are typically the most sequestered of all children, participate in the learning and social activities of inclusive classrooms. This is a startling idea for many people, particularly if they have never seen it in action. In classroom environments such as these, the criteria for demonstrating competence may not be the same for all children, but together the group tackles the subject matter and each child engages with it in a manner consistent with her or his aptitudes and needs. Goals and standards are shifted not downward but out, to a more flexible and broader means of demonstrating competence. The burden to "keep up" is shifted off the individual student, and the whole classroom environment shifts in its overall procedures and expectations to maximize learning for all.

The report of the National Center on Educational Restructuring and Inclusion (1995) on the status of inclusive education in the United States provides qualitative data on the benefits and problems in the transformation of schools to inclusive sites. Multiple examples underscore the positive transformations in the behavior and learning patterns of disabled students who have been transferred from special education classrooms to inclusive ones. Students who had previously required a great deal of adult intervention to sit still, to be quiet, to focus on lessons and not distract other students appear to respond to peer pressure to behave, and teachers are reported to spend much more time on instruction than on "parenting" behaviors such as "setting and enforcing guidelines of appropriate behavior" (226). An example from Burbank, California, describes one way that a school accommodated children who are deaf. The school draws children who are deaf from a wide area and, as a result, from one-third to two-thirds of the students in any given class are deaf. The regular school curriculum is maintained by using a team-teaching approach (one general education teacher and one teacher trained in special education, both fluent in sign language). All students participate in the same classes and recreational activities, with a high degree of social interaction among deaf and hearing students. The district report indicates that "there is no isolation of the deaf students, in the classroom or playground. Hearing students sign . . . and at the eighth-grade graduation ceremony, the three hearing students who were chosen as speakers (the fourth was deaf) each signed their speech" (39).

Inclusion is not an educational plan to benefit disabled children. It is a model for educating all children equitably. The concept of heterogeneous grouping is supported by data from studies of detracking,[2] which indicate that the benefits of detracking accrue to all children. The benefits for the nondisabled children are not solely that they learn tolerance and acceptance. Although I don't want to minimize the importance of that lesson, the benefits are broader than the moral lessons such exposure can offer. For instance, when nondeaf children learn sign language, they are not only exposed to a second language, rare these days in most elementary schools but come to understand something about language itself and how it functions in human experience. The presence, let's say, of children with mental retardation in a classroom not only helps the children who have never had such exposure see the disabled children as complex human beings, recognize their strengths and weaknesses, and learn from their abilities but teach all the children how to interact to solve problems and about the range of ways that people approach a task. The children who learn more slowly can pick up cues from children who have mastered a particular domain, and the children who have mastered it can benefit from explaining it, paraphrasing and highlighting important points, and also, significantly, can benefit from watching the steps that the learners go through in mastering the material. A range of types of learners in the classroom provides teachers with many "teachable moments," the occasions when the spontaneous curriculum that arises in classroom interactions enriches learning.

I want to resist the impulse to overromanticize inclusive education. These described benefits don't always get realized. Inclusion has not been an unmitigated success wherever it has been implemented. Insufficient teacher preparation, overcrowding, and understaffing can interfere with the best of plans. Further, this plan for integrated environments in schools is taking place in a society that is far from integrated. Neither the children nor the teachers and parents have much experience with integrated communities. There have been instances where disabled children have been disruptive, where nondisabled children have rejected disabled children and they remain isolated in the classroom, and where teachers are overwhelmed and underprepared, and resent teaching in this type of heterogeneously grouped

classroom. Those problems may always occur, although there are certainly ways to decrease them.

Although integration is a goal of the disability rights community in education and in society as a whole, it does not stem from a valorization of the nondisabled, nor should it be read solely as a reaction to the quality of special education. "Normalization" is a spurious goal and not a useful way to think about the push to inclusive education. Herbert Kohl (1994) makes a similar point about the misinterpretation of the *Brown vs. Board of Education* decision when he notes that "the specific wording of the decision—'Separate education facilities are inherently unequal'—has racist implications," and he then distinguishes between involuntary and voluntary segregation (92). He reports on the high quality of teaching that occurred in many all-black schools.

What is wrong with special education, then, is not that the quality of instruction is necessarily inferior or that there are only disabled children in the classrooms. What is problematic is that these are often isolated, stigmatized classes, and that placement in special education is not voluntary. Segregated special education is bedeviled by the stigma that all members of the school, whether consciously or not, attach to the designation. All the children in the school, the staff, and parents know which classes are special education classes. No matter what kinds of overt lessons are taught at the school about respect for difference or other such seemingly committed agendas with weak impact, the hidden curriculum, the stronger message, is that children in special education are different, incompetent and unsavory, and, because of their isolation, easily avoidable. Expectations that the school, the disabled and nondisabled children, the parents, and the teachers have are inevitably lowered by these designations. Most damaging of all, the negative expectations are assimilated and internalized by the disabled children with devastating long-term consequences.

Segregated education is not inherently worse than integrated education because it is inhabited by disabled children. It is functionally worse because it is a restricted environment, with classes so small that the benefits of individualized instruction are often overshadowed by the limited types of interactions children can have with one another, and often by the dominance of adults who may interfere with children's opportunities to learn from and with one another. Children in special education may learn a great deal. Indeed, there have been wonderful special education classes with dedicated and knowledgeable teachers, but as

Jeffrey Libby, an integration-support teacher for an inclusive elementary school, points out, "One of the biggest arguments against inclusion . . . is that disabled students can acquire more skills within an isolated setting . . . but you teach things in isolation, and they're only good in isolation" (Casanave 1991, 41).

Although integration is sought for the breadth of educational opportunities offered and other advantages, dismantling special education will, unfortunately, diminish disabled children's opportunities to grow and learn around other children with disabilities, which gives them the opportunity to shape this essential part of their identity in the company of others who share their experience. Children with disabilities are hungry for role models, and other children may be the only disabled people in a child's life. Exposure to other disabled children's adaptiveness, understanding of their social position, sense of self, ability to negotiate in the world, and basic information make these friendships critical in development. In an inclusive setting there may be only one or two children with disabilities in a classroom.

School districts that support inclusion are among the most consciously rendered participatory and accommodating environments known, yet there have been other moments and places in the world where integration has been spotted. For the most part these have been more spontaneous, chance events rather than purposefully constructed environments, and the accommodations are usually not for all disabled people, just groups who achieve certain significance in the culture. It is critical that these be noted. They speak to the human capacity to construct disability very differently than it usually is.

One of the most thoroughly investigated environments is described in a landmark study conducted by Nora Groce (1985) and reported in her book *Everyone Here Spoke Sign Language*. It is an ethnohistory of Martha's Vineyard, where, for more than two centuries ending in the 1950s, a high incidence of hereditary deafness existed. Rather than focus on the condition itself, Groce focuses on the accommodations that some communities on the island made to this subgroup of their population. The deaf and hearing residents lived and worked together as equals, and, as the book's title suggests, most people on the Vineyard were fluent in a signed language that evolved there. It should be noted that although the proportion of deaf residents was larger than usual, in the course of the three centuries in which this hereditary phenomenon occurred only about 72 people with hereditary deafness lived on the island, one in

every 155 people; the typical ratio in the United States in the nineteenth century was one in every 5,728 people. Therefore, the deaf on the island were significantly more proportionately, but the use of sign language by the whole community was in response to a rather small absolute number.

In interviews with members of the community who could remember the time when the deaf residents were still around, what comes across most vividly is the matter-of-fact way that they spoke of their deaf neighbors, and of their own accommodation to their presence. Groce (1985) notes that "the community's attitude can be judged also from the fact that until I asked a direct question on the subject, most of my informants never even considered anything unusual about the manner in which their deaf townsmen were integrated into the society" (51). But a reporter for the *Boston Sunday Herald* knew there was something unusual occurring there. Groce quotes an 1895 story:

The kindly and well-informed people whom I saw, strange to say, seem to be proud of the affliction—to regard it as a kind of plume in the hat of the stock. Elsewhere the afflicted are screened as much as possible from public notoriety. But these people gave me a great lot of photographs, extending back four generations. These pictures of people who have never spoken a word from the day of their birth, create the impression of the invasion by deafness of what might otherwise have been a wonderfully perfect type.

The reporter presaged the deaf pride movement by almost one hundred years and displayed some understanding of the social construction of disability. However, the ableist notion that the deaf people would be perfect if not for their impairments and a later comment that "the mutes are not uncomfortable in their deprivation" (52–53) reveal the limitations of the reporter's insight.

How would a reporter today approach a story on a similar but more circumscribed environment, for instance, the Burbank, California, school, discussed earlier, where hearing and nonhearing students learn and play together and where both groups are fluent in sign language? Would she or he frame the subjects as less than perfect, albeit valiant and plucky, and the hearing kids as generous and good-spirited? Paint the relationships between the two groups in sentimentalized colors? Glorify the accomplishments of the deaf children? Or might a reporter today have the sophistication and insight about disability issues to focus on how an accommodating environment structures equality and motivates both groups to work together utilizing a range of communications media that allows full participation of everyone? Even if a reporter did have that sophistication and insight, she or he would have to contend with the overwhelming tendency of most news stories today to go for the uplifting human interest story rather than an analysis of the structural elements that determine interpersonal relationships. This is true of the media in general, but in the case of disability, the likelihood is magnified a thousand times.

Representations of disability and the representations of disabled people's place in society are largely in the hands of people schooled in a particular vision of disability, one that is saturated with deterministic thinking and characterized by maudlin and morbid sentiments projected onto disabled people's experience. The insistence not just that disability is an unfortunate occurrence but that disabled people are, perforce, "unfortunates" seeps into most reports on the disability experience. Insiders' reports of disability, as seen in some of the best of the disability studies scholarship and in such publications as the *Disability Rag* and the *Mouth*, present a different perspective.

The Martha's Vineyard study also stands in contrast to typical records of disabled people in society because it documents a Participatory and Accommodating environment, focuses on social determinants, and is comprehensive. The dearth of such reports raises a number of questions that I address below. Have there been no other such environments? Does the absence in history of similar environments indicate the impossibility of such integration and equity? Are researchers not interested in such social patterns? Do researchers lack the theoretical tools with which to evaluate such behaviors and practices?

I believe there have been and are places and moments where more equitable and integrated environments are seen. They are not ideal; indeed, Martha's Vineyard is far from ideal because the accommodation made to deaf people did not extend to all disabled people. These are places where the nondisabled center and dominance shifts and greater degrees of accommodation are evident. John Hockenberry (1995) describes the neighborhood around Israel's most famous acute trauma facility, at Tel Hashomer Hospital, where most people who were wounded in the wars or in automobile accidents go for rehabilitation. It seems the disabled men (it is not clear where disabled women go) stay on in the neighborhood after they leave the hospital, and Hockenberry, a reporter for National Public Radio and a wheelchair user, noted a concentration of houses with "newly built wide doors, ramped entrances, and freshly paved driveways," quite different from most Israeli neighborhoods. The area, though, was "something of a crip ghetto, the only place in Israel where I would regularly see people in wheelchairs on the street" (236).

Anyone who has ever visited a well-run independent living center[3] would witness an environment consciously rendered to accommodate all people. In addition to the offices themselves, in the immediate neighborhood of these centers, you are more likely to see ramps to get into stores, accessible bathrooms in local restaurants, and possibly menus in Braille. In some instances, the independent living center has had a strong impact on local policy.

Berkeley, California was the site of the first independent living center in the country (incorporated in 1972), and is notable for its history of strong activism and high degree of local impact. Anyone with an interest in such phenomena would notice the curb cuts on every corner and the ramps into buildings. When I first visited Berkeley in 1975, what was even more striking to me was the degree to which disability had become such a common feature of the landscape that I could move about casually without causing a stir. People, it appeared to me, did not stare nor did they glance and quickly avert their eyes. People were, in general, neither rude nor overly solicitous. The shifts that had occurred in the physical and communications environments, and the strong presence of an active disability community have these kinds of effects on the interpersonal environment.

Granted, there are very few places like independent living centers and their environs where disabled people have much autonomy and freedom of movement. Only a few other examples come to mind. One is some of the newly designed areas in the National Parks System, where disabled people and nondisabled people have worked together to make the environments accessible. Another is a small, rustic resort I visited in Byron Bay, Australia, run by disabled people in a place where pleasure and good times are the order of the day. Other places include meetings of disability rights groups or disability studies conferences.

These places are remarkable for disabled people. They differ from most of the places encountered, in which inequities, discrimination, and marginalization are more likely to occur. These places are so radically different from typical experience and yet so clearly possible that they remind us of the absence of will to create such environments everywhere. Thinking about this situation brings to mind a study reported in the *New York Times* Science section a few years ago. The article (Wilford, 1994) reviewed the results of a two-year investigation by an anthropologist of the sparsely populated island of Vanatinai near Papua New Guinea. Its front-page headline read "Sexes Equal on South Sea Isle." Dr. Maria Lepowsky reported that a unique social arrangement exists: men and women live and work as virtual equals. "It is not a place where men and women live in perfect harmony and where the privileges and burdens of both sexes are exactly equal, but it comes close" (C1). She said that the findings challenge some theorists' position that male dominance is universal or somehow inherent in human cultures.

The value and meaning of Lepowsky's discovery was, I think, apparent to most *Times* readers. Vanatinai differs from other known cultures around the world in its apparently high degree of gender equity. Would the readers have a similarly sophisticated understanding of, let's say, the meaning and significance

of the anthropological data collected on Martha's Vineyard? Are they ready to consider that the social position of disabled people in the United States and in most other known cultures is not inevitable and immutable. It took the tools of women's studies to uncover the key ingredients of the Vanatinai culture. Similarly, disability studies is needed to investigate equitable arrangements and apply that knowledge to the construction of equitable societies. Until disability studies articulated the social and political paradigms, there was little in the way of a theoretical framework from which such research could proceed.

The title of this chapter, "Divided Society," speaks to the fissures between disabled and nondisabled people evident across time and across cultures. I contend these divides are not inevitable; indeed, if we mobilize sufficient intellectual wherewithal, I believe we can unearth other positive arrangements or, at least, envision what they might look like. In the next chapter I turn to the academy to investigate its role in marginalizing the knowledge and the people needed to reposition disabled people in the social and political arena.

Notes

1. See also Eiesland's (1994) *The Disabled God: Toward a Liberatory Theology of Disability* for an overview of religious explanations of disability.

2. For discussions of tracking and detracking, see McLaren (1994); Oakes (1985); and Polakow (1993).

3. Independent living centers are organizations run by and for disabled people, operating on the premise that, as Joseph Shapiro (1993) writes in *No Pity*, no one "knew more about the needs of disabled people than disabled people themselves" (73). The centers provide services that allow people with disabilities to achieve maximum independence in the community and at the same time serve as advocates to change the community to make it more accessible and equitable for disabled people.

Chapter Four

Public Policy Issues

4.1   The Disproportionate Representation of African Americans in Special Education:

Looking Behind the Curtain for Understanding and Solutions

James M. Patton

The overrepresentation of African American children and youth in special education programs for students with learning disabilities, severe emotional or behavioral disabilities, and mental disabilities has remained a persistent reality even after more than 20 years of recognition. After reviewing these recurring patterns, a critical-theory mode of inquiry is used to discuss how certain basic assumptions, worldviews, beliefs, and epistemologies used by some special education knowledge producers serve to perpetuate the disproportionality drama. The author concludes by suggesting that the voices of qualitatively different knowledge producers, who are culturally and interculturally competent, are needed to bring resolution to this persistent challenge.

The overrepresentation of African Americans in certain special education programs (see Note 1) has been a persistent problem negatively affecting large numbers of African Americans and their families, the field of special education, and society at large. The sociopolitical and historical roots of the disproportionate representation problem addressed in this article predate the field of special education, with origins as early as 1619. They can be traced back to the arrival of Africans in America and their subsequent continuous, unequal treatment (Willie, Garibaldi, & Reed, 1991). The current reality of the overrepresentation of African Americans in special education classes perpetuates this sociohistorical legacy by allowing the general and special education enterprises to continue the creation of programmatic and classroom arrangements that jeopardize the life chances of large numbers of African American youth. The fact that disproportionately large numbers of African Americans are being persistently diagnosed as disabled and placed in special education programs con-

stitutes a problem—for many of these students are inappropriately placed. The consequences, however, of such misidentification, classification, and placement are often deleterious. As an example, this problem is exacerbated by the fact that many African American youth today fail to receive a quality and life-enhancing education in precisely those special education programs in which they are often inappropriately placed (Heller, Holtzman, & Messick, 1982; Hilliard, 1992). In addition, the special education label borne by these students often serves as a stigma, producing negative effects on the bearer of the label and others interacting with the stigmatized individual (Goffman, 1963). Furthermore, while these students are in special education programs, they miss essential general education academic and social curricula. This limited exposure with the core academic curriculum continues the spiral of "lower levels of achievement, decreased likelihood of post secondary education, and more limited employment" (Markowitz, Garcia, & Eichelberger, 1997, p. 3).

Concerns about racial discrimination and violations of civil rights are raised when African American youth are consistently misidentified and disproportionately placed in special education programs. Recently, renewed attention has been made regarding these issues. Reschly (1996) observed that this heightened awareness can be seen in recent reports to Congress and several initiatives funded by the

From "The disproportionate representation of African Americans in special education: Looking behind the curtain for understanding and solutions" by J. M. Patton, 1998, *The Journal of Special Education* 32(1), pp. 25–31. Copyright © 1998 by PRO-ED, Inc. Reprinted with permission.

U.S. Office of Education. The first initiative included a study conducted by the National Academy of Sciences of the National Research Council that critiqued the use of intelligence tests in special education and explored alternatives to these tests. This body noted the absence of "benefits" resulting from the use of these tests and their lack of pedagogical utility (Morrison, White, & Fever, 1996). A second initiative involved funding the National Association of State Directors of Special Education to examine policy issues around the disprotortionality problem and to recommend practical solutions. Although interest in this area has been recently piqued, renewed interest without a different analysis and different voices will not resolve this problem.

The purposes of this article are to look behind the special education ontological, axiological, and epistemological "curtain" and address the overrepresentation of African American learners in special education classes. I am convinced that important insights can emerge from exploring the beliefs, assumptions, worldviews, ways of knowing, and cultural inclinations of those writing the special education scripts, rather than perseverating our focus on those acting out various roles. Much has been said about the "actors," and little about the "playwrights." To accomplish this, initially, I will discuss briefly the persistent patterns embedded in the overrepresentation of African Americans in mildly disabled and emotionally disturbed programs in order to provide a convenient context, or marker, for subsequent discussions. Then, employing a critical theory mode of inquiry (Apple, 1990; Arnowitz & Giroux, 1991; Freire, 1970; Giroux, 1988; Skrtic, 1991). I will discuss how the basic assumptions, beliefs, epistempologies, and worldviews employed by the major "script writers" in the field often serve to perpetuate the disproportionality drama. Relatedly, this narrative will be followed with an examination of special education knowledge producers and the role that these script writers play in perpetuating overrepresentation. I will then offer an ethical narrative that I hope will lead to problem solutions.

THE OVERREPRESENTATION PROBLEM: PERSISTENT PATTERNS

The overrepresentation of African American children and youth in special education programs for students with learning disabilities, severe emotional or behavioral disorders, and mental disabilities has remained a persistent reality even after more than 20 years of

recognition. The literature is replete with causal factors that range from failure of the general education system (Artiles & Trent, 1994; Deno, 1970; MacMillan & Hendrick, 1993; McDermott, 1987; Townsend, Thomas, Witty, & Lee, 1996) to inequities associated with the special education referral, assessment, and placement processes (Harry & Anderson, 1994; Mercer, 1973). Yet, the problem of overrepresentation of African Americans persists even after causes have been unequivocally noted. We know and have known for years, for example, that, in spite of all the study and scripting of this issue, the proportion of African Americans identified as mentally disabled has not changed much from 38% in 1975 when those students constituted 15% of the school population. In 1991 they made up 16% of this nation's school population and 35% of the special education population (Harry & Anderson, 1994). Further, it is well documented that African American males are particularly overrepresented both in disciplinary practices (i.e., recipients of corporal punishment and suspension) and in certain special education categories and typically receive their special education in segregated classrooms or buildings (Harry & Anderson, 1994).

We also know that the labels associated with the sociocultural construction of the categories of mild mental disability, learning disability, and serious emotional or behavioral disability (SED) have definitional and validity problems with serious negative implications for African American learners. For example, Ysseldyke, Algozzine, and Thurlow (1992) observed that the arbitrary shifts in diagnostic criteria and frequency rates for the SED label coupled with the extreme variability in placement rates across the states call into question the validity of the SED category. These concerns and the attendant cultural variability of student behavior and teacher judgment place African American youth at great risk of being falsely labeled as SED. Similar arguments have been made for the educable mentally retarded (EMR) and specific learning disability (SLD) categories (Harry & Anderson, 1994).

The literature about this subject is also clear: Given the ambiguity and subjectivity embedded in the mild disabilities categories, teacher judgments in the referral process combined with the inherent biases of the assessment process contribute to the disproportionate referral and special education placement of African American students (Anderson, 1994; Artiles & Trent, 1994; Gould, 1981; Harry & Anderson, 1994; Nobles, 1991). The aspect of assessment has received the greatest attention in the research literature and in the courts in terms of its centrality to the overrepresentation discourse. There appears to be enough theoretical and statistical evidence suggesting that intelligence tests are biased and harmful to many African American learners (Gould, 1981; Hilliard, 1991; Jones, 1988; Patton, 1992). Furthermore, the deleterious effect of standardized intelligence testing is exacerbated by the fact that most of these tests are used for classification purposes rather than for diagnostic or prescriptive reasons. In that regard, these tests contribute very little to curriculum or pedagogical validity (Hilliard, 1991). Recently, the Board of Assessment and Testing (BOTA) of the National Research Council (Morrison et al, 1996) issued a report concluding that "the usefulness of IQ tests in making special education decisions needs reevaluation" (p. 27). Again, the report revealed a lack of connection between assessment practices and effective treatments (Morrison et al., 1996).

In spite of the presence of convincing data on the overrepresentation issue and the extant literature challenging special education processes that lead to identification and placement, this problem continues to persist. Its persistence will continue unless we reanalyze old premises and reconstruct new premises underlying the field of special education. An analysis of the deep structure foundations of special education will be discussed in the next section.

SPECIAL EDUCATION AND ITS SOCIAL SCIENCE UNDERPINNINGS

The dominant mode of inquiry in the field of special education has closely followed the "objectivist," or functionalist, tradition of theory development, paradigm construction, research approach, methodology use, and research applications (Bowles & Gintis, 1976; Skrtic, 1986). As a worldview, functionalism presupposes an objective, rational, orderly interpretation of social reality, whereby deviations to this view are placed under a pathology heading (Foucault, 1976). This functionalist framework leads persons to postulate that schools exist to transmit a body of "prescribed knowledge, skills, values, and norms that are essential for society" (Irvine, 1990, p. 2). Individuals so theoretically predisposed then engage in discourses and practices that lead them to constantly search for the "right" test, the "right" diagnosis, and the "appropriate" pedagogy, within the confines and restraints of their worldview, which often goes uncontested. This functionalist narrative, enjoined by

the medical and psychological grounding of the field of special education, explains deviations from the norm as deficits or pathologies (Skrtic, 1991). Students, then, who fail in general education are viewed as defective and consequently as needing some "special" system to organize itself, develop a different set of norms, values, roles, expectations and procedures to "fix" these "defective" students. Skrtic (1991) pointed out that the creation of the special education system to deal with these "defective" students removed the problem from the general education discourse and compartmentalized it into a separate special education narrative. This special education narrative, according to that author, includes a language that developed four assumptions that have reinforced its functionalist/psychological/medical origins. These mutually reinforcing assumptions are that "a) disabilities are pathological conditions that students have b) differential diagnosis is objective and useful, c) special education is a rationally conceived and coordinated system of services that benefits diagnosed students, and d) progress results from rational technological improvements in diagnostic and instructional practices" (Skrtic, 1991, p. 152). Such, therefore, is the language used by many of the key special education knowledge producers who are writing the scripts for others to play.

CRITICAL THEORY AND SPECIAL EDUCATION

This functionalist, or positivist, view fails to recognize the socioeconomic and political nature of schooling. Nor does it imagine the role played by schools and the special education system in maintaining the existing social and economic stratification order, thereby exerting ideological, social, and political control of African American learners. As previously mentioned, a host of theorists, taking a more critical view, has created a body of literature that links school structures and processes, including those used in special education, with the values, attitudes, and needs that reflect the dominant social, economic, and political groups in this nation (e.g., Apple, 1981; Cherryholmes, 1988; Katz, 1971; Lipsky & Gartner, 1989; Skrtic, 1991). These critical, or conflict, theorists hold that education, and, thus special education, grounded in structured power relationships, is designed to serve the interests of the dominant social, political, and economic classes and to place African Americans in a disvalued position. As such, the structures, processes, assumptions, and beliefs of the dominant classes are deeply embedded in the special education knowledge base and its knowledge producers, thus undermining its theory, research, and practice. These theories, assumptions, and practices also are enormously resistant to change. This coupling of special education with the needs of the dominant social, political, and economic classes in society has resulted in the maintenance of a special education system that is unjust to African Americans. Many of those major knowledge producers, or "gods," in the field of special education have played an essential role in maintenance of this injustice.

SPECIAL EDUCATION KNOWLEDGE PRODUCTION: A MISSING DISCOURSE

The overrepresentation discourse has not, to my knowledge, been discussed within an analysis of the social, political, and cultural contexts of the major knowledge producers in the field and the ontologies, axiologies, and epistemologies they employ. In the main, those who create, manufacture, and produce the knowledge base in special education historically have not included African Americans, especially those directly affected by overrepresentation. There exists in special education a mismatch of chasm proportion between the social, political, and cultural backgrounds and experiences of its knowledge producers and those African American learners studied, placed, and overrepresented in special education classes.

It is axiomatic that knowledge and the production of knowledge is not culture free. In fact, Gordon, Miller, and Rollock (1990) have postulated that social science knowledge production operates within communicentric frames of references, whereby one's own "community" becomes the center of the universe and the conceptual frame that structures thought. Knowledge producers in special education, as in other social science disciplines, shape the explanatory parameters of issues such as paradigm formation, definitional constructs, theory development, and choice of research methods—all important foundational concerns that shape the overrepresentation discourse. The nature of meaning and the stances taken by knowledge producers in the important knowledge production process are influenced by their cultural and ethnic identities, which shape their notions of what is "real," "true," and "good." Accordingly, the "pseudo-objective" nature of knowledge production and of those who produce knowledge is

influenced strongly by the culture, assumptions, and beliefs that knowledge producers hold about the "other." If they lack knowledge, experience, or "insider" insight into the culture of the "other," their theories and constructs face serious construct and predictive validity challenges.

An examination of the special education knowledge base relative to African Americans will reveal that many knowledge producers have attempted to understand and explain the behavior and life experiences of African Americans through their own narrow cultural/ethnic perspectives and against an equally narrowly constructed cultural/ethnic standard (Gordon, 1985). As previously stated, the field's functionalist and positivistic core knowledge base further compounds the problem because of the culture-bound nature of this discourse and the limited explanatory usefulness embedded in this perspective. As such, many researchers and knowledge producers in special education generally explain and interpret the behavior of African Americans based upon their "outsider" beliefs and assumptions about the origins and meanings of behavior and the values placed on that behavior and the behaving person. Some have argued that this perspective represents a form of epistemological racism (Scheurich & Young, 1997; Stanfield, 1985). Underneath the processes of observing, identifying, and interpreting worth and behavior that one might say are deviant or different is the knowledge producer and his or her culturally bound frame of reference. This "filtering" process historically has not displayed enough of a passionate or empathic understanding and respect for the "other." The present critique of knowledge producers and production should better help us to understand the historical, sociopolitical problem of the overrepresentation of African Americans in special education programs. An important and missing context, I believe, is provided by this narrative. A new set of enlightened cultural filters and discourses is needed to replace the current language and narratives used to maintain the legitimacy of current special education social and political arrangements. It is essential that these discourses include important ethical themes heretofore missing from most disproportionality narratives.

NEEDED ETHICAL DISCOURSES

If the social sciences and special education shifted from their rational, functionalist, and positivist grounding, the field of special education would move naturally toward the inclusion of human factors, especially those ethical and moral ones, in its epistemology, ontology, knowledge production, structure, and practices (Starratt, 1991, 1994, 1996). With this transformation, certain ethical themes would prevail and envelope the narratives around disproportionality. Starratt (1991) has synthesized some important and disparate pieces of ethical discourse that can illuminate the problem of overrepresentation. The three ethical themes of critique, justice, and caring, explicated by Starratt (1991, 1994), will be used as a framework for bringing ethical clarification and development to this discussion in the hope of helping to resolve the problem of the overrepresentation of African Americans in special education programs.

As noted, the current special education system is structurally flawed and thus in need of critique. The previously discussed critique of the dogmatic, structuralist grounding of special education and its knowledge producers provided a preliminary lens into an ethic of critique. This ethic of critique employs a frame of reference to uncover the marginalization and dehumanizing effect of a system that disproportionately relegates large numbers of a cultural group into programs largely proven to be dysfunctional to their development. This stance is, by nature, an ethical one as it explores questions of social justice, equity, and human dignity on individual and collective levels (Starratt, 1991). For example, the critical ethicist understands that no knowledge production or the resulting understandings and practices that flow from that produced knowledge is neutral or culture free. Relatedly, no sociopolitical arrangement of human relationships that result from organizational, structural, or practical considerations have neutral antecedents. These arrangements are "usually structured to benefit some segments of society at the expense of others" (Starratt, 1991, p. 189). The application, therefore, of this framework of ethical critique to the disproportionality issue makes it clear that African Americans as a group are not best served by this arrangement and that the will and interests of the dominant social, economic, and political forces are indeed served. The ethical challenge of this ethic of critique is to uncover this inequality, confront, it, and begin to make bold social arrangements that are "more responsive to the human and civil rights of all and that enable those affected by these social arrangements to have a voice in evaluating the results and in altering practice" (Starratt, 1991, p. 190).

This essential ethical challenge has not been met on a grand scale thus far by the field. Heretofore, with few exceptions, deep structure theoretical and conceptual assumptions that drive this disproportionality reality have remained unchallenged. Often using ontologies, epistemologies, and axiologies that emanate from the social histories of the dominant race, the script writers continue to create dramas that have tragic endings for far too many African American learners. Rarely have alternative narratives been offered that make the system of special education and its major players accountable for the unethical consequences of large numbers of misdiagnosed African Americans labeled and placed in special education programs. There is a call, therefore, for some justice in the special education system.

This ethic of critique illuminates injustice and dehumanization and provides some markers for socially responsible corrective action, but an "ethic of justice provides more explicit responses" to these problems (Starratt, 1991, p. 194). In terms of overrepresentation, one might ask, "What common good is served by having disproportionately large numbers of African Americans, especially males, in special education programs?" Whose common good is served and for what purpose? How are the rights of individual African American students served by this arrangement? What kind of disservice does this arrangement, and the subsequent lack of contact with African American students, provide non-African American people individually or collectively? How does society benefit when the potentialities of large numbers of African Americans lie in a program for those with emotional disturbance or mental disability? These are the types of questions asked by special educators who employ an ethic of justice. Are we, as a collective, in all of our various roles as researchers, theorists, and practitioners, asking and struggling with answers to these questions?

Starratt (1991) argued that an ethic of justice can serve a better purpose if it is complemented by an ethic of caring. Nel Noddings (1984, 1988) has offered a compelling discourse on the ethic of caring that has important implications for the present narrative. Grounded in psychological literature, especially that of women's moral development, an ethic of caring calls for its users to create natural relationships with the "other" that display absolute and unconditional regard for the "other." This ethic rejects means-to-end relationships and prefers acts "done out of love and natural inclination" (Noddings, 1988,

p. 219). This ethic honors and extols the dignity, worth, and respect of every human being, individually and collectively, and places human relationships at the center of person-to-person interactions.

Special educators, especially its knowledge producers, can instill into their work and promote an ethic of caring by holding the integrity and goodness of each human relationship and each human being as sacred and by desiring to see individuals enjoy a complete life (Starratt, 1991). The persistent existence and perpetuation of the overrepresentation of African Americans in special education programs serves as counterforce against an ethic of caring. In loving relationships care is taken not to cause harm to the "other" in thoughts or actions. Many African Americans continue to be harmed by the unjust arrangements created by the presuppositions, theories, research, constructs, actions, behaviors, and processes that dominate the field of special education. The ethics of domination, control, oppression, and unjust treatment of African Americans that result in their disproportionate placement in special education programs serve to intrude on and block their human completion. An ethic of caring requires that all persons involved in the education enterprise, whether they are researchers, administrators, special education teachers, college professors, or school psychologists, treat African Americans and their culture with caring and respect and hold them in absolute regard.

With a few exceptions, ethnic minority knowledge producers, especially those of African descent, have largely been absent from writing these new ethical discourses or have been complicitous in their uncritical analysis of the hegemonic cultural base of special education knowledge producers (Gordon et al., 1990). It is essential that more ethnic minorities, from their own ontological, epistemological, and axiological perspectives, begin to write critical narratives about the philosophy, theory, values, methodologies, systems, and processes that undergird the field of special education. Such narratives should seek to amplify the muffled voices of those who seek to expose those ideologies, systems, processes, and practices that continue to marginalize African Americans—and that often culminate in their referral and eventual placement in dead-end special education programs. African American knowledge producers, aligned with culturally sensitive and competent others, have an essential and vital opportunity to clearly identify all inequities in special education, including those epistemologies and axiologies that result from its

functionalistic foundation hegemony of knowledge p distortions of knowledge and lightened knowledge producer a constant, relentless, and cari that can serve as a counterbalanc ideology of the field, which contin and maintain the hierarchical order in society and to ensure that Africa cans, especially males, remain at the bottom o ne social-political–economic heap.

THE NEED FOR NEW SCRIPT WRITERS

The underrepresentation of African Americans and conscious others in the special education knowledge production process has had a strong impact on the character and nature of the knowledge that has been produced. Their relative absence from this story has limited some insightful knowledge production and, accordingly, our deep structure understanding of the disproportionality narrative. The knowledge, meanings, understandings, and principles that have guided the disproportionality discourse have largely been derived from the field's positivistic tradition in the western social sciences. This explanatory framework, largely ahistorical and lacking social, political and economic considerations, has been inadequate in its explanations and solutions relative to the overrepresentation of African Americans in special education programs. New ways of knowing and valuing and new types of knowledge producers are called for. These knowledge producers are called upon to uncover the philosophical underpinnings of special education and replace them with a paradigm that expresses cultural "insider" knowledge, epistemologies, axiologies, and experiences that are social, political, cultural, and economic and that speak in multilectic terms (see Note 2). This grounding, then, by nature would require knowledge producers to understand and "be sensitive to the actual traits of populations under inquiry" (Stanfield, 1985, p. 411). In addition to rigor and methodological soundness in the inquiry process, this change calls for knowledge producers to develop a vast reservoir of cultural knowledge and experiences of African Americans, guided by "insiders" to this culture. This knowledge should serve to guide theory, research design, data collection, and interpretation (Stanfield, 1985). The need for this reformulated paradigm serves, then, as a special challenge to African American knowledge

, as well as sensitive and caring non-Americans knowledge producers.

Knowledge producers who would script the disproportionality problem with an ethic of critique, justice, and caring would offer the hope of replacing special education paradigms of domination and control with ones of liberation and emancipation. Resistance to such a paradigm shift is likely. The knowledge and analysis that have been produced thus far as "scientific," "objective," and "rational" have in the main not served the field well as an explanatory model for problem identification and resolution. New structures, systems, and paradigms are needed that allow for new knowledge producers in special education to make their voices heard and to approach the task of analysis and problem solving in honest ways (Sullivan, 1984). With this perspective, the pitfalls of our current ways of perceiving and dealing with the disproportionately problem will be placed in full view, thus beginning the process of our philosophical liberation.

CONCLUDING STATEMENTS

Artiles and Trent (1994) ended their treatise on the problem of disproportionate representation in special education by stating that some still find themselves asking the same basic question—whether or not overrepresentation is a problem. That is not a question that I have ever heard an African American special educator, sociologist, psychologist, anthropologist, barber, teacher, minister, social worker, custodian, business person, homemaker, or anyone else ask. Nor have I heard Latinos or Native Americans ask that question. We know the answer and it is *yes*. When this question is asked, the individual asking the question is usually from a European cultural background. The challenge and basis of analysis is to determine why this group, especially its knowledge producers, continues to beg the question. What is behind their question? It should be obvious to most people, professional and lay, that African Americans are overrepresented in large numbers in special education classrooms, particularly those for students with mild disabilities or emotional or behavioral disabilities. It is obvious, or should be, that many of these learners are misdiagnosed, mislabeled, and therefore misplaced.

It is obvious, or should be, that this reality has a historical legacy and has been (a) confirmed year after year by numerous scholarly studies, (b) recognized in U.S. law (the Individuals with Disabilities Education Act of 1990; P.L. 94-142), and (c) biannually confirmed by data from the U.S. Office for Civil Rights. It is obvious, or should be, that this reality is a symptom of a special education system run amok with many underlying problems in its deep structure philosophical and theoretical foundation, its ethics, processes, and practices. It is obvious, or should be, that its foundation, ethics, and practices have emanated from a set of knowledge producers outside of the affected population who have all too often created a system of false languages and knowledge production that continue to reinforce the dominant social, political, economic, and ethical order of things. Their beliefs, epistemologies, values, and presuppositions must be unveiled analyzed, and made clear as an absolute precondition for resolving this problem—which has plagued this profession and nation for too many years. There is, however, a way out.

These same knowledge producers can begin to reevaluate their worldview, epistemologies, ethical themes, so-called objectivity, methodology, and practice in light of the many muted voices of African Americans. They could employ a language of ethical critique, justice, and caring in their work and inject social, political, economic, historical, and ethical discourses into all that they do. They could go to those who are "studied" to listen and hear. They could go to "insiders" for critical insights into the "other" and be guided by those insights. They could allow the "other," African American knowledge producers, to teach and lead them in their quest for knowledge production liberation. The challenge is not just with the dominant European knowledge producers. African Americans have an equally large leadership challenge.

A system is needed in special education that nurtures, develops, and allows for the voices of African American knowledge producers to be heard, confirmed, and affirmed. Their voices will more closely represent those who are studied, tested, identified, labeled, and placed in special education programs—often at levels well beyond accepted rates. It is through looking behind the special education ontological, epistemological, and axiological "curtain" and bringing to center stage the voices, narratives, and discourses of African Americans and sensitive and aware others that this problem can be resolved. The criteria needed for these new knowledge producers are the same ones needed for all of those participating in an agenda that turns the corner in resolving the African American special education overrepresentation problem. The training and continual development of liberating knowledge producers and practitioners should be conditioned by these criteria. Out of this reflection, growth, freedom, and progression could emerge a grand story. The denouement to yet another story that threatens this society could conclude in a way that liberates those most negatively affected, as well as those perpetuating these threats.

AUTHOR'S NOTE

Preparation of this manuscript was supported in part by Grant No. H029J60006 from the U.S. Department of Education, Office of Special Education Programs, to the University of Virginia for the Center of Minority Research in Special Education.

Notes

1. The present analysis focuses on the overrepresentation of African Americans in certain special education programs. I have addressed the underrepresentation of African Americans in gifted programs in other writings (Patton, 1992, 1995).

2. The term *multilectic* is used here to refer to a multitude of theses, their opposites, and their syntheses, as opposed to the Hegelian/Marxist dialectic.

References

Anderson, M. G. (1994). Perceptions about behavioral disorders in African American cultures and communities. In R. L. Perterson & S. Ishii-Jordon (Eds.). *Multicultural issues in the education of students with behavioral disorders* (pp. 93–104). Cambridge, MA: Brookline.

Apple, M. W. (Ed.). (1981). *Cultural and economic reproduction in education.* Boston: Routledge & Kegan Paul.

Apple, M. (1990). *Ideology and curriculum.* New York: Routledge.

Aronowitz. S., & Giroux, H. A. (1991). *Postmodern education: Politics, culture, and social criticism.* Minneapolis: University of Minnesota.

Artiles, A. J., & Trent, S. C. (1994). Overrepresentation of minority students in special education: A continuing debate. *The Journal of Special Education, 22,* 410–436.

Bowles, S., & Gintis, H. (1976). *Schooling in capitalist America,* New York: Basic Books.

Cherryholmes, C. H. (1988). *Power and criticism: Poststructuralist investigations in education.* New York: Teachers College Press.

Deno, E. (1970). Special education as development capital. *Exceptional Children, 37,* 229–237.

Foucault, M. (1976). *Mental illness and psychology.* Berkeley: University of California Press.

Freire, P. (1970). *Pedagogy of the oppressed.* New York: Herder & Herder.

Giroux, H. A. (1988). *Teachers as intellectuals: Toward a critical pedagogy of learning.* Granby, MA: Bergin & Garvey.

Goffman, E. (1963). *Stigma: Notes on the management of spoiled identity.* Englewood Cliffs, NJ: Prentice Hall.

Gordon, E. W. (1985). Social science knowledge production and minority experience. *The Journal of Higher Education, 54,* 117–133.

Gordon, E. W., Miller, F., & Rollock, D. (1990). Coping with communicentric bias in knowledge production in the social sciences. *Educational Researcher, 19*(3), 14–19.

Gould, S. G. (1981). *The mismeasure of man.* New York: Norton.

Harry, B., & Anderson, M. (1994). The disproportionate placement of African American males in special education programs: A critique of the process. *Journal of Negro Education, 63,* 602–619.

Heller, K. A., Holtzman, W. H., & Messick, S. (Eds.). (1982). *Placing children in special education: A strategy for equity.* Washington, DC: National Academy Press.

Hilliard, A. G., III. (1991). The learning potential assessment device and instrumental enrichment as a paradigm shift. In A. G. Hilliard, III (Ed.). *Testing African American students: A special re-issue of the Negro education reviews* (pp. 200–208). Morristown, NJ: Aaron.

Hilliard, A. G., III. (1992). The pitfalls and promises of special education practice. *Exceptional Children, 59,* 168–172.

Individuals with Disabilities Education Act of 1990, 20 U.S.C. §1400 *et seq.*

Irvine, J. J. (1990). *Black students and school failure: Policies, practices, and prescriptions.* New York: Greenwood.

Jones, R. L. (Ed.). (1988). *Psychoeducational assessment of minority group children: A casebook.* Berkeley: Cobb & Henry.

Katz, M. B. (1971). *Class, bureaucracy, and schools: The illusion of educational change in America.* New York: Praeger.

Lipsky, D. K., & Gartner, A. (1989). *Beyond separate education: Quality education for all.* Baltimore: Brookes.

MacMillan, D. L., & Hendrick, I. G. (1993). Evolution and legacies. In J. I. Goodlad & T. C. Lovitt (Eds.). *Integrating general and special education* (pp. 23–48). Columbus, OH: Merrill/Macmillan.

Markowitz, J., Garcia, S., & Eichelberger, J. H. (1997). *Addressing the disproportionate placement of students from racial and ethnic minority groups in special ed programs and classes.* Alexandria, VA: National Association of State Directors of Special Education.

McDermott, R. P. (1987). Achieving school failure: An anthropological approach to illiteracy and social stratification. In G. D. Spindler (Ed.), *Education and cultural process: Anthropological approaches* (2nd ed., pp. 173–209). Prospect Heights, IL: Waveland.

Mercer, G. R. (1973). *Labeling the mentally retarded.* Berkeley: University of California Press.

Morrison, P., White, S. H., & Fever, M. J. (Eds.). (1996). *The use of IQ tests in special education decision making and planning: Summary of two workshops.* Washington, DC: National Academy Press.

Nobles, W. (1991). Psychometrics and African American reality: A question of cultural antimony. In A. G. Hilliard, III (Ed.). *Testing African American students: Special re-issue of the Negro education reviews* (pp. 45–55). Morristown, NJ: Aaron.

Noddings, N. (1984). *Caring: A feminine approach to ethics and moral education.* Berkeley: University of California Press.

Noddings, N. (1988). An ethic of caring and its implications for instructional arrangements. *American Journal of Education, 96,* 215–230.

Patton, J. M. (1992). Assessment and identification of African American learners with gifts and talents. *Exceptional Children, 59,* 150–159.

Patton, J. M. (1995). Identifying and transforming the potential of young, gifted African Americans: A clarion call for action. In B. A. Ford, F. D. Obiakor, & J. M. Patton (Eds.). *Effective education of African American exceptional learners: New perspectives* (pp. 27–67). Austin, TX: PRO-ED.

Reschly, D. (1996). *Disproportionate minority representation in general and special education programs: Patterns, issues, and alternatives.* Des Moines, IA: Drake University, Resource Center/MPRRC.

Scheurich, J. J., & Young, M. (1997). Coloring epistemologies: Are our research epistemologies racially biased? *Educational Researcher, 26*(4), 4–16.

Skrtic, T. M. (1986). The crisis in social education knowledge: A perspective on perspective. *Focus on Exceptional Children, 18*(7), 1–16.

Skrtic, T. M. (1991). The special education paradox: Equity as the way to excellence. *Harvard Educational Review, 61,* 148–206.

Stanfield, J. (1985). The ethnocentric bias of social science knowledge production. In E. W. Gordon (Ed.), *Review of research in education* (Vol. 12. pp. 387–415). Washington, DC: American Educational Research Association.

Starratt, R. J. (1991). Building an ethical school: A theory for practice in educational leadership. *Educational Administration Quarterly, 27,* 185–202.

Starratt, R. J. (1994). *Building an ethical school: A practical response to the moral crisis in schools.* London: Falmer.

Starratt, R. J. (1996). *Transforming educational administration: Meaning, community, and excellence.* New York: McGraw-Hill.

Sullivan, E. (1984). *A critical psychology,* New York: Plenum.

Townsend, B., Thomas, D., Witty, J. P., & Lee, R. S. (1996). Diversity and school restructuring: Creating partnerships in a world of difference. *Teacher Education and Special Education. 19*(2), 102–118.

Willie, C. V., Garibaldi, A. M., & Reed, W. L. (Eds.). (1991). *The education of African-Americans.* Boston: William Monroe Trotter Institute.

Ysseldyke, J. E., Algozzine, B., & Thurlow, M. L. (1992). *Critical issues in special education* (2nd ed.). Boston: Houghton Mifflin.

4.2 | Special Education in the Restructured School

Wayne Sailor

Two significant, overriding trends in reform have emerged in special education at all levels from policy to program implementation during the past decade. These are, first, the movement to integrate students with severe disabilities and those with low-incidence disabilities into general education schools and classrooms for their educational programs; second, the effort to retain students with mild and moderate disabilities in the general classroom as an alternative to pull-out programs. These trends are closely associated. Until recently, parallel trends in general education reform have tended to focus on improvement in curriculum and in instructional techniques. Most recently, however, these reform efforts have shifted in the direction of systematic reorganization of school governance structures, policy, and resource utilization at the school site. This shift presents an opportunity for amalgamation of these various related viewpoints through broad-based, school restructuring policy reform. This amalgamation is particularly reflected in those aspects of restructuring that are concerned with regulatory waivers, site-based management and budgetary control, shared decision making, and full infusion, with school site coordination, of federal, categorical program resources into the general education program. Sufficient parallels exist between the general and special education reform agendas to suggest that the time may be at hand for a shared educational agenda.

Significant reform efforts have characterized special education over the past decade. Parallel efforts at reform have also been under way over the same period in general education. Until recently, these separate reform directions have held relatively little significance for one another and, if anything, have tended to increase the separation between the two groups of educators. Very recently, however, the dominant trend of reform in general education has shifted attention to organization and governance issues in an effort to better support the needs of a changing demography, characterized by greater diversity among the nation's collective student body.

Within special education, dominant reform trends have been focused in part on achieving greater social and, to a degree, academic integration of students with wide-ranging types of significant disabilities in general education schools and classrooms. For example, emphasis is frequently placed on partial participation in the general classroom curriculum, assisted by curricular and technological adaptations (e.g., Thousand & Villa, 1989), for students with even the most severe disabilities. A larger and more controversial agenda has been focused on efforts to retain students with milder disabilities, such as learning disabilities, in general education classrooms and to reduce the incidence of utilization of pull-out strategies, such as self-contained classes and resource room configurations for these students.

In general education, reform efforts have shifted recently, from intensive concentration on efforts to improve curriculum and instruction, to efforts in the reorganization of school and district-level governance systems and in the manner in which fiscal and personnel resources are allocated and utilized at the school site. This shift in emphasis in general education reform presents a window of opportunity for the emergence of a shared educational agenda, one that holds potential for capturing the innovative elements of improvement and reform in federal categorical programs such as special education as well as elements in general education reform. In the remainder of this paper, the basis for a shared educational agenda in school reform is examined by considering dominant aspects of special education reform in light of the current school restructuring movement.

TRENDS IN SPECIAL EDUCATION REFORM

The movement of students with significant and multiple disabilities ("severely handicapped") into general educational settings has undeniably represented the hallmark of research and development activity concerned with this population over the past decade. Much of the summative literature base of the 1970s was concerned with how and what to teach, focusing on behavioral teaching technology with its emphasis on task analysis and data management schemes (Haring & Bricker, 1978; Haring & Brown, 1976, 1977; Sontag, 1977; York & Edgar, 1979). In the 1980s the focus shifted palpably to a concern with where to teach and the ramifications of the learning environment. This past decade also witnessed the least restrictive environment (LRE) language in statutory and regulatory language begin to take on a major significance from policy-level decisions to classroom practice (Sailor, Wilcox, & Brown, 1980; Snell, 1978).

The emphasis on social and, to a lesser degree, academic integration of the population with more severe disabilities has been strongly buttressed by positive outcomes in comparative "efficacy" studies (Brinker & Thorpe, 1984; Halvorsen & Sailor, 1990; Meyer, Peck, & Brown, 1990; Sailor et al., 1989) and by legal-policy analytic interpretations of the litigative history of P.L. 94-142 (Gilhool, 1989; Gilhool & Stutman, 1978). The integration thrust has met only token resistance in the research literature (Burton & Hirschoren, 1979; Cruickshank, 1977; Gottlieb, 1981; Haywood, 1981), but no controlled studies have surfaced to date presenting data supportive of separate rather than integrated educational programs (see Halvorsen & Sailor, 1990, for a review of efficacy studies on integration).

Students with Severe Disabilities

Studies of specific issues in the placement of students with severe disabilities are few in number and inconclusive, but seem to suggest increased placements in more integrated educational environments over time (Haring et al., in press) characterized by a great deal of variability across the states (Danielson & Bellamy, 1989). The emphasis on integrated educational placements appears to extend to students with the most severe disabilities, including those with significant health; or behavioral problems (Campbell & Bailey, in press; Sailor, Gee, Graham, & Goetz, 1988), and to encompass a "zero-rejection" philosophy, wherein no student or disability category would be deemed too disabled to be integrated (Sailor, Gerry, & Wilson, in press-b).

Most recently, the emphasis in the literature pertaining to integration of students with severe disabilities has shifted from a discussion of approaches that exemplify special class models within regular

> "In general education, reform efforts have shifted recently, from intensive concentration on efforts to improve curriculum and instruction, to efforts in the reorganization of school and district-level governance systems and in the manner in which fiscal and personnel resources are allocated and utilized at the school site."

schools, where integration occurs primarily in extraneous school settings such as assemblies, recess, and lunch time involving peer tutors, friendship relationships, etc., to a discussion of "full inclusion" models that exemplify placement of these children in the general classroom with some program time in other environments, as needed (Biklen, Bogdan, Ferguson, Searl, & Taylor, 1985; Falvey, 1989; Forest & Lusthaus, 1989; Sailor et al., 1989; Stainback & Stainback, 1990; Stainback, Stainback, & Forest, 1989; Thousand & Villa, 1989). The pros and cons of these relative placement considerations are discussed in Brown et al. (1989a, 1989b) and in Sailor et al. (in press-b).

The full inclusion approach to the provision of integrated special educational services to low-incidence and severe disability populations appears to be gaining strength across the country. A recent study by the California Research Institute (CRI) resulted in the identification of some 15 school districts around the country that are reported by their administrative staff as entirely, or close to being entirely, operated on a full inclusion basis (Karasoff & Kelly, 1989), with the most extensively documented service delivery model to emerge to date being provided by the Johnson City School District in upstate New York (Mamary & Rowe, 1990). Three entire states have now published their intent to commit to some form of a full inclusion delivery system within a short time span: Colorado (McNulty, 1990); Iowa (Hamre-Nietupski, Nietupski, & Maurer, 1990); and Vermont (Williams et al., 1986). Other states, including California, with the impetus provided by their successful competition in the federal Office of Special Education and Rehabilitation Services (OSERS) systems change grants program to enhance less restrictive educational placements (e.g., Winget, 1990), are developing positions of policy and program implementation philosophy that suggest strong trends toward statewide full inclusion practices. Several Canadian models have also emerged, most notably in Ontario and New Brunswick (Forest, 1987; Stainback et al., 1989; Vandercook, York, & Forest, 1989). Finally, within western European countries, Italy stands out as the country with the most visible application of full inclusion educational services, particularly in the northern provinces of Liguria (i.e., Genoa) and Emilia-Romagna (i.e., Bologna) (Gaylord-Ross, 1987; Sailor, 1989; Vitello, 1989).

The basic components that most full inclusion models share include:

1. All students attend the school to which they would go if they had no disability.
2. A natural proportion (i.e., representative of the school district at large) of students with disabilities occurs at any school site.
3. A zero-rejection philosophy exists so that typically no student would be excluded on the basis of type or extent of disability [except, see Sailor, Gerry, & Wilson (in press-a) for a discussion of the implications of these models for children with deafness].
4. School and general education placements are age- and grade-appropriate, with no self-contained special education classes operative at the school site.
5. Cooperative learning and peer instructional methods receive significant use in general instructional practice at the school site.
6. Special education supports are provided within the context of the general education class and in other integrated environments.

Obviously, a school organization that includes these six points can only exist in the context of a unified educational program wherein planning for the education of general as well as special populations at the school site is a shared responsibility of the total professional and administrative staff (Stainback et al., 1989; Stainback & Stainback, 1990), and, conversely, where special education does not function as a "second system" (Gartner & Lipsky, 1990b) with descriptors such as "a school within a school," "side-by-side program," and so on.

Students with Mild or Moderate Disabilities

Although the integration imperative has met with relatively little resistance from the educational research community, efforts to reform service delivery to the population of students with milder disabilities, to the contrary, have generated enormous controversy. These efforts surfaced visibly in 1986 as a federal policy initiative (Will, 1986), called the Regular Education Initiative, or REI, which seemed to suggest that responsibility for the education of these children should best be viewed as a shared responsibility of all educators rather than the sole purview of special education. The initiative quickly gained support from several prominent educational researchers whose data collectively suggested that under certain service delivery models, children with learning disabilities, for example, would do better in mainstreamed educational programs than in pull-out, resource-room, separate classroom-oriented programs (Wang & Peverly, 1987; Wang, Reynolds, & Walberg, 1986, 1988). These publications resulted in an unprecedented entire issue of the *Journal of Learning Disabilities* (January 1988) being devoted to a rebuttal of the Wang and Reynolds research and program development efforts.

Later on, others argued that the REI was "deeply flawed" social policy in that it was a special education initiative rather than a regular education initiative (Singer, 1988; Singer & Butler, 1987), that REI was inappropriate for certain categorical disability groups (Braaten, Kauffman, Braaten, Polsgrove, & Nelson, 1988), and that the REI constituted nothing less than a Republican plot to destroy special education and redirect the funds from P.L. 94-142 to a more socially affluent and high-achieving class of children and youth (Kauffman, 1989). [See also Goetz & Sailor (1990), Kauffman & Hallahan (1990), and McLeskey, Skiba, & Wilcox (1990), for discussions of this article.]

The issue on the special education side is clearly one that evokes strong emotion, even among otherwise sanguine academic researchers. Kauffman (1989), Singer (1988), Vergason and Anderegg (in press), and others have written in highly charged rhetorical terms on the topic, with reference to "throwing the baby out with the bathwater," for example. Opponents of REI have argued that its proponents believe:

1. No truly special instruction is needed by any student.
2. Special training is not required for handicapped students or for their teachers.
3. Specific targeting of funds for specific students is unnecessary.
4. All students can be instructed and managed effectively in general classrooms.

5. The more important equity issue is the site, not the quality of instruction. (Goetz & Sailor, 1990, p. 336)

McClesky et al. (1990) argued that extensive reviews of the literature that examine categorical labeling and grouping in terms of special education effectiveness collectively have revealed a set of conclusions that are at variance with the conclusions of the most vociferous reform opponents, particularly Kauffman (1989).

Goetz and Sailor (1990) argued that the "most radical" suggestions that can be gleaned from the sum total of the reform literature are: (a) Special education may work best in mainstream educational settings; (b) categorical labels and homogeneous special education grouping strategies are nonprescriptive in themselves; and (c) special education may function most effectively as a support to the regular educational program rather than as a second system operating in parallel to regular education, but without sufficient contact and coordination with it. Opponents of special education reform who are focused on students with mild and moderate disabilities tend to view these efforts as an attack on and direct threat to special education, rather than as an attempt to introduce reform into special education that would align its mission more closely with that of the greater body of general education.

Special Education Reform as a Cohesive Trend

In one sense REI is to children with moderate and mild disabilities as the integration imperative (Gilhool, 1989) is to children with low-incidence and severe disabilities. The common denominator is the principle of the least restrictive educational environment, which in turn is born of the recognition that social and communicative development in children with disabilities is predicated on opportunities for mainstream socialization as well as academic experiences and that these experiences are an inherent entitlement of children with disabilities under the constitutional guarantee of freedom of association (Council of Chief State School Officers, 1989; Fine, 1983, 1987; Sailor, Gerry, & Wilson, in press-a). Current reform efforts in special education at both the policy and programmatic levels are aimed, as they are in the case of general educators at redesigning existing statutory and regulatory systems to meet the needs of a changing demography of constituents and to better reflect major technological, curricular, and pedagogical advances over the recent short term (Bauwens, Hourcade, & Friend, 1989).

Lowenbraun, Madge, and Affleck (1990), for example, presented some data that illuminate the perspective of parents of both special and general education students under reformed service models. Their results indicate that both sets of the parents they studied were satisfied with general class placement of special education students and that their degree of satisfaction increased over time. The parents of the special education children were particularly positive concerning friendships and self-esteem factors associated with the general class placement sample. A substantial 8⁻% of the mainstream sample parents indicated that they would choose general class placement again.

Bauwens et al. (1989) reviewed a number of teacher consultation models that are facilitative of the goals of special education reform. They described a particular approach, which they call cooperative teaching, based on the collaborative consultation model of Idol, Paolucci-Whitcomb, and Nevin (1986). These models stress the use of teams made up of special and general education classroom teachers at the school site (a) to determine curricular and pedagogical approaches to be used with mainstreamed students identified for special education support and (b) to facilitate joint planning for utilization of professional resources at the school to best serve all of the students at the school.

Downing and Eichinger (1990) and Slavin, Stevens, and Madden (1988) presented impressive arguments for the extension of cooperative learning strategies to promote mainstream educational programs for students with dual sensory impairments and with "academically handicapped" students, respectively. It is clear from the emergent survey research literature on mainstreaming, however, that although general education principals and other administrators may be quite open to implementation of these kinds of reforms, little of the process will likely occur without efforts to deal specifically with the fear of loss of responsibility for special education students by special education teachers, and fear of lack of adequate classroom support felt by general education classroom teachers (Garvar-Pinhas & Pedhazur Schmelkin, 1989; Knapp & Turnbull, 1990; Vladero, 1990). Gersten and Woodward (1990) and Miller (1990) presented balanced arguments on the reform controversy and suggested that it should best be viewed as that portion of the school restructuring reform movement that is concerned with special education. Semmel and Gerber (1990), in reviewing the collection of papers by general educators that made up the special issue of *Remedial and Special Education* concerned with the REI (May/June 1990), provided a thoughtful focus on the perspective of classroom teachers in the reform process. In the context of expressing the usual caveat of special educators against the potential for cannibalizing P.L. 94-142 to find the money to solve the myriad larger problems of general education (Kauffman, 1989; Kauffman, Gerber, & Semmel, 1989), the authors in this publication have *supported* the reform efforts. This support, however, contains the caveat that at least some teacher collaboration models, which successfully focus efforts on all students in the general education classroom (including special education students), will need to be disseminated as highly visible demonstrations.

Semmel and Gerber (1990) also cited in detail Dolores Durkin's (1990) report of a classroom teacher who failed to benefit from consultation on special education children in her classroom because the general education teacher held "slavishly" to the idea that all of the children in her class should complete a given curriculum at the same minimal level of performance (i.e., mastery). Semmel and Gerber concluded that these kinds of educational reforms can be positive to the extent that

1. Reform focuses on conditions that inhibit successful accommodations of *particular* children in general education classrooms.
2. An ethic of unified, school-based ownership of all children at the school, including ownership of the problems posed by all "difficult-to-teach" children, prevails at the school site.
3. Special education must be focused at the school, not the district level, and a mechanism must exist for shared decision making and joint responsibility for all students at the site (Glatthorn, 1990a, 1990b).

The current wave of school reform in general education is clearly focused less on accelerating students who are already high achievers, and much more on improving the performance of more challenging populations associated with the changing demography of U.S. schools. This circumstance creates a significant window of opportunity for aligning the reform efforts in special education discussed above to those of general education. In the next section, reform efforts in general education are examined with an eye to potential correspondence with parallel efforts in special education reform.

REFORM IN GENERAL EDUCATION

The Problem of Students at Risk

The changing demography of America's school population, coupled with the increasing demands of technological advances in business and industry, have given rise to startling findings in recent analyses of the preparedness of America's schools to adapt to these changes. Among the findings of concern:

- 1 million students drop out of school each year
- 1.5 million teenage women become pregnant each year
- Between ⅕ and ¼ of all U.S. children live below the poverty line
- On any given night it is estimated there are at least 100,000 homeless children
- Every year, more than 5,000 young people take their own lives
- More than 2.2 million cases of child abuse and neglect were reported in 1987
- Fifteen percent of graduates of urban high schools read at less than the 6th grade level
- Almost 10 million children have no regular source of medical care
- About 20 million children under age 17 have never seen a dentist
- An estimated 3 million children have a serious drinking problem. (Davis & McCaul, 1990, p. 4)

If "students at risk" are defined as comprising only those who are likely to leave school prematurely or to graduate without the social, academic, and vocational skills needed to lead a productive life in our society, current estimates would place the figure at about 30% of current enrollment and growing yearly (New Partnerships, 1988). Research on the factors placing students at risk have focused in recent years on the concept of educational disadvantage (Hodginson, 1985; Levin, 1985; McDill, Natriello, & Pallas, 1986) and its implications for the way services are organized at the school site.

The primary indicators of societal factors that place children at risk have been identified as (a) poverty; (b) minority, racial/ethnic group identity; (c) non-

English or limited English background; and (d) specific family configurations, such as single parent households (Davis & McCaul, 1990). These societal factors, which have been extensively documented in, for example, Rose (1989) and Schoor (1988), interact with school organization and environmental factors such as defective student-teacher and parent-teacher communication, low-motivational instructional materials, weak or ineffectual school leadership, and outdated instructional procedures to produce an unbroken cycle of deterioration in American education (MDC, Inc., 1988).

Whether one uses a general definition of at risk such as "unlikely to graduate" (Slavin, 1989) or a more detailed analysis, such as "educationally disadvantaged children" (Levin, 1989), it is clear that the problem is not simply concentrated in and closely associated with areas of inner-city urban decay. A National School Boards Association (1989) study indicated that as many as three-fifths of the at-risk population can be found in rural and suburban areas.

According to Lipsky and Gartner (1989), the present wave of reform in general education is characterized by a focus on higher standards of performance and professionalism at the state and local levels, and or effective schools research-based methods, such as cooperative learning and mechanisms for peer tutorial services (Bickel & Bickel, 1986; Gartner & Lipsky 1990a; Jenkins & Jenkins, 1981), to address primarily the problems presented by the population of student at risk. The hallmark of this reform is community empowerment in the life of the schools (Carnegie Foundation for the Advancement of Teaching, 1988; Committee for Economic Development, 1987). Current school restructuring efforts, for example, are concerned with greater parent involvement in the decision-making apparatus of the schools, and greater community participation in school management, such as is evidenced by the local school governing board experiment currently under way in Chicago. Finally greater flexibility in the integration of resources available to the school site through federal categorical programs is being strongly advanced (Gartner & Lipsky 1987; Lipsky & Gartner, 1989).

One of the principal recommendations of the report by the National Center on Education and the Economy (NCEE), *To Secure Our Future: The Federal Role in Education* (1989), is to restructure schools for high performance. The report stresses incorporation of curriculum and instruction to promote mastery of higher order thinking skills in all students; requiring performance-oriented outcomes for school achievement; upgrading teacher skills and standards; and giving teachers more authority in school decision making. Most important, the NCEE report calls for a comprehensive restructuring of the way categorical programs, such as Special Education, Chapter I, Vocational Education, Adult Education, Bilingual Education, Head Start, and other programs, are operated. Removal of children from opportunities to succeed or even excel in the mainstream, according to the report, is costly and detrimental to all, particularly since the relatively rich resources provided through categorical programs to benefit children who are often inappropriately labeled neither demonstrably improves their educational outcomes in isolation (Lipsky & Gartner, 1989), nor allows for the maximization of educational resources for the good of all.

The categorical restructuring of the type recommended by NCEE can be accomplished within the framework of existing rules, regulations, and waiver processes to permit experiments in school restructuring to be properly evaluated and useful models to be disseminated without throwing various categorical "babies" out with the proverbial bathwater (Vergason & Anderegg, in press). The rules and regulations governing the Individuals with Disabilities Act (IDEA), for example, are specifically designed to protect the rights of children with disabilities and prevent their resources from being redirected to meet the needs of "more capable, but underachieving" populations. Compromising those protections is dangerous, unwise, and unwarranted, particularly if it can be demonstrated that IDEA resources can be harnessed and coordinated in such a manner, at the school site, to actually improve outcomes for students with disabilities while, at the same time, having a positive impact on the total school population through an integrated programmatic structure (California State Department of Education, 1989).

In addition to innovation in assessment, curriculum, and instructional practices, most school restructuring models that have been described in the literature to date have at least three of the following four primary sets of operations in common:

1. School organizational autonomy
2. Site-based management and shared decision making
3. Full infusion and coordination of categorical resources
4. Community participation in the life of the school

School Organizational Autonomy

Elmore and Associates (1990) have argued that school restructuring must concern itself with curriculum and teaching technology issues, but only within the context of school organization, school governance, and the place of the governance structures within the state systems. Cohen (1988) similarly argues that restructuring must be viewed as organizationally multitiered and, most important, must be related in clear, measurable ways to improved school productivity and student performance. States must stimulate restructuring through evolving functional standards of accountability, highly publicized results of accountability data, and by providing rewards and sanctions linked to school/student performance. Concomitant changes at the school, district, and state levels will be required to accomplish restructuring.

David, together with her colleagues (David, 1990; David, Cohen, Honetschlage, & Traiman, 1990), recently provided a set of recommendations to the nation's governors entitled *State Actions to Restructure Schools: First Steps*, a publication of the Center for Policy Research of the National Governors' Association (David et al., 1990). David et al. approach restructuring from a policy analysis perspective, and target specific actions that can be initiated at the level of the state education agency to stimulate action at the district level. Their blueprint for state action includes the following steps:

1. Define restructuring at the state level and create a vision for its outcomes.
2. Initiate conferences, statewide and regional, to inform the educational community and the public about the initiative.
3. Build statewide support for the initiative through networking organizations.
4. Start small with invited or competed pilot demonstration projects.
5. Offer access to waivers from state rules to facilitate demonstration projects (see Table 1 for examples of waiver requests).
6. Provide time for staff development and staff meetings to get restructuring off the ground.
7. Offer technical assistance and training from state and brokered services.
8. Gradually shift the state role from compliance policeman to facilitator and assistance provider.
9. Provide an outcomes-driven philosophy that stresses school accountability and increases student performance.

10. Maintain a clear focus on the specific goals and objectives of a state-level restructuring initiative.

What is clear from the writings of David, and also Skrtic (1988; 1990), is that restructuring is a viable concept and worth retaining as a clearly focused set of goals, objectives, and specifiable outcomes: restructuring cannot be accomplished from either the "top down" by a policy analytic/administrative set of interventions, nor can it effectively proceed from the "ground up" by simply restructuring what goes on within individual schools in isolation. Effective restructuring is organizationally systemic in nature and must proceed from both directions simultaneously. The set of operations required for school organizational autonomy require multilevel policy analyses and clear specifications as to the extent of autonomy and flexibility afforded to the school site.

Site-Based Management and Shared Decision Making

Virtually all of the broad strategies that have emerged in the recent literature of school restructuring have stressed the component of decentralized governance (Sirotnik & Clark, 1988). In these systems, the locus of decision making with regard to the day-to-day operation of school programs is largely shifted from the central district office to the school site administrators, with the result being much more flexibility and autonomy among the schools, both in organization/governance and in program implementation.

Site-based management models allow decisions to be made about how various categorical revenues are to be coordinated and utilized, how instruction is to be organized and delivered, how curriculum and materials are to be selected and staffing arrangements to be made—all concentrated at the level of the building principal (Cohen, 1988). Site-based management can, of course, vary substantially on dimensions of school organization, such as the extent to which the management style is "bureaucratic or adhocratic" (Skrtic, 1988).

Shared decision making is one current focus of site-based management efforts at restructuring. Under this model, teachers, other school staff, administrators, and parents form a group that is charged with the responsibility of making key school decisions in allocating resources. Issues such as how students and staff are assigned to classrooms; how roles of administrators are to be determined; how personnel are evaluated, hired, fired, or promoted; curriculum issues; all can come under the purview of a shared-responsibility, site-management group.

Table 1

Examples of waiver requests.

- Use textbook money for books and materials not on the approved list
- Combine three high school classes into a three-hour block of time
- Allow teachers professional leave time during the school year
- Allow an elementary certified teacher to teach with a ninth-grade team
- Allow secondary teachers to teach subjects other than their certified subject in order to participate on a multidisciplinary team
- Shorten the high school day to allow time for forty-minute special topic seminars for small mixed grade groups taught by teachers, administrators, and clerical staff
- In order to provide additional time for teachers to meet and plan:
  —Reduce student contact hours;
  —Hire a full-time substitute; and
  —Set aside full days without students for teachers
- Ignore state curriculum guidelines in order to implement a cross-disciplinary curriculum
- Ignore class size limits to allow large classes for certain presentations freeing teachers to have small discussion groups
- Remove grade-level restrictions on the use of paraprofessionals to enable schools to use them as needed
- Ignore requirements for specified minutes of instruction by subject area to allow more flexibility in how time is spent
- Redefine high school credits to permit credits for cross-disciplinary courses

Note. From *State Actions to Restructure Schools: First Steps* (p. 21) by J. David, M. Cohen, D. Honetschlager, and S. Traiman, 1990. Washington, DC: National Governor's Association, Center for Policy Research. Reprinted by permission.

The issue of teacher authority in decision-making models at the school site is a second factor in site-based management models that may directly affect teacher motivation and job performance (e.g., Cistone, Fernandez, & Tornillo, 1989). It is axiomatic that "fired-up" teachers produce results that are reflected in a wide range of pupil-focused outcomes. Teacher motivation has long been a critical, neglected, and puzzling variable in the school reform literature, but is clearly linked to teacher perception of professional authority in all aspects of the life of the school (The Holmes Group 1986: McDonnell & Pascal, 1988). The most creative ideas for educational reform at the school site level will have only a fraction of their potential impact under a top-down, administrative-mandate structure, in which teachers are given in-service training in new technologies and configurations and then expected to implement reforms with no particular say in the decisions that led to the mandate. The room for creative restructuring at the level of the school site is clearly at the point of design of organizational schemes that secure teacher buy-in concerning all aspects of educational reform

and resource allocation to implement those reforms (Skrtic, 1988).

Conley (1988) found four critical domains that must be influenced directly by teachers in a shared-decision model: (a) organizational resource allocation; (b) work allocation (e.g., school assignments); (c) professional-organizational interface (i.e., grading policies, staff hiring); and (d) teaching process (curriculum, textbooks, etc.). Greater teacher authority in these realms implies different organizational studies to support the process. Similarly, Lieberman (1988) pointed to the need to pay careful attention to sociological aspects of organization theory in moving toward shared-decision models that emphasize greater teacher authority and professionalism, because some arrangements are likely to operate more effectively than others.

Perhaps the most comprehensive resource to emerge to date on all of the myriad issues that face conversion to shared-decision models is that provided by Marburger (1985). The issue of "management councils" is discussed in detail, with particular concern given to membership; size issues; selection or election processes for membership; processes for selection of membership from the community; relationship of the management council to the district office, school board, and community agencies; the role of the principal and the conflict-resolution issues surrounding the school accountability criteria with respect to the position of the principal and his or her relationship to the management council, council products and procedures, and issues concerned with budgeting and allocation of time for participation on the council (Sailor et al., in press-a, in press-b; Sykes, 1990).

Full Infusion and Coordination of All Available Resources

The third set of operations characterizing some school restructuring models pertains to the issue of resource reconfiguration and management. The best teachers working with the most advanced curriculum and with effective teaching practices still cannot hope to reverse the processes that place students at risk for school failure and dropout without adequate resources, particularly when class sizes are high. The needs of children at risk are many, and human resources in general education are typically too few. Many of those human resources needed for the educational improvement of all children are locked up in federal categorical programs that are designed to benefit relatively few students, and often historically in isolation. The major policy issue at stake here is whether those students for whom categorical resources are tagged can have their specialized needs met in a manner that allows all students at the school to benefit from those programs (Sapon-Shevin, 1988; Shaw et al., 1990).

An examination of special education resource allocation, as one categorical program, provides a case in point. In fiscal year 1987, 4.4 million students were served in special education in the U.S. at an annual cost for that year of $1.338 billion (Lipsky & Gartner, 1989). The process of referral and placement of these students varies so widely and haphazardly around the country, according to one report, that at times it seems to approximate pure chance (Ysseldyke, 1983). The Council of Great City Schools in 1986, for example, reported that referral rates for special education programs in the nation's large cities varied between 7.8% and 91.8% (Council of Great City Schools, 1986). The problem of identifying who is truly in need of special education resources is significant, and raises serious questions as to whether expensive resources are being largely mismanaged or misapplied. For example, as a category, learning disabilities (LD) increased 142% between 1977 and 1987, whereas special education as a whole increased

only 20% in the same period. LD now describes around 44% of all students identified nationally for special education services.

- More than 80% of the student population could be classified as learning disabled by one or more definitions presently in use (Ysseldyke, 1987)
- Based upon the records of those already certified as learning disabled and those not, experienced evaluators could not tell the difference (Davis & Shepard, 1983)
- Students identified as learning disabled cannot be shown to differ from other low achievers on a wide variety of school-related characteristics (Algozzine & Ysseldyke, 1983; Bartoli & Botel, 1988; Ysseldyke, Algozzine, Shinn, & Mcgue, 1982). (U.S. Department of Education, 1989, p. 9)

A further complication in the referral and placement of students for special education services is to be found in the continuing overrepresentation of students of various racial and ethnic groups. In the 1986–1987 school year, minority populations represented 30% of all U.S. public school students, but made up 42% of special education students labeled as educable mentally retarded (EMR). This proportion was particularly overbalanced for students of African-American descent, who made up 16% of the public school population but 35% of the EMR subpopulation within special education, according to a 1988 national survey (Hume, 1988d, 1988e).

The question of misidentification of pupils for specialized resources might not present such a monumental concern for school restructuring if these students' educational needs were being met in the mainstream, but such is not the case. In the 1985–1986 school year, barely one-fourth of all students served in special education nationally received those services in general education classrooms and other general instructional environments (Hume, 1988a, 1988b, 1988c). For most special education students, their program is a separate pull-out or send-off effort for most of the school day. If special education students and their relatively rich mix of resources are pulled out of mainstream education, the relevant question of interest becomes, do they so benefit from this educational apartheid? Lipsky and Gartner (1989) in a review of the literature on special education efficacy concluded:

Reviews and meta-analyses . . . consistently report little or no benefit for students of all levels of severity placed in special education settings (Carlberg & Kavale, 1980; Cegelka & Tyler, 1970; Epps & Tindal, 1987; Glass, 1983; Kavale & Glass, 1982; Leinhardt & Pallay, 1982; Madden & Slavin, 1982, 1983; Semmel, Gottlieb, & Robinson, 1979; Ysseldyke, 1987). Even the authors of a petulant attack on challenges to present special education practices offer little to defend them (Kauffman, Lloyd, & McKinney, 1988). (Lipsky & Gartner, 1989, p. 19)

If special education in separate pull-out programs is a relative failure (Lipsky & Gartner, 1989), and, conversely, the success rate is demonstrably higher in general education program applications (Hagerty & Abramson, 1987; Slavin & Madden, 1989), then the question arises as to whether coordinating special education resources within the general education program might indeed benefit all students. Slavin (1990), for example, showed that special education students profited significantly in a range of educational outcomes from inclusion in cooperative learning groups at the elementary school level when compared with similar students in a special class situation, and without any loss to the general education students in the group. In a report that generated much controversy. Wang (1988) found similar results in a comprehensive series of studies of the Adaptive Learning Environments Model (ALEM), a general education–based delivery system.

Resource infusion as a set of restructuring operations thus reflects the existing knowledge base concerning the comparative efficacy of keeping federal categorical programs within their diverse resources, such as represented by special education, closely coordinated with and infused into the general education program so that benefits might accrue to both general education and categorically identified students. As yet, however, there is no data base with which to refute or support the attribution of benefits for general education students resulting from a full infusion of special education resources. Finally, there is an obvious need to protect the statutory and regulatory requirements, including due process mechanisms in P.L. 94-142 and P.L. 99-457, within the specified operations of resource infusion. School restructuring efforts are a failure if there are no demonstrable improvements in the educational programs and performances of special education students, as well as the general student population at the school. Some states (e.g., California) have passed laws designed to facilitate these kinds of school restructuring efforts in a manner that protects the specific federal requirements for each program category.

Community Participation in the Life of the School

The fourth component of typical school restructuring models involves the extent to which the school can successfully regain its all-but-lost status as a fundamental mainstay of the community it serves (Sailor, 1990). This component has a particular relevance for the potential of its impact on children at risk for school failure and dropout. The work of Clark (1983, 1989) presents an example of community participation in restructuring. Clark developed strategies to involve the families, single parents, and foster care providers of African-American children in predominantly poor, multiethnic, minority school districts in their children's academic life in the school. His efforts, particularly in math and reading through parent involvement in homework, paid off in greatly improved test performances of his subjects and reduced status for being at risk. Clark (1989) was able to show that illiterate parents can nevertheless stimulate a child's reading and writing skills by, for example, focusing the child's attention on stories invented by the parents to nonword picture story books.

Many community involvement strategies are focused on the problem of high school dropout. Among the factors most closely associated with high school dropout has been the perception of school as a relatively valueless place in the eyes of families of children at risk in earlier grade levels (Council of Chief State School Officers, 1989). If school is a place where children of poverty are viewed negatively by teachers and administrators, and where parents are held accountable for these perceived problems by being furnished with detention slips, requests to come in for disciplinary discussions, threats of suspension, and so on, then parents will come to view the school as mainly a place of bad news and harassment. Such a view is soon communicated to the child, and the school comes to have a negative value.

Community involvement is required, as a key component of restructuring, in such diverse areas as improved health care for young children, provision of preschool and infant support services, case management and child protective services (Hickey, Lockwood, Payzant, & Wenrich, 1990), parent involvement in school decision-making councils, community volunteer participation in middle and junior high schools (Vasquez, 1990a, 1990b), and the involvement of business and industry in the process of transition from school to adult status at the secondary school level (Sailor et al., 1989). This list taps but a few of the significant ways that members of the community can enhance the life of a school under restructuring and identification of services to meet children's specific health care needs (Hickey et al., 1990).

A number of federal programs are now under way that significantly augment the community involvement effort through the restructured school. For example, the Comprehensive Child Development Program will supply $19,760,000 per year through fiscal year 1993 for the funding of 10 to 25 projects for intensive, comprehensive, integrated, and continuous support services for low-income infants, toddlers, preschoolers, parents, and other household members. Under the Medicaid expansion program, pregnant women and young children under the age of 1 year who have poverty-level income will be eligible for Medicaid. P.L. 99-457, which extends Individuals with Disabilities Act (IDEA) entitlements to early childhood at-risk (for disability) children, and the Family Support Law of 1989 greatly augment services potentially harnessed through the schools to young children. The latter requires the states to provide more systematic support to recipients of Aid to Families with Dependent Children (AFDC) and to establish a Basic Skills (JOBS) program. Under this law, states are required to evaluate the level of child care necessary to permit parents to engage in education, training activities, or work.

The critical need to expand and coordinate children's services through the schools is highlighted by the extent to which many children eligible for entitlement programs are not presently recipients of these programs (Kagan, 1989; Leichter, 1979; Lightfoot, 1987; McLaughlin & Shields, 1987; Seeley, 1981). Sixty percent of families headed by single mothers with children under 6 are living in poverty. These children are three times more likely to die in infancy than are other children; four times more likely to become pregnant as teenagers; far more likely to suffer serious illness, abuse, neglect, and to drop out of school than are their economically sufficient counterparts. Yet, in California research shows that less than half of all eligible children in that state receive AFDC income (Wald, Evans, & Ventresca, 1989).

Community Involvement In Secondary Education

Community involvement at the high school level is often heavily focused on the foundation of new partnerships between business/industry and the schools to facilitate the transition of students into adult status. Central to high school restructuring

around transitional services is the regrouping of traditional vocational educational programs (Kadamus & Daggett, 1986). Examples of restructuring in high schools in Boston (Dentzer & Wheelock, 1990) and in New York (Kadamus & Daggett, 1986) have indicated how vocational education resources can be effectively reorganized to facilitate the movement of students into the workplace or into higher education through partnership arrangements between high schools and business industry councils, or between high schools and higher education agencies.

Integrated learning environments, for example, can provide a vehicle for blending community and school resources into a common planning framework that has a significant, measurable impact on the reduction of high school dropout (Fillmore, in press; Flynn, 1989). Collaboration between high schools and such agencies as the Department of Vocational Rehabilitation (DVR) and Department of Developmental Services (DDS) or their equivalents, together with business and industry groups, has led to recent strong movements in vocational education to create direct community job experiences within career employment opportunities for high school students (Siegel, 1988; Siegel & Gaylord-Ross, 1991), and the creation of transition specialists within high schools whose jobs call for the development of career-linkage plans for categorical students and students at risk for dropout (Sailor et al., 1989).

Comprehensive Local School (CLS)

The California Research Institute (CRI) at San Francisco State University began the development of an approach to school restructuring in 1985, which was widely disseminated in 1989 with the publication of the text. *The Comprehensive Local School: Regular Education for All Students with Disabilities* (Sailor et al., 1989). This model, which began with efforts to socially integrate students with severe disabilities into the life of regular schools, has expanded over the past 3 years to a model of school restructuring that is strongly geared to coordinated management of categorical resources to the collective advantage of all students at the school site; hence, the term *comprehensive* local school.

The CLS approach has five distinct components, each of which is geared to a specific age group in the educational continuum. School organization and restructuring is thus examined in terms of issues affecting (a) early childhood programs, (b) elementary programs, (c) middle school or junior high school programs, (d) secondary programs, and (e) postsecondary educational programs.

Comprehensive Local School as an approach to school restructuring has two principal features that distinguish it from many other models. First, CLS envisions the school as the coordinating vehicle for all children's services, going beyond traditional educational issues to encompass health and social service issues as well (Kirst & McLaughlin, 1990; Morrill & Gerry, 1990). Schools under this model gradually progress toward becoming comprehensive, interdisciplinary children's service centers, with education making up the primary service around which other services, including case management and health-related services, are configured according to need (Hickey et al., 1990). Second, CLS functions as a comprehensive, unified educational vehicle with all categorical programs reconfigured and coordinated at the school site under a strong site-based management system characterized by a shared decision-making process.

CONCLUSIONS

Those special educators associated with, or indeed committed to the current directions in reform, such as those indicated by the LRE mandate for social and academic integration and the retention of special education students in general education classrooms, might well consider forming a strong alliance with the school restructuring process under way in the dominant reform movement within general education. With an increasing likelihood of further progress in special education reform being closely linked with (if not co-opted by) processes of change in the bigger picture of general school organizational reform, an opportunity exists to realign all educational systems to work more effectively and efficiently for all children at the school site. The inherent danger to special educators who choose to maintain the status

quo and to wait this one out is to ultimately witness the possibility of a take-over of special education programs and funding by an increasingly troubled and strained general education system that is ill-equipped to utilize effectively special education and other federal categorical resources to benefit the increasingly diverse population it is intended to serve.

In terms of federal policy, special education, as a field, is at a crossroads. The pressing reform movement in general education can result in an expanded use of special education as a separate system (Lipsky & Gartner, 1989). An expansion in eligibility of the number of types of categorically defined students with special needs, for example, offers one possibility. The present debate over whether Attention Deficit Disorder (ADD) should be included is a case in point. Expansion in special education eligibility could lead to a condition under which as many as 25% to 30% of public school enrollment is served by a separate special education delivery system.

Alternatively, reform efforts within special education to achieve greater levels of integration within general education offer the more attractive possibility for a shared educational agenda for all students. By a more judicious and efficient application of special education and other federal, categorical program resources at the local school site level, these resources might well be reconfigured under school restructuring efforts to better meet the needs of all students at the school.

AUTHOR'S NOTES

1. Preparation of this manuscript was supported in part by the Office of Special Education & Rehabilitation Services (GOO87-C3056). No official endorsement should be inferred.
2. The author gratefully acknowledges the contributions of Lorie Goetz and Tricia Karasoff in the development of this manuscript.

References

Algozzine, B., & Ysseldyke, J.E. (1983). Learning disabilities as a subset of school failure: The over-sophistication of a concept. *Exceptional Children, 50,* 242–246.

Bartoli, J., & Botel, M. (1988). *Reading learning disability: An ecological approach.* New York: Teachers College Press.

Bauwens, J., Hourcade, J.J., & Friend, M. (1989). Cooperative teaching: A model for general and special education integration. *Remedial and Special Education, 10*(2), 17–22.

Bickel, W.E., & Bickel, D.D. (1986). Effective schools, classrooms, and instruction: Implications for special education. *Exceptional Children, 52,* 189–500.

Biklen, D., Bogdan, R., Ferguson, D., Searl, S., & Taylor, S. (1985). *Achieving the complete school: Strategies for effective mainstreaming.* New York: Teachers College Press.

Braaten, S., Kauffman, J.M., Braaten, B., Polsgrove, L., & Nelson, C.M. (1988). The Regular Education Initiative: Patent medicine for behavioral disorders. *Exceptional Children, 55*(1), 21–27.

Brinker, R.P., & Thorpe, M.E. (1984). *Evaluation of the integration of severely handicapped students in regular education and community settings* (Research Rep.). Princeton, NJ: Educational Testing Service.

Brown, L., Long, E., I'dvari-Solner, A., Davis, L., Van-Deventer, P., Ahlgren, C., Johnson, F., Gruenewald, L., & Jorgensen, J. (1989a). The home school: Why students with severe intellectual disabilities must attend the schools of their brothers, sisters, friends, and neighbors. *The Journal of The Association for Persons with Severe Handicaps, 14,* 1–7.

Brown, L., Long, E., Udvari-Solner, A., Schwarz, P., Van-Deventer, P., Ahlgren, C., Johnson, F., Gruenewald, L., & Jorgensen, J. (1989b). Should students with severe intellectual disabilities be based in regular or in special education classrooms in home schools? *The Journal of The Association for Persons with Severe Handicaps, 14,* 8–12.

Burton, T., & Hirschoren, A. (1979). *Education of severely and profoundly handicapped children: Are we sacrificing the child to the concept?* Paper presented for the Council of Exceptional Children, Reston, VA.

California State Department of Education. (1989, December). *The challenge for the '90s: The California framework for special education programs and services* (Draft). Sacramento: California State Department of Education.

Campbell, P.H., & Bailey, K. (in press). Issues in health care in the education of students with the most severe disabilities. In M. Wang, H. Walberg, & M. Reynolds (Eds.). *Handbook of special education* (vol. IV) Oxford, England: Pergamon Press.

Carlberg, C., & Kavale, K. (1980). The efficacy of special versus regular class placement for exceptional children: A meta-analysis. *The Journal of Special Education, 14,* 295–309.

Carnegie Foundation for the Advancement of Teaching. (1988). *An imperiled generation: Saving urban schools.* Princeton, NJ: Carnegie Foundation.

Cegelka, W.J., Tyler, J. (1970). The efficacy of special class placement for mentally retarded in proper perspective. *Training School Bulletin: 66,* 33–66.

Cistone, P.J., Fernandez, J.A., & Tornillo, P.L. (1989). School-based management/shared decision making in Dade County (Miami). *Education and Urban Society, 21*(4), 393–402.

Clark, R.M. (1983). *Family life and school achievement: Why poor black children succeed or fail.* Chicago: University of Chicago Press.

Clark, R.M. (1989). *The role of parents in assuring education success in restructuring efforts* (Draft). Washington, DC: Council of Chief State School Officers.

Cohen, M. (1988). *Restructuring the education system: Agenda for the 1990s.* Washington, DC: National Governor's Association.

Committee for Economic Development. (1987). *Children in need.* Washington, DC: Committee for Economic Development.

Conley, S. (1988). Reforming paper pushers and avoiding free agents: The teacher as a constrained decision-maker. *Educational Administration Quarterly, 24*(41), 393–404.

Council of Chief State School Officers. (1989, November). *Success for all in a new century: A report by the Council of Chief State School Officers on Restructuring Education.* Washington, DC: Author.

Council of Great City Schools. (1986). *Special education: Views from America's cities.* Washington, DC: Council of Great City Schools.

Cruickshank, W.M. (1977). Least restrictive placement: Administrative wishful thinking. *Journal of Learning Disabilities, 10,* 193–194.

Danielson, L.C., & Bellamy, G.T. (1989). State variation in placement of children with handicaps in segregated environments. *Exceptional Children, 55*(5), 398–455.

David, J. (1990, February). What is restructuring? *Work-America, 7*(2), 1.

David, J., Cohen, M., Honetschlager, D., & Traiman, S. (1990). *State actions to restructure schools: First steps.* Washington, DC: National Governor's Association, Center for Policy Research.

Davis, W.A., & Shepard, L.A. (1983). Specialists' use of test and clinical judgment in the diagnosis of learning disabilities. *Learning Disabilities Quarterly, 19,* 128–138.

Davis, W.E., & McCaul, E.J. (1990, January). *At-risk children and youth: A crisis in our schools and society* [Monograph]. Orono: Institute for the Study of At-Risk Students, Maine Department of Educational Services and the College of Education, University of Maine.

Dentzer, E., & Wheelock, A. (1990, March). *Locked in/locked out: Tracking and placement practices in Boston Public Schools.* Boston: Massachusetts Advocacy Center.

Downing, J., & Eichinger, J. (1990). Instructional strategies for learners with dual sensory impairments in integrated settings. *The Journal of The Association for Persons with Severe Handicaps, 15*(2), 98–105.

Durkin, D. (1990). Matching classroom instruction with reading abilities: An unmet need. *Remedial and Special Education, 11*(3), 23–28.

Elmore, R.F., & Associates. (1990). *Restructuring schools: The next generation of educational reform.* San Francisco: Jossey-Bass.

Epps, S., & Tindal, G. (1987). The effectiveness of differential programming in serving students with mild handicaps: Placement options and instructional programming. In M.C. Wang, M.C. Reynolds, & H.J. Walberg (Eds.), *The handbook of special education* (vol. 1, pp. 213–248). New York: Pergamon Press.

Falvey, M.A. (1989). *Community-based curriculum: Instructional strategies for students with severe handicaps* (2nd ed.). Baltimore: Brookes.

Filmore, L.W. (in press). Now or later? Issues related to the early education of minority group children. In C. Harris (Ed.), *Children at risk* (pp. 110–133). New York: Harcourt Brace Jovanovich.

Fine, M. (1983). Perspectives on inequity: Voices from urban schools. In L. Bicklman (Ed.), *Applied social psychology annual IV.* Los Angeles: Sage.

Fine, M. (1987). Silencing in public schools. *Language Arts, 64*(2).

Flynn, G. (1989, October). *The Waterloo story.* Paper presented at the annual meeting of TASH, Chicago.

Forest, M. (1987). *More education integration.* Downsview, Ontario: G. Allan Rocher Institute.

Forest, M., & Lusthaus, E. (1989). Promoting educational equality for all students: Circles and maps. In W. Stainback, S. Stainback, & M. Forest (Eds.), *Educating all students in the mainstream of regular education* (pp. 43–57). Baltimore: Brookes.

Gartner, A., & Lipsky, D.K. (1987). Beyond special education: Toward a quality system for all students. *Harvard Educational Review, 57,* 367–395.

Gartner, A., & Lipsky, D.K. (1990a). Students as instructional agents. In W. Stainback & S. Stainback (Eds.), *Support networks for inclusive schooling: Interdependent integrated education* (pp. 81–93). Baltimore: Brookes.

Gartner, A., & Lipsky, D.K. (1990b). *The yoke of special education: How to break it* (Paper, Federal Role Series). Rochester, NY: National Center on Education and the Economy.

Garvar-Pinhas, A., & Pedhazur Schmelkin, L. (1989). Administrators' and teachers' attitudes toward mainstreaming. *Remedial and Special Education, 10*(4), 38–43.

Gaylord-Ross, R. (1987). School integration for students with mental handicaps: A cross-cultural perspective. *European Journal of Special Needs Education, 2*(2).

Gersten, R., & Woodward, J. (1990). Rethinking the Regular Education Initiative: Focus on the classroom teacher *Remedial and Special Education, 11*(3), 7–16.

Gilhool, T.K. (1989). The right to an effective education: From Brown to PL 94-142 and beyond. In D. Lipsky & A. Gartner (Eds.), *Beyond separate education: Quality education for all* (pp. 243–253). Baltimore: Brookes.

Gilhool, T.K., & Stutman, E.A. (1978). Integration of severely handicapped students: Toward criteria for implementing and enforcing the integration imperative of PL 94-142 and Section 504. In *Developing criteria for the evaluation of the least restrictive environment provision.* Washington, DC: State Program Studies Branch, Division of Innovation and Development, Bureau of Education for the Handicapped, U.S. Department of Education.

Glass, G.V. (1983). Effectiveness of special education. *Policy Studies Review, 2,* 65–78.

Glatthorn, A.A. (1990a). Cooperative professional development: Facilitating the growth of the special education teacher and the classroom teacher. *Remedial and Special Education, 11*(3), 29–34.

Glatthorn, A.A. (1990b). Cooperative professional development: A tested approach, not a panacea. *Remedial and Special Education, 11*(4), 62.

Goetz, L., & Sailor, W. (1990). Much ado about babies, murky bath water, and trickle down politics: A reply to Kauffman. *The Journal of Special Education, 24*(3), 334–339.

Gottlieb, J. (1981). Mainstreaming: Fulfilling the promise? *Journal of Mental Deficiency, 86*(2), 115–126.

Hagerty, G.J., & Abramson, M. (1987). Impediments to implementing national policy change for mildly handicapped students. *Exceptional Children, 53*(4), 315–324.

Halvorsen, A.T., & Sailor, W. (1990). Integration of students with severe and profound disabilities: A review of research. In R. Gaylord-Ross (Ed.), *Issues and Research in Special Education* (vol. 1, pp. 110–172). New York: Teachers College Press.

Hamre-Nietupski, S., Nietupski, J., & Maurer, S. (1990). A comprehensive state education agency plan to promote the integration of students with moderate/severe handicaps. *The Journal of The Association for Persons with Severe Handicaps, 15,* 106–113.

Haring, K., Farron-Davis, F., Karasoff, P., Zeph, L., Goetz, L., & Sailor, W. (in press). *LRE and placement.* Manuscript submitted for publication, San Francisco State University, Department of Special Education, California Research Institute.

Haring, N., & Bricker, D. (Eds.). (1978). *Teaching the severely handicapped* (vol. III). New York: Grune & Stratton.

Haring, N.G., & Brown, L. (Eds.). (1976). *Teaching the severely handicapped* (vol. I). New York: Grune & Stratton.

Haring, N., & Brown, L. (Eds.). (1977). *Teaching the severely handicapped* (vol. II). New York: Grune & Stratton.

Haywood, H. (1981). Reducing social vulnerability is the challenge of the eighties (AAMD Presidential Address). *Mental Retardation, 19*(4), 190–195.

Hickey, N.W., Lockwood, J., Payzant, T.W., & Wenrich, J.W. (1990, July). *New beginnings: A feasibility study of integrated services for children and families* (Final report). San Diego, CA: City, County of San Diego, San Diego City Schools, San Diego Community College District.

Hodginson, H.L. (1985). *All one system: Demographics of education—Kindergarten through graduate school.* Washington, DC: Institute for Educational Leadership.

The Holmes Group. (1986). *Tomorrow's teachers: A report of The Holmes Group.* East Lansing, MI: Author.

Hume, M. (1988a, March 4). Another year increases the demands on special education, report shows. *Education Daily, 21*(43), 7–8.

Hume, M. (1988b, March 15). Despite progress, states have problems to overcome in special education. *Education Daily, 21*(50), 1–3.

Hume, M. (1988c, June 29). Experts debate progress in mainstreaming handicapped children. *Education Daily, 21*(125), 3–4.

Hume, M. (1988d, August 16). Found violating disabled students' rights, Chicago could lose $117 million. *Education Daily, 21*(158), 3–4.

Hume, M. (1988e, February 17). OCR data shows minorities overrepresented among disability groups. *Education Daily, 21*(31), 5–6.

Idol, L., Paolucci-Whitcomb, P., & Nevin, A. (1986). *Collaborative consultation.* Austin, TX: PRO-ED.

Jenkins, J.R., & Jenkins, L.M. (1981). *Cross-age and peer tutoring. Help for children with learning problems.* Reston, VA: The Council for Exceptional Children.

Kadamus, J.A., & Daggett, W.R. (1986). *New directions for vocational education at the secondary level* (Information Series No. 311), Columbus, OH: ERIC Clearinghouse on Adult, Career, and Vocational Education.

Kagan, S.L. (1989, October). Early care and education: Beyond the schoolhouse doors. *Phi Delta Kappan,* pp. 107–112.

Karasoff, P., & Kelly, D. (1989). What makes integration work? *STRATEGIES Bulletin, 1*(1), 1–2.

Kauffman, J.M. (1989). The Regular Education Initiative as Reagan-Bush education policy: A trickle-down theory of education of the hard-to-teach. *The Journal of Special Education, 23*(3), 256–278.

Kauffman, J.M., Gerber, M.M., & Semmel, M.I. (1989). Arguable assumptions underlying the Regular Education Initiative *Journal of Learning Disabilities, 21,* 6–11.

Kauffman, J.M., & Hallahan, D.P. (1990). What we want for children: A rejoinder to REI proponents. *The Journal of Special Education, 24*(3), 340–345.

Kauffman, J.M., Lloyd, J.W., & McKinney, J.D. (Eds.). (1988). *Journal of Learning Disabilities, 2*(1). [Special issue].

Kavale, J.A., & Glass, G.V. (1982). The efficacy of special education interventions and practices: A compendium of meta-analysis findings. *Focus on Exceptional Children, 15*(4), 1–14.

Kirst, M.W., & McLaughlin, M. (1990). Rethinking policy for children: Implications for educational administration. In D. Mitchell & L.L. Cunningham (Eds.), *Educational leadership in changing contexts of families, communities, and schools, 89th Yearbook of the National Society for the Study of Education (Part II)* (pp. 69–90). Chicago: University of Chicago Press.

Knapp, M.S., & Turnbull, B.J. (1990, January). *Better schooling for the children of poverty: Alternatives to conventional wisdom* (vol. I: Summary). Study of Academic Instruction for Disadvantaged Students by SRI International and Policy Studies Associates (Contract No. LC88054001). Washington, DC: U.S. Department of Education, Office of Planning, Budget & Evaluation.

Leichter, H.J. (Ed.). (1979). *Families and communities as educators.* New York: Teachers College Press.

Leinhardt, G., & Pallay, A. (1982). Restrictive educational settings: Exile or haven? *Review of Educational Research, 52,* 557–578.

Levin, H.M. (1985). *The educationally disadvantaged: A national crisis* (The State Youth Initiatives, Project Working Paper No. 6). Philadelphia: Public/Private Ventures.

Levin, H.M. (1989). Cost-effectiveness and educational policy. *Educational Evaluation and Policy Analysis, 10*(1), 51–69.

Lieberman, A. (Ed.). (1988). *Building a professional culture in schools* (Report). New York: Teachers College Press.

Lightfoot, S.L. (1987). *Worlds apart: Relationships between families and schools.* New York: Basic Books.

Lipsky, D.K., & Gartner, A. (1989). *Beyond separate education: Quality education for all.* Baltimore: Brookes.

Lowenbraun, S., Madge, S., & Affleck, J. (1990). Parental satisfaction with integrated class placements for special education and general education students. *Remedial and Special Education, 11*(4), 37–40.

MDC, Inc. (1988). *America's shame, America's hope: Twelve million youth at risk* (Report prepared for the Charles Stewart Mott Foundation). Chapel Hill, NC: Author.

Madden, N.A., & Slavin, R.L. (1982). *Count me in: Academic achievement and social outcomes of mainstreaming students with mild academic handicaps.* Baltimore: The Johns Hopkins University Press.

Madden, N.A., & Slavin, R.L. (1983). Mainstreaming students with mild handicaps: Academic achievement and social outcomes. *Review of Educational Research, 53,* 519–569.

Mamary, A., & Rowe, L. (1989, January). *The outcome-driven developmental model (A program for comprehensive school improvement).* Johnson City, NY: Johnson City Central School District.

Marburger, C.L. (1985). *One school at a time: School based management, a process for change.* Columbia, MD: National Committee for Citizens in Education.

McDill, E.L., Natriello, G., & Pallas, A.M. (1986). A population at risk: Potential consequences of tougher school standards for student dropouts. In G. Natriello (Ed.), *School dropouts: Patterns and policies* (pp. 106–147). New York: Teachers College Press.

McDonnell, L., & Pascal, A. (1988). *Teacher unions and educational reform* (Rep. No. FRE-02). Santa Monica, CA: RAND Corp., Center for Policy Research in Education Center for the Study of the Teaching Profession.

McLaughlin, M.W., & Shields, P.M. (1987). Involving low-income parents in the schools: A role for policy? *Phi Delta Kappan,* October, 156–160.

McLeskey, J., Skiba, R., & Wilcox, B. (1990). Reform and special education: A mainstream perspective. *The Journal of Special Education, 24*(3), 319–325.

McNulty, B.A. (Producer). (1990). *Learning together* [Videotape]. Denver: Colorado Department of Education.

Meyer, L., Peck, C., & Brown, L. (1990). *Critical issues in the lives of persons with disabilities.* Baltimore: Brookes.

Miller, L. (1990). The Regular Education Initiative and school reform: Lessons from the mainstream. *Remedial and Special Education, 11*(3), 17–22.

Morrill, W.A., & Gerry, M.H. (1990, February 6). *Integrating the delivery of services to school-aged children at risk: Toward a description of American experience and experimentation.* Paper presented at Conference on Children and Youth at Risk sponsored by the U.S. Department of Education and the Organization for Economic Cooperation & Development, Washington, DC.

National Center on Education and the Economy. (1989). *To secure our future: The federal role in education.* Rochester, NY: National Center on Education and the Economy.

National School Boards Association. (1989). *A equal chance: Educating at-risk children to succeed* [Monograph]. Alexandria, VA: Author.

New Partnerships: Education's Stake in the Family Support Act of 1988. (1988). Washington, DC: WTG.

Rose, M. (1989). *Lives on the boundary: The struggles and achievements of America's underprepared.* New York: The Free Press (Macmillan).

Sailor, W. (1989). Transition in Italy. *New Ways,* Fall, 10–11, 13.

Sailor, W. (1990). Community school: An essay. In L. Meyer, C. Peck, & L. Brown (Eds.), *Critical issues in the lives of persons with disabilities* (pp. 379–385). Baltimore: Brookes.

Sailor, W., Anderson, J., Halvorsen, A.T., Doering, K., Filler, J., & Goetz, L. (1989). *The comprehensive local school: Regular education for all students with disabilities.* Baltimore: Brookes.

Sailor, W., Gee, K., Graham, N., & Goetz, L. (1988). Progress in educating students with the most severe disabilities: Is there any? *The Journal of The Association for Persons with Severe Handicaps,* 13(2), 87–99.

Sailor, W., Gerry, M., & Wilson, W.C. (in press-a). Disability and school integration. In T. Husen & T.N. Postlethwaite (Eds.). *International encyclopedia of education: Research and studies* (2nd suppl.). New York: Pergamon Press.

Sailor, W., Gerry, M., & Wilson, W.C. (in press-b). Policy implications of emergency full inclusion models for the education of students with severe disabilities. In M. Wang, H. Walberg, & M. Reynolds (Eds.), *The handbook of special education* (vol. IV). Oxford, England: Pergamon Press.

Sailor, W., Wilcox, B., & Brown, L. (Eds.). (1980). *Methods of instruction for severely handicapped students.* Baltimore: Brookes.

Sapon-Shevin, M. (1988). Working towards merger together: Seeing beyond distrust and fear. *Teacher Education and Special Education,* 11, 103–110.

Schoor, L.B. (1988). *Within our reach: Breaking the cycle of disadvantaged.* New York: Doubleday.

Seeley, D. (1981). *Education through partnership: Mediating structures and education.* Cambridge, MA: Ballinger.

Semmel, M.Y., & Gerber, M.M. (1990). If at first you don't succeed, bye, bye again: A response to general educators' views on the REI. *Remedial and Special Education,* 11(4), 53–59.

Shaw, S.F., Biklen, D., Conlon, S., Dunn, J., Kramer, J., & DeRoma-Wagner, V. (1990). Special education and school reform. In L.M. Bullock & R.L. Simpson (Eds.), *Critical issues in special education: Implications for personnel preparation* (pp. 12–25). Denton: University of North Texas.

Siegel, S. (1988). The career ladder program: Implementing re-ED principles in vocational settings. *Behavioral Disorders,* 14(1), 16.

Siegel, S., & Gaylord-Ross, R. (1991). Factors associated with employment success among youth with learning disabilities. *Journal of Leraning Disabilities,* 24, 40–47.

Singer, J.D. (1988). Should special education merge with regular education? *Educational Policy,* 2, 409–424.

Singer, J.D., & Butler, J.A. (1987). The Education for All Handicapped Children Act: Schools as agents of social reform. *Harvard Educational Review,* 57, 125–152.

Sirotnik, K.A., & Clark, R. (1988, May). School-centered decision making and renewal. *Phi Delta Kappan,* pp. 660–664.

Skrtic, T.M. (1988). The organizational context of special education. In E.L. Meyen & T.M. Skrtic (Eds.), *Exceptional children and youth: An introduction* (pp. 479–517). Denver: Love.

Skrtic, T. (1990). *Behind special education: A critical analysis of professional culture and school organization.* Denver: Love.

Slavin, R.E. (1989). Students at risk of school failure: The problem and its dimensions. In R. Slavin, N. Karweit, & N. Madden (Eds.), *Effective programs for students at risk* (pp. 3–19). Boston: Allyn & Bacon.

Slavin, R.E. (1990). General education under the Regular Education Initiative: How must it change? *Remedial and Special Education,* 11(3), 40–50.

Slavin, R.E., & Madden, N.A. (1989). What works for students at risk: A research synthesis. *Educational Leadership,* 46, 14–20.

Slavin, R.E., Madden, N.A., Karweit, N.L., Livermon, B.J., & Dolan, L. (1990). *Success for all: First-year outcomes of a comprehensive plan for reforming urban education.* Baltimore: The Johns Hopkins University, Center for Research on Elementary and Middle Schools.

Slavin, R.E., Stevens, R.J., & Madden, N.A. (1988). Accommodating student diversity in reading and writing instruction: A cooperative learning approach. *Remedial and Special Education,* 9(1), 60–66.

Snell, M.E. (Ed.). (1978). *Systematic instruction of the moderately and severely handicapped.* Columbus, OH: Merrill.

Sontag, E. (Ed.). (1977). *Educational programming for the severely and profoundly handicapped.* Reston, VA: Council for Exceptional Children.

Stainback, S., Stainback, W., & Forest, M. (1989). *Educating all students in the mainstream of regular education.* Baltimore: Brookes.

Stainback, W., & Stainback, S. (Eds.). (1990). *Support networks for inclusive schooling: Interdependent integrated education.* Baltimore: Brookes.

Sykes, G. (1990). Fostering teacher professionalism in schools. In R. Elmore (Ed.), *Restructuring schools: The next generation of educational reform* (pp. 59–98). San Francisco: Jossey-Bass.

Thousand, J.S., & Villa, R.A. (1989). Enhancing success in heterogeneous schools. In S. Stainback, W. Stainback, & M. Forest (Eds.), *Educating all students in the mainstream of regular education* (pp. 89–104). Baltimore: Brookes.

U.S. Department of Education. (1989). *Tenth annual report to Congress.* Washington, DC: U.S. Department of Education.

Vandercook, T., York, J., & Forest, M. (1989). The McGill Action Planning System (MAPS): A strategy for building the vision. *The Journal of The Association for Persons with Severe Handicaps, 14,* 205–215.

Vasquez, B.T. (1990a). *A generic model of school-wide collaboration.* San Francisco: San Francisco Unified School District and San Francisco School Volunteers.

Vasquez, B.T. (1990b). *Effective placement of students with special needs in the regular classroom through organizational development and cooperative learning.* San Francisco: San Francisco Unified School District and San Francisco School Volunteers.

Vergason, G., & Anderegg, M.L. (in press). Save the baby!: An answer to integrating children of the second system. *Phi Delta Kappan.*

Vitello, S.J. (1989). *Special education in integration in Italy: Parent and teacher viewpoints.* Unpublished manuscript, Rutgers University. New Brunswick, NJ.

Vladero, D. (1990, June 6). Learning-disabled students found to fare poorly. *Education Week, IX(37).* pp. 23, 25.

Wald, N.S., Evans, J.H., & Ventresca, M.J. (1989). Economic status. In M.H. Kirst (Project Director). *Conditions of children in California.* Berkeley: Policy Analysis for California Education.

Wang, M.C. (1988). Weighing the "Regular Education Initiative." *Education Week, 7,* 28, 36.

Wang, M.C., & Peverly, S. (1987). The role of the learner: An individual difference variable in school learning and functioning. In M. Wang, M. Reynolds, & H. Walberg (Eds.), *Handbook of special education: Research and practice, Vol. I: Learner characteristics and adaptive education* (pp. 59–92). Oxford. England: Pergamon Press.

Wang, M.C., Reynolds, M., & Walberg, H.J. (1986). Rethinking special education. *Educational Leadership, 44*(1), 26–31.

Wang, M., Reynolds, M., & Walberg, H. (1988, November). Integrating the children of the second system. *Phi Delta Kappan,* pp. 248–251.

Will, M. (1986). Educating children with learning problems: A shared responsibility. *Exceptional Children, 52*(5), 411–415.

Williams, W., Fox, W., Christie, L., Thousand, J., Conn-Powers, M., Carmichael, L., Vogelsberg, R.T., & Hull, M. (1986). Community integration in Vermont. *The Journal of The Association for Persons with Severe Handicaps, 11,* 294–299.

Winget, P. (Ed.). (1990). Education programs must integrate to benefit all students at every school, says Honig. *The Special Edge, 4*(7), 1, 3–4.

York, R., & Edgar, E. (Eds.). (1979). *Teaching the severely handicapped* (vol. IV). Seattle, WA: American Association for the Education of the Severely/Profoundly Handicapped.

Ysseldyke, J.E. (1983). Current practices in making psycho-educational decisions about learning disabled students. *Journal of Learning Disabilities, 16,* 29–31.

Ysseldyke, J.E. (1987). Classification of handicapped students. In M. Wang, M. Reynolds, & H. Walberg (Eds.), *Handbook of special education: Research and practice* (Vol. 1, pp. 253–271). New York: Pergamon Press.

Ysseldyke, J.E., Algozzine, B., Shinn, M.R., & Mcgue, M. (1982). Similarities and differences between low achievers and students classified as learning disabled. *The Journal of Special Education, 16,* 73–85.

4.3   Beyond Special Education:

Toward a Quality System for All Students

Alan Gartner
Dorothy Kerzner Lipsky

A review of a decade's experience with the implementation of PL 94-142 provides an opportunity to assess the process of providing education to students with handicapping conditions and to study the larger general education system. In addition, such a review offers an opportunity to examine changes in the place of persons with disabilities in American society. Alan Gartner and Dorothy Kerzner Lipsky find both the practice and conceptualization of a separate special education system wanting, and they propose a single system, special for all students.

Thank you for your letter in which you ask about data concerning children who had been certified as handicapped and have returned to regular education.

While these are certainly very interesting data you request, these data are not required in State Plans nor has the Office of Special Education Programs collected them in any other survey.

—Letter to Alan Gartner from Patricia J. Guard, Deputy Director, Office of Special Education
Programs, U.S. Department of Education, November 7, 1986.

The decision not to collect "interesting data" can conceivably be made for various reasons. For instance, policymakers may believe that the data are not important, or they may fear the results, or believe that the collection process is not worth the potential benefit. No doubt collecting decertification data might be difficult, and most likely would show an embarrassingly low level of return to general education. We believe, however, that the major reason such data are not collected has to do with beliefs and attitudes—some implicit, some explicit—generally held about the purposes of special education and about special education students.

The faults of current special education practice, as we will detail in the following pages, are myriad. It incorporates a medical view of disability which characterizes the disability as inherent in the individual and thus formulates two separate categories of people, handicapped and nonhandicapped, as useful and rational distinctions. This arbitrary division of students provides the rationale for educating students with handicapping conditions[1] in separate programs, and even in completely separate systems. The assumptions underlying separate programs have produced a system that is both segregated and second class.

The needs of students with handicapping conditions have led some parents and professionals to accept the notion of separate, if quality, education. We will argue that the current system has proven to be inadequate because it is a system that is not integrated, and that we must learn from our mistakes and attempt to create a new type of unitary system, one which incorporates quality education for all students.

It is our belief that the attitudes and assumptions about the disabled and disability require change, as do the inadequacies in general and special education practice. The need for such changes is both consequence and cause of a unitary system, thereby encouraging the production of an education model for all students—supple, variegated, and individualized—in an integrated setting.

Gartner, A. & Lipsky, D.K. (1987). "Beyond special education: Toward a quality system for all students." *Harvard Educational Review*, 57:4, pp. 367–395. Copyright © 1987 by the President and Fellows of Harvard College. All rights reserved.

While special education programs of the past decade have been successful in bringing unserved students into public education and have established their right to education, these programs have failed both to overcome the separation between general and special education and to make the separate system significant in terms of student benefits. This article first examines developments of the past decade, then analyzes the current failures, and, finally, formulates recommendations that will improve these programs in the future.

BACKGROUND TO THE LAW

There are many possible beginnings for a discussion of the current status of education of students with handicapping conditions. We start with *Brown v. Board of Education* (347 U.S. 483). In doing so, we wish to make three points: (1) to note the importance of education to the "life and minds" of children; (2) to set the framework concerning the inherent inequality of separate education; and (3) to recognize that advocacy efforts in the 1960s and 1970s on behalf of persons with disabilities were drawn from the context of the Civil Rights movement. One of the tactics which the disability rights movement learned from the Black Civil Rights movement was how to produce change in policies and practices through use of both the legal system and the legislature. Indeed, many see developments in special education as the logical outgrowth of civil rights efforts of an earlier period.

Between 1966 and 1974, a series of federal laws focusing on children with disabilities and the services they needed were enacted. Together, these laws can be seen as capacity building: preparing personnel, launching a set of discretionary grant programs, establishing the Bureau of Education for the Handicapped in what was then the U.S. Office of Education, providing capital funds, developing regional centers for deaf-blind children, and establishing authority for research and demonstration projects.

The concerns of adults with disabilities were addressed in the Rehabilitation Act of 1973. The Act provided a comprehensive program of vocational rehabilitation and independent living, established a federal board to coordinate and monitor access to public buildings and transportation, prohibited discrimination in employment, required affirmative action by federal agencies and federal contractors, and, almost as an afterthought, proclaimed a national mandate prohibiting discrimination against the handicapped by recipients of federal assistance (Section 504).[2]

Parents of children with disabilities were essential contributors in the legislative strategy and took the lead in litigation. Here the parent groups followed the precedent of *Brown* in its assertion of the essential importance of education. Two key decisions, *Pennsylvania Association of Retarded Citizens (PARC) v. Commonwealth* (334 F. Supp. 1257) and *Mills v. Board of Education* (348 F. Supp. 866), in 1971 and 1972, respectively, rejected reasons school districts had given for excluding students with handicapping conditions. In *PARC*, the federal district court overturned a Pennsylvania law that had relieved schools of the responsibility of enrolling "uneducable" or "untrainable" children. Basing its opinion on extensive expert testimony, the court ruled that mentally retarded children could benefit from education. In *Mills*, the federal district court ruled that a district's financial exigencies could not be the basis for excluding students with handicaps; they could not be made to take last place in the queue for funds.

The process of enacting PL 94-142, The Education for All Handicapped Children Act, began in the spring of 1974. Building both on the earlier legislative efforts and court cases, as well as a growing number of state laws extending the right to attend school to students with disabilities, Representative John Brademas (DIND) introduced H.R. 7217, and six months later Senator Jennings Randolph (DWV) introduced S. 6. The Senate bill was passed by a vote of 83 to 10 on June 18, 1975, and the House bill by a vote of 375 to 44 on July 29th. The key issues in the conference committee were: (1) funding levels, involving a cap on the number of students who could be counted as handicapped for funding purposes (as well as an internal cap on the number of learning disabled students); (2) the respective roles of state education departments and local school districts; (3) services for children aged three to five; (4) the requirement of an individualized education plan (IEP) for each student; and (5) the date for full implementation of the law. The conference report was passed in the House on November 18 and in the Senate the next day with overwhelming majorities (only seven votes against in each chamber). After some suspense about whether President Gerald Ford would veto the bill because of its cost, he signed it into law ten days later.[3]

PUBLIC LAW 94-142

As it presently exists, there is a duality inherent in PL 94-142. It contains a mixture both of attention to the needs of individual students and of provisions designed to solve problems that children with handicapping conditions experienced because the public school system, and other public agencies, failed to address the issue properly. One of its authors suggests that six basic principles are incorporated in the law: (1) the right of access to public education programs; (2) the individualization of services; (3) the principle of "least restrictive environment"; (4) the scope of broadened services to be provided by the schools and a set of procedures for determining them; (5) the general guidelines for identification of disability; and (6) the principles of primary state and local responsibilities.[4]

In the previous decade, federal law, state statutes, and court decisions had begun to reduce the exclusion of children with disabilities from public education programs or the charging of their parents for services otherwise provided at no cost to non-disabled children. Often, exclusions were based on categorical statements about classes of "uneducable" children or in deference to professional judgments on a child's educability. The law eliminated this exclusion of children with disabilities: it stated in the unambiguous language of its title that "all handicapped children" were to be provided with a free public education. Henceforth, no child was to be rejected as uneducable.

Once students with handicaps were included in public education, Congress wanted to assure that each student, particularly one with severe handicaps, would receive services based upon individual need, not upon categories of handicap or pre-existing service offerings. The law explicitly required a multidisciplinary individual evaluation that was nondiscriminatory, and the development of an individualized education plan (IEP).

While each student's placement was to be individually determined, the law, in keeping with its philosophic acceptance of the concepts of "normalization,"[5] expressed a strong presumption that students with disabilities be placed in regular classes whenever possible, where they could receive specialized services as necessary. Only when regular classroom placements did not meet individual students' needs would they be placed in separate classes or settings. This was expressed in the law's requirement that students be educated in the "least restrictive environment" (LRE).

The law, while rejecting the traditional medical model of disability,[6] recognized that some of these students needed more than educational services alone to be successful in school. Hence the concept of "related services" was developed, incorporating those

services—including counseling, physical and occupational therapy, and some medical services—necessary to enable students to take advantage of and benefit from the educational program. In addition to describing the scope of services to be provided, the law established a process for determining students' handicapping condition, educational placement, and related services, which incorporated parental involvement and required substantial due process procedures and appeal rights.

During the course of the congressional debate, there was considerable dispute about the total number of students who would be eligible for services, and, foreshadowing a continuing issue, the number of those defined as having specific learning disabilities within that overall figure. For funding purposes, caps of 12 and 2 percent of the total school population, respectively, were set. Procedural guidelines were set for identification, assessment, and placement of students, with particular emphasis on nondiscrimination and procedural due process.

As was to be expected, the respective roles of the state and local educational agencies and the flow of money were key issues in the congressional consideration. While the House bill required that funds go directly to local educational agencies (LEAs), the Council of Chief State School Officers argued in favor of state responsibility for monitoring local school districts and gained a victory for the state educational agencies (SEAs). Funds were to flow through SEAs, with requirements that annual increasing percentages be passed on to the local level. Also, while recognizing that other state agencies might provide services to the students, particularly the severely impaired, the SEA had responsibility for assuring that the educational services were provided, regardless of who provided or paid for them or where the student received them.

THE CURRENT SITUATION

While there was considerable concern about the feasibility of implementing PL 94-142, and some difficulty in doing so at the compliance level, by and large it has been accomplished.

- Over six hundred and fifty thousand more students are being served now than when the law was enacted. During the 1985–86 school year, somewhat over 4.37 million students received services under the provisions of PL 94-142.[7] This comprised approximately 11 percent of the total public school enrollment (a slight drop from the previous year), with percentages in some states pushing against the 12 percent cap. Generally, educators believe that few, if any, students needing services have not been identified.

- There has been a substantial increase in the funds devoted to special education, from $100 million in FY 1976 to $1.64 billion in FY 1985, for PL 94-142. However, the promised federal contribution (40 percent of the average per pupil cost by 1982) has never been met. Current figures are around 8.5 percent,[8] with states (54 percent) and local governments (37 percent) providing the difference.
- While there are some exceptions, such as students in prisons, from migrant families, and in some institutional settings, for the most part location of the student does not seem to be a factor in the availability of services. The overall responsibility of SEAs has been achieved, perhaps more so in special education than in other areas of SEA-LEA joint responsibility. With New Mexico's submission of a state plan in August, 1984, all fifty states are presently participating under PL 94-142.

In these areas, the implementation of the law has been successful. And to turn now, more extensively, to areas of lesser achievement is neither to gainsay that achievement nor deny its rightness.

While consideration of each of the issues in the conduct of special education is required, we will focus here on only those areas in special education that have emerged as the most troubling. These include referral and assessment procedures, placement options, educational programs, Least Restrictive Environment (LRE), and parental participation.

Referral and Assessment Procedures

Perhaps no area in special education has received as much concern as have procedures used for the referral, assessment, and eventual placement of students. Together, these activities raise substantive issues: (1) cost, a key factor in the congressional capping of the number of students (at 12 percent) who could be counted for funding purposes; (2) professional judgment, particularly with regard to identification of students with learning disabilities; and (3) discrimination, as seen in the disproportionate number of minority and limited-English-proficient students referred for evaluation and placed in certain cate-

gories. These issues can be framed as a sequence of questions:

1. Who is being referred and on what basis?
2. What is the nature of the assessment?
3. What are the bases of the placement?
4. What is the likelihood, once a student is placed in a special education setting, that appropriate programs and services will be provided?
5. What is the likelihood, once these programs are provided, that the student will return to general education?

Aside from those students with obvious physical handicaps who are identified before entering a classroom, referral occurs, for the most part, "when student behavior and academic progress varies from the school norm. . . ."[9] The assumption in such cases is that there is something wrong with the student. In particular, referral is more likely to occur in cases where the student is a member of a minority group or from a family whose socioeconomic status varies from the district's norm.[10] Further,

decisions about special education classification are not only functions of child characteristics but rather involve powerful organizational influences. The number of programs, availability of space, incentives for identification, range and kind of competing programs and services, number of professionals, and federal, state, and community pressures all affect classification decisions.[11]

Referral rates vary widely. This is apparent from examining two different sets of data from twenty-eight large cities. As a percentage of total student enrollment, referral rates range from 6 to 11 percent. The figures for assessment vary even more widely. For the same twenty-eight cities, the percentage of students who are referred and then placed in special education ranges from 7.8 percent to 91.8 percent.[12]

The most extensive study of the evaluation process reports that results are barely more accurate than a flip of the coin, with the evaluation process often providing a psychological justification for the referral.[13] The leading researchers conclude that current classification procedures are plagued with major conceptual and practical problems.[14]

While PL 94-142 includes eleven different classifications of handicapping conditions,[15] "most diagnoses of students placed in special education programs are based on social and psychological criteria. These include measured intelligence, achievement, social behavior and adjustment, and communication and language problems. Furthermore, many of the measuring criteria used in classification lack reliability or validity. . . ."[16] According to one observer, when test results do not produce the desired outcome, evaluators often change the yardstick: "If the test scores indicate the child is ineligible, but the teacher really feels the child needs help, we try to select other tests that might make the child eligible. . . ." The tests then become "a means of corroborating referral decisions. Testing, therefore, does not drive decisions but is driven by decisions."[17]

The major classification problems concern those students labeled as learning disabled. The number of students classified as learning disabled rose 119 percent between 1976–77 and 1984–85, at a time when the overall special education population rose 16 percent. The growth has been slowed in the past two school years. In 1985–86, students labeled as learning disabled accounted for 42.8 percent of the students—aged three through twenty-one—receiving special education services.[18] The percentage of special education students labeled as learning disabled varied from 30 to 67 percent among the fifty states, and from 0 to 73 percent among thirty large cities.[19]

In what can be fairly called a form of classification plea bargaining, this growth in those labeled as learning disabled has been accompanied by a decline (by some 300,000 between 1976–77 and 1983–84) in those labeled as mentally retarded. The Department of Education gently explains, "These decreases in the number of children classified as mentally retarded are the result of an increasing sensitivity to the negative features of the label itself and to the reaction on the part of local school systems to allegations of racial and ethnic bias as a result of the use of discriminatory or culturally biased testing procedures."[20]

The problem is not only the excessive numbers of students classified as learning disabled; there are even more troubling issues as to the accuracy of the label:

- More than 80 percent of the student population could be classified as learning disabled by one or more definitions presently in use.[21]
- Based upon the records of those already certified as learning disabled and those not, experienced evaluators could not tell the difference.[22]
- Students identified as learning disabled cannot be shown to differ from other low achievers with regard to a wide variety of school-related characteristics.[23]

- A study of special education in Colorado concluded: "The single most important finding is that more than half the children do not meet statistical or valid clinical criteria for the identification of perceptual or communicative disorders."[24]

Summarizing national data on the subject, the authors of one study remarked, "At least half of the learning disabled population could be more accurately described as slow learners, as children with second-language backgrounds, as children who are naughty in class, as those who are absent more often or move from school to school, or as average learners in above-average school systems."[25]

Such results are not surprising, given reports concerning the inadequacy and inappropriateness of the measuring instruments, the disregard of results in decisionmaking, and, often, the evaluators' incompetence and biases.[26] A decade later, there is nothing to warrant changing Nicholas Hobbs's assessment that the classification system of students with disabilities is "a major barrier to the efficient and effective delivery of services to them and their families and thereby impedes efforts to help them."[27] The standard for assessment, in special education as elsewhere, should be validity and reliability on a series of axes.

Placement Options

While referral and assessment procedures vary widely, and students are "placed" in special education programs based upon such discrepant outcomes, PL 94-142 is clear concerning least restrictive environment (LRE) criteria, namely, that "removal from the regular education environment" is to occur "only when the nature and severity of the handicap is such that education in regular classes with the use of supplementary aids cannot be achieved satisfactorily" [Sec. 612 (5) (B)]. There is, however, wide variability in the implementation of the federal law at the local level. This is shown in Table 1, which presents data showing the percentage of students with the four most frequent handicapping conditions who are placed in regular classes, the placement favored by the law. These four categories together account for 95 percent of all students classified as "handicapped."

Overall, 74 percent of special education students are in pull-out or separate programs. For each handicapping condition the variation among states is substantial. For the students labeled as learning disabled (LD), 16 percent are in regular classes,

Table 1

Percent of students with handicapping conditions in regular classes.

	All Conditions	Learning Disabled	Speech Impaired	Mentally Retarded	Emotionally Disturbed
U.S. average	69	78	96	31	44
State with highest percent in regular classes	90	99	100	84	86
State with lowest percent in regular classes	36	35	75	3	8

Source: Seventh Annual Report to the Congress on the Implementation of the Education of the Handicapped Act, Table 6C3.

with a range from 0.06 to 98 percent—in effect, from a bare handful in Arizona to nearly all students in Alabama. For those students labeled as speech-impaired, the national average is 64 percent of the students in regular classes, ranging from zero percent in Mississippi to nearly all in Alabama. For those students labeled as mentally retarded (MR), the national average is 5 percent in regular classes, and ranges from zero percent in five states to 50 percent in New Hampshire. Finally, for those students labeled emotionally disturbed (ED), the national average is 12 percent in regular classes, and ranges from zero percent in four states to 74 percent in Alabama.

Such results indicate that students with seemingly identical characteristics qualify for different programs, depending on where they reside and how individuals on school staffs evaluate them. Most often, these are pull-out programs, despite evidence about their lack of efficacy.[28]

Patterns of service often appear to relate more to the systems of funding than to indices of pupil benefit. For example, each of the states with the highest percentage of the students in these four categories placed in regular classes used the same type of funding formula ("cost" basis), while in all but one case the states with the lowest percentage of students in the four categories in regular classes used another type of formula ("unit" basis).[29]

The consequence in New York, for example, was to reward LEAs for assigning students to more-rather than less-restrictive placements, and for assigning them outside of the public school system to private schools.[30] In other words, rather than encouraging and supporting the mandate of the law to

place students in the least restrictive environment, current New York State Education Department practice rewards the opposite.

Some have argued that such funding practices explain both the growth of special education and the absence of decertification or the return of students to general education once they have met their IEP objectives in special education. While funding patterns no doubt have their consequences, we will argue that a set of attitudes is more important in producing the current pattern. Here it is sufficient to note that among twenty-six large cities, fewer than 5 percent of students in special education return to general education, with a range of zero to 13.4 percent.[31] No national figures, however, have been collected on the number of students who were certified as handicapped and who have returned to general education.

Educational Programs

The basic premise of special education is that students with deficits will benefit from a unique body of knowledge and from smaller classes staffed by specially trained teachers using special materials. We will address these assumptions of a segregated special education system in the concluding section of this paper; here we cite recent research findings that support an integrated setting.

There is no compelling body of evidence that segregated special education programs have significant benefits for students. On the contrary, there is substantial and growing evidence that goes in the opposite direction.[32] In fifty recent studies comparing the academic performance of mainstreamed and segregated students with handicapping conditions, the mean academic performance of the integrated group was in the 80th percentile, while the segregated students scored in the 50th percentile.[33]

A review of programs for academically handicapped students found no consistent benefits of full-time special education programs. Rather, it found full- or part-time regular class placements more beneficial for students' achievements, self-esteem, behavior, and emotional adjustment.[34] A study in one state found that 40 to 50 percent of students labeled as learning disabled did not realize the expected benefits from special education.[35]

In summarizing impediments to achieving national policy in the education of students with mild handicaps, a recent study rejects the prevalent "pull-out" strategy as ineffective, and concludes, "This split-scheduling approach . . . is neither administratively nor instructionally supportable when measured against legal requirements, effective schools research or fiscal consideration."[36]

A careful review of the literature on effective instruction strongly indicates that the general practice of special education runs counter to the basic effectiveness tenets in teaching behaviors, organization of instruction, and instructional support.[37] Furthermore,

> there appear to be at least three discrepancies between the suggestions for best practice and the observation of actual teaching practice for mildly handicapped students: (a) there is almost no instruction presented to these students that might be classified as involving high level cognitive skills, (b) there is a small amount of time spent in activities that could be considered direct instruction with active learner response and teacher feedback, and (c) students receive a low frequency of contingent teacher attention.[38]

While these shortcomings are true as well in general education classes, the needs of students appropriately classified as handicapped make the absence of the desired practices even more consequential.

At the classroom level, the time special education students spend on academic tasks is not greater than that for general education students: about forty-five minutes of engaged time per day.[39] And, most often, there is little qualitatively different in special education instruction in the areas of additional time on task, curriculum adaptation, diverse teaching strategies, adaptive equipment, or advanced technology. Classrooms, despite their small size, remain "teacher-centric."

The limited expectation for student learning in special education programs is reflected in the following results of a study of special education in large cities: (1) only seven of thirty-one cities evaluate "student achievement/outcomes"; (2) only three of thirty-one cities conduct "longitudinal student outcome studies"; and (3) only nine of the twenty-four special education directors whose districts do not conduct such evaluations believe "student achievement/outcome studies" are needed.[40] Thus, combining the numbers of special education directors whose districts conduct such evaluations and those who do not, but say they are needed, fifteen of the thirty-one directors of large-city special education programs neither collect student outcome data nor believe that such evaluations are needed. While the failure to evaluate outcomes does not in and of itself indicate limited expectations, at the least it does indicate a lack of concern with outcomes, which we believe comes from limited expectations of student capacity.

Least Restrictive Environment

We have previously addressed the topic of separation in the context of instructional placement; in this section, we will focus on separation as one aspect of the overall least restrictive environment (LRE) mandate. The two are inextricably entwined: LRE placement is not a mandate in itself; rather, students are to receive services in an appropriate placement in the least restrictive environment.

This formulation is based on the premise that while many types of placement might be appropriate for a student, the one to be chosen should be the least restrictive, that is, the one which allows maximum integration of students with their peers. Putting it the opposite way, the Sixth Circuit Court of Appeals directed: in situations "where a segregated facility is considered superior, the court should determine whether the services which make that placement superior could feasibly be provided in a non-segregated setting. If they can, the placement in the segregated school would be inappropriate under the Act."[41] Further, the Department of Education has stated that the type of placement must not be based on any of the following factors, either alone or in combination: category of handicapping condition, configuration of the service delivery system, availability of educational or related services, availability of space, or curriculum content or methods of curriculum delivery.[42]

Despite such statements from the Office of Special Education and Rehabilitation Services, the reality in schools turns out to be far different. When the first figures were collected in 1976–77, 67 percent of the students who were served under PL 94-142 were served in general classes, 25 percent in special classes. A decade later, the figures were essentially the same.[43] While overall there have been no changes in the direction of increasing the proportion of students receiving services in general education, the change has been in the opposite direction for the mentally retarded.[44]

The New York State Association for Retarded Children (NYSARC) has charged the State Education Department (SED) with failure to enforce the law, noting, among other charges, that in Nassau County on Long Island, "out of 320 special education classes, 308 are in segregated facilities." The response of the official charged with enforcing the law gives a somewhat peculiar reading to the SED's sense of its obligations here. "It's a question of where do you draw the line. . . . [While NYSARC is strongly in favor of placing students in integrated settings], many other people in New York State feel differently."[45] The continuing support in New York of its Board of Cooperative Education Services (BOCES), and similar intermediate units in other states, which cluster special education students in separate settings, no doubt will be an arena of future contention about the least restrictive environment.

An extensive study in Massachusetts not only mirrors the national data on the absence of integrated placements, but also reveals a significant trend toward more restrictive placements, especially in the past five years.[46] In its most recent report to Congress on the implementation of PL 94-142, the Department of Education, reporting on the eighteen states reviewed in the past year, indicated that "virtually every state had significant problems in meeting its LRE requirements. . . ."[47] Indeed, all eighteen states were out of compliance with the law in this area. Despite such findings, only seven states reported a need to improve their LRE performances.[48]

As we have learned in the area of race relations, integration is a more complex matter than achieving mere physical proximity. Not only are there administrative barriers when one organization operates its programs in the buildings of another, but there is also the day-to-day, period-to-period reality of the students' education. A unique analysis of "mainstreaming" in the Pittsburgh schools gives dramatic evidence of its actual limitations.[49] The district classifies approximately 6 percent of its students as mildly to moderately disabled, serving them in thirty-eight of the district's fifty-six elementary schools. Based on an examination of their academic schedules, "the percent of [special] students assigned to regular classes ranged from 3 to 7 percent. This

means that over 90 percent of the mildly handicapped elementary students . . . were *never* assigned to regular education academic classes" (emphasis in the original).[50] Participation is limited in three ways: (1) scheduling students for fewer than the full number of periods in the week, (2) having students attend several different general education classes for the same subject, and (3) assigning students to inappropriate (by age or level) general education classes.[51] Thus, fewer than one-tenth of mildly handicapped students participated in the mainstream, and of this small number, less than half participated in the mainstream class on a full basis. Given such program limitations, it is no surprise that only 1.4 percent of the students return to general education.[52]

In a review of mainstreaming in high schools, there was a large discrepancy between reported availability and actual utilization of general classroom education. Although special education teachers indicated that general classroom opportunities were available for their students with disabilities, according to the students' parents only one-third of the students were actually benefiting from this opportunity. Teachers cited the following impediments to mainstreaming special education students: (1) students lack entry-level skills required in general education classrooms; (2) general education classroom teachers resist mainstreaming efforts; and (3) supportive resources, such as modified curricula, are not available.[53]

Parental Involvement

Parents were central to the passage of PL 94-142—to the enactment of prior and subsequent state laws as well as to the maintenance of strong regulations to implement them. While their rights are specifically cited in federal and state laws, parental involvement in student assessment, program development, and the evaluation of students' progress is limited.[54]

Research studies report that most parents are far from fulfilling their roles of providing information, participating in decisions, or serving as advocates.[55] One study reported that in 70 percent of the cases, parents provided no input to IEP development.[56] A more recent study reports that only half of the parents attended IEP meetings,[57] and that when they did, professionals believed they contributed little.[58] Other professionals suggest that perhaps parents "feel intimidated or are provided only limited opportunity" to become involved.[59] This point is emphasized in the most recent Department of Education report to Congress which notes, "several studies have reported that in the majority of IEP conferences, the IEP was completely prepared prior to the meeting. . . ." The report concludes, "presenting parents with what may appear to be decisions the school has already reached rather than recommendations, and the failure to directly communicate and provide appropriate opportunities for involvement, can obviously limit parent participation in the IEP decision making process."[60]

Parents of children with disabilities often feel as if they share their children's labels[61] and are thereby perceived by others as part of the overall problem and in need of professional services for themselves. Thus, should parents at an IEP conference express frustration or anger at the lack of educational or related services being provided to their children, professionals, rather than addressing the specific problem areas or providing the required services, are often quick to "diagnose" the parent as overwhelmed and overprotective and in need of psychological services to combat "their problems." If, on the other hand, parents lead an active life and have less time to devote to their children's education or therapeutic program than the professionals deem appropriate, this behavior is often diagnosed as a form of parental denial that requires psychological treatment for the family members. In addition:

The belief that parents displace their anger onto the professional is a kind of "Catch-22." That is, whenever the parent disagrees with or confronts the professional, that behavior can be dismissed as an expression of inadequate adjustment, frustration, displaced anger, or a host of psychological problems. Any interpretation is possible other than that the parent may be correct![62]

The narratives of parents of children with disabilities repeatedly describe the power struggles surrounding their involvement in the students' education[63] and the devaluing or denigration of their knowledge about their children. Their concerns are often dismissed, their requests are often patronized, and their reports of the child's home behavior are often distrusted.[64] While not all parent-professional relationships are characterized by these factors, the pattern does appear to be endemic, in keeping with the historic role of the clinical or medical model in special education. Further, this attitude often leads to an over-valuing of the knowledge of so-called experts. Thus, professionals invariably refer children with problems and their parents to specialist rather than generalist service providers or mutual support groups. Summarizing the growing parent literature: "The nar-

ratives repeatedly express anger, frustration, and resentment . . . at the unnecessary burdens they and their children face because of social attitudes and behavior toward disabilities."[65]

A WORLD OF DISABLING ATTITUDES

The National Council on the Handicapped, appointed by President Reagan, has reiterated what people with disabilities have been saying for years: their major obstacles arise from external rather than internal barriers. The Council cites with approval the statement of an expert United Nations panel:

Despite everything we can do, or hope to do, to assist each physically or mentally disabled person achieve his or her maximum potential in life, our efforts will not succeed until we have found the way to remove the obstacles to this goal directed by human society—the physical barriers we have created in public buildings, housing, transportation, houses of worship, centers of social life and other community facilities—the social barriers we have evolved and accepted against those who vary more than a certain degree from what we have been conditioned to regard as normal. More people are forced into limited lives and made to suffer by these man-made [sic] obstacles than by any specific physical or mental disability.[66]

Individuals with disabilities make the point even more directly:

In his classic article entitled "What does it mean when a retarded person says, 'I'm not retarded'?" Bogdan tells of people labelled retarded who say, "I have never really thought of myself as retarded. I never really had that ugly feeling deep down," and another who says. "The worst word I have been called is retarded." The single largest self advocacy organization of people labelled retarded calls itself "People First." Marsha Saxton, a person with Spina Bifida, reports, "As I see it, I'm not lucky or unlucky. I'm just the way I am. But I'm not disabled, I always thought. Or handicapped." Denise Karuth, who also has a physical disability, . . . writes, "Put your handkerchiefs away. I'm a lot more like you than you probably imagine." The message in each of these instances . . . is that a disability is only one dimension of a person, not all-defining and not inherently a barrier to being recognized as fully human.[67]

A quarter of a century ago, Erving Goffman addressed this issue. He wrote, "By definition, of course, we believe the person with a stigma is not quite human."[68] The point has been made more recently by Ved Mehta. "You see, we are confronted with a vast ignorance in the world about the handicapped [so that] they would not understand if we acted like normal people."[69]

In a variety of ways, persons with disabilities are neither treated like nor viewed as "normal people." More often, they are treated "specially" either for their own good or for someone else's, but always according to an externally imposed standard. From the many examples of this, two are noted here.

Airlines have asserted that for the safety of passengers who are blind (and sometimes, they argue, for the safety of non-disabled passengers), persons with disabilities *must* preboard, wait to deplane, sit in special seats and not in others, and receive special briefings. To the extent that any database is used to justify these requirements, it was created using blindfolded sighted persons in trial evacuations of planes. One need not suggest the likelihood that persons who are blind would be more rather than less able to maneuver in a smoky airplane than sighted persons (blindfolded or not!) to see that the requirements as to special treatment are both unnecessary and demeaning.[70]

The cases of "Baby Doe" in Indiana and "Baby Jane Doe" in New York have drawn considerable attention to professional attitudes toward disability and how they affect the treatment of newborns. Among the major issues raised is "quality of life." For example, in order to determine, which babies with spina bifida should be provided "active vigorous treatment" as opposed to "supportive care only," doctors at the University of Oklahoma Health Sciences Center reported in 1983 on a formula they used to determine quality of life: $QL - NE \times (H + S)$. "QL" stands for quality of life; "NE" for natural endowment; "H" for contribution from home and family; and "S" for contribution from society.[71] Those infants for whom the equation predicted a high quality of life were given "active" medically indicated treatment; those for whom it predicted a low score received "no active" medical treatment, no surgery to close the spinal lesion or to drain fluid from the brain, no antibiotics to treat infection. "Of the 24 infants who did not get active, vigorous treatment, none survived. . . . All but one of the infants who received active, vigorous treatment survived. The exception was killed in an automobile accident."[72] What we have here, masquerading as an objective medical judgment, is a means test for care and a determination about one person's quality of life based on an outside person's assessment of a family's and society's "contribution."

Given public attitudes and policies such as these, persons with disabilities have increasingly developed a new perspective. This has been reflected recently in writings by disability rights activists[73] and others in the independent-living movement. For them, "the problem of disability is not only of physical impairment but also of unnecessary dependence on relatives and professionals, of architectural barriers and of unprotected rights."[74] This formulation is echoed in the report of the first national survey of self-perceptions of Americans with disabilities.[75]

- An overwhelming majority, 74 percent, say they feel at least some sense of common identity with other people with disabilities. (Table 56)
- Nearly half, 45 percent, feel that disabled persons are a minority group in the same sense as Blacks and Hispanics. This figure rises to 56 percent of those disabled between birth and adolescence and 53 percent of those 44 years of age and younger. (Table 57)

This emerging and growing involvement of adults with disabilities can have a major impact in the field of special education. These individuals will be less likely to tolerate an educational system that fails to recognize the capabilities of handicapped students and to prepare them to deal with the realities of the outside world.

SPECIAL EDUCATION: DISABLING ATTITUDES IN PRACTICE

It is the attitudinal milieu more than the individual's physical condition that influences society's response to persons with disabilities. An all-or-nothing concept of disability requires proof of total incapacity in order to gain entitlement to various benefit programs.[76] Further, the media portrays disabled persons as either the heroic individual or the pathetic cripple, rather than as a human being with a multiplicity of qualities. Together these images of disability burden policy, including the education of students with disabilities.[77]

This point was recognized by Justice William Brennan, writing for the Supreme Court in *School Board of Nassau County v. Arline,* who said, "Congress acknowledged that society's accumulated myths and fears about disability and disease are as handicapping as are the physical limitations that flow from actual impairment."[78]

Society's attitudes toward disability are deeply ingrained in professional practice. This is particularly evident in the social-psychological literature, where disability is based on the following assumptions: (1) disability is biologically based; (2) disabled persons face endless problems, which are caused by the impairment; (3) disabled persons are "victims"; (4) disability is central to the disabled person's self-concept and self-definition; and (5) disability is synonymous with a need for help and social support.[79]

Similar assumptions hold true in special education. Here the child and family are considered impaired, instruction is disability-focused, professional personnel are often trained and certified to work with specific disabilities, and attention to societal issues is often considered too political and not the business of educational institutions. The assumptions underlying such beliefs can be tersely summarized: "(1) Disability is a condition that individuals have; (2) disabled/typical is a useful and objective distinction; and (3) special education is a rationally conceived and coordinated system of services that help children labeled disabled.... "[80] This view of students labeled as handicapped, however, adversely affects expectations regarding their academic achievement. It causes them to be separated from other students; to be exposed to a watered-down curriculum; to be excused from standards and tests routinely applied to other students; to be allowed grades that they have not earned; and, in some states, to be permitted special diplomas.[81]

The rationale given for such watered-down expectations is that they are in the best interest of the child. Professionals often suggest that a child be placed in an environment where he or she will be "safe...because he would never be asked to do things there 'we know he cannot do.'" Many parents recognize, however, that a "safe" place may not be the best learning environment. Writing about their experience with Chicago-area schools, which identified their young son as being in need of special education, Lori and Bill Granger conclude:

The trap of Special Education was now open and waiting for the little boy. It is a beguiling trap. Children of Special Education are children of Small Expectations, not great ones. Little is expected and little is demanded. Gradually, these children—no matter their IQ level—learn to be cozy in the category of being "special." They learn to be less than they are.[82]

Not only do "small expectations" excuse students from academic performance; they have also led state education departments, school systems, and the courts to excuse them from the social and behavioral expectations and standards set for other students. The medical or clinical model that undergirds special education inextricably leads to the belief that persons with a handicap, especially the severely disabled, are not capable of making choices or decisions. This conceptualization diminishes "our ability to see them as individuals capable of ever making a choice, let alone the right choice. Seldom, if ever, is the person with the handicapping condition involved in the process of determining how their behavior, or the behavior of those around them, will be modified. The end result is more control for the care-givers and less control for the person being cared for."[83] Having denied individuals with disabilities autonomy and decision-making authority—in effect denying them the respect given to people whom society respects—we then excuse their behavior, ascribing it to the disability.[84]

GENERAL EDUCATION

It is not special education but the total educational system that must change. The origin, growth, and shape of special education have in many ways been defined by general education and the attitudes and behaviors of mainstream educators toward students with handicapping conditions. Whatever the rationale or the benign purpose claimed, children with disabilities have been denied access to public education, or, when given access, have received an education that is not equal to that given other children.

The growth of special education in the past decade has occurred not only in response to the exclusion of students with handicapping conditions. Additional factors have fueled this growth, including: (1) cutbacks in Chapter 1 (formerly Title 1) programs and other school remedial efforts that strained local school system resources (in the same period as and coincidental with the implementation of PL 94-142); (2) the development of remedial and pull-out programs for students with "problems"—slow learners, "disadvantaged," limited-English proficient (miscalled bilingual), new immigrants, and gay and lesbian students;[85] and (3) given the increased emphasis on accountability, the referral of "low achievers" to special education programs, thus excluding them from test-score analyses in school districts.

Another factor promoting exclusion has been a narrowing of the definition of what is considered "normal." In special education, "this often means referral based on race, sex, physical appearance, and socioeconomic status...."[86] A recent study in ten states noted that referral occurs when student behavior and academic achievement vary negatively from the school norm, and for minority students, when their socioeconomic status is lower than the norm of the community.[87] Additionally, the role of school psychologists, given their training and the present educational philosophy, gives professional rationale for special education placements and for the ever-growing identification of deviant, or to use the more recent term, "at-risk" students.[88] The obverse of this has consequences for those students who remain in regular classroom programs. "Every time a child is called mentally defective and sent off to the special education class for some trivial defect, the children who are left in the regular classroom receive a message: no one is above suspicion; everyone is being watched by the authorities; nonconformity is dangerous."[89]

The problem is not special education or general education alone. "In a sense, regular and special education teachers have colluded to relieve regular teachers of responsibilities for teaching children functioning at the bottom of their class."[90] The pressure to "succeed" with high test scores, and with the very large class sizes that make individual attention extremely difficult, makes it more likely that teachers will seek uniformity of students rather than diversity. To put it more sharply, there is, in effect, a "deal" between special and general education. The former asserts a particular body of expertise and a unique understanding of "special" students, thus laying claim both to professional obligation and student benefit. The latter, because of the lack of skills and resources or prejudice, is often happy to hand over "these" students to a welcoming special education system. This includes not only those with the traditional handicapping conditions, but increasing numbers of students labeled "learning disabled," a category that, at present, incorporates such a multitude of students that, under one or another definition, it may incorporate as many as 80 percent of the general education student body. The "deal is sanctioned, on one hand, by the clinicians who provide an intrapsychic justification for the referral, and, on the other hand, by those in the role of advocacy who see increasing numbers of students in special education as providing evidence of their effectiveness."[91]

NEXT STEPS

No discussion of a future education system for students with handicapping conditions can begin without acknowledgment of what has been achieved. As one of the PL 94-142 drafters writes, however, "If the law has been massively successful in assigning responsibility for students and setting up mechanisms to assure that schools carry out these responsibilities, it has been less successful in removing the barriers between general and special education. It did not anticipate that the artifice of delivery systems in schools might drive the maintenance of separate services and keep students from the mainstream."[92]

A part of this separation is revealed in special educators' decrying the absence of attention to special education in the raft of national reports about education. Indeed, nearly an entire issue of *Exceptional Children* addressed this topic. The inattention to special education is described and the alleged trade-off between excellence and equity deplored.[93] Stephen Lilly suggests, however, that the reason special education is ignored is that "current special education policies and practices for students labelled mildly handicapped are neither conceptually sound nor of sufficient quality to be included in the 'ideal' educational system described by these authors." Thus, rather than deploring the inattention, he applauds it, saying that "until we are willing to examine our flawed assumptions about children and teachers and become integral members of the general education community, we cannot expect either to be featured in reform reports or to be involved in construction of the next era of public education in the United States."[94]

We have, in the preceding pages, examined some of the flawed assumptions about disability. Before turning to ideas for reform, this section will highlight some critiques of special education that are pertinent to the development of new designs. On the one hand, the Heritage Foundation has criticized the very promises of PL 94-142 by saying that it "rests on the questionable assumption that the responsibility for disabled individuals is primarily society's as a civil right," and has questioned its major program direction, saying that "public schools should not be required to educate those children who cannot, without damaging the main purposes of public education, function in a normal classroom setting."[95] At the opposite extreme, the National Coalition of Advocates for Students criticized the lack of access to education for various groups, including students with handicaps. They did so, however, without questioning "the underlying separateness of regular education and special education systems."[96]

A different level of critique is represented by those who argue that the current pattern of special education, by serving some inappropriately, "robs the genuinely handicapped of funds and services they need to deal with their very real problems."[97] In particular, for those labeled learning disabled, inappropriate expenditures are claimed, both in the cost of assessments and in the expense of providing low student-teacher ratios and individualized programs.[98]

In a seeming backlash against the poor quality of services for those with low-incidence handicaps, there is a call from some for a return to separate services. These include: a proposed resolution at the annual convention of the National Federation of the Blind to (re)establish specialized schools for the blind; a proposal from a group of superintendents of residential schools and state directors of special education to (re)establish residential schools for deaf and blind students;[99] the accreditation for the first time of a special education school by a regional accrediting association;[100] and the approval by the New York State Education Department for the construction of a segregated high school for students with physical disabilities.

While the return to more restrictive settings may be understood in light of current special education services, the more predominant reaction of professionals and parents is to propose reforms designed to preclude or limit services to inappropriately labeled students and/or to lower the "barriers" between general and special education.

While no one can argue for the inappropriate labeling of students, one can also empathize with the directors of special education programs who see such students "dumped" into their programs. More disturbing, however, are efforts to impose an arbitrary "cap" on the number of students referred, to cut a "bargain" with general education, or to tighten criteria. While "tightening eligibility criteria may seem to make the problem go away . . . the main effect might be either to (a) redirect referred students into other categorical services or programs; or (b) disguise as nonhandicapped the portion of students for whom technical eligibility cannot be demonstrated."[101]

ALTERNATIVE DELIVERY SYSTEMS

An alternative way to serve students with mild and moderate handicaps is to integrate them into general education programs at the building level. Indeed, a number of states and districts are implementing experimental programs using such an approach,[102] especially for students categorized as having "learning problems." A report to the Secretary of the U.S. De-

partment of Education noted that present practices suffer from (1) fragmented approaches ("Many students who require help and are not learning effectively fall 'through the cracks' of a program structure based on preconceived definitions of eligibility. . . ."); (2) a dual system ("The separate administrative arrangements for special programs contribute to a lack of coordination, raise questions about leadership, cloud areas of responsibility, and obscure lines of accountability within schools."); (3) stigmatization of students (producing in students "low expectations of success, failure to persist on tasks, the belief that failures are caused by personal inadequacies, and a continued failure to learn effectively"); and (4) placement decisions becoming a battleground between parents and schools. In light of such practices, the panel called for experimental programs for students with learning problems, which incorporate increased instructional time, support systems for teachers, empowerment of principals to control all programs and resources at the building level, and new instructional approaches that involve "shared responsibility" between general and special education.[103]

While clearly an improvement over the present special education practice, this broad proposal nonetheless continues a dual system approach for a smaller (more severely impaired) population.[104] As described a decade ago, such students will continue to be faced with consequences of negative attitudes and lowered expectations, with teachers making comparisons between them "in relation to degrees of handicap rather than comparing [their] skill levels to the criteria of nonhandicapped skill performance."[105]

The data in the earlier sections of this article concerning least restrictive environment and mainstreaming focused on students with mild and moderate handicapping conditions. This reflects both the preponderance of students in special education and the major emphasis in the research literature. There is, however, an increasing body of work concerning the integration of students with severe handicaps into regular schools.[106] The Association for Persons with Severe Handicaps (TASH) has been in the forefront of these efforts,[107] and a recent book gives guidance on the conduct of programs to integrate severely impaired students into regular programs,[108] as does a recent Council for Exceptional Children report.[109]

According to this research, the education of students with severe disabilities in an integrated setting requires first and foremost an attitude change from seeing the education of students with disabilities as different or "special" and the education of "non-disabled" students as normal and expected.

Major work in the integration of students with severe multiple disabilities in classes at age-appropriate schools has been carried out by the California Research Institute on the Integration of Students with Severe Disabilities (CRI). In the past five years, they have worked with over two hundred classes serving more than two thousand students with severe handicaps in twenty San Francisco Bay Area school districts. By integration, CRI means: (1) placement of classes in general school buildings which are the chronologically age-appropriate sites for the students; (2) a balanced ratio (from 5 to 20 percent) of such classes in a school; (3) structured opportunities for regular and sustained interactions between severely disabled and nondisabled students; (4) participation of the severely disabled students in all non-academic activities of the school; and (5) implementation of a functional life-skills curriculum for severely disabled students. The rationale for educating students with severe disabilities in integrated settings is to ensure their normalized community participation by providing them with systematic instruction in the skills that are essential to their success in the social and environmental contexts in which they will ultimately use these skills. Thus, a key feature of the CRI model is the mixing of classroom, school, and community-based learning situations.[110]

This type of integration is a far cry from the "dumping" of students back into general education settings, rightly decried by parents and advocates after their long-fought battles. It is also vastly different from the segregated programs that have proven ineffective for many students.

A new framework for education is needed; its entire organization must be reconceptualized. Within this new framework, it would be appropriate to question programs of special education as a separate means of educating students who are deemed unable to profit from school simply because of their handicapping conditions. The growth in the numbers of those categorized as having handicapping conditions was coincidental with the past Sputnik concern for American competitiveness in the Cold War; young people who failed to keep up with rising standards were categorized as "slow learners," "mentally retarded," "emotionally disturbed," "culturally deprived," and "learning disabled." There was a disproportionate percentage of students from minority and low-income families in the first four categories, while White and middle-class students constituted the bulk of students in the last category.

This discriminatory way of categorizing served the function of preserving class and skin color privileges as the schools performed their assigned sorting function. And, in the current wave of school reform, "members of advantaged social groups will still advocate treating their failing children in ways that maintain their advantaged status as much as possible."[111] In essence,

we are talking about the distribution of advantage and disadvantage in society through the differential provision of opportunities to acquire knowledge or to acquire the status that goes with having been exposed to a certain kind of knowledge. There is no question of simply doing it more or less effectively. Effectiveness in such situations only has a meaning when it relates to some set of recognized values or ideals.[112]

It is not simply a matter of using the present measurement instruments more sensitively or more discretely. Nearly three quarters of a century ago, in a series of essays concerning the use of new I.Q. tests to measure officer candidates for World War I, Walter Lippmann wrote of his fear that these tests would be used to label children as inferior, and consign them to a second-class life. "It is not possible, I think, to imagine a more contemptible proceeding than to confront a child with a set of puzzles, and after an hour's monkeying with them, proclaim to the child, or to his parents, that here is a C-minus individual. It would not only be a contemptible thing to do. It would be a crazy thing to do. . . ."[113]

Drawing from an older history, one can learn from the experience on Martha's Vineyard in the eighteenth and nineteenth centuries, when it was the home of the highest concentration in the United States of people who were deaf. They were full participants in community life as workers, friends, neighbors, and family members.

The fact that a society could adjust to disabled individuals, rather than requiring them to do all the adjusting, as is the case in American society as a whole, raises important questions about the rights of the disabled and the responsibilities of those who are not. The Martha's Vineyard experience suggests strongly that the concept of a handicap is an arbitrary social category. And if it is a question of definition, rather than a universal given, perhaps it can be redefined, and many of the cultural preconceptions summarized in the term "handicapped," as it is now used, eliminated.

The most important lesson to be learned from Martha's Vineyard is that disabled people can be full and useful members of a community if the community makes an effort to include them.[114]

How then does one shape an educational system to include students with disabilities, one which is both consonant with and builds toward an inclusive society? Clearly, it is not done by taking students from the general education setting and labeling them as "deficient," nor is it done, as in special education, by focusing on the setting in which instruction takes place. Rather, research indicates that we must focus on the features of instruction that can produce improved learning for students.[115] Current practices, however, mean the "dumbing down" of the curriculum: "Instead of adapting instruction to individual differences to maximize common goal attainment . . . special education programs . . . in the extreme, become merely dead ends where common goals have been dropped altogether."[116]

An important step toward a restructured unitary system is expressed in a concept called "Rights without Labels": namely, the provision of needed services for students without the deleterious consequences of classification and labeling. A joint statement issued by the National Association of School Psychologists, the National Association of Social Workers, and the National Coalition of Advocates for Students suggests guidelines to encourage the education of (at least mild to moderately handicapped) students in general education settings.[117]

Regardless of the conceptual undergirding or the organizational arrangements of education for students with handicapping conditions, special education practice needs substantial improvement. In maintaining a separate special education system; however, no matter how refined or improved, education will continue to operate based on a set of organizational and individual assumptions that disabled and nondisabled youngsters require two distinct sets of services, which in turn require distinct funding, service delivery, and organization. While PL 94-142 requires educational services for students with handicapping conditions, it does not require a special education system.

There is an alternative to separate systems: a merged or unitary system. The conception of a unitary system requires a "paradigm shift,"[118] a fundamental change in the way we think about differences among people, in the ways we choose to organize schools for their education, and in how we view the purpose of that education. It rejects the bimodal division of handicapped and nonhandicapped students, and recognizes that individuals vary—that single-characteristic definitions fail to capture the complexity of people. Moreover, it rejects the belief, common to all human services work that incorporates a medical or deviancy model, that the problem lies in the individual and the resolution lies in one or another treatment modality. The unitary system, in contrast, requires adaptations in society and in education, not solely in the individual.

No longer would there be a need to approach differences in human capabilities or characteristics as disabilities on which to base categorical groupings. In a merged system, an individual difference in visual ability, for example, could be viewed as only one of numerous characteristics of a student, rather than the over-riding educational focus of a student's life. . . . It would not dictate differential placement and treatment according to a categorical affiliation which is often inherent in the disabilities approach to education.[119]

In a merged or unitary system, effective practices in classrooms and schools would characterize education for all students. No longer would there be an education system that focuses on the limitations of "handicapped" students, a teacher's incapacity to teach students because of a lack of special-credentials, or instruction that is determined by the label attached to students. Nor would blame be placed on students or on family characteristics. Rather, the focus would be on effective instruction for all students based on the belief that "substantial student improvements occur when teachers accept the responsibility for the performance of all their students and when they structure their classrooms so that student success is a primary product of the interaction that takes place there."[120]

At present, students are hampered in their intellectual growth by the lack of appropriate supports available to them and their families. Appropriate supports could include: assessment based on multidimensional axes; psychosocial evaluations directed toward instruction; instructional practices that utilize current research; classrooms and schools designed to incorporate effective schools research; enhanced staff and curriculum development; early intervention and transition programs; and postsecondary education, training, work, and community living options.[121] A new system means curriculum adaptations and individualized educational strategies that would allow both general and special education students to take more difficult courses. Another phenomenon that now distinguishes general from special education is that in general education, "in order to help young people make wise course choices, schools are increasingly requiring students to take courses that match their grade level and abilities. Schools are also seeing to it that the materials used in those courses are intellectually challenging." Moreover: "the more rigorous the course of study, the more a student achieves, within the limits of his capacity. Student achievement also depends on how much the school emphasizes a subject and the amount of time spent on it: the more time expended, the higher the achievement. Successful teachers encourage their students' best efforts."[122]

Fundamental to the work in school effectiveness (exemplified best by the late Ron Edmonds's efforts in New York City's public schools) is the principle that school improvement must involve both quality and equity. In other words, the results of school reform must benefit *all* students. The effective schools research identified five factors that characterize schools that achieve quality and equity: (1) high expectations for all students, and staff acceptance of responsibility for students' learning; (2) instructional leadership on the part of the principal; (3) a safe and orderly environment conducive to learning; (4) a clear and focused mission concerning instructional goals shared by the staff; and (5) frequent monitoring of student progress.[123] Work on effective instructional techniques, including teacher-directed instruction, increased academic engaged time, use of reinforcement, and individual instruction has paralleled much of the effective schools research.

While tutoring programs have involved students with handicaps for some time,[124] more recently, programs have been developed in which students with handicaps serve as tutors for other students with handicaps and for those without.[125] This serves to integrate students with handicaps, to promote respect for their capacity, and to enable them to learn by teaching.[126]

Recent reports on cross-cultural education can provide additional features worth emulating in a new unitary system. In Japan, for example, reports note the importance of clear purpose, strong motivation, and high standards; the importance of parental involvement and reinforcement between home and school; and the importance of maximum time devoted to learning and its effective use. Perhaps most central is the belief that differences in student achievement come not from innate differences in ability but from level of effort, perseverance, and self-discipline, each of which the school can encourage and teach.[127] While innate differences are limiting for some students appropriately labeled as handicapped, they are not limiting for most students in special education today.

In the United States, there is a body of "adaptive education" approaches and specific educational practice attuned to individual differences that have been shown to be effective for students with handicapping conditions.[128] Asserting the legal duty to provide effective schooling, lawyers at the Public Interest Law Center of Philadelphia put it succinctly: "Play school is out. Schooling is a profession. The law requires that practice in the schools measure up to the art of what has been demonstrated by the professional to be possible. What is done must be calculated to be effective."[129] In the Adaptive Learning Environments Model (ALEM) and similar programs, there is a design that integrates both those who are labeled as handicapped and those who are not and that benefits both.[130]

The ultimate rationale for quality education of students in an integrated setting is based not only on law or pedagogy, but also on values. What kinds of people are we? What kind of society do we wish to develop? What values do we honor? The current failure to provide a quality education to all students and the perpetuation of segregated settings expresses one set of answers to these questions. To change the outcome, we need to develop another set of values. As Walter Lippmann said in 1922, "If a child fails in school and then fails in life, the schools cannot sit back and say: 'You see how accurately I predicted this.' Unless we are to admit that education is essentially impotent, we have to throw back the child's failure at the school, and describe it as a failure not by the child but by the school."[131]

While there is neither agreement among educators nor commitment by policy-makers to a unitary system of quality education for all students, especially commitment in terms of money, we believe "we can, whenever and wherever we choose, successfully teach all children whose schooling is of interest to us. We already know more than we need in order to do this. Whether we do it must finally depend on how we feel about the fact that we haven't done it so far."[132]

Notes

1. Nomenclature in the filed of disability is often confusing and changing. Generally, disability refers to the individual's condition, while handicap refers to the consequence in society. Thus, for example, the individual with quadriplegia is disabled by the paralysis of his or her legs, but handicapped by the absence of a ramp to the local library. In special education, however, given the title of the major federal law PL 94-142, "The Education for All Handicapped Children Act," the term, "handicapped" is used synonymously with disabled. We will, therefore, use the terms "students with handicapping conditions" and "persons with a disability" interchangeably. We do not use the words handicapped or disabled, nor refer to a particular condition, such as deaf or blind, as an adjective. Rather than saying "The deaf boy," we say, "The boy who is deaf." This makes the point that deafness is but one of the boy's characteristics, and not the most important.

2. For a study of the passage of Section 504, and the tortuous process of the issuance of regulations implementing it, see Richard K. Scotch, *From Good Will to Civil Rights: Transforming Federal Disability Policy* (Philadelphia: Temple University Press, 1984).

3. There is not one in-depth study of the law's development and passage. For a brief survey, see Roberta Weiner, *P.L. 94-142: Impact on the Schools* (Washington, DC: Capitol Publications, 1985).

4. Lisa J. Walker, "Procedural Rights in the Wrong System: Special Education Is Not Enough," in *Images of the Disabled/Disabling Images,* ed. Alan Gartner and Tom Joe (New York: Praeger, 1987), pp. 98–102.

5. Coined in 1959, normalization as a concept was introduced in the United States a decade later. Generally, it means giving people with disabilities opportunities to live in as normal a fashion as possible. See, in particular, R. B. Kugel and W. Wolfensberger, *Changing Patterns in Residential Services for the Mentally Retarded* (Washington, DC: President's Committee on Mental Retardation, 1969) and W. Wolfensberger, *The Principle of Normalization in Human Services* (Toronto: National Institute on Mental Retardation, 1971).

6. The medical model views disability as located within the individual, and, thus, primary emphasis is devoted to the etiology or causes of conditions and the placement of persons in separate diagnostic categories. From this perspective, efforts to improve the functional capabilities of individuals are regarded as the exclusive solution to disability.

7. *Ninth Annual Report to the Congress on the Implementation of the Education of the Handicapped Act* (Washington, DC: U.S. Department of Education, 1987), Table EA1.

8. *Ninth Annual Report,* Table EJ1.

9. *Walker,* "Procedural Rights in the Wrong System," p. 105.

10. Among myriad studies, see especially Patricia Craig. *Status of Handicapped Students* (Menlo Park, CA: SRI,

1978) and *Barriers in Excellence: Our Children at Ried,* report of the National Coalition of Advocates for Students (New York, 1985).

11. B. K. Keogh, "Learning Disabilities: Diversity in Search of Order," in *The Handbook of Special Education Research and Practice,* vol 2., *Mildly Handicapped Conditions,* ed. Margaret C. Wang, Maynard C. Reynolds, and Herbert J. Walberg (Oxford: Pergannon, in press).

12. *Special Education: Views from America's Cities* (Washington, DC: The Council of Great City Schools, 1986), Tables 8 and 9.

13. James E. Ysseldyke et al., "Generalizations from Five Years of Research on Assessment and Decision-Making," *Exceptional Education Quarterly, 4* (1983), 75–93.

14. James E. Ysseldyke et al., "A Logical and Empirical Analysis of Current Practice in Classifying Students as Handicapped," *Exceptional Children, 50* (1983), 160–166.

15. Deaf, deaf-blind, hard of hearing, mentally retarded, multihandicapped, orthopedically impaired, other health impaired, seriously emotionally disturbed, specific learning disabled, speech impaired, and visually handicapped.

16. Margaret C. Wang, Maynard C. Reynolds, and Herbert J. Walberg, "Rethinking Special Education," *Educational Leadership, 44* (1986), 27.

17. Richard White and Mary Lynne Calhoun, "From Referral to Placement: Teachers' Perceptions of Their Responsibilities," *Exceptional Children, 53* (1987), 467.

18. Keogh, "Learning Disabilities."

19. Betty Binkard, "State Classifications of Handicapped Students: A National Comparative Data Report," *Counter-Point 12* (1986), and *A Study of Special Education,* Table 2. Both the state and city data are for the 1984–85 school year but are not strictly comparable.

20. *Seventh Annual Report to Congress on the Implementation of the Education of the Handicapped Act* (Washington, DC: U.S. Department of Education, 1985), p. 4.

21. James E, Ysseldyke, "Classification of Handicapped Students," in *Handbook of Special Education: Research and Practice,* vol. 1. *Learner Characteristics and Adaptive Education,* ed. Margaret C. Wang, Maynard C. Reynolds, and Herbert J. Walberg (Oxford: Pergamon, in press).

22. W. A. Davis and L. A. Shepard, "Specialists' Use of Test and Clinical Judgment in the Diagnosis of Learning Disabilities," *Learning Disabilities Quarterly, 19* (1983), 128–138.

23. James E. Ysseldyke et al., *Similarities and Differences between Underachievers and Students Labelled Learning Disabled: Identical Twins with Different Mothers* (Minneapolis: University of Minnesota, Institute for Research and Learning Disabilities, 1979) and James E. Ysseldyke et al., "Similarities and Differences between Low Achievers and Students Classified as Learning Disabled," *Journal of Special Education, 16* (1982), 73–85.

24. Lorrie A. Shepard and L. A. Smith, *Evaluation of the Identification of Perceptual Communicative Disorders in Colorado* (Boulder: University of Colorado, 1981), p. 28.

25. Lorrie A. Shepard, L. A. Smith, and C. P. Vojir, "Characteristics of Pupils Identified as Learning Disabled," *Journal of Special Education*, 16 (1983), 73–85.

26. Davis and Shepard, "Specialists Use of Tests and Clinical Judgment in the Diagnosis of Learning Disabilities": James E. Ysseidyke et al., "Technical Adequacy of Tests Used by Professionals in Simulated Decision-Making," *Psychology in the Schools, 17* (1980), 202–209; James E. Ysseldyke et al., "Declaring Students Eligible for Learning Disability Services: Why Bother with the Data?" *Learning Disability Quarterly, 5* (1982), 37–44; James E. Ysseldyke and B. Algozzine, "LD or not LD: That's Not the Question!" *Journal of Learning Disabilities, 16* (1983), 29–31; James E. Ysseldyke and B. Algozzine. *Introduction to Special Education* (Boston: Houghton Mifflin, 1984).

27. Nicholas Hobbs, "An Ecologically Oriented Service-Based System for Classification of Handicapped Children," in *The Ecosystem of the "Risk" Child*, ed. E. Salzmeyer, J. Antrobus, and J. Gliak (New York: Academic Press, 1980), p. 274.

28. C. Carlberg and Kenneth Kavale, "The Efficacy of Special versus Regular Class Placement for Exceptional Children: A Meta Analysis," *Journal of Special Education, 14* (1980), 295–309. See also P. Johnston, R. L. Allington, and P. Afflerbach, "The Congruence of Classroom and Remedial Reading Evaluation," *Elementary School Journal, 85* (1985), 465–478.

29. "Funding formulas that create incentives for more restrictive and separate class placement or that support particular configurations of services based on special education teacher allocations maintain an inflexible program structure and fail to allow models that encourage students to remain in general classrooms with resource room or individualized help.... States that provide financial incentives for separate placements, or which traditionally have had dual systems of services, place students disproportionately in more restrictive placements." Walker, "Procedural Rights in the Wrong System," p. 110.

30. Based upon a study of the effects of the state's funding formulae on the New York City public schools conducted by Lynn Weikart, Chief Administrator, Office of Finance and Management, Division of Special Education, 1981–83. The study found that the net cost to the school system—that is, program cost less state reimbursement—was greater when the student was placed in a more rather than less restrictive environment. In other words, while (generally) more restrictive placements cost more, the reimbursement was sufficiently greater so that the net cost to the school system favored more restrictive placements.

31. *Special Education*, Table 13. Again, these numbers must be viewed with some skepticism. Internal evidence suggests that the figures on students exiting from special education may, at least in some instances, be too high by at least half.

32. Dorothy Kerzner Lipsky and Alan Gartner, "Capable of Achievement and Worthy of Respect: Education for the Handicapped as if They Were Full-Fledged Human Beings," *Exceptional Children, 54* (1987), 61.

33. Weiner, *PL 94-142*, p. 42.

34. Nancy A. Madden and Robert L. Slavin, *Count Me In: Academic Achievement and Social Outcomes of Mainstreaming Students with Mild Academic Handicaps* (Baltimore: The Johns Hopkins University Press, 1982), p. 1.

35. R. Bloomer et al., *Mainstreaming in Vermont: A Study of the Identification Process* (Livonia, NY: Brador Publications, 1982).

36. George J. Hagerty and Marty Abramson, "Impediments to Implementing National Policy Change for Mildly Handicapped Students, *Exceptional Children, 53* (1987), 316.

37. William E. Bickel and Donna Diprima Bickel, "Effective Schools, Classrooms, and Instruction: Implications for Special Education," *Exceptional Children, 52* (1986), 489–500.

38. Catherine V. Morsink et al., "Research on Teaching: Opening the Door to Special Education Classrooms," *Exceptional Children, 53* (1986), 38.

39. James E. Ysseldyke, "Current Practices in Making Psychoeducational Decisions about Learning Disabled Students," *Journal of Learning Disabilities, 16* (1983), 226–233.

40. *Special Education*, Table 21.

41. Roncker v. Walter 700 F. 2d 1058 (1983), *cert. denied*, 104 S. Ct. 196 (1983).

42. *Standards and Guidelines for Compliance with Federal Requirements for the Education of the Handicapped* (Washington, DC: Office of Special Education Programs, U.S. Department of Education, 1986), p. 24.

43. Walker, "Procedural Rights in the Wrong System," p. 104.

44. National Center for Education Statistics, *The School-Age Handicapped* (Washington, DC: Government Printing Office, 1985), p. 20.

45. "Special Ed Students Kept in Restrictive Environments, Disability Groups Say," *Education of the Handicapped* (29 October 1986), pp. 5–6.

46. *Out of the Mainstream: Education of Disabled Youth in Massachusetts* (Boston: Massachusetts Advocacy Center, 1987).

47. "Improved Special Education Monitoring Unearthing More Flaws, ED Says," *Education Daily* (21 April 1987), p. 3.

48. *Ninth Annual Report*, p. 166.

49. Janet Sansone and Naomi Zigmond, "Evaluating Mainstreaming through an Analysis of Students' Schedules," *Exceptional Children, 52* (1986), 452–458.

50. Sansone and Zigmond, "Evaluating Mainstreaming," p. 455.

51. The opportunity "to provide preparation periods for special education teachers ... seems to be the decisive factor in these assignments." Sansone and Zigmond, "Evaluating Mainstreaming," p. 455.

52. *Special Education*, Table 13.

53. Andrew S. Halpern, "Transition: A Look at the Foundations," *Exceptional Children, 51* (1985), 483.

54. Despite myriad studies concerning PL 94-142, there has not been a systematic study nor an in-depth evaluation of parental involvement in the education of their children. Rick Rodgers, *Caught in the Act: What LEA's Tell Parents under the 1981 Education Act* (London: Centre for Studies on Integration in Education, 1986) is a model for this.

55. B. L. Baker and R. P. Brightman, "Access of Handicapped Children to Educational Services," in *Children, Mental Health, and the Law,* ed. N. D. Repucci, L. A. Withorn, E. P. Mulvey, and J. Monahan (Beverly Hills, CA: Sage, 1984), p. 297.

56. *A National Survey of Individualized Education Programs (IEPs) for Handicapped Children* (Triangle Park, NC: Research Triangle Institute, 1980).

57. C. A. Scanlon, J. Arick, and N. Phelps, "Participation in the Development of the IEP: Parents' Perspective," *Exceptional Children, 47* (1981), 373.

58. S. Goldstein, B. Strickland, A. P. Turnbull, and L. Curry, "An Observational Analysis of the IEP Conference," *Exceptional Children, 46* (1980), 278–286.

59. C. E. Meyers and Jan Blacher, "Parents' Perception of Schooling for Severely Handicapped Children: Home and Family Variables," *Exceptional Children, 53* (1987), 441.

60. *Ninth Annual Report,* p. 71.

61. See, for example, Philip M. Ferguson and Dianne L. Ferguson, "Parents and Professionals," in *Introduction to Special Education,* ed. Peter Knoblock (Boston: Little, Brown, in press); Seymour B. Sarason and John Doris, *Educational Handicap, Public Policy, and Social History* (New York: Free Press, 1979); H. Rutherford Turnbull, III, and Ann P. Turnbull, eds., *Parents Speak Out: Then and Now,* 2nd ed. (Columbus, OH: Charles C. Merrill, 1985); Philip M. Ferguson and Adrienne Asch, "What We Want for Our Children: Perspectives of Parents and Adults with Disabilities," in *Schooling and Disability,* ed. Douglas Biklen, Philip M. Ferguson, and Allison Ford (Chicago: National Society for the Study of Education, in press).

62. Dorothy Kerzner Lipsky, "A Parental Perspective on Stress and Coping," *American Journal of Orthopsychiatry, 55* (1985), 616.

63. Ferguson and Asch, "What We Want for Our Children."

64. A recent version of this is reported in Lori Granger and Bill Granger, *The Magic Feather* (New York: E. P. Dutton, 1986). Diagnosticians, having decided that the Grangers' child could not read, refused to heed the parents' report that he read at home; therefore, they failed to ask him to read, but rather only subjected him to batteries of tests to explain why he could not read.

65. Ferguson and Asch, "What We Want for Our Children."

66. "Report of the United Nations Expert Group Meeting on Barrier-Free Design," *International Rehabilitation Review 26* (1975), 3.

67. Douglas Biklen, "The Culture of Poverty: Disability Images in Literature and Their Analogies in Public Policy," *Policy Studies Journal,* forthcoming.

68. Erving Goffman, *Stigma: Notes on the Management of Spoiled Identities* (Englewood Cliffs, NJ: Prentice-Hall, 1963).

69. Ved Mehta, "Personal History," *The New Yorker, 60,* 53 (1985), 61.

70. A new law, PL 99-435, states: "No air carrier may discriminate against any otherwise qualified handicapped individual, by reason of such handicap in the provision of air travel." Of course, the question here is the interpretation, should differential service be provided, as to whether it is "by reason of such handicap." *The Braille Monitor,* the National Foundation of the Blind's publication, provides extensive treatment of this topic from the perspective of an organization of the blind.

71. Richard Gross, Alan Cox, and Michael Pollay, "Early Management and Decision Making for the Treatment of Myelomeningocele," *Pediatrics* (1983).

72. Nat Hentoff, "The Awful Privacy of Baby Doe," *Atlantic Monthly* (1985), 59.

73. See particularly, Michelle Fine and Adrienne Asch, "Disability beyond Stigma: Social Interaction, Discrimination, and Activism," *Journal of Social Issues,* forthcoming; William Gliedeman and William Roth, *The Unexpected Minority: Handicapped Children in America* (New York: Harcourt Brace Jovanovich, 1980); Harlan Hahn, "Paternalism and Public Policy," *Society* (1983), 36–42; Robert Funk, "Disability Rights: From Caste to Class in the Context of Civil Rights"; and Harlan Hahn, "Civil Rights for Disabled Americans: The Formulation of a Political Agenda," in *Images of the Disabled/Disabling Images,* ed. Alan Gartner and Tom Joe (New York: Praeger, 1987).

74. Gerben DeJong and Raymond Lifchez, "Physical Disability and Public Policy," *Scientific American, 248* (1983), 40–49.

75. Louis Harris and Associates, *Disabled Americans' Self-Perceptions: Bringing Disabled Americans into the Mainstream* (New York: Louis Harris and Associates, 1986).

76. National Council on the Handicapped, *Toward Independence: A Report to the President and to the Congress of the United States* (Washington, DC: The Council, 1986), pp. 22–29.

77. For a description of these images as expressed in literature, the press, television, and the movies and a discussion of the ways in which the images play themselves out in policies in employment, education, health care, everyday living, and the treatment of newborns, see *Images of the Disabled/Disabling Images,* ed. Alan Gartner and Tom Joe (New York: Praeger, 1987).

78. "On Cases of Contagion," *New York Times,* 4 March 1987, p. A21.

79. Fine and Asch, "Disability beyond Stigma."

80. Robert Bogdan and J. Kugelmass, "Case Studies of Mainstreaming: A Symbolic Interactionist Approach to Special Schooling," in *Special Education and Societal Interests*, ed. L. Barton and S. Tomlinson (London: Croom-Helm, 1984), p. 173.

81. These are annotated "regular" diplomas which denote that the student has achieved the goals and objectives of her/his IEP. Such diplomas may reduce the pressure upon school districts to provide educational services that enable all students, including those labeled as handicapped, to earn a diploma.

And where so-called minimum competency tests are used as diploma requirements, there are questions as to adequate notice, common courses of study, and the appropriateness of the competencies used, as well as test validity. Martha M. McCarthy, "The Application of Competency Testing Mandates to Handicapped Students," *Harvard Educational Review*, 53 (1983), 146–164.

82. Granger and Granger, *The Magic Feather*, pp. 26, 27.

83. Doug Guess, Holly Anne Benson, and Ellin Siegel-Causey, "Concepts and Issues Related to Choice-Making and Autonomy among Persons with Severe Disabilities," *Journal of the Association for Persons with Severe Handicaps*, 10 (1985), 83. The authors' suggestion that the opportunity for choice-making may have a positive effect upon an individual's learning appears to be correct. Analysis of programs involving persons with severe handicaps indicates that those which involve opportunities for choice are more effective; that is, increase the subject's learning. Alan Gartner, "TASH Reflects Changes," *TASH Newsletter* (October, 1986), p. 12.

84. The approved process in carrying out disciplinary action for students with handicapping procedures involves the same clinical procedure which labeled the child; it must be used to determine whether the misconduct in question was a manifestation of the handicapping condition.

85. We favor the inclusion of all children in the public schools and believe that all can and should be educated in integrated settings. We oppose segregated schemes, such as that developed recently by the New York City Board of Education, which responded to the abuse of gay and lesbian students by setting up a separate and segregated school for them, rather than by meeting its obligation to provide safe settings for all students.

86. Walker, "Procedural Rights in the Wrong System," p. 105.

87. *A Policy-Oriented Study of Special Education's Service Delivery Systems Research* (Triangle Park, NC: Research Triangle Institute, 1984).

88. *School Psychology: A Blueprint for Training and Practice* (Minneapolis: National School Psychology Inservice Training Network, 1984), pp. 7–9.

89. Granger and Granger, *The Magic Feather*, p. xii.

90. Shepard. "The New Push for Excellence," p. 328.

91. Lipsky and Gartner, "Capable of Achievement," p. 59.

92. Walker, "Procedural Rights in the Wrong System," p. 109.

93. Marleen Pugach and Mara Sapon-Shevin, "New Agendas for Special Education Policy: What the National Reports Haven't Said," *Exceptional Children*, 53 (1987), 295–299, and Mara Sapon-Shevin, "The National Education Reports and Special Education: Implications for Students," *Exceptional Children*, 53 (1987), 300–307.

94. M. Stephen Lilly, "Lack of Focus on Special Education in Literature on Educational Reform," *Exceptional Children*, 53 (1987), 326, 327.

95. Heritage Foundation, "The Crisis: Washington Shares the Blame," *The Heritage Foundation Backgrounder* (Washington, DC: The Heritage Foundation, 1984), pp. 1, 12.

96. Sapon-Shevin, "The National Education Reports," p. 304.

97. Granger and Granger, *The Magic Feather*, p. xi.

98. *Special Education*, p. 52.

99. "Deaf, Blind Need Both Segregated and Mainstreamed Services, Experts Say," *Education Daily*, 9 December 1986, p. 4.

100. "Kennedy Institute First Special Ed School to Receive Accreditation," *Education Daily*, 26 November 1986, p. 2.

101. Michael M. Gerber, "The Department of Education's Sixth Annual Report to Congress on PL 94-142: Is Congress Getting the Full Story?" *Exceptional Children*, 51 (1984), 213.

102. Margaret C. Wang, Maynard C. Reynolds, and Herbert J. Walberg, "Rethinking Special Education," *Educational Leadership* (1986), 26–31.

103. *Educating Students with Learning Problems—A Shared Responsibility*, A Report to the Secretary (Washington, DC: Office of Special Education and Rehabilitative Services, 1986), pp. 7–9.

104. See Susan Stainback and William Stainback, "Integration versus Cooperation: A Commentary on 'Educating Children with Learning Problems: A Shared Responsibility,'" *Exceptional Children*, 54 (1987), 66–68.

105. L. Brown et al., "Toward the Realization of the Least Restrictive Educational Environments for Severely Handicapped Students," *AAESPH Review*, 2 (1977), 198.

106. "Integration is *not* mainstreaming. . . . Children [with severe handicaps] who are integrated spend the majority of each school day in a special education classroom, although they join nonhandicapped peers for certain nonacademic activities. The education needs of the two groups are too disparate to warrant putting them together for academic activities. But integration provides a supportive environment in which nonhandicapped children and severely handicapped youngsters can play and grow as well as learn from one another." Mary Frances Hanline and Carola Murray, "Integrating Severely Handicapped Children into Regular Public Schools," *Phi Delta Kappan* (December 1984), 274.

107. Bud Fredericks, "Back to the Future: Integration Revisited," *TASH Newsletter, 13,* No. 6 (1987), 1.

108. Douglas Biklen, *Achieving the Complete School: Strategies for Effective Mainstreaming* (New York: Teachers College Press, 1985).

109. Susan Stainback and William Stainback, *Educating Students with Severe Handicaps in Regular Schools* (Reston, VA: The Council for Exceptional Children, 1985).

110. Wayne Sailor, Lori Goetz, Jacki Anderson, Pam Hunt, and Kathy Gee, "Integrated Community Intensive Instruction" in *Generalization and Maintenance in Applied Settings,* ed. R. Horner, G. Dunlap, and R. Koegel (Baltimore: Paul H. Brookes, in press); Wayne Sailor, Ann Halvorsen, Jacki Anderson, Lori Goetz, Kathy Gee, Kathy Doering, and Pam Hunt, "Community Intensive Instruction" in *Education of Learners with Severe Handicaps,* ed. R. Horner, L. Meyer, and H. Fredericks (Baltimore: Paul H. Brookes, 1986).

111. Christine E. Sleeter, "Learning Disabilities: The Social Construction of a Special Education Category," *Exceptional Children, 53* (1986), 52.

112. F. Inglis, "Ideology and the Curriculum: The Value Assumptions of Systems Builders," *Policy Sciences, 18* (1985), 5.

113. Cited in Granger and Granger, *The Magic Feather,* p. v.

114. Nora Ellen Groce, *Everyone Here Spoke Sign Language: Hereditary Deafness on Martha's Vineyard* (Cambridge: Harvard University Press, 1985), p. 108.

115. Sapon-Shevin, "The National Education Reports," p. 303.

116. R. E. Snow, "Placing Children in Special Education: Some Comments," *Educational Researcher, 13* (1984), 13.

117. The statement is available from the Advocacy Center for the Elderly and Disabled, 1001 Howard Avenue, New Orleans, LA 70113.

118. Thomas S. Kuhn, ed., *The Structure of Scientific Revolutions* (Chicago: University of Chicago Press, 1962).

119. William Stainback and Nancy Stainback, "A Rationale for the Merger of Special and Regular Education," *Exceptional Children, 51* (1984), 109.

120. B. Algozzine and L. Maheady, "When All Else Fails, Teach!" *Exceptional Children, 52* (1985), 498.

121. Our focus in this article has been on school services. However, we cannot fail to note that whatever the many inadequacies of the education for students with handicapping conditions, services for those who have "aged out" of the PL 94-142 entitlement are far fewer. For example, a recent article notes that while approximately 50,000 mentally impaired students, those with IQs of 70 and below, leave school each year, there are only "roughly 5,000 places in training and support programs nationwide. . . ." William

Celis, III, "Generation of Retarded Youth Emerges from Public Schools—But Little Awaits," *Wall Street Journal,* 16 January 1987, p. 25.

122. *What Works: Research about Teaching and Learning* (Washington, DC: U.S. Department of Education, 1986), p. 59.

123. Ronald Edmonds, "Effective Schools for the Urban Poor," *Educational Leadership, 37* (1979), 15–27, and "Some Schools Work and More Can," *Social Policy, 9,* No. 5 (1979), 26–31.

124. Joseph R. Jenkins and Linda M. Jenkins, *Cross Age and Peer Tutoring Help for Children with Learning Problems* (Reston, VA: The Council for Exceptional Children, 1981).

125. R. T. Osguthorpe and T. E. Scruggs, "Special Education Students as Tutors: A Review and Analysis," *Remedial and Special Education, 7,* No. 4 (1986), 15–26.

126. Alan Gartner, Mary Conway Kohler, and Frank Riessman, *Children Teach Children: Learning by Teaching* (New York: Harper & Row, 1971).

127. *Japanese Education Today* (Washington, DC: U.S. Department of Education, 1987).

128. Margaret C. Wang and Herbert J. Walberg, eds., *Adapting Instruction to Individual Differences* (Berkeley, CA: McCutchan, 1985).

129. Frank J. Laski, Thomas K. Gilhool, and Stephen F. Gold, "A Legal Duty to Provide Effective Schooling," Adaptive Instruction Conference, 3 June 1983, p. 8.

130. Margaret C. Wang, Stephen Peverly, and Robert Randolph, "An Investigation of the Implementation and Effects of a Full-Time Mainstreaming Program," *Remedial and Special Education, 5* (1984), 21–32. The authors of this article were responsible for the introduction of the Adaptive Learning Environments Model (ALEM) program into the New York City public schools when, respectively, they were Executive Director and Chief Administrator for Program Development, Division of Special Education. We did this at the behest of the Chancellor, Frank J. Macchiarola, whose support of the program expressed his belief that all students can learn and that it was the obligation of the school system to enable that to happen. Basically, the ALEM program involved the full-time mainstreaming of students certified as handicapped in a program that adapted curricula to each student's needs, paced learning at an individual rate, and taught students to take responsibility for their own learning.

131. Walter Lippmann, "The Reliability of Intelligence Tests," *The New Republic* (1922), reprinted in *The I.Q. Controversy,* ed. N. J. Block and Gerald Dworkin (New York: Random House, 1976), p. 17.

132. Edmonds, "Some Schools Work and More Can," p. 29.

Part Two

Issues and Innovations in Special Education Practice

Chapter Five

Transition Issues and Practices

5.1

Generations of Hope:

Parental Perspectives on the Transitions of Their Children With Severe Retardation From School to Adult Life

Philip M. Ferguson, Dianne L. Ferguson, and David Jones

Transitions within families are socially constructed processes that need to be understood in both their historical and their cultural context. This study explored how parents interpret the events and relationships surrounding the transition of their children with severe disabilities from school to adult life. The study used qualitative techniques to collect and analyze data from two sets of parents grouped according to their children's ages. Results indicated that the parents interviewed tended to perceive three distinct types of transition: bureaucratic, family life, and adult status. Generational patterns of parental response to these transitions are discussed in terms of professional relationships and self-reliance. A matrix of these response patterns is presented. The findings suggested several ways in which parent-professional cooperation around transition events might be improved.

DESCRIPTORS: families, parent-professional relations, parents, qualitative research

The transition from childhood to adulthood is an important process that occurs, in some form or other, in almost every culture. The rituals change and the expectations vary, but members of a society seem to need some method of demarcating for themselves just who is an adult and who is not. In our own culture, graduation from high school has come to serve as one of the more significant rites of passage indicating a commencement of life as an adult. Currently, around 75% of the students who start high school finish, although the figures remain troublingly skewed along racial lines (Boyer, 1983). Even with youth whose formal schooling will continue for many

more years, most parents still find the transition of a child from high school to be a time of important symbolism and strong emotions. Immense pride in "launching" a new adult into the world must often compete with a sense of uneasiness about the future and a certain wistfulness for the child who has grown up so quickly. As with all rites of passage, it is a stressful time.

For parents of children with severe disabilities, the stress associated with the process of transition from high school to work and adult life can become even greater. For these parents, graduation of a child from the public school system is a prospect whose risks often seem to overshadow the rewards (Searl, 1985). In our society, most individuals with severe disabilities face an adult world of "make work" day programs and endless wait lists. However, the challenge of inadequate services is not new, for parents have faced these issues in schools as well. What is new for parents in the transition of their children to adult status is the combination of erratic or nonexistent community services with the application of cultural norms that typically include less active parental involvement in the daily life of the child (Ferguson & Ferguson, 1986).

This complicated challenge of greater need and reduced involvement is one of the reasons why the transition of children with severe disabilities to adult status is uniquely stressful within the life-span of each family. However, the transition experience is also historically new for this specific generation of

This research was supported in part by the U.S. Department of Education Grant G008430061, Office of Special Education and Rehabilitation Services, Division of Personnel Preparation. The content and opinions expressed herein do not necessarily reflect the position or policy of the U.S. Department of Education and no official endorsement should be inferred.

Ferguson, P., Ferguson, D., and Jones, D. (1988). Generations of hope: Parental perspectives on the transitions of their children with severe retardation from school to adult life. *Journal of the Association for Persons with Severe Handicaps, 13*(3), 177–187. Reprinted by permission.

parents. There are at least two aspects to this generational difference. First, historians tell us that the cultural norms surrounding the transition of adulthood have themselves changed dramatically over time (Anderson, 1971; Modell, Furstenberg, & Hershberg, 1978). As part of the larger society, parents of children with severe disabilities presumably do not escape the influence of these more general historical patterns. Second, and more narrowly, this is probably the first generation of parents to have their children's transition to adult status emphasized as important despite the presence of severe disabilities. Until recently, many families presumably experienced very little expectation that such a transition would occur at all as their children approached the age of 21. Instead, the child might attend a series of "cradle to grave," segregated programs provided by either state agencies or private, nonprofit organizations (often begun by parent advocates). The point is certainly not that earlier generations of parents had an easier time of it. The absence of culturally normative transitions within the life course of a family creates its own kind of stress (Neugarten, 1976). Rather, the point is simply that raising a child is not a timeless process, once and for all the same. Perhaps even more than for the general population, the transition expectations and experiences of parents with children labeled severely retarded may differ not only across families, but across decades as well.

The study reported here explored the differences in interpretation of transition between two generations of families. The study did not go more than two or three decades into the past. However, those 20 or so years have seen momentous changes in the policies and programs that govern educational services for people with severe disabilities. Indeed, the advent of the Education for All Handicapped Children Act (P.L. 94-142) arguably provides the most obvious and the most important single reference point for the sociohistorical study of the family and disability since World War II. The study also explored the interpretations of parents currently involved in the events of leaving school and entering adult life. The aim of the study was three-fold: (a) to describe how at least some parents of children with severe disabilities constructed the meaning of events by which those children became adults, (b) to compare any changes in those constructed meanings over two generations of parents, and (c) to consider how this knowledge of parental perspectives might lead to better parent-professional collaboration in planning successful transitions.

METHOD

The terms "qualitative" or "ethnographic research" are by now probably well known to most researchers and practitioners within special education and mental retardation. However, for scholars and practitioners professionally trained in the dominant tradition of quantitative techniques, the theoretical heritage of "naturalistic inquiry" (Lincoln & Guba, 1985), as well as the details of how such research actually gathers and analyzes data, may be less familiar. This section cannot provide more than a cursory reference to many of the fundamental assumptions and procedural conventions of qualitative research. Fortunately, there are now available a number of excellent articles and texts that cover both theory and practice in much more detail (Agar, 1980; Blumer, 1969; Bogdan & Biklen, 1982; Glaser & Strauss, 1967; Lincoln & Guba, 1985; Lofland & Lofland, 1984; Smith & Heshusius, 1986; Taylor & Bogdan, 1984).

Generally speaking, the techniques used in qualitative research are not efficient ways to produce predictive, generalizable statements about how to better control designated outcomes. Although there is some debate among qualitative researchers themselves about how "testable" a "grounded theory" should be (Glaser & Strauss, 1967; Lincoln & Guba, 1985), this type of research generally does not try to operationalize the world. What the techniques can do is provide the kind of information that anthropologists have called "thick description" (Geertz, 1973): a multilayered account that relishes complexity, recognizes nuance, and strives for understanding over prediction.

A prominent educational anthropologist has described ethnography as simply "the science of cultural description" (Wolcott, 1975, p. 111). Although not an ethnography as such, our study did use "ethnographic" or "qualitative" techniques to interview parents of children with severe disabilities about their perspectives on the events surrounding their children leaving school and/or turning 21.

Participants

Fifteen families agreed to be interviewed for this project. One of the families had three children labeled severely retarded, so the 15 families included a total of 17 youth or adults with such a label. For 11 families, the mother was the sole interviewee, although in five of these this was because the mother was either divorced or widowed. In one case a single father was the only interviewee. In the three remaining cases, both parents were interviewed together. An initial list of potential families was identified through several sources: a state-wide parent advocacy group, adult service agencies, and personal knowledge of the investigators. Additional families were identified through the "snowball effect" of asking initial participants for names of others who might be interested in being interviewed. All of the families had at least one child who at some time had been described as "severely mentally retarded" or a roughly equivalent term (e.g., "trainable" or "profoundly retarded"). In the case of the family with three identified children, the initial recruitment was prompted by the two younger children who were both labeled severely retarded. The older labeled child in this family actually fell between the two age ranges sought, but was viewed as developmentally disabled and was discussed as part of the interview along with the other two children.

For the historical comparison, the families were divided into two "generations" based on the age of the labeled child. Six families composed the "pre-P.L.

94-142" generation; their children ranged in age from 34 to 40. Two of these parents still worked at least part time and two others did volunteer work for programs involving their adult children. The "post-P.L. 94-142" generation included nine families whose children ranged in age from 15 to 23 (not counting the individual mentioned previously, who was 30 years old). The participants in this study were not randomly chosen. On the contrary, the research design used a process of "purposive sampling" (Glaser & Strauss, 1967), whereby key informants are selected precisely because they possess certain characteristics and information. Nonetheless, the final group of participants did represent a fairly broad range of socioeconomic backgrounds, and lived in urban, suburban, and rural settings. Their participation in parent groups varied across both generations. One parent in each group had a child with physical as well as mental disabilities. All of the families were Caucasian. Information about the people interviewed, listed by pseudonyms and grouped by generation, is presented in Table 1.

Table 1

Participant descriptions.

Pseudonym	Age of child	Comments	No. of interviews	Interviewer
Margaret Lewis[a]	40	Retired. Single. Began a provider agency.	1	PF
Paula Rice[a]	38	Single. Works part-time in an office.	1	DF
Lori Sargent[a]	35	Single. Began a provider agency.	1	DJ
Pam Wilson[a]	34	Retired.	1	DJ
Bill/Betty Frank[a]	40	Retired.	1	PF
Joe/Peg Sanders[a]	34	Retired professionals.	1	DJ
Rose Tillman[b]	22	Professional couple.	2	DF
Janet Swinburne[b]	21, 23, 30	Works in family.	1	PF
Diane Mitchell[b]	22	Returned to school. Does not work.	2	PF/DJ
Gwen Simpson[b]	22	Works part-time.	2	DF
Steve/Betty Richards[b]	18	Both work.	2	DF/DJ
John Thompson[b]	18	Retired. Single.	1	DJ
Amy Roberts[b]	22	Single. Does not work.	1	PF
Karen Baker[b]	15	Single. Domestic worker.	1	DF
Sharon Davis[b]	21	Married. Does not work.	1	PF

[a]Pre-P.L. 94-142 generation.
[b]Post-P.L. 94-142 generation.

Data Gathering Procedures

Data were collected over a period of about 1 year, primarily through the use of in-depth, semistructured interviews. All of the interviews were conducted by one of the three authors, with each doing at least five. The interviews were structured in two ways. First, parent and interviewer agreed in advance that the main topic was to be the general "transition" experience surrounding a child leaving school and/or becoming an adult, or the participation and planning for such events. Second, each of the interviewers used a very general "interview guide," to ensure that all three interviewers covered more or less the same basic information. Following an initial round of interviews, a more specific interview guide was constructed to gain better topical continuity as themes began to emerge. This latter guide is presented in Table 2. Beyond this, there was no interview protocol. Specific questions were not structured, and the sequence and format of the interview questions were determined by context and the experiences of the individual families, together with the judgment of the

Table 2

Expanded interview guide.

1. Changes in program or routine at transition.
2. Changes in agencies and bureaucracies.
3. Changes in perception of person's status as adult.
4. Relations with current professionals.
5. Characterization of history of experiences with professionals.
6. Changes in person's family role.
7. Changes (or lack thereof) in parent roles: person and professionals.
8. Daily schedule.
9. How describe/explain person to new acquaintances and neighbors.
10. Probe "helpfulness" of professionals.
11. Characterize (list adjectives) person's life.
12. Expectations of parent involvement/activity and responsibility: current and in 10 years.
13. Relations, perceptions, and "transition" of siblings.
14. Changes in the field and parents' response.

interviewer about how best to proceed at any given moment in the interview.

Most interviews lasted at least 1½ hours. Four families were interviewed twice. All families were contacted again for the member check interviews described below. Most of the interviews occurred in the parents' homes, with a few taking place in settings such as coffee shops or restaurants and one done at the home of the interviewer. In some cases, the interviewers wrote field notes or extended "observer comments" about something that occurred during the interview, a description of the setting, or other observations and reactions. All of the interviews and field notes were tape recorded and transcribed into a mainframe computer. Altogether, over 480 single-spaced pages of interview transcripts and observations were gathered for analysis.

The analysis of the transcripts and field notes adhered to the procedures commonly associated with the sociological tradition of symbolic interactionism (Blumer, 1969; Bogdan & Biklen, 1982; Taylor & Bogdan, 1984). Unlike most quantitative research, qualitative data analysis usually begins while the data are still being collected (Lofland & Lofland, 1984). Each step of analysis, then, helps shape and focus subsequent data collection. For example, the expanded interview guide was revised from the initial guide along lines suggested by an analysis of some of the initial interviews.

Data Analysis Procedures

The interviews were repeatedly sorted into increasingly theoretical categories identified by the researchers. This analytic process used a powerful software program called *QUALOG* (Shelly & Sibert, 1983), which is specially designed to handle the steps of categorizing mountains of words into more manageable piles. As with statistical analysis, the use of such powerful computers in textual analysis does not in and of itself increase the rigor of the techniques. However, the increasing availability of these relatively sophisticated text editors in qualitative research does save enormous amounts of time and thereby makes additional analysis more practicable. Moreover, the program creates a type of "audit trail" (Lincoln & Guba, 1985), whereby the various stages of indexing and analysis can be reproduced to show how the categorization of individual sections of data changed and interpretation evolved. Although not precisely analogous to the notions of reliability, audit trails do allow the potential for an independent analyst to recreate the steps of analysis followed in a qualitative research project and then make a judgment of the reasonableness of those steps.

The analysis proceeded through three separate levels of sorting and interpretation during this project. First, after completing two or three interviews, each researcher indexed the initial transcripts using descriptive labels and concrete properties. These independently derived sets of categories were then compared and collapsed into a single index jointly agreed upon by all three researchers. A second stage of indexing included additional interviews and began the search for "grounded theories," looking for recurrent properties and more abstract themes that ran throughout the transcripts. Again, each interviewer indexed his or her own transcripts. However, this time we also exchanged the transcripts as we identified themes, and double-checked the "trustworthiness" (Lincoln & Guba, 1985) of each other's reading. This is actually one of the modes of "triangulation" suggested by Denzin (1978) as a way of producing more credible results. Finally, a third stage of analysis began late in the data collection and continued after all interviews were completed. These themes were even more abstracted from the data and were the product of weekly project meetings, where proposed theories were discussed and defended through reference to the transcripts.

At the heart of this process is the interpretivist's conviction that facts are always silent. They never speak for themselves; we always give them voice in the language of our assumptions. Theories emerge from our data only as we ask them to, grounded in the transcripts but nurtured into patterns of insight and explanation that we admittedly help create. It was only at this third stage, for example, that the patterns of interaction among the types of transition described later were fully perceived.

Member Checks

Once the tentative final coding was completed, participants were contacted again, either by phone or letter. Each was asked to react to a summary of our findings. Did the analysis seem to fit their own experience? How did it differ? Did it "ring true" to them? These member checks were short and confirmatory. It should be noted as well that careful interviewers conduct "member checks" constantly during their actual interviews, verifying interpretations, returning to questions, probing for expanded answers to confirm an impression. However, using member checks as a final stage of analysis provides an essential technique for making sure one's grounded theories do not take flight. In this project, none of the participants disputed the findings, and aside from a few questions regarding emphasis or wording, most found the analysis useful.

RESULTS

We commonly refer to *the* transition process of a child becoming an adult. For the parents interviewed in this research project, however, there were three distinct but simultaneous transition processes associated with their children turning 21: (a) bureaucratic transitions, (b) family life transitions, and (c) status transitions. Each transition seems better understood as a separate process, rather than as one aspect of a singular course of events. Moreover, the bureaucratic and family life transitions each encompassed its own continuum of parental response patterns. Figure 1 presents these types of transition together with their associated issues and parental response continua.

Bureaucratic Transitions

Of the three types of transition that parents discussed, bureaucratic transitions showed the strongest evidence of generational variation. By bureaucratic transition we mean the process whereby the agencies and professionals involved with a family change from representatives of the special education system to representatives of the adult service system. Included here were all of the parents' descriptions of professional relationships with their families and the patterns of parental responses to these professionals.

The generational variation in this category demonstrates how the absence of a transition process can be as disruptive and powerful as the presence of

1. Bureaucratic Transitions and Patterns of Response to Professionals

| Abandonment | Surrender | Assimilation | Engagement |

2. Family Life Transitions and Patterns of Response to Family Needs

| Passive/Resigned | Forced/Resentful | Collective |

3. Status Transitions
   Adulthood and Control

Figure 1
Transition types and patterns of parental response.

an unsatisfactory outcome to that process. Parents in the older generation often recalled this bureaucratic transition as either noticeable in its absence or persistent in its ambiguity. For many of these parents, the problem was not the change in professional relationships, but rather the lack of any relationship at all. At best the process was ambiguous: repeated exclusions from existing services followed by ad hoc accommodations by the parents. When new agencies entered it tended, in parental recollections, to be in a tentative manner with professionals who were often pessimistic that anything could be done.

There is much more clarity to the bureaucratic processes faced by parents of the newer generation. Unfortunately, from the parents' perspective, the clarity has more to do with endings than beginnings; that is, there is certainty that special education services will end, but great uncertainty that adult services will begin to fill the gap. In comparing the two generations, we detected a sense among some of the older parents that the ambiguity and instability of the services, or even their total absence, at least lent an ironic consistency to the process with which they could approach their children's needs as they grew older. For the newer generation, the incomplete reforms and the partial service mandates seemed to end suddenly, if predictably, when the child turned 21. In response to their experiences with bureaucratic transitions, parents described at least four patterns of how they interpreted their relationships with professionals: abandonment, surrender, assimilation, and engagement. These are best conceived as continuous rather than discrete patterns, with many of the interviews encompassing elements of more than one pattern. Keeping the patterns conceptually separate for description, however, will allow a subsequent comparison of bureaucratic and family life transitions.

Surrender to professionals. Although not as extreme as the "abandonment" response, surrender to expertise needs to come first in historical order. Some parents described a relationship pattern with professionals that involved their repeated deferrals to professional opinion and explanation for what might otherwise have appeared to be inadequate services. Elements of this pattern emerged in the relationships described by parents from both generations. Indeed, given the aura of expertise and "professionalism" that envelopes special education, rehabilitation, and family support in general (Lasch, 1977; Sarason, 1981), it would be surprising if evidence of such parental submission had not been fairly common. Nonetheless, it is also true that this pattern was much stronger in the older generation than the newer. The strength

was not a numerical one; nearly the same number of parents from each generation expressed at least some versions of this surrender pattern. When parents from the older generation described this type of response, however, it tended to be more pervasive as an interpretive framework for all professional relationships.

Bill and Betty Frank exemplified this unquestioning acceptance of professional opinion. Their son was not in any day program at all. Moreover, the Franks were admittedly not pushing very hard to find one unless it was recreational. After all, said Betty, "they [children with severe retardation] will always be childlike—and this is from people that know, that are in this field, that are experts." Of course, most current professionals would respond that such attitudes are at least 20 years out of date, which is precisely when the Franks were in the midst of an ambiguous bureaucratic transition where the service "system" presented few options for programs and even fewer hopes of success. It was a formative time for the Franks as far as establishing a pattern within which to react to the professionals' involvement in the adult life of their son. Surrender, once offered, is hard to withdraw.

Abandonment by professionals. The Franks received little help and accepted the explanation that little could be given. They reported the lack of services for their son not so much with anger as with a kind of solemn acquiescence. Other parents, especially some from the newer generation, interpreted the lack of assistance during this period of change as an intentional abandonment by professionals who could have helped but chose not to do so.

Diane Mitchell, a newer generation parent, typified this pattern of relationship. Her child, like the Frank's son, was also at home with no day program. However, Diane actively rejected the professionals' explanations of failure. What the two types of relationship have in common is the implicit powerlessness of the parent in any relationship with the service bureaucracy. For the Franks that was proper; for Diane Mitchell it was improper but inevitable.

Mitchell repeatedly voiced her disinclination to work with the agencies who would normally develop program placements for her son. From her interpretation, the bureaucratic transition was marked by professionals who gave up:

I don't know, it just seems real sad to me that they didn't help me. I don't know . . . but what we should chuck the whole system. . . . I just got so burned out, it's a wonder it didn't drive me nuts. . . . I haven't done anything in years because there was no place he could go. I mean I've taken him to my mother-in-law's funeral and he sat in the car. He's been to my oldest boy's wedding and he sat in the car. I would have liked to have gone out and, you know, just done something. But there was never anywhere to leave him.

Assimilation with professionals. Often associated with an absence of a bureaucratic transition, a third pattern of response found some parents who felt forced to become professionals themselves. Of the four patterns of professional relationships, this was the one most clearly associated with one generation over the other. Parents belonging to the older generation repeatedly described how they responded to the scarcity or absence of professionals by gradually assuming that role in the provision of needed services.

The individual stories varied in specifics but followed a similar pattern. Margaret Lewis started a program in a basement and now runs Comfort Haven, a "lifetime care" facility that serves over 70 people with mental retardation. Paula Rice helped start a workshop, mainly for her son, that eventually ended up with over 60 "clients." Laurie Sargent began a recreation program for her multiply handicapped son. She moved on to establish two group homes and become one of the major residential service providers in her community. Her explanation is simple: "If you wait for the bureaucracy to come to you, they might not ever get there. And then, if they do come to you, they might not do it the way you want it done."

Engagement with professionals. There was a tendency for this final relationship pattern to emerge more often in the interviews with newer generation parents. The pattern took one of two forms. On the one hand, there were parents who saw themselves working eagerly with professionals in constructive patterns of active involvement. In such cases, the similarity with assimilation response patterns became much closer. On the other hand, there were parents who tended to see the process in much more adversarial terms. In fact, many of these parents' accounts switched from one form of engagement to the other, but reported consistent activity in the process as both an advocate and parent. The unity in this pattern came in the interpretive division that ultimately persisted in expectations of separate but equal parent and professional responsibilities. In some cases, the perceived loss of clarity in the distribution of professional responsibilities in the transition process evoked strong statements of engagement regardless

of how specific professionals behaved in specific situations. As Gwen Simpson stated,

I've heard [a case manager] say that "these parents need to back off at this [transition] stage of the kid's life." But if you do, nothing is going to happen for your kid. You can't afford to back off at this point. This is when your kid needs you more than ever. . . . I mean I feel like we're a threat to these professionals. And it's very understandable. . . . I mean, they're not doing their job.

Family Life Transitions

The bureaucratic transition process, whether clear or ambiguous, symmetrical or skewed, was seen by the parents we talked to as something that occurred outside the family. It was something done by professionals and the agencies for whom they worked. Parents had to relate to those professionals, but the key stages of the process were essentially extrafamilial. A second major type of transition might be understood as the intrafamilial counterpart to the bureaucratic transition.

Family life transitions cover all the changes and/or disruptions in established routines and accepted responsibilities that make daily life manageable within family units. In the context of this study, the relevant changes and/or disruptions were those associated with or occasioned by a young person's move from school to adult services. If parents have organized their schedules around a child being in school for 6 to 8 hours a day, the sudden need to change that schedule can be extremely disruptive to family routines. Schools are required to provide transportation; adult programs are not. That aspect alone can radically alter the demands upon a parent's time.

Unlike the examples of generational variation that characterized the parental construction of bureaucratic transitions, the response to family life disruptions remained fairly constant across the two groups of parents. Certainly, the two generations differed in the clusters of specific changes that occurred within family life. The continuity arose in the disruptive significance of those changes for families in which they occurred. Even parents whose children were still in school often anticipated this type of disruption as the most upsetting transition of all. Words such as "panicky" and "scared" were often used by these parents when wondering what they would do if no acceptable day program were found. Steve and Betty Richards both work. As is true of many families these days, both incomes were necessary. The Richards had only recently learned how long the wait list for vocational services was in their community. They discussed the prospect of their 18-year-old leaving school in 3 years with no day program of any kind in brief but plaintive desperation. "It would be very, very difficult. It just can't be." Rose Tillman, who also works, wondered aloud about what the options would be in such a situation. "What would I do if I got Mike back home without a day program? Would I have to quit work?"

The greatest fear of the Richards and Tillman was of the disruption to their lives that would occur if there were no day programming at all for their children. A failure in the move of their daughter or son from school to work would lead to a failure in the routine of family life. What was most important about the process of family life transitions, however, was that even "successful" program outcomes did not guarantee successful outcomes for family life. Upon graduation from high school, Gwen Simpson's daughter, Mary, began a model program of supported employment, working in the community for meaningful wages. By all the usual standards, Mary's transition outcome was judged a success. However, the changing hours of Mary's job played havoc with the Simpson household routine. From this perspective, Gwen found the outcome to Mary's graduation much less successful:

The hours [of Mary's job] are just obnoxious. I mean my husband can't even keep track of them. . . . It makes our whole life so much more hectic than it was before, trying to arrange our life around her schedule, while before, when she was in school, it was kind of all set and you knew. She was gone during the day when we were gone during the day, and it was nice.

Just as parents related to professionals within the context of bureaucratic transitions, they interpreted their own responsibilities within the context of the transitions of family needs. All parents face inevitable changes with their children's departure from school. For most of the parents we interviewed, those changes usually were seen as imposing new burdens on themselves. The individual perceptions of these burdens were certainly associated with the pattern of relationships that a parent reported having (or anticipating) with the various professionals. However, there also emerged a distinct continuum of parental response patterns to these perceived intrafamilial burdens. The responses almost always involved some aspect of a parent's interpretation of self-reliance. We detected three separate patterns of self-reliance woven through the parents' discussion of the family life transition process.

Again, the claim is not that each parent verbalized only one pattern of self-reliance, or that the patterns themselves were clearly divided. Rather, the conceptual separation remains useful for understanding any of the larger generational variations or similarities.

Resigned and passive self-reliance. Some parents from both generations reacted to the turmoil and disruptions of post-school services (or lack thereof) with fatigue and resignation. The new set of problems created by an adult service system that seemed chaotic compared with the mandated procedures and programs of the public school system struck them as one more phase of never ending isolated struggles. When we talked to Janet Swinburne, her third child with severe disabilities was about to graduate from school. The second child had graduated a year earlier and was sitting at home. One job placement had failed, but another had been promised. It had been months since the Swinburnes had heard any news of a new placement: "The case manager told me to just keep calling them every so often. . . . But I don't like to complain. I really don't. My husband might disagree, because I do complain to him." Such a reaction is more passive than blasé. It is not that Ms. Swinburne is apathetic about her son's life, but just that "deep inside of me . . . I feel like I ought to be able to solve my own problems."

Sharon Davis provided another example with even clearer expressions of the "burnout" that seemed to accompany this pattern of self-reliance. She anticipated that burdens of care and advocacy would fall to her once more when her son graduated from school. Her remarks illustrate the resignation, tinged with resentment, with which she approached that eventuality:

[I] have been involved with John's programs—really, I think, one of the most involved parents all along. And I don't regret it because our primary focus as parents is that I would be there [taking care of] the children's educations and their growing up. But as he is reaching adulthood, I am tired of it. I don't look forward to this level of involvement through his entire life. When he graduates, my goal is that I graduate. I'm hanging by my fingertips right now. . . . We need to be in there, but it isn't with the fervor, enthusiasm, and joy that I approached preschool things or early education things. I am doing it because I have a responsibility to do it. I want his future to have some solid foundations, but I want my involvement to end also.

After her son graduated, Sharon Davis' fears seemed justified. An initial vocational placement fell through. She felt forced to find a solution, any solution, that would address her family's basic need of daytime "coverage" for her son. Collective advocacy for integrated supported work became a luxury. Self-reliance came in the form of an isolated scramble to get something stable and secure for her son. Perhaps nothing symbolized Sharon Davis' sense of resignation as well as her actual resignation from the advocacy group to which she had belonged. The failed process of family life transition forced her to abandon her dreams for her son's future and accept the logic of the status quo: Something is better than nothing. In the end, it is important to recognize that this pattern of resigned and passive self-reliance is not so much an example of learned helplessness as of "learned isolation."

Forced and resented self-reliance. The comments of Sharon Davis also suggest a second pattern of self-reliance. This pattern maintains the isolation of the previous pattern, but replaces the passivity with an active sense of injustice. This pattern also cuts across generational lines. Specifics of the family disruption vary, but both older and newer parents often interpreted the process as one of exploitation and necessity. These parents reported working very hard and aggressively to create their own family solutions to the disruptions created by inadequate services. They said they did it (or would when the time came) because they had to. They saw the problem as theirs to deal with, but resented the isolation and effort that continually was required of them. Many parents said similar things in slightly different ways. "They're always laying it on me." "If I don't do it, it won't get done." "I guess it's true that a kid like mine will take my involvement for the rest of my life. It feels like a lot of work. I really do want somebody else to do that at some point in time."

One of the themes that emerged in this pattern of resented self-reliance was that parents felt confused about the loss of cultural norms that could otherwise have guided their continued involvement in their adult child's life. It has long been culturally normative for parents, especially mothers, to be involved with schools on behalf of their school age children (Arnot, 1984; Lightfoot, 1977). The perceived necessity for their continued resolution of the problems in the lives of their adult children, however, runs counter to many of these parents' assumptions about the accepted outcome of child rearing. When, they ask, will my nest be empty? Given that the nest remains at least partially full, where are the role models for these parents to follow?

Natural and collective self-reliance. This final pattern of self-reliance also occurred among parents of both generations. The main difference in this pattern was the replacement of the sense of isolation with a strong sense of social support. When following this pattern, parents spoke of reliance as part of a group rather than individually. These parents said they sought informal solutions by calling upon the resources of their social network when facing transitions in family life. The self-reliance in this pattern was the mutual reliance of parents on each other instead of upon professionals. Rose Tillman addressed the disruptions in her family life as systemic problems that require long-term group advocacy as well as short-term, immediate responses. "Bill calls it my cheerleading routine: I get on the phone and that's what I have to do. I'm encouraging people." Laurie Sargent, one of the older generation, said her approach has not changed for 20 years. As she saw it, "Parents have all these support systems out there. . . . I really think people need to be more involved and not let the professionals do it."

For some parents, this collective self-reliance seemed to have the character of a crusade. This "crusadership" (Darling & Darling, 1982) continues to promise eventual relief; that is, the group's efforts will improve the system so that family life is not so unnecessarily disrupted. But the "rightness" of the crusade also implies the responsibility to make the effort. Relying on others to help address the disruptions in your own family entails the willingness to reciprocate when other families need your support. Gwen Simpson captured this mixture of reliance and responsibility by imbuing the informal efforts of herself and her friends with a sense of community and determined pragmatism. The immediate topic of conversation was finding jobs for their sons and daughters:

I think parents have just as much responsibility in finding work placements as professionals do. I really do. . . . We would never have had any jobs [for adults with disabilities] in this community if we didn't have this network system working out there, telling people about supported work. . . . An organization can't do it. . . . They don't know the people. They don't have the networking system that parents do. I just really think it takes parents to make some of these things happen.

Status Transitions

Parents interpreted the bureaucratic transition process as something that happened to the professionals with whom they or their children were involved. Parents interpreted the process of family life transitions, on the other hand, as something that happened to them as the head of their families. Regardless of what happened to professionals or themselves, however, the parents we spoke to also discussed a third type of transition. This transition was the process as constructed by the parent whereby the status of a son or daughter changed from child to adult.

This type of transition was complicated in the parents' interpretations. Adulthood is a cultural status as well as a familial one; there are both public and private criteria, official and unofficial perceptions. Parents found adulthood for their young people with disabilities to be more than a simple outcome to a straightforward series of events. Yet they also recognized those events (e.g., leaving school, turning 21, getting a job, and perhaps moving away from home) as important cultural markers of passage in children's lives.

For the parents with whom we talked, the adult status for their children with disabilities was not something that they, as parents, could permit or deny; professionals could not award it or take it away. For some parents this adult status was prevented by physiology. For others this status was gradually built up by the young people themselves and for others still, it was a complex amalgamation of parental feelings that wanted to encourage independence without ignoring vulnerability; to applaud the adult and protect the child (Ferguson, Ferguson, & Jones, 1987).

For most of the parents we interviewed, the issue of adult status was really an issue of control, not independence. That is, as parents interpreted the process, the status transitions of their sons and daughters often became translated from a "child-or-adult" question to a "parent control-or-professional control" question. Margaret Lewis talked of the pressure the county case managers placed on her and other parents to move their children out into community group homes and apartments. For Ms. Lewis it was a question of stability and loss of control. Once "locked" into the system, the children were at the mercy of professional strangers, not family and friends:

> I don't think any of us want to totally control our children's lives as far as what they do by the day. But for the future, we do. . . . Ultimately the family has to be involved. This total schism between family and the retarded person is unnatural. It doesn't happen in any other part of your family.

DISCUSSION

It is important to be clear about what the interviews show. Not every parent talked about all three types of transitions. Even when parents did talk about two or three different types of transition, as most did, they usually would emphasize one or another as paramount in their memory or anticipation. Finally, in some cases the parents were much more ambiguous than the categorization scheme presented here might indicate. However, by outlining the sometimes fuzzy distinctions of parental interpretation, the categorization scheme presented does serve to highlight both directions for future research and directions for defining new roles between parents and professionals that will facilitate productive engagement.

Generational Variation

For most of the parents we interviewed, the events involved in bureaucratic transition and family life transition processes described here held much more practical significance than the more abstract passage of a son or daughter from child to adult status. The status of the child with severe disabilities was certainly important to the parents; usually, it proved to be the most inclusive context in which they framed their discussions. However, the more pragmatic concerns of how the family will cope (family life transitions) and who will be there to help (bureaucratic transitions) seemed ultimately much more revealing of how families really differ in their approaches to the post-school lives of their children. Furthermore, the generational variation of those patterns of parental interpretations underscores the importance of a historical context for our professional approaches to families.

A Matrix of Transition Patterns

Within both the bureaucratic and the family life transitions there were characteristic patterns of parental interpretations of events and responsibilities. Those patterns themselves were related to each other; that is, the pattern of professional relationships described by a parent tended to be associated with the pattern of self-reliance described by that parent. The association of those two patterns provides a typology of generational change in how these two classes of transition have been interpreted by parents. This typology is presented as a generational matrix in Figure 2.

Within each of the "cells" of the matrix appear the initials of the parents who provided examples of the combination of response patterns of that cell. Again, the force of the analysis is not numerical. Many parents appear in more than one cell. Theoretically, a cell with only one parent example could be just as "significant" qualitatively as another cell with 15 different parents. The listing does show how the analysis broke down parents' response patterns to

		Abandonment	Surrender	Assimilation	Engagement
Response Patterns to Family Needs	Collective			* L. S. * M. L.	** R. T. ** G. S. ** K. B. * J/P. S. ** A. R.
	Forced/ Resentful	** S/B. R. ** D. M. ** S. D. * L. S. * P. W.	* P. W. * M. L.	* L. S. * M. L. * P. R. * J/P. S.	** R. T. ** G. S. ** K. B. ** S. D. * P. W.
	Resigned/ Passive	** D. M. ** S. O. ** J. S. ** A. R.	* B/B. F. ** J. T. ** J. S. ** S/B. R.		

* = PRE-P. L. 94-142 GENERATION   ** = POST-P. L. 94-142 GENERATION

Figure 2

Generational variation in patterns of parental response to bureaucratic and family life transitions

professionals and adds some weight to the interpretation of generational trends presented here.

As discussed earlier, the most distinct patterns of generational variation occurred in parental descriptions of their relationships with professionals from the human service bureaucracies. The tendency of parents in the generation whose children left school before P.L. 94-142 was either surrender or assimilation. For parents whose children had just left school or soon would, the tendency was toward abandonment or engagement. On the other hand, parental patterns of self-reliance cut across the two generations. Within both generations there were instances of all three patterns of parental responsibilities for family adaptation. What Figure 2 illustrates is how the specific pattern of self-reliance was associated with the specific pattern of professional relationships of that same parent. The matrix suggests several topics that need further exploration.

Increased Risks and Rewards

The distribution of parental interpretations in Figure 2 suggests that contemporary relationships of parents and professionals may be more contentious than they used to be. Compared with the patterns of the earlier generation, the outcome of that contention seems a mixture of promise and threat. The potential for parents to view their relationship with professionals as one of productive, engaged interdependence seems greater than ever. In such a relationship neither side overwhelms the other. Instead, a flexible interaction, sometimes adversarial, sometimes collegial, structures the relationship, with each side bringing a distinct perspective and function to the process. However, the threat of isolation of parent from professional also seems greater than ever. There needs to be more research into this historical evolution of parent-professional relationships. Along with special education professionals' increasing emphasis on the importance of "parental involvement" (Ferguson & Ferguson, 1987), they may have increased the sense of professional abandonment perceived by some parents when they must deal with the lack of procedural mandates and program entitlements that unfortunately still characterize the adult service system. Can interventions in the transition processes affecting families reduce that risk of isolation without weakening the growth of healthy engagement?

Formal and informal support systems. A second topic suggested by Figure 2 is the need for an improved understanding of how to balance the perception and use of formal and informal support systems. Figure 2 is arranged so that there is an increased involvement with the formal support system of professionals as one moves from left to right. Moving from bottom to top there is increased involvement with the informal support system of friends, neighbors, and fellow parents. The example of parents who combine the patterns of collective self-reliance and engagement with professionals demonstrates that the use of formal and informal supports does not have to be a zero sum equation; that is, increasing one does not presume the reduction of the other. Parents should be able to actively seek informal solutions to various transition problems without feeling they have simultaneously reduced the responsibilities of the formal service system to address these problems. The understanding of how to increase reliance on informal resources while also improving formal services would make such a balanced approach more likely.

Redefining Transition Success

One implication of this research is that parents and professionals seem to spend at least some of their time in transition planning talking past each other. Professionals need to recognize the different types of transition processes that affect families. Collapsing all of these separate processes into a single transition too often leaves only the rubble of miscommunication. A parent may be talking about disruptions to a harmonious family life when he or she refers to problems in a supported work placement. Professionals may respond with explanations of how the parent needs to recognize the changed status of the young person from child to adult. Without the appropriate distinctions, both parties to the conversation may think they are talking about the same transition when in fact they are not. Implicit in this recognition of multiple transition processes is the possibility that there can be a combination of success and failure for a single family. The bureaucratic transition may result in healthy engagement, while the family life transition leaves the parent resentful of the level of individual self-reliance still required. An absence of status transition may persist with the collective support of other parents who share a "Peter Pan" interpretation of retardation. There needs to be a redefinition of transition success to encompass these related but separate processes.

CONCLUSION

It is appropriate to conclude this exploration of parents' interpretations with a comment from one of the parents. Regardless of whether professionals agree with the various estimations of transition success that parents may have, they need most of all to appreciate the concern and purpose that drive parents to make those estimations. Normalization suggests the need for a weaning away of the individual from the daily protection and restrictions of parental control. Reality suggests the need for even greater parental advocacy and over-sight when the individual faces the tremendous inadequacies of adult services. It is a dilemma for parents as well as for the professionals who must work with them. It is a dilemma created by the fundamental desire of parenthood. Rose Tillman expressed it best:

> I think if I could say anything that is broad (about parents), it would be that they want a life for their kid where this person looks secure and happy. And that means a variety of things to people. I mean you can break that down a lot of ways . . . but basically what we're talking about is quality of life. And those things boil down to having a place to live. Having money. Having friends. And having a job to do that either earns them a living or is something to do every day that has some dignity and worth, instead of just sitting around. So it breaks down a lot of different ways, but I think the overall heading would be something trite like "a happy life."

References

Agar, M. H. (1980). *The professional stranger*. New York: Academic Press.

Anderson, M. (1971). *Family structure in nineteenth century Lancashire*. Cambridge, England: Cambridge University Press.

Arnot, M. (1984). A feminist perspective on the relationship between family life and school life. *Journal of Education, 166*(1), 5–24.

Blumer, H. (1969). *Symbolic interactionism: Perspective and method*. Englewood Cliffs, NJ: Prentice-Hall.

Bogdan, R. C., & Biklen, S. K. (1982). *Qualitative research for education: An introduction to theory and methods*. Boston: Allyn and Bacon.

Boyer, E. L. (1983). *High school: A report on secondary education in America*. New York: Harper & Row.

Darling, R. B., & Darling, J. (1982). *Children who are different: Meeting the challenges of birth defects in society*. St. Louis: C. V. Mosby Co.

Denzin, N. (1978). *The research act: A theoretical introduction to sociological methods* (2nd ed.). New York: McGraw-Hill.

Ferguson, D. L., & Ferguson, P. M. (1986, May). *Families in transition: A qualitative study of parents' perceptions of the move from school to adult life for their severely retarded children*. Paper presented at the AAMD Annual Conference, Denver, CO.

Ferguson, P. M., & Ferguson, D. L. (1987). Parents and professionals. In P. Knoblock (Ed.), *Understanding exceptional children and youth* (pp. 346–391). Boston: Little, Brown & Co.

Ferguson, P. M., Ferguson, D. L., & Jones, D. (1987). Generations of hope: Parental perspectives on the transitions of their severely retarded children from school to adult life. In P. Ferguson (Ed.), *Transition planning and adult services: Perspectives on policy and practice* (pp. 81–123). Eugene: Specialized Training Program, University of Oregon.

Geertz, C. (1973). *The interpretation of cultures.* New York: Basic Books.

Glaser, B., & Strauss, A. (1967). *Discovery of grounded theory.* Chicago: Aldine.

Lasch, C. (1977). *Haven in a heartless world: The family besieged.* New York: Basic Books.

Lightfoot, S. L. (1977). Family-school interactions: The cultural image of mothers and teachers. *SIGNS: Journal of women in culture and society, 3*(2), 395–408.

Lincoln, Y. S., & Guba, E. G. (1985). *Naturalistic inquiry.* Beverly Hills, CA: Sage.

Lofland, J., & Lofland, L. H. (1984). *Analyzing social settings: A guide to qualitative observation and analysis* (2nd ed.). Belmont, CA: Wadsworth.

Modell, J., Furstenberg, F. F., Jr., & Hershberg, T. (1978). Social change and transitions to adulthood in historical perspective. In M. Gordon (Ed.), *The American family in social-historical perspective* (2nd ed.) (pp. 51–68). New York: St. Martin's Press.

Neugarten, B. (1976). Adaptations and the life cycle. *The Counseling Psychologist, 6*(1), 16–20.

Sarason, S. B. (1981). *Psychology misdirected.* New York: The Free Press.

Searl, S. J., Jr. (1985). *Thinking about the future: A manual for parents about transitions.* Syracuse, NY: The Center on Human Policy, Syracuse University.

Shelly, A., & Sibert, E. (1983). *The QUALOG user's manual.* Syracuse, NY: School of Computer and Information Services, Syracuse University.

Smith, J. K., & Heshusius, L. (1986). Closing down the conversation: The end of the quantitative-qualitative debate among educational inquirers. *Educational Researcher, 15*(1), 4–12.

Taylor, S. J., & Bogdan, R. (1984). *Introduction to qualitative research methods.* New York: Wiley.

Wolcott, H. F. (1975). Criteria for an ethnographic approach to research in schools. *Human Organization, 34,* 111–127.

5.2 School-to-Work Transitions for Youth With Disabilities:

A Review of Outcomes and Practices

L. Allen Phelps and Cheryl Hanley-Maxwell

This review examined employment and postsecondary education outcomes for youth with disabilities leaving secondary schools, as well as studies of educational practices reporting high-quality outcomes. Analytical considerations included the current initiatives in educational reform that emphasize the improvement of career-related outcomes for all students and the inclusion of youth with disabilities in regular classes. While school- and employment-related outcomes for youth with disabilities continue to be problematic when compared with those for nondisabled youth, two educational practices appear to consistently align with higher-quality outcomes for students. The promising practices that merit attention in improving programs and in advancing the knowledge base include school supervised work experiences and function-

The research reported herein was supported in part by the Offices of Vocational and Adult Education and Special Education and Rehabilitative Services of the U.S. Department of Education through grants respectively to the National Center for Research in Vocational Education (NCRVE) at the University of California, Berkeley, and the National Center to Improve the Tools of Educators (NCITE) at the University of Oregon. The opinions expressed do not necessarily reflect the positions of the supporting agencies, and no official endorsement should be inferred.

Phelps, L. A., & Hanley-Maxwell, C. 1997. School-to-work transitions for youth with disabilities: A review of outcomes and practices. *Review of Educational Research, 67*(2), 197–226. Reprinted by permission of the publisher.

ally oriented curricula in which occupationally specific skills, employability skills, and academic skills are systematically connected for students. The educational reform literature indicates that valued outcomes for all students are focusing more prominently on workplace and transition outcomes, and that educational practices supported with documented evidence from the secondary special education literature are viewed by many authors as promising directions for improving secondary education for all students.

The civil rights era of the 1960s generated new social commitments to improving and expanding educational opportunities for youth from poor and ethnic minority backgrounds. Federal statutes that grew out of several Supreme Court decisions (e.g. Brown v. Board of Education in 1962) were viewed as central to strengthening the economic and employment prospects of special population groups. In the 1970s, federal and state statutes extended similar benefits to youth with disabilities, the most prominent of these being the Education for All Handicapped Children Act of 1975. Paradoxically, the rapid advancement of workplace skill requirements and global competition has focused the decade of the 1990s on similar issues for all students leaving high school. Since the late 1980s, the successful transition of youth from high school into an established adult working life has been a central focus of the widespread educational reform movement in the United States (National Center on Education and the Economy, 1990; William T. Grant Foundation, 1988).

This review is designed to document and synthesize the knowledge base regarding youth with disabilities and their transition to work roles in the community. To address the rising and rapidly changing economic and societal expectations for schools, the knowledge base examined is grounded in the learning and educational outcomes deemed appropriate for all students, as envisioned by the Goals 2000: Educate America Act, the School-to-Work Opportunities Act, and other conceptions of high-quality teaching and learning at the secondary level (e.g., National Council of Teachers of Mathematics, 1989; Newmann & Wehlage, 1995). Rather than suggesting differentiated approaches and outcomes for youth with disabilities, these initiatives suggest a more inclusive approach in which all students, regardless of their economic, social, or learning difficulties, are educated in integrated school and workplace settings.

Consistent with this national trend, the enactment of the Individuals With Disabilities Education Act of 1990 focuses on ensuring that students with disabilities receive a coordinated education designed to enhance the transition to employment, further education and training, and independent living. The parallels between the design and delivery of services for youth with disabilities over the past two decades and those being undertaken in the educational reform movement are indeed striking. Thus, this review is based on the assumption that restructured schools will incorporate all students with disabilities in ways that maximize their learning as well as the learning and achievement of their nondisabled peers.

Several observations on the importance of joining the analysis of secondary special education and educational restructuring as a framework for future research were outlined by Johnson and Rusch (1993). They note that mainstream education reformers have not adequately addressed the inclusion of students with disabilities and that special educators have not addressed the failure of public schools to improve learning and educational outcomes for nondisabled students where possible. In terms of common ground, both general and special educators have concerned themselves with low expectations and the devaluation of specific groups, as well as the transition from school to adulthood. For all educators, the issues of access for youth with disabilities and other special groups have abated, while concerns for the overall quality and effectiveness of education have come to the forefront.

In this review, the research on the educational and employment outcomes for youth with disabilities are examined, drawing primarily on the large number of follow-up studies of the past decade. Second, the research literature on educational skills required in the contemporary workplace provides a backdrop for examining efficacy studies of educational practices that are linked to the documented, aforementioned skills and competencies. Finally, we provide a discussion and synthesis of the extant knowledge base that charts research directions for the future and suggests the relative importance of various research questions for teachers, administrators, policymakers, parents, and employers.

In constructing this review, we examined research literature that centered on school-based special education programs, with particular attention to those students served in regular classes or special education resource rooms, who comprise 68% of the school-age special education population (U.S. Department of Education, 1992, p. 23). Literature was gathered using computer-based searches of several electronic databases covering the past 10 years, including the ERIC database and psychological abstracts. Search descriptors were delimited to include attention to employment and postsecondary education outcomes for youth. The primary focus on economic outcomes is predicted here in the belief that income and involvement in work (paid and unpaid) are primary concerns that directly affect other important outcomes—for example, quality of life and living independently. Further, the review was delimited to include only the literature documenting educational practices that were explicitly linked to the economic outcomes of graduates. The content of articles, reports, and chapters deemed pertinent to the central questions of the review was systematically analyzed.

TRANSITION OUTCOMES

A variety of authors in both general and special education have attempted to define the goals of schooling, and thus the goals of transition. Seigel and Sleeter (1991) describe the mission of education in this way:

> The mission of special (or general) education is not restricted to the teaching of academic subjects, nor is it to protect students from a harsh adult environment. It is to prepare them to participate fully in the mainstream adult world. (p. 27)

Copa and Pease (1992) include "a guaranteed set of learner outcomes closely linked to present and future life roles and responsibilities for all students" (p. 2) as an important feature of the 21st-century high school. Glasser (1992) defines the quality of a curriculum by the usefulness of the content to the student, now or in the future. This utility is individually determined. And, to ensure its usefulness, students should be taught how, when, where, and why to use the knowledge provided through curricular content (Hanley-Maxwell & Collet-Klingenberg, 1995).

Regardless of the specific view, Ysseldyke, Thurlow, and Bruininks (1992) indicate that an educational outcome should be

> valued by society; reflect... cultural expectations [for] participation and achievement in normal social,

educational, training, employment, leisure, and community environments; include both direct and indirect results of educational experiences; be relevant to all individuals... ; [and] be a product of learning and experience (what has been learned) rather than how learning occurred. (p. 27)

Outcomes in terms of societal value (what we want) and what exists are described in the following sections.

Educational Outcomes: The Expectations

Desired outcomes for students can be specified for all students and tailored to meet the needs of students with disabilities. Current reports and research target both areas. It is debatable whether the authors and sponsors of many of the educational reform initiatives (e.g., Goals 2000 and the Secretary's Commission on Achieving Necessary Skills [SCANS]) intended to include students with disabilities in their references to *all* students. However, the outcomes identified for students without disabilities are also relevant to those who have disabilities (see Table 1 for a comparison of common themes of the major reports). Thus, reviewed first in this section are recent federal policy initiatives and studies that relate to identifying outcomes for students with and without disabilities. Work that has targeted only students with disabilities is reviewed in the next section.

Outcomes for All Students

Recent reports and new federal legislation have focused the education community clearly on the matter of ensuring learning by all students, with particular attention to the skills and knowledge required to be

Table 1
Common themes from targeted outcome reports.

Theme	SCANS	Goals 2000	NCEO
Literacy	X	X	X
Independence	X		X
Citizenship		X	X
Behavior	X		X
Mental health	X		X
Basic academic skills	X	X	X
Critical thinking	X	X	X

successful beyond school. These initiatives and the accompanying research form a consistent picture of skills needed by workers as they enter and stay in the job market. The reports and research reviewed in this section include Goals 2000: Educate America Act (1993; U.S. Department of Education, 1994), *What Work Requires of Schools: A SCANS Report for America 2000* (U.S. Department of Labor, 1991), and the School-to-Work Opportunities Act (STWOA; 1994). Goals 2000 is the overarching framework under which all other efforts can be nested. These broad goals are further defined through the greater detail identified in the SCANS report. Finally, STWOA is the articulation of the parameters and experiences that enable students to reach the goals and skills identified in Goals 2000 and the SCANS report.

Goals 2000. The Goals 2000: Educate America Act (1993) codifies eight national education goals. Three of these goals relate to the outcomes of schooling for all students, while the others address educational inputs and schooling processes. Goal 2 addresses the need to increase the high school graduation rate to at least 90% by the year 2000. Goal 3 deals with the development of academic competencies

> in challenging subject matter including English, mathematics, science, history, and geography; and every school in America will ensure that all students learn to use their minds well, so they may be prepared for responsible citizenship, further learning, and productive employment in our modern economy. (p. 9)

Finally, Goal 6 draws the connection between educational achievement and adult roles. This goal identifies the need to prepare students to "be literate and... possess the knowledge and skills necessary to compete in a global economy and exercise the rights and responsibilities of citizenship" (p. 9). Among the objectives for this goal is the expectation that every major American business will be involved in strengthening the connection between education and work.

Other goals that pertain to building the capacity for schools to assist students with disabilities are the goals pertaining to teacher education and professional development (Goal 4) and parental participation (Goal 8). The teacher education goal notes that the nation's teaching force will have access to programs for the continuous improvement of teaching skills required to prepare all students for the 21st century. Finally, all schools are charged with the responsibility for developing partnerships with

parents that promote the social and academic growth of children.

What Work Requires of Schools: A SCANS Report for America 2000. The authors of this report (U.S. Department of Labor, 1991) identify competencies, foundational skills, and personal qualities that are essential for work. The competencies and foundational skills, described in the paragraphs that follow, are examples of how the outcomes specified in Goals 2000 can dictate content or skills requirements. The skills identified in the SCANS report represent the content broadly identified in Goals 3 and 6 (of the national education goals codified in Goals 2000).

The SCANS report reflects one way to identify what skills might meet the national education goals. Members of the SCANS were prominent business leaders representing a variety of industry sectors. The research undergirding this taxonomy of skills and competencies is drawn, in part, from a comprehensive analysis of 50 contemporary entry-level occupations across eight major industry sectors (see U.S. Department of Labor, 1991, Appendix D). The use of this forum and information reflects the clear expectation articulated in Goal 6: that business be involved in connecting school and work.

Foundational skills refer to basic academic and thinking skills. Included within basic academic skills are the areas of reading (finding, comprehending, and applying printed information), writing to communicate, arithmetic and mathematical operations (basic computational skills, using reasoning to select an appropriate operation and applying it to practical problems), listening (receiving, attending to, interpreting, and responding to verbal messages and other cues), and speaking (organizing ideas and communicating orally). Thinking skills include generating new ideas, decision making and acting, problem solving and implementing, visualizing (to organize, understand, and respond), reasoning to find connections and relationships necessary for problem solving, and continued self-learning. Personal qualities were also deemed essential in this schema for new skills. The following personal qualities are specifically identified in the SCANS report as critical for success in today's labor markets: responsibility as shown in effort and perseverance, self-esteem as reflected in self-value and self-view, interpersonal skills that allow effective working with others, self-management (self-assessment, self-monitoring, self-control, and goal setting), and integrity and honesty as shown in using ethics to make decisions. Foundational skills and personal qualities are combined to form the underlying structure for the specific competencies.

The workplace competencies identified in the SCANS report build on the foundational skills and apply those skills in various combinations. The competencies are (a) identifying, organizing, planning, and allocating resources (time, money, human, and material/facilities); (b) working with other people (i.e., working in a team, sharing information and skills, responding to customer needs, self-advocating, using negotiation and conflict resolution, and responding appropriately to individual differences); (c) acquiring, organizing, interpreting, and communicating information (includes use of computer technology); (d) understanding inter-relationships of complex social, organizational, and technological systems; and (e) securing, applying, and maintaining a variety of technologies. Although aspects of these competencies are difficult for some students with special needs to attain, they provide a clear frame-work for skills needed in a variety of work environments.

The School-to-Work Opportunities Act (STWOA). The STWOA, enacted in 1994, authorized state funding for the development of programs that improved the work-related skills of school leavers. This law also provides the beginnings of the organizational structure needed to meet Goals 3 and 6 of the national education goals. School-to-work programs must include the following activities: help students with career selection through the provision of career awareness, exploration, and counseling services (with career major selected no later than 11th grade); connect school-based learning (designed to meet the criteria of Goals 2000) and work-based learning (preemployment and employment skills, workplace mentoring); and provide instruction in work attitudes, employability skills, and participation skills (the skills identified in the SCANS report). STWOA program decisions for individual students must be based on ongoing evaluation. Regardless of individualized program, all students must receive work experience, a planned program of job training and experiences, and workplace mentoring. If appropriate for individual communities and learners, these programs should also offer instruction in skills needed for employment in local industry and job-based experiences (e.g., paid work, on-the-job training). Finally, STWOA programs must ensure that students are matched with appropriate work-based learning opportunities, that each student has a school mentor who serves as the central link in the process, and that employers are provided with necessary technical assistance to facilitate their participation in the program.

Outcomes Specific to Children With Disabilities

Several authors have considered outcomes as they relate to students with disabilities. The outcomes sought specifically for students with disabilities go beyond those identified in Goals 2000 (see Table 1). The specific skills are similar to those identified in the SCANS report. However, emphasis and degree of specification are often different. Two notable efforts that reflect current thinking are discussed below. The first, the National Center on Education Outcomes (NCEO; Ysseldyke, Thurlow, Bruininks, Gilman, et al., 1992) reflects several years of work by multiple researchers in conjunction with focus groups. The second, the quality of life (QOL) framework described by Halpern (1992), provides the context in which outcomes should be nested.

NCEO. Work conducted by NCEO researchers has led to the identification of important educational outcomes for students with disabilities. The attainment of these outcomes is influenced by the presence or absence of four enabling outcomes that are processes or idiosyncratic aspects of schooling.

Enabling outcomes include student presence and participation in educational activities as a contributor to successful education outcomes. This outcome is similar to Goal 2 of the national education goals, which seeks to raise graduation rates to 90%. However, this outcome takes Goal 2 a step further by moving beyond presence into participation. Students with disabilities need to access and become actively engaged in the educational opportunities available to their nondisabled peers.

Compensatory and accommodation skills, as well as adaptive behavior, enable the individual to respond to varying environmental demands and to meet disability-specific needs. As enabling outcomes, these areas are essential in assisting the learner to develop the skills which enhance their flexibility and independence as adults. This NCEO area parallels Goals 3 and 6 and the foundational skills identified in the SCANS report.

Finally, family coping and support skills are identified as a composite enabling outcome. The lifelong needs of learners with disabilities mandate the need to attend to the development of active support systems. And, since adults with disabilities are more likely to continue to reside at home, attention to the family as a specific source of these supports is justifiable. Family skills in coping with the support needs of the student will influence both the progress toward educational outcomes and the overall success of the individual in the adult community.

The enabling outcomes contribute to the success in attaining the six educational outcomes described in NCEO reports. The educational outcomes are literacy, self-dependence, social/behavioral, contribution/citizenship, satisfaction, and physical/mental health. These outcomes parallel a combination of skills and goals targeted in the national education goals and the SCANS report (see Table 1).

Similar to the skill areas identified in the SCANS report, literacy in the NCEO report is broader than the acquisition and use of reading skills. Within the context of these outcomes, literacy refers to gathering and applying information to survive in the adult world, attain goals, and continue learning. Independence/responsibility relates to the behavior of the individual. This outcome reflects the ability of the individual to direct, monitor, and amend behavior, solve problems, and successfully use other metacognitive strategies. Social/behavioral skills, the third outcome, further refines the parameters of the individual's behavior. While the performance of behavior must be independent, it must now be socially acceptable as well.

Socially acceptable behavior includes contribution/citizenship, also found in the SCANS report and Goals 2000. If an individual is behaving in responsible and socially acceptable ways, that individual must also consider ways in which he or she can give something back to society by participating as a citizen or general community member. This outcome stresses the performance of those behaviors.

The fifth outcome, satisfaction with the results of the educational process, is also considered an educational outcome. Satisfaction must be experienced by the individual as well as the broader community.

Finally, physical/mental health is considered to be an important educational outcome (and is reflective of needs identified by employers in the SCANS report). This outcome is demonstrated by the individual's knowledge, attitudes, and engagement in behaviors that contribute to her or his physical and mental well-being.

Quality of life framework. Quality of life (QOL) can serve as a conceptual framework for examining educational outcomes for students with disabilities. It is another application of the outcomes and skills identified in the national education goals, the SCANS report, and the NCEO framework. Quality of life considerations include both personal needs and social expectations. These needs and expectations are classified into three basic domains. The initial domain is physical and material well-being, which includes physical and mental health; food, clothing, and lodging; financial security; and safety from harm. Another domain, performance of a variety of adult roles, includes mobility and community access; vocation, career, and employment; leisure and recreation; personal relationships and social networks; educational attainment; spiritual fulfillment; citizenship (e.g., voting); and social responsibility (e.g., law abiding behavior). The final domain, personal fulfillment, includes happiness, satisfaction, and sense of general well-being.

EDUCATIONAL OUTCOMES: THE REALITIES FOR YOUTH WITH DISABILITIES

Do outcomes for students with disabilities match the outcomes specified in the national education goals, the NCEO report, or the QOL framework? Are students with disabilities acquiring the skills identified in the SCANS report and making the transitions from school to the workplace envisioned by the STWOA? The answers to these questions are critical. Unfortunately, they can be answered only partially. Most studies of youth with disabilities have focused on specific groups or special programs with small-scale interventions, which limits the quality of the responses to these important questions.

Provided in this section is an overview of the data related to employment and educational outcomes for students with disabilities. This is followed by a more indepth examination of the nation's largest follow-up study, the National Longitudinal Transition Study of Special Education Students (NLTS: Wagner, Blackorby, Cameto, & Newman, 1993). Finally, the section concludes with a discussion of factors that appear to contribute to improved outcomes for students with disabilities.

Overall Statistics

Data indicate that students with disabilities have poor postschool outcomes. Just getting to the point of graduation may be difficult for them. Benz and Halpern (1987) report that an average of 22% of all students with disabilities drop out of school, while only 12% of their peers without disabilities drop out. In a study of students in the state of Washington, Edgar (1988) found dropout rates that varied according to disability classification: 42% for students with learning disabilities or behavior disorders, 18%

Table 2

Summary of selected data from the National Longitudinal Transition Study (NLTS).

Outcome	Disability category			
	Learning disabled	Emotionally disturbed	Speech or language impaired	Mentally retarded
Drop out	28%	48%	23%	30%
Enrolled postsecondary academic	19%	15%	37%	2%
Enrolled postsecondary vocational	18%	13%	18%	6%
Competitively employed	63%	52%	58%	41%
Living independently	34%	21%	36%	15%
Full community participation	74%	56%	79%	42%
Self-care rated highly	98%	96%	99%	85%
Functional mental skills rated highly	68%	66%	68%	40%

for students with mild mental retardation, and 16% for students in regular education. Graduation rates for students with disabilities need to exhibit substantial improvement if they are to meet the 90% target specified in the national education goals.

Unfortunately, while graduation improves outcomes, follow-up studies continue to indicate poor postschool outcomes for students with disabilities who do graduate. Edgar (1988) found that while 84% of graduates who had learning or behavioral disabilities were working or in school, only 18% earned more than minimum wage. Furthermore, for graduates with mild mental retardation, 41% were working or going to school, but only 5% earned more than minimum wage. While other follow-up studies vary in their exact percentage of graduates who begin working immediately after graduation, postschool employment data consistently reflect poor outcomes for a large portion of all former students with disabilities (Hasazi, Gordon, Roe, Hull, et al., 1985; Hasazi, Gordon, & Roe, 1985; Kortering & Edgar, 1988; Mithaug, Horiuchi, & Fanning, 1985; Neel, Meadows, Levine, & Edgar, 1988; Scuccimarra & Speece, 1990; Sitlington, Frank, & Carson, 1992). These data indicate that students with disabilities have not been provided with the necessary skills (e.g., those identified in the SCANS report and in the national education goals) or the connections to postschool employment and/or college settings envisioned by the STWOA.

NLTS Data

The NLTS (Blackorby & Wagner, 1996; Wagner et al., 1993) provides the most comprehensive data set regarding outcomes for students with disabilities and the strongest evidence that students with disabilities are not achieving the expected outcomes discussed earlier. Beginning in 1987, this longitudinal study conducted by SRI International examined the 5-year educational and postschool performance of 8,000 youth of ages 13 to 21 with a variety of disabilities. Data from students who were within 3 years of leaving school depict a variety of outcomes. These outcomes vary dramatically based on student disability label. Outcomes for students with mild disabilities (learning disability, emotional disability, speech impairment, mild/moderate mental retardation) are discussed in the following paragraphs and summarized in Table 2. The NLTS data depicting outcomes based on ethnicity and gender are also examined.

Students with learning disabilities. Over 28% of students with learning disabilities dropped out of high school. Data for graduates and dropouts reveal that 19% enrolled in postsecondary academic programs, 18% enrolled in postsecondary vocational programs, and 63% obtained competitive employment (average annual compensation = $11,671). Furthermore, 34% were living independently, and 74% were fully participating in at least two aspects of community life (i.e., work or education outside home, independent residential settings, social activity). Performance of survival skills by students with learning disabilities varied. While most were highly rated on self-care tasks (98%), mixed ratings on functional mental skills (i.e., time telling, reading common signs, counting change, using phone book and phone) were provided by parent respondents (68% rated as highly skilled and 32% rated moderately skilled). These data reflect positive trends for former students with learning disabilities in the areas of employment, wages earned, attendance in postsecondary education, and independent living. However, these same individuals are not making gains as rapidly as their peers without disabilities and continue to reflect the significant gaps that exist between individuals with disabilities and the general population (Blackorby & Wagner, 1996). This continuing disparity is also reflected in other outcomes, including information on parenting rates and arrest records. The parenting rate for youth without disabilities was 21%. This is compared to a parenting rate of 50% for youth with learning disabilities. Arrest rates across the postschool years show a steady increase for youth with learning disabilities: 9% for in-school youth, 19.9% for youth who had been out of school for less than 2 years, and 31% for youth within 5 years of exiting school (Wagner et al., 1993).

Students with emotional disturbance. Outcomes for students with emotional disabilities followed a similar profile. The data revealed that 48% dropped out of high school, 15% enrolled in postsecondary academic programs, 13% enrolled in postsecondary vocational programs, 52% were competitively employed (average compensation = $11,267), 21% lived independently, and 56% were fully participating in at least two aspects of community life. Performance of survival skills by students with emotional disabilities varied but was similar to the performance ratings of students with learning disabilities. Most were highly rated on self-care tasks (96%). However, mixed ratings on functional mental skills were provided by parent respondents— 66% received high ratings, and 30% received moderate ratings. As time since leaving school passes, trends for former students with emotional disturbance show significant gains only in the percentage who earn greater than minimum wage and in the percentage living independently. Despite these gains, they continue to lag behind peers in the general population and many of their peers with other disabilities (Blackorby & Wagner, 1996).

Students with speech impairments. Students with speech impairments had slightly different postschool outcomes. Fewer of them, only 23%, dropped out of high school. Compared to other youth with disabilities, more of these students enrolled in postsecondary academic programs (37%). Other outcomes included: 18% enrolled in postsecondary vocational programs, 58% became competitively employed (average compensation = $8,145), 36% were living independently, and 79% were fully participating in at least two aspects of community life. Performance of survival skills by students with speech impairments varied but was similar to the performance ratings of students with learning or emotional disabilities. Nearly all were highly rated on self-care tasks (99%). However, as with the other students with mild disabilities, mixed ratings on functional mental skills were provided by parent respondents; 68% rated these skills as high, and 30% rated them as moderate. Positive postschool trends in all areas of adult life are evident for these individuals. However, like their peers with other disabilities, they continue to lag behind their nondisabled peers in all areas (Blackorby & Wagner, 1996).

Students with mental retardation. Students with mild or moderate mental retardation had significantly poorer outcomes when compared with other students with mild disabilities: 29.9% dropped out of high school, only 2% enrolled in postsecondary academic programs, 6% enrolled in postsecondary vocational programs, 41% were competitively employed (average compensation = $8,274), 15% were living independently, and 42% were fully participating in at least two aspects of community life (work or education outside the home, independent residential, social activity). Their performance of survival skills and functional mental skills was also rated as poorer than that of their peers with other mild disabilities: 85% were highly rated on self-care tasks, 13% received a medium rating, 40% were rated highly in relation to functional mental skills, 46% received medium ratings. Research examining trends after school leaving reveals positive changes in the percentage of individuals working competitively and in the percentage of individuals living independently (Blackorby & Wagner, 1996).

Gender and ethnicity. Reexamination of follow-up data on the basis of gender and ethnicity reveals clear trends in each area. Young women with disabilities are more likely to live independently but less likely to be employed than their male counterparts or their peers in the general population (Blackorby &

Wagner, 1996). Levine and Edgar (as cited in Blackorby & Wagner, 1996) and Wagner (as cited in Blackorby & Wagner, 1996) have found that young women with disabilities are primarily wives and mothers. Thus, postschool patterns of adult life are drastically different for young women with disabilities than for all other age peers.

Ethnicity has a slightly different impact. Comparison of outcomes for (a) African American and Hispanic students with disabilities and (b) White students with disabilities reveals that from the initial point of leaving school, the former are less likely than their White counterparts to be competitively employed (25.5% and 49.4%, respectively, versus 53.1%). Although African Americans make the largest gains over the postschool years in the percentage of individuals competitively employed, they continue to lag behind their White peers and are relatively even with their Hispanic peers. Interestingly, African Americans with disabilities are more likely to initially receive jobs that pay above minimum wage. However, this initial condition drastically changes as time passes. Within 3 to 5 years after graduation, students who are White have made dramatic gains in wages earned, as revealed by a significant gain in the percentage of individuals with earnings greater than the minimum wage. Former Hispanic students have also made large but nonsignificant gains in the percentage of individuals who are advancing by making greater than minimum wage. Former African American students show no gains in wages earned.

Trends in independent living are slightly different, but continue to demonstrate a more positive pattern for former White students. Immediately following school, former students who are Hispanic are more likely than their White or African American counterparts to live independently (15.2% versus 13.4% and 5.1%, respectively). This pattern changes as time passes. Although there is significant growth in the percentage of former students living independently for all ethnic groups, White students have shown the greatest gains 3 to 5 years after leaving school. At this point, White students are more likely to be living independently than their Hispanic or African American peers (42.3% versus 33.1% and 25.5%, respectively) (Blackorby & Wagner, 1996).

Other Factors Affecting Outcomes

A mix of activities and factors are correlated with successful vocational or employment outcomes for students with disabilities. Some of these factors include individual characteristics which are correlated with differing postschool outcomes: family charac-

teristics (Fourqurean & LaCourt, 1991; Heal & Rusch, 1995); socioeconomic status (Edgar, 1988); IQ and type of handicap (Fourqurean & LaCourt, 1991); and, as discussed above, ethnicity and gender (Blackorby & Wagner, 1996; Heal & Rusch, 1995). Other factors include skills that when acquired appear to positively affect community adjustment and job acquisition: independent living skills and academic skills (Fourqurean & LaCourt, 1991; Heal & Rusch, 1995); high math ability (Fourqurean, Meisgeier, Swank, & Williams, 1991); reading, math, and writing (Carnevale et al., as cited in White, 1992; McCrea, 1991; Okolo & Sitlington, 1988; Shapiro & Lentz, 1991); and the application of academic skills in problem solving and communication (Smith & Trist, as cited in White, 1992).

Analysis of NLTS (Wagner et al., 1993) data also identified several factors that were related to positive outcomes for students with mild disabilities. These factors are similar to those targeted in the SCANS report and the outcomes targeted in the national education goals, the NCEO report, and the QOL framework. Competitive employment was correlated with functional mental skills, participation in vocational courses, and school-supervised work experiences. Functional mental skills and the completion of occupation-specific vocational education courses were also correlated with higher wages. Participation in advanced math and foreign language classes was related to enrollment in postsecondary academic programs. Teen parenting by the mother appeared to produce mixed results. It was related to higher levels of independent living and community participation but lower rates of competitive employment and lower wages.

Some of the other factors identified in the NLTS (Wagner et al., 1993) data are supported by additional follow-up studies. These include the following: method of school leaving, dropping out versus graduation (e.g., Fourqurean & LaCourt, 1991); type of special education placement, percentage of time in the regular education program (e.g., Fourqurean & LaCourt, 1991); and involvement in vocational education and training and employment during the high school years (e.g., Hasazi, Gordon, Roe, Hull, et al., 1985; Hasazi, Gordon, & Roe, 1985; Mithaug et al., 1985). However, more recent work (Heal & Rusch, 1995; Sitlington & Frank, 1990) has found that when other factors were controlled for, existing data did not support the connection between improved employment outcomes and vocational training during high school. Despite the conflicting results related to vocational training, employment during the high school years (e.g., summer jobs, school-year jobs) has been consistently related to better postschool employment outcomes (Fourqurean & LaCourt, 1991; Fourqurean et al., 1991; Hasazi, Gordon, Roe, Hull, et al., 1985; Hasazi, Gordon, & Roe, 1985; Scuccimarra & Speece, 1990; Sitlington & Frank, 1990).

EDUCATIONAL PRACTICES ALIGNED WITH VALUED OUTCOMES

In addition to the program and demographic factors cited from in-depth analyses of the NLTS data set (Gierl & Harnisch, 1995; Heal & Rusch, 1995), a series of recent articles have examined and summarized studies focused on program and curriculum effects (Chadsey-Rusch, Rusch, & O'Reilly, 1991; Phelps & Wermuth, 1992). Further, studies and national surveys of managers of federally funded transition programs have suggested important relationships between selected practices and positive employment outcomes for youth with disabilities (Rusch, Enchelmaier, & Kohler, 1994).

As DeStefano and Wagner (1993) indicated, educators are increasingly focusing attention on postsecondary education and employment outcomes related to education, and on interventions that produce desired or valued outcomes. In their recently completed analysis of restructured schools in the United States, Newmann and Wehlage (1995) make clear the need to differentiate means from ends in studying the effects of schooling: "The recent education reform movement gives too much attention to changes in school organization that do not directly address the quality of student learning" (p. 51). However, since the vast majority of curriculum and educational practice literature in secondary special education is descriptive and theoretical in nature (Hanley-Maxwell & Collet-Klingenberg, 1995), the number of studies examining practices or instructional activities that are aligned with explicit and observable learner outcomes is quite limited (Chadsey-Rusch et al., 1991; Kohler, 1994).

The lack of research that links educational practices with learning outcomes suggests that a broad-based framework is required to seek out possible interactions. A massive analysis of research on learning was conducted recently using meta-analyses and other techniques to construct a knowledge base for school learning (Wang, Haertel, & Walberg, 1993). As these authors sought to estimate the influence of educational, psychological, and social factors on learning, the following universe of constructs was examined: state and district governance and organization (e.g., district policies, teacher licensure requirements); home and community contexts (e.g., use of out-of-school time, socioeconomic level of community); school demographics, culture, climate, policies, and practices (e.g., size of school, discipline policy, emphasis on recognition of academic achievement); design and delivery of curriculum and instruction (e.g., size of instructional group, alignment of goals, content, instruction, and evaluation); classroom practices (e.g., classroom management, use of assessment); and student characteristics (e.g., student demographics such as gender and social and behavioral development of learners). Such comprehensive frameworks, which examine broadly the variables and factors that could potentially influence student learning and postschool outcomes, are an essential beginning point for documenting the effects of practices on the attainment of valued outcomes. If a large array of variables are considered, the search for significant relationships among the multitude of complex factors is more likely to bear fruit.

Phelps and Wermuth (1992) offer a framework for examining effective educational practices from studies of programs that produced high levels of learner outcomes. These program effectiveness studies included both research studies and large-scale evaluations. Since the number of intervention-outcome studies pertaining directly to youth with disabilities was limited, studies of programs serving economically disadvantaged and limited English proficient youth were included in formulating this preliminary framework. In all cases, each of the studies reviewed met two or more of the following criteria, which emphasize student learning: (a) programs included in the studies had operated for a minimum of 5 years; (b) programs had relatively high completion rates for enrollees; and (c) programs produced relatively high postprogram placement rates for graduates. In addition, studies of program effects drawn from recently gathered longitudinal databases were included in the analytical framework. Across eight major effectiveness studies (six of which included programs serving youth with disabilities), 20 program components and practices were identified. The resultant analytical framework is provided in Table 3.

The following sections examine selected program components and practices from the framework. Attention is given to recently published studies that address explicitly the educational effects of programs serving youth with disabilities.

Table 3
Framework of clusters and components
of programs and services providing effective
outcomes for students with special needs.

Program administration

Administrative leadership and support

Sufficient financial support

Formative program evaluation

Summative program evaluation

Staff development

Curriculum and instruction

Individualized curriculum modifications

Integration of vocational and academic curricula

Appropriate instructional settings

Cooperative learning experiences

Comprehensive support services

Career guidance and counseling

Instructional support services (e.g., aides and
resources)

Assessment of individual career interests and
abilities

Formalized articulation and communication

Family/parental involvement and support

Early notification of vocational opportunities

Vocation and regular educators' involvement in
individualized planning

Formalized transition planning

Intra- and interagency collaboration

Occupational experience, placement, and follow-up

Work experience opportunities

Job placement services

Follow-up

PROGRAM ADMINISTRATION

Studies of programs focused on student learning reveal that the support of building and program administrators for the inclusion of youth with disabilities is evident. In programs focused specifically on vocational skills development, close attention is given by principals, as well as directors of special education and vocational education, to the enrollment, retention, and appropriate placement of youth with disabilities (Eagle, Choy, Hoachlander, Stoddard, & Tuma, 1989; Gugerty, Tindall, Heffron, & Dougherty, 1988; Hoachlander & Stoddard, 1987). Another indicator of programs producing positive student outcomes was substantial expenditures for youth with disabilities placed in regular secondary education. The average per-pupil expenditures for youth with disabilities exceeded the spending for nondisabled youth in four studies (Eagle et al., 1989; Gugerty et al., 1988; Hoachlander & Stoddard, 1987; Parks, McKinney, & Mahlman, 1987). Typically, the additional costs were required for modified instruction, special equipment, and staff development.

The capacity of regular and vocational education teachers to successfully accommodate and teach youth with disabilities has been a prominent issue in the literature since the mid-1970s (Phelps & Frongillo, 1986). A recent study of practicing vocational educators in Ohio documents the critical need for staff development efforts. In the teaching of youth with disabilities and other at-risk conditions (in comparison to nondisabled students), the following aspects of the instructional process were rated as significantly important to effective instruction: assessment and evaluation, counseling and referral, program placement, remediation, tutoring, specialized services, job placement, and follow-up (Burrell, 1993).

For youth with disabilities who are placed in regular classes for their instruction, collaboration and consultation between special and regular educators is central to the delivery of instruction. Evans (1991) reviewed the research base for collaboration in special education and found that few studies are able to report changes in client (student) performance as a result of collaboration. However, studies do find that intervention plans (e.g., individualized education plans, or IEPs) are more likely to be carried out when they are developed jointly by the consultant and the consultee, that is, when facilitative rather than authoritative consultation skills are employed. Additionally, according to Evans, studies suggest that following training and practice in peer collaboration, teachers' tolerance of learning and behavior problems was increased considerably.

The research on effective schools (Little, 1982, 1984; Rosenholtz, Bassler, & Hoover-Dempsey, 1986) suggests that collegiality and cooperation among teachers are vital aspects of the culture. Effective schools are characterized by high levels of teacher-teacher and teacher-principal collaboration, as well as extensive commitments to staff development, much of which is conducted through consultation among teachers. In schools where collegiality is the norm; Little (1982) found that teachers interact frequently about teaching, jointly plan and evaluate instructional materials, and are often cast in the role of instructing other teachers. Close program monitoring is evident in programs as well. Students, parents, and employers have opportunities to frequently assess the quality of programs and services. Additionally, monitoring systems in effective programs pay close attention to outcome and performance data, including completion rates, program-related job placement, earnings, and program compliance with accreditation standards (Gugerty et al., 1988; Hoachlander & Stoddard, 1987; Parks et al., 1987; Wagner, 1991).

CURRICULUM AND INSTRUCTION

Curriculum Content

As noted earlier in the section on outcomes, the scope and content of secondary school curricula continue to be debated intensely in regular education and, in different yet parallel ways, in programs designed to serve youth with disabilities. Gajar, Goodman, and McAfee (1993) identify three basic models of curriculum found in secondary school programs serving youth with disabilities: functional skills models (i.e., vocational/employment preparation and independent adult living skills), process models (i.e., learning strategies), and academic skills models (i.e., tutorials, completing regular education requirements, basic skills, functional literacy). The authors suggest that most schools offer choices between the functional skills and the academic skills curriculum in the same way that high schools offer nondisabled students the vocational/career track or the college prep track. This "forced choice" stirs emotionally charged debate in relation to functional versus academic curricular foci and learning experiences. Advocates of academic skills or process approaches to curriculum selection contend that without emphasis on academic skills, students with disabilities are not being held to the same standards as their peers without disabilities. These students are not achieving their fullest potential and may have reduced occupational aspirations (Rojewski, 1996). The result is that students with disabilities are not participating in postsecondary education. This nonparticipation is resulting in poorer short-term and long-term employment outcomes

(Blackorby & Wagner, 1996). Advocates for the functional skills approach argue that curriculum content should (a) include consideration for generalizing and maintaining functional skills beyond school, (b) be taught in community and work settings, and (c) offer a means for understanding or grounding academic skills (math and communication skills) in a practical context (Clark, 1994; Halpern, 1992). Furthermore, Kohler's (1994) review of follow-up studies, quasi-experimental studies, and theory-based literature reveals that more than 50% of 49 studies cited vocational training as central to successful transition to adult life beyond high school.

Data collected through SRI's national longitudinal study of youth with disabilities (Wagner, 1991) suggests that students who participated in occupationally oriented vocational education during their last year in school were more likely than nonparticipating special education youth to register positive outcomes (e.g., employment or attending postsecondary education programs). When demographic and disability differences were controlled for, students who had completed occupationally oriented vocational courses had significantly lower absenteeism from school, as well as a lower probability of dropping out. Further, students in these courses also had a higher likelihood of finding a job and enrolling at a postsecondary vocational school in the period immediately following high school (Wagner, 1991).

Another blending of the functional and academic skills approaches to curriculum is found in studies of the integration of academic and vocational education (e.g., Grubb, 1995). Studies of several programs serving youth with disabilities (Eagle et al., 1989; Gugerty et al., 1988; Hayward & Wirt, 1989; Wagner, 1991) have reported that the integration of math, English, and basic science skills content with the development of specific occupational skills (e.g., building trades, home health assistant) maximizes learning of both kinds. Especially for students with learning disabilities and mild cognitive limitations, these studies suggest that learning traditional academic skills in ways that illustrate their immediate and direct application within a job aids in comprehension and generalization. Conversely, the acquisition of advanced occupational skills is mediated by students' understanding of the importance of written communication, the application of advanced measuring skills, and the use of similar academic skills in the context of their application. In a reanalysis of 1,358 NLTS interviewees who left school but had a job in 1987, a community-focused curriculum (e.g., one in which academic and vocational skills were integrated through coordinated school and work-based learning) was one of three predictor variables (from among 74 studied) found to contribute significantly to postschool employment (Heal & Rusch, 1995).

Extensive research has shown that the lack of appropriate social skills will have a dramatic impact on the success of any individual in any adult life role, especially in employment roles. This is demonstrated by the following: (a) The most common reason for termination is inappropriate social skills (Greenspan & Shoultz, 1981; Hanley-Maxwell, Rusch, Chadsey-Rusch, & Renzaglia, 1986); (b) the most commonly reported problems in the work environment are related to interpersonal communication (Chadsey-Rusch & Gonzalez, 1988); and (c) the most common interaction in the work environment is joking and teasing (Chadsey-Rusch & Gonzalez, 1988).

Curriculum Planning

Several studies of extant programs producing high-quality outcomes reveal the importance of individualized curriculum planning, including the modification or supplementation of curriculum goals within the students' individualized education plan (IEP; Eagle et al., 1989; Gugerty et al., 1988; Parks et al., 1987). In these programs, general and vocational educators, along with guidance counselors and special educators, meet frequently to plan and deliver instruction based on assessment data depicting the performance of individual students with disabilities. In these programs, instruction is matched carefully to the learning styles of individuals or small groups of learners.

Recent studies have suggested a progressive use of the IEP, especially among adolescent students, to ensure that the process enhances the control these youth exert over their own futures (Micheals, 1994; Wehmeyer, 1994). In addition to guiding the determination of curriculum and instructional planning, the IEP should be used as a tool to assist students in planning learning, addressing self-advocacy skills, and assuming responsibility for their future transitions to working and independent living (Hanley-Maxwell & Collet-Klingenberg, 1995).

Appropriate Settings

Students with disabilities at the high school level who are successful in postschool outcomes are educated in age-appropriate settings, most often in regular classrooms during the latter school years. Evidence from an analysis of high-quality programs (Phelps &

Wermuth, 1992) suggests that both the assessment process and placement decisions are crucial. In-depth program evaluations and case studies reveal that students are carefully assessed and subsequently placed in vocational-technical programs based on IEP team analyses of their individual needs, family and academic backgrounds, abilities, and career interests. Among the various practices reported by these studies are use of career exploration programs in middle schools (Gugerty et al., 1988), career interest measures (Eagle et al., 1989), and bilingual assessment procedures and instruments (Parks et al., 1987).

COMPREHENSIVE SUPPORT SERVICES

Studies of programs with high-quality outcomes suggest that three integrated support services are present in such programs (Eagle et al., 1989; Gugerty et al., 1988; Parks et al., 1987). Instructional support services (including teacher aides, special materials, assistive technology, interpreters, and peer tutors) are present in the specific forms needed to address the learning of particular students with disabilities. Also noted in these studies is a close link to delivery of these instructional services in regular classes that are focused directly on occupational preparation and transition (e.g., business occupations, food service occupations, job seeking classes).

Career Guidance and Counseling

Career guidance services are included in many of the high-quality programs. These services are usually configured so that guidance counselors, rehabilitation counselors, and teachers provide career and labor market information to students and parents beginning in the early years of high school. As postschool transition plans are developed and formalized for students, this information is included more extensively in IEPs and classroom instruction.

The National Center for Research in Vocational Education is currently testing the viability of a set of criteria for identification of effective career guidance and counseling programs designed to meet the needs of diverse student populations. The preliminary framework is gleaned from an analysis of studies of programs that provide school-based guidance services to youth with disabilities and other special groups. The provisional criteria for documenting a specific guidance program include the program's capacities to assist students with self-assessment, deliver educational and occupational exploration and lifelong career planning, address the needs of diverse groups of learners, provide support services (e.g., child care), and create career information delivery systems (Maddy-Bernstein, 1994).

Continuous Assessment

Assessment of students' career interests and abilities is a component in many of the programs with positive student outcomes. A wide range of teacher-developed and commercially developed instruments and procedures are used to assess and monitor the development of career interests, aptitudes, informal work or volunteer experiences, and related academic skills (writing, oral communication, math, and reading skills).

Hanley-Maxwell and Collet-Klingenberg (1995) argue that ecological assessment is integral to the development of curriculum and instruction that facilitate transition. Ecological assessments take into account the broad array of concerns that professionals and parents must address, including the assessment of potential skill needs (task-specific and social skills), individual assessment (e.g., measures of future goals and aspirations, learning history, likes and dislikes), and support systems (e.g., existence of a family/friend network, community and employment services, independent living options). While not fully evident and identified as such, aspects of continuous ecological assessment systems can be found in many of the effective transition programs.

FORMALIZED ARTICULATION AND COMMUNICATION

Programs with documented transition outcomes for graduates are well connected to institutions and agencies beyond the school, as well as coordinated across different groups and departments within the school. For example, regular math and English teachers and vocational educators are involved directly in IEP meetings and transition planning discussions with personnel from rehabilitation agencies, community colleges, and adult service agencies. In many cases, formal systemic arrangements have been developed via intra- or interagency agreements to ensure that in-school instructional and transition planning is maximized, and to make cost-effective use of government and private services once students exit high school (Phelps & Wermuth, 1992).

Several programs feature extensive parental involvement in planning and evaluating the progress of their child's program, as required by federal legisla-

tion. Additionally, these programs make extensive use of parents on program advisory committees and special task forces, plan and conduct parent training workshops, and arrange support networks for parents whose children are leaving school (Eagle et al., 1989).

Early notification of parents and students regarding career education options and support services is required by the Perkins Vocational Education Act. Studies of programs with documented high-quality learner outcomes suggest that consultation with parents and middle school and early high school students is essential for students to gain access to the full range of services. Further, since most career options require concentrated and focused training, early planning helps to ensure that in-depth occupational programs can be completed (Gugerty et al., 1988; Parks et al., 1987).

As noted earlier, students with disabilities are to be provided with formalized transition planning under the Individuals With Disabilities Education Act (IDEA) Amendments of 1990 (section 602). However, prior to the enactment of the transition planning provisions of the IDEA, selected programs were providing coordinated services designed to move students and graduates successfully and systematically from one level of education to the next or to an appropriate postschool setting. Indicators of the scope and quality of the transition planning services included consultation with vocational rehabilitation and other nonschool agencies, frequent contact with representatives of the education or workplace settings being considered, involvement of parents and guardians, and consideration of a range of transition placements. However, it should be noted that the NLTS data on youth with disabilities do not confirm a positive relationship between formal transition planning (i.e., the presence of a formal plan with specified postschool goals and school-initiated contacts with potential placements) and positive postschool outcomes. While having a specific goal (e.g., academic postsecondary education, employment, or postsecondary vocational training) had a positive impact on attaining that goal, it was significant only for those students who chose to pursue academic postsecondary work. The presence of transition planning, formal goals, and school-initiated contacts for placement did not affect employment rates, compensation, or independent living status (Wagner et al., 1993).

Finally, most carefully evaluated programs have plans for internal and external coordination (Phelps & Wermuth, 1992). Internally, schools have well defined relationships between special education, at-risk services, vocational-technical education departments, and guidance and pupil services. Beyond the program or school, coordinated service arrangements often specify vocational assessment and job coaching services to be provided, referral and eligibility determination policies, job placement services, and additional training services to be provided by employment and training agencies.

OCCUPATIONAL EXPERIENCE, PLACEMENT, AND FOLLOW-UP

The most substantial and compelling evidence linking educational practices and positive learning outcomes for youth with disabilities can be found in the literature describing programs making extensive use of instruction in the workplace, direct job placement, and the provision of follow-up services. Research on this set of practices is extensive, in part because these approaches were instrumental in the early development of the field of secondary special education (e.g., adaptation of the vocational rehabilitation model to schools). Further, this arena of program practice focuses directly on the preferred outcome (e.g., employment), which is seen by many policymakers, educators, and parents as the central purpose of the secondary special education and transition enterprise (Clark, 1994; Edgar, 1988).

Work Experience Opportunities

The National Longitudinal Study of Youth With Disabilities (Wagner, 1991) confirmed several of the positive benefits of work experience. After all other variables were controlled for, students who had taken vocational education during their last year in high school were 9% more likely to be competitively employed. If youths' secondary vocational education involved work experience, the likelihood of employment was 14% higher than for students who had not been engaged in work experience. In a follow-up study of former special education students in Vermont, Hasazi, Gordon, Roe, Hull, et al. (1985) found that vocational training experiences, including part-time and summer work were significant predictors of employment.

Gierl and Harnisch (1995) examined the NLTS database on students participating in work experience programs more closely and found that (a) only 40% of students with disabilities had exposure to these programs, (b) students with mental retardation were much more likely to be engaged in work experi-

ence (45% compared to 38% for students with learning disabilities and 30% for students with emotional disturbance), and (c) significant differences in access to work experience favored Whites over African Americans of Hispanics.

Each of the programs with high-quality graduate outcomes (Phelps & Wermuth, 1992) featured supervised work experience programs wherein all students gained varying amounts of on-the-job experience during the program. In these programs, employment and work assignments were coordinated directly with instructional and career exploration goals for individual students.

Job Placement Services

Studies confirm the importance of providing youth with disabilities direct assistance in locating employment; however, there appear to be a variety of potentially effective approaches to job placement. In studying 54 matched pairs of young adults with mental retardation (half of whom had been successfully employed for 10 or more hours per week for more than 6 months), Heal et al. (1990) found that the support and services provided by employment placement agencies, parents, and employers were more extensive for those who had sustained employment.

Wehman, Kregal, and Barcus (1985) found that students with disabilities who were successful in gaining employment beyond high school seldom or never used a job placement service, but relied instead on friends or family members. This observation is substantiated by others (Hasazi, Gordon, & Roe, 1985; Schalock & Lilley, 1986; Schalock et al., 1986) who have documented the pervasive influence of the family and friend network in gaining employment.

However, programs with high-quality employment outcomes do make job placement services available to students with disabilities prior to and following completion of the vocational education programs. These services assist students in finding part-time and summer employment while still in school, and several were associated with the local job service offices operated by state and federal agencies.

SUMMARY AND DISCUSSION

This review suggests two primary concerns relative to improving the school-to-work transition for youth with disabilities. First, the general expectations for educational achievement by youth, including those with disabilities, are changing markedly as we approach the 21st century. The resulting uncertainty regarding valued knowledge and competence creates new dilemmas for both defining and assessing student learning for youth with disabilities. Addressing these dilemmas is especially critical for these youth, who traditionally have not fared well in terms of postschool outcomes—for example, employment, earnings, and further education. Second, the review of educational practices that are associated with positive learning outcomes for youth with disabilities appears to align with at least two of the proposed components of reforms in the national school-to-work movement: (a) integrating academic and vocational learning and (b) providing expanded opportunities for work experience.

Addressing New Outcomes and Measures of Achievement

Kagan (1990) reminds us of the importance of student achievement in educational research:

> For the most part, the public knows but one sign of good teaching—student achievement. Any agenda of research on teaching that ignores this variable must seem a pointless intellectual exercise. In refusing to acknowledge the importance of student achievement, educational researchers forfeit any chance of changing public opinion. Worse still, they must appear arrogant and nonresponsive to key constituencies— certainly unfit to decide how future teachers should be educated. (p. 458)

Studies reported herein reveal the abysmal record of achievement for youth with disabilities. The dropout rates for youth with disabilities exceed those of nondisabled students by nearly a factor of two. The lack of a high school diploma for nearly half of the students with emotional and behavioral difficulties is particularly problematic. For all students with disabilities who do complete high school, access to employment and postsecondary education still falls substantially below the levels attained by their nondisabled peers. In general, when students with disabilities do find employment, their earnings tend to be only slightly above the minimum wage in entry-level jobs, and they are faced with limited prospects for promotion and personal growth.

A less problematic but still pessimistic view is provided when one examines the transitional experiences of nondisabled youth. The National Longitudinal Survey of Youth reveals that the typical high school graduate between the ages of 18 and 27 who

did not enroll in postsecondary education held six different jobs and spent almost 35 weeks unemployed (Veum & Weiss, 1993). During the mid-1980s, employers expressed considerable concern regarding the competencies acquired by students in high school. Reports and studies sponsored by national business organizations and federal agencies (e.g., SCANS) focused attention on the reported lack of foundational or basic skills, as well as the general inability to function in the new workplace. Success in today's work environments requires teamwork and problem solving, as well as understandings of systems and new technologies. The introduction of national education goals and the initiation of a system of voluntary industry skills standards bode well for future efforts to delineate the new learning outcomes for secondary education. Despite these initiatives, to date the national dialogue has been limited concerning issues that are likely to affect employment outcomes for youth with disabilities in this forthcoming era of widespread educational reform. For example, the extent to which employment legislation such as Title I of the Americans With Disabilities Act (which provides mechanisms for reasonable accommodation in the workplace) assists employers in maintaining a competitive workforce in an era of new standards for workplace organization is not addressed in research to date. The new competencies sought by employers and colleges have created wide interests in alternative forms of assessment, including performance assessment and portfolio review. The appropriate use of these processes with youth with disabilities will require research exploring the influence of disabilities on the fairness and reliability of measurement techniques, privacy of information, and other related concerns. As schools shift more of the curriculum to include learning in the workplace, research on the effects of employment barriers encountered by youth with disabilities will be central to maximizing their participation.

Considering the Effects of Educational Practices for All Students

The evidence suggesting that special education placement and other pull-out or specialized interventions have substantial effects on learning is, at best, limited (Gamoran & Berends, 1987; Wang, Reynolds, & Walberg, 1988). As Oakes (1985) argues, these well-intentioned efforts to create responsive educational tracks have had substantial deleterious effects on learning and achievement for many students.

Combined with the evidence that inclusive programs and practices appear to have small to moderate beneficial effects on both academic and social outcomes for children with disabilities (Baker, Wang, & Walberg, 1994), the merger of special education with general education appears to be well underway nationally. The key consideration for educators and researchers becomes determining which educational practices serve all students' learning—and, in this case, with attention to outcomes and practices associated with employment and postschool transition.

From the five clusters of 20 educational practices considered in this review, two practices are found prominently and consistently in the research on school-to-work transition initiatives: functional curriculum and work experiences. These experiences have produced positive effects for students with a variety of disabilities.

The integration of vocational and academic skills to create a functional curriculum is intended to address the workplace demand for improved and broadened skills. As reflected in studies of cognitive learning psychology (e.g., Resnick, 1987), students' competencies relative to measuring and mathematics or science are likely to be increased if students are taught these skills in the context of their application and use beyond school (Newmann & Wehlage, 1995). A multitude of models are being developed and implemented that are each designed to achieve some level of integration. The range of approaches encompasses classroom integration (vocational teachers emphasizing more math, science, and writing; math and science teachers expanding the use of applications and real-world problems), team teaching models, the use of broad career clusters to orient high school curricula, and whole school reforms (for example, magnet and charter schools with occupation or career themes) (Grubb, 1995). While relatively little evidence exists to document the effects of these approaches on student learning, some of the findings from qualitative analyses of student experiences appear promising (Phelps, Hernandez-Gantes, Jones, & Holub, 1995).

The NLTS provides a more quantitative look at the impact of school experiences on vocational outcomes. This database provides estimates of the long-term effects of different types of school programs on outcomes for youth with disabilities from comparable family, ethnic, and economic backgrounds (Wagner

et al., 1993). The economic and educational benefits were substantial for students who had classes in regular education (but not advanced math or foreign language), concentrated in vocational education with work experience, and graduated. Compared to students with disabilities who graduated with an "academic only" preparation, these students were more likely to be competitively employed (78% to 71%), had higher annual wages ($10,141 to $8,750), and were much more likely to be pursuing postsecondary technical education (54% to 29%). The various studies cited in this review suggest further that a functionally oriented curriculum—that is, one which bridges academic, vocational, and independent living concerns—is frequently associated with positive employment and postschool outcomes.

Future research needs to address the variation in student learning and outcomes achieved by students from diverse backgrounds as they gain access to these integrated curricula that are enriched with work and community experience at the high school level. The evidence to date suggests that such approaches have been relatively successful for youth with mild disabilities. However, the question of whether or not similar approaches are able to reflect relationships to important employment and postsecondary education outcomes when delivered in the community of all students is of crucial importance.

School-supervised work experience has also been related to positive employment outcomes for youth with disabilities (Hasazi, Gordon, & Roe, 1985) and is experienced by nearly 40% of special education youth sometime during four years of high school (Wagner et al., 1993). Participation in work experience programs was associated with a number of positive secondary school outcomes, most notably a reduction in the dropout rate. While it is difficult to separate the effects of vocational education from work experience programs, it is clear that work experiences have profound effects on employment and earnings for youth with physical disabilities who were out of school for approximately 2 years (Wagner et al., 1993).

The use of programs linking school with a structured work experience is prominent among the ideas for improving education and work connections for all students (Stern, Finkelstein, Stone, Latting, & Dornsife, 1995). Among the most visible examples are youth apprenticeship programs, cooperative education, and school-based enterprises: unfortunately, the documented accounts of these model programs (e.g., Pauly, Kopp, & Haimson, 1994; Stern, Stone, Hopkins, McMillion, & Crain, 1994) fail to cite or discuss the participation of youth with disabilities in any of the programs studied. Stern et al. (1995) summarize the research on these programs as follows:

Students who work during high school obtain higher earnings in the first few years after leaving high school. In addition, students who work only a moderate number of hours per week have been found to perform better in school than those who do not work at all. However, students who work more hours per week perform less well in high school and obtain less postsecondary education. It is difficult to say how much these correlations represent the effect of working, or how much they reflect pre-existing differences among students. An important question, as yet unanswered, is whether providing some school supervision for jobs that are not now supervised by the school would mitigate some of the negative relationship between working and school performance. (p. 3)

Over the past 30 years, substantial federal investments have been made in advancing the quality of education for youth with disabilities, vocational education, and, more recently, school-to-work systems development at the state and local levels. However, the array of federal work-related education and training programs and special population targeting have created a fragmented, disjointed quagmire of programs and services for the populations most in need of effective schooling, transition, employment, and postsecondary education (Grubb, 1996). This review suggests that federal policy should be focused on both (a) a clear, explicit set of educational goals and performance standards (designed for all youth, including those with disabilities) and (b) consistent and tightly linked policies that include making richly integrated curricula (connecting academic, occupational, and employability outcomes) available to all students along with school-supervised work experiences. Policies should also be formulated at the federal and state levels to implement large-scale, promising practices that are potentially capable of significantly increasing post–high school employment and postsecondary education outcomes. However, such policies must provide for systematic and longitudinal evaluation measures.

Changes in teacher education and professional development systems are also crucial to advancing the quality of programs and outcomes for youth with disabilities. The results of this review suggest that all educators (including counselors and administrators) working in secondary schools must develop a critical understanding of the new workplace skills required of students. Additionally, professional preparation and development programs should enable educators to develop comprehensively integrated curricula employing both school- and work-based learning experiences. Strategies for accommodation and inclusion of youth with disabilities in these restructured education-and-work programs must be a high priority for redesigned teacher education programs at the undergraduate and graduate levels. Both future and practicing teachers need to be educated using approaches which integrate curriculum with real-world experiences and which, in turn, demonstrate the importance of these integrated perspectives for all students, especially those with disabilities.

The current research base provides limited information on which to develop transition practices. While school work experiences and functional curricula appear to positively influence immediate postschool outcomes for all students, specific practices and content remain unclear. To bring greater clarity to the efforts to improve postschool outcomes for youth with disabilities, future research needs to focus on two important arenas, as suggested above. First, the knowledge base must include a deeper understanding of the emerging skills and knowledge that employers indicate are integral to high performance in workplaces. Without a continuing assessment of employment requirements and accommodation strategies used by employers and individuals with disabilities, the match between educational competence and successful participation in the economy and community will remain problematic at the individual, program, community, and societal levels. Second, research endeavors need to explore the direct connections between practices and valued postschool outcomes. In addition to carefully designed longitudinal studies, efforts are needed to involve practitioners more extensively in conducting evaluations, inquiries, and applied research within the context of their communities and programs. To ensure that research efforts affect practices for high school-age youth with disabilities, practitioners, administrators, and researchers need to be engaged collaboratively in the search for teaching and learning experiences that produce high-quality postschool outcomes for all youth with disabilities.

References

Americans with Disabilities Act of 1990, 104 U.S.C. chap. 327.

Baker, E. T., Wang, M. C., & Walberg, H. J. (1994). The effects of inclusion on learning, *Educational Leadership, 52*(4), 33–35.

Benz, M. R., & Halpern, A. S. (1987). Transition services for secondary students with mild disabilities: A statewide perspective. *Exceptional Children, 53,* 507–514.

Blackorby, J., & Wagner, M. (1996). Longitudinal post-school outcomes of youth with disabilities: Findings from the National Longitudinal Transition Study. *Exceptional Children, 62,* 399–413.

Burrell, L. P. (1993, December). *A study of the preparation of vocational teachers for teaching mainstreamed at-risk special needs students.* Paper presented at the American Vocational Association Convention, Nashville, TN.

Chadsey-Rusch, J., & Gonzalez, P. (1988). Social ecology of the workplace: Employers' perceptions versus direct observation. *Research in Developmental Disabilities, 9,* 229–245.

Chadsey-Rusch, J., Rusch, F. R., & O'Reilly, M. F. (1991). Transition from school to integrated communities. *Remedial and Special Education, 12*(6), 23–33.

Clark, G. (1994). Is a functional curriculum approach compatible with an inclusive education model? *Teaching Exceptional Children, 26*(2), 36–39.

Copa, G. H., & Pease, V. H. (1992). *New designs for the comprehensive high school.* Berkeley: National Center for Research in Vocational Education, University of California, Berkeley.

DeStefano, L., & Wagner, M. (1993). *Outcome assessment in special education: Lessons learned.* Unpublished manuscript, University of Illinois.

Eagle, E., Choy, S., Hoachlander, E. G., Stoddard, S., & Tuma, J. (1989). *Increasing vocational options for students with learning handicaps: A practical guide.* Berkeley: University of California, National Center for Research in Vocational Education.

Edgar, E. (1988). Employment as an outcome for mildly handicapped students: Current status and future directions. *Focus on Exceptional Children, 21,* 1–8.

Education for All Handicapped Children Act of 1975, 20 U.S.C. chap. 33.

Evans, S. B. (1991, Summer). A realistic look at the research base for collaboration in special education. *Preventing School Failure, 35*(4), 10–13.

Fourqurean, J. M., & LaCourt, T. (1991, January/February). A follow-up of former special education students: A model for program evaluation. *Remedial and Special Education, 12*(1), 16–23.

Fourqurean, J. M., Meisgeier, C., Swank, P. R., & Williams, R. E. (1991). Correlates of postsecondary employment outcomes for young adults with learning disabilities. *Journal of Learning Disabilities, 24,* 400–405.

Gajar, A., Goodman, L., & McAfee, J. (1993). *Secondary schools and beyond: Transition of individuals with mild disabilities.* New York: Macmillan.

Gamoran, A., & Berends, M. (1987) The efforts of stratification in secondary schools. *Review of Educational Research, 57,* 415–435.

Gierl, M. J., & Harnisch, D. L. (1995, April). *Factors associated with dropping out for students with disabilities: A latent variable analysis using data from the National Longitudinal Transition Study.* Paper presented at the Annual Meeting of the American Educational Research Association, San Francisco.

Glasser, W. (1992). The quality school curriculum. *Phi Delta Kappan, 73,* 690–694.

Goals 2000: Educate America Act, 20 U.S.C. § 5801 (1993).

Greenspan, S., & Shoultz, B. (1981). Why mentally retarded adults lose their jobs: Social competence as a factor in work adjustment. *Applied Research in Mental Retardation, 2,* 23–38.

Grubb, W. N. (Ed.). (1995). *Education through occupations in American high schools: Vol. I. Approaches to integrating academic and vocational education.* New York: Teachers College Press.

Grubb, W. N. (1996, Fall). Creating coherent workforce preparation systems from the quagmire of education and job training. *CenterFocus, 13.* (National Center for Research in Vocational Education)

Gugerty, J. J., Tindall, L. W., Heffron, T. J., & Dougherty, B. B. (1988). *Profiles of success serving secondary special education students through the Carl D. Perkins Vocational Education Act: 12 exemplary approaches.* Madison: University of Wisconsin, Vocational Studies Center.

Halpern, A. S. (1992). Transition: Old wine in new bottles. *Exceptional Children, 58,* 202–211.

Hanley-Maxwell, C., & Collet-Klingenberg, L. (1995). *Research synthesis on the design of effective curricular practices in transition from school to community* (Tech. Rep. No. 9). Eugene: University of Oregon, National Center to Improve the Tools of Educators. (ERIC Document Reproduction Service No. ED 386 857).

Hanley-Maxwell, C., Rusch, F. R., Chadsey-Rusch, J., & Renzaglia, A. (1986). Reported factors contributing to job terminations of individuals with severe disabilities. *Journal of the Association for Persons With Severe Handicaps, 11*(1), 45–52.

Hasazi, S., Gordon, L., Roe, C., Hull, M., Fink, R., & Salembier, G. (1985). A statewide follow-up on the post high school employment and residential status of students labeled "mentally retarded." *Education and Training of the Mentally Retarded, 20,* 222–234.

Hasazi, S. B., Gordon, L. R., & Roe, C. A. (1985). Factors associated with the employment status of handicapped youth exiting high school from 1979 to 1983. *Exceptional Children, 51,* 455–469.

Hayward, B. J., & Wirt, J. G. (1989). *Handicapped and disadvantaged students: Access to quality vocational education.* Washington, DC: U.S. Department of Education, National Assessment of Vocational Education.

Heal, L. W., & Rusch, F. R. (1995). Predicting employment for students who leave special education high school programs. *Exceptional Children, 61,* 472–487.

Heal, L. W., et al. (1990). A comparison of successful and unsuccessful placements of youths with mental handicaps into competitive employment. *Exceptionality, 1*(3), 181–195.

Hoachlander, E. G., & Stoddard, S. (1987). *What works and why: Employment and training programs in the Bay area.* Berkeley, CA: Institute for the Study of Family, Work, and Community.

Individuals With Disabilities Education Act, 20 U.S.C. chap. 33 (1990).

Johnson, J. R., & Rusch, F. R. (1993). Educational reform and special education: Foundations for a national research agenda focused on special education, In P. D. Kohler, J. R. Johnson, J. Chadsey-Rusch, & F. R. Rusch (Eds.), *Transition from school to adult life: Foundations, best practices, and research directions.* Champaign: University of Illinois, Transition Research Institute. (ERIC Document Reproduction Service No. ED 358 607)

Kagan, D. M. (1990). Teacher cognition. *Review of Educational Research, 60,* 419–469.

Kohler, P. D. (1994). *A taxonomy for transition programming.* Champaign: University of Illinois, Transition Research Institute.

Kortering, L., & Edgar, E. (1988). Special education and rehabilitation: A need for cooperation. *Rehabilitation Counseling Bulletin, 31,* 178–184.

Little, J. W. (1982). Norms of collegiality and experimentation: Workplace conditions of school success. *American Educational Research Journal, 19,* 325–340.

Little, J. W. (1984). Seductive images and organizational realities in professional development. *Teachers College Record, 86*(1), 84–102.

Maddy-Bernstein, C. (1994). *Exemplary career guidance and counseling programs for the nation's diverse student population: A preliminary framework.* Berkeley: University of California, National Center for Research in Vocational Education.

McCrea, L. (1991). A comparison between the perceptions of special educators and employers: What factors are critical for job success? *Career Development of Exceptional Individuals, 14*(2), 121–130.

Micheals, C. A. (1994). *Transition strategies for persons with learning disabilities.* San Diego, CA: Singular.

Mithaug, D. E., Horiuchi, C., & Fanning, P. (1985). A report on the Colorado statewide follow-up survey of special education students. *Exceptional Children, 51,* 397–404.

National Center on Education and the Economy. (1990). *America's choice: High skills or low wages!* Rochester, NY: Author.

National Council of Teachers of Mathematics. (1989). *Curriculum and evaluation standards for school mathematics.* Reston, VA: Author.

Neel, R., Meadows, N., Levine, P., & Edgar, E. (1988). What happens after special education: A statewide follow-up study. *Behavior Disorders, 13,* 209–216.

Newmann, F. M., & Wehlage, G. G. (1995). *Successful school restructuring.* Madison: University of Wisconsin, Center on Organization and Restructuring of Schools.

Oakes, J. (1985). *Keeping track: How schools structure inequality.* New Haven, CT: Yale University Press.

Okolo, C., & Sitlington, P. (1988). The role of special education in learning disabled adolescents' transition from school to work. *Learning Disability Quarterly, 11,* 292–306.

Parks, M. A., McKinney, F. L., & Mahlman, R. A. (1987). *Characteristics of effective secondary vocational education programs for special populations.* Columbus: Ohio State University, National Center for Research in Vocational Education.

Pauly, E., Kopp, H., & Haimson, J. (1994). *Home-grown lessons: Innovative programs linking work and high school.* New York: Manpower Development Research Corporation.

Phelps, L. A., & Frongillo, M. C. (1986). Preparing vocational educators to serve special population youth: An exploratory evaluation and follow-up study. *Journal of Vocational and Technical Education, 3*(1), 33–44.

Phelps, L. A., Hernandez-Gantes, V., Jones, J., & Holub, T. (1995). Students' indicators of quality in emerging school-to-work programs. *Journal of Vocational Education Research, 20*(2), 75–101.

Phelps, L. A., & Wermuth, T. R. (1992). Effective vocational education for students with special needs: A framework. Berkeley: University of California, National Center for Research in Vocational Education.

Resnick, L. B. (1987). Learning in school and out. *Educational Researcher, 16*(9), 13–20.

Rojewski, J. W. (1996). Educational and occupational aspirations of high school seniors with learning disabilities. *Exceptional Children, 62,* 463–476.

Rosenholtz, S. J., Bassler, O., & Hoover-Dempsey, K. (1986). Organizational conditions of teacher learning. *Teaching and Teacher Education, 2*(2), 91–104.

Rusch, F. R., Enchelmaier, J. F., & Kohler, P. D. (1994). Employment outcomes and activities for youths in transition. *Career Development for Exceptional Individuals, 17,* 1–16.

Schalock, R. L., & Lilley, M. A. (1986). Placement from community-based mental health programs: How well do clients do after 8 to 10 years? *American Journal of Mental Deficiency, 90,* 669–676.

Schalock, R. L., Woltze, B., Ross, I., Elliott, B., Werbel, G., & Peterson, K. (1986). Postsecondary community placement of handicapped students: A five year follow-up. *Learning Disability Quarterly, 9,* 292–303.

School-to-Work Opportunities Act of 1994, 20 U.S.C. chap. 69.

Scuccimarra, D., & Speece, D. (1990). Employment outcomes and social integration of students with mild disabilities: The quality of life two years after high school. *The Journal of Learning Disabilities, 23,* 213–219.

Seigel, S., & Sleeter, C. E. (1991). Transforming transition: Next steps for the school-to-work transition movement. *Career Development for Exceptional Individuals, 14*, 27–41.

Shapiro, E. S., & Lentz, F. E. (1991). Vocational-technical programs: Follow-up of students with learning disabilities. *Exceptional Children, 58*, 47–59.

Sitlington, P. L., & Frank, A. R. (1990). Are adolescents with learning disabilities successfully crossing the bridge into adult life? *Learning Disabilities Quarterly, 13*(2), 97–111.

Sitlington, P. L., Frank, A. R., & Carson, R. (1992). Adult adjustment among high school graduates with mild disabilities. *Exceptional Children, 59*(3), 221–233.

Stern, D., Finkelstein, N., Stone, J. R., Latting, J., & Dornsife, C. (1995). *School to work: Research on programs in the United States*. London: The Falmer Press.

Stern, D., Stone, J., Hopkins, C., McMillion, M., & Crain, R. (1994). *School-based enterprise: Productive learning in American high schools*. San Francisco: Jossey-Bass.

U.S. Department of Education. (1992). *To assure the free and appropriate public education of all children with disabilities: Fourteenth annual report to Congress on the implementation of the Individuals With Disabilities Education Act*. Washington, DC: Author.

U.S. Department of Education (1994). *Changing education: Resources for systemic reform*. Washington, DC: Author.

U.S. Department of Labor. (1991). *What work requires of schools: A SCANS report for America 2000*, Washington, DC: Author.

Veum, J. R., & Weiss, A. B. (1993, April). Education and the work histories of young adults. *Monthly Labor Review*, pp. 11–20.

Wagner, M. (1991, April). *The benefits of secondary vocational education for young people with disabilities*. Paper presented at the Annual Meeting of the American Educational Research Association, Chicago.

Wagner, M., Blackorby, J., Cameto, R., & Newman, L. (1993). *What makes a difference? Influences on postschool outcomes of youth with disabilities*. Menlo Park, CA: SRI International.

Wang, M. C., Haertel, G. D., & Walberg, H. J. (1993). Toward a knowledge base for school learning. *Review of Educational Research, 63*, 249–294.

Wang, M. C., Reynolds, M. C., & Walberg, H. J. (1988). Integrating the children of the second system. *Phi Delta Kappan, 70*, 248–251.

Wehman, P., Kregal, J., & Barcus, J. M. (1985). From school to work: A vocational transition model for handicapped students. *Exceptional Children, 52*(1), 25–37.

Wehmeyer, M. L. (1994). Self-determination and the education of students with mental retardation. *Education and Training in Mental Retardation, 27*, 303–314.

White, W. J. (1992). The postschool adjustment of persons with learning disabilities: Current status and future projections. *Journal of Learning Disabilities, 25*, 448–456.

William T. Grant Foundation. (1988). *The forgotten half: Non-college youth in America*. Washington, DC: Author.

Ysseldyke, J. E., Thurlow, M. L., & Bruininks, R. H. (1992). Expected outcomes for students with disabilities. *Remedial and Special Education, 13*(6), 19–30.

Ysseldyke, J. E., Thurlow, M. L., Bruininks, R. H., Gilman, C. J., Deno, S. L., McGrew, K. S., & Shriner, J. G. (1992). *An evolving conceptual model of educational outcomes for children and youth with disabilities* (Working Paper No. 2). Minneapolis: University of Minnesota, National Center on Educational Outcomes.

Chapter Six

Relationships Between Schools and Parents, Families, and Communities

6.1 Making Sense of Disability:

Low-Income, Puerto Rican Parents' Theories of the Problem

Beth Harry

Abstract: This article reports findings from an ethnographic study of the views of 12 low-income Puerto Rican parents whose children were classified as learning disabled or mildly mentally retarded. Different cultural meanings of disability and normalcy led parents to reject the notion of disability and focus on the impact of family identity, language confusion, and detrimental educational practices on children's school performance. Parents' views were in line with current arguments against labeling and English-only instruction.

In the face of the rapidly increasing cultural diversity of the United States, the special education system is faced with the challenge of explaining its services and practices to people who may hold radically different types of cultural understanding, assumptions, and expectations regarding education. Current demographic projections for the 21st century (Hodgkinson, 1985) have underscored the urgency of finding radical solutions for the evident mismatch between school systems and many of those they serve.

This article is concerned with one aspect of this mismatch—the potential impact on parents of cross-cultural misunderstanding. The mandate for the participation of parents in the placement process should serve as a protection to students who might be inappropriately placed in special education programs and should provide assistance to educators in the decision-making process. However, unless professionals working with culturally different parents can find effective means of ensuring a shared understanding of the meaning of special education placement, the intent of the law will be seriously undermined.

Using the findings of an ethnographic study of low-income Puerto Rican parents' views, this article demonstrates both the impact of cross-cultural misunderstanding and the tremendous potential of parents as effective collaborators in the education process. The concerns of the parents centered on conflicting interpretations of the concept of disability and on parents' provision of alternative explanations for their children's learning difficulties. Cultural differences notwithstanding, the parents' explanations of their children's difficulties were very much in line with some of the major debates current in the field, that is, arguments concerning labeling as well as the debate on appropriate assessment and instruction of cultural and linguistic minority students.

PARENTS' VIEWS OF LABELING

Official definitions of *mild mental retardation* emphasize that the concept does not include the expectation of biologically based, permanent, and comprehensive incompetence. Nevertheless, the term continues to evoke such an impression, partly because the same term is used for individuals with much more severe intellectual limitations (Reschly, 1987), and partly because the term *disability* inevitably suggests a deficit within the individual.

A small but consistent body of literature on parents' reactions to labeling reflects this concern. Parents have been shown to be more accepting of terms such as *brain injured* (Barsch, 1961), *learning disabled,* and *slow learner* (Wolfensberger & Kurtz, 1974) than of retardation-related labels. The greater social desirability of the term *learning disabled* generally reflects the notion of an impairment that is specific rather than global in nature and therefore less stigmatizing to the image of the child as a whole person. Parents' preference for this type of description was observed by Smith, Osborne, Crim, and Rhu (1986). These researchers compared the definitions of learning disability given by 129 parents and 137 school personnel and found that parents tended to describe their children's difficulties in terms of physical disorders and attention span. The authors interpreted this tendency as a protective device on the part of parents to "neutralize" the social stigma attached to broader interpretations. On the other hand, Pollack (1985) pointed to potential negative effects if parents cling to such definitions to escape facing children's real needs. In case studies of upper-middle-class professional families, Pollack found that parents actively sought the "learning disabled" label, in what seemed to be an effort to deflect responsibility for negative familial dynamics underlying the child's difficulties.

Meanwhile, it is also likely that parents might be influenced by terminology they perceive to be negative. For example, Coleman (1984) found that mothers of children labeled learning disabled estimated their children's self-concept to be lower than the ratings actually given by the children themselves, perhaps because of the mothers' knowledge of social judgments. In addition, Kaufman (1982) found that mothers rated videotaped children more negatively when they were informed that the children were labeled mentally retarded rather than developmentally delayed.

It is important to distinguish between parents' reactions to the labels per se, and their estimations of their children's capabilities. Wolfensberger and Kurtz (1974) found that although parents' estimations of children's mental age and functioning agreed with those of professionals, they tended to reject retardation-related labels. Thus, parents' disagreement over any particular label does not necessarily mean that they do not recognize their children's difficulties, but rather that they interpret and name them differently.

These findings are in keeping with commonsense expectations of parents' need to protect their children and families from stigma. Further, it is in keeping with Goffman's (1963) well-known consideration of stigma, in which he observes that labeled persons themselves may engage in actions designed to camouflage their difference so as to "pass" for normal. This theory was applied by Edgerton (1967) to his findings that previously institutionalized persons labeled mentally retarded rejected the label and expended considerable energy in disguising their deviance. Edgerton referred to this self-defensive mechanism as a "cloak of competence." His follow-up study 10 years later, however, found that this concern was no longer central in the lives of these persons; he concluded that this related to their increased distance from the stigma of the institution. More recently, Zetlin and Turner (1984) identified different types of self-perceptions among such persons, which included both "acceptors" and "deniers" of the label, and argued that one significant source of such reactions was the way parents had explained their children's limitations to them.

It is important to understand the meaning of the concept of "passing." A standard that has been established by society for the identification of deviance does not represent objective reality or "truth," but simply a social agreement as to the definition of deviance. Indeed, labeling theory, as set forth by theorists such as Lofland (1969) and Becker (1963), emphasizes that definitions of deviance are social constructions negotiated by those with official power to label. Bogdan and Taylor's (1982) life histories of persons labeled mentally retarded have demonstrated that such persons' self-identifications may differ sharply from the way society has identified them. Bogdan and Taylor pointed out that these individuals' rejection of society's label simply reveals the existence of differing perspectives, thus underscoring the socially negotiated nature of the labeling process. In other words, because a person engages in denial, one cannot assume that the denier is inherently wrong, and the official labeler is right, since the application of the label is but a social decision reflecting a societal value. To attempt to "pass" is simply to assert one's self-definition over the definition imposed by society.

Parental rejection of labels for their children underscores the highly differentiated response of individuals to their loved ones, whom they see as individuals with behaviors that may be recognizably different, but which do not necessarily render the whole individual "deviant" and therefore warrant a deviant classification. Thus, when professionals say that parents do not accept a child's classification, it should not be assumed that the professional is right and the parent wrong, but rather that both are using different criteria for describing the child. It would be more appropriate to describe the parent as disagreeing with the label than as failing to accept it.

Most studies of parents' views of labeling were either conducted with white populations, or else did not specify differences in responses between racially different groups. Studies of non-white parents' views of the mental retardation label per se are few, the best known being Mercer's (1972) report of interviews with Black and Hispanic parents who explicitly rejected the appropriateness of the label for their children. These parents felt that the special education classes into which the children were placed offered no remediation to their learning difficulties. Marion (1980) has also reported that Black parents have expressed resentment at the disproportionate classification and special education placement of their children.

Although the impact of the "mild mental retardation" label is important for all students and their families, the decades-long controversy has been fueled by the overrepresentation of minority students in special education programs (Dunn, 1968; Mercer, 1973). This continuing concern has more recently focused on the pressing need for more appropriate and effective methods of assessment and instruction for cultural and linguistic minority students (Duran, 1989; Figueroa, 1989; Ortiz & Polyzoi, 1986). The intensity of the debate reflects the elusive nature of the search for a dividing line between special and regular education, while the arbitrariness of the designation "disability" for many students with mild learning disorders illustrates that the concept is more a reflection of social values than of objective reality. For many minority students, underachievement is the point at which regular and special education meet, with many students from what has been called the "mental withdrawal—grade retention—drop-out syndrome" (Stein, 1986), crossing the border from "normalcy" to "disability."

HISPANIC PARENTS AND SPECIAL EDUCATION

Since Mercer's (1972) study of parents' opinions, which was conducted before the passage of Public Law 94-142, literature focusing on Hispanic parents has centered on their knowledge of and participation in the education process. Documentation so far indicates that parents place great value on education and express faith in the schools, but that their knowledge of what actually goes on in schools in the United States may be minimal (Condon, Peters, & Sueiro-Ross, 1979; Delgado-Gaitan, 1987). Studies focusing on special education show a similar pattern, indicating that there is often no parallel in the families' home countries (Figler, 1981; Lynch & Stein, 1987) and that cultural meanings attached to concepts of disability may be very different from those in the United States (Condon et al., 1979; Correa, 1989; Figler, 1981). Further, a recent ethnographic study by Bennett (1988) concluded that the discourse of parent-professional interactions is so structured as to render parents effectively powerless as partners in their children's educational careers.

The present study offers an additional dimension to the literature on Hispanic families' interaction with special education by seeking parents' actual definitions of disability, as well as their reactions to the experience of their children's classification and placement in special education programs. Further, the study shows that such parents can be very perceptive about their children's difficulties and, therefore, have a great deal to contribute to an effective parent-professional partnership.

DESIGN OF THE STUDY

The findings reported in this article are part of a larger data set from an ethnographic study of low-income, Puerto Rican-American parents' views of special education (Harry, 1992). The primary aim of the study was to examine the role of culture in parents' interpretations of their children's special education placement. A secondary aim was to examine the extent and quality of the parents' interaction with the special education system, as well as factors that facilitate or obstruct their participation. This article addresses only the findings related to the first of these aims.

Participants were 12 Puerto Rican-American families residing in a low-income, largely Hispanic community, in a medium-sized city in the northeast. In three families, both fathers and mothers were participants, while in the other nine, only mothers and one grandmother participated. Spanish was the language of the homes; only one mother, who was born on the mainland, was a native speaker of English. The families had lived between 2 and 12 years on the mainland, and 11 families were currently receiving welfare benefits. Only two of the mothers had completed high school, most having left school between the fourth and ninth grades, while few of the fathers had gone beyond the fifth grade.

Although the sample number was small, these 12 families represented 17 children in special education programs, which amounted to 35% of the 48 Puerto Rican students enrolled in special education programs in the school district. All but one of these 48 were classified as having mild disabilities, while among the sample children 6 were classified as mentally retarded and 11 as learning disabled.

The parents were contacted by two Hispanic social workers affiliated with a neighborhood voluntary agency. This approach was important because it allowed the researcher to be presented as an independent agent, not affiliated with or accountable to the school system and therefore in a better position to gain parents' honest opinions of the system. Selection of the families was based on personal judgments by the social workers concerning which families they felt would be most accessible and most willing to participate. Families were not chosen because of any prior knowledge regarding the parents' experiences with the school system. The researcher was introduced to the parents by the social workers and subsequently proceeded independently of them.

Over a period of 9 months, information was collected through repeated unstructured interviews, conducted in the ethnographic tradition (Spradley, 1979; Bogdan & Biklen, 1982), with recurring feedback from researcher to participants to ensure accuracy and correct interpretation. At least three taped interviews were held with each family. The interviews were conducted by the researcher in participants' homes in Spanish or a mixture of Spanish and English, as appropriate; further, additional informal interviews were held with most parents. A second method of data collection was participant observation, conducted primarily in the style of "observer as participant" (McCall & Simmons, 1969). These included seven meetings between parents and school personnel, as well as a variety of family and community activities. Triangulation of data was achieved by examination of students' school documents and by interviews with 12 district professionals involved in special education policy or service delivery to Spanish-speaking families.

The findings of this study are based on the views of a small group of parents from a particular background, that is, Puerto Rican families of low income and relatively little formal education, who might be described as being in the early stages of acculturation to the culture of the U.S. mainland. Their voices cannot be expected to be representative of all culturally different parents, or even of all Hispanic parents. However, though the study cannot claim to be generalizable to other populations, the in-depth, recursive nature of the interview and observation methodology ensures that an accurate picture of parents' views has been obtained. In other words, one of the main strengths of this methodology lies in its claim to validity—the notion that what it claims to demonstrate is in fact what has been studied, and therefore that one might expect similar findings with a similar population under similar circumstances.

Patton (1980) has offered a thoughtful discussion of the relevance of generalizability to qualitative data and concludes that the strength of the method lies in the provision of perspective and of well-grounded information that can lead to action. In the case of this study, the clarity of participants' perspectives demonstrates the principle of cultural relativity, which goes beyond the particular views of a given group and which can serve as a guide for professionals working with any significantly different cultural group.

FINDINGS

This article focuses on two central findings: first, important ways in which the meaning of disability differed along cultural lines for these families and, second, that the parents held their own theories explaining their children's difficulties. With regard to the issue of culturally based meanings of disability, the data showed two particular trends:

1. The parameters of "normalcy" in terms of children's developments were much wider than those used by the educational system.
2. Different designations for disability led to parents' confusion of terms like *handicapped* and *retarded* with more extreme forms of deviance.

This section outlines, first, the meaning of the labels and, second, parents' theories of their children's problems.

The Meaning of the Labels

Francisca, a woman of 55, had years of experience with the special education system. Her daughter, Angelica, had been placed in a program for children labeled "educable mentally retarded" when she was between the ages of 8 and 13. At the time of the study, she had returned to the regular class, but Francisca's granddaughter, Rosita, was currently in special education, classified as "mildly mentally retarded." The following is Francisca's account of her daughter's initial referral to special education. This story is representative of the way in which many families described the initial referral of a child for special education services. For many it was a moment of crisis, marking the onset of a period of confusion and distress.

When the children were small I always used to go and collect them from school. One day, when my youngest daughter was in the second grade, I went to get her and as I was walking along Spruce Street the child came running toward me screaming. I was very frightened and thought that something terrible had happened. When she got close to me she grabbed me and threw herself on me and shrieked, "Mammi!" I said, "My God! What has happened to you?" And she said to me, "The teacher told me that I must not come to her class anymore, that she is not going to struggle with me anymore because I am crazy!"

So I went to the school and I told them the child is not crazy but they started sending me these letters and I took them to the Latin American Association and asked someone what they said and they told me it said the child is retarded. They put her in the special class although I told them at the meeting that no person who is retarded, who does not have a good mind, can do the hard school work she does. I told them to stop sending these letters because the child sees them, she knows English and she reads them and she gets very upset and says, "I am not going back to the school unless they stop saying I am crazy because I am not crazy."

Now they are saying the same thing about my granddaughter, but she has nothing wrong with her mind either. She behaves well and she speaks clearly in both Spanish and English. Why do they say she is retarded? . . .

They say that the word "handicap" means a lot of things, it doesn't just mean that a person is crazy. But for us, Puerto Ricans, we still understand this word as "crazy." For me, a person who is handicapped is a person who is not of sound mind or has problems in speech or some problem of the hands or legs. But my children have nothing like that, thanks to God and the Virgin! (Francisca)

Most parents were initially as incredulous as Francisca at the assignment of the label "mentally retarded." Coming from a background where daily affairs can be managed by a healthy body, common sense, and elementary academic skills, parents explained that the label "retarded" or "handicapped" would be applied only to someone whose competence is severely impaired or who is considered mentally deranged. Thus, the labeling of Francisca's daughter and granddaughter seemed a contradiction in terms: How could a person who is retarded read and become incensed by the very letter that describes her as retarded? How could a 6 1/2-year-old who speaks both English and Spanish be retarded?

In addition to different parameters for normal development, the word "retardado" was tied to the general category of mental illness—a tremendously stigmatized form of social deviance. Thus the term would only be used to denote behavior and a functional level seriously different from the norm. One mother, Ana, speaking in terms very similar to those of Francisca, made a clear distinction between "retarded" and "handicapped":

For me, retarded is crazy; in Spanish that's "retardado." For me, the word "handicap" means a person who is incapacitated, like mentally, or missing a leg, or who is blind or deaf, who cannot work and cannot do anything . . . a person who is invalid, useless. . . . But for Americans, it is a different thing—for them, "handicap" is everybody! (Ana)

For parents to accept the use of the word *retarded* they had to start by differentiating it from the word *loco/crazy*, and most parents who made this transition substituted the word *slow*. However, to reach this level of agreement with the school, parents would still need to see the child as significantly different from their own expectations. This became confusing for parents whose own level of education was at the third or fourth grade and who had a child already in the fifth or sixth, or who was bilingual while the parent found English difficult to learn. One mother, Carmen, exclaimed angrily that the work her daughter was doing was sometimes so hard that "neither her father nor I can do it!"

The term *learning disabled* did not evoke the same confusion for parents, but neither did they accept it as an appropriate description of their children's difficulties. They readily understood the intent of the term, and did not find it offensive since it acknowledged the overall developmental competence of the children. However, with only one exception, the notion of a deficit intrinsic to the child was rejected by the parents; in other words, they did not interpret the difficulty as a "disability." Their explanations are described in the next section.

Parents' Theories

Parents' interpretations of their children's difficulties varied in specific ways; but from all the interviews there emerged three distinct themes: the importance of family identity in the interpretation of a child's developmental patterns; the detrimental effects of second-language acquisition on school learning; and the detrimental effects of educational practices such as frequent changes in placement, out-of-neighborhood placement, an unchallenging curriculum, and inflexible reading instruction.

Family Identity. The strong familism of Hispanic cultures is well documented (Condon et al., 1979). With reference to Puerto Rican people in particular, Canino (1980) has described the typical family as tending to show an "enmeshed" rather than a "disengaged" structure. In this pattern, there is a strong emphasis on the family's identity as a group rather than as a collection of individuals, which, Canino says, may lead to features such as, "prolonged mother-child interaction," overlapping of nuclear and extended family roles, and a perception of illness as a problem that resides within the family rather than solely within the individual.

This concept of the family became a crucial factor in some parents' interpretations of their children's being described as "handicapped." For example, some parents said they felt that their families had been disgraced because the social histories written about the children gave the impression that the children's difficulties resulted from immorality in the family. In addition to these families' traditional association of "retardation" with mental illness, disability thus took on an extra stigma, that of being tied to bad family character.

Parents' comments also demonstrated that although a strong concept of group identity makes the whole group vulnerable, there is a resilience created by these same assumptions. That is, inasmuch as the individual may bring shame to the group, so may aspects of the groups's identity serve to protect the individual. Thus, all parents spoke of their children's strengths and weaknesses in terms of family characteristics.

There is a certain acceptability in a child's difficulties "coming from the father," or being "just like his aunt." Some mothers modified the term "retarded" and other rejected it outright; but in either case they described the children in terms of marked family traits not considered to be outside the range of normal behavior. Thus, they felt that the school's labeling process did not recognize the child's individuality and family identity. Francisca, for example, explained both her daughter's and her granddaughter's difficulties at school in terms of the school's preference for more expressive types of personality. Her children, she said, were very quiet, both by heredity and because of the family's life style:

As I told them at the school, the only problem my child has is that she is very quiet. She does not talk much. But this quietness comes from the family because the father of these children is very silent. If you speak to him he speaks, if you greet him he greets you, if not, nothing! . . . So this is by heredity; the child has no problem in speech nor is she retarded or anything. . . .

And my granddaughter—she is very timid, you know. I brought her up here and she does not play with other children outside, only at school. At home I only let her go outside if she goes with the family, but alone, no. (Francisca)

In a similar vein, another mother, Ramona, acknowledged that her 10-year-old daughter was progressing more slowly than most children in academic work, but did not agree that this meant she was mentally retarded. Rather, she described her daughter as very unsure of herself because of extreme shyness, similar to that of her "father's family" and of Ramona herself. Ana, whose 9-year-old, Gina, was also classified as "mentally retarded," agreed that her daughter needed a special class because she was slow in learning and her behavior was very erratic. Ana understood what "Americans" mean by "retarded" but considered it irrelevant: Gina, she said, is simply "like her father." He never did learn to read and write and has a quick temper. He has always been like that, and she feared that Gina would be too:

I think she won't change because she is the same thing as my husband. He is always "con coraje" (quick to anger). You tell him something, he talks to you back. He can't stay quiet. He spoils Gina—he says, "I love her because she is just like me!" (Ana)

Learning Disability: "A causa del idioma/Because of the language." Parents of children in both learning disability and mental retardation classifications tended to place their children's difficulties in the context of family identity. Beyond this, however, parents also placed a great deal of responsibility for children's difficulties on the school. Here a noticeable pattern emerged regarding the disability label. Parents of children labeled learning disabled focused on the common theme of "confusion" resulting from the change from Spanish to English, and one parent specifically charged the method of teaching reading as the source of her daughter's difficulties. Parents of children labeled mentally retarded, however, focused on other detrimental educational practices.

Because Spanish was the primary language in all homes in the study, even those children born in the United States learned Spanish as their first language. Thus, English became a requirement only upon entrance into school, which, for most, was between kindergarten and the third grade. These children were placed directly into regular education English-speaking classes with varying amounts of "pull-out" for the "English as a Second Language" (ESL) program. Those labeled mentally retarded were identified within a year or two, and those labeled learning disabled were referred to special education between the second and sixth grades. All of the latter group had repeated one or, in several cases, two grades before being referred.

Parents said that the children had been "doing fine" in prekindergarten and kindergarten and that their problems began when the child entered the elementary grades. Of those children who had started school in Puerto Rico, most of the parents said that the child had no problem in school there. Only two children, who had behavior problems, had been considered for special education placement in Puerto Rico.

Some parents interpreted the second-language difficulties in school as a reflection of teachers' intolerance and unreasonable expectation. Josefina, for example, whose 14-year-old son had been in a special education class since the fourth grade, pointed to an undue focus on students' accents, a point which has also been made by researchers Moll and Diaz (1987). To quote Josefina:

It is all because of the language—nothing more! At first my son did not know English, but he had to learn to read it and write it. Then when he learned it, his pronunciation was not perfect like an American because he must have a Puerto Rican accent, but they wanted him to know it correctly. When I went to the meeting they said that the child is at a high level in math but the reading. . . . So I told them that I suppose that a child from Puerto Rico could not learn English so quickly—he can learn to read it but not so perfectly as an American! (Josefina)

Another mother, Delia, illustrated the impact of the language problem by drawing a comparison between her older children, who began school in Puerto Rico and were doing "all right" until they entered the first and second grades in the United States, and her youngest child, who was born in the United States and went to prekindergarten here. She said that at the end of the semester there was a family joke when the little girl came home from her kindergarten class with a certificate for good reading; the older children laughed, but were really embarrassed because they were behind in reading. Delia concluded that the difference was that "the little girl started here in the pre-k, not like the others starting in Puerto Rico and then coming to this country to meet with a new language."

Although parents were adamant regarding the role of language confusion, it was evident that they did not have a clear idea of exactly how this worked in school. Parents used the terms *ESL* and *bilingual* interchangeably and expressed the belief that this program was the source of the children's confusion. However, none of the children in the study were old enough to have been in the district's bilingual program, which had been discontinued about 8 years before the study began.

Another aspect of the comment that "bilingual or ESL" classes confused children is that this belief presented a dilemma for most of the parents: They felt that a choice had to be made between English and Spanish, and all were adamant that they would choose English for their children. Yet they thought it a shame that the children were not learning to read and write in Spanish, and might even forget the language after a while. For families who thought they might like to return to Puerto Rico, this was particularly worrying. Others simply felt that the ability to speak two languages should be an advantage.

Teaching of Reading. The teaching of reading became the focus of one mother's concern. Dora, whose daughter, Maria, was labeled learning disabled, was pursuing an understanding of the methodology used to teach reading and had concluded that inflexible use of a direct-instruction, phonic method, along with repeated grade retention, had compounded her daughter's language-induced difficulties. Dora did not consider her daughter as learning disabled, because, she said:

When I started teaching her to read in kindergarten, I taught her to read the whole word and she was learning, but the way they are teaching her now is confusing her. All children are not the same, and she is not learning by this method. For one thing, it is only phonetics; and she became confused when she started school and had to learn the difference between the letters ABC, and the sounds you have to say in English. (Dora)

Both Dora's account and her daughter's school records showed that although Maria had passed the first reading level at the end of the second grade, in repeating the grade she had, somehow, been put back to the same level. Toward the end of her repeating year, Maria's report indicated that she still had not mastered this reading level. Her mother was incredulous:

It is a very hard thing to understand! It is impossible that Maria could stay a whole year on the same reading level, especially when she had passed it the year before! (Dora)

Placement and Curriculum in the Special Class. Although parents of children labeled mentally retarded generally agreed that their children were slow in development, they argued that two aspects of special education programming had exacerbated their children's difficulties and, in Ana's words, had done the children "a lot of harm." The detrimental practices identified were, first, frequent changes of school and, second, an infantile and repetitive curriculum in the special class.

The frequent changes of placement reflected the school district's pattern of moving children labeled mentally retarded to whatever was considered the most appropriate self-contained program. This was devastating for some children and for their parents, who, for the most part, spent most of their time in their own neighborhood and generally considered the city at large dangerous and alien. Rita's daughter, Marta, for example, had been moved to five different schools between ages 6 and 9, and had finally been placed in a school where the district said she would remain until age 12. Similarly, Francisca's grand-daughter, Angelica, had been placed in three different schools between the ages of 5 and 7, and Francisca had recently refused to allow her to be moved to a fourth. Ana's daughter, Gina, had experienced four school changes by the age of 9. The parents were angry about the moves and about the children's being placed in schools outside of the neighborhood.

These parents were also angry about the nature of the curriculum in special classes, which they all said taught only kindergarten activities such as painting and coloring. In Francisca's words:

> They give her a little paper with animals and she has to mark if it is a cow or a dog, and things like that! I see her as much more alert than that and she could learn to count and write. . . . All day long she is wasting time, because they are not teaching her anything. If she needs to learn to paint I could teach her at home! (Francisca)

Ana had encountered the same problem when her son had been placed in special education some years before in another city. Upon relocating, she found her own way of solving the problem:

> When I moved down here I was tired of José staying down in the special class. He was always in kindergarten; they never let him pass to the first grade because they say he doesn't know the work. But how can José know something if you don't tell him how to do it? All they did was painting and some little stuff—every day the same thing. So when I came here I told them I lost the school papers and I put him in regular first grade. He failed one year, but the next year he passed. . . . He never failed since then, and he gets As and Bs in the regular class because he is very intelligent. (Ana)

Parents' Views of Children's Progress

Despite disagreement with the school's interpretations of the meaning of their children's difficulties, parents' satisfaction with the effectiveness of special education varied. As indicated previously, the exigencies of special class placement were generally seen as a deterrent to children's progress for those labeled mentally retarded. On the other hand, some parents of children labeled learning disabled felt that the resource room program was helping their child. Margarita

and Delia, for example, who both explained their children's problems in terms of second-language "confusion," said that the children were progressing better as a result of the special attention. Inés, the only mother who said she had come to the United States because of her son's learning difficulties, felt that the school was doing its best and she was getting the services she came for. Others, however, such as Dora and Josefina, were skeptical, believing that a combination of intolerance and inappropriate methods continued to hold the children back.

Yet it is important to note that the parents did not object to special assistance as such. On the contrary, they all said that small-group instruction should be the main benefit of special education. Even parents who considered the curriculum or the teaching methods inappropriate also felt that the child "would not make it" in a large class. In sum, parents mostly agreed that the children were having difficulty and were willing to accept appropriate and effective help from special education, but varied in their assessment of the actual success of these programs.

DISCUSSION

This study of parents' views makes two crucial points for professionals in special education: first, it illustrates the argument that conceptions of disability are socially constructed (Bogdan & Knoll, 1988) and that, in the words of Irving Goffman, "The normal and the stigmatized are not persons but rather perspectives" (Goffman, 1963, p. 138). Second, the study shows a cluster of folk theories that are very much in line with certain current arguments in the field of special education.

Parents' Theories as Cultural Perspectives

The perspectives of these 12 Puerto Rican families should sharpen educators' awareness of the potential for cross-cultural misunderstanding inherent in the culturally specific classification system used by special education. As professionals, we need to be reminded that any deviance classification is based on the values and expectations of a society in a particular era. Indeed, it is likely that, in a more rural and less technological America, mainstream conceptions of disability may have been considerably different.

The language of the law (the Individuals with Disabilities Education Act), however, and the medical model it espouses, reflect none of this ambiguity. Indeed, the process of reification, by which a theoretical construct is treated as objective reality (Bowers, 1984), is evident in the conception of disability inherent in special education theory and practice—the belief that a child's failure to master certain skills is indicative of an objectively identifiable intrinsic deficit. The limitations of the assessment process are recognized by the law in its call for measures to ensure unbiased assessment, yet the subjective nature of the process is inescapable and becomes most evident with students from culturally diverse backgrounds.

The interpretation of parents' disagreement as a reflection of cultural difference may be challenged in a number of ways. First, it is appropriate to ask whether these parents' views differ significantly from those of mainstream American parents; second, whether parents are simply engaging in a process of denial to protect their children's and their families' identities; third, whether parents' disagreement simply represents a difference in nomenclature—in this case, a mistaken translation of the term *retarded* to mean *crazy*.

Wolfensberger (1983) described the process of stigmatizing in terms of the negative valuing of a characteristic, the subsequent attribution of that characteristic as the defining feature of an individual, and, hence, the ultimate devaluing of the whole individual. Similarly, Goffman (1963) spoke of this process as the "spoiling" or "disgracing" of individual identity. As was indicated by the earlier review of literature, parents' desire to protect their families from such stigma could explain the commonly observed preference for milder, more specific, rather than global labels. The literature also showed that parents disagreed with professionals mostly at the level of naming the problem, not at the level of describing children's performance or behavior. In this regard, the parents in this study showed a pattern similar to what is known about mainstream parents, in that they rejected the labels while acknowledging that their children have difficulties. The reasons for their rejection of these labels, however, were complex.

First, like the mainstream parents in the literature, they found the label "mental retardation" too stigmatizing. This was exacerbated by the fact that the traditional Spanish used by these families does not have a word for *retarded*, but rather identifies mental disability with mental retardation, under the vernacular term *loco* (*crazy*). It is not simply a matter of mistranslation, but a reflection of an absence of distinction between mental illness and intellectual impairment, the latter being considered an impairment only at the more extreme end of the spectrum.

The avoidance of stigma, however, is not the only reason that parents may reject a label. The parents in this study genuinely disagreed that deficits in mastering academic skills were tantamount to a handicap, as was made clear by Francisca's incredulity that a child who can read and who can speak two languages could be considered retarded. The use of academic learning as a criterion for normalcy is clearly related to differing societal norms.

Beyond the issues of stigma and varying societal norms, there is also the question of assumptions about etiology in mild disabilities. The concept of disability, by definition, suggests some impairment intrinsic to the individual. Mainstream parents have argued for more restricted, less global interpretations of children's difficulties, but have not rejected the notion of disability as such. Indeed, it is well known that parents have been a powerful force in the recognition of the existence of learning disabilities. In this study, parents of children labeled mentally retarded, when they accepted their children's delay as an intrinsic characteristic, tended to accept it as falling within the normal framework of the family's identity, and did not define it as a disability. Parents of children labeled learning disabled, on the other hand, explicitly rejected the notion of within-child etiology, identifying the source as extrinsic to the child. This is in keeping with the previously mentioned work of Mercer (1972) and of Marion (1980) with Black and Hispanic parents.

Thus, the views of culturally different parents may differ in some important ways from those of mainstream parents. This study shows how intense can be the stigmatizing effects on families whose cultural base is different, whose knowledge of the school system is minimal, and who already feel powerless and alienated. Correa (1989) made the point that acculturation must be a two way, "reciprocal" process, with professionals in education becoming sensitized to the values and norms of the cultures from which their students come. First, however, professionals must become aware of their own values, and of the fact that most human values are not universal but are generated by the needs of each culture. Such awareness is not too much to ask: It is through the eyes of the school that a child officially comes to be defined as a success or a failure; the school system must, therefore, accept the tremendous responsibility that accompanies such power.

Folk Theories and Professional Arguments

The ability of these parents to identify weaknesses in the education system exemplifies the validity of the law's intention to include parents in the decision-making process, yet it is notable that the discourse between parents and professionals provided no forum for parents' theories to be heard. Indeed, as has been observed elsewhere (Harry, 1992), such discourse is structured so as to exclude and delegitimate views that fall outside the framework of the law's conception of disability.

Marion (1980), in discussing the subordinate role often accorded minority parents, stated that professionals often withhold information on the assumption that such parents are too unsophisticated to benefit from much professional information. Similarly, Sullivan (1980) charged professionals with assuming that low-income parents will accept any evaluation of their children. This study illustrates the perceptiveness of a group of low-income parents who spoke neither the literal nor the metaphorical language of the school. The study offers a small but effective challenge to the recent charge of Dunn (1988) that Hispanic parents' lack of interest is partly responsible for the poor performance of their children. The theories of these parents reflect ongoing debates current among professionals in the field—debates on labeling, on appropriate instruction for bilingual students, and on the efficacy of special class placement.

Labeling. Arguments against the current classification system are no less than 20 years old (Dunn, 1968; Mercer, 1973) and have continued to gain momentum (Gardner, 1982; Reynolds & Lakin, 1987) with regard to both the mild mental retardation construct and learning disabilities. One recommendation for change has been a call for new designations, such as "educational handicap" (Reschly, 1987), or "educationally delayed" (Polloway & Smith, 1987), reflecting the fact that students' difficulties are largely related to academic learning. Indeed, Reschly's argument that students classified as mildly retarded are "inappropriately stigmatized by implicit use of the same continuum for all levels of mental retardation" (Reschly, p. 37) is identical to that of the parents in this study. Goodman (1989), in a study of thirdgraders' perceptions of the term *mentally retarded*, has recently demonstrated that this label is a "poor diagnostic term . . . embedded in erroneous thinking" (p. 327) and has called for new terminology or classification criteria.

More radical, however, are challenges that call for rejection of categorical eligibility criteria based on the concept of within-child deficits. Such arguments call for a system of service that would reflect the programmatic needs of students or that rely on curriculum-based approaches and dimensional rather than categorical diagnosis (Gerber & Semmel, 1984; Reynolds & Lakin, 1987).

These arguments are even more urgent when applied to students from racially and culturally diverse backgrounds. It is not enough to say that many people misunderstand disability classifications and that it is therefore simply a matter of nomenclature. It is now widely acknowledged that our assessment system is severely limited in its ability to identify the true nature of students' learning difficulties, especially when these students' cultural experiences predispose them to linguistic, cognitive, and behavioral styles that may differ in important ways from what is considered normative on most assessment instruments (Cummins, 1984; Figueroa, 1989). Particularly relevant to the views of parents in this study is the observation that the "learning disability" label is often applied to children whose difficulties are really a reflection of normal second-language development (Ortiz & Polyzoi, 1986).

This study supports the argument that it is time for us to abandon our reliance on a model whose main effect is to locate the source of failure in the child. The concept of disability in the case of underachieving children is simply inadequate and inappropriate in the context of the tremendous diversity of American schools.

Instruction and Efficacy. Research on instruction and efficacy in special education also parallels the interpretations of parents in this study. Cummins (1979, 1984) has argued convincingly that children may demonstrate adequate basic interpersonal competence in a second language while their level of cognitive academic language proficiency may be inadequate to the task of literacy or psychological assessment in the second language. Indeed, the literature on this topic overwhelmingly concurs that to move children to second-language literacy too soon is to set them up for failure in both languages, thus preparing them for low-status roles in the host society, as well as alienation from their native culture (Cordasco, 1976; Lewis, 1980; Ovando & Collier, 1985; Spener, 1988; Stein, 1986).

A crucial outcome of the premature introduction of children to instruction in the second language is grade retention, a feature frequently observed among bilingual students, with a common pattern of "overage" students (Walker, 1987). Among the families in this study, it was not uncommon to find children as much as 3 years older than the usual age for their grade, and it was the rare child who had not repeated at least one grade level.

Besides language of instruction, research is increasingly focusing on the need for culturally sensitive instructional approaches. In contrast to the direct instruction, phonic-based approach used with

Dora's daughter in this study, are more holistic, meaning-based approaches recommended currently for students from different cultures (Au, 1981; Ruiz, 1989). Indeed, Figueroa, Fradd, and Correa (1989), in summarizing the findings on assessment and instructional services, call for a paradigm shift from "decontextualized, acultural and asocial" interventions, toward conditions of high context, both in assessment and instructional approaches. Along with this shift, other researchers recommend targeting curricula toward the "upper range of bilingual children's academic, linguistic, and social skills" (Ruiz, p. 130), and viewing the culture from which students come as a resource rather than a deficit (Moll & Diaz, 1987). Like the parents in this study, professionals in the field of special education are calling for effective, challenging, and culturally appropriate programs.

The Role of Parents in Empowerment

In his proposed framework for the empowerment of minority students. Cummins (1989) has used a sociohistorical perspective to analyze the underachievement of students from what John Ogbu (1978) has called "caste-like minorities." Cummins argued that only through holistic interventions, incorporating cultural/linguistic, community, pedagogical, and assessment needs, will minority students be empowered to achieve to their potential. The input of parents is essential in this process.

Most of the parents in this study said that their children were fine until they started school. This should not be relegated to the status of parent/folk lore: It is, increasingly, the comment of careful scholars who have focused their attention on students from low-status minority groups. Henry Trueba (1989) has put the case succinctly:

These disabilities are an attribute of schools. Children's seeming "unpreparedness" for mainstream

schooling is only a measure of the rigidity and ignorance of our school system, which creates handicap out of social and cultural differences. (p. 70)

This study shows that the power of parents may be seriously undermined by culturally different ways of understanding. Yet it also shows that poor parents, with little formal education, and a different language and culture, may, through their own analysis of their children's difficulties, have a significant contribution to make to current debates in the field of special education. This can only underscore Cummins' (1989) call for a collaborative versus an exclusionary approach to defining the roles of families. Students from widely differing cultural backgrounds already comprise the bulk of the population in certain school systems; in the coming century they will no longer be in the minority nationwide. If their parents' voices cannot be listened to, vast numbers of students will be caught between irreconcilable worlds of home and school.

Two years after the completion of this study, a limited follow-up revealed that parents' opinions of their children's performance had not changed. In the words of one mother, Dora, whose apparently very bright 6-year-old was about to fail kindergarten:

Algo está pasando en la enseñanza, porque la chiquilla es muy normál, y después de un año, no pudo aprender a leer ni una palabra! Yo lo siento, pero, es imposible que yo crea una cosa así! Y siempre la mayoría de los niños Hispanos tienen problemas en la lectura. Eso yo no comprendo!

(Something is going wrong in the teaching, because the little girl is very normal, and after one year, she has not been able to learn to read even one word! I am sorry, but it is impossible to believe such a thing! And the majority of Hispanic children continue to have problems in reading. I do not understand it!) (Dora)

References

Au, K. (1981). Teaching reading to Hawaiian children: Finding a culturally appropriate solution. In H. T. Trueba, G. P. Guthrie, & K. Au (Eds.), *Culture and the bilingual classroom* (pp. 139–154). Rowley, MA: Newbury House.

Barsch, R. H. (1961). Explanations offered by parents and siblings of brain-damaged children. *Exceptional Children, 27,* 286–291.

Becker, H. S. (1963). *Studies in the sociology of deviance.* New York: Free Press.

Bennett, A. T. (1988). Gateways to powerlessness: Incorporating Hispanic deaf children and families into formal schooling. *Disability, Handicap & Society, 3* (2), 119–151.

Bogdan, B., & Biklen, S. (1982). *Qualitative research for education.* Boston: Allyn & Bacon.

Bogdan, R., & Knoll, J. (1988). The sociology of disability. In E. L. Meyen & T. M. Skrtic (Eds.), *Exceptional children and youth: An introduction* (3rd ed., pp. 449–478). Denver, CO: Love.

Bogdan, R., & Taylor, S. J. (1982). *Inside out: Two first-person accounts of what it means to be labeled "mentally retarded."* Toronto: University of Toronto Press.

Bowers, C. A. (1984). *The promise of theory: Education and the politics of cultural change.* New York: Longman.

Canino, I. A., & Canino, G. (1980). Impact of stress on the Puerto Rican family: Treatment considerations. *American Journal of Orthopsychiatry, 50*(3), 535–541.

Coleman, J. M. (1984). Mothers' predictions of the self-concept of their normal or learning-disabled children. *Journal of Learning Disabilities, 17* (4), 214–217.

Condon, E. C., Peters, J. Y., & Sueiro-Ross, C. (1979). *Special education and the Hispanic child: Cultural perspectives.* New Brunswick, NJ: Teachers' Corp. Mid-Atlantic Network.

Cordasco, F. (1976). *Bilingual schooling in the United States.* New York: McGraw-Hill.

Correa, V. I. (1989). Involving culturally different families in the educational process. In S. H. Fradd & M. J. Weismantel (Eds.), *Meeting the needs of culturally and linguistically different students* (pp. 130–144), Boston: College-Hill.

Cummins, J. (1979). Linguistic interdependence and the educational development of bilingual children. *Review of Educational Research, 49* (2), 222–251.

Cummins, J. (1984). *Bilingualism and special education: Issues in assessment and pedagogy.* San Diego, CA: College-Hill Press.

Cummins, J. (1989). A theoretical framework for bilingual special education. *Exceptional Children, 56,* 111–120.

Delgado-Gaitan, C. (1987). Parent perceptions of school: Supportive environments for children. In H. T. Trueba, (Ed.), *Success or failure? Learning and the language minority student* (pp. 131–155). New York: Newbury House.

Dunn, L. M. (1968). Special education for the mildly retarded: Is much of it justifiable? *Exceptional Children, 35,* 5–22.

Dunn, L. M. (1988). *Bilingual Hispanic children on the U.S. mainland: A review of research on their cognitive, linguistic, and scholastic development.* Honolulu: Dunn Educational Services.

Duran, R. P. (1989). Assessment and instruction of at-risk Hispanic students. *Exceptional Children, 56,* 154–159.

Edgerton, R. (1967). *The cloak of competence: Stigma in the lives of the mentally retarded.* Berkeley: University of California Press.

Figler, C. S. (1981). *Puerto Rican families with and without handicapped children.* Paper presented at the Council for Exceptional Children Conference on the Exceptional Bilingual Child, New Orleans. (ERIC Document Reproduction Service, ED 204 876)

Figueroa, R. A. (1989). Psychological testing of linguistic-minority students: Knowledge gaps and regulations. *Exceptional Children, 56,* 145–153.

Figueroa, R. A., Fradd, S. H., & Correa, V. I. (1989). Bilingual special education and this special issue. *Exceptional Children, 56,* 174–178.

Gardner, W. I. (1982). Why do we persist? *Education and Treatment of Children, 5*(4), 360–362.

Gerber, M. M., & Semmel, M. I. (1984). Teacher as imperfect test: Reconceptualizing the referral process. *Educational Psychologist, 19*(3), 137–148.

Goffman, E. (1963). *Stigma: Notes on the management of spoiled identity.* New York: Simon & Schuster.

Goodman, J. F. (1989). Does retardation mean dumb? Children's perceptions of the nature, cause, and course of mental retardation. *Journal of Special Education, 23*(3), 313–327.

Harry, B. (1992). *Culturally diverse families and the special education system.* New York: Teachers College Press.

Hodgkinson, L. (1985). *All one system: Demographics of education.* Washington, DC: Institute for Educational Leadership.

Kauffman, A. L. (1982). Mothers's perceptions of the developmentally delayed label. *Dissellation Abstracts International, 43*(6), 2017B.

Lewis, E. G. (1980). *Bilingualism and bilingual education.* Albuquerque: University of New Mexico Press.

Lofland, J. (1969). *Deviance and identity.* Englewood Cliffs, NJ: Prentice-Hall.

Lynch, E. W., & Stein, R. C. (1987). Parent participation by ethnicity: A comparison of Hispanic, Black and Anglo families. *Exceptional Children, 54,* 105–111.

Marion, R. (1980). Communicating with parents of culturally diverse exceptional children. *Exceptional Children, 46,* 616–623.

McCall, G. J., & Simmons, J. L. (Eds.). (1969). *Issues in participant observation.* Reading, MA: Addison-Wesley.

Mercer, J. R. (1972). *Sociocultural factors in the educational evaluation of Black and Chicano children.* Paper presented at the 10th Annual Conference of Civil Rights Educators and Students, National Education Association, Washington, DC. (ERIC Document Reproduction Service No. ED 062 462)

Mercer, J. R. (1973). *Labeling the mentally retarded.* Berkeley: University of California Press.

Moll, L. C., & Diaz, S. (1987). Change as the goal of educational research. *Anthropology and Education Quarterly, 18,* 300–311.

Ogbu, J. (1978). *Minority education and caste: The American system in cross-cultural perspective.* San Francisco: Academic Press.

Ortiz, A. A., & Polyzoi, E. (Eds.). (1986). *Characteristics of limited English proficient Hispanic students in programs for the learning disabled: Implications for policy, practice and research.* Part 1, Report Summary. Austin: University of Texas. (ERIC Document Reproduction Service No. ED 267578)

Patton, M. Q. (1980). *Qualitative evaluation methods.* Beverly Hills, CA: Sage.

Pollack, J. M. (1985). Pitfalls in the psychoeducational assessment of adolescents with learning and school adjustment problems. *Adolescence, 20*(78), 479–493.

Polloway, E. A., & Smith, J. D. (1987). Current status of the mild mental retardation construct: Identification, placement, and programs. In M. C. Wang, R. C. Reynolds, & H. J. Walberg (Eds.), *Handbook of special education: Research and practice. Vol. 1: Learner characteristics and adaptive education* (pp. 7–22). New York: Pergamon Press.

Ovando, C. J., & Collier, V. P. (1985). *Bilingual and ESL classrooms.* New York: McGraw-Hill.

Reschly, D. J. (1987). Minority overrepresentation: Legal issues, research findings, and reform trends. In M. C. Wang, R. C. Reynolds, & H. J. Walberg (Eds.), *Handbook of special education: Research and practice, Vol. I: Learner characteristics and adaptive education* (pp. 23–42). New York: Pergamon Press.

Reynolds, M. C., & Lakin, C. K. (1987). Non-categorical special education: Models for research and practice. In M. C. Wang, R. C. Reynolds, & J. J. Walberg (Eds.), *Handbook of special education: Research and practice. Vol. 2: Mildly handicapped conditions* (pp. 331–356). New York: Pergamon Press.

Ruiz, N. (1989). An optimal learning environment for Rosemary. *Exceptional Children, 56*(2), 130–144.

Smith, R. W., Osborne, L. T., Crim, D., & Rhu, A. H. (1986). Labeling theory as applied to learning disabilities: Findings and policy suggestions. *Journal of Learning Disabilities, 19*(4), 195–202.

Spener, D. (1988). Transitional bilingual education and the socialization of immigrants. *Harvard Educational Review, 58,* 133–152.

Spradley, J. (1979). *The ethnographic interview.* New York: Holt, Rinehart and Winston.

Stein, C. B. (1986). *Sink or swim: The politics of bilingual education.* New York: Praeger.

Sullivan, O. T. (1980). *Meeting the needs of low-income families with handicapped children.* Washington, DC: District of Columbia Public Schools. (ERIC Document Reproduction Service No. ED 201 091)

Trueba, H. T. (1989). *Raising silent voices.* New York: Newbury House.

Walker, C. L. (1987). Hispanic achievement: Old views and new perspectives. In H. T. Trueba (Ed.), *Success or failure?* (pp. 15–32). Cambridge, MA: Newbury House.

Wolfensberger, W., & Kurtz, R. A. (1974). Use of retardation-related diagnostic and descriptive labels by parents of retarded children. *Journal of Special Education, 8*(2), 131–142.

Wolfensberger, W., & Thomas, S. (1983). *Program analysis of service system's implementation of normalization goals (PASSING)* (2nd ed.). Toronto: National Institute on Mental Retardation.

Zetlin, A. G., & Turner, J. L. (1984). Self-perspectives on being handicapped: Stigma and adjustment. In R. B. Edgerton (Ed.), *Lives in process: Mildly retarded adults in a large city.* Washington, DC: American Association on Mental Deficiency.

6.2   Parents and Inclusive Schooling:

Advocating for and Participating in the Reform of Special Education

Leslie C. Soodak

Several recurring themes emerge from recent discussions of educational reform, one of which is the importance of parental involvement in the education of their children. Research has shown that parental involvement benefits children's learning and school success (Chavkin, 1993; Eccles & Harold, 1993; U. S. Department of Education, 1994). The notion that schools would be more effective if parents partici-

Soodak, L. (1998). Parents and inclusive schooling: Advocating for and participating in the reform of special education. In S. J. Vitello and D. E. Mithaug (Eds.), *Inclusive schooling: national and international perspectives* (pp. 113–131). Mahwah, NJ: Lawrence Erlbaum Associates. Reprinted by permission.

pated in the education of their children is appealing. However, establishing meaningful partnerships with parents remains an elusive goal in many schools. Even when parental participation in decision making is mandated, as in the education of students with disabilities, collaborative decision making is often difficult to achieve (Hilton & Henderson, 1993; Turnbull & Turnbull, 1997). In special education, parents' rights to participate as members of the team responsible for decisions pertaining to the diagnosis, placement, and instruction of their children are protected by federal mandates that were initially included in PL94-142 (later renamed the Individuals with Disabilities Education Act [IDEA]). The rights of parents of children with disabilities have been reaffirmed and strengthened in the 1997 reauthorization of IDEA. However, although proponents of school improvement advocate for parental involvement in education, and parents of children with disabilities have secured the right to participate in decisions pertaining to their children, parents' perspectives on their children's education are not always adequately understood or sufficiently considered in educational planning. The former situation calls for greater understanding of parents' perspectives; the latter suggests the need to rethink policies and practices supporting (or hindering) collaboration.

Parents' perspectives on inclusive education can provide rich information regarding what parents value in the education of their children, and what they perceive their role to be in obtaining the desired schooling for their children. The move toward inclusive education is an important and relevant context within which to explore parents' perspectives for several reasons.

First, parents are among the primary stakeholders in the success of inclusive education. Whereas parents have the most to gain in terms of their children being accepted as respected members of their schools and communities, they also risk losing access to educational services that they fought hard to obtain for their children. Interestingly, despite their concerns, most parents support the goals of inclusive education, and feel strongly that children with and without disabilities will benefit from shared educational experiences (Erwin & Soodak, 1995; Guralnick, 1994; Ryndak, Downing, Jacqueline, & Morrison, 1995; Turnbull, Winton, Blacher, & Salkind, 1982). In fact, parent advocacy has been largely responsible for the move toward inclusive education in many schools throughout the country (Lipsky & Gartner, 1997).

Second, proponents of inclusive education maintain that effective schooling is a collaborative endeavor involving all stakeholders, including parents (Lipsky & Gartner, 1997; Stainback & Stainback, 1996). Inclusive schools are characterized by collaborative problem solving reflecting a belief that professionals are not the only experts in the education of diverse student groups. Thus, parental participation in inclusive schools is not limited to consent giving. Rather, parents are considered to be an integral part of school planning and service delivery.

Parents' perspectives on inclusive education are also revealing because, despite general support for the values underlying inclusive schooling, parents have assumed diverse roles in its implementation. Whereas some parents have served as catalysts for reform, other parents have assumed less active roles in initiating change. Variability in parents' involvement in their children's education may reflect underlying differences in their beliefs about themselves, their children, and their children's schooling. Hoover-Dempsey and Sandler (1997) proposed a model of parent involvement in which they suggest that parents elect to be involved in their children's education based on their construction of the parental role; their sense of efficacy for helping their children succeed; and their perceptions of the school's willingness, demands, and opportunities for parental participation. According to Hoover-Dempsey and Sandler, these three constructs have an additive effect on parents' decisions to become involved (i.e, parents must first believe they should be involved, and they must feel both capable of helping their children, and welcome to participate). The unique experiences of parenting a child with disabilities may complicate this model. Mandates requiring parent involvement in special education may encourage parents to be involved or, as MacMillan and Turnbull (1983) suggested, may place them in an inappropriate, unrealistic, or overly professionalized role. Furthermore, the issues that limit the participation of some parents may be exacerbated when parents from minority backgrounds and those new to the U.S. educational system are involved (Harry, Allen, & McLaughlin, 1995). Therefore, to understand parents' perspectives on inclusion, and to understand why some parents may take greater initiative than others in pursuing change, it is necessary to explore the reasons underlying their beliefs and actions.

Parents' perspectives on inclusion are not only likely to be diverse, but due to the dynamic nature of reform, are also likely to change over time. Clearly, the movement toward inclusive education is a process involving considerably more than the placement of children in general education classes. In inclusive schools, individual differences in all children are recognized and accepted, and instructional methods vary to meet the needs of all students. Attitudes, expectations, and classroom practices change slowly, and changes in thinking and behavior are influenced by a number of personal and situational factors. For example, parents may be more willing to place their children in inclusive settings following positive experiences with students and teachers in heterogeneous classrooms. On the other hand, parents may become disillusioned following negative experiences with inclusion. An understanding of changes in parents' perspectives may shed light on the nature of the reform process, and may provide direction for developing strategies to facilitate collaboration.

In this chapter, I explore the beliefs, motivations, and concerns of parents who have advocated for inclusion, as well as those who have served as participants in this reform. Parents' perspectives on their child's schooling, and their role in their child's education, are explored as dynamic phenomena in which roles and responsibilities are likely to change over time. In the first section, I focus on the reasons underlying parents' decisions to advocate for inclusive education for their children, their experiences in doing so, and their perceptions of the outcomes of their efforts. The second section synthesizes research on the perspectives of parents who may be effected by, but who have not advocated for, inclusion. Specifically, parents' perspectives on the benefits and drawbacks of inclusive education are explored and factors underlying differences in attitudes toward inclusion are discussed. In the last section, I draw on the research presented in the prior sections to reflect on how schools may facilitate collaboration with parents. Several key questions guide this chapter:

- What do parents value in the education of their children with disabilities?
- How and why do parents differ in their support of, and advocacy for, inclusive education?
- How do parents' perspectives on inclusion change over time?
- What are parents' perspectives on the outcomes of inclusive education?
- How can parental involvement in inclusive education be fostered so as to benefit students and their families?

PARENT SATISFACTION, INVOLVEMENT, AND ADVOCACY

Parents of children with disabilities have been a major force in making inclusive education possible for their children. Although many parents recognize the benefits of educating their children in general education classrooms, few parents take on the role of advocate and reformer. What motivates parents to move from a concerned parent to advocate for change? Of the many factors that are needed to inspire advocacy, parents' dissatisfaction with special education is the most documented explanation for parents' involvement in their child's education (Meyers & Blacher, 1987; Plunge & Kratochwill, 1995) and in their advocacy for inclusion (Bennett, Deluca, & Bruns, 1997). In a survey of 200 parents of children receiving special education services, Plunge and Kratochwill found a negative relation between parents' level of involvement in their child's education and their level of satisfaction with their child's educational plan, special education services, and school personnel. The 18 parents who participated in follow-up interviews unanimously agreed they had become more involved in their child's education as a result of their dissatisfaction, and to ensure that their child received adequate services. Similarly, Meyers and Blacher's study of 99 families of school-age children with disabilities indicated that the least satisfied parents were among those who were most likely to be highly involved in school activities, suggesting that parents seek to address perceived inadequacies through their involvement. In a more recent study of 48 parents of children with disabilities in preschool programs through Grade 7, Bennett and his colleagues (1997) found that parental advocacy for inclusion increased as positive experiences with members of the multidisciplinary team responsible for educational planning decreased.

Inclusive education may be an appealing option for parents who are dissatisfied with their child's education because of the high priority placed on the social and emotional development of their children, and their belief that segregated special education classes hinder such growth. Research suggests that parents regard social integration as a primary goal for their children, irrespective of the child's age or disability. Plunge and Kratochwill (1995) selected parents for their study so as to represent the characteristics of all children receiving special education in the school district. When questioned about their concerns, parents indicated that they were least satisfied with the lack of opportunities for social integration. Parents of children with reading disabilities who were interviewed by Green and Shinn (1994) considered affective factors, such as self-esteem, as being more important than skill acquisition in their evaluation of their child's progress in the resource room. Parents of preschool children have consistently cited opportunities for interaction with same-age peers without disabilities as the primary factor in their support of inclusive education (Bailey & Winton, 1987; Green & Stoneman, 1989; Guralnick, 1994; Guralnick, Connor, & Hammond, 1995).

Thus, parental involvement is related to parents' dissatisfaction with their children's education, and those dissatisfied with special education may seek inclusive education in order to promote the goals that they value for their children. Although results of these studies offer a possible explanation for parental involvement, the relation between satisfaction and involvement is unclear because the findings were based on correlation data only. Thus, parental dissatisfaction may motivate parents to become advocates for inclusion or, conversely, their dissatisfaction may have resulted from their having assumed adversarial positions. Furthermore, these studies considered several degrees of involvement, ranging from support for inclusion to advocacy for reform, making it difficult to understand the unique experiences of parent advocates, (i.e., those who actively pursue systems change). The factors that underlie parents' decisions to advocate for inclusive education, their experiences in "taking on the system," and the degree to which their efforts lead to satisfaction with their child's education, are explored more fully in the following section.

PARENTS AS ADVOCATES FOR REFORM

Two research projects have been conducted to explore the motivations and experiences of parents who have actively pursued, and obtained, inclusive education for their children. In Soodak and Erwin (1995), we interviewed nine parents who advocated for inclusion to understand their perspectives on special education and their experiences in pursuing inclusive education (Erwin & Soodak, 1995). Similarly, Ryndak and her colleagues interviewed 13 parents who advocated for inclusion regarding their perceptions of their children's education in self-contained and integrated settings (Ryndak, Downing, Morrison, & Williams, 1996), and their perceptions of the outcomes of having their children in general education classes (Ryndak, Downing, Jacqueline, & Morrison, 1995). Parents in both research projects were re-

cruited through parental advocacy organizations and were not identified through schools. Thus, both samples were intentionally biased to include parents who were extremely knowledgeable about inclusion, and who were actively involved in promoting inclusive education, at least for their own children.

The nine mothers who participated in the Soodak and Erwin Research lived in New York City and the surrounding suburbs, and were from diverse ethnic and socioeconomic backgrounds. All but one of these mothers were married and employed. Their children ranged in age from 5 to 19 years old, and were reported to have disabilities in the moderate to severe range. Five of the nine children spent some or all of the school day in special education classes. Of the four children who were in general education classes, one child was in a class with his same-age peers, and three children were in classes with students who were between 1 to 2 years their junior.

The 13 participants in the study conducted by Ryndak and her colleagues lived in western New York. They were white, comprised two-parent families, and were from diverse socioeconomic backgrounds. Children of parents in this study ranged in age from 5 to 19 years old, attended schools in urban, suburban, and rural districts, and were considered to have moderate, severe, or multiple disabilities. All of the children had been in inclusive educational settings between 1 and 5 years, and had previously spent between 0 and 13 years in self-contained, special education classrooms. Five children were in classes with same-age peers and the remaining eight students were in classes with students who were 1 to 2 years younger than themselves. All of the children attended their neighborhood school or school of choice.

There are interesting similarities among the participants in both studies. First, almost all families were comprised of two parents, and, although the researchers in both studies invited mothers and fathers to participate, it was primarily mothers who elected to be interviewed. (Three fathers participated with their wives in the interviews conducted by Ryndak and her colleagues.) Perhaps the large representation of two-parent families suggests that specific resources are needed for advocacy, such as emotional and financial support. The large representation of mothers is consistent with previous observations that, traditionally, mothers are more involved than fathers in their children's education (Hoover-Dempsey & Sandler, 1997). In fact, the mothers that were interviewed described themselves as the parent who more actively pursued inclusion (i.e., attended meetings, visited classrooms, even when both parents were equally supportive of it). A second similarity among the participants in both studies is that all parents described their children as being moderately, severely, or multiply disabled. Perhaps parents of children with severe disabilities are more likely to advocate for inclusion. However, it is also possible that parents of children with more challenging behaviors were more likely represented in the particular advocacy organizations through which participants were recruited.

Parents' Perspectives on Their Motivations for Advocating for Inclusion

There was considerable consistency among the parents in the two studies regarding their reasons for becoming advocates for inclusion. The two primary reasons underlying parents' decisions to pursue inclusive education were their desire for their children to fit in as members of their communities, and their negative perceptions of their child's experiences in special education (Ryndak et al., 1996; Soodak & Erwin, 1995). Parents wanted their children to "have the same opportunities that we've given everybody else" (Soodak & Erwin, 1995, p. 265). However, they felt that school personnel did not see the need for their children to have natural support networks or interactions with nondisabled peers. Parental dissatisfaction with their child's participation in segregated special education classes emerged as an important theme in both studies. Parents did not want their children to attend schools apart from their own siblings or neighbors, and they resented special education classes being situated in undesirable locations within the school. Several parents drew parallels to racial segregation. One mother remarked: "How far have we come? So we've had the segregation of the races at one point. It is exactly the same thing" (Soodak & Erwin, 1995, p. 266). Thus, according to parents, inclusion is based on the fundamental right of all children to the same opportunities, and experiences and the belief that this right is violated by the practice of educating students in segregated, special education classes.

Parents were motivated to integrate their children into general education because they felt that educators maintained a deficit orientation toward children in special education. Specifically, parents indicated that special education teachers held low expectations for their children, focused on problems that the parents did not recognize as being important, and

provided far too much supervision for their children. Whereas these problems were noted by parents of children of all ages, the issues were most pronounced when discussed in relation to older students. For example, one mother remarked: "There was open lunch for the other high school kids [without disabilities]. The kids in the special education class, though, stood and waited in line . . . What message does that give to the other professionals the other students when you have to take a 17-, 18-, 19-, or 20-year-old kid to the bathroom?" (Ryndak et al., 1996, p. 115). Furthermore, parents who advocated for inclusion felt there was a pervasive lack of individualization in special education, and they cited examples in which all students attending the same program received identical related services, students were assigned goals irrespective of their needs, and goals were repeated regardless of student progress.

An additional area of concern for parents in both studies pertained to their own roles in their child's special education. Parents described feeling powerless when interacting with school personnel, leaving them to defer to "expert judgments" even when they disagreed with the decisions being made. One mother commented that she "had absolutely no control over what schooling [her son] was getting" (Soodak & Erwin, 1995, p. 270). The Individualized Education Program (IEP) meeting was particularly difficult for many of the parents. During these meetings parents were consistently outnumbered by school personnel, and were often unable to understand the professional jargon being used. The interactions between parents and professionals, as described by these parent advocates, are consistent with what Biklen (1992) referred to as the "myth of clinical judgment" in which parents' options for recourse are limited by shared and erroneous assumptions regarding the accuracy of professional expertise.

Findings of these studies support the notion that parental advocacy results, in part, from parents' perceptions of the incongruity between the goals they have for their children and what they perceive to be the goals of special education. Consistent with the findings of research on parent satisfaction and involvement cited earlier, parents who strongly advocate for inclusive education are extremely dissatisfied with the services their children receive in special education, and the limited opportunities they have to collaborate with school personnel in the planning of their child's education. Although caution is needed in the interpretation of findings based on a limited number of parents (23 mothers) and a limited data source (each parent was interviewed once), the consistency of findings within and across studies suggests that, at least for this group of parents, issues of equality and acceptance led them to pursue changes in their child's education.

Parents' Perspectives on the Pursuit of Inclusion

Parents in both studies stood up to the system in order to make inclusive education available to their children. In doing so, each took a unique and difficult journey that not only had an impact on their child, but on their families, and on their perceptions of themselves. Despite sometimes powerful resistance from professionals, parents employed numerous strategies to obtain what they believed to be best for their children. These strategies, detailed in Erwin and Soodak (1995), included involving schools in due process hearings, obtaining media attention, lobbying key players in the school district, becoming involved as a parent member of the interdisciplinary team, removing their children from school, and relocating their families to an area with a more receptive school district. Many parents used multiple strategies simultaneously. For example, one mother kept her child out of school for several years in order to accept no less than an inclusive education for the child. While providing home instruction for her child and being employed full-time, this parent sought media attention, engaged in due process hearings, and tried to educate school personnel about the goals of inclusion. For all parents, the pursuit of inclusive education was undertaken at great expense, in terms of time, money, and emotional well-being.

Despite parents' willingness to fight for what they believed to be best for their children, many grew to resent the role they felt forced to assume. Many parents were angry and frustrated at having to devote significant time and energy to obtain an appropriate education for their children. One parent felt that the pursuit of inclusion had been more difficult for her to endure than dealing with complications arising from her son's medical condition: "Sometimes you have to fight for medication. To me, it is a right. I should not have to fight for this—it's his right." (Erwin & Soodak, 1995, p. 143). However, despite their anger and frustration, many parents noted they had developed an awareness of their own strengths as a result of their advocacy efforts. Several comments reflected the personal transformations that had been experienced. For example, one mother remarked that the experience of advocating for the inclusion of her child "probably affected me more than any one thing in my whole life" (Erwin &

Soodak, 1995, p. 143). Another mother concluded that the experience left her feeling good about herself, whereas another attributed her satisfaction to making others "stop and think" (Erwin & Soodak, 1995, p. 143).

Thus, parents who strongly desire inclusive education for their children are willing to struggle long and hard to obtain it. However, regardless of the parents' success in securing inclusive education, they feel angry at having to assume the role of advocate. Similar findings were reported by Hanline and Halvorsen (1989) in their study of parents' perception of the transition from special to general education. Seven of the 13 parents in this study who were considered to be the prime advocates for the inclusion of their children in general education expressed resentment at having to assume the role of advocate. One mother commented that "One of the hardest parts is having people not like you. . . . Parents should not have to go through some of the things we've had to go through" (p. 488). Furthermore, several parents felt that the role of advocate was more appropriately assumed by school personnel, as noted in one parent's question: "Why wasn't it done by the people who's job it is?" (p. 489). Hanline and Halvorsen suggested that educators who feel powerless to make changes in service delivery may encourage parents themselves to pursue inclusion rather than work collaboratively with them to ensure that districts provide integrated services.

Parents' Perspectives on the Effects of Their Advocacy Efforts

Parents who advocated for, and obtained, inclusive education for their children readily reflected on the positive outcomes of their efforts. All parents who participated in the research conducted by Ryndak and her colleagues cited benefits of having their children in inclusive settings. Unlike the parents in this study, however, most of the parents who participated in the research conducted by Erwin and me had not yet secured inclusive education for their children at the time of the initial interviews. Rather, these parents were still actively in pursuit of the expected benefits of inclusion. Follow-up interviews that were conducted 3 years after the initial interviews (Soodak, 1997) indicated that nearly all of the nine parents who participated in the original study had secured inclusive educational placements for their children within that time and that many of them also felt that their children were benefiting from the experience in general education. At the time of the follow-up interviews, seven of the parents reported their children were in general education classes full time (three of whom were in age-appropriate classes), one child was spending a half day in general education, and one child had "aged out" of school. Only half of the school-age children were attending classes in their neighborhood schools.

Parents who successfully advocated for inclusive education cited specific benefits of such placements both to their children and to their families. Ryndak et al. (1995) found that parents were satisfied because they felt that their children had increased opportunities to interact with nondisabled peers, and had greater access to the general education curriculum when in inclusive settings. Each of the parents reported that their children had made significant gains in the acquisition of academic, communication, and social skills. Positive effects of integration on the children who were included were also reported by the parents interviewed by Hanline and Halvorsen (1989). Specifically, parents in this study (the majority of whom had advocated for their child's integrated placement) reported that their children had enhanced their social skills and self-esteem as a result of their participation in general education. I also found parents to be satisfied with their child's inclusion in general education. Almost all the parents interviewed felt their children were benefiting socially and academically from their involvement in general education. The only parents who were unable to identify benefits of inclusion for their children were those who also indicated that their child's placement was not truly inclusive (i.e., the child was only attending general education classes part time or was not placed in a class with his or her age-mates).

Positive effects of inclusion on families were also noted by parents. The mothers and fathers interviewed by Hanline and Halvorsen indicated that their own expectations for their children had been raised after the children had participated in integrated settings. One father stated that expecting any less than "a perfectly normal life" for his 9-year-old daughter would be his own "artificial barrier" (Hanline & Halvorsen, 1989, pp. 490–491). Parents in this study also noted that their families had benefited from integration, in that siblings were less concerned about issues of long-term care and that the families' focus had shifted away from the child's disability. For these families, community acceptance of children with disabilities reinforced their commitment to inclusion, encouraged parents to be less overprotective

of their children with disabilities, and strengthened family ties.

The follow-up interviews conducted indicated that the roles parents assume in their child's education change once inclusive education is made available to their children. Although no less committed to inclusion, many of the parents interviewed noted that their advocacy efforts had diminished the longer their children participated in general education. Several parents no longer actively participated in advocacy organizations, and instead were involved in established and mainstream parent organizations, such as the parent–teacher association and the local school board. The more secure parents were that the school was truly committed to inclusive education, the more they were able to retreat from their advocacy roles. However, they did not terminate their involvement in their child's education. Parents indicated they remained involved to ensure their children were given a reasonable opportunity to learn and interact in general education.

In summary, studies that have explored the motivations and experiences of parents who advocate for inclusion indicate that parents' commitment to inclusive education overrides their reluctance to challenge the system. In fact, parents who advocate for inclusion seem willing to persist in their efforts to seek change in their child's education despite the financial and emotional costs to themselves and their families. Furthermore, parents who advocate for inclusive education, or at least those who had agreed to participate in these studies, are likely to be successful in securing inclusive education for their children, and to be generally satisfied with the effects of inclusive education on their children and their families. However, despite the success of their advocacy efforts, parents unanimously agree that they should not have had to challenge schools to be more inclusive.

PARENTS AS PARTICIPANTS IN REFORM

Although the progress made toward inclusive schooling during the 1990's has been attributed, in part, to parent advocacy, there are far more parents who assume less active roles in this movement. Research on parents' perspectives on inclusive education suggests that differences in parents' involvement is not a function of differences in attitudes toward inclusive education. In fact, the most consistent finding to emerge from 10 years of research is that most parents of children with disabilities are supportive of the goals of inclusion. Parents want their children to learn and socialize with typically developing children, and they believe that all children are likely to benefit from integration. However, parental support for inclusion is tempered by their perceptions of barriers to successful inclusion. In this section, research on parents' attitudes toward inclusive education is reviewed to understand parents' expectations and concerns regarding the education of their children, and to identify factors that mediate their perspectives on this initiative.

Perceived Benefits Of Inclusion

Considerable support for inclusive education is found among parents of children ranging in age and ability. Interestingly, the largest body of research to emerge on this topic pertains to the attitudes of parents of preschool children. The preponderance of data pertaining to the inclusion of preschoolers, and specifically parents' responses to inclusive education, may be due to the relevance of this issue to children entering the educational system. As children enter school, parents are able to see their children in a new context, one that incorporates a given set of goals and expectations for their children that may or may not match their own. In addition, research on parents of preschoolers may have flourished because of the specific focus on parental involvement at this level of service.

Parents of preschoolers with disabilities consistently support inclusive education for their children. Positive attitudes toward inclusion have been found among parents with children in segregated programs (Diamond & LeFurgy, 1994; Guralnick, 1994; Miller et al., 1992), those with children in the process of transitioning to integrated preschool programs (Bailey & Winton, 1987; Reichart et al., 1989), and those with children who have participated in inclusive preschool programs (Bailey & Winton, 1987; Diamond & LeFurgy, 1994; Guralnick, 1994; Miller et al., 1992). Most of these studies surveyed more than 100 parents, and employed questionnaires to assess parental attitudes toward integration. Regardless of the specific instrument employed, the vast majority of parents in each study were found to be supportive of inclusive education. For example, approximately 85% of 222 mothers surveyed by Guralnick (1994) indicated they perceived either probable or definite benefits of inclusion to children with and without disabilities. Specifically, parents noted that inclusion would promote the acceptance of children with dis-

abilities, prepare children for real-world experiences, and provide children with greater opportunities for learning. In addition, Miller and her colleagues (1992) found that parents of preschoolers with disabilities were optimistic about the integration of children with disabilities into school-age programs, suggesting that parents of preschool children believe that the benefits of inclusion will endure as children continue their education.

Parents of school-age children are also supportive of inclusive education. Interviews with parents of children ages to 20 years with moderate to severe disabilities have demonstrated that both parents who have had their children in inclusive settings, and those who have not, are able to cite benefits of integration (Bennett et al., 1997; Reichart et al., 1989; Ryndak et al., 1995; Turnbull et al., 1982). A recent study of 48 parents of school-age children with a broad range of disabilities who were participating to varying degrees in general education indicated that parents felt strongly that inclusion represented a positive change in the educational system, and that it would likely benefit all children (Bennett et al., 1997). Furthermore, parents' positive attitudes were associated with their having had positive experiences with inclusion. Nearly two thirds of the parents whose children were in inclusive settings indicated that they were generally satisfied with their child's experiences in these settings.

Parents of children with mild disabilities who receive special education services in resource-room programs also hold positive attitudes toward inclusion. However, it is noteworthy that parents and professionals representing students with learning disabilities have been among those who are most resistant to the idea of full inclusion (Skrtic, 1995). Research indicates that, although parents believe that reintegrating students from pullout programs into general education classrooms will likely improve the academic abilities of children with learning disabilities (Abramson, Willson, Yoshida, & Hagerty, 1983; Mlynek, Hannah, & Hamlin, 1982), they are less likely to perceive benefits of inclusion for their own children (Abramson et al., 1983; Green & Shinn, 1994; Simpson & Myles, 1989). It seems that parents of children with learning disabilities are in agreement with the goals inclusive education, but that they are not confident that their own children will benefit from the experience. Green and Shinn (1994) suggested that parents' reluctance to include their children with reading disabilities in general education may be a function of parents' satisfaction with the pull-out services their children have received, and conversely, their fear of relinquishing services that they feel have been beneficial to their children.

Although parents of children with mild disabilities may be reluctant to include their children initially (or more accurately, they may be less likely to recognize the benefits of doing so), their hesitancy seems to diminish as inclusion moves closer to becoming a reality. Specifically, parents are more likely to endorse inclusion once they have been informed that their children will begin receiving instruction in the regular classroom (Green & Shinn, 1994), and following their child's involvement in integrated settings (Lowenbraun, Madge, & Affleck, 1990). Although it is unclear whether parents held more favorable attitudes as a result of the inclusion of children in general education classes, or whether changes in parental attitudes played a role in their child's move to inclusive education, attitudes among parents of children with learning disabilities seem to become more favorable over time.

There is considerable consistency among parents regarding their perceptions of the benefits of inclusion. The two reasons parents offer most often for their support of inclusion are increased opportunities for friendships with nondisabled children, and increased opportunities for learning (Bailey & Winton, 1987; Guralnick, 1994; Reichart et al., 1989; Turnbull et al., 1982). Specifically, parents feel that interactions among students with differing abilities will facilitate the acceptance of children with disabilities, and will provide opportunities for friendships among children. Furthermore, parents feel that the availability of role models will be an asset to their child's education and social development. In terms of academic benefits, parents believe that their children will be exposed to, and benefit from, a richer and more varied curriculum in general education. Parents are also supportive of inclusive education because they feel that integrated educational experiences will provide better preparation for participation in mainstream activities outside of school, and in later life. Indeed, research on parental perspectives of the outcomes of inclusion indicate that, for most parents, the expected benefits are realized. Although there have been only a limited number of studies that directly explore parents' perceptions of the success of inclusion, parents of children who have experienced inclusive education readily identify gains made by their children in integrated settings (Bennett et al., 1997; Guralnick, 1994; Guralnick et al., 1995;

Shinn, Powell-Smith, Good, & Baker, 1997; Ryndak et al., 1995; Soodak, 1997). Parents of preschoolers report their children show gains in social, communication, and motor skills after participation in integrated programs. Parents of school-age children report their children benefit in terms of social skills, preacademic and academic skills, and communication skills. In all studies, parents specifically noted that, much to their satisfaction, inclusion facilitated the development of friendships, and promoted acceptance of their children among their peers.

Sources Of Concern

There are two concerns that predominate parents' thinking about the integration of their children. First, parents are concerned about the possibility of their children experiencing rejection, and second, they are concerned about the quality of the education their children will receive in integrated programs. Issues pertaining to attitudinal barriers are important to both parents of preschoolers (Bailey & Winton, 1987; Diamond & LeFurgy, 1994; Guralnick, 1994; Peck, Hayden, Wandschneider, Peterson, & Richarz, 1989), and parents of school-age children (Bennett et al., 1997; Green & Shinn, 1994; Hanline & Halvorsen, 1989; York & Tundidor, 1995). Interestingly, these concerns reflect the same values that underlie parents' perspectives on the potential benefits of inclusion. In other words, whereas parents long to have their children fit in with typically developing children, they also fear that those in the mainstream (i.e., students and teachers), may be less than welcoming to their children.

As is the case with all parents, parents of children with disabilities desire to protect their children from social isolation and ridicule. Although parents' concern about their child's rejection in inclusive settings is an important and recurring theme, it is a concern that may not be consistent with what actually happens in integrated classes. In fact, research indicates that integrated settings promote positive peer relationships among children with and without disabilities (Green & Stoneman, 1989; Guralnick et al., 1995). However, it is presently unknown whether children with disabilities are more likely to be rejected in integrated settings than in segregated settings, and if so, what strategies may be employed to minimize problems for children. Regardless of the basis for parents' fears, efforts must be made to address parents' concerns about their child's sense of security in integrated settings. As suggested by parents in one study, perhaps children with special needs in integrated programs should have access to others with similar abilities to reduce feelings of isolation, and encourage greater tolerance of differences (Guralnick et al., 1995).

Parental concerns about the educational opportunities provided to their children in integrated settings must also be addressed. Presently, not all parents believe that the individual needs of their children will be adequately addressed in inclusive settings. Specifically, at issue is the availability of instructional and related resources, and teachers' ability to adapt instruction to the needs of the child with disabilities. In addition, parents of typically developing children are concerned that the inclusion of children with disabilities will limit the educational resources (such as teacher attention) available to their children. Because of these concerns, teachers are seen by parents as being vital to the success of inclusion (Reichart et al., 1989; York & Tundidor, 1994) Interestingly, the concerns parents have regarding their child's access to instruction with the necessary adaptations, supports, and related services are most often cited by parents of children who have not yet been included. Parents of children who have participated in inclusive settings, on the other hand, often perceive adequate learning opportunities for their children (Bennett et al., 1997; Ryndak et al., 1995; Shinn et al., 1997). Therefore, it may be beneficial for parents with concerns about including their children to observe in inclusive programs, or to speak with parents whose children have had experience in included settings. Furthermore, because program quality varies, parents' concerns may be indicative of poor instructional practices that require interventions, such as teacher training or the reallocation of support services.

Thus, in general, parents hold positive attitudes toward inclusion because they want all children to be accepted (and accepting) and they want all children to have the same learning opportunities. However, parents are mindful of potential threats to their child's psychological well-being and intellectual development. Whereas parents who strongly advocate for their children to be in inclusive settings focus on their child's right to be in general education classes, parents who are less actively involved in the pursuit of inclusion focus on their child's right to an appropriate education. In both cases, parents agree that all children are likely to benefit from participating in inclusive schooling.

Factors Mediating Parents' Attitudes Toward Inclusion

Although both parents who advocate for inclusive education and those who serve as participants in this reform indicate support for inclusion, an understanding of factors that mediate parents' attitudes may help explain why parents assume different roles in this reform. The factors that have been found to mediate parents' attitudes inclusion fall into three categories (i.e., setting characteristics, child characteristics, and family characteristics).

First, parents with children in inclusive settings hold more positive attitudes toward inclusion than do parents of children in segregated settings (Diamond & LeFurgy, 1994; Green & Stoneman, 1989; Guralnick et al., 1995; Lowenbraun et al., 1990; Miller et al., 1992). This finding is consistent with research that indicates that parents' concerns lessen as soon as an inclusive placement is recommended for their children. Two factors that do not appear to influence parental attitudes are the length of time children participate in mainstream settings (Miller et al., 1992), and whether the parent had requested that their children be placed in an inclusive setting (Lowenbraun et al., 1990). Although research indicates a relation between experience with and attitudes toward inclusion, many questions remain unanswered. First, do parents develop more positive attitudes toward inclusion as a result of their child's experience in inclusion, or are attitudes and experience determined by other factors? Second, are parents' attitudes influenced by their perceptions of the quality of their child's experiences in inclusive education, and if so, would perceptions of negative experiences undermine parents' attitudes toward inclusion? Third, do findings of increased support for inclusion following placement indicate a preference for inclusion, or do the findings indicate that parents tend to be satisfied with the services their children receive at a given time?

In terms of child characteristics, research suggests that the age of the child may underlie differences in parental attitudes. Attitudes toward inclusion appear to be more favorable among parents of younger children than among parents of older students (Green & Stoneman, 1989; York & Tundidor, 1995). Parents may be more reluctant to integrate their children into school-age programs because they recognize that, in the upper grades, there is less attention given to a child's social and emotional development, and a greater emphasis on academic achievement. Furthermore, the reluctance of parents of school-age students to include their children may reflect the specific concerns of parents of children with learning disabilities discussed earlier. These parents seem to be hesitant to give up services they find beneficial to their children and, because children with mild disabilities often receive instruction in the mainstream for part of the school day, parents may be less likely to perceive their children as being isolated from their nondisabled peers as are parents of preschoolers attending specialized programs.

There is little evidence to suggest that the developmental characteristics of the children to be integrated influence parents' attitudes toward inclusion. No relation between the level of developmental functioning of preschool children and parental attitudes toward inclusion was found in the two studies that explored such differences (Guralnick, 1994; Miller et al., 1992). In addition, Guralnick (1994) did not find a relation between the type of disability and parental attitudes, except for mothers of children with behavior disorders. Mothers of preschool children with behavior problems were more concerned about the drawbacks of inclusion than were mothers of other preschoolers. These mothers seem to be particularly concerned that their children will be rejected in mainstream settings, suggesting that the integration of preschool children with behavior problems may pose a challenge for integration, or that parents of these children need to be reassured that efforts will be made to facilitate acceptance.

There are virtually no studies that have directly explored family characteristics as an explanation of differences in attitudes toward inclusion. However, there is an emerging body of research that has investigated the relation between family background and parental participation in special education. Researchers have documented that some parents, particularly those from diverse linguistic and cultural backgrounds, tend not to participate in or challenge educational decisions pertaining to their children because they feel disengaged and powerless when interacting with school personnel. In a study of 24 African-American families whose children were in special education, half of whom were interviewed over 3 years (Harry et al., 1995) revealed the process by which parental involvement and advocacy is diminished. Specifically, the bureaucratic and overly professionalized structure of meetings between school personnel

and parents resulted in frustration and passivity on the part of the parents, several of whom were initially advocating for a change in placement for their children. Similar feelings of mistrust and withdrawal were observed in an earlier study that explored the experiences of Puerto Rican families in the special education system (Harry, 1992). One mother in this study noted that "Our opinions are not valued. Many parents do not want their child in a special class or in a school so far away, but they keep quiet. It is very hard to struggle with these Americans. In America, the schools are for Americans" (p. 486). Thus, the suggestion that parents from minority backgrounds tend to be trusting of decisions made by educators and satisfied with the services their children receive may be misleading (Lynch & Stein, 1987).

Research on factors mediating parental attitudes toward inclusion is beginning to shed light on the complex nature of parents thinking about inclusion. In summary, research conducted to date indicates that parents are most favorable following their child's placement, and when young children, and those without behavior problems, are being included. Parents' attitudes seem to be unaffected by the child's developmental functioning, and the length of time the child is in an included setting. Research has not, however, explored whether setting variables, such as program quality, influence parents' judgments. In addition, research has not directly explored how family background, and other personal attributes, interact with setting and child characteristics in mediating parents' attitudes.

CONCLUSIONS AND IMPLICATIONS

Perhaps the most important finding to emerge from research on parents and inclusive education is that, regardless of whether or not parents actively seek to reform special education, all parents want their children to be accepted by others, to develop friendships, and to have an opportunity to learn. Most importantly, the vast majority of parents are confident that these goals are most likely to be met by educating children in general education settings. Parental support for inclusion seems to evolve into advocacy for reform when dissatisfaction, frustration and hope exist simultaneously. However, although these conditions may motivate some parents to fight for change, they may encourage others to withdraw from participation in their children's education. Clearly, for parents, educators, and children, neither extreme is desirable. Therefore, the question that remains to be answered is: "How can parental involvement in inclusive education be fostered so as to benefit students and their families?"

The answer is both simple and complex. First, parents' perspectives on their children's education must be understood, respected, and considered before decisions are made. Second, opportunities for interactions cannot be limited to formal meetings that focus on obtaining consent to important educational decisions. Third, parents should be involved in the development and evaluation of program changes, so that their goals and concerns are addressed prior to implementation. These suggestions, however, represent some of the simpler changes that are needed for effective collaboration in inclusive schools. The more complex changes involve modifications in attitudes and behaviors among both parents and professionals that presently act as obstacles to collaboration.

Based on the data reviewed in this chapter, many parents lack trust in the educational system, believing, for example, that educators underestimate their children or that the services their children receive are provided at the school's discretion. School personnel, on the other hand, often view parents as adversaries (Turnbull & Turnbull, 1997), and tend to attribute a student's learning and behavior problems, that are otherwise unexplained, to conditions within the child's home (Soodak & Podell, 1994). Distrust clearly undermines collaboration. However, to counter feelings of distrust, schools need to create an empowering context for both parents and professionals. Kalyanpur and Rao (1991) defined the attributes of empowerment in this way:

> Empowerment signifies changing the role of a service provider from that of an expert to that of an ally or

friend who enables families to articulate what they need ... [Empowerment] involves caring, which builds supportive relationships; respect, which builds, reciprocity; and the acceptance of differences, which build trust ... Such empathy involves the acceptance and open acknowledgment of the parents' competence, the willingness to interact with them on equal terms, and the adoption of a nonjudgmental stance. (p. 531)

According to Turnbull and Turnbull (1997), professionals can build reliable alliances that empower parents by understanding their own perceptions; understanding families' characteristics, interactions, functions, and life cycle issues; honoring cultural diversity; building on family strengths; promoting family choices; encouraging high expectations; practicing positive communication skills; and warranting mutual trust and respect.

The possibility for meaningful collaboration is enhanced by the move toward inclusive education. As schools become more inclusive, there may be a change in the continuum of parental involvement, such that a greater number of parents will participate with educators in fostering students' learning and school success. On one end of the continuum, parents who presently advocate for change may be able to assume less adversarial roles. On the other end of the continuum, parents who presently feel disenfranchised may become more engaged in their children's education once their children become members of mainstream classes. The research presented in this chapter suggests that parents are mindful of the opportunities and problems associated with inclusive education. Future research should explore changes in parents' perceptions of their children, their perceptions of inclusion, and their relationship with school personnel as inclusive education continues to develop as an accepted practice in U.S. schools.

References

Abramson, M., Willson, V., Yoshida, R. K., & Hagerty, G. (1983). Parents' perceptions of their learning disabled child's educational performance. *Learning Disability Quarterly, 6,* 184–194.

Bailey, D. B., Jr., & Winton, P. J. (1987). Stability and change in parents' expectations about mainstreaming. · *Topics in Early Childhood Special Education, 7,* 73–88.

Bennett, T., Deluca, D., & Bruns, D. (1997). Putting inclusion into practice: Perspectives of teachers and parents. *Exceptional Children, 64*, 115–131.

Biklen, D. (1992). *Schooling without labels: Parents, educators, and inclusive education.* Philadelphia: Temple University Press.

Chavkin, N. F. (Ed.). (1993). *Families and schools in a plauralistic society.* Albany: State University of New York Press.

Diamond, K. E., & LeFurgy, W. G. (1994). Attitudes of parents of preschool children toward integration. *Early Education and Development, 5*, 69–77.

Eccles, J. S., & Harold, R. D. (1993). Parent-school involvement during the early adolescent years. *Teachers College Record, 94*, 568–587.

Erwin, E. J., & Soodak, L. C. (1995). I never knew I could stand up to the system: Families' perspectives on pursing inclusive education. *The Journal of the Association for Severe Handicaps, 20*, 136–146.

Green, A. L., & Stoneman, Z. (1989). Attitudes of mothers and fathers of nonhandicapped children. *Journal of Early Intervention, 13*, 292–304.

Green, S. K., & Shinn, M. (1994). Parent attitudes about special education and reintegration: What is the role of student outcomes. *Exceptional Children, 61*, 269–281.

Guralnick, M. J. (1994). Mothers' perceptions of the benefits and drawbacks of early childhood mainstreaming. *Journal of Early Intervention, 18*, 168–183.

Guralnick, M. J., Connor, R. T., & Hammond, M. (1995). Parent perspectives of peer relationships and friendships in integrated and specialized programs. *American Journal on Mental Retardation, 99*, 457–476.

Hanline, M. F., & Halvorsen, A. (1989). Parent perceptions of the integration transition process: Overcoming artificial barriers. *Exceptional Children, 55*, 487–492.

Harry, B. (1992). An ethnographic study of cross-cultural communication with Puerto Rican-American families in the special education system. *American Educational Research Journal, 29*, 471–494.

Harry, B., Allen, N., & McLaughlin, M. (1995). Communication versus compliance: African-American parents' involvement in special education. *Exceptional Children, 61*, 364–377.

Hilton, A., & Henderson, C. J. (1993). Parent involvement: A best practice or forgotten practice? *Education and Training in Mental Retardation, 28*, 199–211.

Hoover-Dempsey, K. V., & Sandler, H. M. (1997). Why do parents become involved in their children education? *Review of Educational Research, 67*, 3–42.

Kalyanpur, M., & Rao, S. S. (1991). Empowering low-income black families of handicapped children. *American Journal of Orthopsychiatry, 61*, 523–532.

Lipsky, D. K., & Gartner, A. (1997). *Inclusion and school reform: Transforming America's classrooms.* Baltimore: Paul H. Brookes.

Lowenbraun, S., Madge, S., & Affleck, J. (1990). Parental satisfaction with integrated class placements of special education and general education students. *Remedial and Special Education, 11*, 37–40.

Lynch, E. W., & Stein, R. C. (1987). Parent participation by ethnicity: A comparison of Hispanic, Black, and Anglo families. *Exceptional Children, 54*, 105–111.

MacMillan, D. L., & Turnbull, A. P. (1983). Parent involvement in special education: Respecting individual preferences. *Education and Training of the Mentally Retarded, 18*, 4–9.

Meyers, C. E., & Blacher, J. (1987). Parents' perceptions of schooling for severely handicapped children: Home and school variables. *Exceptional Children, 53*, 441–449.

Miller, L. J., Strain, P. S., Boyd, K., Hunsicker, S., McKinley, J., & Wu, A. (1992). Parental attitudes toward integration. *Topics in Early Childhood Special Education, 12*, 230–246.

Mlynek, S., Hannah, M. E., & Hamlin, M. A. (1982). Mainstreaming: Parental perceptions. *Psychology in the Schools, 19*, 354–359.

Peck, C. A., Hayden, L., Wandschneider, M., Peterson, K., & Richarz, S. (1989). Development of integrated preschools: A qualitative inquiry into sources of resistance among parents, administrators, and teachers. *Journal of Early Intervention, 13*, 353–363.

Plunge, M. M., & Kratochwill, T. R. (1995). Parental knowledge, involvement, and satisfaction with their child's special education services. *Special Services in the Schools, 10*, 113–138.

Reichart, D. C., Lynch, E. C., Anderson, B. C., Svobodny, L. A., DiCola, J. M., & Mercury, M. G. (1989). Parental perspectives on integrated preschool opportunities for children with handicaps and children without handicaps. *Journal of Early Intervention, 13*, 6–13.

Ryndak, D. L., Downing, J. E., Jacqueline, L. R., & Morrison, A. P. (1995). Parents's perceptions after inclusion of their children with moderate or severe disabilities. *Journal of the Association for Persons with Severe Handicaps, 20*, 147–157.

Ryndak, D. L., Downing, J. E., Morrison, A. P., & Williams, L. J. (1996). Parents' perceptions of educational settings and services for children with moderate or severe disabilities. *Remedial and Special Education, 17*, 106–118.

Shinn, M. R., Powell-Smith, K. A., Good, R. H., & Baker, S. (1997). The effects of reintegration into general education reading instruction for students with mild disabilities. *Exceptional Children, 64*, 59–79.

Simpson, R. L., & Myles, B. S. (1989). Parents' mainstreaming modification preferences for children with educable mental handicaps, behavior disorders, and learning disabilities. *Psychology in the Schools, 26*, 29–301.

Skrtic, T. M. (1995). The special education knowledge tradition: Crisis and opportunity. In E. L. Meyen & T. M. Skrtic

(Eds.), *Special education and student_disability: Traditional, emerging, and alternative perspectives* (pp. 609–672). Denver, CO: Love Publishing.

Soodak, L. C. (1997, March). *Parents as advocates for inclusion: A three-year follow-up study.* Paper presented at the annual conference of the American Educational Research Association, Chicago.

Soodak, L. C., & Erwin, E. J. (1995). Parents, professionals, and inclusive education: A call for collaboration. *Journal of Educational and Psychological Consultation, 6,* 257–276.

Soodak, L. C., & Podell, D. M. (1994). Teachers' thinking about difficult to teach students. *Journal of Educational Research, 88,* 44–51.

Stainback, S., & Stainback, W. (Eds.). (1996). *Inclusion: A guide for educators.* Baltimore: Paul H. Brookes.

Turnbull, A. P., & Turnbull, H. R. (1997). *Families, professionals, and exceptionality: A special partnership* (3rd ed.). Columbus, OH: Merrill.

Turnbull, A. P., Winton, P., Blacher, J., & Salkind, N. (1982). Mainstreaming in the kindergarten classroom: Perspectives of parents of handicapped and nonhandicapped children. *Journal of the Division of Early Childhood, 6,* 14–20.

U.S. Department of Education. (1994). *Strong families, strong schools: Building community partnerships for learning.* Washington, DC: Author.

York, J., & Tundidor, H. (1995). Issues raised in the name of inclusion: Perspectives of educators, parents, and students. *Journal of the Persons with Severe Handicaps, 20, Association for* 31–44.

Chapter Seven

Instructional Practices

7.1   The Real Challenge of Inclusion

Confessions of a 'Rabid Inclusionist'

Dianne L. Ferguson

The new challenge of inclusion is to create schools in which our day-to-day efforts no longer assume that a particular text, activity, or teaching mode will "work" to support any particular student's learning, Ms. Ferguson avers.

About a year ago, a colleague told me that my work was constrained by the fact that "everyone" thought I was a "rabid inclusionist." I was not exactly sure what he meant by "rabid inclusionist" or how he and others had arrived at the conclusion that I was one. I also found it somewhat ironic to be so labeled since I had been feeling uncomfortable with the arguments and rhetoric of both the anti-inclusionists and, increasingly, many of the inclusionists. My own efforts to figure out how to achieve "inclusion"—at least as I understood it—were causing me to question many of the assumptions and arguments of both groups.

In this article, I wish to trace the journey that led me to a different understanding of inclusion. I'll also describe the challenges I now face—and that I think we all face—in trying to improve our schools.

THE LIMITS OF OUR REFORMS

Despite our best efforts, it was clear to my husband and me that even the possibility of "mainstreaming" was not open to our son Ian. Although mainstreaming has been a goal of the effort to change the delivery of special education services since the late 1960s, the debates never extended to a consideration of students with severe disabilities. Indeed, it was only the "zero reject" provisions of the Education for All Handicapped Children Act (P.L. 94-142) in 1974 that afforded our son the opportunity to attend school at all—albeit a separate special education school some 20 miles and two towns away from our home. What that landmark legislation did not change,

however, were underlying assumptions about schooling for students designated as "disabled."

Since special education emerged as a separate part of public education in the decades spanning the turn of the century, the fundamental assumptions about students and learning shared by both "general" and "special" educators have not changed much. Despite periodic challenges, these assumptions have become so embedded in the culture and processes of schools that they are treated more as self-evident "truths" than as assumptions. School personnel, the families of schoolchildren, and even students themselves unquestionably believe:

- that students are responsible for their own learning;
- that, when students don't learn, there is something wrong with them; and
- that the job of the schools is to determine what's wrong with as much precision as possible, so that students can be directed to the tracks, curricula, teachers, and classrooms that match their learning profiles.

Even our efforts to "integrate" and later to "include" students with severe disabilities in general education failed to challenge these fundamental assumptions. Indeed, these special education reform initiatives have served more to reinforce them.

Unlike mainstreaming, which was grounded in debate about where best to provide the alternative curricular and instructional offerings that students with disabilities need, the reform initiatives of integration and later of inclusion drew much more heavily on social and political discourse. From a democratic perspective, every child has a right to a public education. For those moderately and severely disabled students who had previously been excluded

Ferguson, D. (1995). The real challenge of inclusion: Confessions of a 'rabid inclusionist.' *Phi Delta Kappan* 77(4), 281–287. Reprinted by permission.

from schooling on the ground that they were too disabled to benefit, the application of a civil rights framework gave them the same status as any minority group that was widely disenfranchised and discriminated against.[1] The essential message of integration was to remediate social discrimination (not so much learning deficits) by ending stigmatizing and discriminatory exclusion.

We sought this more "normalized" schooling experience for Ian, advocating actively for placement in a typical public school rather than in a separate school. Unfortunately, the efforts of professional educators to balance the right of students to be educated with the still unchallenged and highly individualized deficit/remediation model of disability most often resulted in the delivery of educational services along some continuum of locations, each matched to the constellation of services believed to "fit" the identified type and amount of student deficit and disability.

For someone like our son, with multiple and severe disabilities, the result was self-contained classrooms that afforded only the briefest contact with nondisabled students. The integrationists' promise that the mainstream would tolerate and perhaps even incorporate more differences in abilities remained largely unfulfilled. Even when some students found themselves integrated into general education classrooms, they often did not reap the promised rewards of full membership.

Yet we could see the promise of something else. Ian's first experience in a *public* school was when he was about 10. He was assigned to a new self-contained classroom for "severely and profoundly handicapped" students. This new classroom was located in the "physically handicapped school," where all students with physical disabilities were assigned because the building had long ago been made accessible, unlike most other school buildings in town.

Because we hoped he would have some involvement with nondisabled peers, we lobbied the school administration for a policy that permitted two kinds of "mainstreaming": one kind for students who could learn alongside their peers with some extra teaching help and another kind for students like Ian, who could not learn the same things but might benefit by learning other things. It took months of discussion, but finally the grade 5 class down the hall from Ian's self-contained room invited him to join it for the "free" times during the day when students got to pick their own games and activities. The teacher was skeptical but willing and

sent students to collect him for some part of nearly every day.

One day a small group of students invited Ian to join them in a Parcheesi game. Of course, he had no experience with the game and probably didn't grasp much of it. It could be argued, I suppose, that his lessons (at the separate school and class) on picking things up and putting them into cans offered him some ability to participate, but he would not be just another player like the other fifth graders. The students, with no adult intervention, solved this participation problem by making him the official emptier of the cup of dice for all the players—something he could not only do, but relished. His role was critical to the game, and he got lots of opportunities to participate, since he was needed to begin every player's turn.

Ian's experience in Parcheesi expanded over the year to include some integration in music, lunch, and recess with these same students: More important were the lessons his participation began to teach us about the possibilities of integration that we and others had not yet fully explored, especially regarding the ways that learning, participation, and membership can mean different things for very different children in the same situation.

However it was being implemented, integration also contained a critical flaw in logic: in order to be "integrated" one must first be segregated. This simple point led to the first calls for inclusion. According to this new initiative, all students should simply be included, by right, in the opportunities and responsibilities of public schooling. Like integration, however, these early notions of inclusion focused primarily on students with moderate to severe disabilities who most often were placed along the continuum of service environments furthest from general education classrooms.

Unfortunately, neither integration nor inclusion offered much practical guidance to teachers who were engaged in the daily dynamics of teaching and learning in classrooms with these diverse students. The focus on the right to access did not provide clear direction for achieving learning outcomes in general education settings. Essentially, both of these reform efforts challenged the logic of attaching services to places—in effect challenged the idea of a continuum of services. However, the absence of clear directions for how services would be delivered instead and the lack of information about what impact such a change might have on general education led some proponents to emphasize the importance of social rather than learning outcomes, especially for students with severe disabilities.[2] This emphasis on social outcomes certainly did nothing to end the debates.

INCLUSION AS 'PRETTY GOOD' INTEGRATION

The inclusion initiative has generated a wide range of outcomes—some exciting and productive, others problematic and unsatisfying. As our son finished his official schooling and began his challenging journey to adult life, he enjoyed some quite successful experiences, one as a real member of a high school drama class, though he was still officially assigned to a self-contained classroom.[3] Not only did he learn to "fly," trusting others to lift him up and toss him in the air (not an easy thing for someone who has little control over his body), but he also memorized lines and delivered them during exams, learned to interact more comfortably and spontaneously with classmates and teachers, and began using more and different vocal inflections than had ever before characterized his admittedly limited verbal communications. Classmates, puzzled and perhaps put off by him at the beginning of the year, creatively incorporated him into enough of their improvisations and activities to be able to nominate him at the end of the year not only as one of the students who had shown progress, but also as one who showed promise as an actor. He didn't garner enough votes to win the title, but that he was nominated at all showed the drama teacher "how much [the other students] came to see him as a *member* of the class."

Ian's experiences in drama class helped me begin to understand more fully that *learning* membership was the most important dimension of inclusion and that it was an extraordinarily complex phenomenon, especially within classrooms.[4] It also prompted me to question other bits of the conventional wisdom about inclusion: Is inclusion all about place? Must it be full time? Is it okay for learning to take second priority to socialization and friendship? Does one always have to be traded for the other? Will students learn things that they can use and that will make a difference in their lives? Who will teach, and what will happen to special educators? And so on.

A three-year research effort followed, during which I learned a good deal about what inclusion is and isn't. Perhaps the most troubling realization was that—even when students were assigned to general education classrooms and spent most (or even all) of their time there with various kinds of special education supports—their participation often fell short of the kind of social and learning membership that most proponents of inclusion envision and that Ian achieved in that one drama class. Even to casual observers, some students seemed set apart—immediately recognizable as different—not so much because of any particular impairment or disability but because of what they were doing, with whom, and how.

During the years of our research, my colleagues and I saw students walking through hallways with clipboard-bearing adults "attached" to them or sitting apart in classrooms with an adult hovering over them showing them how to use books and papers unlike any others in the class. Often these "Velcroed" adults were easily identifiable as "special education" teachers because the students called them by their first names while using the more formal Ms. or Mr. to refer to the general education teacher. The included students seemed *in,* but not *of,* the class. Indeed, we observed teachers who referred to particular students as "my inclusion student." It seemed to us that these students were caught inside a bubble that teachers didn't seem to notice but that nonetheless succeeded in keeping other students and teachers at a distance.

We also saw other students "fitting in," following the routines, and looking more or less like other students. But their participation seemed hollow. They *looked* like they were doing social studies or math, but it seemed more a "going through the motions" than a real learning engagement. Maybe they were learning in the sense of remembering things, but, we wondered, did they know what they were learning? Or why? Or whether they would use this learning in their lives outside of school?

Even the protection of an individualized education program (IEP)—a key component of P.L. 94-142 and now of the updated Individuals with Disabilities Education Act (IDEA)—seemed yet one more barrier to real membership. Special education teachers became "teachers without classrooms," plying their skills in many places, following carefully designed and complicated schedules that deployed support personnel in the form of classroom assistants to teach, manage, and assist the "inclusion students" so that they could meet the goals and objectives of their IEPs. Classroom teachers struggled to understand how to "bond" with their new students.

Even more challenging was how to negotiate teaching. The peripatetic special educator usually remained primarily responsible for writing IEPs that only distantly related to the classroom teacher's curriculum and teaching plans. At the same time the general educator would strive to assume "ownership" of the shared student's teaching, often by following the instructions of the special educator. Special educators who were successful at moving out of their separate classrooms struggled with the sheer logistics of teaching their students in so many different places. They also struggled with whether they were teachers of students or teachers of other teachers. And some wondered what would happen to them if the general educators ever "learned how" to include students without help.

BURSTING BUBBLES

Gradually I came to see these examples and the experiences that have been detailed elsewhere as problematic for everyone precisely because they failed to challenge underlying assumptions about student learning differences.[5] Too much inclusion as implemented by special education seems to succeed primarily in relocating "special" education to the general education classroom along with all the special materials, specially trained adults, and special curriculum and teaching techniques. The overriding assumptions remain unchanged and clearly communicated.

- These "inclusion" students are "irregular," even though they are in "regular" classrooms.
- They need "special" stuff that the "regular" teacher is neither competent nor approved to provide.
- The "special" educator is the officially designated provider of these "special" things.

In trying to change everything, inclusion all too often seems to be leaving everything the same. But in a new place.

My colleagues and I also saw lots of examples of things that did not remain the same, examples like my son's experience in drama class. The challenge was to try to understand what made these experiences different.

Gradually I began to realize that, if inclusion is ever to mean more than pretty good integration, we special educators will have to change our tactics. To resolve the debates about roles, ownership, accountability, student learning achievements, the meaningfulness of IEPs, and the achievement of genuine student membership in the regular classroom, we must begin with the *majority* perspective and build the tools and strategies for achieving inclusion from

the center out rather than from the most exceptional student in. Devising and defining inclusion to be about students with severe disabilities—indeed, any disabilities—seems increasingly wrongheaded to me and quite possibly doomed to fail. It can only continue to focus everyone's attention on a small number of students and a small number of student differences, rather than on the whole group of students with their various abilities and needs.

Inclusion isn't about eliminating the continuum of placements[6] or even just about eliminating some locations on the continuum,[7] though that will be one result. Nor is it about discontinuing the services that used to be attached to the various points on that continuum.[8] Instead, a more *systemic* inclusion—one that merges the reform and restructuring efforts of general education with special education inclusion—will disassociate the delivery of supports from *places* and make the full continuum of supports available to the full range of students. A more systemic inclusion will replace old practices (which presumed a relationship between ability, service, and place of delivery) with new kinds of practice (in which groups of teachers work together to provide learning supports for all students).

Inclusion isn't about time either. Another continuing debate involves whether "all" students should spend "all" of their time in general education classrooms.[9] One form of this discussion relies largely on extreme examples of "inappropriate" students: "Do you really mean that the student in a coma should be in a general education classroom? What about the student who holds a teacher hostage at knife point?" Other forms of this argument seek to emphasize the inappropriateness of the general education classroom for some students: "Without one-to-one specialized instruction the student will not learn and his or her future will be sacrificed." Another version of the same argument points out that the resources of the general education classroom are already limited, and the addition of resource-hungry students will only further reduce what is available for regular education students.

Of course these arguments fail to note that labeled students are not always the most resource-hungry students. Indeed, when some students join general education classrooms, their need for resources diminishes. In other instances, the labeled student can bring additional resources that can be shared to other classmates' benefit. These arguments also fail to note that the teaching in self-contained settings, as well as the resource management, can sometimes be uninspired, ordinary, and ineffective. Consider how many students with IEPs end up with exactly the same goals and objectives from year to year.

Like the debates about place, debates about time miss the point and overlook the opportunity of a shift from special education inclusion to more systemic inclusion. *Every* child should have the opportunity to learn in lots of different places—in small groups and large, in classrooms, in hallways, in libraries, and in a wide variety of community locations. For some parts of their schooling, some students might spend more time than others in some settings. Still, the greater the number and variety of students learning in various locations with more varied approaches and innovations, the less likely that any student will be disadvantaged by not "qualifying" for some kind of attention, support, or assistance. If all students work in a variety of school and community places, the likelihood that any particular students will be stigmatized because of their learning needs, interests, and preferences will be eliminated. All students will benefit from such variety in teaching approaches, locations, and supports.

THE REAL CHALLENGE OF INCLUSION

Coming to understand the limits of inclusion as articulated by special educators was only part of my journey. I also had to spend time in general education classrooms, listening to teachers and trying to understand their struggles and efforts to change, to help me see the limits of general education as well. The general education environment, organized as it still is according to the bell curve logic of labeling and grouping by ability, may never be accommodating enough to achieve the goals of inclusion, even if special educators and their special ideas, materials, and techniques become less "special" and separate.

It seems to me that the lesson to be learned from special education's inclusion initiative is that the real challenge is a lot harder and more complicated than we thought. Neither special nor general education alone has either the capacity or the vision to challenge and change the deep-rooted assumptions that separate and track children and youths according to presumptions about ability, achievement, and eventual social contribution. Meaningful change will require nothing less than a joint effort to reinvent schools to be more accommodating to all dimensions of human diversity. It will also require that the purposes and processes of these reinvented schools be organized not so much to make sure that students

learn and develop on the basis of their own abilities and talents, but rather to make sure that all children are prepared to participate in the benefits of their communities so that others in that community care enough about what happens to them to value them as members.[10]

My own journey toward challenging these assumptions was greatly assisted by the faculty of one of the elementary schools in our research study on inclusion. Most of our research had really centered on the perspectives of special educators. While we talked with many other people in the schools, our access had always been through the special educator who was trying to move out into the school. Finally, however, we began to shift our attention to the *whole* school through the eyes of *all* its members. For me, it was a shift from *special education research* to *educational research* that also happened to "include" special education teachers and students. I began to learn the language of schooling, became able to "talk education" rather than just talk special education, and sought that same bilingualism for my students and colleagues through a series of reframed research and demonstration projects.

Learning about various reform agendas within education that support and facilitate systemic inclusion enormously reassured and encouraged me, and I have begun to refocus my efforts toward nurturing them. For example, in response to the changing demands of work and community life in the 21st century, some initiatives within general education reform and restructuring are focusing on students' understanding and use of their own learning rather than on whether or not they can recall information during tests. Employers and community leaders want citizens who are active learners and collaborators as well as individuals who possess the personal confidence and ability to contribute to a changing society.[11]

In response to these broader social demands, teachers at all levels of schooling are trying to rethink curriculum. They are looking for ways to help students develop habits of learning that will serve them long after formal schooling ends. In pursuit of this goal, they are moving from seeking to cover a large number of "facts" to exploring in more depth a smaller number of topics of interest and relevance to students.[12] An important aspect of this curriculum shift is that not all students will learn exactly the same things, even within the same lesson or activity.

These changes in general education are being pursued because of increasing social complexity and student diversity. Educators are less and less confident that learning one standard, "official" curriculum will help students achieve the kind of competence they need to lead satisfactory lives. Greater numbers of educators are concerned not so much that some bit of content knowledge is learned, but rather that students use their learning in ways that make a difference in their lives outside of school. The difficulty in making this happen in classrooms is that students bring with them all manner of differences that teachers must take into consideration. These include different abilities, of course, but also different interests, different family lifestyles, and different preferences about schools and learning. Students' linguistic backgrounds, socioeconomic status, and cultural heritage must also be considered when making curriculum and teaching decisions. Finally, some students have different ways of thinking and knowing—sometimes emphasizing language, sometimes motor learning, sometimes artistic intelligence, and so on.[13]

To general education teachers who are experimenting with these kinds of curricular and teaching reforms, students with official disabilities become different in degree rather than in type. Tailoring the learning event for them might require adjustments or supports not needed by some other students. But the essential process remains the same for all. Fear of "watering down" the official curriculum remains only for those classrooms that have not responded to the need for more systemic reform of curriculum and teaching. Classrooms and teachers seriously engaged in preparing students for the future have already expanded and enriched the curriculum to respond both to the demands for broader student outcomes and to the different interests, purposes, and abilities of each student.

A NEW INCLUSION INITIATIVE

These are just a few of the ongoing discussions within general education. There are many more. Some, like the pressure to articulate new national standards and benchmarks, are less clearly supportive of student diversity. Reform initiatives are emerging from all parts of the system—from the efforts of small groups of teachers to those of state and federal policy makers. Often these various pressures for change contradict one another, but in the end all will have to be accommodated, understood, and transformed into a single whole.

Changing schools at all, never mind actually *improving* them, is an extraordinarily complex and

arduous task. Public education is like a web: each strand touches many others, depending upon as well as providing support for the entire structure. Any change, even a small one, ripples through the web, sometimes strengthening, sometimes weakening the whole. When many things change at once, it is a time of both great risk and great energy.

Public education is in just such an exciting period of change. Perhaps for the first time, changes in all parts of the system can begin to converge. My own journey to understand inclusion has led me to propose my own definition of inclusion:

Inclusion is a process of meshing general and special education reform initiatives and strategies in order to achieve a unified system of public education that incorporates all children and youths as active; fully participating members of the school community; that views diversity as the norm; and that ensures a high-quality education for each student by providing meaningful curriculum, effective teaching, and necessary supports for each student.

Perhaps there are "rabid inclusionists," foaming at the mouth over some specific change and having but little awareness of the challenge their agenda represents to fundamental assumptions. I suppose that there are also "rabid separatists," just as fanatically insisting on preserving the present system and similarly unaware of the fundamental assumptions that influence their positions.

My own journey led me to a different destination. It led me to take the risk of admitting that I have changed my mind about many things. (Perhaps it would be more accurate to say that I have not so much "changed" my mind as "clarified" and expanded my thinking.) I am still an advocate for inclusion, but now I understand it to mean much more than I believed it meant when I first began to study and experience it through my son. As I and others who share this broader understanding work to create genuinely inclusive schools, we will be encouraging people in schools, on every strand of the complex web, to change in three directions.

The first shift involves moving away from schools that are structured and organized according to ability and toward schools that are structured around student diversity and that accommodate many different ways of organizing students for learning. This shift will also require teachers with different abilities and talents to work together to create a wide array of learning opportunities.[14]

The second shift involves moving away from teaching approaches that emphasize the teacher as disseminator of content that students must retain and toward approaches that emphasize the role of the learner in creating knowledge, competence, and the ability to pursue further learning. There is a good deal of literature that seeks to blend various theories of teaching and learning into flexible and creative approaches that will accomplish these ends. The strength of these approaches is that they begin with an appreciation of student differences that can be stretched comfortably to incorporate the differences of disability and the effective teaching technology created by special educators.[15]

The third shift involves changing our view of the schools' role from one of providing educational *services* to one of providing educational *supports* for learning. This shift will occur naturally as a consequence of the changes in teaching demanded by diversity. Valuing diversity and difference, rather than trying to change or diminish it so that everyone fits some ideal of similarity, leads to the realization that we can *support* students in their efforts to become active members of their communities. No longer must the opportunity to participate in life wait until some standard of "normalcy" or similarity is reached. A focus on the support of learning also encourages a shift from viewing difference or disability in terms of individual limitations to a focus on environmental constraints. Perhaps the most important feature of support as a concept for schooling is that it is grounded in the perspective of the person receiving it, not the person providing it.[16]

The new challenge of inclusion is to create schools in which our day-to-day efforts no longer assume that a particular text, activity, or teaching mode will "work" to support any particular student's learning. Typical classrooms will include students with more and more kinds of differences. The learning enterprise of reinvented *inclusive* schools will be a constant conversation involving students, teachers, other school personnel, families, and community members, all working to construct learning, to document accomplishments, and to adjust supports. About this kind of inclusion I can be very rabid indeed.

Notes

1. John Gliedman and William Roth, *The Unexpected Minority: Handicapped Children in America* (New York: Harcourt Brace Jovanovich, 1980).

2. Jeff Strully and Cindy Strully, "Friendship as an Educational Goal," in Susan Stainback, William Stainback, and Marsha Forest, eds., *Educating All Students in the Mainstream of Regular Education* (Baltimore: Paul H. Brookes, 1989), pp. 59–68.

3. Dianne L, Ferguson et al., "Figuring Out What to Do with Grownups: How Teachers Make Inclusion 'Work' for Students with Disabilities," *Journal of the Association for Persons with Severe Handicaps*, vol. 17, 1993, pp. 218–26.

4. Dianne L. Ferguson, "Is Communication Really the Point? Some Thoughts on Interventions and Membership," *Mental Retardation*, vol. 32, no. 1, 1994, pp. 7–18.

5. Dianne L. Ferguson, Christopher Willis, and Gwen Meyer, "Widening the Stream: Ways to Think About Including Exceptions in Schools," in Donna H. Lear and Fredda Brown, eds., *People with Disabilities Who Challenge the System* (Baltimore: Paul H. Brookes, forthcoming); and Dianne L. Ferguson and Gwen Meyer, "Creating Together the Tools to Reinvent Schools," in Michael Berres, Peter Knoblock, Dianne L. Ferguson, and Connie Woods, eds., *Restructuring Schools for All Children* (New York: Teachers College Press, forthcoming).

6. Michael Giangreco et al., " 'I've Counted on Jon': Transformational Experiences of Teachers Educating Students with Disabilities," *Exceptional Children*, vol. 59, 1993, pp. 359–72; and Marlene Pugach and Stephen Lilly, "Reconceptualizing Support Services for Classroom Teachers: Implications for Teacher Education," *Journal of Teacher Education*, vol. 35, no. 5, 1984, pp. 48–55.

7. Russell Gersten and John Woodward, "Rethinking the Regular Education Initiative: Focus on the Classroom Teacher," *Remedial and Special Education*, vol. 11, no. 3, 1990, pp. 7–16.

8. Douglas Fuchs and Lynn S. Fuchs. "Inclusive Schools Movement and the Radicalization of Special Education Reform," *Exceptional Children*, vol. 60, 1994, pp. 294–309.

9. Lou Brown et al., "How Much Time Should Students with Severe Intellectual Disabilities Spend in Regular Education Classrooms and Elsewhere?," *Journal of the Association of Persons with Severe Handicaps*, vol. 16, 1991, pp. 39–47: and William Stainback, Susan Stainback, and Jeanette S. Moravec, "Using Curriculum to Build Inclusive Classrooms," in Susan Stainback and William Stainback, eds., *Curriculum Considerations in Inclusive Classrooms: Facilitating Learning for All Students* (Baltimore: Paul H. Brookes, 1992), pp. 65–84.

10. Dianne L. Ferguson, "Bursting Bubbles: Marrying General and Special Education Reforms," in Berres, Knoblock, Ferguson, and Woods, op. cit.: and Terry Astuto et al., *Roots of Reform: Challenging the Assumptions That Control Change in Education* (Bloomington, Ind.: Phi Delta Kappa Educational Foundation, 1994).

11. See, for example, Anthony D. Carnevale, Leila J. Gainer, and Ann S. Meltze. *The Essential Skills Employers Want* (San Francisco: Jossey-Bass, 1990).

12. David T. Conley, *Roadmap to Restructuring: Policies, Practices, and the Emerging Visions of Schooling* (Eugene: ERIC Clearinghouse on Educational Management. University of Oregon, 1993); Robin Fogarty, "Ten Ways to Integrate Curriculum." *Educational Leadership,* October 1991, pp. 61–65; Jacqueline G. Brooks and Martin Brooks, *In Search of Understanding: The Case for Constructivist Classrooms* (Alexandria. Va.: Association for Supervision and Curriculum Development, 1993); Nel Noddings, "Excellence as a Guide to Educational Conversations." *Teachers College Record,* vol. 94, 1993, pp. 730-43; Theodore Sizer, *Horace's School: Redesigning the American School* (Boston: Houghton Mifflin, 1992); and Grant Wiggins. "The Futility of Trying to Teach Everything of Importance," *Educational Leadership,* November 1989, pp. 44–59.

13. Thomas Armstrong, *Multiple Intelligences in the Classroom* (Alexandria, Va.: Association for Supervision and Curriculum Development, 1994); Howard Gardner, *Multiple Intelligences: The Theory in Practice* (New York: Baste Books, 1993); and Gaea Leinhardt, "What Research on Learning Tells Us About Teaching," *Educational Leadership,* April 1992, pp. 20–25.

14. Linda Darling-Hammond, "Reframing the School Reform Agenda: Developing Capacity for School Transformation," *Phi Delta Kappan.* June 1993, pp. 753–61: Jeannie Oakes and Martin Lipton, "Detracking Schools: Early Lessons from the Field." *Phi Delta Kappan,* February 1992, pp. 448–54; and Thomas M. Skrtic, *Behind Special Education: A Critical Analysis of Professional Culture and School Organization* (Denver: Love Publishing, 1991).

15. Conley, op. cit.: Robin Fogarty, *The Mindful School: How to Integrate the Curricula* (Palatine, Ill.: IRI/Skylight Publishing, 1991); Brooks and Brooks, op. cit.: Nel Noddings, *The Challenge to Care in Schools* (New York: Teachers College Press, 1992); Sizer, op. cit.; and Wiggins, op. cit.

16. Philip M. Ferguson et al., "Supported Community Life: Disability Policy and the Renewal of Mediating Structures," *Journal of Disability Policy,* vol. 1, no. 1, 1990, pp. 9–35; and Michael W. Smull and G. Thomas Bellamy, "Community Services for Adults with Disabilities: Policy Challenges in the Emerging Support Paradigm," in Luanna Meyer, Charles A. Peck, and Lou Brown, eds., *Critical Issues in the Lives of People with Severe Disabilities* (Baltimore: Paul H. Brookes, 1991), pp. 527–36.

7.2 Visions and Revisions:

A Special Education Perspective on the Whole Language Controversy

Russell Gersten and Joseph Dimino

This article discusses the conflict between emerging conceptions of literature-based or whole language approaches to reading literacy instruction and the direct instruction approach that was widely advocated in the 1980s. The conceptualizations underlying each approach are delineated, as are the limitations. The essay concludes with a depiction of each approach as an idealized vision of the teaching-learning process and the assertion that, in practice, these approaches often overlap. It concludes with a call for research that examines issues in literacy instruction, in a nonpolemic fashion, through careful observation of actual teaching.

In the past several years, the whole language or literature-based approach to reading and language arts instruction has been dramatically altering the shape of reading instruction in many American classrooms.

Hoffman (1989) noted that "the whole language movement in reading and language arts instruction is so contrary to prevailing norms for schooling that it must be regarded as revolutionary. . . . For some it is a rallying cry for reform. For others it is an illusion of promise that misrepresents what classroom research has demonstrated to be effective . . . " (p. 112).

In our conversations with special educators over the past 2 years—both those in higher education and those in the field—we have found that many view whole language as, at best, a fad and, at worst, an assault on what they know about effectively teaching students with disabilities. The whole language movement is viewed as an affront not only to the knowledge base of effective teaching (Brophy & Good, 1986), but also to many of the key concepts of special education practice (e.g., direct instruction, teaching to mastery, curriculum-based assessment, the use of explicit reinforcement procedures).

The strong antiskills bias in whole language, the emphasis on motivation over mastery, and the movement's antipathy toward sequenced, systematic instruction are all anathema to conventional special education doctrine. The tendency to ask low-achieving students to silently read material that is far too difficult for them, in the hope that they will get the gist of the passage, seems but one more example of unsound instructional practice.

In the current atmosphere of increased interest in collaboration between teachers of special and general education to better meet the needs of students with handicaps, anxiety over the whole language movement is particularly intense. Calls for increased collaboration come at a time when the philosophies of optimal reading instruction between special and general education seem in stark conflict.

After several years of both formal (Gersten, 1991; Gersten & Jiménez, 1993) and informal observations of whole language instruction in elementary classrooms and a close look at the emerging literature on whole language, we have concluded that special educators should seriously consider the issues raised by whole language advocates. We believe that much can be learned by observing whole language programs in operation. We also believe that the emotional tenor of the whole language debate has curtailed genuine dialogue between advocates of whole language and those who advocate other approaches to reading instruction. The purpose of this article is to begin that process.

In deference to the whole language tradition, we begin with a poem by William Butler Yeats. In what some consider to be his greatest poem, Yeats (1955) confronted the issue of how writers learn to write. He did this in the form of a somewhat rancorous dialogue

between two men that reads like a turn of the century Siskel and Ebert dialogue. One claims that "style is found by sedentary toil/And by imitation of great masters" (p. 159); alluding to the fact that good, clear writing always requires great quantities of hard work and that even the most stylistically mature artists often begin their careers by writing in the style of past masters.

His counterpart rather heatedly replies that it takes more than imitation and toil to develop a personal style and write well. He asserts that in order to write, one must first discover one's true self. "Art is but *a vision* [italics added] of reality," he states (Yeats, 1955, p. 159). Formulating the vision is essential.

His friend then vigorously attacks this assertion, arguing that great technical skill and facility is necessary for great writing. Without skill, he claims, people are unable to express their thoughts and ideas clearly. Without toil, practice, and systematic feedback, writing style and ability cannot develop.

The two concur that good writing involves personal vision as well as high levels of technical ability, but they disagree as to how individuals develop the accompanying maturity, insight, and skill. Their debate continues unresolved as night turns into morning.

Though nothing is resolved, the reader is left with deep insights into what great writing is, and some reasonable, if contradictory, ideas as to how writers learn to write. The reader is also left knowing that both men are "right" even though both overstate their cases. The "answer" lies in the dialogue.

The debate about how to effectively teach reading to students experiencing difficulties, including those with learning disabilities or who are at risk, has remained unresolved for almost a century. There is every reason to believe that it will continue so throughout our lifetimes. In no way do we hope to resolve the endless debate about reading instruction. Rather, like in the Yeats poem, we wish to explore two of the positions in this debate so as to provide greater insights into the complex problem of teaching reading to low-performing students.

This article explores the two seemingly divergent approaches for teaching reading: whole language and direct instruction. Our major concern is how to implement aspects of each approach so that all students succeed, even those diagnosed as learning disabled or at risk. We present each approach as a vision of instruction, and then analyze what we see as the relative strengths and weaknesses of each.

WHOLE LANGUAGE/LITERATURE-BASED APPROACHES

Whole language proponents (e.g., Goodman, 1990; Harste, 1989) vehemently attack the orientation of many remedial and compensatory instructional programs in discrete comprehension or word attack skills. They decry the overreliance on worksheets in remedial instruction, and the contrived nature of student textbooks that use controlled vocabulary. They decry most strongly the paucity of interesting literature and the lack of enjoyment and excitement in remedial reading programs for at-risk students. They argue that if reading instruction were more spontaneous, integrated, and authentic, virtually all children would learn to read. Reading ability, then, would evolve in a relatively natural, developmental fashion, much as these children's oral language developed when they were younger (Altwerger, Edelstein, & Flores, 1987).

An example from Routman (1988) nicely exemplifies the problem with basal readers. She presented two pages from a story—first the original version:

> A long time ago there was an old man.
> His name was Peter, and he lived in an old,
> old house.
> The bed creaked.
> The floor squeaked.
> Outside, the wind blew the leaves through
> the trees.
> The leaves fell on the roof. Swish. Swish.
> The tea kettle whistled. Hiss. Hiss.
> "Too noisy," said Peter. (p. 22)

and then the adapted version that appears in a basal reader (Holt, Rinehart, & Winston, 1986):

> Peter was an old man
> Who lived in an old, old house.
> There was too much noise in Peter's house.
> The bed made noise.
> The door made noise.
> And the window made noise.
> Peter didn't like all that noise. (pp. 22–23)

Routman concluded,

> Beginning readers love reading the original version and read it easily and eagerly. The six lines beginning with "The bed creaked. . . . The floor squeaked. . . . "

appear nine times in this short, delightful story. The magic of the language, the rhyme and rhythm, the repetition of the above passage and others throughout the book, and the noisy words themselves (Swish, Swish, and Hiss, Hiss) make it fun to read and *actually easier* than the basal version.

> The original version deals with non-concrete imagery of the sounds of the wind blowing leaves through the trees, leaves falling on the roof, and a whistling tea kettle—rich language which leads children to form mental images of the sounds. By contrast, the story language in the basal reflects only concrete objects and then only to make "noise." The poetic language is gone. The child has been deprived of exposure to literary language so necessary for the development of imaginative writing and a love of literature. (p. 23)

Routman (1988) illustrated this point with a personal experience as a remedial reading teacher. She had just finished reading the students a beautifully illustrated children's book, which they loved. They wanted to read it, but she refused to let them, because it was too hard for them. They insisted, she gave in, and with adequate practice, they were able to read the entire book. She cited how differently the students responded to reading this book, with its rhymes and large, pretty pictures—as compared to their desultory response to standard remedial reading fare. For the first time, they became interested in reading.

The widespread acceptance of whole language among teachers and administrators can be traced in large part to a dissatisfaction with conventional reading instruction. Duffy (1983) noted that many teachers are almost obsessed with establishing and maintaining routines for "getting through" all the skill sheets and the round-robin reading activity. He found that discussion of comprehension questions was almost always done in a rush, and that teachers spent hardly any time explaining concepts, probing students, providing feedback, or clarifying. Duffy also noted that teachers virtually never stopped to listen to what students thought about a story, or even to see if they understood it. Similar problems were noted by Durkin (1978–79); Stallings (1975); and Ysseldyke, O'Sullivan, Thurlow, and Christenson (1989).

Research on the instruction of students placed in "low ability" groups and/or remedial pull-out groups presents other distressing findings. Much of this research points out that year after year, the students in these groups receive massive amounts of practice in marginally useful skills, at the expense of real comprehension instruction (Allington, 1983; Moll & Diaz, 1987). In contrast, whole language advocates eliminate ability grouping, so that all students, not just the brightest, are given opportunities to discuss and think about what they read.

A major goal of whole language instruction is to bring a sense of wonder and joy back into reading instruction for at-risk students (Routman, 1988)—to eradicate the emotionally flat, routinized instruction that Duffy (1983) and Moll and Diaz (1987) observed. Teachers are encouraged to authentically share experiences with students (Garcia & Pearson, 1989), to "give up control" and celebrate risk-taking (Routman, 1988).

Whole language instruction is viewed as a process, not as a particular method. The belief is that students will emulate the risk taking, the probing, and the sense of experimentation that the teacher provides. Teachers will demonstrate that questions often have many correct answers. They will utilize literature that deals with complex human issues. Real books, not simplified, abridged versions, are recommended as the "texts" to be used in the classroom.

Research on Whole Language and At-Risk Students

McCaslin (1989) praised the whole language movement for revealing that "something is amiss in reading instruction that has no vision of the constructive and predictive capacity of the learner" (pp. 226–227). Whole language has assisted teachers in developing a more dynamic, richer view of the student—especially the at-risk student—as an active learner. This view of students was demonstrated in a recent study by Fisher and Hiebert (1990).

After extensive observations of 40 days of instruction in classrooms implementing whole language programs in Grades 2 and 6, Fisher and Hiebert (1990) observed many aspects of instruction that seemed far superior to conventional basal instruction. They found that students spent significantly more time on literacy and writing tasks than students in traditional basal programs. They noted that the literacy assignments and projects were more cognitively demanding than those in the classes taught with basal programs, and that students had much more say about the type of reading or writing activity in which they were involved. All these would seem to contribute to enhanced growth in literacy and/or improved or more sophisticated attitudes toward reading and writing.

Their research also raised several specific concerns. First, they found that virtually all the material read was narrative. They saw the lack of any exposure to expository material as posing a serious threat to students' intellectual growth, especially in sixth grade. Fisher and Hiebert's research also revealed a paucity of small group, teacher-led instruction in the whole language classrooms. Students spent most of the time in either whole class instruction or individual seatwork. (They remind us that it is *long-term* ability grouping, not ability grouping per se, that has been viewed as detrimental to students' self-esteem.) They concluded that "teacher-led small groups . . . are in danger of being a baby thrown out with the bath water" (p. 63) and urged teachers to utilize temporary small groups for a wide range of activities.

Whereas Fisher and Hiebert (1990) focused on all students in the class, Lindsey's (1990) observational research focused on students with learning disabilities and those being considered for referral and/or grade retention. She noted that when given the option of either writing a story or copying a story written by the teacher and the class, these students invariably copied the teacher's story, thus spending a good deal of time each day performing a task with little meaning and little potential for cognitive development. (Subsequent research by Gersten and Jiménez, 1993, noted this as a frequent phenomenon. Only the most highly skilled teachers preempted this possibility.) Lindsey also noted problems in the practice of allowing students to select books for extended periods of silent reading. Two of the three targeted low-achieving students consistently picked books that were too difficult for them, and had little success reading them. Finally, the observational data demonstrated that most teacher–student interactions were brief and infrequent, rarely lasting for more than 1 minute.

The practices described in these studies raise concerns regarding the suitability of the whole language approach for students with learning disabilities or those with limited motivation or skill.

A meta-analysis of research on holistic approaches to reading instruction in the primary grades (both whole language and earlier language experience approaches) by Stahl and Miller (1989) found that, overall, holistic approaches were *no more effective* than conventional basal reading approaches. This was true on standardized measures of reading achievement, as well as for more naturalistic measures (such as oral reading miscue analyses and attitude measures). Stahl and Miller did find that holistic approaches seemed to have a positive effect in the area of reading and reading readiness activities in kindergarten. The effects were reversed, however, in first grade. (The latter finding was recently replicated by Freppon, 1991.) The authors presented several plausible explanations for these findings. They concluded that the emphasis on listening to and writing stories may serve a useful function for at-risk kindergarten students, in that they are able to see the many purposes of reading and experience the pleasures associated with reading and writing.

On the other hand, the reversal in first grade may be largely due to the limitations of whole language as a *total* reading program. Whereas whole language approaches may effectively increase students' motivation to read, they do not seem to provide systematic instruction in *how* to read.

Nagging Concerns About Whole Language

Although most whole language advocates realize that students need to spend some time on word analysis skills in the early grades (California State Department of Education, 1988; Goodman, 1990), they believe that this instruction should *always* be integrated with the literature being read and *never* taught in isolation. The following excerpt from a whole language manual gives readers a sense of this approach:

The teacher reads the story aloud and points to the words. Next, the group reads the story through several times in unison, *although some students may join in only on repetitive refrains* [italics added].... As children repeatedly hear the words and see the print, they make associations between letters and sounds; *many children figure out the code by themselves* [italics added]. Teachers ask students to point to words that begin alike or ones that have similar parts; phonics is taught in context, not in isolation. (Cullinan, 1987, pp. 8–9)

In a critique of the whole language approach, Chall (1989) concluded that

to say that teachers should teach phonics only as needed is to put a greater burden of responsibility on teachers and children than theory, research, and practice support. *And it puts at even greater risk those children who need the instruction most—low income, minority, and learning-disabled children* [italics added]. (p. 532)

Chall's conclusions parallel observations made by Stahl and Miller (1989) that whole language does not make sense as a *comprehensive* approach to teaching reading to students with potential reading disabilities. There is no *system* for these students to learn how to break the code, but many need systematic instruction as part of their reading program (Adams, 1990; Beck, 1990; Stahl, 1992).

Several recent commentaries provide other perspectives on whole language. Delpit (1988) observed that holistic process-oriented approaches to literacy instruction give many mainstream students an opportunity to demonstrate what they have already learned at home, while depriving minority students of the explicit instruction they need. She noted how each culture has many implicit rules, and that the rules of the culture of power need to be explicitly shared with minority students:

In some instances adherents of process approaches to writing create situations in which students ultimately find themselves held accountable for knowing a set of rules about which no one has ever directly informed them. Teachers do students no service to suggest, even implicitly, that "product" is not important. In this country, students will be judged on their product regardless of the process they utilized to achieve it. And that product, based as it is on the specific codes of a particular culture is more readily produced when the directives of how to produce it are made explicit. (p. 287)

Reyes's (1991, 1992) observational research of Latino and Hmong students in whole language instructional programs also found that lack of explicitness and clarity impeded some of the lower performing students' growth in reading.

Pearson (1989) raised several germane issues about authenticity and real world literacy tasks. His analysis of whole language concluded, "We should encourage students to read more authentic texts than are found in many basals. . . . We should ask students to read and write for real reasons (the kind real people in the real world have) rather than fake reasons we give them in school" (p. 235). But he cautioned that "compared to some real worlds, the simulated world of schools may seem pretty exciting. . . . An *ideal* real world may contain many opportunities for exciting applications of reading and writing, but there are many *real* worlds that possess either drab applications, or even worse, no applications" (p. 238). Finally, he expressed the fear that "whole language scholars will not tolerate . . . modeling, error correction, and task sequencing as important components of cognitive apprenticeship models" (p. 23). And yet, research on comprehension consistently shows that teachers' explanations and models—their "public sharing of cognitive secrets" (Paris, Lipson, & Wixson, 1983)—are essential for low-achieving students to develop comprehension abilities (Gersten & Carnine, 1986; Pearson & Dole, 1987). Thus, from very different vantage points. Chall, Delpit, Reyes, and Pearson conclude that whole language is not a comprehensive model for reading instruction.

THE DIRECT INSTRUCTION TRADITION

Stein, Leinhardt, and Bickel (1989) summed up the legacy of direct instruction research as follows: "Mastery does not materialize from brief encounters, but rather develops with (systematic instruction)" (p. 164). Their assertion highlights the fundamental difference between the direct instruction and whole language traditions.

Many educators believe that the best approach for teaching reading to students at risk for failure involves a strong, systematic component of word attack strategy instruction during the early stages of reading, and comprehensive, systematic instruction throughout the more advanced strategies. Adherents of direct instruction assert that unless students can read fluently and accurately, they will be unable to comprehend what they read (Engelmann & Carnine, 1982; Reith, Polsgrove, & Semmel, 1982). This group, too, decries the quality of conventional basal instruction, largely because it is not systematic and rarely provides lower performing students with successful reading experiences. They point out that conventional basal instruction programs are geared to the average student. As Idol (1988) commented: "If concepts are presented briefly and are not followed by sufficient practice opportunity, the poor reader is likely to flounder" (p. 10).

It is important to note that advocates of direct instruction do not necessarily stress only phonics during the initial stages of reading instruction; they recognize that systematic instruction in comprehension is also an essential part of direct instruction (Carnine & Kinder, 1985; Idol, 1988). However, work is appreciably less developed in this area than in breaking the code. Whereas much of the writing about whole language takes on a visionary tone and tends to discuss the world of teaching and learning as it ought to be, writing about direct instruction tends to be much more down-to-earth, procedural, pragmatic, and—arguably—mechanistic (see, e.g., Anderson, Evertson, & Brophy, 1979; Carnine, 1983). Yet, direct instruction advocates also often adopt a visionary tone in their advocacy. Because direct instruction is so

often perceived as a set of procedures and techniques, it seems important to discuss it, too, as a vision.

Our description of direct instruction is culled from research, theoretical writings, informal discussions with some key figures, and a decade's worth of systematic observation (Gersten, Carnine, & Williams, 1982; Gersten, Carnine, Zoref, & Cronin, 1986). To understand the term *direct instruction* and the evolution of the concept, it is necessary to go back to its roots in the Bereiter-Engelmann preschool (Bereiter & Engelmann, 1966) and the U.S. Department of Education's Project Follow Through.

Follow Through was implemented in some of the poorest communities in the United States; students entered the program in kindergarten, many with limited exposure to essential literacy and language concepts. In these communities, large numbers of children typically fail in school. The major operating principle behind the Direct Instruction Follow Through model was that if these students experienced unremitting success in all their academic work, very different things would happen. According to this principle, if, when learning to read, students experience success each day at a high rate and receive clear feedback when they experience difficulty, their self-confidence, attitudes toward reading, and reading ability would all increase. Conventional basal readers could not provide this level of support, so new curricula were developed. The direct instruction model can be viewed as an attempt to radically reform the defects in conventional reading instruction.

The key belief system underlying this approach is that at-risk students will more often learn to read when they receive instruction that is clear and well designed, when they are given many opportunities to participate, and when they are provided with clear feedback. The planned curriculum involves what some educators perceive as mundane details (e.g., the best wording for teachers to use in demonstrating a concept, the number of examples necessary for low-performing students to truly understand a concept, specific suggestions for dealing with student misconceptions). Professional development activities stressed high levels of teacher–student interaction, emphasizing the role of the teacher as not only a conveyor of information, but also a provider of feedback and guidance to students.

In the Follow Through study (Becker, 1977; Stebbins, St. Pierre, Proper, Anderson, & Cerva, 1977) the principles of direct instruction were field-tested, revised, and evaluated in 20 low-income communities between 1969 and 1977, and were found to be effective in raising the reading performance of thousands of low-income students to levels close to their middle class peers'. The effectiveness of the essentials of the direct instruction approach was corroborated by a host of independent researchers (e.g., Christenson, Ysseldyke, & Thurlow, 1989). Stein et al. (1989) noted that the findings were remarkably uniform across settings (mainstreamed classroom, special pull-out program) and across grade levels.

Nagging Concerns About Direct Instruction

Many educators express concern about the conception of direct instruction and the kind of effective teaching described above. Some feel that with direct instruction, the teacher is *always* in control because he or she constantly controls the flow of information to students. Others feel that this method does not seem democratic or natural, and they wonder how kids who are taught with the direct instruction model will ever learn to function independently (Palinesar, David, Winn, & Stevens, 1991; Peterson, 1979). The amount of drill and practice necessary for teaching to mastery is upsetting to some. Cazden (1983) expressed the sentiments of many when she concluded that direct instruction "can only be implemented in an authoritarian, manipulative, bureaucratic system" (p. 33).

There is also a serious concern about the efficacy of direct instruction as a comprehensive means of helping students read independently and comprehend and analyze what they have read (Heshusius, 1991; Palinesar et al., 1991). Some researchers (Duffy, 1983; Rosenshine, 1991) have called for an expanded view of direct instruction, noting that classic views of direct instruction require a teacher to break each learning activity into a series of small steps and that the process of comprehension is often not amenable to this approach.

CONCLUSIONS

In the midst of a recent debate. Pearson (cited in Rothman, 1989) declared that *"reading is more a religion than a science* [italics added]" (p. 7). We would agree, pointing out that advocates of each of the major approaches to reading instruction take on a zealous tone in their communications. Compromise is rarely possible. Yet, we would also point out that reading research is gradually becoming more of a science, though it has been slow in its evolution (for example, it is only in the last decade that researchers have begun to explore the relative effectiveness of various strategies for teaching comprehension).

Systematic instruction appears to be important for students who fail to develop phonemic awareness—or other important aspects of breaking the code—on their own (Adams, 1990). Research evidence strongly suggests that these students need well-sequenced, clear assistance in how to break the code. In her comprehensive synthesis of research on beginning reading, Adams stressed that the use of *isolated* phonics exercises, without the reading and discussion of real stories, is counterproductive, and that learning to read must be an interplay between instruction in word analysis and oral reading, and engagement in emergent literacy listening comprehension activities and reading comprehension activities. We suspect that the ideal mix that Adams calls for is not typical of the major basal reading series.

Though there is evidence that systematic instruction in word analysis and oral reading should be an essential component of beginning reading, there is no evidence that these same students need 10 years of skills-based direct instruction. A great deal of research points to the futility of breaking reading into discrete skills and objectives that are taught in a series of sequenced activities (Anderson et al., 1979).

After extensive observational study of whole language instruction, Fisher and Hiebert (1990) concluded that whole language was optimal once students could read on their own, but probably of little use for students who could not read. Thus, although further inquiry is needed to explore the extent to which their assertion is true for lower performing students, there is no question that holistic approaches can appreciably benefit students with disabilities. Whole language, in some instances, has made reading instruction come alive in schools (Englert, Garmon, Mariage, Rozendal, & Tarrant, 1993; Fisher & Hiebert, 1990; Gersten, 1993; Palinesar, 1993).

There also appear to be far too many instances of low-achieving students floundering in whole language contexts (Reyes, 1991). Much needs to be learned about the exact balance between explicitness and discovery, between the use of well-sequenced activities and naturally occurring texts. As researchers, we need to more carefully examine which contexts make sense for which sets of instructional strategies. This type of precise research is in its infancy.

McCaslin (1989) articulated a major concern regarding whole language, held by many in the field of special and remedial education. She noted that

whole language advocates seem to equate the lack of instruction in comprehension with the futility of instruction in comprehension. With whole language, students are rarely taught "how to comprehend." [Therefore] learning to comprehend essentially becomes discovery learning. Some students, especially those of higher ability, can self-instruct.... Other [low-performing] students who were unable to self-instruct ... engage in a variety of coping strategies aimed at pleasing teachers, staying out of trouble or saving face rather than learning what it is to comprehend the written word. (p. 226)

In the past 10 years, a variety of approaches for improving comprehension have been developed and researched. They fall under a confusing rubric of categories—cognitive strategy instruction (Harris & Pressley, 1991), explicit strategy instruction (Duffy et al., 1987; Pearson & Dole, 1987), scaffolded instruction (Palinesar, 1986). As Harris and Pressley noted, strategy instruction "is neither fully constructed ... nor completely understood.... More needs to be known about how to teach strategies so that durable use and transfer is maximized" (p. 401).

Many of these approaches are derived, in part, from the work of the Russian psychologist Vygotsky, as well as other cognitive psychologists. The goal is typically to develop abilities and skills that are *emerging* in the students' repertoires but that are as yet immature (Palinesar, 1986). In scaffolded instruction, the teacher often "thinks aloud," explaining to students in a step-by-step fashion how he or she reached a specific conclusion. Gradually, the temporary structure, or "scaffold," is removed and students perform independently. Many of these approaches involve the use of cooperative and collaborative learning (e.g., Armbruster, Anderson, & Meyer, 1991; Palinesar et al., 1991).

We see no reason why these approaches to helping students understand what they read cannot be integrated into whole language frameworks or direct instruction frameworks. The effective use of these strategies can address some of the nagging concerns raised about each model.

A FINAL NOTE

We intentionally began with a poem by Yeats. The poem reached no conclusion but revealed and illuminated much about the process of writing and creativity. Delpit, McCaslin, Pearson, Fisher, Routman, Adams, Palinesar, Carnine, Harris, and Pressley all offer some insights into *certain aspects* of teaching reading to low-performing students. Many years ago, Baker and Brown noted that the goal of reading instruction should be the "click of comprehension," alluding to the somewhat mystical moment we have all experienced at some time, and which is the aim of much of the reading instruction we hope to provide.

Both the direct instruction and the whole language approaches can be distilled into images. Whole language proponents imagine a classroom where students are genuinely interested in what they read, where teachers often experiment, and where freedom is reflected in a dynamic class atmosphere. Intrinsic rather than extrinsic motivation is fostered.

Direct instruction presents a very different type of image. Rather than the image of authentic, intuitive instruction, it is an image of students learning in highly interactive instructional groups, in which they experience consistent success and are provided with immediate feedback when they encounter problems. The role of the teacher is, in part, to demystify the process of reading—to show the students that there are rules and principles and that by learning the system, they will read with understanding.

One of the most prominent empirical researchers, Brophy (1985), concluded that one thing he learned from decades of classroom research is how deceptive labels can be. When observing classrooms using approaches based on a complex Vygotskian model of scaffolded instruction, he still observed a good deal of direct instruction. On the other hand, in direct instruction classrooms, Brophy observed a lot of time devoted to comprehension activities and higher order analytic processes, a good deal of reading of "real," unedited literature, and a lot of scaffolded instruction. If nothing else, empirical research should enable us to move beyond statements of philosophy and toward a serious analysis of the type of learning situations teachers actually create with children.

AUTHORS' NOTES

1. This research was supported, in part, by the following grants from the Office of Special Education Programs, U.S. Department of Education: 11023F80018 and 11023H00014.

2. An earlier version of this article was presented at the National Reading Conference in December 1990.

3. The authors wish to thank the following individuals for insightful feedback on earlier versions of the manuscript: Sharon Vaughn, Gary Davis, Bonnie Grossen, Robert Jimenez, Jean Osborn, and, especially, Martha Morvant.

References

Adams, M.J. (1990). *Beginning to read: Thinking and learning about print.* Cambridge, MA: MIT Press.

Allington, R.I., (1983). The reading instruction provided readers of differing reading abilities. *Elementary School Journal, 83,* 548–559.

Altwerger, B., Edelstein, C., & Flores, B.M. (1987). Whole language: What's new? *The Reading Teacher, 11,* 144–154.

Anderson, L., Evertson, C., & Brophy, J. (1979). An experimental study of effective teaching in first-grade reading groups. *Elementary School Journal, 79,* 193–223.

Armbruster, B.B., Anderson, T.H., & Meyer, J. (1991). The framing project: Collaboration to improve content area reading using instructional graphics. *Reading Research Quarterly, 26,* 393–417.

Baker, L., & Brown, A.L. (1981), Metacognitive skills and reading. In P.D. Pearson (Ed.), *Handbook of reading research* (pp. 353–391). New York: Longman.

Beck, I. (1990, December). *Response to "Beginning to read: Thinking and learning about print."* Paper presented at the National Reading Conference, Miami, FL.

Becker, W.C. (1977). Teaching reading and language to the disadvantaged: What we have learned from field research. *Harvard Education Review, 47,* 518–543.

Bereiter, C., & Engelmann, S. (1966). *Teaching disadvantaged children in the preschool.* Englewood Cliffs, NJ: Prentice-Hall.

Brophy, J.E. (1985, April). *Conceptualizing instruction in reading.* Paper presented at the meeting of the American Educational Research Association, Chicago.

Brophy, J., & Good, T.L. (1986). Teacher behavior and student achievement. In M. Wittrock (Ed.), *The third handbook of research on teaching* (pp. 328–375). New York: Macmillan.

California State Department of Education. (1988). *California language arts framework.* Sacramento, CA: Author.

Carnine, D. (1983). Direct instruction: In search of instructional solutions for educational problems. In *Interdisciplinary voices in learning disabilities and remedial education* (pp. 1–60). Austin, TX: PRO-ED.

Carnine, D., & Kinder, B.D. (1985). Teaching low-performance students to apply generative and schema strategies to narrative and expository material. *Remedial and Special Education, 6*(1), 20–30.

Cazden, C.B. (1983). Can ethnographic research go beyond the status quo? *Anthropology and Education Quarterly, 14,* 33–41.

Chall, J.S. (1989). Learning to read: The great debate 20 years later—a response to "Debunking the Great Phonics Myth." *Phi Delta Kappan, 70,* 521–538.

Christenson, S.L., Ysseldyke, J.E., & Thurlow, M.L. (1989). Critical instructional factors for students with mild handicaps: An integrative review. *Remedial and Special Education, 10*(5), 21–31.

Cullinan, B.E. (1987). Inviting readers to literature. In B.E. Cullinan (Ed.), *Children's literature in the reading program* (pp. 2–14). Newark, DE: International Reading Association.

Delpit, L.D. (1988). The silenced dialogue: Power and pedagogy in educating other people's children. *Harvard Educational Review, 58,* 280–298.

Duffy, G.G. (1983). From turn-taking to sense-making: Broadening the concept of teacher effectiveness. *Journal of Educational Research, 76,* 134–139.

Duffy, G.G., Rochter, L.R., Sivan, E., Rackliffe, G., Book, C., Meloth, M., Vavrus, L., Wessellman, R., Putnam, J., & Bassiri, D. (1987). The effects of explaining the reasoning associated with using reading strategies. *Reading Research Quarterly, 22,* 347–368.

Durkin, D. (1978–79). What classroom observations reveal about reading comprehension instruction. *Reading Research Quarterly, 14,* 481–533.

Engelmann, S., & Carnine, D. (1982). *Theory of instruction.* New York: Irvington.

Englert, C.S., Garmon, A., Mariage, T., Rozendal, M., & Tarrant, K. (1993, April). *Beyond skills instruction: The effects of discourse communities in special education classrooms on literacy performance.* Paper presented at the annual meeting of the American Educational Research Association, Atlanta.

Fisher, C.W. & Hiebert, E.H. (1990). Characteristics of tasks in two approaches to literacy instruction. *Elementary School Journal, 91*(1), 3–18.

Garcia, G.E., & Pearson, P.D. (1989). *Modifying reading instruction to maximize its effectiveness for "disadvantaged" students.* Manuscript submitted for publication.

Gersten, R. (1991, November). *Research issues in the education of limited English proficient students in special education.* Paper presented at the Council for Exceptional Children Conference on At-Risk Children and Youth, New Orleans, LA.

Gersten, R. (1993, April). *The language minority student in transition: Exploring the parameters of effective literacy instruction.* Paper presented at the annual meeting of the American Educational Research Association, Atlanta.

Gersten, R., & Carnine, D. (1986). Direct instruction in reading comprehension. *Educational Leadership, 43*(7), 70–78.

Gersten, R., Carnine, D., & Williams, P. (1982). Measuring implementation of a structured educational model in an urban setting: An observational approach. *Educational Evaluation and Policy Analysis, 4,* 67–79.

Gersten, R., Carnine, D., Zoref, L., & Cronin, D. (1986). A multifaceted study of change in seven inner city schools, *Elementary School Journal, 86,* 257–276.

Gersten, R., & Jiménez, R. (1993). *A delicate balance: Enhancing literacy instruction for language-minority students.* Manuscript submitted for publication.

Goodman, K. (1990). Whole-language research: Foundations and developments. *Elementary School Journal, 90,* 207–221.

Harris, K., & Pressley, M. (1991). The nature of cognitive strategy instruction: Interactive strategy construction. *Exceptional Children, 57,* 392–401.

Harste, J. (1989). The future of whole language. *Elementary School Journal, 90,* 243–249.

Heshusius, L. (1991). Curriculum-based assessment and direct instruction: Critical reflections on fundamental assumptions. *Exceptional Children, 57,* 315–328.

Hoffman, J.V. (1989). Introduction. *Elementary School Journal, 90,* 111–112.

Holt, Rinehart, and Winston, (1986). *A place for me.* New York: Author.

Idol, L. (1988). Johnny can't read: Does the fault lie with the book, the teacher, or Johnny? *Remedial and Special Education, 9*(1), 8–25.

Lindsey, M. (1990, December). *Case studies of the experiences of three low achieving first graders in an integrated literacy curriculum.* Paper presented at the National Reading Conference, Miami.

McCaslin, M. (1989). Whole language: Theory, instruction, and future implementation. *Elementary School Journal, 90,* 223–229.

Moll, L., & Diaz, S. (1987). Change as the goal of educational research. *Anthropology & Education Quarterly, 18,* 300–311.

Palinesar, A.S. (1986). The role of dialogue in providing scaffolded instruction. *Educational Psychologist, 21*(1 & 2), 73–98.

Palinesar, A. (1993, April). *Designing best contexts for learning.* Paper presented at the annual meeting of the American Educational Research Association, Atlanta.

Palinesar, A.S., David, Y.M., Winn, J.A., & Stevens, D.D. (1991). Examining the contexts of strategy instruction. *Remedial and Special Education, 12*(3), 43–53.

Paris, S.G., Lipson, M.Y., & Wixson, K.K. (1983). Becoming a strategic reader. *Contemporary Educational Psychology, 8,* 293–316.

Pearson, P.D. (1989). Reading the whole-language movement. *The Elementary School Journal, 90,* 231–241.

Pearson, P.D., & Dole, J.A. (1987). Explicit comprehension instruction: A review of research and a new conceptualization of instruction. *The Elementary School Journal, 88,* 151–165.

Peterson, P.L. (1979). Direct instruction reconsidered. In P.L. Peterson & H.J. Walberg (Eds.), *Research on teaching: Concepts, findings, and implications* (pp. 57–69), Berkeley, CA: McCutchan.

Reith, H.L., Polsgrove, L., & Semmel, M.I. (1982). Instructional variables that make a difference: Attention to task and beyond. *Exceptional Children Quarterly, 2,* 61–71.

Reyes, M. de la Luz. (1991). A process approach to literacy using dialogue journals and literature logs with second language learners. *Research in the Teaching of English, 25,* 291–313.

Reyes, M. de la Luz. (1992). Challenging verable assumptions: Literacy instruction for linguistically different students. *Harvard Educational Review, 62*(4), 427–446.

Rosenshine, B. (1991, April). *The use of scaffolds for teaching higher-level cognitive strategies.* Paper presented at the annual conference of the American Educational Research Association, Chicago.

Rothman, R. (1989). NAEP board is seeking a consensus on reading. *Education Week, 9*(4), 7.

Routman, R. (1988). *Transitions: From literature to literacy.* Portsmouth, NH: Heinemann.

Stahl, S. (1992). Saying the "p" word: Nine guidelines for exemplary phonics instruction. *The Reading Teacher, 45,* 608–617.

Stahl, S.L. & Miller, P.D. (1989). Whole language and language experience approaches for beginning reading: A quantitative research synthesis. *Review of Educational Research, 59*(1), 87–116.

Stallings, J. (1975). *Follow through program classroom observation evaluation.* Menlo Park, CA: Stanford Research Institute.

Stebbins, L., St. Pierre, R.G., Proper, E.L., Anderson, R.B., & Cerva, T.R. (1977). *Education as experimentation: A planned variation model* (Vols. 4 A–D). Cambridge, MA: Abt Associates.

Stein, M.K., Leinhardt, G., & Bickel, W. (1989). Instructional issues for teaching students at risk. In R.E. Slavin, N.L. Karweit, & N.A. Madden (Eds.), *Effective programs for students at risk.* (pp. 145–194). Boston: Allyn and Bacon.

Yeats, W.B. (1955). *The collected poems of W.B. Yeats* (7th Ed.). New York: Macmillan.

Ysseldyke, J., O'Sullivan, P.J., Thurlow, M., & Christenson, S. (1989). Qualitative differences in reading and math instruction received by handicapped students. *Remedial and Special Education, 10*(1), 14–20.

7.3 ▌ Communication Unbound:

Autism and Praxis

Douglas Biklen

Douglas Biklen has done extensive research into a method for facilitating communication for people with autism. His article is a rich qualitative study of a facilitative communication method developed by Rosemary Crossley and her colleagues at the Dignity through Education and Language Communication Centre in Melbourne, Australia. This method challenges both Biklen's assumptions and those widely held in the field about the ability of people with autism to communicate. He demonstrates how people who have been labeled severely autistic can selectively communicate with certain facilitators, and in certain circumstances. In so doing, they not only challenge our widely held assumptions about autism, but also illustrate the effectiveness of an "education-through-dialogue approach" in which teachers and students learn from each other and where school validates personal expression.

Jonothan Solaris cannot speak. David Armbruster can say a few words, usually unintelligible. Both are young adolescents classified as autistic. I first met them in Melbourne, Australia, at the Dignity through Education and Language (DEAL) Communication Centre, an independent, government-funded organization established by educator Rosemary Crossley and her colleagues to assist people who are unable either to talk or to do so clearly. Jonothan seemed full of nervous energy and he got up from his seat frequently. His way of walking on the balls of his feet was akin to prancing. David gazed at the ceiling light, reaching toward it with his hands. Both boys relied heavily on peripheral vision. Even when spoken to, I felt like they listened to me "sideways." Also, their facial expressions didn't correspond with the conversation, although David smiled a lot.

I was not surprised by how either of them appeared. Theirs were the behaviors of autism. But what I did not anticipate was that their communication with me would assault my assumptions about autism and ultimately yield important lessons for education.

On the day of my visit, Jonothan and David were present to demonstrate a method that Crossley had developed called "facilitated communication." I spent fifteen or twenty minutes speaking with David's mother and several DEAL staff members, occasionally directing my statements to Jonothan and David. Then, when Crossley asked if they had anything to tell me, Jonothan began to type on a Canon Communicator (a small electronic typing device with a dot matrix tape output). With a staff member's hand on his shoulder, Jonothan typed, "ILIKEDOUGGBUTT-HHEISMAAD."[1] Seeing what Jonothan had written, Crossley asked why he thought I was "maad," whereupon he typed, "HETALKSTOMELIKEIMHUMAN." By "MAAD" he had meant "crazy."

Jonothan and David produced only a few sentences in the several hours that we were together. But when they typed, they did so fairly quickly, without hesitation, and independently (with just the hand on the shoulder). I asked David and Jonothan if I could take some pictures of them communicating. I explained that people in the U.S. would be interested in seeing what they were doing. They both agreed, typing "y" for "yes" on their Canons. David added, "NOSEY PEOPLE TO EVEN WANT TO SEE ME." Unlike Jonothan, he had put in spaces between the words. During this session, Crossley described the method of facilitated communication that had allowed David and Jonothan to communicate. In the midst of her enthusiastic and lengthy discourse, David revealed his sense of humor, typing, "TURN HER OFF."

Crossley's first attempt at facilitation with a person with autism had been Jonothan, not an "easy" student. For over a month he had resisted typing. When I asked him what had finally caused him to communicate on a regular basis, he did not answer. Then, several minutes later, he typed, "IMNOTVERYQUIT-RHIGHTNOWBECIGOTSATONBYROSIE." Translated, he said, "I'm not very quiet right now because I got sat on by Rosie." Hearing this, Crossley asked, "Do you mean that literally or metaphorically?" Jonothan responded by typing "MET."

Jonothan's easy grasp of this abstract concept, "metaphorical," and David's facile sarcasm struck me as extraordinary. The content of their communication was "normal," not what one expects from children with autism. A year and a half earlier I had been similarly, if not so vividly, shocked by a letter from Australia that described Crossley's success in using a new technique to allow people with autism to communicate. The letter claimed that Crossley was eliciting "high-level" communication from her students. "Sophisticated written (typed) communication at sentence level," I was told. I didn't know what to think about this claim. It seemed conceivable to me that Crossley and her colleagues had happened on a *few* people with autism for whom such communication was possible. But it made no sense that people with autism who had been classified as severely intellectually disabled would have normal or even near-normal literacy skills. By definition, people with autism who do not speak or who speak only a small range of phrases are referred to as "low functioning" and are thought to have a severe intellectual disability as well (Rutter, 1978). Of course, one possible explanation was that Crossley's students were actually mildly disabled; in other words, perhaps they had autism but were among the group commonly called "high functioning." This term is often applied to those people with autism who have usable, easily understood speech. Yet the letter described the method as working with students who typically might be called "low functioning," and included some who were previously thought to be severely intellectually disabled. The letter about Crossley was baffling, so much so that, whether consciously or not, I put it out of my mind for a year and a half. But when I knew I would be in Melbourne I arranged to visit DEAL. Then, seeing David and Jonothan type sophisticated thoughts, I could not ignore the many questions their communication posed.

How, why, and with whom does facilitated communication work? Does facilitated communication work anywhere or is it more effective in certain settings, under specific educational or social conditions, and with certain people more than with others? If there were preferred conditions, how would these compare to prevailing notions about "good" school-

ing? Presumably, the DEAL students themselves would be able to comment on many issues, such as how society treats them and how they want to be treated. Would the DEAL students change as a result of their new-found communication and, if so, how? Equally important, would the ability to communicate lead to changes in their families, schools, and other environments? Did the success of students like David and Jonothan portend a dramatic transformation in how we think about and define autism?

In July of 1989, seven months after the session with Jonothan and David, I returned to Melbourne to study Crossley's work more systematically. I observed nearly all the students Crossley worked with both at DEAL and in the community over a four-week period. I also observed the two part-time speech therapists working with other children at DEAL, interviewed parents, and visited schools. My discussion in this article is based upon communication efforts by twenty-one individuals served by the Dignity through Education and Language Centre.[2] All twenty-one are nonspeaking or speak only with echolalic expressions (echoes of phrases they have previously heard); all have been labeled autistic or display autistic behaviors. Observations and interviews were audio-recorded; thus students' typed words were recorded as facilitators read them aloud.

ORIGINS OF CROSSLEY'S DISCOVERY

Crossley's discovery of literacy skills among nonspeaking people or people who have disordered speech because of autism and other developmental disabilities occurred by accident. During the 1970s, when she worked at the St. Nicholas Institution, she had used hand support or arm support to help people with cerebral palsy achieve greater control over their movements, to slow them down, *and* to give them more likelihood of hitting an intended target (for example a switch, key, button, letter, or picture on a board). The method was controversial (Crossley & McDonald, 1980) because it raised the possibility that the people's choice of letters from a language board, for example, might reflect the facilitator's rather than the learner's choice. The controversy ultimately subsided somewhat when, through message-passing tests (for instance, Crossley left the room and returned to facilitate communication about something that had transpired in her absence), the Supreme Court of Victoria sided with Crossley, recognizing the students as authors of such communication (Crossley & McDonald, 1980). Application of this method to people with autism and similar conditions was unplanned although, Crossley now believes, logical. She began with Jonothan.

By every account, Jonothan was a handsome but challenging child. He was not toilet trained. He fidgeted. To get things, he simply grabbed them. He did not look people in the eye. He nearly skipped when walking, on the balls of his feet. He had a history of fits of screaming, regurgitating food, scratching, and running away from people. In March of 1985, when Jonothan was seven, Rosemary Crossley invited his mother to leave him with her for an afternoon. That afternoon, after watching Jonothan's stereotyped repetitive play with a squeeze mop, Crossley managed to settle Jonothan on her sofa, first interesting him in a speech synthesizer and then in a Canon Communicator. With wrist support, he pressed buttons that she touched. Occasionally he pressed buttons without any assistance. She typed "JONOTHAN," followed by "MUM," and then asked him for "Dad." He went straight to the D, without wrist support and then to A, where he hesitated.

"I think he completed 'DAD' with no prompting but with wrist support," she wrote later in her notes that day. If she had "prompted" him, she would have actually moved his wrist toward the letter or letters; instead, she merely supported his wrist as he moved his hand toward the letters. She typed "JONATHAN," whereupon he typed "JONOTHAN." Crossley later checked the spelling with his mother. Jonothan had been correct. Crossley asked him if the mop was a plane when he was playing with it. He typed "MOP." She guided him through the entire alphabet on the keyboard, then asked him what letter the word good starts with. He pressed G. She asked how many fingers she had on one hand. He pressed 5. She asked how many on two hands; he pressed 10. "If you took 5 from 10, how many would you have left?" she then asked. He typed 5. She continued, 5 plus 3? He gave 8. For 3 plus 4, he pressed 6. She said try again. He got 7. She observed, over time, that Jonothan often veered to the side of a character at the last moment, resulting in a typographical rather than a cognitive error, presumably the result of cerebellar damage to judgment of distance. Crossley asked if Jonothan had anything he would like to say. He spelled "STOP." He was reluctant to finish the word; he made several tries and erasures before completing it.

Coincidentally, on the afternoon I interviewed Crossley about how she had discovered that this

method worked with Jonothan, he came to visit DEAL. Crossley told him that we had just been talking about the first time he had typed on the Canon. She asked him if he remembered what his first word had been. As she asked the question, she held out a Canon Communicator. Independently, he typed "DAD." Then he typed, "JONOTHAN NOT JONATHAN." This is one child who remembers his first words.

When Jonothan's mother returned to Crossley's home that afternoon in 1986, Crossley presumed that Jonothan wanted to show her what he had been doing. But, in Crossley's words, "he completely gummed up . . . [He] was quite unable or unwilling to give so much as a 'yes' or 'no' with her there." Jonothan's inability to communicate with his mother continued until she died in 1989. While Jonothan communicates with several other people now, much of it independently or with only a hand on the shoulder, his communication with his mother was basically unsuccessful, a fact she found "discouraging."

Why people who regularly communicate independently with a few people but not at all or only with support to the wrist and forearm with others is mysterious. Is it difficult for some students to communicate with people with whom they feel a close personal bond? In other words, is it harder to reveal yourself and your skills to those whose judgment you especially value? Are some people better at facilitation than others? Must the student believe that the person is an effective facilitator? Is the willingness or ability to communicate with particular people reflective of the "autistic" quality of wanting order and sameness?

OBSERVATIONS OF FIRST ASSESSMENTS

Among the DEAL students I observed were people whom Crossley was seeing for the first time. They included school-age children and young adults, and ranged in age from five to twenty-three. Like my first meeting with Jonothan and David, these first sessions startled me. Crossley's assessment of Louis is a case in point.

Louis is twenty-four years old, with reddish-brown hair and gold metal-rimmed, rectangular-shaped glasses with thick lenses. He was wearing a black and white sweater, black jeans, and white tennis shoes when we met him at an adult training center (ATC)–ATCs are considered one step less demanding than sheltered workshops–which are designed specifically for people with disabilities who are presumed unable to work in competitive employment but capable of working under supervision, albeit often at less than average productivity rates and for less than the minimum wage. People who attend ATCs are generally considered too disabled to qualify for admittance to a sheltered workshop. Louis had very little facial expression. He does not speak, except for a few phrases that seem involuntarily uttered and are out of context. As he entered the room where Crossley was to conduct the assessment, he said: "Excuse me. Get mommy on the bus. Excuse me," which didn't make sense to me. Attempts at answering his statements by saying, for example, "There is no need to be excused, you are fine," did not quiet him. He repeated the phrase.

Crossley introduced herself and me to Louis, who sat between us. She described her work to him as helping people who don't speak find other ways to communicate. She apologized in advance for her assessment approach: "Louis, I ask people a lot of really silly questions." She commenced the session by asking him to press down on various pictures on a talking computer, a children's toy with a voice output that requests the person using it to press various pictures or letters and which announces the user's choice, for example, "Right, that's the apple."

As Crossley asked questions, tears began to roll down Louis's face. He was crying silently. She reassured him, telling him that she would do it with him. She held her hand on top of Louis's right arm. In response to the command, "Press the red car," Louis put his index finger on it and Crossley helped him push it down. Louis was moving slowly. He seemed tentative. The machine instructed him to find the circle, which he did. He followed with correct answers to square, triangle, circle, and triangle. He hit them all, five of five.

Crossley changed the display page on the talking computer. This time he was asked for the small rectangle. Louis started to go for the big one. She held him back and said, with emphasis, "*Small* rectangle." He then went for it correctly. She reassured him, "Yes." Louis had struggled with the demands of the machine; with Crossley's help he had gotten the right answers. When asked for the "big square," Louis hesitated. As he hovered over it, Crossley encouraged him, "Go on, you've got it." He did. Next he was asked, "Find the small yellow rectangle." His hand wobbled between the brown triangle and blue circle. Crossley pulled him back and Louis uttered the words, "That one," and hit the small yellow rectangle.

The next screen displayed a picture of grass, a tree, a car, a house, and a cat. He pressed the car on demand. He got the tree. Then he was asked to locate the word "tree" as distinct from the picture. He did. Again he got five out of five. On another screen he had to choose pictures to go with the words "yacht," "fish," "dog," "girl," "bird," and "boy." For "girl" he started to move away from the picture of a girl. Crossley pulled his hand back and asked, "Where are you going?" With the exception of this help, he pressed the words independently.

The next sheet included only words. When Crossley asked Louis to identify the clock, his finger seemed to drop to flower. She said, "Hold on," and asked, "Can you point to clock?" He did. She followed by asking him to point to the words "hand," "eye," and "fish." He identified each. For these, she was holding the top of his sleeve above his wrist. Louis was seemingly expressionless throughout. Next, Crossley read five sentences aloud to Louis and asked him to find words in the sentences, including, for example, "our," "on," "and," "is," and "the." He got them all. She was pleased. "Terrific. That's great, mate," she declared.

Finally, she switched to a page displaying the alphabet and asked Louis to point to specific letters, including, for example, *v, g, a,* and *z.* He got them all. Less than half an hour had elapsed and Crossley was ready to introduce Louis to the Canon Communicator. At this point, I wrote in my notebook, "He's sailing." Except for minor stumbling with the geometric figures, Louis had cruised through the questions. Also, he now had a slight smile at the corner of his mouth. He had relaxed.

Crossley showed Louis the Canon and went through the alphabet and numbers with him. "For starters," she asked, "can you type your name?" At this point, her hand was stretched out flat, on top of, but not actually touching, his. He typed "LOUIS." As he finished, she asked if there was anything else he wanted to say. Louis started typing again. First he typed an "O," then "PC." Crossley pulled his hand back from the keys, saying, "I'm not sure I follow. Let's start over." This time he typed "POCCO." She was confused. Then we realized what he was typing. *Pocco* is his last name. He was still responding to Crossley's first request, to type his name.

Crossley asked again if there was anything else Louis wanted to say. He typed, "IM NOT RETARDED," to which she remarked, "No, I don't think you are. Keep going." Louis continued, "MY MOTHER FEELS IM STUPID BECAUSE IH [he back-spaced this and crossed out the *h*] CANT USE MY VOICE PROPERLY." A tear rolled down his left cheek as he typed. And Crossley said to me and to Louis, "A lot of people believe that what people say is what they're capable of."

Louis was not done. He typed, "HOW MUCH IS A CANON?"

"They're dear," Crossley answered.

"I SAVE A BIT BUT NOT ENOUGH" Louis typed.

Crossley explained that she would continue to work with Louis in conjunction with the Adult Training Center and that she would try to get him a Canon. Then she congratulated him on his work in the session and said to me, for Louis to hear, "Anybody who starts off typing, 'I'm not retarded' isn't retarded. First rule!"

The words of other first-time communicators, meaning those who communicated neither with echolalia or by physical manipulation of objects, were no less astonishing. One young man typed "I CAN READ" for his first sentence. He had learned to read by being around words and by watching television. Crossley's students and their parents typically report that the students had had incidental exposure to language through television, magazines, and books, or with labels on foods and other items. Some were reported to have been in formal reading programs as part of early intervention and developmental training efforts. Yet until Crossley elicited typing from them, the assumption for all of them was that they had *not* learned to read.

Margaret, a seventeen-year-old young woman referred to DEAL by an autism center, also surprised me with her performance in her first session at DEAL. Except for the word "no" and an approximation of "hello," she is mute. During a two-hour assessment session, though I addressed her several times, she never once looked at me. Her first sentence, typed independently, save Crossley's hand on her shoulder, was a question: "CAN I COME AGAIN?" Sessions with younger children were often much shorter, with the students unable or unwilling to cooperate for such long stretches.

DOUBTS: FACILITATION OR MANIPULATION?

Despite the seeming ease with which Crossley assesses some new students, she and her colleagues admit that communication is not always so easily facilitated. Initially, it has often proved difficult for students to communicate with more than one or two facilitators, especially when they are new to DEAL. They may refuse to communicate at particular moments, in particular situations, with certain people, or for specific time periods as, for example, Jonothan

did. Some are independent in some situations, but dependent or noncommunicative in others, whether with the same or other people. Some then will produce obviously incorrect information. Related to this, facilitators often find themselves inadvertently cueing their nonspeaking partners to letters and therefore to words or statements. This is particularly true with people who are just learning to communicate by typing with facilitation. Occasionally, people who have previously demonstrated excellent facility will type only repetitions of specific letters and phrases or will produce unintelligible sequences of letters or words. All of the people I observed typing "independently," with just a hand on the shoulder, did not type as well or sometimes at all for me alone or for other new facilitators. Jane Remington Gurney, a speech therapist at DEAL, recounted that she worked with several students for "months," unsure whether the students' output was anything more than a reflection of her own manipulation of their arms. She recalled that ". . . gradually I began to receive words from clients that were not in my vocabulary, were phonetically spelled or were . . . spelled better than I could spell." She also found that when she tried "too hard" she was even less successful.

Several facilitators, including speech therapists, teachers, and parents, encountered difficulty in identifying the source of certain communication: either it had been generated by the person being supported or by their own unconscious selection or cueing. They reported instances where they had believed the communication to be genuine, only to discover that it reflected their own subtle cues. I asked a teenager, Bette, for example, "What is your full name? Is it Beth, Elizabeth, or Bette?", to which she answered "Elizabeth." She also declared that she prefers the name Bette. Later I learned that her full name is Beth and that her family and friends call her Bette. Another student, Geraldine, gave a staff member her family's address incorrectly. Such miscues have caused facilitators to wonder about the validity of other communication. Were the words the students' own? Or were they the facilitators'? Or were there perfectly reasonable explanations for the "incorrect" communication? Did Bette think "Elizabeth" sounded better and therefore claim it as her name? Did Geraldine not know her address and decide simply to provide any address in order to at least answer the question asked? Or had she heard the address previously—was this a typed version of echolalia, like the advertising jingles that people with autism have been known to type? Both girls who provided "incorrect" information in these instances communicated independently in other conversations, with only the support of a hand on the shoulder or a finger touching the thread of a sweater.[3]

Within the professional community there has also been a mixed reception to Crossley's work. In 1988, an ad hoc group of psychologists, speech specialists, educators, and administrators calling themselves the "Interdisciplinary Working Party" issued a critique of "assisted communication" (Interdisciplinary, 1988).

The Working Party report cited major contradictions between the nature of communication content being claimed for people with autism and prevailing theories of autism. A letter and assessment statement on DEAL prepared by staff of the Victorian Autistic Children's Association, Eastern Centre, stated, for example, "Well recognized characteristics of autism bring into question much of the assisted communication of autistic children" (p. 91). The assessment, dated September 1, 1987, argues that children with autism would need "far more time to learn the task procedure" than just the brief moments given by Crossley, that the children would have a hard time remembering the sequence of letters they had typed into the Canon Communicator ("short-term sequential memory tasks are particularly difficult for autistic children"), and that Crossley's prompts of counting to ten or saying "Get on your bike" would cause students with autism to forget the task and instructions. This evaluation of Crossley's work also stated that "the sentence structure used by all the children via assisted communication was not characteristic of the 'different' language used by autistic children." Only the most advanced would be capable of using "I"; they would not typically be able to use the word "by" correctly; and "why" questions would "involve cognitive processes well beyond the ability of all but a few autistic children" (p. 93). The Working Party report led to a state government inquiry entitled, *Investigation into the Reliability and Validity of the Assisted Communication Technique* (Intellectual Disability Review Panel, 1989).

The Review Panel report noted that people with intellectual disabilities are "extremely susceptible to influence by people who may be unaware of the extent to which they may be influencing decisions." The panel's charge was to ensure clients' "maximum control" of decisions—in other words, communication and the decisions made on the basis of communication. The panel argued, "given the conflict that the

'assisted communication technique' has engendered and the consequences for the client if doubt exists about his/her communication," it was essential for any disputes over communication to be resolved (p. 18).

In the Review Panel's studies of facilitated communication, the findings were equivocal. The study involved two different procedures, one in which people were given questions that were the same as those given to the facilitator and different from those given the facilitator (the facilitator wore earphones that transmitted the same or different information). The second procedure involved message passing. In this latter approach, people were given gifts. The facilitator did not know about the gifts. The people were then asked to tell the facilitators what they had been given. Since the Review Panel chose not to describe its subjects in any detail, the conclusions others are able to draw from the study are limited. The results of both parts of the study were summarized by the Review Panel in the following manner:

> The validity of the communication while using the "assisted communication technique" was demonstrated in four of the six clients who participated in the two studies. Under controlled conditions the data clearly indicated that the communication of one of the three clients was validated using the "assisted communication technique." The communication of the three clients who participated in the message passing exercise was also validated. The validity of the remaining two clients' communication when using the "assisted communication technique" was not established. However, the absence of data on these occasions does not automatically imply that the clients are not capable of communication. In all three cases of the controlled study, client responses were influenced by the assistant. Influence occurred with a client who demonstrated valid, uninfluenced responses to other items. It appeared that a given assistant could influence some client responses and leave others uninfluenced. (p. 40)

The Panel also noted that assistants appeared unaware of when they might be influencing communication. Also some of the uninfluenced correct responses were correct in general information (category) but were not as specific as anticipated. The Panel concluded that the two parts of the study had produced support from those who claimed facilitated communication had validity *and* for those who doubted it.

BEHAVIOR AND THE PERSON

The behaviors of people labeled autistic are often unusual and appear to reflect lack of attention and/or awareness of social and communication cues and/or severe intellectual disabilities. Perhaps it is such behaviors, including the on-again, off-again ability or willingness of students to communicate, that cause some people to worry that facilitated communication is no more real than a Ouija board.

Polly is a fifteen-year-old high school student who attends regular tenth-grade classes. Before being mainstreamed for the first time in ninth grade, Polly had attended a special school for students with severe disabilities. As her mother rushed to catch her up on math and other school content areas, Polly grasped concepts quickly. Given a subtraction problem that would yield only a negative answer, Polly hesitated momentarily and then typed, "BUT IT IS LESS THAN NAUGHT." I asked one of the teachers to describe Polly's best and worst days at the high school. The teacher explained that Polly had attended the school for three months before being willing or able to communicate with her, and that her "best day" was "when she typed for me!" The "worst" day was when Polly climbed a tree and pulled her skirt up over her head. Another bad day was when Polly urinated in the playground. Her mother believes Polly was testing whether the school would accept her *and* that she was saying, "Look, I'm retarded—do you still want me?"

Polly has several behaviors that are not uncommon for a person labeled autistic, including a tendency to walk on the balls of her feet and sometimes clap her hands together. At school, she will occasionally pace from her locker about fifteen feet to the top of the steps and back. She has had a habit of picking up items such as a wad of dried gum off the ground and putting them in her mouth; if asked, however, she'll stop this particular behavior. When she's seated, she sometimes places her hands between her legs and rocks forward. When she types on the Canon or on an electric typewriter she frequently appears to be looking off into space, horizontally rather than forward. When I would meet her at school or at DEAL I would extend my hand to shake hers. As I grasped her hand, she would pull back, smiling.

Another DEAL student, Bette, could be observed typing independently while simultaneously grimacing and nervously flicking her fingers between words. On one occasion she wanted to stop doing fill-in-the-blanks type "set work" and demonstrate to her parents that she could say what she wanted. She typed the words, "LET ME SHOW THEM WHAT I CAN REALLY DO." As she finished typing, she slapped the table hard. It was startling and incongruous. At home, her mother explains, even since Bette has begun to type with her mother's facilitation, "it's a little bit puzzling that . . . she can . . . have these intelligent thoughts, and yet she will . . . wet . . . the bed or [do] something like that. It's puzzling for us." Bette often needs to be prompted to keep eating or to use a bathroom; otherwise she will sometimes not eat and has toileting accidents. The same seems true of her communication. She will not initiate it. But when her mother, her teacher, or a DEAL staff person begins a conversation with her and provides some support, such as a hand on her sleeve, she will usually communicate.

Such unusual behavior was typical of the people I observed. When I reached out to shake Amanda's hand as I was saying goodbye for the day, she reeled back on the sofa, made a high pitched scream and put one leg up in the air as her arms reached backward. Another student, Robert, smacked himself on the head with his open hand in the middle of a communication exercise. Then he typed to Crossley, "IM NERVOUS." When she asked him, "Are you prepared to fight your nerves?", he responded, "IM FINE." Tommy, age twelve, screamed intermittently while typing. His typed communication was quite normal. Joshua, age six, cried sharp, high-pitched cries off and on during the session. When he typed, he did so quickly. He would type the letter *z* repetitively unless stopped. At the same time, he could answer questions that Crossley posed. She asked him what a cowboy does and he answered, "RIDES." He typed the letters very quickly. Eric had a habit of clipping the output tape off the Canon Communicator. As he typed, he occasionally stopped to slap the table and kick at it. He also kept repeating over and over "McDogs," which his mother said meant McDonalds. It appeared to be echolalic speech.

A young man, Paul, had sores and scratches on his face one day when he came to DEAL. When Crossley asked him what had happened, he responded enigmatically, typing, "I hurt my face. I bashed myself. I do things I don't want to." Throughout the session he held a handful of cloth strips. He brushed the ends of these against his nose and face. He moaned while writing captions for a cartoon and also scrunched his face into a severe grimace. In the middle of the writing, Paul got up from his chair, reached under his black sweater and ripped his undershirt off. When Crossley asked, "Now Paul, what brought that on?" he responded, "I felt hot." Later his mother told me that when she has asked him why he grabs pieces of cloth, he has responded, "Because I can't help myself."

Edward, a high school student who is mute, implied that he could use his behavior calculatingly, refusing to type for his teachers and teaching assistants, holding out for his mother to be his facilitator. When Crossley asked him what he thought his teachers should do about him, he responded with humor: "SHOOT ME."

AUTISM AS WE HAVE UNDERSTOOD IT

My initial difficulty in understanding and *accepting* the claim that children with autism who were mute or highly echolalic could be literate was undoubtedly influenced by what I knew about autism. Results from Crossley's work challenged current theories; she was getting results that no one else had.

The literature on autism is complex and sometimes contentious. (For discussions of the controversies, see, for example, Donnellan, 1985; Rimland, 1964; and Rutter, 1968.) Hypotheses about its cause have ranged from the psychogenic (Bettelheim, 1967), in which mothers are blamed for treating their children so coldly as to cause them to turn inward, to the physiological (Ornitz & Ritvo, 1968; Wetherby, 1984). Yet for all the struggles waged about the "true" nature of this baffling condition or set of behaviors, there is a great deal of agreement about the behavior of people labeled autistic. Autism is characterized by problems of speech, language, and communication, including mutism, echolalia, and perseverative speech, difficulties with social interaction, stereotyped activity, a seeming concern for sameness or constancy of order, and lack of response or unusual response to external events or actions (see, for example, Rutter, 1978; Wetherby, 1984). There is less unanimity, however, about the implications of the behavior.

Language behaviors associated with autism include delay in the development of language and atypical expressions of language. Capturing the range of communication (or absence of it) that characterizes people labeled autistic, over a decade ago Wing summarized the work of Kanner (1943, 1971), Rutter (1968, 1978), and Eisenberg (1956), concluding that "simple stereotypes of the less able child have their counterparts in the elaborate repetitive routines and the stereotyped speech of the more able children" (Wing, 1978, p. 40). When some children labeled autistic develop more elaborate speech, she notes, "it is

characterized by very special abnormalities, suggesting that it is learned by rote without understanding of the rich and subtle associations of words" (p. 40)—in other words, what we might call delayed, transplanted, or recurrent echolalia. Children with autism are assumed to have difficulty understanding abstract concepts "such as time, color, size, and feelings. . . . Questions such as who, what, where, when, and why are confusing" (Schopler, Reichler, & Lansing 1980, p. 29).[4]

To use an analogy from electronics, the brain of a person with autism has been characterized more like a tape recorder and playback device than a computer. Those who display echolalia typically produce words that are phonologically correct, but which appear to be repetitions of other people's phrases or chunks of phrases rather than the person's own creation (Baltaxe & Simmons, 1977; Tager-Flusberg, 1981a,b). A number of such children echo television advertisements, seemingly without linking the words to content. Often, they repeat phrases heard much earlier, producing a delayed echo. Prizant (1983) calls such learning and expression a "gestalt style of language acquisition," a "gestalt mode of cognitive processing," and "gestalt forms" of expression.

Until fairly recently, the assumption has been that though the range of children labeled autistic includes some who perform in the normal range, those who do not communicate or who communicate only very limited numbers of echolalic phrases, often seemingly out of context, and who have a variety of other unusual and seemingly asocial behaviors, in the main are not smart (see, for example, Bartak, Rutter, & Cox, 1977; James & Barry, 1983; and Ricks & Wing, 1975). Language in the form of stereotyped phrases, incorrect semantics, and the ability of some children to "parrot back long phrases" (Schopler et al., 1980, p. 29) were presumed to be the trademarks of incompetence. If they used words appropriately, this was thought to result from "accidental operant conditioning because these words are closely connected with rewards, especially food" (Ricks & Wing, 1975, p. 209).

More recently, Prizant and Rydell have suggested that the language of people with autism occurs along a continuum from little or no symbolic or abstract activity to higher-order thinking and therefore more normal language, though they caution that even in its most flexible form, echolalic language "rarely approaches the flexibility of 'normal' language forms and use" (1984, p. 191). It is presumed that "highly echolalic autistic people use echoes as a means of engaging in ongoing discourse" (Paul, 1987, p. 77), the facility of which is tempered by their less-than-normal comprehension/communicative knowledge (Mirenda & Schuler, 1988, p. 25). In a discussion of echolalic expressions, Wetherby (1984) hypothesizes that the person with autism relies on the limbic system for language, accounting for the person's "proficient use of communication to achieve environmental needs, and deficient use of communication for social purposes" (p. 29); more complex, intentional communication would require cortical control.

Other important developments in recent years concern eye use and communication methods. Assumptions about poor eye contact, for example, are being challenged by the growing realization that people with autism may not lack eye-to-face contact, but may use it differently than "normal" people (Mirenda, Donnellan, & Yoder, 1983; see also Rutter, 1978). Additionally, a wide array of communication literature supports teaching alternative modes of communication to people whose speech is limited. Wetherby (1984), for example, advocates gestural rather than vocal communication training for people with severe autism. She believes that instruction in manual language builds on existing strengths; "the autistic child's use of communicative gestures (for example, giving, pointing, pushing away, head shaking, and nodding) should be the primary consideration in language intervention and should form the foundation for teaching words, whether through speech or signs" (p. 31). Similarly, Schuler and Baldwin (1981) also note that nonspeech methods allow easier, quicker access to communication where there has been a breakdown in speech: "techniques that can be used effectively to teach nonspeech responses, such as prompting or 'molding,' by guiding the student's hands through the required responses can't be used to teach speech" (p. 250).

Despite these changing perspectives on autism, scholars continue to ask several questions similar to the ones Kanner (1943, 1971) raised thirty years after his original elaboration of the condition or set of behaviors. Is autism attended by a global intellectual deficit? Is autism a combination of specific acquisition/detection or receptive deficits? Is it reflective of processing deficits? Does autism reflect some other problems?

AN ALTERNATIVE INTERPRETATION OF UNUSUAL COMMUNICATION

In light of the natural language produced by Crossley's students through typing, we are compelled to search for an alternative explanation for their mutism and unusual speech. The obvious interpretation is that they have a neurologically based problem of expression. In other words, their difficulty with communication appears to be one of praxis rather than cognition. Here, I use the term *praxis* not as a technical term but merely to refer to the problem of people with autism speaking, or enacting their words or ideas. In contrast with the recording and playback metaphor used earlier, that person's speech ability is more like a "dedicated" computer or language device, capable of expressing phrases that have already been introduced aurally; the more advanced version of this speech output device can select segments of phrases and join them with others, though it generally lacks the program to "output" verb tense and pronouns correctly. With facilitation, the person can bypass his or her problem of verbal expression and type natural language.

By saying that the person with autism has a problem with praxis we do *not* presume a deficit in understanding, but rather in expression. This interpretation also presumes that while there may be peculiarities in vision and learning, such as involuntary attention to light or acute sensitivity to certain sounds, these do not necessarily reflect or create cognitive problems.

There is a small body of generally ignored literature on educational methods that, at minimum, does not contradict and may well support this praxis theory. In the late 1960s, two pediatricians in upstate New York employed the Edison Response Environment (ERE), "a cubicle enclosing a multiphase electric typewriter, projector, and programming device that could respond to or direct the user in a variety of ways," also called the "talking typewriter" (Goodwin & Goodwin, 1969), to teach children with disabilities, including learning disabilities and physical disabilities. Sixty-five of their students had been diagnosed as autistic. Some students who were generally nonspeaking, except for some nonfunctional or echolalic speech, produced individual words and echolalic-like phrases. In some instances, the typing was followed by speech development. One child, for instance, is described as using the ERE

in a sporadic and explosive fashion, often dashing up the stairs and into the booth in which it was installed, sometimes falling down en route, jumping up on the chair, lifting up the plastic lid and typing a few keys, then tearing off the paper and rushing downstairs. This continued over a period of several months. Efforts to slow him down were only partially successful. (p. 558)

One day, this student, Malcolm, seemed to change. He typed his name and then the word "cow" and left the room. On subsequent visits he seemed to recognize letters and words, "but still did not talk." He was four at the time. With his acquisition of words, he also began to talk. "At eight, he has a large vocabulary, speaks intelligently with slight articulation defect, and is doing well in the second grade of a home instruction program" (p. 558). Another student, John, also with obvious autism, first produced only stereotyped typing. His teacher had described him as "hyperactive, jams food in his mouth, laughs in a peculiar cackle, won't mind, pushes other children, mimics, screams, never says I" (p. 560). At the Goodwins' clinic he typed labels or sign names, for example "UTICA CLUB" (a regional beer) and "WORK ZONE AHEAD." Later, John successfully completed the fifth grade.

It is difficult to discern from the Goodwins' notes and article how unusual or typical of their total subject group these students may have been. Many of the children with whom they worked remained institutionalized, were placed in special schools, or stayed at home with no education. In their concluding remarks on the ERE treatment and studies, the Goodwins argued that the ERE did not cause the students' intelligence, but rather provided the means of expressing their intelligence: "The E.R.E. was the instrument that showed us abilities not measured by conventional psychological tests" (1969, p. 562).

Another approach to teaching academic and communication skills seems to have coincidentally built upon and confirmed the Goodwins' experiences. In her book *Effective Teaching Methods for Autistic Children*, Oppenheim (1974) describes "hand-over-hand" work with autistic children as a crucial aspect of first efforts at manual communication with students at the Rimland School for Autistic Children. Oppenheim's approach apparently used hand writing rather than typing, but the support she provided closely resembles Crossley's facilitated communication. She concluded that "the autistic child's difficulties with writing stem from a definite apraxia just as the nonverbal child's troubles with articulation do when speech finally develops" (p. 54). This communicative apraxia to which she referred has been described in a rare autobiographical account by Temple Grandin, a person with autism: "Up to this time, communication had been a one-way street for me. I could understand what was being said, but I was unable to respond. Screaming and flapping my hands was my only way to communicate" (Grandin & Scariano, 1986, p. 21). To overcome the student's apparent problem with "motor expressive behavior," Oppenheim found that it was "usually necessary to continue to guide the child's hand for a considerable period of time" (p. 54). She reported:

> Gradually, however, we are able to fade this to the mere touch of a finger on the child's writing hand. "I can't remember how to write the letters without your finger touching my skin," one nonverbal child responded when he was asked why he would not write unless he was touched. (p. 55)

Oppenheim concluded that students' problem with communication was "not recognition, but rather execution, in retaining the mental image of required motor patterns. Ultimately . . . finger-touching can be eliminated, and the child does write without it, *although some children want the touch of a finger on some other bodily surface such as the head, in order to write*" (Oppenheim, 1974, p. 55, emphasis mine).

Typing overcomes many of the difficulties of hand writing by simplifying the communication motion to pointing at or pressing letters or numerals. Oppenheim used some pointing at pictures and multiple choice captions and some typing, although it appears that she used typing mainly with the students whose "eye-hand coordination is sufficiently developed" (p. 58). Some educators have encouraged the use of language boards or symbol systems as other accessible means of communicating, but typing has the advantage of giving people access to nonprogrammed, non-preselected communication symbols (for instance, the alphabet and numbers); and the communication becomes their own.

Like the Goodwins, Oppenheim presumes a potential competence in her students, no matter how stereotyped or unusual their behavior. She suggests that teachers ignore the behaviors and focus on teaching academics.

> The immaturities and/or deficiencies in the child's general functioning—including the fact that the child may be nonverbal or noncommunicative—should never be used as an index of the likelihood of his being able to absorb and benefit from teaching at higher cognitive levels—specifically, his ability to learn reading, writing, and mathematics. (1974, p. 90)

PRINCIPLES OF FACILITATED COMMUNICATION

Crossley's interactions with nonspeaking and aphasic people reflect a certain attitude.[5] Like Oppenheim and the Goodwins she expects her students to communicate. She seems to admire them. She anticipates their producing interesting or even unique statements. Table 1 shows the attitudinal dimensions of facilitated communication.

Facilitated communication practices vary considerably with the student's disability, behavior, style of interaction, personality, and other factors. Consequently, the method is not a uniform approach to teaching or supporting communication that can be used with each person, but rather a range of skills as described in Table 2.

CONVERSATIONAL COMMUNICATION: A MAINTENANCE SESSION

One Saturday morning, four students who communicate with facilitation (a facilitator gives wrist, arm, or hand-on-shoulder support) gathered at DEAL for a "maintenance" session.[6] Jane Remington Gurney, a speech therapist, had arranged an activity to focus the group. "It's your task to find out as much as you can about Doug," she explained. She wanted them to practice interviewing, to "try to get . . . [their] questions out as quickly as" they could "in the most direct way." This skill, she believed, would help them engage in school classroom discussions more effectively, allowing them to ask questions before "the teacher's passed on to the next thing." She asked the students to figure out signaling devices to indicate when they wanted their printouts from the Canon Communicators read aloud by their facilitators. Polly was to put up her hand. Amanda would speak the word "ready." Peter would make a sound that approximates "ya." And Bette would tap the table where she was typing. Peter has a severe tremor and required arm support as he typed.

Amanda, Beth, and Polly did most of their typing independently, with support by a hand on a shoulder, or hand on a sleeve, leg, or elsewhere. Jane began the interview by telling the group that my full name is "Professor Doug Biklen."

Amanda spoke first: "Professor of what?" she asked.

"Of special education," I explained, "at Syracuse University, in Syracuse, New York."

Peter asked me what I thought about "each area of Australia." I said that I had not actually seen each area, but that Queensland had beautiful fish, warm weather, and overly conservative politics. I was admittedly clichéd about Sydney, calling it gorgeous but "too fast moving," and a little more detailed on Melbourne, singling out its array of ethnic restaurants, beautiful flowers, Victorian architecture, and a quaint but efficient tram system.

Amanda then asked, "Why are you here?"

I explained my interest in facilitated communication.

Table 1
Attitudinal dimensions of facilitated communication.

Presentation/Intention

---

1. Don't patronize people with nervous jokes, excessive familiarity, or babying. Be candid.

2. Be reasonably vulnerable and self-effacing (e.g., make note of your own errors, personal limitations, etc.).

3. Be apologetic about the assessment process. Invariably it involves asking questions that are too simple for the person being queried; apologize for speaking about the person in front of him or her (e.g., when asking a speaking person something about the person who is nonspeaking).

4. Being a dynamic support means being able to suborn your own ego or, at the very least, being able to carry on a two-sided conversation rather than imposing a one-sided, dominant relationship. You have to be comfortable touching, being close to people, and supporting without taking over.

5. Don't use labels; e.g., talk about "students like so-and-so," rather than referring to people as having a particular disability.

Assumptions/Beliefs

---

6. Assume the person's competence. "It's far better to overestimate than underestimate a person's ability."

7. Believe communication is important; conveying this belief will help convey to the person that you see him or her as important, as your peer, as someone worthy of being "heard." Respond to what is typed as if it were spoken.

Table 2
Facilitated communication practices.

Physical Support

1. Attend to the person's physical location: feet on ground, typing device slanted (e.g., at 30 degree angle), stabilized table, non-slip pad under device and person, relaxed atmosphere, etc.

2. Initially, and only where necessary, provide physical supports under the forearm, under or above the wrist, or by helping a person to isolate the index finger to facilitate use of communication aid.

3. Pull back the hand or arm after each choice so that the person takes enough time to make a next selection and also to avoid repeating selections.

Being Positive

4. Progress through *successful* choices of pictures, words, sentences, letters, name spelling, first sentence, pulling back and reminding the person of the question or request whenever an incorrect or nonsensical choice is about to be made. Use semantic common sense (e.g., *n* does not come after *w*). In other words, help the person avoid errors.

5. Provide encouragement verbally and avoid telling the person that he or she has made an error or mistake during assessment (i.e., Don't say "No," "That was wrong," or "Incorrect"). Relate to the person naturally, conversationally.

6. Be direct and firm about the tasks: the need for practice, staying on task, focusing eyes, etc. Redirect the person to the tasks (e.g., "I'm going to count to 10—1, 2, 3, 10" or, "You know the house rules, Work before play.").

Other Support

7. Keep your eyes on both the person's eyes and on the target (e.g., letter keys). This helps you identify and prevent errors caused by hand/eye coordination problems. It also helps you monitor whether the person is attending to the task.

8. Facilitated communication often requires the facilitator to do several tasks at once, for example, carrying on a verbal conversation with the person being assisted or with others in the room, watching the person's eyes, looking at the printed output, thinking of the next question or activity and at the same time keeping your mind on the present activity, and so forth, in addition to providing physical support and encouragement.

Achieving Communication/Overcoming Problems

9. Communication is a process, including support, fading, training receivers, etc. It is important to see it as a process and to recognize that people generally get better (i.e., faster and more independent) at it over time. Ongoing support increases a person's speed; thus, independence is balanced by need for speed. Encourage lots of practice; practice builds accuracy and speed!

10. If a person is not communicating, is producing nonsensical communication, or is producing questionable or wrong communication (e.g., when you doubt the communication and believe that it might be you, the facilitator, who is initiating the choices of letters and words), revert to set, structured curricula (e.g., fill in blanks, math drills).

11. Look for small differences in communication style or behavior, such as 1) radial ulnar instability—when a person's index finger swings to one side when approaching a letter, thus consistently getting a typographical error; 2) habitual, meaningless repetitions of certain letters; or, 3) the tendency to revert to familiar, echolalic words or phrases.

12. Stop stereotyped utterances by ignoring them and focusing on the task of manual communication.

13. Ignore "behavior" such as screeches, hand slapping on desk, pushing desk away, and getting up by asking, for example, "What's the next letter you want?"

Table 2
(Continued)

Curriculum

14. Don't use teaching or communication situations to "test" the person (e.g., "Is this a cup or a dollar bill?")

15. Give the student choices of work to do.

16. Use interesting materials: cartoons to be filled in, caption-less magazine pictures, crossword puzzles, and other activities that would not offend adults, teenagers, or other age groups with whom you are working.

17. Don't start communication work by focusing on the expression of feelings; wait for feelings to come. Allow the person with whom you are working to initiate feelings at his or her own choosing.

18. Get nonspeaking people working together; group sessions can be encouraging and motivating as well as interesting to people who are developing familiarity with facilitated communication. It is often helpful for facilitators (also called receivers) to work with people other than their usual partners in group sessions.

Next, Polly, who had heard me lecture several days earlier on the topic of integrating students with disabilities in typical schools, challenged me. "You put emphasis on integration," she noted. "What really does integration have to offer to some terribly retarded people?" Her question was a variation on the theme, "I'm not retarded," and at the same time a question about what I believe.

"It offers the chance to be seen as an ordinary person. Of course that depends on other people being able to see them in this way," I responded.

"You must be so idealistic," she accused me.

"I think I'm optimistic," I countered. "I think if I were to call my attitudes 'idealistic' I would be . . . saying that I don't quite believe them."

Amanda entered the conversation, seeming to argue at once with Polly and with society. "Too mean to judge people by ability," she typed.

I returned to Polly's original question: "I don't know if it's fair to call someone 'so terribly disabled.' "

Peter returned us to personal details. "Are you married?" he had typed.

"I am," I answered.

"What's your wife's name?" he asked.

"Sari," I told him.

"Funny name," Peter commented, with a loud, nearly laughing sound.

"I prefer to call it unusual," I joked.

Amanda returned the conversation to ideas. "Tell me how really retarded people get people to see them as ordinary human beings," she typed.

"We might ask the question differently," I countered. "Why is it that so-called ordinary people do not see people who are so-called 'really retarded' as ordinary?"

Amanda found my question a non-answer: "that gives me the question back, not answer it," she complained.

"What I meant by posing another question was to say that maybe the problem of gaining acceptance is not . . . owned by people labeled different but is a problem for those who do the labeling."

"Most people need proof," Polly declared. "How can the disabled meet such a gauntlet?"

Polly seemed to be challenging my ideas about the social construction of reality specifically concerning disabilities, but also agreeing with me—the gauntlet is not the disability as much as it is society's demand for proof that people meet a standard of normality.

Amanda accused me of being glib: "If you had that problem you would believe that the problem was yours."

I didn't give up the argument, though in retrospect I could have been more sympathetic and less chidingly argumentative. "I guess I'm saying that all of us need to force society to abandon the gauntlet. And I do consider it a problem of mine," I added.

"Not realistic," Polly insisted.

At this point, Peter reentered the conversation, relating our discussion of acceptance to his own situation. Peter lives in an institution for people presumed intellectually disabled. "Do you really feel there's a future for us out of institutions?" he asked.

"Yes, absolutely," I responded, "for everyone."

"You'll still have to make concessions," Polly typed.

"What do you mean by concessions?" I asked.

Jane tried to turn us away from the conversation to something more concrete. "Let me just remind you people to stick to the task which is to find out something about Doug."

Of course they were finding out a lot about me, albeit what I believe rather than the usual details.

Responding to my question about concessions, Polly explained, "unless people suborn their own wishes, it will fail." In other words, people with disabilities can only be accepted if society makes accommodations.

I agreed. The state builds roads for car drivers and airports for people who want to fly. These seemed analogous; "society can take communication seriously; it can encourage facilitated communication by training communicators and by making communication devices available." Similarly, I offered, "society can organize schools to serve *all* students."

Polly was unconvinced. She brought in economics: "You are illogical because there is no profit in disability."

At this point, Bette asked a seemingly unrelated question. She wanted to know if she would ever be able to communicate. Peter told her she did "not have to worry."

Amanda, still focused on the airports analogy, accused me of naiveté: "That falls down," she reasoned, "because people can worry about us but still not have enough money to build airports." Society might insist on funding airports before human services.

Amanda then returned the conversation to Bette's question about talking. Speaking to Peter, she declared, "To you it may not be, but to me it is and I think it is to Bette, to [a] person who wants to be like others."

Next, Amanda questioned my thoughts on deinstitutionalization. "Have you thought about people wanting to be in institutions?" she challenged.

"I believe in self-determination" I told her. "People should have choices. My experience has been that when people have the option to live outside the institution, they choose it. But society often doesn't create those options."

As I spoke, Polly was writing about Bette's desire to speak. I was now getting used to this on-again-off-again style of conversation, delayed by the timing of speaking through typing devices. Polly had typed, "Not important [to speak] if you have typing. Just tell yourself that daring to reach out is more important."

Jane interjected a bit of humor: "Now who is idealistic?"

Now it was Bette's turn. "I want to ask Doug if people like me will ever be normal . . . able to do more things that other people do?" I told her that I considered her normal in the sense that she has good ideas, lots of interests, especially an interest in other people, and that other people could come to see what I saw.

I am not sure if this comment triggered Peter's next remark or whether his statement was just a general sally. He asked, "Why do you make people believe they can do the impossible?"

"There is a consistency about this conversation," I joked. "I'm constantly being told by school people that I'm 'unrealistic' [in reference to school integration], by which they mean 'We don't want to hear what you say' or 'It's not going to work.' And then I come here and you say the same thing, except you are saying, 'They are not going to let it work.' "

Jane came to my defense. "Is this the way the group really feels or the way you've been conditioned to feel by the response you've had?"

Peter answered, "I've tried for thirteen years to be normal and I'm still where I started."

Polly typed that she did not object to the principle of integration, "but the distaste that has to be broken down in each case."

"Why am I arguing with all of you?" I asked.

Bette returned the conversation to the question about being normal. "I do not think that. I am not able to do many things." Then she asked, "Can Doug be out of America for very long?"—That is, would I be around to facilitate her communication, and to be a friend?

Polly typed about her own struggle for integration and acceptance. "Some really terrible kids have no responsibility." Her mother explained that Polly was referring to the fact that the other students in her school don't have to forge their way in school or society; they can fool around, make nuisances of themselves, and act immature. Polly added that she and other students with autism have a responsibility "thrust on us. Just want to be like those terrible kids."

I told her I understood.

Ever the detail person, Peter asked me if I make a lot of money. Bette asked if my job makes me happy. I answered "yes" to both.

Finally, Amanda gave in and joined my side of the integration argument. "Help get the skeptics to think like you. We are so cheesed [fed up]. At least I am."

THE QUESTION OF PROOF

Inevitably, an element of my examination of facilitated communication involved looking for proof that the words were the students' own. Proof took two forms: 1) some students were able to type independently, either without physical contact or with a hand on the shoulder, leg, thread of the sleeve, or other location; and 2), for those who lacked independent communication, the nature of communication varied across individuals, despite the fact that a single facilitator might be facilitating; there were facial expressions, verbal noises, including laughter, or other signs of a person's understanding of communication; and/or in some instances, the content of the communication suggested that it *really* came from the person communicating, not from the facilitator.

Instances of independent communication were numerous. A dozen students were observed typing phrases independently. Six of them communicated independently (without hand support on the arm or hand) much of the time, with at least two different facilitators. Of those who typed independently less often or not at all, nearly all had only recently been introduced to facilitated communication. Yet, one of the people who was independent had only recently been introduced to facilitated communication. While it is possible in any instance of facilitation involving the forearm, wrist, or hand for the person's communication to be influenced by a facilitator, presumably such instances could be double-checked at another time without support if they were particularly important. Independent communication of a similar level of literacy and content to that which was observed being physically facilitated was taken as validating a person's communication.

Petrov is an adolescent who attends a school for deaf and hearing impaired students. He wears hearing aids, but he is not deaf. For years, people assumed he was deaf. As I observed him in a class at the deaf school in which other students were all either profoundly deaf or hearing impaired, Crossley held just the cloth of his sweatshirt, not even resting her hand on his shoulder. He typed answers to math problems. I asked why he had hearing aids. He typed, "I excuse myself, helping myself by pretending to be deaf." In sociological terms, he was "managing stigma"; his reasoning seems to be that his hearing aids imply a hearing loss which explains his not speaking and also suggests that his absence of speech is not due to an intellectual disability. He had typed this independently, but the originality and unexpected character of his answer also seemed a kind of "proof" that the words were his.

In instances where the person did not type independently, without support under the forearm or on the hand, there was often evidence that the person worked independently. Brian, for example, has little affect in his expressions. Yet he has a slight smile at appropriate moments. In my conversations with him, his mood and comfort changed as we communicated. Initially, his responses to me were quite formal. He said, for example, "I AM ACHIEVING A GREAT DEAL ALREADY AND I AM HOPING TO ACHIEVE MUCH MORE." His teacher told me it took her six months of trying before she became able to facilitate for Brian. She held her hand on his. When I asked what it was like before he learned to type, he abandoned his formalism: "IT WAS HELL AND I COULD NOT EVEN BEGIN TO MAKE MY NEEDS KNOWN." At one point, his teacher and Crossley left the room. I asked Brian if his mother and father would be coming to the center to talk to us or if just one of his parents was coming. I asked him to type "B" for both or "O" for one. He typed "B." Both arrived a little while later. Toward the end of our conversation, with his father facilitating him in his conversation, Crossley asked Brian if he had anything he wanted to say to her. He responded, "I'VE TALKED A LOT ABOUT YOU (he had been speaking with me). I DONT NEED TO TALK *TO* YOU." Characteristically, Brian's face displayed its usual nearly expressionless facade, with just a slight smile at the corner of his mouth. Independently, Brian turned off the Canon.

Clearly, the level of proof for those people who were not communicating independently was less "ironclad." Yet, the indicators that communication was the person's own were strong enough, in my view, to justify the continuing assumption of its validity.

CONCLUSION

The implications of the DEAL students' communication are enormous. Among other things, it forced me to redefine autism. While the students in this study included some who previously had been thought of as severely intellectually disabled and autistic, they demonstrated unexpected literacy skills. The Saturday morning group, for example, instead of querying me about the concrete facts of my life, were far more focused on my beliefs. They chose to converse about concepts. Each of them obviously engages in internal conversations; each had thought about the issues we discussed. Also, they had chosen to speak about their feelings. Obviously their problem was neither in cognition nor affect. Rather, their difficulty has been in sharing what they know and feel.

Readers of this article will naturally ask, "Will facilitated communication allow all people labeled autistic to communicate at high levels of literacy?" This question is not easily answered. First, the category of autism, like many disability categories, is not as precise or as uniformly applied as we might imagine or desire. A broad range of behaviors are defined as autistic, with the result that people who seem quite different one from another share the label of autism. Second it is of course not possible to prove that *all* people so labeled will achieve a particular level of communication. We can learn about their potential only through practice. Third, it is quite possible, even expected, that within the group of those categorized as autistic, there will be a very wide range of intellectual ability, as there is in the general population. Nevertheless, it is especially noteworthy and encouraging that among those for whom facilitated communication has allowed high levels of literacy and numeracy are people who were previously presumed to be among the "lowest" intellectually functioning persons labeled autistic.

Before they could communicate, these students were evaluated primarily by their repertoires of unusual behaviors. Now that they *do* communicate, schools, families, and society ask: Will the stereotyped and other behaviors associated with autism diminish or even disappear as students become more fluent communicators? This is not known. While there is observational evidence that some bizarre behaviors decline—Polly does not make a habit of climbing trees at her high school and pulling her skirt up—others persist. Paul did rip his teeshirt off during a communication session, and he still clutches strips of cloth, occasionally brushing them against his face; Polly still puts objects in her mouth, but less often than in previous years; and Bette still slaps her work table periodically. It is noteworthy that at the time of these observations, Bette had begun communicating fluently only a few months earlier and Paul was living in a locked ward of an institution where he had no opportunities to communicate. Crossley believes that students who have been able to use facilitated communication at home and in school over a period of months and even years demonstrate fewer unusual behaviors than when they first came to

DEAL. "We never could have mainstreamed [in school] so many of the students if they hadn't changed," she argues.

The question of how much acceptance Crossley's students will find in their families and schools cannot be separated from their behavior or from the perceptions and attitudes of people around them. Students in Polly's high school English class regularly volunteer to be in discussion groups with her; the teacher says they recognize that Polly has creative ideas about the readings they discuss. But she still does not have classmates who she considers her friends. Polly told me that she worries about the idea of possibly having friends. She has not yet had one, other than her mother, her siblings, Rosemary Crossley, and people like herself who use facilitated communication. She is afraid. "I don't know what to feel," she told me. David Armbruster said he wanted girls at his school to stop "mothering" him. "I want a girlfriend," he declared. Not surprisingly, the degree to which DEAL students can or will reach out and communicate to others seems to depend on how others receive them.

Awareness of that fact pervades Crossley's work. She embraces the age-old, but not always honored, belief in students' capacity to learn and express themselves. From her first interaction with students, where she uses no-fail and always open-ended assessments, to her unstructured dialogues with students about their lives, she engages them, speaking personally and directly to them, never patronizing. Her purpose, after all, is not to test their competence but to find ways for them to reveal their competence. She warns us against the persistent tendency to impose low expectations on students. Their poetry, their letters, and their statements are the text of her work and comprise both the product and the material of her teaching.

Perhaps more than most students, the students described in this article *demand* an education-through-dialogue approach, where teachers and students learn from each other and where schooling validates personal expression. It is as if this group of people, labeled autistic, by *not* communicating except with certain facilitators and in certain, supportive circumstances, is saying what all students at one time or another have said, if less obviously: We will reveal ourselves, we will show our creativity, when we feel appreciated, when we are supported.

Notes

1. Jonothan left out spaces between words and repeated several letters without correcting the errors, although he later demonstrated the ability to put in spaces and to make his own corrections; the Canon Communicator is like any electric typewriter such that if the person typing lingers on a key, it will produce the same letter more than once.

2. In all I observed twenty-seven people, nine of whom were being seen by DEAL staff for the first time and who had not previously communicated more than single words or signs or echolalic phrases. The six people observed at DEAL that are not included in this account had a variety of other disabling conditions, including Down Syndrome, cerebral palsy, and other physical and intellectual disabilities.

3. Crossley's recommendation in instances of doubt over the communication is for facilitators to return to "set work" in which the correct answers are known, at least until the person's facility with communication increases and becomes more independent.

4. The assumption has been that children with autism are unable "to analyze and categorize both linguistic and nonlinguistic data" (Menyuk, 1978, p. 115). This inability has been thought to limit the person's "performance in certain intellectual tasks and social adaptation" (pp. 114–115). Consistent with this interpretation, Wing explains the apparent "social avoidance and poor eye contact . . . as arising from the absence of any mechanism for understanding the environment" (Wing, 1978, p. 41).

5. The principal differences between Crossley's approach and that of most other educators of children with autism is her addition of hand-over-hand, wrist, or arm facilitation in the initial stages of typed communication *and* the expectation that students are capable of sophisticated communication.

6. As with all observations and interviews, this session was audio-recorded. Since facilitators spoke the students' words aloud, it was possible to develop a verbatim transcript of the entire conversation.

References

Baltaxe, C. A. M., & Simmons, J. Q. (1977). Bedtime soliloquies and linguistic competence in autism. *Journal of Speech and Hearing Disorders, 42,* 376–393.

Bartak, L., Rutter, M., & Cox, A. (1977). A comparative study of infantile autism and specific developmental receptive language disorders. III. Discriminant function analysis. *Journal of Autism and Childhood Schizophrenia, 7,* 383–396.

Bettelheim, B. (1967). *The empty fortress: Infantile autism and the birth of the self.* New York: Free Press.

Crossley, R., & McDonald, A. (1980). *Annie's coming out.* New York: Penguin.

Donnellan, A. M. (Ed.). (1985). *Classic readings in autism.* New York: Teachers College Press.

Eisenberg, L. (1956). The autistic child in adolescence. *American Journal of Psychiatry, 112,* 607–612.

Goodwin, M. S., & Goodwin, T. C. (1969). In a dark mirror. *Mental Hygiene, 53,* 550–563.

Grandin, T., & Scariano, M. M. (1986). *Emergence labeled autistic.* Novato, CA: Arena Press.

Intellectual Disability Review Panel. (1989). *Investigation into the reliability and validity of the assisted communication technique.* Melbourne: Department of Community Services, Victoria.

Interdisciplinary Working Party on Issues in Severe Communication Impairment. (1988). *D.E.A.L. Communication Centre Operation: A Statement of Concern.* Melbourne: Author.

James, A. L., & Barry, R. J. (1983). Developmental effects in the cerebral lateralization of autistic, retarded, and normal children. *Journal of Autism and Developmental Disorders, 13,* 43–55.

Kanner, L. (1943). Autistic disturbances of affective contact. *Nervous Child, 2,* 217–250.

Kanner, L. (1971). Follow-up study of eleven autistic children originally reported in 1943. *Journal of Autism and Childhood Schizophrenia, 1, 2,* 119–145.

Menyuk, P. (1978). Language: What's wrong and why. In M. Rutter & E. Schopler (Eds.), *Autism* (pp. 105–116). New York: Plenum Press.

Mirenda, P., & Schuler, A. L. (1988). Augmenting communication for persons with autism: Issues and strategies. *Topics in Language Disorders, 9,* 24–43.

Mirenda, P. L., Donnellan, A. M., & Yoder, D. E. (1983). Gaze behavior: A new look at an old problem. *Journal of Autism and Developmental Disorders, 13,* 397–409.

Oppenheim, R. (1974). *Effective teaching methods for autistic children.* Springfield, IL: Charles C. Thomas.

Ornitz, E. M., & Ritvo, E. R. (1968). Perceptual inconsistency in infantile autism. *Archives of General Psychiatry, 18,* 76–98.

Paul, R. (1987). Communication. In D. J. Cohen, A. M. Donnellan, & R. Paul (Eds.), *Handbook of autism and pervasive development disorders* (pp. 61–64). New York: John Wiley & Sons.

Prizant, B. M. (1983). Language acquisition and communication behavior in autism: Toward an understanding of the "whole" of it. *Journal of Speech and Hearing Disorders, 48,* 286–296.

Prizant, B. M., & Rydell, P. J. (1984). Analysis of functions of delayed echolalia in autistic children. *Journal of Speech and Hearing Research, 27,* 183–192.

Ricks, D. M., & Wing, L. (1975). Language, communication, and the use of symbols in normal and autistic children. *Journal of Autism and Childhood Schizophrenia, 5,* 191–221.

Rimland, B. (1964). *Infantile autism.* New York: Appleton-Century-Crofts.

Rutter, M. (1968). Concepts of autism: A review of research. *Journal of Child Psychology and Psychiatry, 9,* 1–25.

Rutter, M. (1978). Etiology and treatment: Cause and cure. In M. Rutter & E. Schopler (Eds.), *Autism* (pp. 327–335). New York: Plenum Press.

Schopler, E., Reichler, R. J., & Lansing, M. (1980). *Individualized assessment and treatment for autistic and developmentally disabled children.* Baltimore: University Park Press.

Schuler, A. L., & Baldwin, M. (1981). Nonspeech communication and childhood autism. *Language, Speech, and Hearing Services in Schools, 12,* 246–257.

Tager-Flusberg, H. (1981a). On the nature of linguistic functioning in early infantile autism. *Journal of Autism and Development Disorders, 11,* 45–56.

Tager-Flusberg, H. (1981b). Sentence comprehension in autistic children. *Applied Psycholinguistics, 2,* 5–24.

Wetherby, A. M. (1984). Possible neurolinguistic breakdown in autistic children. *Topics in Language Disorders, 4,* 19–33.

Wing, L. (1978). Social, behavioral, and cognitive characteristics: An epidemiological approach. In M. Rutter & E. Schopler (Eds.), *Autism.* New York: Plenum Press.

7.4 Citizenship in the Literate Community:

An Ethnography of Children with Down Syndrome and the Written Word

Christopher Kliewer

Abstract: In school, children with Down syndrome have historically been separated from literacy opportunities and expectations. In this ethnography, the school literacy experiences of 10 students with Down syndrome were examined over a 2-year period. Two broad definitions of literacy were uncovered. The first regarded reading as conformity to a hierarchy of psychologically-deduced subskills. Children with Down syndrome had difficulty conforming and were separated from Citizenship in the classrooms' literate communities. The second definition regarded literacy as the construction of shared meaning in specific contexts. In these classrooms, students with Down syndrome were valued as symbolic beings and engaged literacy as a communication tool. The implications for reconceptualizing Down syndrome are discussed.

In school, children with Down syndrome have traditionally been separated from literacy opportunities and expectations (Buckley, 1995). Two premises serve as the basis for this partial or complete separation of child from printed language: (1) That reading is a curricular end-product requiring students to master a set of isolated subskills in an age-normed, linear sequence (Adams, 1990; McKenna, Robinson, & Miller, 1994); and (2) that children with Down syndrome intrinsically lack the cognitive capacity necessary to master the literacy subskills at an age-normed pace (Cicchetti & Beeghly, 1990).

Though both premises represent prevailing educational assumptions, neither is reflective of an essential reality. For instance, competing interpretations of literacy have been presented which deemphasize reading as a hierarchy of isolated subskills and instead, focus on all children "as active sense makers" (Crawford, 1995, p. 82) who construct meaning through symbol systems in specific contexts at specific times (Crawford, 1995; Goodman, 1992; Goodman & Goodman, 1979; Harste, Woodward, & Burke, 1984; Shannon, 1990). Within this framework, separating children from literacy is not a logical consequence of the child's lack of cognitive ability; rather, it is a moral choice made when particular student-constructed meanings are misunderstood and devalued (Smith, F., 1992).

Interpreting literacy as a social process in which children make sense of a particular context has educational consequences. Based on this definition, children often excluded from reading and writing have entered into literate relationships as acknowledged creators of complex symbolic language. This has occurred for children whose exclusion was race and class based (Ashton-Warner, 1963; Solsken, 1993), and disability based (Koppenhaver, Pierce, & Yoder, 1995).

This study is an ethnographic exploration (Ferguson, Ferguson, & Taylor, 1992) of the meaning of literacy for children with Down syndrome in 10 preschool and elementary school classrooms. Over the course of 2 school years, it became apparent that classroom conceptualizations of reading influenced the meaning of Down syndrome, and that children with Down syndrome could influence how literacy itself was defined in particular classrooms.

METHOD

Theoretical Approach

This is a qualitative study conducted in an interpretivist tradition (Ferguson, Ferguson, & Taylor, 1992; Smith, J. K., 1993). Interpretivism rejects the assumption that social realities exist as objective states. Instead, ideas like Down syndrome and literacy are recognized as social constructions: culturally-bound, historically situated perspectives that are constantly being negotiated and renegotiated by individuals in interaction with one another (Ferguson et al., 1992). For instance, not so many years ago, to have Down syndrome meant that one was considered "hardly human" (Spock, 1949, p. 478) and was likely incarcerated into a custodial institution for life (Blatt, 1987). Nothing about trisomy of the 21st chromosome inherently required this treatment, as is evidenced in the level of community participation enjoyed by many people with Down syndrome today (Nadel & Rosenthal, 1995). However, dehumanizing treatments were accepted at one time as the logical response to the differences associated with Down syndrome.

In this example, it becomes clear that to understand Down syndrome may require as much a focus

on the context in which the meaning of Down syndrome is constructed as on the chromosomal anomaly itself. Refocusing the researcher's gaze on context has had profound implications for both disability and literacy theory. Qualitative inquiry has influenced the rejection of custodial warehousing of people with disabilities (Blatt & Kaplan, 1966; Bogdan & Taylor, 1994) and has shown the humanness of people historically interpreted to be less-than-human (Bogdan & Taylor, 1989). Ethnographic research has also opened up whole new interpretations of literacy development reflected, for example, in "emergent literacy" first described naturalistically by Marie Clay (Clay 1967; Teale & Sulzby, 1986).

Recognizing that reality is "a multiple set of contextually-bound social constructions" requires that the researcher enter into the relationships in which people create and enact meaning (Bogdan & Biklen, 1992). Therefore, in order to understand literacy in relation to children with Down syndrome, I followed the school lives of 10 students with Down syndrome across 12 classrooms over a 2-year period.

Settings and Participants

Originally, the settings were chosen out of an interest in the meaning of Down syndrome in classrooms that included children without disabilities. Literacy quickly emerged as an important school theme differentiating students into separate categories. With an invigorated focus on literacy, the principle of theoretical sampling (Glaser & Strauss, 1967) led to the inclusion of other settings that would develop insight into the understanding of printed language in the lives of children with Down syndrome. Table 1 describes the settings and participants.

Data Collection and Analysis

In the tradition of qualitative research, data took the form of richly descriptive field notes and transcripts based on participant observation and indepth interviews with members of each setting (Bogdan & Biklen, 1992; Denzin & Lincoln, 1994). Over the course of 2 school years, I conducted and tape recorded 45 observations and 12 interviews, resulting in 1,300 pages of field notes. The notes reflected detailed accounts of the interactions observed in multiple classrooms as children and teachers constructed meaning in their everyday lives.

As field notes and observations accumulated, particular patterns of understanding began to emerge within and across settings. These patterns formed primary codes and subcodes through which data

Table 1
Summary of the research settings and participants.[a]

Student		Teachers[b]		Classmates		Perceived Literacy Level	
Age	Grade	No. Assistants	No. Student Teachers	No. Non-disabled	No. Disabled	Teachers	Psychologist
L. Larson		*C. Madison*					
9	FT 2nd	2	1	24	3	Average	Moderate MR/Illiterate
M. Jersey		*J. McClanahan*					
10	5th/6th I.D	1	—	—	12	Semiliterate	
S. Loveland		*J. Lyle & S. O'Malley*					
9	PT SPED. PT 2nd	2	1	—	8	Average	Severe MR/Illiterate
J. Sylvester		*M. Baily*	*R. Collins*				
9	FT 2nd	1	—	28	5	Illiterate	
I. Johnson		*B. Chandler*	*L. Morgan*				
2	Toddler Rm.	1	—	5	5	Semiliterate	Illiterate
I. Johnson		*S. Robbins*					
3	3/4-yr.-old Pre-K	2	1	10	6	Average	Illiterate
L. Kelly		*B. Chandler*	*L. Morgan*				
2	Toddler Rm.	1	—	5	5	Average	
L. Kelly		*S. Robbins*					
3	3/4-yr.-old Pre-K	2	1	10	6	Average	
A. Carpenter		*S. Robbins*					
3	3/4-yr.-old Pre-K	2	1	10	6	Average	Semiliterate
G. Lafrey		*D. Jorgenson*					
4	4-yr.-old Pre-K	2	—	6	6	Semiliterate	
V. Schroeder		*D. Jorgenson*					
4	4-yr.-old Pre-K	2	—	6	6	Illiterate	
J. Frederickson		*J. A. Latoya*					
4	4-yr.-old Pre-K	2	—	6	6	Semiliterate	

Note: FT = Full time; PT = Part time.
[a]All names have been changed to protect confidentiality.
[b]Teacher in charge.

Table 2
Primary code analysis second stage.

Primary Code	Secondary Codes	Data Vignette
Direct Classroom Imposed Illiteracy	(a) Reading lesson separation (b) Other content area separation (c) Denial of materials (d) In-lesson reduced expectation (e) In-lesson no expectation (f) Lesson participation requiring speech/no accommodation (g) Lesson participation requiring line motor/no accommodation	Mrs. O'Malley looked at the clock, "O.K. kids," she said. "Put away your books and I want to see your spelling." Shelly L. had just entered the room from her self-contained class (a). She sat at the empty desk assigned her (c), and Diane, her assistant, pulled up a chair. Mrs. O'Malley said, "Nice to see you Shelly. Kids are getting to spelling. Diane, why don't you have Shelly spend this time at the computer?" (a) Diane takes Shelly's hand, and they sit at the computer. Diane choses a program that creates intricate designs that move when Shelly touches the mouse (a, c, d).

were constantly organized, reorganized, and analyzed (Bogdan & Biklen, 1992). Ultimately, I arrived at seven primary codes related to literacy which are later described as interrelated themes. The seven codes included the following:

1. Direct classroom imposed illiteracy.
2. Indirect classroom imposed illiteracy.
3. Interpreting behavior as illiterate.
4. Direct support of literacy acquisition.
5. Indirect support of literacy acquisition.
6. Assumption of literacy in student behavior.
7. Literacy as negotiation tool.

For further clarification, Table 2 demonstrates the second level of analysis (among several levels) imposed on one primary code, and provides a brief data vignette related to the primary code.

Data Credibility Procedures

Efforts to achieve credibility of the themes presented include both qualitative triangulation (Bogdan & Taylor, 1982; Denzin, 1978; Janesick, 1994) and meeting criteria of data trustworthiness (Kincheloe & McLaren, 1994; Lincoln & Guba, 1985). Triangulation assures a thorough analysis of the contexts studied through the extensive and long-term use of multiple ethnographic methods and data sources. Triangulation leads to trustworthiness when the empirical portrayals of the constructed realities are descriptively credible to both the study's participants and the research audience. In studying literacy and children with Down syndrome, the following data checks were employed to assure credibility:

- A disciplined approach to coding required conceptualizations be grounded in the empirical observations recorded (Huberman & Miles, 1994; Strauss & Corbin, 1994).
- Extensive observations over 2 school years recorded in 1,300 pages of field notes reflective of a deep understanding of the contexts studied (Bogdan & Biklen, 1992).
- Consistent discussions and the sharing of field notes, codes, and essays on emerging themes with experienced qualitative and quantitative researchers (Bogdan & Biklen, 1992).
- Consistent discussions with adult research participants on interpretations of the observations (Janesick, 1994).
- Multiple data gathering techniques including participant observation, in-depth interviews, unstructured group interviews, and document and record analysis (Bogdan & Biklen, 1992).
- Multiple data sources (Lincoln & Guba, 1985).

RESULTS: INTERPRETATIONS OF THE DATA

Definitions of Literacy

In the classrooms observed, two broad definitions of literacy were evident, each with implications for positioning children with Down syndrome as literate, semiliterate, or illiterate. The first conceptualized literacy as one strand of a linear curriculum requiring student *conformity* to an objectively identified sequence of technical skills or cognitive concepts. The second defined literacy as the construction of meaning in an evolving web of relationships connecting student, teachers, and classroom materials.

Literacy of Conformity

Several classrooms observed defined literacy as student conformity to a sequence of isolated subskills either transmitted directly by teachers or discovered by children in teacher-contrived activities. Students' literacy was judged by measuring the degree of conformity demonstrated through written work and tests, completed workbook pages, oral discussion, oral reading, teacher-structured play, or developmental assessments.

The Dilemma of Conformity for Students with Down Syndrome

For students with Down syndrome, requiring conformity placed them at a distinct disadvantage for inclusion into the literate community. Each child with Down syndrome in this study exhibited idiosyncratic communication and behavior that, when viewed through the cultural lens of Down syndrome as an automatic cognitive impairment, made the child appear intellectually incompetent.

Communication and Behavior Separating Students with Down Syndrome. Joanna Sylvester's (all names have been changed to protect confidentiality) speech and movement control looked very different from that of her classmates' who participated in a three-tiered reading instruction format. Each tier was represented by a single reading group composed of children thought to be reading and writing at a particular level.

Joanna was nonspeaking. Her movements were slow and awkward. When she walked, Joanna alternated attention between moving her limbs and avoiding obstacles. She formed a fist to grasp a pencil, and had difficulty regulating the pressure necessary to write. Her papers ended up ripped and uninterpretable.

Joanna's movement and speech did not conform to traditional expectations for student competence in reading. In turn, she was separated with four peers into a "print awareness" group which meant listening to the assistant teacher read a book, and then doing a daily coloring activity. Joanna colored poorly, and was regarded as the lowest functioning child in this group of presumably illiterate children.

On several occasions, however, Joanna softly articulated the final word in sentences shown her previously, or in unison with the assistant teacher. This suggested that Joanna was able to read words and her speech was cued by print, a common finding in the research literature on Down syndrome (see Buckley, 1995). The assistant teacher disagreed. She explained, "Joanna wasn't reading then. She makes those sounds like a kid playing school."

Mark Jersey had greater control over his speech and movement than did Joanna. Correspondingly, he was recognized as reading at a higher, second-grade level. Yet, at silent reading times, Mark was engaged for extended periods of up to 20 min reading *Dirt Biker* magazines written, on average, at a fifth-grade level. Based on one-to-one discussions with Mark, it was clear he understood the content of the stories. Mark's teacher, Jim McClanahan, lamented, "That's the thing. I haven't even really had a chance to sit down and hear him read or anything like that." Mr. McClanahan had primarily judged Mark's reading level based on his group participation, which was hindered by ridicule Mark received from his peers due to his poor articulation.

Consequences of Nonconformity: The Stratified Classroom. Requiring conformity to a predetermined set of subskills resulted in the formation of a stratified literate social structure. Those students who conformed to expectations belonged, as Citizens, to a privileged literate community. Other students who struggled to conform, including those with Down syndrome, were sifted to the classrooms' reading margins. Here, existing in relation to the literate community as Squatters or Aliens, the children did not merely languish, but entered instructional practices that solidified their separation from privilege. Table 3 describes the stratified literate social structure and how particular students in the study were represented apart from valued literacy opportunities.

Literacy as a Web of Constructed Relationships

Certain teachers in this study rejected the definition of reading as an end-element to a sequence of isolated subskills requiring student conformity. In these

Table 3
Relationship of student to literate community in stratified classrooms.

Name	Conformity	Rights	Justification	Student Status
Citizen	At age-normed pace to linear sequence of transmitted subskills or developmental scheme.	Opportunity for full curricular participation leading to increasingly complex knowledge recognized as school success.	Conformity recognized as cognitive ability.	
Squatter	Partial at a reduced pace to linear sequence of transmitted subskills or developmental scheme.	Participation in reme-dial practices that focus on low-level concepts or diminished subskills.	Limited ability to conform is basis for reduced curriculum.	M. Jersey, S. Loveland, G. Lafrey, J. Frederickson
Alien	Lacking in relation to linear sequence of transmitted subskills or developmental scheme.	Separation from literate community.	Idiosyncratic behavior interpreted as cognitive incompetence.	V. Schroeder, J. Sylvester

classrooms, teachers defined literacy as an evolving dimension intrinsic to each strand of the web of shifting relationships that made up a classroom community. Children engaged symbolic tools, at varying levels of effectiveness, as they constructed understanding through constant negotiation and renegotiation of relationships with peers, adults, and materials.

The negotiation process was guided by teachers as they fostered culturally-valued connections between children and classroom materials. Within this framework, all children, including students with Down syndrome, were recognized as symbolic beings, and written language was recognized as a useful symbolic tool for constructing progressively enhanced relationships.

Recognizing the Symbolic Value of Students with Down Syndrome. Teachers who recognized their students as literate appeared to value each child as a fully symbolic being, albeit in a constantly evolving web of relationships with the wider context. Shayne Robbins, whose classroom community included three children with Down syndrome, explained. "I see all my kids as incredible readers. Every one of them." She rejected the interpretation of teaching as transmitting skills, saying. "My sense is not that I'm teaching anyone to read, but I'm showing them that they do know how to read—to have them feel comfortable that they do read."

Establishing a value that all children were competently symbolic impacted on teachers' interpretations of student behavior and communication. Ms. Robbins demonstrated this during a conflict with a school psychologist over an assessment of her student, Isaac Johnson, who was nonspeaking and had Down syndrome. The psychologist asked Isaac to sort spoons and blocks into various containers. Isaac placed all the blocks to the side of a container, then tasted from each spoon before throwing it across the room, one after the other. He was not given credit. The psychologist used Isaac's response, in effect, to represent disengagement and incompetence from what the assessment defined as normaley in development.

Shayne Robbins argued, "He didn't get credit for it because he didn't do it right, but he clearly knew which was the block, which was the spoon. And he followed directions in an organizing sense." Ms. Robbins recognized that Isaac was extremely focused on stories, both at home and at school, and that he engaged in pretend play based on stories he enjoyed most. His licking each spoon as he separated the objects was according to Ms. Robbins, an act of pretending.

In engaging in symbolic play, Isaac recontextualized the assessment task into one of meaning based on experience, materials available, and performance comfort. What the psychologist saw as an act separating Isaac from normality, Ms. Robbins suggested, was actually a complex, symbolic response creating a more thoughtful and meaningful context.

Literacy as a Tool for Enhanced Connection. Though certain teachers valued each student as symbolic, they also realized that to enter relationships of meaning required shared patterns for communicating ideas. Rather than dismissing to the classroom margins children with Down syndrome whose behavior was idiosyncratic, or allowing students to exist in relationships of misunderstanding leading to stagnation in the construction of meaning, teachers saw worth in symbols and print as a tool for connecting students to the wider classroom community. So, when Lee Larson responded to a reading workbook page by scribbling the word "Exit" over the entire page, Colleen Madison did not respond by interpreting Lee as incompetent, but rather saw in his relationship to the materials at hand a mismatch between expected behavior and Lee's manner for conveying meaning. Ms. Madison viewed her role as one of problem-solving to establish paths of connection, not as one of laying blame on children for the mismatch. She noted, "I really think teaching is problem-solving. That you deal. And that's what you model to kids because that's what learning is."

Establishing Symbol Systems to Construct Relationships. Lee Larson entered Colleen Madison's classroom unable to speak which, Ms. Madison felt, left him frustrated. Lee's preclusion from participation resulted in a context of trepidation. "We were always walking on pins and needles waiting for the shoe to drop," Ms. Madison explained. "We never knew when he was going to erupt."

Ms. Madison noted, "We knew communication was the big piece missing. He was frustrated. We quickly saw that he gestured to try to tell us things. We understood him best through motion and movement." Based on his manner of performance, Ms. Madison invited a parent of one of her students to come each week to the class to teach signed English.

Instructors in the class began to sign keywords in lessons, and, as comfort with signs developed, in conversation, Lee quickly began to gesture with close approximation to symbols in the signed English script. Ms. Madison said, "We thought, 'Wow! We can understand Lee better when he's signing and doing these motions. It sort of clicked with him."

In providing Lee with a set of shared symbols to convey ideas, Ms. Madison recontextualized the communicative context of the classroom. Rather than interpreting symbols as an end to be used only after appropriate subskills were demonstrated, she saw the system as a means towards relationship building.

Though signing was of critical importance to Lee and other children with Down syndrome, the system had limitations. Both Ms. Madison and Shayne Robbins noted that the fine motor control of their students with Down syndrome posed an obstacle to clear use of a symbol system that demanded minute finger manipulations.

Establishing Print Systems to Construct Relationships. For those children with Down syndrome whose performance difficulties precluded efficient use of speech or sign, teachers in classrooms that recognized students as symbolic beings were open to their students' use of printed language to build relationships. For instance, based both on Lee's quick ability to use gestural symbols, and the limitations that system held for him, his teachers introduced written words for communication purposes. Initially, Ms. Madison and the language therapist created a series of communication boards with sets of words and phrases they felt would be useful in different classroom situations. For instance, a "math board" included a number line, equation symbols, and words and phrases such as: yes, no, I don't know, need a break, bathroom, and all done.

In using the communication board, Ms. Madison did not require that Lee demonstrate subskills presumably required for print decoding. Instead, she introduced the written options in the context of real choices and told Lee to point to the word representing his request. Lee quickly found success in recognizing and making use of the print.

This led to the instructional team introducing the use of a keyboard for communication purposes. Rather than pointing to prearranged options controlled by adults, Lee was asked to spell choices. Spelling was a challenge for Lee because his movement patterns were explosively impulsive. His finger would come down on the keyboard with a bang, and remained fixed to the key causing multiple letters to appear.

Rather than focusing on Lee's movement as a manifestation of incompetence, Ms. Madison altered the typing context. She placed a key guard over the keyboard to assist Lee in hitting isolated keys, and she supported his arm with her hand to remind him to slow his gesture and target his pointing. This type of support, recently described as an element of "facilitated communication" (Biklen, 1993; see discussion) was first explored for children with Down syndrome by Feuerstein, Rand, and Rynders (1988). They pointed out that "many children who manifest impulsivity fail in tasks even though they know what they need to do to respond correctly" (p. 75). In describing the teacher as a "mediator," Feuerstein et al. (1988) suggested:

> At certain stages in the development of control over impulsivity, the mediator may need to use physical means to keep the child from impulsive responding—perhaps holding the child's hands (for asking the child to sit on his own hands)—so that he won't point to an answer before looking carefully at the situation and thinking about it. (p. 75)

Ms. Madison explained, "It occurred to me [Lee] really needed the processing time, delay time, lag time. Overcome that impulsivity. And then stuff took off from there."

What took off was Lee's ability to express himself through print. Again, Ms. Madison opened up the option of print for communication purposes in day-to-day situations and relationships. In this way, Lee used print to build meaning with his peers. For instance, Lee and a classmate, Laura, got into an altercation on the classroom's couch. Laura shouted out, "Lee hit me. I didn't do nothing." Lee, however, disagreed. He typed, "I HIT LAR MAKE ME MOVE." Ms. Madison, who had entered the situation, asked Laura, "Did you make Lee move?" Laura said, "I didn't make him. I ASKED him." Lee typed, "LARA MEAN," but the two quickly joined each other, giggling, in a bean bag chair.

By introducing Lee and his classmates to signing, then to the use of words and print for Lee's expression, the meaning of literacy was constructed as a tool for connecting children with the wider context. It was within this connection that relationships were negotiated and renegotiated as the children's web of meaning constantly evolved.

The Meaning of Citizenship for Children with Down Syndrome

Conceptualizing all students as symbolic people and providing them with tools for creating meaningful relationships, had consequences for students with Down syndrome. Participation as a member of the literate community was fostered. Opportunities to demonstrate friendship were expanded, and the image of Down syndrome as an inherent deficiency was reconceptualized.

Opportunities for Participation. Children with Down syndrome participated as full members of the literate community in classrooms that recognized the community as a web of relationships involving each student. Idiosyncratic behaviors did not separate children from the curriculum, but helped make up the community's ever-shifting boundaries.

For instance, Isaac Johnson entered Shayne Robbins classroom with a love from home for Maurice Sendak's (1963) picture book *Where the Wild Things Are.* For years Ms. Robbins' classes had made panoramas based on Max's journey, but this was difficult for Isaac who had problems creating, cutting, and gluing recognizable figures. However, Isaac had a dramatic flair and a love for pretending. This led Ms. Robbins to support her class in developing a play based on the book. The students created dialogue, scenery, and costumes. Isaac played the lead role as Max. He was unable to speak his lines, but gestured to the printed line on a communication board with the facilitated support of an adult. A peer then read the line to the audience.

Ms. Robbins, recognizing Isaac's symbolic and literate presence, had effectively altered the context of her classroom in a direction that supported Isaac's participation. In doing so, she had opened up a rich literacy experience for all her children.

Opportunities to Demonstrate Friendship. When a child was conceptualized as literate and symbolic, all behavior was supported as an effort to build relationships of meaning. April Carpenter was observed placing her arm around a sleeping friend during a van ride back to school following a field trip. Though she was unable to speak, her voice was clearly humming in varying pitches as she moved her hand close to the boy's face. Ms. Robbins glanced into the rearview mirror, and said, "April, you're singing William a lullaby. You're singing him the alphabet song." Ms. Robbins recognized April's hand movements to be the signed alphabet. April released William, tapped him on the head, and gestured towards Ms. Robbins the sign for "sleep."

Reconceptualizing Down Syndrome. Interpreting children with Down syndrome as symbolic, and providing children with tools to construct meaningful relationships, reconceptualized Down syndrome from a traditional context of global intellectual deficiency to one in which each child was recognized as uniquely valuable to the classroom community. Shayne Robbins, in thinking about her three students with Down syndrome, explained:

> I don't tend to see Down syndrome as something. If you look at those three kids running around the room, they're incredibly different from each other. They're different in terms of what their bodies are like, how they best communicate, what they're like socially, their interests. And with those three kids in the room

it would be hard to say, "This is how you should teach kids with Down syndrome." They are not at all alike.

Resisting the interpretation of difference as deficit, Colleen Madison, in describing Lee Larson, said:

> If you came into the room and were told there was a retarded child in the class, a child with special needs, I don't think you would pick Lee out. The kids really agree that he's as capable as they are. Intellectually the same.

These teachers effectively repositioned students with Down syndrome from a location of deficiency to one of value in the classroom.

DISCUSSION

Citizenship in the literate community for children with Down syndrome is based on two conclusions established in the research literature on literacy and disability. The first suggests all students are symbolic beings motivated to connect with the wider community (Ashton-Warner, 1963; Cunningham & Allington, 1994; Gardner, 1991; Koppenhaver, Coleman, Kalman, & Yoder, 1991; Smith, F., 1992). The second recognizes that written language must be incorporated into the classroom as a tool for connecting children with the wider community (Cunningham & Allington, 1994; Goodman, 1992; Goodman & Goodman, 1979; Oelwein, 1995; Smith, F., 1988a, 1988b; Solsken, 1993). Cunningham and Allington (1994) note, "Children who are successful at becoming literate view reading and writing as authentic activities from which they get information and pleasure and by which they communicate with others" (p. 21).

In establishing literacy as a mode of communication and connection, the idiosyncrasies associated with Down syndrome must be accounted for. Disability researchers have accumulated a mass of data noting a peculiar intensity in motor dilemmas expressed by people with Down syndrome which significantly affect their speech and movement (Anwar & Hermelin, 1979; Elliott, 1985; Frith & Frith, 1974; Henderson, Illingsworth, & Allen, 1991; Henderson, Morris, & Frith, 1981; LeClair, Pollock, & Elliott, 1993). Henderson et al. (1981) note that "There is some evidence to suggest that within the retarded population Down's syndrome children are less well-coordinated than their non-D.S. peers" (p. 233) intensifying the perception of intellectual disabilities.

Certain teachers involved in this study viewed "problem-solving" as central to their profession, and worked to support their students with Down syndrome to overcome performance and communication difficulties. One method described involved elements of what has recently been termed "facilitated communication training." Controversy surrounds this process of developing controlled gestures (see, for example, a series of opinions published in 1994 in the American Association on Mental Retardation's journal *Mental Retardation, 32*[3]). The question of authorship arises: "When Colleen Madison supports Lee Larson's typing gestures, is she actually manipulating his hand to construct words?" Several studies suggest that in experimental and quasi-experimental situations, the words purportedly typed by students are, in fact, authored by the support person facilitating the typing (e.g., Eberlin, McConnachie, Ibel, & Volpe, 1993; Hudson, Melita, & Arnold, 1993; Moore, Donovan, & Hudson, 1993; Simon, Toll, & Whitehair, 1994; Simpson & Myles, 1995; Szempruch & Jacobson, 1993; Wheeler, Jacobson, Paglieri, & Schwartz, 1993).

A number of studies, however, contradict the above findings, and suggest that people with disabilities are authoring the facilitated text. This has occurred in:

- Experimental and quasi-experimental conditions (e.g., Biklen & Cardinal, 1997; Cardinal, Hanson, & Wakeham, 1996; Crossley & McDonald, 1984; Intellectual Disability Review Panel, 1989; Marcus & Shevin, 1997; Sheehan & Matuozzi, 1996; Steering Committee, 1993; Weiss, Wagner, & Bauman, 1996).
- Through outside corroboration of typed statements (e.g., Botash et al., 1994; State of Kansas v. Warden, 1995).
- Through progressive independence in typing skills (e.g., McCarthy, Blackman, & Blackman, 1996).

Researchers have yet to sort out the facilitated communication controversy, but Colleen Madison noted that Lee's progressive independence with controlled gestures and his ability to express information unknown to the support person served to assure the instructional team and Lee's family that Lee's typed words were his own.

Recently, several efforts have been described in the research literature which successfully incorporate literacy as a communication tool connecting students with Down syndrome to the wider community (Buckley, 1985, 1995; Meyers, 1986, 1988, 1990; Oelwein, 1995). This insightful work builds on a small body of often ignored research and biography that has resisted the larger cultural logic resulting in the separation of people with Down syndrome from written language (Buck, 1955; Butterfield, 1961; Hunt, 1967; Pototzky & Grigg, 1942; Seagoe, 1964). In the 1940s, at the Bancroft School in Haddonfield, NJ, students with Down syndrome were recognized as extremely literate. Of 11 children with Down syndrome, 2 scored at the 6th-grade reading level, 7 ranged from 1st-through 5th-grade levels, and 2 were considered prereaders (Pototzky & Grigg, 1942). The authors concluded, "We propose, therefore, that the term 'Mongolian idiocy' so frequently found in the literature be discarded, and the term 'Mongolism' which more accurately describes the physical and not the mental status, be substituted" (Pototzky & Grigg, 1942, p. 510).

In the 1960s, two journals typed by people with Down syndrome were published as autobiographies (Hunt, 1967; Seagoe, 1964). Seagoe (1964) recounts how Paul Scott's wealthy father brought his son, born with Down syndrome, to a California teacher, Hellen Bass Keller. On meeting Paul, Keller assumed he could never become literate: "He spoke no intelligible words or sentences and asked no questions. He made incoherent sounds" (p. 12). However, in part because of the family's wealth, Keller worked with Scott beginning when he was 7 years old. She focused her efforts on developing his movement control, and introduced writing and typing as a means for conveying everyday information. Still at the age of 7, Paul quickly began to write notes such as: "I love you. Will see you soon. Paul." During that first year, Keller brought in a typewriter for Paul to see. Seagoe wrote: "That was the beginning of his self-taught use of the typewriter, a consuming interest and an indispensable tool" (p. 16).

Similarly, Nigel Hunt's father noted that his son "taught himself to type. I showed him how to use the shift key for capital letters, and that is all" (Hunt, 1967, p. 16). Nigel's literacy developed as he helped his mother around the house. She would spell out common items as they used them in the kitchen, connecting literacy to everyday life, and he would recreate the words using magnetic letters and the item labels as models. To the surprise of his parents, when Nigel was first given a book to read, he did so without hesitation or difficulty, and soon asked for books on poetry and a dictionary.

The students at the Bancroft School, as well as Paul Scott and Nigel Hunt, all succeeded as members of the literate community for the two reasons certain children in this study achieved membership: (1) They were valued as symbolic beings, not devalued as intellectually deficient, and (2) it was recognized they needed a tool for connecting symbolically with the wider community. Constructing relationships of connectedness through literacy reconceptualizes the understanding of children with Down syndrome as Citizens of the privileged literate community.

IMPLICATIONS FOR PRACTICE

Teachers described in this study actively connected children with Down syndrome to the literate community. This occurred only when the students were involved as full participants in the regular routines and general lessons of classrooms made up of children with and without disabilities. Restructuring classrooms to support all students' participation appears fundamental to realizing individual children's literacy capacities. Physical presence, however, is not enough. Restructuring must also involve redefining literacy from a consequence of isolated subskill mastery to a tool for communication. In doing so, teachers have turned written language into a path students might choose to solve problems, accomplish learning goals, express emotions, empathize with peers, gather and convey information, form friendships, and resolve conflicts.

References

Adams, M. J. (1990). *Beginning to read: Thinking and learning about print.* Cambridge, MA: MIT Press.

Anwar, F., & Hermelin, B. (1979). Kinaesthetic movement after-effects in children with Down's syndrome. *Journal of Mental Deficiency Research, 23,* 287–297.

Ashton-Warner, S. (1963). *Teacher.* New York: Simon & Schuster.

Biklen, D. (1993). *Communication unbound: How facilitated communication is challenging traditional views of autism, and ability/disability.* New York: Teachers College Press.

Biklen, D., & Cardinal, D. N. (Eds.). (1997). *Contested words, contested science: Unraveling the facilitated communication controversy.* New York: Teachers College Press.

Blatt, B. (1987). *The conquest of mental retardation.* Austin, TX: Pro-Ed.

Blatt, B., & Kaplan, F. (1966). *Christmas in purgatory,* Boston: Allyn & Bacon.

Bogdan, R. C., & Biklen, S. K. (1992). *Qualitative research for education: An introduction to theory and methods.* Boston: Allyn & Bacon.

Bogdan, R., & Taylor, S. J. (1982). *Introduction to qualitative research methods.* New York: Wiley.

Bogdan, R., & Taylor, S. J. (1989). Relationships with severely disabled people: The social construction of humanness. *Social Problems, 36*(2), 135–148.

Bogdan, R., & Taylor, S. J. (1994). *The social meaning of mental retardation.* New York: Teachers College Press.

Botash, A. S., Babuts, D., Mitchell, N., O'Hara, M., Lynch, L., & Manuel, J. (1994). Evaluations of children who have disclosed sexual abuse via facilitated communication. *Archives of Pediatric and Adolescent Medicine, 148,* 1282–1287.

Buck, J. N. (1955). The sage: An unusual Mongoloid. In A. Burton & R. Harris (Eds.), *Clinical studies of personality. Vol III* (pp. 455–481). New York: Harper and Row.

Buckley, S. (1985). Attaining basic educational skills: Reading, writing, and numbers. In D. Lane & B. Stratford (Eds.), *Current approaches to Down's syndrome* (pp. 315–343). New York: Praeger.

Buckley, S (1995). Teaching children with Down syndrome to read and write. In L. Nadel & D. Rosenthal (Eds.), *Down syndrome: Living and learning in the community* (pp. 158–169). New York: Wiley-Liss.

Butterfield, E. C. (1961). A provocative case of overachievement by a Mongoloid. *American Journal on Mental Deficiency, 66,* 444–448.

Cardinal, D. N., Hanson, D., & Wakeham, J. (1996). Investigation of authorship in facilitated communication. *Mental Retardation, 34,* 231–242.

Cicchetti, D., & Beeghly, M. (Eds.). (1990). *Children with Down syndrome: A developmental perspective.* Cambridge: Cambridge University Press.

Clay, M. M. (1967). The reading behavior of five-year-old children. *New Zealand Journal of Educational Studies, 2,* 11–31.

Crawford, P. A. (1995). Early literacy: Emerging perspectives. *Journal of Research in Childhood Education, 10*(1), 71–86.

Crossley, R., & McDonald, A. (1984). *Annie's coming out.* New York: Penguin.

Cunningham, P. M., & Allington, R. L. (1994). *Classrooms that work: They can all read and write.* New York: Harper Collins College.

Denzin, N. (1978). *The research act* (2nd ed.). New York: McGraw-Hill.

Denzin, N. K., & Lincoln, Y. S. (Eds.). (1994). *Handbook of qualitative research.* Thousand Oaks, CA: Sage.

Eberlin, M., McConnachie, G., Ibel, S., & Volpe, L. (1993). Facilitated communication: A failure to replicate the phenomenon. *Journal of Autism and Developmental Disorders, 23,* 507–530.

Elliott, D. (1985). Manual assymetries in the performance of sequential movement by adolescents and adults with Down syndrome. *American Journal of Mental Deficiency, 90*(1), 90–97.

Ferguson, P. M., Ferguson, D. L., & Taylor, S. J. (1992). *Interpreting disability: A qualitative reader.* New York: Teachers College Press.

Feuerstein, R., Rand, Y., & Rynders, J. E. (1988). *Don't accept me as I am: Helping "retarded" people to excel.* New York: Plenum.

Frith, U., & Frith, C. D. (1974). Specific motor disabilities in Down syndrome. *Journal of Child Psychology and Psychiatry, 15,* 283–301.

Gardner, H. (1991). *The unschooled mind.* New York: Basic Books.

Glaser, B. G., & Strauss, A. I. (1967). *The discovery of grounded theory: Strategies for qualitative reseach.* New York: Aldine de Gruyter.

Goodman, K. S. (1992). I didn't found whole language. *The Reading Teacher, 46,* 188–199.

Goodman, K. S., & Goodman, Y. M. (1979). Learning to read is natural. In L. B. Resnick & P. A. Weaver (Eds.), *Theory and practice of early reading. Vol. 2.* Hillsdale, NJ: Erlbaum.

Harste, I. C., Woodward, V. A., & Burke, C. L. (1984). *Language stories and literacy lessons.* Portsmouth, NH: Heinemann.

Henderson, S. E., Illingsworth., S. M., & Allen, J. (1991). Prolongation of simple manual and social reaction times in Down syndrome. *Adapted Physical Activity Quarterly, 8,* 234–241.

Henderson, S. E., Morris, J., & Frith, U. (1981). The motor deficit in Down's syndrome children: A problem of timing: *Journal of Child Psychology and Psychiatry, 22*(3), 233–245.

Huberman, A. M., & Miles, M. B. (1994). Data management and analysis methods. In N. K. Denzin & Y. S. Lincoln (Eds.), *Handbook of qualitative research* (pp. 428–444). Thousand Oaks, CA: Sage.

Hudson, A., Melita, B., & Arnold, N. (1993). Brief report: A case study assessing the validity of facilitated communication. *Journal of Autism and Developmental Disorders, 23,* 165–173.

Hunt, N. (1967). *The world of Nigel Hunt: The diary of a Mongoloid youth.* New York: Garrett.

Intellectual Disability Review Panel, (1989). *Investigation into the reliability, and validity of the assisted communication technique.* Victoria, Australia: Department of Community Services.

Janesick, V. J. (1994). The dance of qualitative research design: Metaphor, methodolatry, and meaning. In N. K. Denzin & Y. S. Lincoln (Eds.), *Handbook of qualitative research* (pp. 209–219), Thousand Oaks, CA: Sage.

Kincheloe, J. L., & McLaren, P. L. (1994). Rethinking critical theory and qualitative research. In N. K. Denzin & Y. S. Lincoln (Eds.), *Handbook of qualitative research* (pp. 138–157). Thousand Oaks, CA: Sage.

Koppenhaver, D. A., Coleman, P. P., Kalman, S., & Yoder, D. E. (1991). The implications of emergent literacy research for children with developmental disabilities. *American Journal of Speech-Language Pathology, 1*(1), 38–44.

Koppenhaver, D. A., Pierce, P. L., & Yoder, D. E. (1995). AAC, FC, and the ABCs: Issues and relationships. *American Journal of Speech-Language Pathology, 4*, 5–14.

LeClair, D. A., Pollock, B. J., & Elliott, D. (1993). Movement preparation in adults with and without Down syndrome. *American Journal on Mental Retardation, 97*(6), 628–633.

Lincoln, Y. S., & Guba, E. G. (1985). *Naturalistic inquiry.* Beverly Hills, CA: Sage.

Marcus, E., & Shevin, M. (1997). Sorring it out under fire: Our journey. In D. Biklen & D. N. Cardinal (Eds.), *Contested words, contested science: Unraveling the facilitated communication controversy* (pp. 31–58). New York: Teachers College Press.

McCarthy, M. K., Blackman, L., & Blackman, M. (1996, July). *Sensation and its effects on development of Language and adaptive behaviors.* Keynote Address at the American National Conference on Autism, Autism Society of America. Milwaukee, WI.

McKenna, M. C., Robinson, R. D., & Miller, J. W. (1994). Whole language and research: The case for caution. In C. B. Smith (Ed.), *Whole language: The debate.* Bloomington, IN: "EDINFO Press."

Meyers, L. F. (1986). Teaching language. *Exceptional Parent, 16*(7), 20–23.

Meyers, L. F. (1988). Using computers to teach children with Down's syndrome spoken and written language skills. In L. Nadel (Ed.), *The psychobiology of Down's syndrome* (pp. 247–265). New York: NDSS.

Meyers, L. F. (1990). Language development and intervention. In D. C. Van Dyke, D. J. Lang, F. Heide, S. van Duyne, & M. J. Soucek (Eds.), *Clinical perspectives in the management of Down's syndrome* (pp. 153–164). New York: Springer-Verlag.

Moore, S., Donovan, B., & Hudson, A. (1993). Facilitator suggested conversational evaluation of facilitated communication. *Journal of Autism and Developmental Disorders, 23*, 541–551.

Nadel, L., & Rosenthal, D. (1995). *Down syndrome: Living and learning in the community,* New York: Wiley-Liss.

Oelwein, P. L. (1995). *Teaching reading to children with Down syndrome.* Bethesda, MD: Woodbine House.

Pototzky, C. & Grigg, A. E. (1942). A revision of the prognosis in Mongolism. *American Journal of Orthopsychiatry, 12*(3), 503–510.

Seagoe, M. V. (1964). *Yesterday was Tuesday, all day and all night: The story of a unique education.* Boston: Little Brown.

Sendak, M. (1963). *Where the wild things are.* New York: Harper and Row.

Shannon, P. (1990). *The struggle to continue: Progressive reading instruction in the United States.* Portsmouth, NH: Heinemann.

Sheehan, C., & Matuozzi, R. (1996). Validation of facilitated communication. *Mental Retardation, 34*, 94–107.

Simon, E. W., Toll, D. M., & Whitehair, P. M. (1994). A naturalistic approach to the validation of facilitated communication. *Journal of Autism and Developmental Disorders, 24*, 647–657.

Simpson, R. L., & Myles, B. S. (1995). Effectiveness of facilitated communication with children and youth with autism. *Journal of Special Education, 28*, 424–439.

Smith, F. (1988a). *Joining the literacy club.* Portsmouth, NH: Heinemann.

Smith, F. (1988b). *Understanding reading* (4th ed.). Hillsdale, NJ: Erlbaum.

Smith, F. (1992), Learning to read: The never ending debate. *Phi Delta Kappan, 73*(6), 432–441.

Smith, J. K. (1993). *After the demise of empiricism: The problems of judging social and educational inquiry.* Norwood, NJ: Ablex.

Solsken, J. W. (1993). *Literacy, gender, and work: In families and in schools.* Norwood, NJ: Ablex.

Spock, B. (1949). *The pocket book of baby and child care.* New York: Pocket Books.

State of Kansas v. Warden, No. 70.377, 1995, LEXIS 41, (S. Ct. 1995).

Steering Committee, (1993). *The Queensland report on facilitated communication.* Queensland, Australia: Department of Family Services and Aboriginal and Islander Affairs, Division of Intellectual Disability Services.

Strauss, A., & Corbin, J. (1994). Grounded theory methodology: An overview. In N. K. Denzin & Y. S. Lincoln (Eds.), *Handbook of qualitative research* (pp. 273–285). Thousand Oaks, CA: Sage.

Szempruch, J., & Jacobson, J. W. (1993). Evaluating the facilitated communications of people with developmental disabilities. *Research in Developmental Disabilities, 14*, 253–264.

Teale, W. H., & Sulzby, E. (Eds.). (1986). *Emergent literacy: Writing and reading,* Norwood, NJ: Ablex.

Weiss, M. J. S., Wagner, S. H., & Bauman, M. I. (1996). A validated case study of facilitated communication. *Mental Retardation, 4*, 220–230.

Wheeler, D. L., Jacobson, J. W., Paglieri, R. A., & Schwartz, A. A. (1993). An experimental assessment of facilitated communication. *Mental Retardation, 31*(1), 49–60.

Chapter Eight

Social, Emotional, and Behavioral Issues in the Classroom

8.1 ▌ The Life-Space Interview

David Wineman

The present article describes an interview approach—the life-space interview—originated by Fritz Redl under specific conditions of practice with ego-disturbed children—and contrasts it with traditional interview techniques found in clinical social work practice.

The greatest single influence on the interview method in clinical social work has come, of course, from classical psychoanalytic treatment practice. *Content* most eagerly sought by the classical therapist is that which refers to the libidinal relationship to the parents and siblings of the client, on both conscious and unconscious levels. Interview *relationship and role structure* are most carefully guarded against contamination from either the therapist's or client's ongoing life experiences; neither the therapist nor the client may have such ties with each other as could involve either or both with the opportunity for gratification of the other or direct power over each other's behavior away from the interview setting. Finally, the *time-space conditions* under which all clinical events take place are strictly defined in an appointment hour (time) and in the therapist's office (space).

The original psychoanalytic model from which this is borrowed is best suited, and was originally developed clinically, for the classical adult neurotic. Although complexly disturbed, he sacrifices the least of his ego to his illness, as compared with other disturbance syndromes, and his principal *ego strain* is experienced in connection with his specific conflicts, leaving him free to cope with most other adjustive tasks in a normal way. However, when we come to the child neurotic, things are a little different—even with the "classical" child neurotic. Redl[1] reminds us that Anna Freud herself explicitly recognized that certain modifications of adult therapy techniques were necessary because of the incompleteness in ego development and the nature of the child's relationship to the adult world. These modifications raised the ceiling on how far the therapist could directly invade libidinal, reality, and value spheres, as compared with adult therapy. Thus, one of Miss Freud's girl patients was seriously advised by her that while it was perfectly all right to use obscene language in telling her fantasies to Miss Freud, this was "out" anywhere else. Specific directions and suggestions of a management or training type could be made to parents. On the gratification level, candy bars, soft drinks, and cookies are far from infrequent in orthodox therapy with children of less than pubertal age.

Yet, in spite of these shifts toward more involvement in the libidinal, reality, or value zones of the child's life, classical child therapy—casework or psychoanalytic—sticks with *content* focus on libidinal materials of a historically determined type, becomes involved in ongoing reality areas only to "save" the therapy from oblivion, and, while permitting gratifications to the child, holds these down to the bare minimum required to involve the child in a relationship. Also the classical *space-time* condition of the office appointment is preserved.

So much for a brief structural analysis of the "classical" interview concept and its modifications for work with children. Now let us examine the origin and development of the "life-space" concept which in some ways only carries further the modifications begun by Anna Freud, and in others is clearly different along qualitative lines.

LIFE-SPACE CONCEPT

In the early 1940's, Fritz Redl was operating both summer camp and winter club groups in the city for severely ego-disturbed children, who had been referred by various Detroit social agencies with whom the children were simultaneously in individual therapy. As experience accumulated in these projects, it was noticed that frequently a child might produce behavior (temper tantrums, swiftly appearing sulks and

Wineman, D. (1959). The life-space interview. *Social Work, 4*(1), 3–17. Copyright © 1959, National Association of Social Workers, Inc., Social Work.

withdrawals, stealing, fighting) that required on-the-spot handling of an interview-like type, the responsibility for which was assumed by the adult in charge, usually a group worker or a group work–field work student. Upon analysis, the types of interviews[2] that grew out of this proved to hold a technical complexity and meaning that any good casework or psychiatric interview might have, even though the locus of interview was much more a part of the *life-space* of the child, its content released by a piece of unplanned *life-space* dynamics and was being performed by an *"out-of-role" person who had direct life-experiential meaning for the child on reality, value, and libidinal terms.* Thus, while the classical approach would specify that reality issues should be handled only when they endanger therapy, the life-space approach would insist that with severely ego-damaged children they provide some necessary materials without which therapy could not go on. Yet—and this is important—it does not argue that traditional methods cannot also be of powerful assistance and readily concedes that both methods can be applied in the service of therapy with the same child. Thus, for instance, many of the episodes that were the target of life-space interviewing in the club groups were also picked up by the agency therapist later on, either being brought in by the child himself or raised by the worker who was always in communication with the project leader.

Beginning in this way, the life-space approach was further experimented with at Pioneer House (1946–48),[3] a residential treatment home for boys, at the children's ward and residence at National Institute of Mental Health in Bethesda (1953–present),[4] and at the University of Michigan Fresh Air Camp, a summer camp for disturbed boys (1950–present)[5] from which setting the clinical material for the present paper is drawn.

GOALS, TASKS, AND LEVELS OF FUNCTION

The type of child around whose treatment life-space interviewing has been developed finds it virtually impossible to manage himself for a single day without the eruption of behavioral episodes representing in one way or another his disturbances in ego functioning. In this section we shall try to examine the ways in which these episodes may be used by the clinician as potential content for life-space interviewing, and the kinds of goals, tasks, and levels of function that have been tentatively worked out for this style of interview. As an opening illustration, let us take a look at Ricki,[6] one of our last season's Fresh Air campers in one of his "bad" moments.

> Ricki, an 11-year-old boy with a chainstyle history of broken foster home placements, was a terribly deprived, bitter child with an insatiable, violent hunger for proofs of affection from the adult and an equally intense expectation of treachery and deceit. Imagine, then, his reaction when one day, after an acrimonious dispute between himself and another camper over the ownership of a walking cane which had been made in the camp craft shop, the facts supported the other child and we had to take the cane from Ricki and give it to the other youngster. He blew up immediately, had to be physically prevented from slugging the other boy, accused us of being in league with the other boy, and so on.

At the point of eruption of this "symptomatic" behavior, the adult on the scene will have to decide in which of two basic directions Ricki's interview handling should go:

1. He may simply try to "pull him through" the behavioral storm and sit it out with him until he is controlled enough to go about his regular business of life at camp. In addition to this protective waiting it out with him, we would also try to take the edge off his suspicion about our being in "cahoots" with the other boy by going over the facts again of how the mixup in the craft shop had occurred so that the other boy's cane had been mistakenly given to Ricki. And we would display our eagerness for him to have a cane by offering immediately to detail a staff member to help him start a new one, thus alleviating his frustration in having to wait until the next morning when the craft shop would be open again.

2. Our on-the-scene adult, instead of merely sitting it out with Ricki and getting him started on a new walking cane, might see this as a good opportunity to pick up this particular blow-up (which was a repetition of many that Ricki had already had) as a typical instance of his "problem," point out that this was the way he reacted *whenever* things didn't go the way he wanted them to, that we knew that even back in the foster homes he had these blow-ups, and so on. In other words, in Step 2 the adult tries to use this situation toward the realization of a long-range clinical "improvement goal." (Actually in this case we went only as far as Step 1 because Ricki was still too confused about himself and his problems to have enough "uninfected ego" on tap for use in picking up a useful perception of any part of the self in relation to a long-range goal.)

Redl has given these two major uses of the life-space interview characteristically descriptive titles.[7] Simply pulling a child through a tough spot (our Step 1) he calls "emotional first aid on the spot." If, in addition, the incident is tactically aimed at the long-range goal (our Step 2) he calls it "clinical exploitation of life events." However, the dichotomy is anything but a tight one. Not infrequently, there may be a coupling of the two functions or a switch midstream in the interview. Following the dichotomy with this warning in mind, let us now examine some of the subfunctions of these two basic functions.

CLINICAL EXPLOITATION OF LIFE EVENTS

Clinical "exploitation"[8] is a broad term. A clinical goal, upon inspection, becomes a network of sub-goals or tasks which therapy is trying to achieve. Interviews along the way serve now one, now another, of these subgoals. In the category under discussion, the following separate subheadings are aimed at demonstrating this discreteness of function in the life-space interview.

1. Reality "Rub-In"

Many ego-damaged children are perceptually confused as to what goes on around them either because they have already woven together a "delusional"[9] system of life interpretation or because they suffer from a peculiar "drag" of a structural type in their ego development. In either case, many times they don't seem to "get the hang" of a social interaction web unless one puts it together for them with the special magnification aids of the "on-the-spot" style of interview.

Hank, 8½, is removed from his cabin at bedtime in screaming, hitting rage, having already socked his counselor twice in the side. "She didn't have no right to flip me on the floor," he yells, as we take him to the main lodge of the camp, giving in this way his rationale for hitting her. In the lodge, he sits broodingly in a thirty-minute sulk before he will say anything at all, while the counselor and I sit with him, the latter having been relieved by another staff member so she can stay with Hank and me. As his rage drains out and in response to our encouragement, he blurts out again, "She didn't have to flip me to the floor!" Then commenced a four-way interview between Hank, Lorie (the counselor), myself, and Dr. Albert Cohen, the camp sociologist.[10]

LORIE: (*replying to Hank's statement that she "flipped" him*) This is not the way it really hap-

pened, Hank. Remember you've been jumping on me, poking me, and pulling on me most of the afternoon and evening.

HANK: (*somewhat defiantly but smiling a little*) Aw, that was just in fun. You didn't even care about *that*.

LORIE: I asked you to stop many times.

HANK: Well, yeah, but you really didn't care though.

COHEN: Hank, let's talk about what happened in the cabin tonight. Here was Lorie trying to get you guys to bed—right?

HANK: Right.

COHEN: And what were you doing?

HANK: I was holdin' on to her.

COHEN: How?

HANK: I was grabbin' her around the middle from behind. I had my arms around hers (*pinning her arms*).

COHEN: And Lorie is busy trying to help the other guys get ready for bed.

HANK: Yeah.

COHEN: And the other guys may need things that she has to get or want her to do some things for them, too.

HANK: Yeah.

COHEN: Lorie is tired and she's been asking you to quit jumping on her most of the afternoon and evening but you're still grabbing her and won't let her go.

HANK: Guess so—but she didn't have to flip me.

COHEN: Did she *ask* you to let her go?

HANK: Yeah.

COHEN: How many times?

HANK: Three or four.

COHEN: So she *asks* you to let go. But you keep hanging on to her. Now, (*gently and emphatically*) she's asked you many times but you still hang on. She wants you to let go because she is tired of all the jumping and hanging on and has all these things to do which she can't because you're dragging on her. What do you think she should do?

HANK: Dunno.

COHEN: She has to get loose, doesn't she?

HANK: Guess so.

COHEN: So she spreads her arms forcing you to let go—right?

HANK: Yes.

COHEN: Could she have done it any other way?

HANK: (*without anger and quite readily*) No—guess not.

WINEMAN: Then you fell to the cabin floor?

HANK: Yeah.

WINEMAN: Then what happened?

HANK: The kids laughed and I got mad.

WINEMAN: I guess we can all see that that would be hard to take. And then?

HANK: I socked Lorie.

WINEMAN: Hank, right after you socked Lorie, how did you expect she felt toward you?

HANK: Sore at me.

WINEMAN: And because you thought she was sore at you, what else did you think about her and you?

HANK: That she wouldn't like me.

WINEMAN: And then?

HANK: I got mad all over again.

WINEMAN: That's about when I came into the cabin, isn't it? (*He nods.*) And she was havin' to hold you because you were so sore. Then I took you over here and at first you were still so sore you wouldn't talk or anything and still kept thinking that she had tried to flip you on purpose—right?

HANK: Yeah. (*By now he is smiling rather brightly; his mood has changed from sullen and defiant to cheerful agreement; actually he seems to enjoy the careful empathic unraveling of the episode.*)

At this point, it seems that Hank has a much clearer perception of his own role in the production of the cabin situation and the "flip" by Lorie. At first he sees her as an aggravator and rejector, blots out entirely his own persistent, somewhat erotic, pestering of her and his blocking of her carrying out of her duties in the cabin in relation to the whole group. This series of perceptions is the target of the first part of the interview. Next he sees that the group reaction to his unfortunate fall "burns him up" and grasps the relation between this and slugging the counselor the first time. Finally, he understands that once he has "socked her" he expects retaliation from her in the form of rejection (Note: He does not expect to get "socked" in return, showing his basically *correct* understanding of our policy against physical punishment). This, he sees, makes him even more angry *so he hits her again.* Then comes the finale in the lodge.

In terms of *goal,* this type of interview is both short-range and long-range in its intent: short-range, we want to help Hank stop mauling the counselor *as soon as possible.* Long-range, through the "injection" of many such interview episodes, we want him (1) to become more habituated and skilled in self-observation and (2) to step up his sensitivity to the feelings and emotions of people upon whom he is acting in an interpersonal chain. Hank's postinterview behavior in relation to this single item—mauling the counselor—improved, by the way, so that the short-range goal can be said to have been achieved. Obviously, as stated, only multiple exposure can attack the long-range problem but this may be seen as a link along the way.

2. Symptom Estrangement

Another characteristic of the children in connection with whose treatment the life-space interview has been developed is that instead of finding any part of their functioning strange or bothersome (as does the conventional "treatment-prone" neurotic) they have invested heavily in secondary gain ventures to such an extent that the whole ego seems to be allied with their central pathology rather than any part of the ego taking a stand against it. While this does not mean that the whole ego is sick with the same disease that we are trying to cure, unless its "uninfected" part can be "estranged" from the core pathology and converted into an allegiance to seeing that "something is wrong," the clinical battle cannot even get started. The life-space interview has shown itself to be peculiarly fitted for this crucial, initial task.

Don, 10 years old, is so intensely driven toward the image of a teen-age "hood" that he seems to have stepped out of a "cornier-than-life" Hollywood movie of this type of kid. He has been an addict smoker since the age of 6, steals, knows all of the crude sex terms and practices, and lies with the aplomb of an Alcatraz lifer when "caught with the goods." An adopted child of a near-to-middle class family, he has overwhelmed his adoptive father with the force of his "delinquent" identification, spurring the father into alternating fits of brutality and mawkish, sentimental surrender of a defeatist type. Any admitted perception on Don's part that he is ever scared, might need protection against more powerful kids, or that he might, in any cell of his being, have a "little boy" part seems to have been ruthlessly ground out of awareness. The following episode was one of the first clinical demonstration chances we had at camp to trap his ego into what might be considered a potentially "treatment positive" perception. It all happened as a result of Don's having sadistically teased one of his cabin mates by shaking a tree branch that this boy was perched on, in spite of the other one's terrified screams for Don to stop, and, then later on the same day, ripping up another cabin mate's Sorry cards because the second boy would not give Don a snake he had caught. These two seemingly unrelated events were "stitched" together in the following interview in such a way that Don's fear motivation was made visible to him.

INTERVIEWER: Don, do I have this straight—when Terry was yelling for you to stop shaking the branch, you kept on doing it anyway?

DON: Yep.

INT.: And then what would Terry do?

DON: Keep yellin' for me to stop.

INT.: But the more he yelled the more you what——?

DON: Shook'im.

INT.: Why do you suppose he was yelling?

DON: Because he was scared.

INT.: Yet the more scared he got, the more it seems you felt like shaking him.

DON: That's right.

INT.: I wonder why you'd want to do that—make him scared?

DON: I dunno.

INT.: That'd be something I should think you'd want to know about yourself—don't you agree?

DON: (uneasily) Yeah.

The interview then moves on to the second incident of the same day—tearing up the Sorry cards.

INT.: Don, how come you ripped up Rusty's Sorry cards?

DON: (indignantly) Heck—he promised me the next snake he caught and after he caught this here snake he never gave it to me.

INT.: Well, I guess he should've gone through with his deal, although I'm not saying you had the right to tear up his cards because he didn't. Anyway, how come you don't catch your own snakes?

DON: (indignantly again) I'll bet you'd like to get bit by a snake on yer finger?

INT.: No, I wouldn't. You mean you are scared enough of snakes that you try to get Rusty to give you one of his? Not take the risk of catching one yourself?

DON: Yeah, boy.

INT.: And yet when Terry is up in the tree you do everything you can to make *him* more what——?

DON: (disgustedly) Scared!

INT.: That's right Don, scared. So now I begin to wonder to myself. Maybe Don wants to make other guys scared because if he can be such a guy as *can* scare other guys, then he doesn't have to be so what——?

DON: (spits it out) Scared!

INT.: Yep—that's right again—scared.

DON: (blustering) Yeah—yeah. (in his most "gravelly" voice) Next time my ma comes I'm gonna ask her to bring two of my buddies, *they'll* tell you I don't get scared.

INT.: Easy, boy, easy! I'm not saying you're chicken or that you get scared all the time. Heck, anybody gets scared about certain things—there's nothing wrong with that. But you—you don't like to admit you get scared hardly at all. Go around actin' like you're a teen-ager, smoking, stealing and all that. You *do*, don't you? We've been through that before.

DON: Yeah.

INT.: So all I'm sayin' now is that maybe some of that stuff is mixed up with your tryin' to make out that you don't scare easy—see? That's about all I'm saying. And you're already in plenty of trouble back home on account of doin' that, aren't you?

DON: (unhappily) Yeah.

Don, of course, is far from happy with any of this. In fact, he is "burned up." The clinical issue, however, is the question: is he any *wiser?* We think he may be—a wee, but crucial, bit. Also, it puts us in a much more favorable position to urge Don to take more seriously the camp caseworker's attempts to get at his problem as well as to take a new look at what his worker in the city is trying to do for him. This, followed by continuing interview coverage which explores his fear motivation, is an important step in working back to his whole tough-guy reaction formation against being little and helpless. (Of course, there is a hard possibility that Don cannot be helped by anything short of residential treatment anyway, but that is another story and not for these pages.)

3. Value Repair and Restoration

The ego-disturbed child handles still another major adjustive task very unskillfully: that of bringing about a proper balance or synthesis between values and behavior. This is a complicated issue and there is not enough space to give it the "phenomenological respect" it deserves. Briefly, with the children under consideration, there are three aspects of this problem:

a. There may be some *deficiencies* in value content: certain pieces of superego have never been formed.

b. There may be some *uniquenesses* in value content: certain pieces of superego are formed but are different, sometimes to the point of opposition, from the value pattern of the dominant, surrounding social environment.

c. Regardless of what value content there may be to begin with, the *superego is incompletely introjected*, still depends in its functioning upon the presence of "adult enforcers," and is feared and fought by the ego.

These three possibilities are not necessarily mutually exclusive; in fact, with the type of children being discussed they are usually interwoven. The resulting clinical challenge involves us in the task of helping them become more sensitive to the demands of whatever superego has already been built into the personality, or rebuilding it or modifying it as the case may be. Since the admission of guilt is often fought off by these children out of fear of peer-group derision or rejection as "adult lovers," it is especially important to reconnoiter their myriad interpersonal squabbles and feuds for "clean" issues where potentially culpable children can be spared this expensive prestige payment in front of their buddies.

A group of 11-year-olds was being seen with the purpose of trying to help them figure out why they were continually at each other's throats, battling, cursing, teasing each other with cruel tricks, and, in general, unmanageable by their counselors. As typically happens, at the outset they all heaped responsibility on a particular youngster who served as chief scapegoat.

INT. (AL COHEN): What are some of the things Larry does that make you guys think he causes all the trouble?

CHORUS OF VOICES: Calls us "mother names,"[11] spits at us, wakes up early in the morning and yells—stuff like that.

INT.: Tell me about the last time he did that.

JOE: This morning I was sitting on my bunk before flag-raising—and I asked him for one of his comics—so he says: "Yer mammy."[12]

INT.: And what did you do?

JOE: I says, "Yer sister."

INT.: And then?

JOE: He throws a shoe at me.

INT.: And then?

JOE: I climbs up on his bunk and slugs him—that's what!

CHUCK: *(a third boy)* Yeah, and he *always* does stuff like that. That's how we get in trouble.

INT.: Who else had fights today?

SAM: *(a fourth boy)* I did—with Chuck!

INT.: How come?

SAM: Aw, we come out of the swim and he calls my mother a name.

INT.: Chuck, is that right?

CHUCK: Yeah—'cause that bastard [Sam] flicked his towel at me!

SAM: The hell I did—I just threw it over my shoulder!

BILL: *(a fifth boy)* 'n this so-an-so *(pointing at Jim, a sixth member of the group)* flicks his towel at *me.*

INT.: What was Larry doing all this time?

GROUP: *(Silence)*

INT.: You mean he wasn't involved at all?

VOICES: Naw!

INT.: Look. First you guys start off by saying that Larry starts all the trouble, but here are Joe, Chuck, Bill, Sam, and Jim all at each other, yelling mother names, slugging with towels, spitting—and Larry wasn't in on it at all. He sure couldn't have started this one, could he? I wonder how fair it is to accuse him of starting "everything."

GROUP: *(Amazed silence, then agreement.)*

JOE: *(his principal accuser)* Boy, it sure wouldn't be easy to be him!

It is clear that this quite amazing pinpointing of a piece of group unfairness could hardly have emerged so cleanly without a close "life-space probe" resulting in clarification of the behavior chain involved in this particular incident. That the original goal of the interview (to help them achieve some insight into their mutual goading of each other) was only lightly covered detracts hardly at all from the unexpected value lesson so deftly pulled out of the interview by the interviewer. In fact, it hit at one of the contributing factors to the group control problem which was one of tax-exempt shifting away of blame from the self on to the scapegoat. This evasion became much harder for them after such a clear admission of unfairness. The reader may be reminded by this spontaneous interview development of an earlier comment (see page 325) about the difficulty of deciding ahead of time as to exactly which goal a given life-space interview is to be focused upon.

4. New Tool Salesmanship

In this very aptly named subfunction of the life-space interview, Redl has emphasized that one of the severe hazards faced by the ego-disturbed child is linked to the marked impoverishment of his reaction techniques. An important clinical goal, then, is defined by this particle of his pathology: situations must be salvaged from his ongoing experience which can be used to give him a vista of "new tools" that may be applied in moments of problem-solving breakdown.

Chick, a delinquent boy of 9½, who had been booked by the police many times in his short life for larceny and armed robbery—among lighter offenses such as truancy—was a very assaultive child. Early in the camp season, we faced a critical problem in his tendency to slug his female counselors on what appeared to be light provocation. Detailed exploration of these encounters proved that the attacks upon the counselors took place when sudden floods of rage and fear confronted the ego based upon Chick's anticipation of rejection or physical attack from the counselors whom he really liked very much. This seemed to be a severe transference style reaction stemming from a lifetime of exposure to violence and fear at home. However, complex though it was, the transference reaction was not the immediate problem but rather that when Chick was in a fear state, reality-justified or not, the only thing he seemed to be able to do was to use his fists or a nearby weapon. Thus, the first problem we attacked was not the reality distortion of his counselors' feelings and motives toward him, but his need to use his fists to begin with whenever he had such feelings. Partly he was *aware* that he was caught in a web of confusion to begin with, which fact he conveyed to us directly once after we had said, "Chick, you know the counselors aren't like *that*" (meaning that the counselors neither wanted to hurt nor reject him). To which he replied, "Yeah, but sometimes you just *can't believe it.*" Our tack with him then became: "Chick, whenever you have those kinds of feelings, use *this (smiling and lightly putting a finger on his mouth)* instead of *these (touching his fists).*" He gave his "crooked" smile and seemed to understand.

Of course this had to be repeated many times—it was not easy to wean Chick from using his fists. Ironically enough, the very next incident, after the above attempt to sell him "word tools" in exchange for slugging, involved his being brought in for *biting* the counselor and then claiming he was using his mouth instead of his fists as he had been asked to! But gradually, and ultimately with pride, he substituted crude verbal statements of fear and rage for action demonstrations as far as the adult was concerned at least.

5. Manipulation of the Boundaries of the Self

One of the job achievements that proper ego development assures to the individual is that of helping him to learn effectively where he "ends" and other people and/or their rights, privileges, and processes "begin." This is one sector of the larger process of distinction between the self and the non-self that developmental theory posits as one of the major critical achievements of ego growth. Unclear and complex as this process is, it is a certain fact that it is blocked and hamstrung in the type of children under discussion. Thus, in addition to having a core pathology of severe, uncheckable impulsivity, they seem to have much more than a peripheral, additional problem in dealing with other people and situations with the proper degree of autonomy and self-determination. Breakdown of this ego subfunction results in two widely opposite responses: (a) either other people's excitement quickly becomes theirs, other kids' mischief or aggression quickly racing toward them and covering them as a leaping flame with a gasoline-soaked rag; or (b) quite the reverse, their own feeling tone, whim, or prejudice is narcissistically, sometimes even megalomaniacally, forced upon another individual with no apparent awareness of or concern about the boundary between the own self and the other person, his rights, privileges, and so on.

In other words, in the first reaction, (a), the ego permits itself to be invaded by a "foreign" ego and then functions as though the motivational trend of the invading ego were its own. In the second reaction, (b), the ego invades a "foreign" ego and then functions as though it were the motivational trend of the invaded ego. The pathology is the same, the direction reversed, just as having the delusion that one is dead or is the last person on earth who is living are examples of the same pathology.

An interesting example of the second reaction, as well as a beginning attempt at influencing it, may be found in the following fragment of a long interview with Slim, a violent, but verbal and intelligent 13-year-old. It so happened that Slim intensely disliked a peculiar trait of one of his cabin mates: a habit of walking on his toes whenever he was barefoot.

SLIM: He *(other boy)* always stands and walks on his tiptoes. I don't like that. I don't know why but it seems to be just one more reason for not liking him. So I decided, and I told him, that every time I caught him doing that I would snap him with my towel. I'm trying to break him of the habit.

INT.: Do you really feel you have the right to inflict pain upon him just because you don't like it.

SLIM: Yeah *(slowly and deliberately).* I really think I do.

INT.: You mean your conscience goes along with this?

SLIM: No, it doesn't. I know it's wrong to do but sometimes when I don't like something I feel I have the right to attack it.

INT.: Even though you know it isn't right according to your conscience.

SLIM: My conscience can't control me when I get mad.

INT.: I guess that's the real problem, isn't it, Slim? You really can't control this, even when your conscience tells you it's wrong. Seems to me that this is where you need special help.

SLIM: I know it. . . .

In this interview the goal is to stake out the problem as clearly as possible when Slim is not caught in one of his megalomaniacal episodes and to promise "lend-lease" to the superego-identified part of the ego in its struggle with the narcissistic infantile part. Obviously, there will be a need in the long-range treatment of Slim to attack many more issues than this one. Thus, the special motives and feelings into which this particular ego weakness plays and which form the central core pathology have, of course, to be dealt with. However, this narcissistic blurring of ego boundaries does stand as a formidable clinical problem on its own and there is a question as to whether entree can be gained or waited for into the deeper pathology without tackling this piece of it first. Thus, for instance, by talking with Slim about Whitey's walking habit, it was possible to explore with him the possibility that Whitey was disliked by him for still other reasons, or served as a target for other problems, and in this way Slim's pubertal, phallic competitiveness with Whitey came out. Then it was suggested to him that perhaps his dislike of Whitey's walking on his toes was based upon a fear that Whitey would leap upon him and hurt him—in this way proving he was stronger than Slim. It was interesting that this markedly paranoid boy was relieved by this "theory" which reduced his fear of Whitey. Now of course this does not cure his ego-boundary problem or his paranoia, but it does aim at giving help to the uninvolved part of the ego for dealing with both if continued in balanced doses over a long enough time.

These have been some few, rough illustrations of the use of life-space interview on the level of "clinical exploitation of life events." There is no implication that a completely investigated instrument of change has been evolved or that any of the children

in this setting are being treated until the correct terminal point in their therapy will have been reached. In each case, only a *piece* of the total pathology is being demonstrated as it has been contacted through the interview by picking up a life event or a series of life events packed together in a relatively short time exposure.

EMOTIONAL FIRST AID ON THE SPOT

As mentioned earlier, another major function of the life-space interview is that of simply pulling a youngster through a tight spot without any specific intention or clinical motive toward cure. Its aim is to offer to the ego hygienic protection and support which aid it in overcoming a temporary, sometimes critical, loss of function. Here, too, Redl has offered tentative categories aimed at clarifying some of the subfunctions of this style of life-space interview. Broadly, these differentiate between interviews which aid the ego in moments of (1) acute frustration, fury, guilt, or panic; (2) throw support around the ego when it is faced by sudden violent retreat from relationship; and (3) help a child steer his way safely through some complicating and confusing "social and behavioral traffic jams" and decision-making crises. For space reasons, we shall confine ourselves to samples showing two different subfunctions classifiable within these three groups. The apparent simplicity of such moments conceals their complexity and to some of our more orthodox clinical brethren may make them "undeserving" for admission to the elite status of "the interview."

INTERVIEW SUPPORT IN AN EPISODE OF PANIC

Chick, whom we have had occasion to describe a few short examples back, was watching a camp movie, "Bad Day at Black Rock," when his counselor observed him get up in a restless, agitated way and walk out of the lodge with the kind of expression that she had learned to read as "trouble." Tipped off by her I followed him out. He said nothing when I asked, "Hey, Chick, what's the trouble?" but strode purposefully along to his cabin. I jogged along by his side in as friendly and relaxed a way as I could. He got into his cabin, climbed up in a bunk, pulled up his blankets to his chin. "I ain't goin' back to that movie or the campfire later or nuthin'." "How come?" No answer. I stretched out on an empty bunk across from his, leaned back, folded my arms under my head and waited. A few minutes later, he got up just as purposefully as he had come in, pulled his blanket back, got down, strode out of the cabin. There I was again by his side. Not a word between us. He walked to the boys' "john." I waited. He came out and went back to the lodge. Instead of going in, he sat down on a bench near the door. I sat down next to him. About a minute passed. Then he said, "Some Western that is... no shootin' or anything!" "Oh" I said, "there'll be shootin'—wait 'till that one-armed guy catches up with the bad guy. The one that killed his buddy which is why he came to this town." "Oh," says he, "that I gotta see," and walked in. I went with him and sat by him in the movie. In a low voice I sketched out what was happening in more detail: how Spencer Tracy, the "one-armed guy," had this friend in the army who had come to this town and been killed by a gang of crooks. Some men in the town who had gone along with the killing—like a weak sheriff—had a bad conscience but were afraid to do anything about it. Now the one-armed guy was going to show them that they didn't have to be scared. He was "giving them back their guts." Then they would take care of the bad guys. Chick relaxed, exchanged comments with me, and appeared to enjoy what was happening. After a bit I "faded" away, leaving him on his own. The rest of the evening was uneventful—campfire and all.

In this encounter, Chick seems to be upset by the subtle violence of this movie as contrasted with the explicit violence of the usual Western—"ain't no shootin' or nothin'." He withdraws and finally returns after two clear-cut "regression" behaviors: climbing into bunk and urinating. In making the plot and actions *explicit* for him—like an interpretive subtitle—and throwing "proximity" protection around him, the ego is able to recontact the fear-inspiring situation and master it. This illustration would seem to be in line with Redl's category of interview helps in the management of "panic, fury, and guilt."

Is this really a "simple" situation that could have gone unhandled? Far from it! Chick, on his own, would have parlayed this momentary threat into an aggressive attack on somebody during the balance of the evening. Yet no attempt is made here to deal with any underlying causality for the ego's inability to meet this situation without fear—this is what differentiates this type of life-space interview from "clinical exploitation."

INTERVIEW SUPPORT IN MOMENTS OF "RELATIONSHIP DECAY"[13]

One of the most dangerous maneuvers of the sick ego is its tendency to draw back into the communication-bereft world of autism. While the more intactly delin-

quent child rarely finds this complete a retreat necessary, using mainly aggressive exploitation of the surrounding world as his major approach to all problems, there is a category of prepsychotic-like disturbances marked by explosive types of acting out intermixed with dependency and passivity, with strong superego and id forces pressing against a thin, underskilled ego, where sudden psychological retreat happens more easily than the clinician finds comfortable to behold. Such a boy was Jon, 13.

Whenever Jon became threatened by aggressive or sexual feelings regardless of whether they were set off by some action or language of other boys in the cabin or from "within" by his own feelings or fantasies, he acted like a virtual hebephrenic: cackled like a rooster, smirked, rolled his eyes, screamed wildly, attacked stronger boys recklessly, shouted obscenity. One day, after a day and a half of such behavior which was almost virtually impossible to bring under control, his whole cabin blew up at him and in their words: "We're goin' to kill the bastard!" The whole gang came in for a talk about it and in the interview room Jon continued to display the whole panorama of behavior described. Finally I asked him in a firm, decisive way: "Look, do you want to work this out or not?" He looked at me and said very calmly, "Well, Dave, you see I've been like this for three years" and then, bang! He was "off" again. Only this time he added to his previous paraphernalia of "goofiness": running out of the room, coming back, hiding under the table, getting back out again and throwing some sunflower seeds he was eating at one of the toughest kids in the cabin. Then, in response to my pressure, he would "come back again" with a few rational statements about himself and his feelings only to follow this with a fit of wildness.

After this happened about six times and it was all we could do to keep the other kids away from him, we let them go and kept him with us since it was dangerous to release him under these conditions. Dr. Phil Spielman, a visiting participating psychiatrist (on a busman's holiday from Dr. Redl's residential treatment unit at Bethesda) and known to all the boys, had been sitting in with us during the group talk and at this point said to Jon: "How come, every time you make a sensible statement about yourself, you immediately go off your rocker and act like a wild man? There is something that is bothering you but you can't come close to it without running away. Why don't you tell us what it is?" At this point I left "Phil" (as he was known to all campers) alone with Jon.

About an hour and a half later, I saw them coming down to the waterfront for a swim. Jon was literally like another person. Phil had "got to him." This particular episode, Jon had finally told Spielman, was caused by his fear of Biff, a much tougher, more primitive adolescent from a neighboring cabin who had come into Jon's cabin one day when the counselor was out for a brief while and started some rough sexual horseplay with him which involved grabbing for his genitals. Jon, quite calm now, told me later that this scared him—that he had never seen "stuff like this before." I told him I would talk to Biff and make clear that we would not tolerate anybody forcing other kids into play like that which, in my role as one of the "camp bosses," it was possible to do as far as Biff was concerned.

In this sequence of events, neither the interviewer nor I made any attempt to get at the reason as to why this upset Jon so much. This would have involved opening up on a deeper clinical level than the camp was able to engage in with Jon. The whole purpose was simply to try to get him back into communication and relationship which necessitated that he face his sexual excitement and fear that Biff had released. Also, obviously, it was important, then and there, to prove to him that we could *protect* him from Biff, which also played a decisive role in the restoration of control and the relinquishing of the bizarre borderline behavior which masked the anxiety.

In summary, these samples of "emotional first aid on the spot" type of life-space interviews are aimed at demonstrating (1) the difference between this function and "clinical exploitation of life events" and (2) differences between some subfunctions of the "first aid" type. It should be obvious that all the classifications of function are anything but airtight and mutually exclusive, a warning that has been stressed, right along in this discussion. For example, both Chick *and* Jon were involved in panic reactions but Jon's was of a deeper and more devastating type and threw him into a more dangerous channel of defense. The reason for subclassifying them is only to trap the different quality of challenge to the interviewer and not to imply that true compartmentalization of ego pathology and interview function really exists in a rigid sense. This same fluidity exists, as has also been stressed, between the "clinical exploitation" and "first-aid type" of interview, too, and there are many interview moments where the two major functions are converged into a single broad interview effort or alternate with each other at different time segments of the interview. This should not surprise the classicist in therapy because the same procedural fluidity exists there, too. For instance, frequently the neurotic

has to be "soothed" in the very same hour as a dream is interpreted, or he has to be sympathized with or emphatically reassured of the therapist's continued affection and support even though he has death wishes toward the therapist. These are similar to the mixtures of "first aid" and "clinical exploitation" that exist on the terrain of the "life-space" approach.

Finally, it is necessary to point to a serious gap in the present discussion. Again because of space, it has not been possible to describe various critical factors that determine the ways in which the life-space interview is to be used. Issues such as *timing*, the particular *role* of the interviewer in the life of the interviewee, the *nature of the ongoing activity* within which the episode to be used for life-space interviewing may develop or even the *particular physical location* circumscribing such an event are all of vital importance. Beyond offering the assurance that the relevance of all such factors is assessed in relation to each instance of use of life-space interviewing, no more can be described.

IMPLICATIONS FOR PRACTICE

What, if any, of this is translatable for general agency or outpatient clinical social work practice? The fact that life-space interviewing has been developed and tested in a relatively restricted area of institutional or quasi-institutional design and that even in such settings there is much for us to relearn and modify makes this a most speculative and tentative issue.

First, it must be clearly stated that the moment we talk about outpatient practice we should be simultaneously shifting our sites to a different type of clientele than the severely disturbed children described thus far. For them the life-space approach holds no new answers in extramural settings. There is no cheap solution for the grim lethargy of the American community in providing a tragically needed expanding front of intensive inpatient treatment designs of a variety of types for severely disturbed children and adults.

Beyond this, for appropriate practice of a clinically oriented type with properly selected clientele, one general, underlying meaning of the life-space approach would involve the development of a *tool-conscious* interest in the ongoing life experience of the client and how various segments of it may be carried into the therapeutic situation more meaningfully. We must recognize that this has been going on silently for some years in agency practice. However, since many of the life experiences of the client are made known to the worker only through the clients reporting of them, there has been reluctance to rely on these as compared to other forms of more indigenous data about the client—fantasies, fragments of emotion, attitudes toward and perceptions of the worker, behavior in the interview situation, and so on. This is a real problem and cannot be dismissed. Still, much of what we do tactically with the client is governed by what we *believe* is achievable and reachable. If there had been no theory about the importance of dreams, no one would "dream" that such ephemeral and diffuse data could ever be recovered from the far-off corners of the psyche and converted into pragmatic materials for therapy either, and a whole magnificent skill area would not have developed. However, agency practice will, itself, have to define its adaptation of the life-space approach through appropriate experimentation and in advance of this nothing more specific should be said.

Leaving the typical agency setting and thinking of certain special, but still non-institutional designs of practice, life-space findings may hold more concrete applicatory meanings. In *detached worker* settings with the hard-to-reach and in *school social work practice,* a very clear entree for experimentation with these techniques is immediately visible. In such settings, the worker in varying ways and degrees is *already embedded in pieces of the client's life-space to begin with,* is perceived as such by the client, and has available for interview use life events in close proximity to their actual occurrence.

Finally, life-space interview findings remind us once again of the crying need for planned experimentation—and I mean in practice!—with combinations of group work and casework. What *did* happen to casework and group work as a clinical blend anyway? Fritz Redl, Gisela Konopka, and S. L. Slavson have written about it for the last twenty years, at least, in publications too numerous to mention. Yet today there is the most abject resignation in our field to the extinction of professional group work, a shaking of heads over the fact that "Group work is a dying field!" If child guidance and family casework agency practice were widened to articulate these two approaches, a badly needed gap would be filled in treatment resources for certain types of problems. Although they do not require institutional therapy, clients with such problems are still not reachable without making available for treatment life experiences that can be created on the group scene and are clinically useful there as well as in the interview situation. Shall we disentomb group work?

Perhaps most fascinating—and admittedly most speculative—is one last issue: what does life-space interview suggest for a *fact and theory* base in social work? Right now our field is exhibiting a frantic lionization of the social scientist in the parlor and a frosty tolerance of the backyard romance between the kitchen maid and the local psychoanalyst on the beat. This is symptomatic of our embarrassment over having buried ourselves (and *we* did it!) too deeply in the id. There may well be an equal and opposite danger that we may, via social science, launch ourselves too swiftly into space. In either case, the client is still left in the dark where he started, poor fellow! It seems to me that life-space data suggests that in *ego processes* are wrapped up the vital connections between the person and his "inner" and "outer" worlds. The ego seems to be a continuum with one end buried (but alive and "kicking"!) in the slumbering roots of the person and the other proliferated into a sensitive network involved in sleepless radarlike contact with the world around it. The resultant picture is that of an enormous, multifunctional plasticity about which we still know pitifully little. This is where we have found—in the "life-space circuit"—our most fascinating clinical challenge. Obviously, we have had to become involved most elaborately with special features—social and nonsocial—of the environmental terrain. However, *the ego is not its environment,* not even that part that becomes specialized for the task of dealing with it. It is always "attached" to the person who "carries" it—even when its "radar" is madly clicking in space with varying, and variable, influences from without.

In our "knowledge rush" toward social science, are we remembering that ego function is a *personal* function? The gap between the data of social science and individual psychology is by no means closed and it is treacherously possible to intermingle carelessly perceptions arising from these two discrete modes of observation and description. The view, for example, that the proper goal of social work is the "enhancement of social functioning" already seems to carry an imagery leaning toward peace with the offerings (and critiques of social work!) of social science. The auxiliary concepts that are lined up with this goal-concept: *role, interaction, environment,* also speak out for this orientation. What is the view of the person that is coming out of this? It is a view of man as *social-man* as opposed to *id-man.* Ego psychology will not, in a manner of speaking, "have" this. The ego—as a function of mind—is no more "loyal" to social-man than it is to id-man. In short, the type of involvement that social work is developing with social science may leave us—as did our handling of psychoanalysis—with a *half-man.* It portends a violation of the concept of the *total person.* If, as seems to be the case, a smooth conceptual model for the determinants of the total person are not yet deducible from social science and individual psychology, this is our proper cross to bear and, operationally speaking, our practical functioning in relation to the client world must reflect, clumsy though it may seem, a tortuous fidelity to two oracles instead of one.

Notes

1. Fritz Redl, "Strategy and Techniques of the Life-Space Interview," *American Journal of Orthopsychiatry,* Vol. 28, No. 1 (January 1959).

2. Redl first used the term "marginal" instead of "life space" for these interviews. The reasons for this shift are interesting but not crucial to this paper. One reason, as Redl wryly puts it: "The term marginal lost the clarity of its meaning besides the low-status meaning the term 'marginal' seems to hold for some people."

3. Fritz Redl and David Wineman, *Controls from Within* (Glencoe, Ill.: The Free Press, 1951).

4. Fritz Redl, "Strategy and Techniques of the Life Space Interview," *op. cit.*

Joel Vernick, "Illustrations of Strategy Problems in Life Space Interviewing Around Situations of Behavioral Crises," paper presented at the 1957 Annual Meeting of the American Orthopsychiatric Association.

Allen T. Dittmann and Howard L. Kitchener, "Life Space Interviewing and Individual Play Therapy: A Comparison of Techniques," *American Journal of Orthopsychiatry,* Vol. 29, No. 1 (January 1959).

William C. Morse and Edna R. Small, "Group Life Space Interviewing in a Therapeutic Camp," *American Journal of Orthopsychiatry,* Vol. 29, No. 1 (January 1959).

5. William Morse and David Wineman, "Group Interviewing in a Camp for Disturbed Boys," *The Journal of Social Issues,* Vol. 13, No. 1 (1957). Also, for the interested, this issue carries several articles on the University of Michigan camp and its operation.

6. All campers' names are pseudonyms.

7. Fritz Redl, "Strategy and Techniques of the Life Space Interview," *op. cit.*

8. Throughout this article I am following the nomenclature of the life-space interview and its major as well as subfunctions originated by Redl and appearing in his article "Strategy and Techniques of the Life-Space Interview," *op. cit.,* and also, in part, in our joint volume, *Controls from Within, op. cit.*

9. The term "delusional" is used to connote a kind of persistent, perceptual distortion of a somewhat persecutory type which is frequently found in impulse-disordered children. Since, however, many of them have really been badly handled by the adult world, this is not classically paranoid. Yet in treating the "good" adult as though he were the same as the "bad," they commit a delusional error.

10. All examples are drawn from the University of Michigan Fresh Air Camp experience of 1958. In each instance the writer was the interviewer except where otherwise specified. Each interview sample is the product of postinterview "selective" recall. Both individual and group interviews are included and will be identified as such.

11. A complicated form of verbal teasing by accusing each others' mothers of obscene sex practices.

12. The unspoken, but understood ending to this expletive is "Yer mammy is a *whore.*"

13. Fritz Redl, "Strategy and Techniques of the Life Space Interview," *op. cit.*

8.2 Behavioral Support for Students with Severe Disabilities:

Functional Assessment and Comprehensive Intervention

Robert H. Horner
Edward G. Carr

Behavioral support for students with severe disabilities has undergone dramatic advances in the past 15 years. The goals of effective behavioral support, as well as the procedures for reaching those goals, have broadened. Two central advances have been procedures for conducting functional assessment and the design of comprehensive interventions. The research foundation for these advances, implications for clinicians, and future research directions are presented.

The need for effective behavioral support continues to be intense. Problem behaviors, such as aggression (hitting, biting, kicking); self-injury (head banging, self-biting); pica; and property destruction and disruption (screaming, throwing, pounding), have been a major cause of exclusion for students with severe disabilities (Reichle, 1990). Without effective behavioral support, students who exhibit problem behaviors face educational isolation, vocational isolation, community isolation, social isolation, medical risk, and exposure to highly intrusive forms of control and treatment (National Institutes of Health, 1989). Although we are far from delivering a technology that is effective for all students, recent advances in behavioral support have had a tremendous impact on the ability of teachers, parents, and community clinicians to support students with severe disabilities and problem behaviors (Carr et al., 1994; Durand, 1990; L. K. Koegel, R. L. Koegel, & Dunlap, 1996; Lehr & Brown, 1996). These advances have occurred in part due to the careful construction of effective intervention procedures and in part due to a recasting of the focus of behavioral support. Behavioral support for students with severe disabilities is far more than a process of reducing problem behaviors by rewarding desired behavior and punishing (or ignoring) undesirable behavior. To a very great extent, effective behavioral support is about engineering of settings (schools, homes, workplaces) so that problem be-

haviors become less likely. In addition, the teaching of new (socially appropriate) skills has become an integral part of behavioral support. If behavioral support is to result in both reduction in problem behavior and substantive change in how the child lives/learns, then the range of procedures we use must be equally expansive. The outcomes expected from behavior support are much higher than in the past, and past technology is adjusting to these expanded expectations. This article focuses on the impact of two key developments influencing the design and implementation of effective behavioral support: (a) the use of *functional assessment* to guide clinical intervention and (b) the growing emphasis on *comprehensive interventions.*

FUNCTIONAL ASSESSMENT

Functional Assessment Defined

Functional assessment is a method for identifying the variables that reliably predict and maintain problem behavior. The variables consist of consequences (i.e., the purpose, intent, function, motivation, or goal of the behavior, with all these terms being roughly synonymous); antecedents, or discriminative stimuli (i.e., the cues that trigger the behavior); and setting events (i.e., the broad context that influences the likelihood that a specific cue will trigger problem behavior). To illustrate, consider a young girl with autism who sometimes bangs her head when her favorite toy is out of reach. Her mother responds to the self-injurious behavior by providing her with the toy. The antecedent for the girl's self-injurious behavior is "toy out of reach." The consequence of the behavior is "mother provides toy." As noted, however, self-injury occurs only some of the time in the situation described. If the child has just played with the toy for 2 hours, then "toy out of reach" does not set off self-injury. Thus, "amount of time since toy was last played with" is an important setting event that influences whether "toy out of reach" will be more or less likely to trigger head-banging.

Two important implications can be derived from our description of functional assessment. First, the focus is on environmental events (i.e., antecedents, consequences, and setting events). Thus, rather than viewing problem behavior as the result of invisible, dynamic forces residing "within" the child, we see such behavior as the result of challenging social situations for which the problem behavior itself represents an attempted solution (e.g., in our earlier illustration, head-banging represents one way of getting your mother to provide the toy you want). Second, because environmental determinants are so important, intervention is not focused on "managing" or "controlling" the child, but on redesigning the environment and building new skills that make problem behavior irrelevant, inefficient, and ineffective in that environment. The problem behavior becomes irrelevant to the extent that those conditions that set the occasion for the problem behavior are not present (e.g., if toys are available). The problem behavior is inefficient if the child has an alternative (appropriate) way of obtaining the same reinforcer that typically is delivered following problem behaviors. And the problem behavior becomes ineffective to the extent that the typical reward for problem behaviors (e.g., attention, toys, activities, escape) is not provided.

The Function of Functional Assessment

A functional assessment is performed to improve the effectiveness and efficiency of an intervention. This is done through (a) understanding what maintains the problem behavior, (b) predicting when a problem behavior will and will not occur, (c) identifying ways to prevent occurrence of the problem behavior, and (d) designing procedures for responding to the problem behavior when it does occur.

Understanding the consequences that maintain a problem behavior is a key to building effective interventions. Examining consequences makes it possible to hypothesize the purpose of the behavior. Thus, in our earlier example, if the mother consistently provides toys contingent on self-injury but not at other times, then we would say that the likely purpose of the child's display of self-injury is to get the mother to provide the desired toys. Or, more technically, that toys are a positive reinforcer that maintains the self-injury.

Consider the second issue, prediction. By examining antecedents and setting events, it is possible to predict when problem behavior is most and least likely. Again, in our example, if the child has not had access to her favorite toys for a while (setting event) and these toys are currently out of reach (antecedent or discriminative stimulus), then we would predict that the problem behavior is likely to occur.

Combining our knowledge of prediction with our knowledge of what maintains the problem behavior enables us to develop prevention and intervention strategies. With respect to prevention, we could remove the antecedent (i.e., place the toys within the child's reach) and/or alter the setting event (i.e., immediately schedule play time with the preferred toys). The problem behavior should not occur now because we have removed the stimuli that set it off. Next, with respect to intervention, knowing that the purpose of self-injury is to get the mother to provide toys, we could teach the child to request toys, thereby giving her an alternative, more efficient strategy for achieving her goal. If head-banging did occur, it would be physically interrupted, toys would *not* be provided, and a prompt to use the new communication would be delivered. To the extent possible, head-banging would be made ineffective. In sum, the assessment information that pertains to understanding and prediction leads logically to the development of a multicomponent preventive and intervention strategy.

Information Obtained from a Functional Assessment

Thus far, we have described in general terms the role of antecedents, setting events, and consequences. Research allows us to be more specific.

Information About Consequences. Studies have shown that the consequences that maintain problem behavior fall into several different categories. There is an *attention-seeking pattern* wherein a person shows aggression or self-injury, for example, as a way of evoking attention, nurturance, and comfort from others (Carr & McDowell, 1980; Lovaas, Freitag, Gold, & Kassorla, 1965; Martin & Foxx, 1973). There is an *escape/avoidance* pattern wherein a person shows problem behavior in order to terminate or avoid unpleasant situations such as those involving difficult, boring, or arduous academic tasks (Carr & Newsom, 1985; Carr, Newsom, & Binkoff, 1976, 1980). Sometimes, problem behavior helps the individual to gain access to desired *tangible items* (foods, toys) and preferred activities, as illustrated earlier in our example of the girl who banged her head until her mother provided desired toys. There is also an *automatic reinforcement* pattern hypothesized to generate sensory reinforcers based on visual, auditory, tactile, and even gustatory stimulation (Favell, McGimsey, & Schell, 1982; R. L. Koegel & L. K. Koegel, 1989; Rincover, Cook, Peoples, & Packard, 1979; Rincover & Devaney, 1982). Thus, a young boy with mental retardation may flap his hands in front of his face because the behavior produces interesting stroboscopic light effects. *Social avoidance* is still another pattern. In this case, individuals appear to use problem behavior to avoid or terminate interactions with other people (Taylor & Carr, 1992a, 1992b). Finally, there is a presumed *biological reinforcement* pattern. Most notably, some instances of self-injury may function as a form of self-addicting behavior in that each episode of problem behavior results in the release of endogenous opiates into the bloodstream, effectively producing a biological high (Cataldo & Harris, 1982; Sandman, 1991).

For brevity, we speak of consequence patterns as if the person with the disability intentionally planned the aggressive behavior or self-injury with a view to achieving some specific goal. No one knows whether behavior is intentional or not. From research we do know, however, that the various categories of consequences described do appear to be related to maintaining problem behavior. Furthermore, a single behavior may be maintained by multiple functions. For example, aggression may be maintained by access to attention in one situation, escape from tasks in another situation, and access to tangibles (food) in yet a third situation (Day, Horner, & O'Neill, 1994; Haring & Kennedy, 1990; Smith, Iwata, Vollmer, & Zarcone, 1993). Therefore, functional assessment is useful not only because it identifies the categories of consequences that maintain problem behavior but also because it identifies how the consequences (purposes) for problem behavior vary from situation to situation. This information is useful in planning interventions because a teacher, for example, would want to know what purpose a problem behavior served in each different situation so as to be in a position to teach relevant and appropriate replacement behaviors, to change features of the situation in order to eliminate or minimize the maintaining consequences, and/or to seek medical expertise if the problem behavior appears to be biologically maintained.

Information About Antecedents (Discriminative Stimuli). Functional assessment also is useful be-

cause it provides information about the antecedents that trigger problem behavior. Of particular interest to teachers is the voluminous literature documenting the role of instructional demands in evoking aggressive and self-injurious behaviors (see, e.g., Carr & Durand, 1985; Horner, Day, Sprague, O'Brien, & Heathfield, 1991; Iwata, Dorsey, Slifer, Bauman, & Richman, 1982; Mace et al., 1988; Repp, Felce, & Barton, 1988; Wacker, Steege, Northup, Sasso, et al., 1990). In illustration, consider a demand involving a basic self-help skill such as dressing. In a typical case (Carr et al., 1980), the teacher presents the demand (e.g., "button up") and the child responds with high levels of aggressive behavior. However, when the teacher is not presenting the demands, the child is well behaved. The effect on the teacher's behavior is profound. The child trains the teacher to drop those demands associated with aggressive behavior and retain those associated with task compliance (Carr, Taylor, & Robinson, 1991).

Functional assessment can provide even more information than simply whether a demand per se will evoke problem behavior. Certain nuances of the teaching situation involving the presentation of task demands may be critical in predicting the occurrence of problem behavior. Thus, research has demonstrated that the specific nature of the task (e.g., whether it is gross motor or fine motor) may predict problem behavior (Dunlap, Kern-Dunlap, Clarke, & Robbins, 1991). Relatedly, it may not be the task demand that predicts problem behavior but rather instructional cues associated with the task, such as gestural and physical prompts (Carr & Carlson, 1993) and negative feedback (Kemp & Carr, 1995). Information about antecedents is important because it helps the teacher pinpoint those aspects of the instructional situation that will need to be modified or redesigned to avoid future problem behavior.

Information About Setting Events (Broad Contexts). Task demands, prompts, and negative feedback are all examples of discrete antecedents that occur in close temporal proximity to the problem behavior they evoke. A given demand may, however, evoke problem behavior one day but not the next. The explanation for this anomaly is that there are broader contextual influences (setting events) operating (Horner, Vaughn, Day, & Ard, 1996; Kantor, 1959; Michael, 1988, 1993). Setting events refer to classes of variables that can alter the likelihood that specific categories of antecedents will evoke specific categories of responses (Bijou & Baer, 1961). Although the precise relationship between setting events and problem behavior is only now beginning to be explored, the research literature suggests some promising leads as to which variables ought to be examined in a functional assessment (Horner et al., 1996). This information, in turn, could provide additional opportunities for intervention.

Setting events that influence problem behavior can be physical, social, or biological in nature. Physical factors include variables as diverse as environmental enrichment (Horner, 1980) and choice of transportation routes (Kennedy & Itkonen, 1993), as well as less researched factors such as temperature, humidity, noise level, and clothing comfort. Social factors include variables such as the presence or absence of specific people (Touchette, MacDonald, & Langer, 1985), classroom social structures (Repp & Karsh, 1992), crowding (Boe, 1977; McAfee, 1987), and sequencing of social activities (Brown, 1991). Finally, biological factors associated with problem behavior (Carr & Smith, 1995) include constipation (Gunsett, Mulick, Fernald, & Martin, 1989), sleep deprivation (O'Reilly, 1995), hunger (Vollmer & Iwata, 1991), allergies (Gardner, 1985), and middle ear infection (deLissovoy, 1963).

A teacher can use information about setting events to prevent problem behavior. Thus, knowing that a child is sensitive to high or low temperature (a physical setting event), a teacher can monitor room temperature to avoid extremes. If crowding (a social setting event) is at issue, then rearrangement of classroom space may be an important consideration. Finally, the presence of allergies or ear infections (biological setting events) in some children may alert the teacher to the need for close monitoring of these conditions and appropriate medical intervention.

How to Conduct a Functional Assessment

There are three generic methods for carrying out a functional assessment: interview, descriptive observation, and functional analysis.

Interview. Interviewing is the functional assessment method most commonly used by practitioners. The person doing the assessment interviews teachers, family members, or professionals who are most familiar with the individual in question. These people are asked to describe three things: (a) the physical description of the problem behavior, (b) the circumstances that predict occurrence and nonoccurrence of the problem behavior, and (c) the reaction that such behavior evokes from others (Carr et al., 1994; Durand, 1990).

One goal is to provide an operational definition of the problem behavior. Thus subjective definitions are avoided (e.g., "Billy gets angry") in favor of specific, objective descriptions (e.g., "Billy kicks, punches, and bites"). With respect to triggering stimuli, the interviewer asks questions about specific antecedents (e.g., the possible role of task demands, negative feedback, prompts, teasing by others) as well as specific setting events (e.g., noise level, crowding, illness). Finally, with respect to reactions from others, the interviewer asks questions about specific consequences of the behavior (e.g., whether the behavior is followed by task removal, suggesting escape motivation; whether the behavior causes the teacher to give the child a "good talking to," suggesting attention motivation; whether another child responds by surrendering a valued toy, suggesting tangible motivation).

Sometimes the interview process may be less conversational than what has just been described. That is, there also exist highly structured questionnaires and rating scales that help organize assessment more formally (e.g., Axelrod, 1987; Durand & Crimmins, 1988; O'Neill, Horner, Albin, Storey, & Sprague, 1990).

Interviews provide a major advantage and carry a major disadvantage as tools for functional assessment. The advantage is that they allow quick review of a huge number of antecedents *and* consequences that may influence a problem behavior. An interview allows the opportunity to identify which of these many events are relevant in a particular situation. The interview focuses on patterns of behavior across the entire day and over a wide range of conditions. It would be impractical to try to observe or test all of the conditions that can be sampled through the interview. In most cases, a small number of factors are important for a particular problem, but without attending to a large list, it is hard to tease out what is important for an individual. The interview provides a good starting point to identify those conditions in which a problem behavior is most likely, those in which it is least likely, and those consequences that may be maintaining the problem behavior. From this initial interview information we can narrow the number of events that warrant more detailed consideration, and a basic hypothesis can be developed. The hypothesis defines the problem behaviors, the events that predict/trigger the problem behaviors, and the consequences that maintain the problem behavior. In a practical sense, the hypothesis defines the *context* in which problem behaviors occur.

The major disadvantage of using interviews is that they rely on the subjective impressions of people, not on systematic observation of behavior. Given the potential for inaccuracy, impressions must be viewed with great restraint. The time saved by using interviews may be lost if the information from the interview is inaccurate. As a result, it is a basic professional standard to expect all hypotheses developed via interview procedures to be validated through some form of descriptive observation or functional analysis (Carr et al., 1994; Durand, 1990; O'Neill et al., 1990).

Descriptive Observation. Systematic observation of the person can provide extremely valuable information about (a) the context and triggers that covary with a problem behavior, (b) the intensity duration and form of the problem behavior, and (c) the events that follow (and presumably maintain) the problem behavior. Observations typically involve the use of data collection forms organized around events that precede and follow problem behaviors (Bijou, Peterson, & Ault, 1968; Doss & Reichle, 1989; Touchette et al., 1985). The collection of functional assessment observation data may require observations for a short period or across several days/ weeks. The results, however, offer a more objective opportunity to validate the hypotheses developed during initial interviews. There are three important reasons why direct observation data are collected after an interview: (a) Direct observation typically generates more detailed information about the triggers and social reactions for problem behavior; (b) information derived from interviews is sometimes inaccurate; and (c) important variables, not discussed during the interview, are sometimes uncovered during the course of direct observation.

An interview may suggest that presentation of demands evokes problem behavior. However, after following up with direct observation, one may discover that it is not just demands per se that are important but associated features such as voice tone (harsh vs. soft), pacing (fast vs. slow), facial expression (calm vs. agitated), and so on. These subtleties may not come out in the interview, but the improved level of detail obtained from direct observation often proves beneficial in designing effective and relevant interventions. Second, the interviewee may provide inaccurate information. For example, it is not uncommon for a teacher to say that she does not attend to problem behavior. However, a follow-up with direct observation reveals that she does (e.g., the teacher may say to the child, "Jim, I hope I didn't see you hit Sue. I'm not going to talk to you anymore if you keep doing that, and no one will want to be your friend. You have to be more mature"). The teacher's perception is that her speech constitutes an implied withdrawal of attention, but in fact it constitutes one-to-one attention. Finally, because of the influence of child effects on teacher behavior (Carr et al., 1991), certain variables may not be discussed in the interview because they have been withdrawn by the teacher. Thus, if vocabulary building is highly associated with child aggression, the teacher may unwittingly avoid further outbursts by temporarily dropping this task from the curriculum. Then, if an interviewer asks what variables currently set off problem behavior, the teacher may overlook vocabulary tasks because they are no longer present. Direct observation may uncover this variable because other adults (e.g., substitute teachers, parents, other professionals) may be observed to introduce the task occasionally, with resulting episodes of aggression.

Descriptive observation has been considerably refined since its introduction several decades ago (Bijou et al., 1968). Today, a variety of data collection forms and measurement procedures are available that make it relatively easy to collect information about the events that trigger and maintain problem behavior (Arndorfer, Miltenberger, Woster, Rortvedt, & Gaffaney, 1994; Carr & Carlson, 1993; Lalli & Goh, 1993; Mace & Lalli, 1991; O'Neill et al., 1990; Touchette et al., 1985). Like interviews, the end product of descriptive observation is development of hypotheses about when, where, and why the problem behavior occurs, hypotheses that can be used to devise effective and efficient interventions.

Functional Analysis. Functional analysis involves systematic manipulation of specific variables to see whether they influence problem behavior. In other words, functional analysis constitutes a formal experiment in contrast to passive direct observation. In addition to being a useful assessment tool, functional analysis is the primary method used by researchers to demonstrate basic behavioral principles. When the results of interview and/or direct observation are ambiguous, only a formal functional analysis can provide data that definitively identify the critical controlling variables.

One prototype for functional analysis was developed by Iwata et al. (1982). Their method involves four experimental conditions designed to identify specific motivational variables: (a) a condition in which demands are withdrawn contingent on problem behavior (subsequent increases in problem behavior suggest escape motivation); (b) a condition in which attention is made contingent on problem behavior (subsequent increases in problem behavior suggest attention-seeking motivation); (c) an "alone" condition in which toys and people are absent (subsequent increases in problem behavior suggest that the behavior is nonsocially motivated, possibly self-stimulatory in nature or biologically motivated); and (d) a play condition involving access to toys, frequent attention for nonproblem behavior, and no demands (this condition serves as a control for sensory reinforcement, attention, and escape, and would be expected to produce minimal problem behavior). Others (e.g., Carr & Durand, 1985; Vollmer, Marcus, Ringdahl, & Roane, 1995) have explored a fifth condition in which tangible reinforcement is made contingent on problem behavior (subsequent increases in problem behavior suggest tangible motivation). When a student is observed in several of these conditions, one often finds that problem behavior is markedly elevated in one condition (e.g., during demands) but not during other conditions. This highly differentiated pattern of responding confirms the maintaining reinforcer and can help teachers focus on those variables needed to design an effective intervention. Thus, knowing that a child's problem behavior is escape motivated rather than attention motivated would imply the need to alter the demand situation rather than the need to focus on level of teacher attention.

One practical issue relevant to functional analysis is that it can be time-consuming. Importantly, in response to this issue, methods have been developed that make it possible to gather useful information about controlling variables in as little as 90 minutes (Wacker, Steege, Northup, Reimers, et al., 1990). In about half the cases, assessment information derived from brief analysis produces clear patterns that lead to the design of effective interventions. This outcome constitutes a good beginning in terms of forming a basis for the further development of brief analysis procedures. Recently, Vollmer et al. (1995) have proposed a model for functional analysis that integrates brief functional analysis procedures and progressively more controlled experimental procedures. Their approach is to conduct an efficient analysis and determine if a clear pattern of responding emerges. If no clear pattern is identified, then more controlled and more complicated analysis is implemented in progressive steps until there is sufficiently clear data to direct an intervention. This approach holds great promise and is consistent with a growing theme of matching the complexity of the functional assessment

procedures to the complexity of the problem (Harding, Wacker, Cooper, Millard, & Jensen-Kovalan, 1994; Mace & Lalli, 1991; Mace & Roberts, 1993).

Issues in the Use of Functional Assessment

The importance of functional assessment is so well established that it is now expected professional practice and a required element in the regulations of many states (Florida, New York, Minnesota, Pennsylvania, Oregon, California, Washington). There remain, however, a number of questions about how best to use functional assessment.

1. What type of assessment is best? Each type of functional assessment has its limitations. Ultimately, however, the answer to the question depends on one's goals. If the goal is to make a definitive demonstration of what antecedent and consequent variables evoke and maintain the problem behavior, then only a formal functional analysis will do. Definitive demonstrations are typically required, however, only in very complex cases or for research articles that systematically examine a principle of behavior. In community settings, functional analysis is often impractical because of the level of expertise it requires, the time commitment involved, and the disruption it causes when variables that set off problem behavior are purposely introduced to test hypotheses. Direct observation and interview require less expertise to carry out, are not as time intensive, and do not generate problem behavior. Unfortunately, these less rigorous assessment procedures may produce ambiguous results (e.g., interviews and observations of aggression in a classroom may not make it clear whether the aggression is motivated by escape from tasks or attention from the teacher). Only a functional analysis can separate the effects of the different variables when other approaches produce ambiguous results. The message, then, is that the precision of a functional analysis needs to be weighed against the greater efficiency of direct observation and interview. At present, the only rational course of action is to weigh the need to balance precision and efficiency on a case-by-case basis. Given a clear hypothesis developed from interviews and supported by direct observation data, it may be appropriate to move to the intervention. If, however, interview information is conflicting and direct observation results are equivocal, it may be appropriate to conduct a formal functional analysis. In most cases, an interview alone does not constitute an appropriate functional assessment.

2. How often must one conduct assessments? Many people assume, mistakenly, that assessment occurs only before the initial intervention. The limitation of restricting assessment in this manner is that it fails to consider the possibility that, over time, it is typical for schedules, curricula, staff, and composition of the student body to change. Each of these changes, in turn, may precipitate new problem situations that set off aggression, self-injury, and other difficulties. Therefore, functional assessment should be an ongoing process and not simply an initial activity. In most cases, the ongoing assessment involves an efficient system of direct observation during the intervention. The key is that this ongoing data collection includes not just monitoring the occurrence of problem behaviors, but also ongoing monitoring of setting events, triggers, and consequences. If the intervention is not effective, the direct observation information should be useful in redesigning a modified intervention.

3. What level of detail is needed in a functional assessment? If a functional assessment is to improve the effectiveness and efficiency of an intervention, it should provide information that is as specific as possible. It is extremely useful, for example, to learn that screams and bites are maintained by escape from tasks. But it is even more useful to learn what it is about the tasks that make them aversive. A functional assessment should provide information about maintaining consequences at three levels. Level 1 indicates if the problem behavior is maintained by positive or negative reinforcement (*obtaining* social, physical, or material consequences vs. *escape/avoiding* social, physical, or material consequences). Level 2 defines whether the consequence involves social, physical, or material/activity consequences. Level 3 defines what features of the consequences are functional. For example, if a task is aversive, is that because the task is long, physically effortful, associated with failure, boring, or unlikely to lead to reinforcers? Similarly, if attention is reinforcing, is it attention from peers as well as adults? Is there a difference between positive and negative attention? The point is that in developing an intervention, the more detail obtained about the functional features of the trigger stimuli and maintaining consequence, the better.

4. Where should functional assessment information be collected? Should functional assessments be done in the natural classroom, home, or community, or should they be conducted in clinics where greater control can be maintained during data collection?

Cooper, Wacker, Sasso, Reimers, and Donn (1990) have demonstrated that in some instances clinic-based assessments produce very similar outcomes to functional assessments conducted in homes. In general, we believe that assessments conducted under natural conditions provide a better opportunity to observe the natural trigger stimuli and natural consequences that are associated with the problem behavior. Natural conditions may also prove more effective for identifying relevant setting events. At the same time, clinic-based assessments may offer the opportunity for more precise control over events and more safety when one is assessing extremely dangerous behaviors.

5. How can the process by which clinicians move from the functional assessment information to interventions be clarified? If the purpose of a functional assessment is to improve the effectiveness and efficiency of the intervention, then clear procedures should exist for moving from the assessment data to interventions. At this time, the field has a significant number of examples where functional assessment was followed by an effective intervention, but little more than conceptual guidelines for moving from assessment data to clinical interventions (Carr & Carlson, 1993; Horner, O'Neill, & Flannery, 1993; Kemp & Carr, 1995; Mace & Lalli, 1991; Pyles & Bailey, 1990). A significant issue hindering application of functional assessment procedures is the need for a more clearly defined process for using functional assessment information in the construction of comprehensive interventions.

COMPREHENSIVE INTERVENTIONS

The use of comprehensive interventions has long been the goal of teachers and clinicians, but only recently has a coherent technology for designing comprehensive interventions been established (Carr et al., 1994; Durand, 1990; Kemp & Carr, 1995; L. K. Koegel et al., 1996). The goal of a comprehensive intervention is to produce rapid, durable, generalized reduction in problem behaviors while improving the individual's success at home, at school, in the community, or in the work environment. An intervention is comprehensive when it (a) addresses all problem behaviors performed by an individual; (b) is driven by the functional assessment; (c) is applied throughout the day; (d) blends multiple intervention procedures (change in structure, instruction, consequences): and (e) incorporates procedures that are consistent with the values, skills, and resources of the implementors.

Interventions conducted for research purposes often focus on a narrow, tightly controlled context and involve the manipulation of a small number of variables. This is appropriate, and necessary, for detailed examination of specific procedures and for defining the principles of behavior that serve as the foundation for applied behavior analysis. Interventions conducted to assist people, however, need to be more comprehensive in scope, format, and function. They need to be focused on improving the living options of the individual as well as reducing problem behavior. They need to focus on behavior change that is not only clinically important, but also durable and generalized across the full set of conditions in a person's life (O'Neill et al., 1990). Comprehensive interventions combine multiple procedures to address the different problem behaviors, different maintaining functions, and different problem routines a person presents.

The development of comprehensive interventions is at once consistent with recent research on functional assessment and an extension of current interventive research. Demonstrations of comprehensive, multicomponent interventions exist (Berkman & Meyer, 1988; Horner, Close, et al., 1996; Lucyshyn, Olson, & Horner, 1995), but we are just beginning to understand factors such as how multiple intervention procedures interact—for example, functional communication training coupled with extinction (Lalli, Casey, & Kates, 1995; Vollmer et al., 1995) or curriculum revision coupled with task instruction and extinction (Dunlap et al., 1991). We also lack information about the variables that influence the maintenance and generalization of response reduction (Durand & Carr, 1991). As comprehensive intervention research develops, we should expect to see a renewed interest in systematic demonstrations of multicomponent interventions changing multiple patterns of behavior. From these demonstrations we will build the more precise experimental research efforts, just as from the early demonstrations of individual interventions came the more rigorous, experimental analysis of individual procedures.

We can also expect to see continued growth in the array of procedures that are viewed as appropriate for inclusion in comprehensive interventions. Given that the expectation is not that a single procedure must produce the entire clinical effect, there is a growing interest in procedures that can be combined to improve the effectiveness of comprehensive intervention. Four examples of this broadening in behavior support procedures are worthy of note: (a) functional communication training, (b) curricular revision, (c) setting event manipulations, and (d) choice.

Functional communication training involves teaching students a specific communication response that (a) is socially appropriate, (b) produces the same effect (escape for aversive situations or obtaining desired objects/activities), and (c) is as or more efficient than the problem behavior (i.e., requires less time, effort, or repetitions; Carr & Durand, 1985; Durand & Carr, 1991). Functional communication training requires that a functional assessment has identified the conditions that evoke and maintain the problem behavior(s). This information is essential for selecting the new communication to be taught. The intervention, however, always includes *teaching* a new communication skill (often combined with efforts to minimize reinforcement of the problem behavior). Carr and Durand described an example of functional communication training with young children with autism. The functional assessment indicated some problem behavior maintained by escape from demands, and other problem behavior maintained by attention from adults. The children were then taught socially appropriate communication skills to request escape from tasks and to request attention from adults. The results documented substantive reductions in the problem behaviors when functionally equivalent communication skills were taught. This basic approach has been applied successfully with a wide range of problem behaviors, individuals, and contexts (Bird, Dores, Moniz, & Robinson, 1989; Fisher et al., 1993; Lalli, Browder, Mace, & Brown, 1993; Lalli et al., 1995; Wacker, Steege, Northup, Sasso, et al., 1990). More recently, Wacker and his colleagues have demonstrated that this procedure can be used by teachers and families of young students with disabilities to produce change in school and home (Cooper et al., 1990; Derby et al., 1992; Harding et al., 1994). Functional communication training stands as a good example of one approach to making problem behavior inefficient by improving the power and competence of the student. This procedure uses our technology of instruction (teaching the new communication skill) with functional assessment procedures to produce a desirable behavior change.

Curricular revision is a second example of the expanding array of intervention procedures. If a functional assessment indicates that problem behaviors are maintained by avoiding certain instructional tasks, then an element of the comprehensive support plan may involve changing the curriculum (tasks).

The logic involves identifying the features of the task that are aversive and changing the task to minimize these aversive features. Dunlap and his colleagues (Dunlap et al., 1991) have demonstrated the power of this procedure by altering features such as the length of the task, the clarity of instructions, and the practical outcomes of the task, and by documenting significant reduction in problem behavior. It is important to note that curricular revision does *not* mean simply removing all difficult tasks and replacing them with simple tasks. Dunlap et al. emphasized that instructional goals should not be compromised, but that efforts should be made to define the specific features of the tasks that are aversive, and curricular revisions should be made to alter those features.

Setting events are an area of behavioral support that is just beginning to receive practical attention. Recent research (Carr, Reeve, & Magito-McLaughlin, 1996; Horner et al., 1996; Kennedy & Itkonen, 1993; Vollmer & Iwata, 1991) suggests that setting events influence problem behaviors (e.g., headaches or allergies increase the likelihood of problem behaviors) and that intervention strategies can be implemented as part of a comprehensive plan of support to reduce the effects of setting events (Dadson & Horner, 1993). It is unlikely that setting event interventions will prove to be powerful, singular intervention strategies, but it appears very likely that they will be important elements of broader, comprehensive plans of support. An example of the possible role of setting events in comprehensive interventions has been reported by Horner and Day (1995), who described a young man with autism who engaged in kicking during instructional tasks. The functional assessment suggested that (a) kicking was escape motivated and (b) the likelihood of kicking was much greater if earlier in the day one of his preferred events had been canceled. Loss of a preferred activity functioned as a setting event that increased the aversive features of instruction and increased the likelihood that he would kick to escape instruction. The researchers first instituted an intervention in which any cancellation of preferred activities was followed by (a) formal rescheduling of the activity and (b) a period of reviewing the activities on his daily schedule. These steps were recommended by staff as procedures for neutralizing the effect of canceling a preferred activity (e.g., neutralizing the setting event). Results documented that the neutralizing routine was effective at reducing kicking during instruction. Following this demonstration, the staff added curricular revision and functional communication training procedures

to build a comprehensive intervention that not only reduced problem behaviors during instruction but also increased active engagement. One message from this report is that setting event manipulations may be important elements in comprehensive interventions.

Student choice is another element of comprehensive behavioral interventions that may help to make an intervention more effective. Making personal choices has long been identified as a valued feature of individual supports (Bannerman, Sheldon, Sherman, & Harchik, 1990; Shevin & Klein, 1984). Recent research, however, suggests that expanding personal choices also is an effective strategy for reducing problem behaviors (Bambara, Koger, Katzer, & Davenport, 1995; Dunlap et al., 1994; Dyer, Dunlap, & Winterling, 1990; Vaughn & Horner, in press). Student choice appears to reduce problem behaviors through two mechanisms. The first is that choices allow the student to avoid more aversive situations and gain larger rewards (Mace, Neef, Shade, & Mauro, 1996; Newton, Horner, & Lund, 1991; Parsons, Reid, Reynolds, & Bumgarner, 1990; Reid & Parsons, 1991; Wacker, Wiggins, Fowler, & Berg, 1988). When given a choice, the student will select the most preferred (or least unpleasant) option. This reduces the likelihood that the student will be presented with challenges that elicit problem behaviors.

A second mechanism that may make choices effective in reducing problem behaviors has been described by Dunlap et al. (1994), who suggested that when an activity is chosen by a student, it is less likely to evoke problem behaviors than if the same activity is selected and presented by the teacher. Choosing may reduce the aversive properties of tasks and activities. A task that evokes strong escape-motivated problem behavior when teacher selected appears less likely to evoke such behavior when it is student selected. At least two additional reports support this finding (Brigham, 1979; Vaughn & Horner, in press).

The major message from research on choice is not that all students should be allowed to choose all elements of their curriculum, but that (a) teaching students with severe disabilities how to make choice and (b) incorporating choice options into daily schedules may hold promise as useful elements of comprehensive behavioral interventions.

Designing comprehensive interventions continues to be a challenge. Functional assessments provide directive information, but they do not dictate specific intervention strategies. In fact, one of the important understandings for behavioral programming is that there is never only one intervention that is appropriate. It is much more likely that many different intervention packages could be implemented with scientific acceptability and practical results. The real goal is to select the complement of procedures (e.g., setting event manipulations, curricular revisions, communication training, escape extinction, reinforcement) that are technically consistent with the functional assessment, yet practical, given the resources and constraints of the school (Albin, Lucyshyn, Horner, & Flannery, 1996). Carr and Carlson (1993) and Kemp and Carr (1995) provided two examples of comprehensive interventions that were systematically developed based on functional assessment information. In each case, structural features of the environment were modified, new skills were taught, and consequences were arranged to minimize reinforcement of problem behaviors and maximize reinforcement of preferred behaviors. These studies do not allow separation of the independent effects of any single element of the comprehensive intervention, but the assumption is that the combined use of the procedures (a) increases the likelihood that they will be implemented with fidelity, (b) increases the likelihood that behavior change will occur, and (c) improves the generalization and maintenance of positive effects.

Considerable work needs yet to be done on how to build comprehensive interventions (Horner et al., 1993) and on the variables that result in durable, generalized changes in problem behavior. It is quite likely, for example, that teaching general case communication skills in a functional communication paradigm could result in reduction in problem behavior well beyond the conditions in which instruction occurred. We anticipate that a major focus of behavioral support research in the near future will address procedures for maintaining and generalizing reduced patterns of problem behavior.

SUMMARY

Problem behaviors continue to pose an intense barrier for students with severe disabilities. Encouraging gains have been documented over the past 15 years, and these gains are improving both our theoretical understanding of problem behavior and our clinical ability to help students. The practical use of functional assessment in schools, the development of a wider range of intervention procedures, and the move toward comprehensive intervention packages are having an important impact. A vast gap remains, however, between what is known about exemplary behavioral support and the actual delivery of support in schools. To narrow this gap a research agenda is needed with four areas of emphasis: (a) basic research, (b) programmatic research, (c) policy-level research, and (d) dissemination.

Basic Research

Behavioral support has grown from initial efforts to understand the variables that influence the likelihood of problem behavior. This work has been of tremendous value, but a great deal needs yet to be learned about issues such as (a) the maintenance and generalization of response reduction, (b) the role of physiological arousal in the elicitation and duration of problem behaviors, (c) the role of response classes in behavior change, (d) the effects of the matching law and behavioral momentum in efforts to reduce problem behaviors, (e) the effects of biochemical interventions, and (f) the effects of independent versus combined intervention procedures.

Efforts to understand when, where, and why problem behaviors occur has led directly to effective intervention procedures. Now is not the time to assume that we have learned all we need about the mechanisms influencing problem behavior. Now is a time to continue to mature our emerging science.

Programmatic Research

Programmatic research is driven by socially important dependent variables. As the dependent variables associated with behavioral support have widened, so has the need for a wider range of programmatic research. Descriptive examples are needed that document the effects of interventions on the multiple outcomes that make behavior change lead to life-style change. Reduction in problem behavior, acquisition of appropriate behavior, increases in activity options, change in social relationships, and improved health and safety are but a few of the simultaneous outcome measures that should be monitored. Programmatic research is needed to document that intervention procedures can be combined successfully, that clinicians and families are willing and able to implement the procedures, and that the results are durable, over socially important time periods.

Policy Research

In addition to documenting the effectiveness of specific interventions, research is needed at a scale that has relevance for broad policy (Biglan & Hayes, 1996). It is important to examine the variables that affect the behavior of an individual student, but it is also important to examine the variables that make entire schools effective (Sugai & Horner, 1994; Walker et al., 1996). Policy research moves the unit of analysis from the individual to the system. Research at this level should build on success with individuals and should include (a) cost–benefit assessments, (b) analysis of the fidelity with which broad-scale interventions can be implemented, and (c) careful measurement of outcomes. Work referenced by Walker, Colvin, and Ramsey (1995) on violence in schools should serve as a model for the level of research that will elevate behavioral support from a practical technology to an embedded element of schools, workplaces, homes, and communities.

Dissemination

Research also is needed on how best to transfer the technology of behavioral support. Existing strategies of personnel preparation will be valuable, but insufficient, to disseminate behavior support systems on a broad scale. Greater attention needs to be paid to the matching of behavioral interventions to the skills, values, and resources of people in a particular setting. If behavioral support is effective, it works for everyone in a context, not just for the student with problem behaviors. Greater attention is needed on the instruction on behavioral systems in real-world contexts rather than in simulations. Both effectiveness and efficiency of dissemination need to be better understood. At this time, it is too easy to disseminate "information" about behavioral support without disseminating the technology of behavioral support.

Together, efforts to both refine and transfer the emerging technology of behavioral support hold promise that our schools and communities can become environments where all students can be successful.

References

Albin, R. W., Lucyshyn, J. M., Horner, R. H., & Flannery, K. B. (1996). Contextual fit for behavioral support plans: A model for "goodness-of-fit." In L. K. Koegel, R. L. Koegel, & G. Dunlap (Eds.), *Positive behavioral support: Including people with difficult behavior in the community* (pp. 81–98). Baltimore: Brookes.

Arndorfer, R. E., Miltenberger, R. E., Woster, S. H., Rortvedt, A. K., & Gaffeney, T. (1994). Home-based descriptive and experimental analysis of problem behaviors in children. *Topics in Early Childhood Special Education, 14,* 64–87.

Axelrod, S. (1987). Functional and structural analysis of behavior: Approaches leading to reduced use of punishment procedures. *Research in Developmental Disabilities, 8,* 165–178.

Bambara, L. M., Koger, F., Katzer, T., & Davenport, T. A. (1995). Embedding choice in the context of daily routines: An experimental case study. *Journal of the Association for Persons with Severe Handicaps, 20,* 185–195.

Bannerman, D. J., Sheldon, J. B., Sherman, J. A., & Harchik, A. E. (1990). Balancing the right to habilitation with the right to personal liberties: The rights of people with developmental disabilities to eat too many doughnuts and take a nap. *Journal of Applied Behavioral Analysis, 23,* 79–89.

Berkman, K. A., & Meyer, L. H. (1988). Alternative strategies and multiple outcomes in the remediation of severe self-injury: Going "all out" nonaversively. *Journal of the Association for Persons with Severe Handicaps, 13,* 76–86.

Biglan, A., & Hayes, S. C. (1996). Should the behavioral sciences become more pragmatic? The case for functional contextualism in research on human behavior. *Applied and Preventive Psychology, 5,* 47–57.

Bijou, S. W., & Baer, D. M. (1961). *Child development I: A systematic and empirical theory.* Englewood Cliffs, NJ: Prentice-Hall.

Bijou, S. W., Peterson, R. F., & Ault, M. H. (1968). A method to integrate description and experimental field studies at the level of data and empirical concepts. *Journal of Applied Behavior Analysis, 1,* 175–191.

Bird, F., Dores, P. A., Moniz, D., & Robinson, J. (1989). Reducing severe aggressive and self-injurious behaviors with functional communication training. *American Journal on Mental Retardation, 94,* 37–48.

Boe, R. B. (1977). Economical procedures for the reduction of aggression in a residential setting. *Mental Retardation, 15,* 25–28.

Brigham, T. A. (1979). Some effects of choice on academic performance. In L. C. Perlmutter & R. A. Monty (Eds.), *Choice and perceived control* (pp. 131–141). Hillsdale, NJ: Erlbaum.

Brown, F. (1991). Creative daily scheduling: A nonintrusive approach to challenging behaviors in community residences. *Journal of the Association for Persons with Severe Handicaps, 16,* 75–84.

Carr, E. G., & Carlson, J. I. (1993). Reduction of severe behavior problems in the community through a multicomponent treatment approach. *Journal of Applied Behavior Analysis, 26,* 157–172.

Carr, E. G., & Durand, V. M. (1985). Reducing behavior problems through functional communication training. *Journal of Applied Behavior Analysis, 18,* 111–126.

Carr, E. G., Levin, L., McConnachie, G., Carlson, J. I., Kemp, D. C., & Smith, C. E. (1994). *Communication-based intervention for problem behavior. A user's guide for producing positive change.* Baltimore: Brookes.

Carr, E. G., & McDowell, J. J. (1980). Social control of self-injurious behavior of organic etiology. *Behavior Therapy, 11,* 402–409.

Carr, E. G., & Newsom, C. D. (1985). Demand-related tantrums: Conceptualization and treatment. *Behavior Modification, 9,* 403–426.

Carr, E. G., Newsom, C. D., & Binkoff, J. A. (1976). Stimulus control of self-destructive behavior in a psychotic child. *Journal of Abnormal Child Psychology, 4,* 139–153.

Carr, E. G., Newsom, C. D., & Binkoff, J. A. (1980). Escape as a factor in the aggressive behavior of two retarded children. *Journal of Applied Behavior Analysis, 13,* 101–117.

Carr, E. G., Reeve, C. E., & Magito-McLaughlin, D. (1996). Contextual influences on problem behavior in people with developmental disabilities. In L. K. Koegel, R. L. Koegel, & G. Dunlap (Eds.), *Positive behavioral support: Including people with difficult behavior in the community* (pp. 403–423). Baltimore: Brookes.

Carr, E. G., & Smith, C. E. (1995). Biological setting events for self-injury. *Mental Retardation and Developmental Disabilities Research Reviews, 1,* 94–98.

Carr, E. G., Taylor, J. C., & Robinson, S. (1991). The effects of severe behavior problems in children on the teaching behavior of adults. *Journal of Applied Behavior Analysis, 24,* 523–535.

Cataldo, M. F., & Harris, J. (1982). The biological basis for self-injury in the mentally retarded. *Analysis and Intervention in Developmental Disabilities, 2,* 21–39.

Cooper, L. J., Wacker, D. P., Sasso, G., Reimers, T. M., & Donn, L. K. (1990). Using parents as therapists to evaluate behavior of their children: Application to a tertiary diagnostic clinic. *Journal of Applied Behavior Analysis, 23,* 285–296.

Dadson, S., & Horner, R. H. (1993). Manipulating setting events to decrease problem behaviors: A case study. *Teaching Exceptional Children, 25,* 53–55.

Day, M., Horner, R. H., & O'Neill, R. E. (1994). Multiple functions of problem behaviors: Assessment and interventions. *Journal of Applied Behavior Analysis, 27,* 279–289.

deLissovoy, V. (1963). Head banging in early childhood: A suggested cause. *Journal of Genetic Psychology, 102,* 109–114.

Derby, K. M., Wacker, D. P., Sasso, G., Steege, M., Northup, J., Cigrand, K., & Asmus, J. (1992). Brief functional assessment techniques to evaluate aberrant behavior in an outpatient clinic: A summary of 79 cases. *Journal of Applied Behavior Analysis, 25,* 713–721.

Doss, S., & Reichle, J. (1989). Establishing communicative alternatives to the emission of socially motivated excess behavior: A review. *Journal of the Association for Persons with Severe Handicaps, 14,* 101–112.

Dunlap, G., Kern-Dunlap, L. K., Clarke, S., & Robbins, F. R. (1991). Functional assessment, curricular revision, and severe behavior problems. *Journal of Applied Behavior Analysis, 24,* 387–397.

Dunlap, G., dePerczel, M., Clarke, S., Wilson, D., Wright, S., White, R., & Gomez, A. (1994). Choice making and proactive behavioral support for students with emotional and behavioral challenges. *Journal of Applied Behavior Analysis, 27,* 505–518.

Durand, V. M. (1990). *Severe behavior problems: A functional communication training approach.* New York: Guilford.

Durand, V. M., & Carr, E. C. (1991). Functional communication training to reduce challenging behavior: Maintenance and application in new settings. *Journal of Applied Behavior Analysis, 24,* 251–264.

Durand, V. M., & Crimmins, D. B. (1988). Identifying the variables maintaining self-injurious behavior. *Journal of Autism and Developmental Disorders, 18,* 99–117.

Dyer, K., Dunlap, G., & Winterling, V. (1990). The effects of choice-making on the serious problem behaviors of students with severe handicaps. *Journal of Applied Behavior Analysis, 23,* 515–524.

Favell, J. E., McGimsey, J. F., & Schell, R. M. (1982). Treatment of self-injury by providing alternate sensory activities. *Analysis and Intervention in Developmental Disabilities, 2,* 83–104.

Fisher, W., Piazza, C., Cataldo, M., Harrell, R., Jefferson, G., & Conner, R. (1993). Functional communication training with and without extinction and punishment. *Journal of Applied Behavior Analysis, 26,* 23–36.

Gardner, J. M. (1985). Using microcomputers to help staff reduce violent behavior. *Computers in Human Services, 1,* 53–61.

Gunsett, R. P., Mulick, J. A., Fernald, W. B., & Martin, J. L. (1989). Brief report: Indications for medical screening prior to behavioral programming for severely and profoundly mentally retarded clients. *Journal of Autism and Developmental Disorders, 19,* 167–172.

Harding, J., Wacker, D., Cooper, L., Millard, T., & Jensen-Kovalan, P. (1994). Brief hierarchical assessment of potential treatment components with children in an out-patient clinic. *Journal of Applied Behavior Analysis, 27,* 291–300.

Haring, T. G., & Kennedy, C. H. (1990). Contextual control of problem behavior in students with severe disabilities. *Journal of Applied Behavior Analysis, 23,* 235–243.

Horner, R. (1980). The effects of an environmental "enrichment" program on the behavior of institutionalized profoundly retarded children. *Journal of Applied Behavior Analysis, 13,* 473–491.

Horner, R. H., Close, D. W., Fredericks, H. D., O'Neill, R. E., Albin, R. W., Sprague, J. R., Kennedy, C. H., Flannery, K. B., & Tuesday-Heathfield, L. (1996). Supported living for people with profound disabilities and severe problem behaviors. In D. H. Lehr & F. Brown (Eds.),

People with disabilities who challenge the system (pp. 209–240). Baltimore: Brookes.

Horner, R. H., & Day, H. M. (1995, May). *Establishing operations and problem behavior: Advances in positive behavioral support.* Paper presented at the annual meeting of the Association for Behavioral Analysis, Chicago.

Horner, R. H., Day, H. M., Sprague, J. R., O'Brien, M., & Heathfield, L. T. (1991). Interspersed requests: A nonaversive procedure for decreasing aggression and self-injury during instruction. *Journal of Applied Behavior Analysis, 24,* 265–278.

Horner, R. H., O'Neill, R. E., & Flannery, K. B. (1993). Building effective behavior support plans from functional assessment information. In M. E. Snell (Ed.), *Systematic instruction of persons with severe handicaps* (4th ed., pp. 184–214). Columbus, OH: Merrill.

Horner, R. H., Vaughn, B. J., Day, H. M., & Ard, W. R. (1996). The relationship between setting events and problem behavior: Expanding our understanding of behavioral support. In L. K. Koegel, R. L. Koegel, & G. Dunlap (Eds.), *Positive behavioral support* (pp. 381–402). Baltimore: Brookes.

Iwata, B. A., Dorsey, M. F., Slifer, K. J., Bauman, K. E., & Richman, G. S. (1982). Toward a functional analysis of self-injury. *Analysis and Intervention in Developmental Disabilities, 2,* 3–20.

Kantor, J. R. (1959). *Interbehavioral psychology.* Granville, OH: Principia Press.

Kemp, D. C., & Carr, E. G. (1995). Reduction of severe problem behavior in community employment using an hypothesis-driven multi-component intervention approach. *Journal of the Association for Persons with Severe Handicaps, 20,* 229–247.

Kennedy, C. H., & Itkonen, T. (1993). Effects of setting events on the problem behavior of students with severe disabilities. *Journal of Applied Behavior Analysis, 26,* 321–327.

Koegel, R. L., & Koegel, L. K. (1989). Community-referenced research on self-stimulation. In C. Cipani (Ed.), *The treatment of severe behavior disorders: Behavior analysis approaches* (Monograph, pp. 129–150). Washington, DC: American Association on Mental Retardation.

Koegel, L. K., Koegel, R. L., & Dunlap, G. (1996). *Positive behavioral support: Including people with difficult behavior in the community.* Baltimore: Brookes.

Lalli, J. S., Browder, D. M., Mace, F. C., & Brown, D. K. (1993). Teacher use of descriptive analysis data to implement interventions to decrease students' problem behaviors. *Journal of Applied Behavior Analysis, 26,* 227–238.

Lalli, J. S., Casey, S., & Kates, K. (1995). Reducing escape behavior and increasing task completion with functional communication training, extinction, and response chaining. *Journal of Applied Behavior Analysis, 28,* 261–268.

Lalli, J. S., & Goh, H. L. (1993). Naturalistic observations in community settings. In J. Reichle & D. P. Wacker (Eds.), *Communicative alternatives to challenging behavior* (pp. 11–39). Baltimore: Brookes.

Lehr. D. H., & Brown, F. (1996). *People with disabilities who challenge the system.* Baltimore: Brookes.

Lovaas, O. I., Freitag, G., Gold, V. J., & Kassorla, I. C. (1965). Experimental studies in childhood schizophrenia: Analysis of self-destructive behavior. *Journal of Experimental Child Psychology, 2,* 67–84.

Lucyshyn, J. M., Olson, D., & Horner, R. H. (1995). Building an ecology of support: A case study of one young woman with severe problem behaviors living in the community. *Journal of the Association for Persons with Severe Handicaps, 20,* 16–30.

Mace, F. C., Hock, M. L., Lalli, J. S., West, B. J., Belfiore, P., Pinter, E., & Brown, D. K. (1988). Behavioral momentum in the treatment of noncompliance. *Journal of Applied Behavior Analysis, 21,* 123–141.

Mace, F. C., & Lalli, J. S. (1991). Linking descriptive and experimental analyses in the treatment of bizarre speech. *Journal of Applied Behavior Analysis, 24,* 553–562.

Mace, F. C., Neef, N., Shade, D., & Mauro, B. (1996). Effects of problem difficulty and reinforcer quality on time allocated to concurrent arithmetic problems. *Journal of Applied Behavior Analysis, 29,* 11–24.

Mace, F. C., & Roberts, M. L. (1993). Factors affecting selection of behavioral interventions. In J. Reichle & D. P. Wacker (Eds.), *Communication and language intervention: Vol. 3. Communicative alternatives to challenging behavior: Integrating functional assessment and intervention strategies* (pp. 113–133). Baltimore: Brookes.

Martin, P. L., & Foxx, R. M. (1973). Victim control of the aggression of an institutionalized retardate. *Journal of Behavior Therapy and Experimental Psychiatry, 4,* 161–165.

McAfee, J. K. (1987). Classroom density and the aggressive behavior of handicapped children. *Education and Treatment of Children, 10,* 134–145.

Michael, J. (1988). Establishing operations and the mand. *Analysis of Verbal Behavior, 6,* 3–9.

Michael, J. (1993). Establishing operations. *The Behavior Analyst, 16,* 191–206.

National Institutes of Health. (1989, September). *Treatment of destructive behaviors.* Abstract presented at the National Institutes of Health, Consensus Development Conference, Rockville, MD.

Newton, S. J., Horner, R. H., & Lund, L. (1991). Honoring activity preferences in individualized plan development: A descriptive analysis. *Journal of the Association for Persons with Severe Handicaps, 16,* 207–212.

O'Neill, R. E., Horner, R. H., Albin, R. W., Storey, K., & Sprague, J. R. (1990). *Functional analysis of problem behavior: A practical assessment guide.* Sycamore, IL: Sycamore Press.

O'Reilly, M. F. (1995). Functional analysis and treatment of escape-maintained aggression correlated with sleep deprivation. *Journal of Applied Behavior Analysis, 28,* 225–226.

Parsons, M. B., Reid, D. H., Reynolds, J., & Bumgarner, M. (1990). Effects of chosen versus assigned jobs on the work performance of persons with severe handicaps. *Journal of Applied Behavior Analysis, 23,* 253–258.

Pyles, D. A. M., & Bailey, J. S. (1990). Diagnosing severe behavior problems. In A. Repp & N. Singh (Eds.), *Perspectives on the use of nonaversive and aversive interventions for persons with developmental disabilities* (pp. 381–401). Chicago: Sycamore Press.

Reichle, J. (1990). *National working conference on positive approaches to the management of excess behavior: Final report and recommendations.* Minneapolis: University of Minnesota, Institute on Community Integration.

Reid, D. H., & Parsons, M. B. (1991). Making choice a routine part of mealtimes for persons with profound mental retardation. *Behavioral Residential Treatment, 6,* 249–261.

Repp, A. C., Felce, D., & Barton, L. E. (1988). Basing the treatment of stereotypic and self-injurious behaviors on hypotheses of their causes. *Journal of Applied Behavior Analysis, 21,* 281–289.

Repp, A. C., & Karsh, K. G. (1992). An analysis of a group teaching procedure for persons with developmental disabilities. *Journal of Applied Behavior Analysis, 25,* 701–712.

Rincover, A., Cook, R., Peoples, A., & Packard, D. (1979). Sensory extinction and sensory reinforcement principles for programming multiple adaptive behavior change. *Journal of Applied Behavior Analysis, 12,* 221–233.

Rincover, A., & Devaney, J. (1982). The application of sensory extinction procedures to self-injury. *Analysis and Intervention in Developmental Disabilities, 2,* 67–81.

Sandman, C. A. (1991). The opiate hypothesis in autism and self-injury. *Journal of Child and Adolescent Psychopharmacology, 1,* 237–248.

Shevin, M., & Klein, N. K. (1984). The importance of choice-making skills for students with severe disabilities. *Journal of the Association for Persons with Severe Handicaps, 9,* 159–166.

Smith, R. G., Iwata, B. A., Vollmer, T. R., & Zarcone, J. R. (1993). Experimental analysis and treatment of multiply controlled self-injury. *Journal of Applied Behavior Analysis, 26,* 183–196.

Sugai, G., & Horner, R. (1994). Including students with severe behavior problems in general education settings: Assumptions, challenges, and solutions. *The Oregon Conference Monograph, 6,* 109–120.

Taylor, J. C., & Carr, E. G. (1992a). Severe problem behaviors related to social interaction: I. Attention seeking and social avoidance. *Behavior Modification, 16,* 305–335.

Taylor, J. C., & Carr, E. G. (1992b). Severe problem behavior related to social interaction: II. A systems analysis. *Behavior Modification, 16,* 336–371.

Touchette, P. E., MacDonald, R. F., & Langer, S. N. (1985). A scatter plot for identifying stimulus control of problem behavior. *Journal of Applied Behavior Analysis, 18,* 343–351.

Vaughn, B., & Horner, R. H. (in press). Effects of student task selection on problem behavior for students with severe disabilities. *Journal of Applied Behavior Analysis.*

Vollmer, T. R., & Iwata, B. A. (1991). Establishing operations and reinforcement effects. *Journal of Applied Behavior Analysis, 24,* 279–291.

Vollmer, T. R., Marcus, B. A., Ringdahl, J. E., & Roane, H. S. (1995). Progressing from brief assessments to extended experimental analyses in the evaluation of aberrant behavior. *Journal of Applied Behavior Analysis, 28,* 561–576.

Wacker, D. P., Steege, M., Northup, J., Reimers, T., Berg, W., & Sasso, G. (1990). Use of functional analysis and acceptability measures to assess and treat severe behavior problems: An outpatient clinic model. In A. C. Repp & N. Singh (Eds.), *Perspectives on the use of aversive and nonaversive interventions for persons with developmental disabilities* (pp. 349–359). Sycamore, IL: Sycamore.

Wacker, D. P., Steege, M. W., Northup, J., Sasso, G., Berg, W., Reimers, T., Cooper, L., Cigrand, K., & Donn, L. (1990). A component analysis of functional communication training across three topographies of severe behavior problems. *Journal of Applied Behavior Analysis, 23,* 417–429.

Wacker, D. P., Wiggins, B., Fowler, M., & Berg, W. (1988). Training students with profound or multiple handicaps to make requests via microswitches. *Journal of Applied Behavior Analysis, 21,* 331–343.

Walker, H. M., Colvin, G., & Ramsey, E. (1995). *Antisocial behavior in public school: Strategies and best practices.* Pacific Grove, CA: Brookes/Cole.

Walker, H. M., Horner, R. H., Sugai, G., Bullis, M., Sprague, J. R., Bricker, D., & Kaufman, M. J. (1996). Integrated approaches to preventing antisocial behavior patterns among school-age children and youth. *Journal of Emotional and Behavioral Disorders, 4,* 194–209.

8.3   Beyond Bribes and Threats:

How Not to Get Control of the Classroom

Alfie Kohn

In an effort to clarify the basic assumptions that underlie our approaches to children, Alfie Kohn proposes a distinction between *doing to* and *working with*. A *doing to* approach involves the imposition of the adult will on the child; *working with* refers to good listening, responsive teaching, and a collaborative approach of community-building, choices, and a fresh view of the curriculum. Kohn exhorts teachers to improve their craft, moving from *doing to* to *working with*.

DOING TO VERSUS *WORKING WITH*

. . . One way of framing a discussion, is to distinguish between *doing to* and *working with*, two verb phrases that have some heuristic power, at least for me. I find them useful, that is, for sorting through different principles and practices. You decide, obviously, whether it is useful for yourself. The difference between *doing to* and *working with* is important if I am right in my central premise, which is that you can only help kids become independent and compassionate and morally responsible and all the rest of it by *working with them* as opposed to *doing to them*. If that's true, then we ought to be on the lookout for even subtle ways that we might be *doing things to* kids.

Let me offer you this little schema (see Figure 1), then I'm going to ask you to work with me to sort of fill in some of the concrete practices that exemplify these two things. The methods of *doing to* and *working with* are basically the topic for this morning. I'm going to go over them quickly now and then come back to them, focusing on the *doing to* methods now and the *working with* methods after our break.

This is a slightly edited version of a presentation made at the North American Montessori Teachers Association conference titled "The Montessori Approach to Discipline," October 23–25, 1997, in Atlanta, Georgia.

Kohn, A. (1998). Beyond bribes and threats: How not to get control of the classroom. *NAMTA Journal, 23*(1), 7–61. Reprinted by permission.

Methods of Doing To

I propose three ways by which we might do *things to* children. The most obvious is *simple coercion:* We make them act the way we want. My favorite example in the typical elementary school is two kids who are talking to each other, arguing, missing out on what is going on in the rest of the room, perhaps creating a disturbance (at least in the teacher's mind) for those others who are present. So the teacher comes up and says, "You need to sit over there." (I'm always alert for phrases like "you need to," which typically say a lot more about the preferences of the speaker than the genuine needs of the listener.) What has happened as a result of this interaction? Has either child been led to think about how to sit next to somebody she doesn't like? No. Has either child been helped to think about how to solve the problem or negotiate a solution with somebody else? No. Has either child or anybody else within earshot been invited to think about how her behavior affects other people? No. What the children have learned is the message of power. "I have the power. They don't. So I can *make* them sit wherever I damn well please, for any reason or no reason." That is the message that coercion always teaches. It's just not always clear to us that what we're doing is, in fact, simple coercion to achieve some short-term goal.

Closely related to coercion is *punishment*, which I will define as doing something aversive or unpleasant with the express purpose of changing future behavior. I force you to do something you don't want to do, or I prevent you from doing something you *do* want to do in order that you will act differently later. I make you suffer to change what you do. Now you

	Doing to	Working with
Methods	coercion punishment ("consequences") rewards ("positive reinforcement")	mutual problem solving; creation of caring community; choices; engaging curriculum
Focus	behavior	motives, values
Goal	compliance	intrinsic commitment to good values, moral sophistication; genuine concern & empathy for others; social skills problem-solving
Message	power	cooperate (as possible and desirable)
Climate	teacher firmly in control	"Control can't be the goal:" teacher as facilitator, guide, model, fellow learner; classroom belongs to all; unpredictability
View of conflict	distraction from the lesson to be elimiated efficiently	teachable moment; this *is* the lesson
Intellectual influences	F. W. Taylor (student as worker to be controlled), Skinner, Dreikurs	Dewey, Piaget
Academic counterpart	transmission/absorption: drill 'n' skill lectures.	constructivism
Telltale signs	teachers' demands (and definition of misbehavior) accepted uncritically; "discipline;" use of recipes; pseudochoice	emphasis on asking kids; student-to-student discussion

Figure 1

Doing to versus *working with*.

can call that punishment, you can call that "consequences," you can call it a Popsicle—it doesn't matter what euphemism you use.

If you want to know whether it's a punishment, don't read Montessori, don't listen to me; look in the child's eyes and you'll have your answer. These days in many schools, I hope not Montessori schools, to a significant extent, there is a movement toward doing the same thing but dressing it up and making it a little nicer. Hence, we insert the modifier *logical* before the euphemism *consequences* so as to pretend the child is not being punished. The whole procedure I like to refer to as "punishment lite," a slightly less unpleasant way of *doing things to* children. And if you'd like to get into this distinction and the specifics of what are offered as logical consequences in discipline manuals, and the work that I think is profoundly anti-child of Rudolf Dreikurs, who is passed off as being humanistic and democratic, I would be very interested in talking with you about this. But, for the time being, let us simply say that it doesn't matter what you call it; it has the same essential impact on the child and is based on the same set of principles about how to change what someone does, typically for the

convenience of the person administering that "consequence." The fact that the punishment may fit the crime, or the tone of voice may be sweet, does not in any significant way alter what has happened during that exchange.

We love these euphemisms, don't we? In schools sometimes we don't call it *incarceration;* we call it *detention*. One of my personal favorites is the euphemism we give to forcible isolation of young children, and that is *time out*, which you may not know is originally short for "time out from positive reinforcement," and was developed as a means for suppressing certain behaviors in laboratory animals. That's the lineage of that term. There are many others, of course, and I'll come back to the arguments against this and try to put them in a way that might be useful for you to pass on to others, but I hardly think I need to persuade you of the problems of being punitive.

The third approach that's used for *doing things to* children is to offer them *rewards* when they do what we want. For so many parents and so many educators, it is extremely discomfiting to hear the message that rewards and punishments are not opposites. Yet that is what I would strongly argue; they are two sides of the same coin. And that coin doesn't buy very much. Whether I say to you, "Do this or here's what I'm going to do to you," or I say, "Do this and you'll get that," I am engaged in pretty much the same kind of attempt to *do things to* children. It doesn't matter whether it's a bribe or a threat, a reward or a punishment, a carrot or a stick; it's the same idea. Of course, there are examples galore of how this is done in homes and in classrooms. Stickers and stars and extra recess, food, grades in many schools, money. There are parents who actually pay children for good grades, which is a reward for a reward. You can almost watch the interest in learning evaporate before your eyes—and we could go on.

One of the most controversial aspects of this argument is the realization that you might be offering to children what amounts to a *verbal* doggie biscuit—in effect, leaving home the stickers and avoiding the grades, but saying, "Good for you, Diana, I'm really proud of what you did just now," or, worse, saying in front of others, "I like the way Pat has done so many interesting things with her cylinders," or has shared her sandwich—which places another whole twist on it when it is done in front of others, and I'll come back to this.

Whether it's done verbally or tangibly, whether it is done through reward or punishment, we are still firmly on the *doing to* side of the ledger. Thus, if my premise is right, we are making it more difficult, making it less likely, for kids to become the kind of independent, responsible, compassionate life-long learners we want them to be. Something, then, has to give. Either you change your mind about that goal or you question the practice . . .

. . . The question is, "Do you never do this when you have problems with the way kids are acting?" A child who is hitting, a child who is acting out, being intrusive or obnoxious or aggressive, is a child who in many cases has already been over-controlled—though not always. In any case, the last thing that child needs is more control. What that child, in particular, needs is a more successful approach to *working with*. When I hear from people, "Oh, I've tried the *working with* stuff; it doesn't work," I think of the following analogy: "I type and I type and I type and I still can't produce a good novel. Clearly typing doesn't work." In other words, if the way we are trying to respectfully engage a child to solve a problem has not been successful, our only alternative, really, is to find another, better way of engaging with the child. It may be a different arena, it may be with a group versus one-on-one, it may be at the time versus later, it may involve or not involve the parent, it may in-

volve more pointed and directed questioning by us, or a more non-directive approach. We may have to struggle for new techniques.

But what I think the research and our experience indicates pretty clearly is that the *doing to* approach never works, except to get one thing: temporary compliance. For that, punishments and rewards can be enormously effective. If I took a gun out of my pocket right now and said, "If I hear another comment or question, you will get shot," I think I would be successful in cutting off any further conversation. See, punishments or consequences work. Conversely, if I yanked out of my podium a stack of checks made payable to cash in the amount of $2,000, and said, "If you cross your legs for the remainder of this presentation, I will give you such a check," my guess is a lot of legs would be crossed in a hurry. I imagine anyone with two legs would cross one over another for two grand. You see, rewards work. But when anyone says, "Consequences or rewards work," even under specific conditions, I would encourage you to respond with two questions: "Work to do what, exactly?"—and here I'm suggesting that temporary compliance pretty much exhausts the effects—and, second, "At what cost?" I'll come back after I've gone through this list to talk about the cost and indicate with more urgency why we should never use these techniques, even with, or especially with, kids who are making life difficult for themselves, other kids, and us. Then we'll also talk more about the *working with*.

Methods of Working With

Basically, the methods that I'm putting on the other side of this ledger begin with what I've called *mutual problem-solving*. "That's easy to say," the understandable response from you is, "but how do I do it, especially when it hasn't been successful so far?" The commitment to seeing a problematic action as a problem to be solved, rather than an infraction to be punished, is a powerful predictor of a successful classroom and a successful kind of interaction with kids. Notice it is not just a problem to be observed. Notice it is not an error to be fixed. It is a problem to be solved, which often indicates that we cannot predict what is the right way to do it in advance. Nor can we impose, in effect, but it does require an active role for the adult, in *working with*. *Working with* is not the same thing as *doing for; working with* is not the same thing as just observing. It is active, but it is at the same time responsive and reciprocal, respectful and collaborative.

But that's just about solving problems that have already happened. What we're interested in, I think, is preventing most problems from occurring in the first place, and let us not forget, the way most discipline programs forget, that we want to do more than just prevent problems; we want affirmatively to help kids become independent, responsible, caring, and so on. And that requires what I call the *three Cs.* Those three Cs, which will form the backbone of what we talk about after the break, are *community, choices,* and *curriculum.*

The creation of a *caring community*—not a bunch of self-sufficient, independent young people in a room, but rather transforming what that room is, so that it is experienced virtually all the time as a community of learners—requires structuring interdependence instead of getting carried away with self-sufficiency, self-discipline, self-esteem, and otherwise relentlessly promoting the idea of individuals only accidentally connected to others.

The idea of *choices* says that it is important for us to recognize autonomy and support the capacity of kids to make decisions about the things that affect them. But that does not mean autonomy in the sense of privacy. Even here we may be talking about a community making decisions together, so that the idea of choices does not necessarily mean just solitary children figuring out what they want to work on at a given moment. But again, when you combine the idea of choices and community, you get—well, what you get is democracy.

The third C, which can never be far from our minds, is the *curriculum,* which is to say: What are the tasks? How engaging are they? To what extent are they experienced as worth doing? Because even if you are talking or thinking just about kids' social and moral development, even if the topic today and tomorrow is just discipline, how can it be far from your mind that if kids do not find meaning and purpose in what it is they are being asked to do, they are going to act out and cause a problem? Very rare is the classroom management seminar or the book on discipline that says when kids are off-task we should ask, "What's the task?" Instead, the presumption is always, "Whatever the adult wants kids to do, here are some tricks for getting them to do it."

There was a period in my life when I was teaching older kids and I had a big discipline problem. At least that's how I experienced it at the time. Those kids must have gotten together at night to figure out how to make my life a living hell, because they could not have been that good spontaneously. Had anyone asked me, "What do you need, Alfie?"—which no one did, incidentally—I would have said, "I need better techniques of discipline." It took me years to figure

out that I had misdiagnosed the problem. These kids were not deliberately trying to make me miserable; they were trying to make the time pass faster. When I look back at the kinds of tasks I was giving them to do—I remember in particular a unit that might as well have been called "Our Friend the Adverb"—I cannot blame them. The real problem lay not with them but with me—specifically, with what I was giving them to do and with my mistaken assumptions about learning and what a good teacher was. It took me a long time to figure that out, and you can see why that is not as popular a message for educators as the packaged programs and catalogued advice for how to make kids buckle down and "get to work."

Focus of Doing To Versus Working With

I want to continue, with your indulgence, to think about this *doing to* and *working with* distinction in different ways. So far, I've only mentioned the *methods* of each approach. But what is the *focus* of each approach? I'm glad you asked. The focus of a *doing to* classroom is *behavior.* The focus of a *doing to* family is behavior. In a *working with* environment, it is the *motives,* the *values,* the why behind the behavior. Whenever I hear an educator or a parent say, "I've got to do something about this kids behavior," I know we're in trouble because when that's the focus, I can predict what the methods are going to be: some variant of bribes and threats—excuse me, "positive reinforcement" and "logical consequences."

What I care about is not just *what* the child is doing but *why.* A lot of folks have recalled a man named Burrhus Frederic Skinner. You know of whom I speak—a man who did his research with rodents and pigeons and wrote most of his books about people—that B. F. Skinner? We recall him chiefly in terms of the doggie biscuits that are offered, the reinforcers used to shape behavior. But it's not the use of the reinforcer that defines a behaviorist. It's the assumption that all there is, or all that's worth talking about, is measurable, observable behavior. And there are a lot of pop behaviorists running around, regardless of whether they use stickers or pizza parties or praise to control children. To the extent that a directress, a mom, or a dad is focusing on just what the child is doing and how to change that, B. F. Skinner feels right at home. The use of the doggie biscuits or the threats will tend to follow, not because of an *a priori* commitment to those techniques, but because of the start, because of the presumption that behavior is what we're supposed to be focused on.

I don't care about behavior, except insofar as it tells me who this child is. Let me give you a very homey example. This child just gave half her sandwich to the kid sitting next to her. This *other* kid just gave half *her* sandwich to the kid sitting next to *her*. Are you pleased? Me, I don't know yet. Couldn't say yes or no. I want to know why. Well, as it turns out, *this* kid did it hoping that the adult nearby would slather her with praise: "Good for you, Debbie. I really appreciate your sharing like that. I'm so proud of you." *This* child did it without knowing or caring whether an adult saw it. *She* did it because she was afraid that if she hadn't done it, the other child would be hungry. Now which of those two motives do you see as better and more worth supporting? Second, which of those two motives do you think praise is likely to promote and sustain?

As soon as you look underneath observable behavior, you recognize why positive reinforcement may not be so positive, and why a *working with* set of methods is going to be necessary—because you are not just concerned about behavior. And in *working with* environments, people look deeper than that.

Goals of Doing To Versus Working With

The goal in a *doing to* classroom is getting *compliance*. Now don't feel obliged to copy down all of the items in *the working with* set; that's just an example. Use, if you like, the long-term goals that you just shouted out a few minutes ago. What I've put on this list as a *working with* set of goals includes an *intrinsic commitment to good values, moral sophistication, genuine concern and empathy for others, social skills, problem-solving*—these are not controversial in their own right. How many educators or parents would say nix to those? What interests me is what an observer would conclude are the real goals in a classroom. In many classrooms, even those of teachers who say they're looking for kids to become responsible and caring and independent and all the rest of it, the real goal apparently is just to get kids to do what they are told. Sometimes what they're told is great stuff. That's where it becomes even more challenging for us to move beyond compliance. I have seen programs, for example, where I love the goals, where the objectives have to do with being caring and creating a safe environment and figuring stuff out and trying many different, new activities and tasks and materials. But if our basic goal is just to get them to comply with even very desirable, even lofty and ambitious objectives, it is still not about these things on the *working with* side. We have to look at the extent to which we then use subtler methods of *doing to* to get kids basically to obey.

Message of Doing To Versus Working With. In a *doing to* classroom the message is *power*, as I said before with respect to coercion in particular. "I have the power, so I can make you do whatever I want." In a *working with* environment, the message is that *cooperation—among* kids, among adults, or between kids and adults—genuine cooperation is both possible and desirable. That's the message that seeps into the air in a genuinely *working with* environment.

Climate of Doing To Versus Working With

In a *doing to* classroom, the climate is that the *teacher is firmly in control.* In a *working with* place, the first slogan is, *"Control can't be the goal."* In a *working with* environment, the teacher is a facilitator, a guide, sure, I'd add observer, a model, a fellow learner. In a *working with* environment, the classroom belongs to everyone and is somewhat unpredictable. There are various ways that we satisfy our need for predictability, for knowing what's going to happen at a particular time. Some environments do it in a more sophisticated way, some in a rather crude and primitive way. In any case, we're doing it more because of *our* needs, sometimes, to know exactly what will happen. Young children, I know, are comforted by ritual and some degree of predictability. I think often we overdo this and provide them with not just structure, which is useful, but control, which may not be, sometimes over-determining what they do, or with whom, or when, or how.

The real problem is the idea of using rewards and punishments. Actually, though, rewards and punishments are not the problem either, which is a curious thing to say when you've written a 400-page book about rewards and punishments. I have come to realize, and I continue to believe strongly, that the rewards and punishments are just the techniques that flow logically and inexorably from the belief that the adult should be in control of the classroom. And as long as that belief is there, all rewards and punishments could disappear and new ones would pop up like new Kleenexes in the box. I, as a teacher, had unthinkingly accepted what I was told, in no uncertain terms, was my responsibility in the class, which is to have control of the classroom. After all, the alternative to control is chaos. We're all taught that, as if those are the only two possibilities. "Control and chaos," I thought, "where have I heard that before?" And then I remembered: *Get Smart!*

Where I'd really heard that before was from the mouths of dictators through history who have argued, in effect, if I am not in control of this environment there will be bloody anarchy, wild chaos, and so on. It's for your own good that I make all the decisions. When we, from our comfortable vantage point in contemporary America, look over or back at tyrants who have made that claim, our response is, "Hey buddy, you're forgetting a third alternative here. We call it *dem-oc-racy.*" How come we forget that possibility when we look inside classrooms?

I'm not arguing that a 40-year-old and a bunch of 3-year-olds have the same vote, the same voice, the same talents, the same agenda, and are in all respects interchangeable. I don't know anyone who believes that. But I do believe that even with very young children, it behooves us, if we're really looking at those long-term goals, to rethink the idea of control and think about bringing even young children, but especially older children, into the process of making decisions, constructing meaning, and solving problems together. That may mean that the adult provides guidance that the children require, and nurturance, observation, support, limits, and structure. But it does not necessarily mean that we are "in control of the room." Indeed, one might argue that children cannot become responsible members of a democratic society, or agitators to create a democratic society as the case may be, unless from a very young age they have been in an environment where the adult has deliberately and carefully given up some authority to shrewdly, to carefully share the control and create a very different kind of environment than is true of the typical preschool, 9 to 12, high school, or other environment, in which we find ourselves, where pretty soon we learn to take being controlled for granted.

If punishments or rewards are as destructive as I'm going to argue they are, why would they be so popular? One reason is that they work—in the extremely circumscribed sense of getting temporary compliance. And often, we don't know what else *to* do. They are convenient in a convenient society. Also, they are familiar to us. They are the way that most of us *were* raised and taught. One might also say that they are easy. To do the *working with* stuff, to give up control, to create a caring community, to devise an engaging curriculum, this takes time, it takes skill, it takes care, it takes courage because we have to give up the control to which we've become accustomed. But to say, "Do this because I'm the mom," or "I don't care what you think," or "I'll give you an ice cream cone if you do it," takes no time, no care, no skill, no talent, and, above all, no courage. Guess which approach is more popular. That's an argument about the difficulty of moving to *working with*, not an argument about the desirability of continuing to *do to.* . . .

View of Conflict in Doing To Versus Working With. The view of conflict in a *doing to* approach is that conflict is a *distraction from the lesson* and should be ended as swiftly as possible. Conflict is, in this view, rather like dandruff. The only question is how you get rid of it. In a *working with* environment, conflict, putting aside of course the kind that leads to kids getting hurt, is a *teachable moment*. Some kinds of conflict are devoutly to be wished. I know some teachers of young children who deliberately have fewer materials around than there are kids to use them, in the hope that this will provide a kind of conflict that will help children think through issues in a way they wouldn't have otherwise. That's just one example. When kids are arguing about something, and seem unhappy, this is a moment that we should not lose. We should not, I would argue, prepare an environment so carefully as to preclude such conflict from arising because lessons then might be lost that would only happen if we had this conflict. I worry when I walk into a classroom where things are going a little too smoothly . . .

Academic Counterparts of Doing To Versus Working With. The academic counterpart to a *doing to* approach—and here I think I'm speaking especially to those of you who teach 6 to 9 or 9 to 12 or 6 to 50 or whatever—is a *transmission* approach to curriculum, the kind of *"drill and skill"* where you're just supposed to memorize a bunch of facts—more importantly, the idea that the teacher, the directress, whoever, has a bunch of facts and skills that are imparted to or poured into the passive receptacle of the student. Lectures, worksheets, basals, primers, dittos, that sort of thing, are the hallmarks of a *doing to* approach.

A *working with* approach, in the social and moral domain, is consistent with an approach known as *constructivism*, which is not a method of teaching. If you want to be strict about it, there's no such thing as a constructivist classroom. Constructivism is not a prescription; it's a description of how people learn, and it says, in effect, that people don't learn by being filled with or—now I will push my luck further—absorbing things that come from elsewhere, but by actively making meaning around ideas, whether the idea has to do with fractions, written expression, or fairness.

What's interesting to me about this logical match-up is how many classrooms I've been in where there's a disconnect again. I have been in schools where the curriculum is incredibly engaging, where there are projects, where there are hands-on lessons all the way up through high school (though rarely), where kids are not using textbooks except as references like dictionaries, but instead figuring out together and giving meaning to ideas. It's an exciting intellectual atmosphere to be part of. And then you look beyond the academic curriculum, and you find the teacher runs the whole show. The rules are up there that the teacher alone devised for everyone to follow. There's not only praise but public praise to control children, consequences for misbehavior, and all of the rest of it.

Conversely, I have seen classrooms and schools that are devoted to a *working with* approach where there are democratic class meetings and circle times and—heaven knows, not all class meetings are done in a way that *is working with*. I have seen class meetings and circle times where the teacher drives the entire conversation, another major opportunity missed. But I'm talking about classrooms where problems are really solved together by a community of learners. Then you look at the curriculum, and you see SRA Reading Series, you see "Circle the vowel," you see "Read Chapter 9 and answer the even-numbered questions." You see relatively little in terms of deep understanding of ideas, but instead a superficial acquisition of facts and skills very useful for standardized test-taking but not for deep learning.

What those two crosses tell me—that is, a constructivist curriculum with a *doing to* environment, and a *working with* environment connecting to a transmission/superficial curriculum—what this teaches me is humility, because of how incredibly hard it is to do both the constructivist curriculum and the *working with* approach . . .

THE CASE AGAINST PUNISHMENT

Let's go back now, if we can, to the case against punishment—or "consequences." That punishment isn't terribly effective should be clear from the fact that the same kids are punished over and over again without apparent benefit. At some point a bright six-year-old can figure it out: "Duh! Maybe the problem isn't with the kid, but with the act of punishing." We've had research for more than half a century indicating that children who are raised in homes with traditional discipline, where severe punishments are meted out for breaking the rules, tend to be more aggressive and obnoxious than their peers when they're away from home. The implication, of course, is that punishment isn't just ineffective, but actually counterproductive.

Why should this be? First, punishment, or the threat of punishment, ticks people off. It makes people mad, fills them with rage and defiance and a desire to get even. Second, it ruptures the relationship between the person giving and the person getting the punishment. If you come to be seen as someone who imposes "consequences," the kid is going to be about as happy to see you coming as you or I would be to see a police car in our rearview mirror. This compromises the all-important caring alliance between adult and child. Third, punishment focuses attention on avoiding the punishment itself—not on the behavior, much less the reason for the behavior. If I say to you, "Hey! I don't want to catch you doing that again!," your reaction is likely to be, "OK. Next time you won't catch me." That's a perfectly logical response to the perfect illogic of punitive consequences.

Fourth, punishment gets people to think almost exclusively about their own self-interest. Whenever we talk about "consequences," we mean the consequences to the person who did something wrong. Consider the resigned, even sullen question that a child is led to ask in a punitive environment: "What do they want me to do—and what happens to me if I don't do it?" Contrast that with the sort of questions we'd like kids to think about:

"What kind of person do I want be?" or, better yet, "What kind of classroom (or school) do we want to create?" The use of consequences—"logical" or otherwise—actively distracts kids from thinking in those terms.

Go back to that question and let's italicize two words this time: "What do they want me to do—and what happens *to me* if I don't do it?" This is the lowest level of moral development, and any time we threaten punitive consequences for misbehavior, we help to arrest kids at that level.

Speaking of arrest, I'm reminded of a common objection to this argument. People sometimes say, "Well, that sounds nice in theory—although I find that such individuals rarely even like the theory—" . . . but in the Real World, there are consequences to be paid. If a kid grows up and robs a bank, assuming he's caught, he'll be thrown in jail. Kids have to learn that now." Do you see the fatal flaw in the logic here? We want kids not to rob banks because they know it's wrong. No "consequence" ever taught right and wrong, only self-interest. Now, it doesn't put kids at a disadvantage for them to become more morally sophisticated and concerned about the impact of their action on others; they're not going to rob banks either, but they won't rob banks even if they think they can get away with it. If you saturate a child in an environment of so-called logical consequences, that child, if he grows up and thinks he can get away with robbing a bank, has a green light to do so, because there will be no consequence, and that's what you've told him is the reason not to do it. That's not an academic argument. You could fill this room with real bank robbers and wife batterers, and I guarantee you that the great majority of them were consequenced plenty when they were kids.

This is an argument for moral sophistication. Are there people in our society who basically just do the right thing or avoid doing the wrong thing because they're afraid they're going to get caught and punished? Sure. Are those the kind of people we want our kids to grow up to be? If so, then use lots of consequences.

THE ARGUMENT AGAINST REWARDS

The flip side of all of these arguments against punishment is the argument against rewards. Let me start with the research. Two questions: Do rewards change behavior? Do rewards improve performance?

First question: Do rewards change behavior? The answer is, yes, they often can, for as long as the reward keeps coming and not a minute afterward. If you're lucky, behavior will typically revert to what it was before the rewards were used. If you are not lucky, which is most of the time, the behavior will get worse than it was before the rewards started. This rebound effect is found by any number of studies collecting dust on library shelves. Example: Programs to help adults quit smoking have found that if they are paid a reward, a financial incentive for quitting, they will tend to go back to smoking faster than people in other kinds of programs, and also faster than people in the control group—that is, people who are not in any program. You see what that means? The reward, like punishments, was not just ineffective, but counterproductive. It was worse than doing nothing. Example: Two recent studies—and this example may be more relevant to you, unless you're trying to quit smoking at the moment—two studies, one at Arizona State University, and one at the University of Toronto, have found that children who are frequently rewarded or praised are somewhat less generous than their peers. The effect is most pronounced when they are rewarded or praised for being generous. Are you surprised, or does it make sense to you? Present this to a parent who is using reward systems, or slathering kids with praise, and ask why this might be. What the child, it will eventually occur to us, is being led to think about is, "What am I supposed to do and what do I get for doing it?" It's just the flip side of the punishment question. It's also about self-interest. All rewards are about self-interest. It just becomes amusingly paradoxical when the rewards are given for generosity. You can buy the behavior of sharing a sandwich or taking a turn or cooperating with other kids as long as the reward is offered for that. But when the reward is no longer there, the kid is less generous than when she started.

What about the second question: Do rewards improve the quality of performance on various tasks? The answer there, in a nutshell, is that it depends on the task. If you're looking for short-term performance on relatively mindless tasks, like how many envelopes can you lick in an hour, you can get people to lick more envelopes if you give them a reward for doing it. But research has shown that when the tasks require higher-order thinking, problem solving, or some degree of creativity, people who are offered nothing for doing the task tend to do it better than people who are offered a reward, either for doing the task or for doing it well. When those first studies showed that in the early 1960s, they carried the telltale phrase in the results section, "Contrary to hypothesis." Whenever you see that phrase, wake up. It means that even the researcher didn't see this coming, and, more remarkably, admitted it.

There have been at least a couple dozen studies now showing that this is true, with males and females, adults and children, a range of tasks, and every reward that experimenters could think to give. And over and over again—Janet Spence put it best (she later became president of the American Psychological Association). Back in 1971 she wrote that rewards "have effects that interfere with performance in ways that we are only beginning to understand." It's been a quarter of a century since she wrote that, and the 39 people who follow this line of research have some good ideas as to why this happens.

Meanwhile, parents, teachers, and managers continue to dangle goodies in front of people, assuming it will make them work harder, work better, or become better people. The evidence mounts that it's not just ineffective but it moves us in the wrong direction.

WHY REWARDS FAIL

How come? Very quickly, let me suggest a couple of possible reasons. . . .

Rewards Punish

The first reason that rewards don't work very well is because they punish. The paradox is intentional.

They're not just different ways of getting to behavior. In the long run, the reward is punitive. Why? My favorite phrase on this topic comes from two of my mentors in this field: Ed Deci and Rich Ryan at the University of Rochester in New York, who've done a lot of the research. The following phrase leapt off of the page and imprinted itself on my brain: Rewards are just "control through seduction" (1985, p. 70). That's absolutely right. To understand why rewards fail, you have to understand the difference between the goodie itself and using the goodie as a reward. You want to give kids a popcorn party on Friday? I have no objection to that. That sounds like fun. What I hope you would never do is say, "*If you're good this week . . . or* "*If . . .* anything, "*we will have a popcorn party.*" The popcorn is not the problem. It's using the popcorn as a reward. What makes a reward a reward? In one word, contingency. In a more down-to-earth phrase, "Do this and you'll get that."

Now you start to see why praise might be a problem. There is nothing wrong, heaven knows, with love and support and attention and acknowledgment. There is a lot wrong with saying, "Jump through my hoops and only then will you get that stuff. Only when you *share*, only when you *comply*, only when you do what I think is a good job, only when you live up to my expectations will I marinate you in praise and approval." It's not the expressions of love that are problematic; it's the conditionality of them. What kids, especially kids from troubled homes, need is unconditional love and support. Praise is not just different from that. Praise is the opposite of that.

"Do this and you'll get that." Ultimately, that feels punitive. Analogously, I don't have problem with money. As long as it doesn't eclipse other values in your life, money is great. I have a big problem with merit pay, pay for performance, incentive plans, bonuses, and commissions. It's not an argument against compensation; it's an argument against using compensation as a doggie biscuit, which is what the vast majority of American companies do. Just like the popcorn. They punish because they're controlling, and, more concretely, they punish because sometimes kids expect to get a reward and don't get it. That happens invariably in reward systems. Tell me how the kid feels after that, what's the difference between that and punishment.

Rewards Rupture Relationships

Second reason: Rewards fail because of what they do to relationships, beginning with the relationships among the kids themselves. Now I'm going to come back to what I take to be the importance of those relationships among kids, how critical it is to create a caring community and pay attention to how kids feel about each other and learn with and from each other. But assuming I don't have to convince you of that, the next step is to realize how rewards, at best, divert our attention from sustaining those relationships and, at worst, actually undermine them, because now kids are not thinking about *us;* they're thinking about what *I* can get.

Do we solve this problem by giving a group reward? No, we create new problems. If we all do *X*, only then will all of us get *Y*. This is an ugly form of peer pressure we are trying to create, causing kids to become our accomplices in control of each other, which is the very opposite of community. The Geneva Convention forbids collective punishment; I think it's time we take a hard look at collective reward.

The other kind of reward that really makes things worse is when it's done publicly, especially in the case of praise, and I'll come back to that in a moment. There is one way to take a bad thing and make it much worse. You're going to have to bring me back sometime for me to talk about this because I have no time right now. But if you were determined to destroy community, if that was your mischievous Satanic goal, to rip out by its roots any sense of safety or connection among kids, then you would probably want to use the most destructive form of rewards known to humankind: competition. The only thing worse than a reward is an award, which means that the number of them has been artificially limited, so my chance of getting one is reduced or even eliminated if she gets one. So now it's not just a sticker when you do *X*; it's a sticker or whatever (praise, recognition, you name it) for the *best* in this category, for the one who does the most. Pick your superlative. Now the message that everybody present learns can be summarized in a single sentence: Other people are potential obstacles to my success. That is the message in every awards assembly, every classroom graded on a curve, every spelling bee, and every time things like this: "OK, kids, who can get into their pajamas fastest? This is not innocuous. This is creating a world view of artificial scarcity and turning other people, even one's own siblings, not into potential collaborators but into potential rivals. Little by little, with phrases like that and by turning the playing field into a battlefield after school, we create people who do not want to succeed but want to triumph over others. It's not about learning, much less caring. It's about victory. The disadvantages of that I have chronicled in another book (*No Contest: The Case against Competition*, 1992), with respect to one's own psychological development, with respect to relationships, and even, surprisingly, with respect to the quality of one's work or learning.

But, if you say, "I don't believe in competition. I want to give every child a sticker," I would suggest that you've taken a giant step forward but might have further to go, because while you've eliminated the competitive twist, you are still offering what psychologists call an extrinsic motivator, such that the point is the sticker—better than limiting the number available, but not as good as moving away from the reward and punishment approach altogether.

There is, however, another relationship to attend to, and that is between the student and the teacher, the directress, the administrator, the parent, the adult. I said before that if you offer consequences, the child is about as happy to see you coming as you and I would be to see a police car, How, then, does the child view us if we are offering rewards, even praise? I would argue that we then become, in effect, giant goodie dispensers on legs. This is not any closer to the caring alliance I spoke of before as so critical. There is still a gap, a gulf that is opened between us and the kid. We give the punishment or the reward; they get it from us. That's not *working with*; it's still *doing to*. It's just that we can't always see it; we don't always notice it for what it is. . . .

Rewards Ignore Reasons

The third reason that I think rewards have this effect is because rewards ignore the reasons why something happened. Another way of putting that is, rewards tend to focus on behavior, which, as I pointed out before, is a hallmark of a *doing to* environment. You want to solve a problem, you have to know what caused it. You've got a kid in your class who's hitting somebody else? You are not going to begin to make headway until you have some inkling as to why. Then, as best as you can, though it's not always due to factors within your control, but as best as you can, you address the source of the problem. If you don't address the source of the problem, it's not going to work.

Quick story: A woman saw a lecture of mine on videotape and wrote me a letter. "Dear Mr. Kohn, you have taken away all my tricks and techniques"—her phrase, which is an apt one. "So what am I supposed to do," she continued, (reading between the lines

here, ". . . Mr. Smarty Pants") "with my little girl, whom I put to bed at night: 'O.K., sweetie, you've got a big day tomorrow.'" Always a big day tomorrow, never a small or insignificant day. "I love you. See you in the morning." Closes the bedroom door; bang, two minutes later the kid is out of the room: "I can't sleep." Put the kid back to bed: "OK, honey, see you *in the morning,*" close the door again; bam, she's back out of bed again. "What am I supposed to do?" the woman asked.

Well, if you go to the parenting section of Barnes & Noble, or, better yet, an independent bookstore, you will find advice that typically comes in two flavors: threat and bribe. Sometimes, if you spend your money wisely, you can get both in the same book. "Young lady, if you are not back *in* that bed before I count to three, you can forget about that trip to the zoo we talked about." Flip side: "Honey, if you are in bed all night for the next four nights, I'll buy you that giant teddy bear we saw in the toy store window." Notice how fundamentally similar these two approaches really are: two ways of manipulating behavior.

What did I say as an alternative? I said, "Frankly, I would not have the audacity to prescribe a solution unless I had at least some inkling of why your kid—this week—is not staying in bed." There are many possible reasons why this is true, are there not? Like what? Fear: There are monsters in the closet. What else? She had a nap, or maybe she's just not tired because her bedtime is too early. Why else? It's fun to watch mom get so weirded out; she's getting a response from that. What else? Something is going on in the child's life that she has to rehearse, and it's hard to sleep when that's going on, just went on, or is about to go on. What else? Maybe I just want to spend more time with mom. I don't get to see her that often. Or maybe, I can just hear what's going on in the rest of the house. Is anybody here too old to remember how the most exciting stuff happened after we were put to sleep?

My point in this story is a very, very elementary one, yet we tend to forget it. The point of this story is that each of those possible explanations for the problem calls for a completely different course of action. Do you agree with me? Would you try to deal with it the same way if the kid was up because she wasn't tired as opposed to she was up because she had a big event coming up tomorrow or was afraid of monsters? Of course not. But every time we use a reward—here's what you'll get if you comply—or a consequence—here's what will happen to you if you don't—we pretend that the reasons are irrelevant. Here's what I'll give you if the problem magically goes away by itself. I don't know why it's happening; I don't care. Big surprise: In the long run this is not very effective. That's the sense of the argument, and you can use your own examples from a school setting of why a reward for good behavior, including praise, or a consequence for doing something wrong, would be expected to be similarly ineffective because *it* gets nowhere near where the trouble is. It's a one-size-fits-all solution. Many of us know that's a lie in clothing. It's also a lie in behavior.

Rewards Reduce Risk-Taking

The next one, I think, really helps to explain the surprising research showing that performance tends to decline when people are offered rewards for doing a task. B.F. Skinner is dead, but his rats live on. On the sixth floor of William James Hall, Harvard University, Cambridge, Massachusetts, not far from where I live, imagine, if you will, a rat placed in a maze. The rat can smell the brie over here (this is Cambridge, after all). Does the rat pause to reflect on the architecture of the maze? I don't think so. Does the rat say to itself, "You know, I smell the cheese over this way, but I wonder what would happen if I took a chance and went over that way instead. Maybe there'll be a shortcut." Does the rat do that? No indeed. The rat goes in the most obvious, stereotypical, tried-and-true direction as fast as its little legs will carry it toward its breakfast—the reward.

People will do that, too, if you offer them rewards, even verbal rewards. When the reward is the point, people tend not to take unnecessary risks, tend not to play hunches that might not pay off, tend not to play with possibilities or look outside of the task for things that might or might not be useful for solving it. Do you know what I've just described? We have a word in English for this: creativity. I've just given you a working definition of the term. That's what rewards reliably kill—not the wrong kind of rewards, not the wrong amount of rewards, but the very idea of rewards. When you say to people, "Do this and you'll get that," people understandably focus on trying to get the "that" as quickly as they can and with as few risks as possible. That is a mindset that is inimical to creativity and innovation. That helps to explain what the research indisputably finds. Particularly on creative tasks, people don't do as well when you offer them a reward for doing it successfully.

Rewards Undermine Intrinsic Motivation

One more reason: Rewards undermine intrinsic motivation . . .

TWO MYTHS ABOUT MOTIVATION

Two myths about motivation: One myth is that you can motivate other people. I'm sorry; you can't do it. Any time you're offered a seminar or a book or article called "How to Motivate Your Students," you should run screaming in the other direction. All you can do is create a curriculum (that is, a set of tasks or activities), a climate, a relationship, a system, a structure, a culture that allows and encourages kids to act on what motivates them. I say that's all you can do; I say that laughingly—that's a lifetime's work at getting better at how to do those things. It's a lot harder than saying, "I'm gonna motivate you."

You can make people do things. That's what coercion and punishment and rewards are all about. But you can't make them *want* to do things. Does that make sense? Even if you thought it were possible, it's not necessary, given that people are all motivated. I've never met a child who was not motivated. I've met plenty of children who are not motivated to work on *this activity*, to play with *this object*, to work *here, now,* or to sit down and shut up. The problem may be with the environment or the task or the request. It may not be, but that's worth thinking about at least . . .

Finally, even if you thought it were possible or necessary, it's not desirable. Think about how presumptuous it is to say, "I'm going to motivate my kids. I'm going to make them want to do this." Extremely problematic.

Now we get to the other myth, which is going to lead us back to where we started. It took me a number of years to figure out what's up here, and I think that it captures, in rather swift strokes, a problem that explains why we persist in this country in doing things that are so counterproductive. The myth is that there is a thing called motivation—one thing. It can go up, it can come down; you can have a lot of it, you can have a little of it. Imagine a hydraulic lift: more motivation, less motivation. Well, we naturally want kids to have more motivation. So we give them the stickers and the stars, the recess, the popcorn, the payments, and the praise; we give them all the goodies, all the doggy biscuits, verbal or otherwise, because that will make their motivation go up. To read. To share. To think about math. To clean their room. Whatever.

And isn't more motivation what we want? If this were true, it would make perfect sense to follow the Pizza Hut® executives with a program like "Book It!," where kids are essentially bribed with pepperoni instead of doggy biscuits for reading books. And badges.

There's a collective classroom version of this, too, where it just gets worse and worse. Do I have an objection to pizza? No, I do not. Do I have an objection to using pizza as a reward? God, yes. My late friend John Nicholls, originally from New Zealand, who was a very gifted and caring educational psychologist, talked to me about this program some years ago. I said, "John, you're one of the experts in the field. What's the effect of a program like Pizza Hut®'s 'Book It!'?" And he said, "Well, the likely effect, mate, is a lot of fat kids who don't like to read."

But it makes perfect sense to use As and pizza and all of the rest of it to "motivate" kids if this myth were reality, because then you would make them more motivated. Here's the problem: There are different *kinds* of motivation. It's not just one entity that rises or falls. We should never be asking, "How motivated are the students?" We should be asking *how* they are motivated. Just transposing those words changes everything. In other words, to put it plainly, it's not the amount of motivation that matters; it's the kind.

How many of you are already familiar with the words *intrinsic* and *extrinsic* and know what they mean? Intrinsic motivation is a fancy term that means you love what you're doing for its own sake. Extrinsic motivation means you do one thing so that something else will happen. You read a book so you get a pizza. You learn some science fact to please the teacher.

Intrinsic and Extrinsic Motivation

Even this dichotomy is limited, as almost all dichotomies are, but it's a heck of a lot better at explaining the world than the idea of a single entity called motivation. I will make three comments about extrinsic motivation, starting with the most obvious one. It's different from intrinsic. This should not he controversial, and indeed it is not except for a small band of cultist orthodox Skinnerian radical behaviorists in large midwestern state universities. For most people, the idea that intrinsic and extrinsic are different and they both exist makes sense.

Second, I'm saying intrinsic is better, or if you like, extrinsic is worse. No artificial inducement can possibly be as powerful as helping people to find what they're doing intrinsically meaningful. Do you buy that? Also, I hope not too controversial. But

here's the punch line: It's not just that extrinsic motivators—rewards—aren't as good as intrinsic motivation; the point is that they are likely to *undermine* intrinsic motivation. That takes us back, for those of you taking careful notes, to the last reason, number five, on why rewards fail: A good part of the reason that performance declines when you offer rewards is that interest declines. Or, to use my visual aids, imagine two lifts, intrinsic and extrinsic motivation. I am suggesting not merely that they operate independently and that there are two; I am suggesting, on the basis of more than 70 studies—this is one of the most thoroughly researched findings in the field of social psychology—that as extrinsic goes up intrinsic tends to go down. Not all the time—there are no universals in human behavior. Let me summarize the 70 studies in one sentence, a feat never before attempted in Georgia: *The more you reward people for doing something, the more they tend to lose interest in whatever they had to do to get the reward.*

No wonder kids who are praised or given other positive reinforcers for helping or caring tend to become less helpful and caring. No wonder people who are paid for quitting smoking are less likely to stay off the cigarettes. No wonder we find study after study showing that people offered an opportunity to get a reward will then be less interested in the original task when the experiment is over. To illustrate this, I used to describe one of the early experiments that appeared in the *Journal of Personality and Social Psychology* (Deci, 1971). But I find people are more interested, for some reason, in my Oprah story. . . .

A year ago January, I got the call that every author dreams of getting. Authors go to sleep murmuring Oprah's name. "Hello," said the woman, "I'm a producer with the *Oprah Winfrey Show* and we'd like you to come on our show." "Yess!" But it turns out they did not want me to speak about competition or rewards, the subject of the two books of mine that are somewhat better known. This producer had somehow gotten hold of another book I had written back in 1990, called *The Brighter Side of Human Nature*, a book about altruism, which has sold dozens of copies. They were doing a show called "The Kindness of Strangers," in which they were planning to bring on various people who had done amazing things for folks they didn't even know, or who had been the beneficiaries of remarkable acts of kindness. Then they brought me on as the so-called "expert" to talk for about five minutes about why people help and when they don't and how to raise caring children.

Being, as you may already guess, a somewhat mischievous, even perverse, fellow, I came at it the other way in trying to summarize three books in about five minutes. I said, "What if we wanted kids to grow up uncaring and unconcerned about others? How would we do that?" I said, "The first thing we would do is emphasize competition because there's plenty of research to show that the more kids are led to become winners, the more we emphasize the importance of being number one—at school, at home, at play, anywhere—the less sensitive they become to other people's needs, the less likely to imagine how the world looks from another person's point of view." In fact, one study even showed (though I didn't say this on the air because I didn't have time) that you can predict how uncaring a child is from looking at how competitive the parent is. You don't even have to directly expose the child to a competitive activity; just being around somebody who needs to win is enough to reduce the child's concern about other people's well-being.

The second way I said we could make sure to undermine kids' interest in and concern about others is to reward or praise them when they show that interest. Then I proceeded to mention the studies I mentioned to you before. I have to give this woman credit. I had never before seen this show. But I have to give her credit. She was wandering around with her microphone and her jaw sort of dropped when I said these things. And Oprah said (we're on a first-name basis now, of course, because there are no last names on television), "That's really interesting. Isn't that interesting?" And her audience, which will do anything she says, nodded: Yes, that was in fact interesting. She said, "I'm going to have to think about that." And I give her credit. Here she had heard something she had never heard before that was counterintuitive and challenged the American way, and instead of laughing it off or ridiculing it, the way many interviewers have, I have experienced, she said, "I'm going to have to think about this." Anyway, it was a great experience.

Nine months later, almost exactly a year ago, in October of 1996, I got a call from the same producer, who said, "We would like you to come back on the show, this time to talk about the rewards piece. . . . We want to do one thing different this time. We're going to do one of the experiments you describe in your book about rewards, videotape it, and show it, and then ask you to comment on it." And I thought, "Oh my God, this cannot turn out well. These are TV producers.

What do they know about replicating a methodologically rigorous study?" What I said was, "Great idea!" No, I didn't. You know me too well already. I raised objections to it, but frankly they were not asking my opinion; they were informing me of their plans. Happily, as it turned out, they had checked with Ed Deci at Rochester and ended up doing it very well.

So here's what they did, which is the reason I tell this whole story. They brought in 20 children, one at a time, and pretended that they were from a toy company. . . . They brought them into an office and said, "We are from a toy company, and we are planning to introduce some new puzzles which we would like you to evaluate for us." Half the kids, 10 of them individually, were simply asked that: "Could you evaluate these for us? Are they hard or easy, fun or boring?" The other 10 were given the same instructions, with one change: "For every puzzle you evaluate for us, we will reward you with five dollars," which they then conspicuously put on the table right next to the kid.

After they had evaluated the puzzle and been rewarded or not, each child was then left alone in the room for a few minutes under some pretext: "I have to do something else for a few minutes." This, of course, was the whole point of the study because a hidden video camera was taping them. What they found was the following: Of the 10 kids who had just been asked to evaluate the puzzle, all 10 spent at least some time playing with the puzzle after they thought the experiment was over. Of the 10 kids who were rewarded, 9 out of the 10 did not touch the puzzle again. Boy, was I relieved. But given dozens of studies predicting this I was not surprised. Even a brief exposure to a reward (and it does not have to be money) is enough to kill the interest in the task or action itself. You see why I feel so strongly about this?

Substitute for puzzles anything you want kids to do. Or, more importantly, things that you want kids to *want* to do. For example, I don't like the idea of giving kids stickers, stars, or M&Ms to potty train them. I think it's manipulative. I think it often is done because the parent is in a hurry and before the child is able to do it effectively. In order to be potty trained, a child needs to have certain language abilities to be able to talk about the prediction of a coming poop, needs to have sphincter control; certain things have to be in place. But, having said all of that, I don't get all that excited about it. I don't get that upset about people who use rewards to potty train children. Why? Because I am not concerned that kids develop a lifelong love of defecation. I am, however, concerned that kids develop a lifelong love of reading or art or generosity. The rule of thumb is that the more you want kids to *want* to do something, the more you would avoid rewards at all costs because of what they do to intrinsic motivation.

Praise as Extrinsic Motivation

I tossed out the provocative example: "I like the way Melinda is sitting, all nice and quiet and ready to start." I have multiple objections to this practice. Does this hit close to home? Does it really? That's interesting. I did not know that. Here we have one of the strongest features, in my view, of the tradition of Montessori, talking about the destructive and needless use of rewards, and yet we have the practice of rewards, even of this kind, which creates a kind of interesting incongruity in its own right, does it not?

Why do I not like this? First of all, I'm not doing Melinda any favors. You can imagine some of the other kids later: "Miss Nice and Quiet. Dork!" Second, and related to the first, is that what I have done in this classroom is created a competition for nicest, quietest child. The rest of you, besides Melinda, just lost. This is one of the subtle ways that even teachers who would never have a spelling bee, who would never rank-order children on some list (who's done better on something than someone else), teachers who would stop teaching before they would do something that destructive, nevertheless are creating an environment that is really about winning—not about learning, God knows not about caring.

The third reason I don't like this: I am pretending to talk to Melinda, but I am actually *using* Melinda to manipulate the behavior of the other people in the room. And that is just not a respectful way to treat people of any age. If you have done this, it is not because you are a disrespectful or stupid person. My guess is that you simply haven't thought of it this way before. That's why I invite you to think about it this way now. Look at it from the child's point of view.

All three of those disadvantages occur because of the fact that this is not just a reward; it's a public reward. If you find it too difficult to think about what I say concerning praise—you're willing to think about some of this other stuff, but praise is just too deeply in-grained—at least stop doing it in public. Public praise is not about helping children at all. It is about control. If you have to praise, for God's sake do it in private . . .

. . . Assertive Discipline uses public praise as its number one technique. Praise every child every day. That's the poster from Assertive Discipline. So if you have the same reaction in the pit of your stomach that I have in mine to Assertive Discipline, yet you think positive reinforcement is an unalloyed good, I invite you to reconcile that conflict. What's going on here? Who is this really for? I have to tell you that of all of the things I teach about, this is the hardest part for me to put into practice in my own life, because when I don't praise it feels weird to me sometimes. It feels sterile or chilly as though I'm withholding something. I came to realize that I'm doing it more because I have to say it than because the kid needs to hear it. Whenever that's true, boy is it time to rethink our practices.

There's one more little piece of this. Even if I do it in private (none of you can hear this): "Melinda, I really liked the way you came right back from lunch and started to work right away." What is the most important word in that sentence? "I." Even if it works, the way many bribes and threats can work to get temporary compliance, all it has worked to do is to get her more dependent on me. It is not merely a missed opportunity to help her think about the kind of person she wants to be; it is an active way of taking her away from thinking about that and getting her focused on my face.

Some little kids act out worse when you praise them. Have you ever seen that? Why would that happen if praise was so great? I think there are several reasons. I will mention one. On some level, the child knows that the big "thumbs up" signals the possibility of a "thumbs down" tomorrow. To put it differently, the most striking feature of a positive judgment is not the fact that it's positive but the fact that it's a judgment. People, even very short people, do not like to be judged. Some of those kids act out to reclaim some of their autonomy when they've been praised, and I say, "Go, kid!"

Other kids, especially girls in our culture, and especially younger children, will light up with delight when you praise them. They will sparkle and shine and try to figure out how they can get that same reaction from you tomorrow. Those are the kids I'm worried about. It's still *doing* to—even if it's private, even if it's verbal, even if there's no punishment, even if there's no competition. But move in stages here. You can't give up the praise, at least give up the public praise. You can't give up the praise at all, at least give up the stickers. You can't give up the rewards, at least move away from the consequences. You can't do any of that but you're willing to do a little more *working with*, do that. Ride my train as far as you can and get off when you have to. It's not all or nothing.

Alternatives to Praise

. . . A child gives a sandwich away; what's the alternative to praise if that's problematic? Must there be sullen silence? No. This is another one of these false dichotomies: Either you slather them with praise or you just scowl at them. Hardly the case. "What else could you say?" is an interesting question. First of all, the assumption that you must say something and give positive reinforcement when a child does something nice, when you think about it, is predicated on a deeply pessimistic view of children. Positive reinforcement at its core says that kids would never help and do nice things unless they were praised or rewarded for it. Fortunately, as I reviewed in that unpopular book, there is a great deal of research showing that cynicism is not realism and that in fact it is as "natural" to help as it is for us to just look out for number one or to hurt. That does not mean that adults do not play a useful role in helping to nurture and support the helpful part because the hurtful part is there, too. I am not Carl Rogers—I am not Mr. Rogers, more to the point. I do not think that our true nature is exclusively or overwhelmingly pro-social. I merely argue that the antisocial stuff is no more true, no closer to the core than the desire to help.

A lot of the time our felt need to intervene, to reinforce a nice thing may not even be necessary at all when you take a more benign, and I believe more accurate, view of children. But here's something you could say, for example, if you felt it was appropriate to do so:

(She just gave Lynn half of her sandwich.) "Look at Lynn's face. Looks like she's smiling now. Seems like she's pretty happy with this sandwich she's getting to eat because you gave it to her. What do you think?" That's not praise. You're not saying, "*I'm* so proud of you. I approve of what you've done. You've met *my* standards." What you're doing is merely helping her experience information. You are helping her to observe, if you like. She is gathering data about the effects of her actions on other people, which is a vote of confidence in children, saying, in effect, that when they are able to attend to the effects of their actions for good or ill, they are going to want to pick good. There is good reason to expect that that is true when they've been in this kind of environment.

The flip side of this is what Martin Hoffman calls inductive discipline (Hoffman and Saltzstein, 1967). If a kid pushes another kid off of the chair and makes him cry, we don't merely observe, but neither do we get across the message, "No! We don't do that!" ("What do you mean, we don't do that? We just did this!") It's not merely that this is a bad thing to do that is unacceptable that you want to get across. What you want to get across is *why* it's unacceptable. That's the key; that's the gist of the communication that's critical. It's not bad because I say so, it's not bad because it breaks my rule, it's not bad because I'll stop caring about you or punish you; *it's bad because of how it made the other kid feel.* In a nonhumiliating, nonthreatening way, we want to help gently direct the kid's attention to the way this kid feels who's on the floor. With very young children, an analogy to an experience that they've had might be useful. "Remember when you were running and you fell down the stairs last week and you hurt your leg? That's the way Zachary feels right now. I don't think we want to make people feel that way. What do you think you could do now to make him feel better?" So it's turned into a positive, and the kid is empowered by being able to choose a method for helping to reach that goal. You are shaping, you are directing, you are playing an active role, but you are not controlling, unless you choose to define the word very broadly. . . .

. . . If an older child does something that you think is terrific, sometimes I would bite my tongue, but I wouldn't get all tongue-tied and nervous and flustered: "Oh, oh, I said I liked that—oh no; I'm ruining this kid for life." But I think there are two things you can do in response. One is to simply describe what you see. Take a drawing. "I notice you put the moon all the way on the left side instead of the middle. You use a lot of purple." A lot of this comes from Haim Ginott, and, I must say, to some extent, even from Rudolf Dreikurs (this is one of the things that I like that he says, to avoid traditional praise). The other thing is to ask questions, not just how does it make you feel, which can become an affectation very quickly, like, "I'm hearing from you that you're . . . " I have this image in my head of a child who's crying a lot and going, "I hear you saying, 'Aaaaahh.' Do I have that right?" The questions you can ask, though, can deal with what the child has done. "You use a lot of purple. Is that your favorite color?" "Why did you pick this part for the moon?" "What was the most fun about this?" These are responses—the pure description and the questions—that are likely to get kids interested in art. "That's so great! What a terrific artist you are!" is a response likely to diminish the child's interest in art and increase his or her dependence on your judgment of it. So we can describe and we can ask.

If you are giving positive responses, at least they should be private and at least they should be noncompetitive. I would never say, "You're the best one in here." And they should not be global kinds of praise—"You're a great artist." If you have to offer an evaluative response, it should be something like, "This is very impressive, the way you've managed to do *this*," so it's pretty specific—if you *have* to. And also, you should do it in a way that's not gimmicky, that's at least authentic. At least it reflects a genuine excitement on your part as opposed to "catch kids doing something right and give them recognition for it," which is inauthentic by definition because you've determined to do that before you've even set foot in the classroom. And you can tell partly that it's fake because of tones of voice. Three-year-olds *can* smell a rat here.

But even if you do it with a clear conscience and for pure motives, there could still be a problem, so you have to look not only at your motives—are you praising the kid for cleaning up *in order* to get the classroom clean? Is it for you? But even if your motives are pure, you also have to look at the effect. It doesn't take a genius to realize that if the kid is coming up to you, saying, "Is this good?" or is looking at you for approval, you've got a problem. One of the reasons we fail to notice and act on this is because, on some level, for many of us, it makes us feel good; it makes us feel kind of powerful to have a whole bunch of people depending on what we think. We have to introspect to see if that's really true for us. Or they will like us because we're giving them this verbal candy. Or it gets compliance. The "I like the way" is *real* phony when it's done this way: "I like the waaaaaaayyyyyyy . . ." No, you don't like the way. That's a lie. You are saying, "Scramble to be the first one to comply and I will single out one of you as an example to the rest."

But I would say here are two quick criteria for, if you're giving positive responses, whether they are constructive or destructive. I'm not going to give you a script to read; that's disrespectful to you and you should be wary of anybody who does that, which is to say virtually every classroom management consultant. First criterion I would suggest is, are your comments helping kids feel more autonomous, more self-determining, more empowered—or the opposite? Are you helping them to feel like they made a choice, or are you getting them more hooked on what you say? And the second criterion is, are your comments helping the kids become more intrinsically mo-

tivated, that is, more engaged in the task or more committed to the action itself—as opposed to less interested in what the child is doing and seeing it only as a prerequisite for getting that approval? If you can satisfy both of those criteria, that kids are becoming more intrinsically motivated and more autonomous, with the way that you're framing a response, then I think you're doing something right . . .

CONCRETE PRACTICES FOR *WORKING WITH* IN THE CLASSROOM

. . . I heard a second-grade teacher, a teacher of seven-year-olds, tell me a story about how, in the spring, the kids were late coming back from recess, and they were all talking amongst themselves, very animatedly, and she walked over and said, "What's going on?" They said, "We had a problem during recess, so we had a meeting to fix it," which they proceeded to do to their own satisfaction while she finished her coffee. And the point I make about this story is that it's not that these kids dropped down from some teacher heaven. She worked damn hard to get them to that point. Part of it is by letting them own their own problems and solve them, but also by emphasizing the social nature of the solution and of the learning.

That's why one of the Cs for me is the idea of community and collaboration. "What can *we* do?" should be part of each class. Not just you and you and you and you and you, the way cooperative learning is sometimes offered—a technique you haul off the shelf: "Pair up and do this project." Or, if the kid wants to, you could let the other kid help. But rather structuring the opportunity for interdependence, creating through class meetings opportunities to share stuff—albeit not with what Lilian Katz calls "bring and brag," which we know as show and tell. And where kids are constantly working on stuff together, a class mural, a class song, a class name or logo, an opportunity to learn about each other at every opportunity and to think about choices and autonomy as something that is done collectively, not just individually. This is critical. Research has shown that the more kids experience their schools and classes as caring communities, the more excited they are about the academic learning and the more helpful they are toward each other.

I have been to a non-Montessori free school for older kids, where it is basically completely up to the kids to decide what to learn and whether to learn—completely free. People ask me about this school and a similar version of it that's very famous in England called Summerhill, "You talk about choice and not controlling kids; you must love this." I say, "No thank you. This is a bunch of self-interested individuals who don't have anything to do with each other. You need the autonomy, but, equally important, you need the community." And especially with young children, that takes a lot of skillful intervention, not merely passive observation, to help kids feel part of a caring community.

And I have seen, in Montessori classrooms, kids do stuff where, personally, I would have stepped in, and they just let it go—stuff that was hurtful to somebody else—making fun of the way a young kid was pronouncing something, a teacher who asks a question of the whole group, and somebody says, "Oh, that's easy." I would stop the whole lesson right there. Let's talk about how that makes people feel. But do it in a way where you're not humiliating the kid who said it, or bring it up later in a more generalized sense; but you're looking at opportunities, constantly, to figure out how we can help us feel connected to each other: related instead of isolated, part of an *us*, not just kids pursuing individualized lessons. Of course, we have to respond in an individualized way to the needs and talents and interests and skill level of each child, but that's just, for me, the surface part of what has to be a caring community, in deciding what goes on the walls, in deciding how the furniture's going to be arranged, in deciding how to cut up this cake, which is an academic lesson at the same time, in deciding what to do when a substitute comes, in deciding if we're going to take a field trip and what we should do, in deciding what the alternative is to lining up. This is an opportunity for *us* to figure out stuff.

I saw a kindergarten class once where—this was in Missouri—at the class meeting, the kids brought up something that had happened with Legos (substitute, if you would, another set of materials), where one kid was copycatting another kid's design, and it was really ticking this girl off. And so they had a discussion together—not inaction on the teacher's part, not taking over and making the problem go *away for* them—but, "Wow, what a teachable moment," she said, "for a class meeting. Let's talk about that. Is that a legitimate complaint?" She didn't put it that way. In fact, what developed in this meeting of five-year-olds is that a very sophisticated sort of meta-issue began to emerge, which was whether it was fair to have a rule that was applied only to people for whom it was relevant. In other words, you can't copycat people who don't like being copycatted, but

it's OK for people who don't mind. Or did you have to have a one-size-fits-all rule for the whole class? With the teacher's skillful intervention, that began to emerge and the kids began to grapple with this in a way they never would have if the teacher had just left it alone and said, "Solve your own problems," and certainly if the teacher had just come in and said, "Hey, it bothers her. Don't do that." Because they did it as a community.

I was in a classroom of seven-year-olds where they had a class meeting to solve problems where the teacher was not even playing an active role. She had so empowered and skilled them, by this point, which took a lot of doing that I didn't get to watch, that there was a facilitator of the meeting, and it was a seven-year-old. And another seven-year-old was laboriously writing down on a flip chart what had happened, thus making it into a language lesson as well. While I was there, this meeting went on two hours, and the kids were rapt. And if the teacher, who was sitting among them—they were sprawled wherever they found things comfortable—if that teacher had gotten up and gone out of the room, you know what would have happened? Absolutely nothing. It would have continued in exactly the same way.

By the way, the teacher who needs control and uses consequences, you know what happens when that teacher leaves the room? Ka-boom! Then when the teacher comes back and sees what has happened, or, God forbid, is absent for a whole day and learns what has happened, what goes through that teacher's mind, that *doing-to* teacher? Does the teacher say, "Huh. I'm going to have to rethink this control approach?" No, what the teacher says is, "See? See what these kids are like?" And it's a beautiful self-fulfilling prophecy that she never changes. The more her *doing-to* approach elicits rebellion as kids desperately try to reclaim their autonomy, the more she thinks that's the way kids are. I heard a teacher of very little kids outside once. She didn't even know me, but she was apologizing to me, walking by with her kids, because the kids had the nerve to be kids. They were laughing and whooping it up. She said to me, "Give 'em an inch, they'll take a mile." And I thought, "This is mostly true of kids who have only been given inches in their lives." This is not a statement about human nature but about the harms of over-control.

But in this second-grade class, the kids were into this. One kid came up, when it was her turn to speak, and talked about how they were playing a game out at recess called Foursquare, and other kids kept taking the ball away from her. She was recognized by her peer, who was the facilitator, and she came and sat in a big chair and told her problem. And then the facilitator said—and this rotates among all the kids, that is, the role of facilitator—"Thank you. Does anybody have any ideas?" And then the recorder wrote down the various ideas, that ranged from "go tell a grownup" to "find another game" to "talk about it in another class meeting," whatever. And then, again, this interesting meta-issue developed, this time without the teacher's help, analogous to the kindergarten meeting that I had seen, where here the question was, "Do we all have to accept this one solution as the best one, either by voting or consensus?" By the way, I'm not big on voting, which I think has very little to do with democracy. It's adversarial majoritarianism. It does not engage people in what they have to do to listen to each other and take each other's perspectives and hash out a consensus. Anyway, the issue that arose from this was, "Do we have to all decide together what the best solution is, or is it just up to her, the kid who is affected, to decide which of these she wants to apply?" Very interesting discussion. But if the teacher runs the circle time, if every question or response is coming from the teacher, then it's not an opportunity for choice or real community-building . . .

I want to tell you a quick story. A teacher of eight-year-olds told me this story. She said, "You talk about giving kids choices. This one example I wanted to do a long time ago, and it took me a lot of years before I worked up the guts to do it. Very simple. I'm not talking curriculum. Every year, they showed up in the room. I had already designed it. I'd already put up the bulletin boards, the stuff on the walls. I said, 'It's *our* room, boys and girls,' but I was lying. In the most concrete sense, it was *my* room. So I wanted to let them design the whole room. But I didn't have the guts. I thought, Well, what will the parents think, dropping their kids off? 'My God, doesn't she even care?' All the other rooms are brightly festooned with color"—albeit commercially printed posters—"at least until high school, when, apparently, the physical environment ceases to matter.

But finally, one summer, she says, "This is the year. If the parents don't understand, if the principal doesn't get it, I'll explain it." And the room, the walls were completely bare, and the first thing they did, the first week, after learning each other's names, was "How do we want *our* classroom to look?" And she said there was an amazing difference that year, in how the kids felt about it.

But an interesting postscript to this story: They decided together to put blue construction paper up over here on this wall and then to put up the projects or the papers that they were individually proudest of. I don't have to tell you it wasn't just the error-free papers, you know; it was, rather, an idea of "what *I'm* proudest of." It's about learning, where errors are not to be avoided but to be celebrated, including by the teacher, for telling us something about how the child is learning, let alone cases where we impose the notion of error where it's not clear there is a right and wrong anyway. But put that aside. They decided which of their projects they were proudest of, individually, on top of the collective decision to use the wall that way in the first place.

But wait a minute. Back up. They said blue construction paper. They wanted to put it up themselves. But to put it up so it looked halfway decent, they had to measure it. And to measure it, they needed to know fractions. This was the world's fastest and most effective fraction lesson in history. Why? Because they didn't learn fractions just because it was on someone's lesson plan or in someone's book, on some curriculum mandate, or the next chapter in a text. They learned fractions because *they needed fractions* to do something they cared about, and they would not have even had that opportunity had they not had a democratic class meeting about something apparently irrelevant like how do we want to decorate our room. For me, that captures the three Cs.

If you have heard me talk this morning about something that you do, and I have spoken of it critically, and it has flashed through your mind even briefly, "Uh oh. Does this mean I'm a poor educator?," then even to think about that for *a* moment, I would say, suggests that you're probably *a* terrific educator. The people I worry about are those who say, "Ah, that's unrealistic," which is the way people say, "I can't listen to this. It's too threatening." People who are willing to say, "Gulp. Now I'm going to have to rethink some of the things I've been doing, reconsider some of my practices and premises," that's at the top of my list for what makes a terrific educator or a terrific parent. Don't try to do it alone. If you're going to make changes of the magnitude suggested here, get some moral support, have some meetings, have some lunches and dinners and drinks, and work it out with other folks so you get better at your craft, at moving from *doing to* to *working with*. Thanks so much.

References

Deci, E. L. (1971). Effects of externally mediated rewards on intrinsic motivation. *Journal of Personality and Social Psychology, 18*, 105–115.

Deci, E. L., & Ryan, R. M. (1985). *Intrinsic motivation and self-determination in human behavior.* New York: Plenum.

Deci, E. L., & Ryan, R. M. (1990). A motivational approach to self: Integration in personality. In R. Dienstbier (Ed.), *Nebraska Symposium on Motivation, 38.*

Harter, S. (1981). A new self-report scale of intrinsic versus extrinsic orientation in the classroom. *Developmental Psychology, 17*, 300–312.

Hoffman, M. L., and Saltzstein, I. I. D. (1967). Parent discipline and the child's moral development. *Journal of Personality and Social Psychology, 5*, 45–57.

Kohn, A. (1990). *The brighter side of human nature.* New York: Basic Books.

Kohn, A. (1992). *No contest: The case against competition* (Rev. ed). Boston: Houghton Mifflin.

Kohn, A. (1993). *Punished by rewards.* Boston: Houghton Mifflin.

Spence, J. (1971). Do material rewards enhance the performance of lower-class children? *Child Development, 42*, 1461–1470.

Taylor, P.W. (1911). *Principles of scientific management.* New York: Harper.